INVENTING IRELAND

Declan Kiberd

Harvard University Press
Cambridge, Massachusetts

First published in the United Kingdom in 1995 by Jonathan Cape,
Random House, 20 Vauxhall Bridge Road, London SW1V 2SA

Library of Congress Cataloging-in-Publication Data

Kiberd, Declan.
Inventing Ireland: the literature of the modern nation/Declan Kiberd
p.   cm. – (Convergences)
Includes bibliographical references (p.) and index

ISBN 0-674-46363-3 (cloth)
ISBN 0-674-46364-1 (pbk.)

1. English literature–Irish authors–History and criticism.
2. English literature–20th century–History and criticism.
3. Irish literature–20th century–History and criticism.
4. National characteristics, Irish, in literature.
5. Nationalism–Ireland–History–20th century.
6. Ireland–Intellectual life–20th century.
7. Nationalism in literature.   I. Title.
II. Series: Convergences (Cambridge, Mass.)
PR8753. K53 1996
95–40521
820.9'9415–dc20

Convergences
Inventories of the Present
Edward W. Said, General Editor

For Lucy, Amy, Rory — and the coming times.

CONTENTS

Acknowledgements x

Introduction 1
One A New England Called Ireland? 9

IRELAND – ENGLAND'S UNCONSCIOUS?

Interchapter 29
Two Oscar Wilde – The Artist as Irishman 33
Three John Bull's Other Islander – Bernard Shaw 51

ANGLO-IRELAND: THE WOMAN'S PART

Interchapter 67
Four Tragedies of Manners – Somerville and Ross 69
Five Lady Gregory and the Empire Boys 83

YEATS: LOOKING INTO THE LION'S FACE

Interchapter 99
Six Childhood and Ireland 101
Seven The National Longing for Form 115

RETURN TO THE SOURCE?

Interchapter 133
Eight Deanglicization 136

Contents

Nine Nationality or Cosmopolitanism?   155
Ten J. M. Synge – Remembering the Future   166

REVOLUTION AND WAR

Interchapter   191
Eleven Uprising   196
Twelve The Plebeians Revise the Uprising   218
Thirteen The Great War and Irish Memory   239

WORLDS APART?

Fourteen Ireland and the End of Empire   251

INVENTING IRELANDS

Interchapter   263
Fifteen Writing Ireland, Reading England   268
Sixteen Inventing Irelands   286
Seventeen Revolt Into Style – Yeatsian Poetics   305
Eighteen The Last *Aisling* – *A Vision*   316
Nineteen James Joyce and Mythic Realism   327

SEXUAL POLITICS

Interchapter   359
Twenty Elizabeth Bowen – The Dandy in Revolt   364
Twenty-One Fathers and Sons   380
Twenty-Two Mothers and Daughters   395

PROTESTANT REVIVALS

Interchapter   413
Twenty-Three Protholics and Cathestants   418
Twenty-Four Saint Joan – Fabian Feminist, Protestant Mystic   428
Twenty-Five The Winding Stair   438
Twenty-Six Religious Writing: Beckett and Others   454

Contents

UNDERDEVELOPMENT

Interchapter   471
Twenty-Seven The Periphery and the Centre   481
Twenty-Eight Flann O'Brien, Myles, and The Poor Mouth   497
Twenty-Nine The Empire Writes Back – Brendan Behan   513
Thirty Beckett's Texts of Laughter and Forgetting   530
Thirty-One Post-Colonial Ireland – "A Quaking Sod"   551

RECOVERY AND RENEWAL

Interchapter   565
Thirty-Two Under Pressure – The Writer and Society 1960–90 580
Thirty-Three Friel Translating   614
Thirty-Four Translating Tradition   624

REINVENTING IRELAND

Thirty-Five Imagining Irish Studies   641

Notes   655
Index   701

ACKNOWLEDGEMENTS

The author and publishers thank the following: the Society of Authors and the Bernard Shaw Estate for permission to quote from *John Bull's Other Island* and *Saint Joan*; Scribners and Paramount Publishing, and Michael and Anne Yeats for permission to quote from *Collected Poems, Collected Plays, Autobiographies* and *A Vision*; the Macmillan Publishing Company and the Estate of Eileen O'Casey for permission to quote from *The Plough and the Stars* and *The Silver Tassie*; Random House and Sean Sweeney, trustee of the Estate of James Joyce, for permission to quote from *A Portrait of the Artist as a Young Man* and *Ulysses*; Alfred A. Knopf, Inc. and the Estate of Elizabeth Bowen for permission to quote from *The Last September*; the Samuel Beckett Estate and Grove/Atlantic for permission to quote from *Murphy* by Samuel Beckett (copyright © Samuel Beckett 1938, 1963, 1977, and copyright © the Samuel Beckett Estate 1993) from the Beckett Trilogy – *Molloy, Malone Dies,* and *The Unnamable* (copyright © Samuel Beckett 1959, 1976 and copyright © the Samuel Beckett Estate 1994), from *Waiting for Godot* and *Endgame* (copyright © Samuel Beckett 1956 and 1958); Stephen P. Maher, executor and trustee of the late Evelyn O'Nolan and Mercier Press Limited, P.O. Box 5, French Street, Cork, Ireland, for permission to quote from *An Béal Bocht* by Brian O'Nolan, alias Myles na gCopaleen, 1941 and to HarperCollins Publishers and Patrick C. Power for permission to quote from the latter's translation of the aforementioned text *The Poor Mouth*; to the Tessa Sayle Agency and the Estate of Beatrice Behan for permission to quote from *The Quare Fellow* and *The Hostage*; to the Catholic University of America Press and the author for permission to quote from *Translations* 1981 by Brian Friel; to Farrar, Straus & Giroux, Inc. and the author for permission to quote from *Death of a Naturalist, North, Station Island,* and *Seeing Things* by Seamus Heaney © 1966, 1975, 1984, 1991; to Wake Forest University Press and the respective authors for permission to quote from 'The Rough Field' and 'The Siege of Mullingar' by John Montague © 1972, 1978, from 'Belfast Confetti' by Ciaran Carson © 1989, from *Pharaoh's Daughter* by Nuala ní Dhomhnaill © 1990 (with English translations by Ciaran Carson, Paul Muldoon, and Eiléan ní Chuilleanáin), from *Quoof* by Paul Muldoon © 1983; to Thomas Kinsella for permission to quote from *Downstream* © 1962 and *Nightwalker* © 1968 and 'The Divided Mind' 1971, 1972; to John F. Deane and Dedalus Press and the Devlin family for permission to quote from 'Lough Derg' and 'The Colours of Love' by Denis Devlin, ed. J. C. C. Mays 1990; to R. Dardis Clarke, 21 Pleasants Street, Dublin 8, Ireland, for permission to quote from *Collected Poems* of Austin Clarke © 1974; to Michael Smith, New Writers' Press and the Estate of Thomas MacGreevy for permission to quote from '*De Civitate Hominum*' and '*Gloria de Carlos V*' by Thomas MacGreevy © 1971, and to New Writers' Press also for permission to quote from 'Nightfall, Midwinter, Missouri' by Brian Coffey © 1973; to Sáirséal Ó Marcaigh Teoranta and Maire Mhac an tSaoi for permission to quote from *An Cion go dti' Seo* and to the author for her translation of 'Cré na Mná Tí; to Sáirséal Ó Marcaigh Teoranta and the Estate of Seán Ó Ríordáin for permission to quote from *Eireaball Spideoige* and *Brosna* © 1952, 1964; to W. W. Norton & Co. and the author for permission to quote from 'The Woman Turns Herself into a Fish' and 'The Emigrant Irish' © 1987; to Oxford University Press and the author for permission to quote from 'The Mute Phenomena', 'The Spring Vacation', 'Afterlives', and 'A Disused Shed in County Wexford' by Derek Mahon; to Caomh Kavanagh and Dr. Peter Kavanagh for permission to quote from *The Complete Poems of Patrick Kavanagh*, copyright © 1972, 1995, Peter Kavanagh Handpress, New York 10016; to Colin Smythe, Barnes and Noble and the Estate of Lady Gregory for permission to quote from *Selected Plays*. Every effort has been made to identify copyright holders and to secure all necessary permissions. Both the author and publishers will be glad to recognize any holders of copyright who have not been duly acknowledged above.

INTRODUCTION

If God invented whiskey to prevent the Irish from ruling the world, then who invented Ireland?

The obvious answer might be the Irish, a truth suggested by those words *Sinn Féin* (ourselves) which became synonymous with the movement for national independence. That movement imagined the Irish people as an historic community, whose self-image was constructed long before the era of modern nationalism and the nation-state. There are many texts in the Irish language to bear this thesis out (and a few will be surveyed in my opening chapter), but what they also register is the extraordinary capacity of Irish society to assimilate new elements through all its major phases. Far from providing a basis for doctrines of racial purity, they seem to take pleasure in the fact that identity is seldom straightforward and given, more often a matter of negotiation and exchange.

No sooner is that admitted than a second answer to the question suggests itself: that the English helped to invent Ireland, in much the same way as Germans contributed to the naming and identification of France. Through many centuries, Ireland was pressed into service as a foil to set off English virtues, as a laboratory in which to conduct experiments, and as a fantasy-land in which to meet fairies and monsters. The 1916 insurrection was a deliberate challenge to such thinking: though often described by dreamy admirers as well as by sardonic detractors as a poets' rebellion, it was an assertion by a modernizing élite that the time had come to end such stereotyping. One 1916 veteran recalled, in old age, his youthful conviction that the rebellion would "put an end to the rule of the fairies in Ireland". In this it was notably unsuccessful: during the 1920s, a young student named Samuel

Beckett reported seeing a fairy-man in the New Square of Trinity College
Dublin; and two decades later a Galway woman, when asked by an
American anthropologist whether she really believed in the "little people", replied with terse sophistication: "I do not, sir – but they're there
anyway". The underlying process, however, was reciprocal: to the Irish,
England was fairyland, a notion developed by Oscar Wilde to whom the
nobility of England seemed as exotic as the caliphs of Baghdad. If
England had never existed, the Irish would have been rather lonely. Each
nation badly needed the other, for the purpose of defining itself.

This hints at yet a third answer, pithily summed up by those who say
that exile is the nursery of nationality. The massive exodus which
followed the famines of the 1840s left hundreds of thousands of Irish
men and women in the major cities of Britain, North America and
Australia dreaming of a homeland, and committed to carrying a burden
which few enough on native grounds still bothered to shoulder: *an idea
of Ireland*. Wilde believed that it would be, in great part, through
contact with the art of other countries that a modern Irish culture
might be reshaped. The implication was that only when large numbers
of Irish people spoke and wrote in English (and, maybe, French and
German) would a fully-fledged national culture emerge. That analysis,
in its political as well as its cultural implications, was ratified by many
other exiles, who provided a major impetus for the Irish Renaissance
which followed. Though often berated by recent historians for their
fanaticism and simple-mindedness, the Irish exiles of the nineteenth
century were keenly aware of the hybrid sources of their own nationalism. They knew, much better than those who remained at home, that
"the native is, like colonial and creole, a white-on-black negative" and
that "the nativeness of natives is always unmoored".[1]

Benedict Anderson has suggested, as a corollary to those aphorisms
of his, that a similar type of exile in the latter half of the nineteenth
century brought many rural peoples into cities and towns, where their
children, in the course of an ever-extending schooling, were made to
learn a standardized vernacular. For the Irish who stayed in their own
country that language was English, and a life conducted through the
medium of English became itself a sort of exile. The revival of the native
language, led by the Gaelic League in the final decade of the century,
was an inevitable protest against such homogenization, a recognition
that to be anglicized was not at all the same thing as to be English. The
colonial élites who were the result of this flawed mimesis would become
so many white-on-black negatives; and it was from Gaelic Leaguers,
who painfully studied and repossessed Irish, while continuing to speak

English in public life, that much of the impetus for political independence would come.

For all of these persons, nationalism evoked an idea of homecoming, a return from exile or captivity, or what Anderson elegantly calls a "positive printed from the negative in the dark-room of political struggle".[2] The same might be said of the literary artists. W. B. Yeats followed Wilde and Shaw to London in the 1880s, the approved route for an Irishman on the make in England. Once there, however, he grew rapidly depressed at the ease with which London publishers could convert a professional Celt into a mere entertainer, and so he decided to return to Dublin and shift the centre of gravity of Irish culture back to the native capital. Cynics have suggested that a literary revival happened in Dublin at the turn of the century "because five or six people lived in the same town and hated one another cordially". The quip captures the vibrancy and occasional malice of the personal exchanges, but it does scant justice to the collaborative nature of the enterprise.

That enterprise achieved nothing less than a renovation of Irish consciousness and a new understanding of politics, economics, philosophy, sport, language and culture in its widest sense. It was the grand destiny of Yeats's generation to make Ireland once again interesting to the Irish, after centuries of enforced provincialism following the collapse of the Gaelic order in 1601. No generation before or since lived with such conscious national intensity or left such an inspiring (and, in some ways, intimidating) legacy. Though they could be fractious, its members set themselves the highest standards of imaginative integrity and personal generosity. Imbued with republican and democratic ideals, they committed themselves in no spirit of chauvinism, but in the conviction that the Irish *risorgimento* might expand the expressive freedoms of all individuals: *that* is the link between thinkers as disparate as Douglas Hyde and James Connolly, Hanna Sheehy-Skeffington and James Joyce.

My concern has been to trace the links between high art and popular expression in the decades before and after independence, and to situate revered masterpieces in the wider social context out of which they came. Hence, chapters of political and cultural history, analyses of urbanization, of vernacular, of debates about national culture and the programme of the Gaelic League, take their place alongside detailed reexaminations of major texts. Although my book is broadly chronological in structure, it sometimes cuts back and forward in time, recognizing that any age is always "constructed" by another. My aim has been to explore continuities between the Irish past and present, to place the Irish Renaissance in a constellation with the current moment when, it seems, Ireland is about to be reinvented for a new century. Nobody who has lived through the denial or distortion of so much of the Irish past in recent years – as various groupings sought to colonize it for their own short-term purposes – could be unaware of the ways in which an act of criticism may be at the mercy of the present moment. Doubtless, many of my own insights may be conditional on certain blindnesses, which are nonetheless regrettable for all that.

I have tried in what follows to see works of art as products of their age; to view them not in splendid isolation but in relation to one another; and, above all, to celebrate that phase in their existence when they transcend the field of force out of which they came. There will always be a silent reference of human works to human abilities and to the limitations of time and place: but it is wise to recognize – despite current critical fashions – that certain masterpieces do float free of their enabling conditions to make their home in the world. Ireland, precisely because its writers have been fiercely loyal to their own localities, has produced a large number of these masterpieces, and in an extraordinarily concentrated phase of expression.

The imagination of these art-works has always been notable for its engagement with society and for its prophetic reading of the forces at work in their time. Less often remarked has been the extent to which political leaders from Pearse to Connolly, from de Valera to Collins, drew on the ideas of poets and playwrights. What makes the Irish Renaissance such a fascinating case is the knowledge that the cultural revival preceded and in many ways enabled the political revolution that followed. This is quite the opposite of the American experience, in which the attainment of cultural autonomy by Whitman and Emerson followed the political Declaration of Independence by fully seventy-five years. In this respect, the Irish experience seems to anticipate that of the emerging nation-states of the so-called "Third World". Yeats also insisted that art offered this kind of anticipatory illumination: he said that "the arts lie dreaming of what is to come". He wrote for the "coming times", as did his friends and colleagues. They would all have understood the force of Walter Benjamin's observation that "every age not only dreams the next, but while dreaming impels it towards wakefulness". These are the responsibilities that begin in dreams.

In restoring writers to the wider cultural context, I have been mindful of the ways in which some shapers of modern Africa, India and the emerging world looked at times to the Irish for guidance. Despite this, a recent study of theory and practice in postcolonial literature, *The*

Empire Writes Back, passes over the Irish case very swiftly, perhaps because the authors find these white Europeans too strange an instance to justify their sustained attention.[3] I hope that this book might prompt a reassessment. All cases are complex, but it is precisely the "mixed" nature of the experience of Irish people, as both exponents and victims of British imperialism, which makes them so representative of the underlying process. Because the Irish were the first modern people to decolonize in the twentieth century, it has seemed useful to make comparisons with other, subsequent movements, and to draw upon the more recent theories of Frantz Fanon and Ashis Nandy for a retrospective illumination. If Ireland once inspired many leaders of the "developing" world, today the country has much to learn from them. This is in no way to deny the specificity of each particular case; and I have tried, in teasing out some analogies, to render the crucial differences as well as the often-forgotten similarities. In that spirit I have refrained from attempts to "recolonize" Irish cultural studies in the name of any fashionable literary theory, preferring to allow my chosen texts to define their own terms of discussion. My belief is that the introduction of the Irish case to the debate will complicate, extend and in some cases expose the limits of current models of postcoloniality. If nationalism is most often invoked in western Europe nowadays by those who wish to defend the *status quo,* in eastern Europe and in the wider decolonizing world it may equally be an inspiration to those who wish to change it: the Irish case, as always, exhibits both tendencies at work, often simultaneously.[4]

A few definitions may be helpful at this point. 'Imperialism' in this text is a term used to describe the seizure of land from its owners and their consequent subjugation by military force and cultural programming: the latter involves the description, mapping and ecological transformation of the occupied territory. "Colonialism" more specifically involves the planting of settlers in the land thus seized, for the purpose of expropriating its wealth and for the promotion of the occupiers' trade and culture. Students of these processes have traditionally devoted most of their attention to the economic and political ramifications, and have tended to underestimate the cultural factors. Recent work by Edward Said, C. L. R. James, Albert Memmi, Aimé Césaire, as well as by Fanon and Nandy, has helped to illuminate the cultural politics of resistance movements, but there is still much to be done on the implications of empire for the life of the "home country". Because Ireland, unlike most other colonies, was positioned so close to the occupying power, and because the relationship between the two countries was one of prolonged if forced intimacy, the study of Irish writing and thought in the English language may allow for a more truly contrapuntal analysis. In my judgement, postcolonial writing does not begin only when the occupier withdraws: rather it is initiated at that very moment when a native writer formulates a text committed to cultural resistance. By this reckoning, Seathrún Céitinn and W. B. Yeats are postcolonial artists, as surely as Brendan Behan.

As far as the Irish were concerned, colonialism took various forms: political rule from London through the medium of Dublin Castle; economic expropriation by planters who came in various waves of settlement; and an accompanying psychology of self-doubt and dependency among the Irish, linked to the loss of economic and political power but also the decline of the native language and culture. Although imperial rule in twenty-six counties ceased in 1921, many descendants of settler families continued to hold much land and wealth. In the ensuing decades, Ireland became part of a new world system, which saw the collapse of colonialism in most of its outposts. That new system was, of course, dominated by the Americans who, learning from the mistakes of predecessors, concluded that there was no need to rule vassal states and so were content simply to "own" them. Once again Ireland, because of its strategic position in the northern hemisphere as a major supplier of American immigrants, found itself in a complex relationship with a great power, and one which was on this occasion also a republic. The resulting ambivalence is traced in later stages of this book, which shows that the effects of cultural dependency remained palpable long after the formal withdrawal of the British military: it was less easy to decolonize the mind than the territory. Such a programme was made even more difficult by the persistence of British rule over six counties of northern Ireland: even today the unionist élites remain committed to an "England of the mind" which has long ceased to have any meaning for most inhabitants of a multicultural Britain.

Inventing Ireland, though long, is bound together by recurring and developing themes. It begins with an outline of the Anglo-Irish antithesis as a slot-rolling mechanism devised by the English; against its either–or polarities both Wilde and Shaw offered a more inclusive philosophy of interpenetrating opposites. This became the Yeatsian method, defined most fully in *A Vision*. The androgynous hero and heroine represented natural refinements of such thinking, to be explored in the very different works of Augusta Gregory, Yeats, Joyce, Synge and Elizabeth Bowen. A corollary was the notion of the self-invented man or woman. Nietzsche had said that those who haven't had a good father are compelled to go out and invent one: taking him at his word, this generation of Irishmen and Irishwomen fathered and mothered themselves, reinventing parents in much the same way as they were reinventing the Irish past. Throughout that process, as Synge saw more clearly than most, there were major reversals in the relations between mothers and daughters, fathers and sons: families split into their constituent parts and the free person was born. The link between such self-invention and a Protestant spirituality was explored in a whole set of texts produced in the 1920s and 1930s, as an implicit critique of the alarming new tendency of Catholic Ireland to equate itself with nationalist Ireland in the early years of the Free State.

All of this put into even sharper focus the meaning of the debate about national identity, which had been initiated by Douglas Hyde and the Gaelic League in 1893 and which registered the choice as one between nationality or cosmopolitanism by the turn of the century. Were the Irish a hybrid people, as the artists generally claimed, exponents of multiple selfhood and modern authenticity? Or were they a pure, unitary race, dedicated to defending a romantic notion of integrity? These discussions anticipated many others which would be heard across the "Third World": in Ireland, as elsewhere, artists celebrated the hybridity of the national experience, even as they lamented the underdevelopment which seemed to be found alongside such cultural richness. At the level of practical politics, the 'green' and 'orange' essentialists seized control, and protected their singular versions of identity on either side of a patrolled border, but the pluralist philosophy espoused by the artists may yet contain the shape of the future. The century which is about to end is once again dominated by the debate with which it began: how to distinguish what is good in nationalism from what is bad, and how to use the positive potentials to assist peoples to modernize in a humane fashion. Each section of my narrative opens with an italicized 'Inter-chapter' which briefly sketches political developments, so that readers who wish can map literature against the blunter realities of history.

I owe thanks to many more people than can be mentioned here. Some of the deepest debts go back farthest: to inspiring teachers Brendan Kennelly, the late Dick Ellmann, the late Máirtín Ó Cadhain, Barbara Wright and Paddy Lyons; to generous colleagues Lyn Innes, Terence McCaughey, Richard and Anne Kearney, Angela Bourke, Liz Butler-Cullingford, Chester Anderson, Porter Abbott and Seamus Deane; and to helpful friends Ulick O'Connor, the late Eilís Dillon, Tony Coughlan, Carol Coulter, Adrian and Rosaleen Moynes, Joan Hyland, Dillon

Johnston, Tim Pat Coogan, Rand Brandes, Patrick Sheeran, Richard Murphy, Roy and Aisling Foster, Gabriel and Brenda Fitzmaurice, Desmond Fennell, Nina Witoszek, Nicky and Eleanor Grene, Phil O'Leary, Máirín Ní Dhonnchadha, Séan Ó Mórdha, Liz Curtis, Owen Dudley Edwards, Anthony Roche, Janet Clare, Michael D. Higgins and Rob Garrett. I recall with fondness many inspiring conversations with my dead friend Vivian Mercier: in all the richness of his tragic being, he was a model of the old-fashioned philologist who took for his home the entire world. Edward Said, another such, has been unstinting in his encouragement: his own work is a touchstone in these endeavours. Brian Friel's kindness and encouragement over the years have been more helpful than he knows. Neil Belton's editorial work has been a constant illumination, all the more helpful in coming from a publisher who is not in full accord with many of my interpretations. Antony Farrell was also most supportive.

The School of Irish Studies, Ballsbridge, and the Faculty Research Fund and Academic Publications Committee of University College Dublin offered financial support and this is gratefully acknowledged. I am also very thankful to Beverly Sperry, Clodagh Murphy and Ciara Boylan of the Night Owl Bureau in Dublin for their most professional and friendly help in preparing this rather long work. A deep debt is also owed to many gifted students – Debbie Reid, Dermot Kelly, Emer Nolan, Carol Tell, Lance Pettitt, Ronan MacDonald, John Redmond, Caitriona Clutterbuck, Glenn Hooper, Brendan Fleming, Declan Collinge, Jeff Holdridge, Fuyuji Tanigawa, Minako Okamura, Clíona ó Gallchóir and Taura Napier – who have gone on to teach others what first they imparted to me. Many friends overseas have also been of great assistance: Krista Kaer in Estonia; Muira Mutran in Brazil; Maria Kurdi in Hungary; Chen Shu in China; Carla de Petris and Rosangela Barone in Italy; Shaun Richards in England; Ihab Hassan and David Lloyd in the United States; Mary Massoud in Egypt.

Since this book is finally a personal statement about the Irish imagination, it would have been unthinkable without the support of my beloved wife, who has greatly complicated and enriched my understanding of my country. My gratitude also to Damien Kiberd and Marguerite Lynch for lively and irreverent debate over more than a quarter of a century about "the matter with Ireland"; and to my father and mother for sharing memories of the old days with me.

Declan Kiberd
Clontarf, Dublin, 1995

One

A New England Called Ireland?

If Ireland had never existed, the English would have invented it; and since it never existed in English eyes as anything more than a patch-work-quilt of warring fiefdoms, their leaders occupied the neighbour-ing island and called it Ireland. With the mission to impose a central administration went the attempt to define a unitary Irish character. Since the first wave of invaders was little more than an uneasy coalition of factions, its members had no very secure identity of their own, in whose name they might justify the incursion. Many Norman settlers gradually became "more Irish than the Irish themselves": many others became hybrids, who partook fully in Irish cultural life, while giving political allegiance to London. So the makers of Crown policy in Ireland made ever more strenuous attempts to define an English national character, and a countervailing Irish one.

Ireland was soon patented as not-England, a place whose peoples were, in many important ways, the very antitheses of their new rulers from overseas.[1] These rulers began to control the developing debate; and it was to be their version of things which would enter universal history. At the outset, they had no justification other than superior force and cohesive organization. Later, an identity was proposed for the natives, which cast them as foils to the occupiers, thereby creating the impres-sion that those who composed it had always been sure of their own national character. What began as a coalition of diverse interests, banded together for purposes of territorial expansion into places like Ireland and the Americas, was later homogenized for reasons of imperial efficiency.

From the later sixteenth century, when Edmund Spenser walked the plantations of Munster, the English have presented themselves to the world as controlled, refined and rooted; and so it suited them to find the Irish hot-headed, rude and nomadic, the perfect foil to set off their own virtues. No sooner had these stereotypes taken their initial shape than they were challenged by poets and intellectuals writing in the Irish

language, and they rapidly learned to decode those texts which pre-
sumed to decode them. Spenser was astute enough to sense the immense power of the poets, who stood second only to their chieftains in
the political pecking-order; and he was also impressed by the "pretty
flowers" and beauty of their imagery. This was precisely why he called
for the removal of their heads, because "by their ditties they do
encourage lords and gentlemen", which was to say Gaelic lords and
Gaelic gentlemen.[2] During his sojourn in Munster, many ancient
manuscripts of the province were cut up to make covers for the English-language primers then being circulated among schoolchildren. "We
must change their course of government, clothing, customs, manner of
holding land, language and habit of life", wrote Sir William Parsons, "it
will otherwise be impossible to set up in them obedience . . . ."

   In his *View of the Present State of Ireland* (1596), Spenser outlined his
programme. The Gaels must be redeemed from their wildness: they
must cut their glibs of overhanging hair (which concealed their plotting
faces); they must convert their mantles (which often concealed offensive
weapons) into conventional cloaks; above all, they must speak the
English tongue. "The speech being Irish", he wrote, "the heart must
needs be Irish". The native poets knew ruin when they saw it staring
them in the face. So they replaced the old word *gaill* for *foreigner* with a
new one *Béarla*, meaning "English language", and this they employed
as a metonym for the new element in population. One wrote

> Is treise Dia ná fian an Bhéarla . . .
> (God is stronger than the English-speaking churls . . .)[3]

   The Norman invaders had lost their will to extirpate native traditions and had lived happily among the Irish, among whom they were
known as Old English: they became the real villains of Spenser's Irish
writings, which obsessively insist that on this occasion the programme
for cultural cleansing must be completely achieved. The fear of hybridity assailed many of the new settlers who worried that, becoming
neither Irish nor English, they might fall into the chasm of barbarism
which all too easily could open between two discrepant codes. A
portrait of Sir Thomas Lee made in 1594 depicted a physically as well
as spiritually hyphenated man: conventionally Elizabethan in apparel to
his waist, but bare-legged and bare-footed as any Irish kern, the
implication being that he might lapse into utter savagery unless the
erasure of Irish culture was completed. For their part, the native poets
had similar worries. They denounced the exponents of cultural fusion,

sarcastically addressing audiences of whose loyalty they could no longer
be sure as "a dhream Ghaoidhealta ghallda" (O people Irish-English); or
they berated an ambivalent leader "lena leath-bhróig Ghaelach agus a
leath-bhróig Ghallda" (with one shoe Gaelic, and the other shoe English).
They reserved their most bitter mockery for the broken English spoken
by those apers of the new fashions, whose abjection illustrated their
theory that to be Anglicized was not at all the same thing as to be English.

The sheer ferocity of Spenser's writings on the Irish resistance – a
ferocity quite at odds with the gentle charm of his poetry – can only be
explained as arising from a radical ambivalence. He wished to convert
the Irish to civil ways, but in order to do that found that it might be
necessary to exterminate many of them. He marvelled at the capacity of
Ireland to enforce a gentle man to violence, a violence which "almost
changed his very natural disposition".[4] Already, this seductive island
was manifesting its fatal tendency to convert even the most rational and
cultivated of Englishmen into arrant tyrants. This tyrannizing may have
owed much to the remarkable *similarity* of the two opposed peoples.
The Irish, despite their glibs and mantles, actually looked like the
English to the point of undetectability; their poets were court poets,
whose duties were, like those of Spenser himself, to praise the sovereign, excoriate the kingdom's enemies, and appeal in complex lyrics to
the shared aesthetic standard of a mandarin class. Just as Spenser
attributed the woes of England to the irreligious behaviour of its
people, so did the Irish poets absolve God of all blame for the calamity
now overtaking them. In the words of Seathrún Céitinn (Geoffrey
Keating), a poet-turned-priest:

> Éigceart na nÉireannach féin
> Do threascair iad do aoinbéim.

> (The wrongs of the Irish themselves
> Are what overturned them in a single moment.)[5]

It was, perhaps, a subliminal awareness of this resemblance which
distressed Spenser, as it would so many of his contemporaries and
successors. One English scholar has marvelled at the way in which Sir
Walter Ralegh's sophisticated tolerance, "so notable when he spoke
about the native inhabitants of the Orinoco or Virginia, dried up very
rapidly at the edge of the Pale".[6]

The struggle for self-definition is conducted within language; and
the English, coming from the stronger society, knew that they would be

the lords of language. Few of their writers considered, even for a passing moment, that the Irish might have a case for their resistance. Henceforth, Ireland would be a sort of absence in English texts, a utopian "no place" into which the deepest fears and fondest ideals might be read. The two major Irish stereotypes on the English national stage embody those polarities of feeling: on the one hand, the threatening, vainglorious soldier, and, on the other, the feckless but cheerily reassuring servant. They have survived into the modern period in such identifiable forms as O'Casey's Captain Boyle and Joxer, or Samuel Beckett's Didi and Gogo: but they were cleverly and soothingly conflated by Shakespeare in the sketch of Captain Macmorris in *Henry the Fifth*.

The scene is a clear instance of English wish-fulfilment in a play written not long after the defeat of the Queen's men at the Battle of the Yellow Ford. Anti-Irish feeling was high in Elizabethan London, as the danger of an Irish-Spanish alliance grew weekly; so Shakespeare causes his Irishman to allay all fears of treachery. When a Welsh comrade-at-arms seems to question Irish fidelity to the crown, Macmorris explodes:

Flauellen: Captain Macmorris I thinke, looke you, under your correction, there is not many of your Nation –

Macmorris: Of my Nation? What ish my Nation? Ish a Villaine, and a Bastard, and a Knave, and a Rascal. What is my Nation? Who talks of my Nation?[7]

In other words, the captain says that there is no Irish nation. The word is mentioned for the good reason that Hugh O'Neill, the earl of Tyrone, had just called and led the first nationwide army of resistance against the English in the field of battle. He had welded rival princes into a coherent force, by appealing to them with such sentences as "it is lawful to die in the quarrel and defence of the native soil". "We Irishmen", he told them, "are exiled and made bond-slaves and servitors to a strange and foreign prince".[8]

The captain's name indicates that he is a descendant of the Norman settlers of the Fitzmaurice clan, some of whom changed their surnames to the Gaelic prefix "Mac": they remained politically loyal to the crown, despite their identification with Irish culture. Macmorris chides his colleagues for retreating when "there is throats to be cut", but his very emphasis has its roots in his pained awareness that a figure of such hybrid status will forever be suspect in English eyes. In Shakespeare's rudimentary portrait are to be found those traits of garrulity, pugnacity and a rather unfocused ethnic pride which would later signalize the stage Irishman – along with a faintly patronizing amusement on the part of the portraitist that the Irish should be so touchy on questions of identity. Even more telling, however, is the fact that some of the Irishman's first notable words in English literature are spoken as a denial of his own otherness. On Shakespeare's stage only fresh-faced country colleens are permitted to lisp charmingly in the patois "Cailín ó cois tSiúire me" (I am a girl from the banks of the Suir). Macmorris is the first known exponent on English soil of a now-familiar literary mode: the extracted confession. So he is made to say what his audiences want to hear.

If colonialism is a system, so also is resistance. Postcolonial writing, in a strict sense, began in Ireland when an artist like Seathrún Céitinn took pen in hand to rebut the occupier's claims. He had been reading those texts which misrepresented him, and he resolved to answer back. He represented the Old English, those Gaelicized Normans who were especially demonized as hybrids in Spenser's *View*: but his ambition was to clear the reputation of the native Irish as well. This gives his comments a certain objectivity: and he is honest enough to tell much that is not flattering. His scholarly scruple is clear in the tentative title which he appended to his text *Foras Feasa ar Éirinn* (A *Basis* for the Knowledge of Ireland), which was assembled mainly after the publication of Spenser's *View* in 1633. A Tipperary man who was born in 1570 and educated at Bordeaux, Céitinn returned in 1610 to witness Gaelic Ireland dying on its feet after the crushing defeat of O'Neill at Kinsale a decade earlier and the subsequent Flight of the Earls. He might properly be seen as one of the first counter-imperial historians, in that his object was not only to reply to Spenser, Stanyhurst and the English writers, but more particularly to save the lore of ancient Ireland from passing into oblivion. Like the revivalists of three centuries later, Céitinn feared that the national archive had been irretrievably disrupted and that his country, to all intents and purposes, was about to disappear. He mocked the ambitious young English historians who had endlessly recycled the same clichés current since the time of Cambrensis, in a tyranny of texts over human encounters:

> ... óir atáim asoda, agus drong díobh-san óg; do chonnairc mé agus tuigim prímh-leabhair an tseanchusa, agus ní facadarsan iad, agus dá bhfacdís, ní tuigfidhe leo iad. Ní ar fhuath ná ar ghrádh droinge ar bioth seach a chéile,

ná ar fhuráileamh aon duine, ná do shúil re sochar d'fháil uaidh, chuireas romham stair na hÉireann do scríobh, ach de bhrí gur mheasas nár bh'oircheas chomh-onóraighe na hÉireann do chrích, agus comh-uaisle gach fóirne d'ar áitigh í, do dhul i mbáthadh, gan lua ná iomrádh do bheith orthu.

(. . . I am old, and a number of these people are young. I have seen and understood the chief books of history, and they have not seen them, and if they had seen them they would not have understood anything. It was not for hatred or love of any tribe beyond another, nor at the order of anyone, nor in hope to get gain out of it, that I took in hand to write the history of Ireland, but because I thought it was not fitting that a country like Ireland for honour, and races as honourable as every race that inhabited it, should be swallowed up without any word or mention to be left about them.)[9]

In the Díonbhrollach or introduction, Céitinn (sounding at times like the Edward Said of his era) laments the fact that "truth" has now become a function of learned judgement rather than the sum of a whole people's wisdom. "Ireland", he complains, is never to be seen in itself, but as a flawed version of England, as a country still entrapped in the conditions from which England liberated itself in 1066. With devastating wit, Céitinn proceeds to show how, even on a purely textual level, the English writers have been amazingly selective in what they have culled from one another, and he unsparingly exposes the contradictions which nonetheless mar their testimonies. Accusing them of writing to a formula – blame the Irish – he compares them to the beetle, which disdains to alight on summer flowers but joyfully rolls itself in dung. Marvelling at Spenser's ignorance of the history of the Irish nobility, he jocosely concludes that, on the score of being a poet, the man allowed himself the licence of invention

. . . mar ba ghnáth leisean agus le na samhail eile iomad finnsgéal filíochta a chumadh agus a chóiriú le briathra blasta, do bhréagadh an léitheora.

(as it was usual with him and with others like him, to frame and arrange many poetic romances with sweet-sounding words to deceive the reader.)[10]

This is, of course, a tongue-in-cheek rebuttal of the very terms in which Spenser castigated the native poets as practised liars, embellishing truth for their own self-interest. By rights Céitinn could have enjoyed the traditional status of a "saoi re héigse" (a man of learning): it was the collapse of the Gaelic order in 1601 which had prevented this. But he was acute enough to sense in Spenser his own mirror-image: a court poet deprived of a court, a learned man who had somehow lost his full entitlements. If *history* is what gets written in books by life's winners and *tradition* is what gets remembered and told among the common people, then Spenser must finally be rated an historian and Céitinn a traditionalist. Lacking a printing press, Céitinn had no opportunity to publish *Foras Feasa* on its completion in 1640; but hundreds of copies circulated in manuscript, and the book became much admired for its lucid style and for the feelings of self-worth which it instilled in Irish speakers. Throughout the same period, after its publication in an abbreviated version in 1633, Spenser's *View* was widely available in Ireland and in England in printed form.

A major part of Céitinn's project was his demonstration that the Irish were not foils to the English so much as mirrors. Against the view of them as hot-headed, rude and uncivil, Céitinn offered a portrait of the ancient Irish as disciplined, slow to anger but steadfast thereafter in pursuit of their rights, urbane and spare of utterance, and so on . . . to all intents, the very model of an English knight or squire. To scant avail. In centuries to come, English colonizers in India or Africa would impute to the "Gunga Dins" and "Fuzzi-Wuzzies" those same traits already attributed to the Irish. The fact that the Irish, like the Indians, can on occasion be extremely cold, polite and calculating was of no great moment, for their official image before the world had been created and consolidated by a far greater power. The occupiers also projected many of their own flaws onto the Irish and then, like parents who are dismayed to find their weaknesses repeated in their own children, felt nonetheless quite at liberty to criticize the Irish for these failings. English understanding of Ireland based itself on a limited number of ideas; as Céitinn feared, such ideas fed off one another far more than they drew sustenance from actual life.

Eventually, Irish intellectuals deduced that the intent of English policy was straightforward: to create a "Sacsa nua darb anim Éire" (a new England called Ireland). This was undeniably true: but, because it remained an open space in which all kinds of desires and loathings might find their embodiment, Ireland also began to appear to English persons in the guise of their Unconscious. In that covert sense, the *effect* of official policy was the creation of *a secret England called Ireland.* The notion had obvious dangers, especially if Ireland were to be imagined as a feminine landscape, whose contours needed only to be laid bare: but as the seventeenth century gave way to the eighteenth, it also revealed its positive literary uses. In George Farquhar's and Richard Brinsley Sheridan's plays, Anglo-Irish gentlemen returned in dishevelled desperation to remind the London smart-set of the cultural price being paid for empire by its sponsors on the periphery, a place often repressed from official consciousness. Oliver Goldsmith in *The Deserted Village* could, in a somewhat ironic manner, bring the consequences of rural clearances to the attention of his more sensitive metropolitan readers; and Jonathan Swift could write of Ireland as a laboratory in which the discrepancies between official pretence and raw underlying realities were starkly posed. In the *Drapier's Letters* Swift asked how a free man in England could lose his autonomy simply by crossing the Irish Sea. His *Modest Proposal* that Irish children under six be roasted as meat for English tables, though seriously discussed by some myopic readers, was for many a sharp reminder of the way in which English policy was viewed in Ireland. For here was a land where the difference between latent and manifest content had to be constantly negotiated by all writers.

Throughout the eighteenth century, this gap exercised the framers of legislation as well as the authors of literature. On the ascendancy side, the Penal Laws implemented against Catholics who refused to work on their church holidays were somewhat undercut by a rider, to the effect that justices and constables who refused to implement the law would be jailed. The verbal harshness of the statutes was a reflection of their inoperability in a country lacking a comprehensive police force or a system of prisons. The very edict which repressed the Catholics into the official unconscious, supposing such persons not to exist, seemed to concede the impossibility of its own consistent application. It implicitly acknowledged that it afforded only one perspective and that another, contrary view would be taken by many.[11]

On the native side, poets writing in Irish showed a penchant for covert statement. They praised the beauty of Cathleen Ní Houlihan when they really meant to celebrate Ireland. In what seemed like harmless love songs, they besought girls to shelter gallants from the storm, gallants who turned out on inspection to be rebels on the run from English guns. They decried the felling of the woods, but in this they were actually bemoaning the fall of the Gaelic aristocracy, whose evicted leaders often took refuge in the woods from which they launched revenge attacks. In both Irish and English writings of the period, the woods appear increasingly often as the unconscious, sheltering kerns, rebels and exponents of those desires punished by the

Puritans (many of whom came to Ireland with Cromwell in the 1640s and later). In the settlers' texts, the clearing represented the daylight world of civilization and the conscious: and so the native who stumbled into the settlement and was promptly killed off became a metaphor for the occupier's need to negate all illicit desires.

In no set of writings is the notion of Ireland as England's unconscious more deeply or more sustainedly explored than in those of Edmund Burke.[12] He contended that what happened to the native aristocracy in Ireland under Cromwell and the Penal Laws befell the nobility of France in the revolution of 1789: an overturning of a decent moral order. He believed that the same sickness lay not far beneath the composed surface of English civil society, and that it was his duty to warn people of its likely long-term effects. Under the Penal Laws in Ireland a son, simply by converting to Protestantism, could usurp his father's prerogatives, or a wife her husband's, and this Burke saw as a blueprint for revolution. Within the Irish Anglican minority, for whom all the better postings were reserved, something like a career open to talents was possible: hence a coachmaker's son like Wolfe Tone, the Jacobin and rebel, could become a barrister-at-law. Burke was profoundly unimpressed by all this, seeing the Protestant ascendancy as nothing more than "a junto of robbers", a mercantile class which displayed the *hauteur* and ruthlessness of a fake aristocracy.

Burke's empathy with India under occupation was also expressed in terms which vividly recalled the extirpation of Gaelic traditions by adventurers and planters. Few people were as rooted in custom as the Indians, but Burke complained that all this had been callously swept aside by Warren Hastings and the East India Company. "The first men of that country", "eminent in situation"[13] were insulted and humiliated by "obscure young men", pushing upstarts who "tore to pieces the most established rights, and the most ancient and most revered institutions of ages and nations".[14] It was the same humiliation known by the princely Gaelic poets-turned-beggars; and Burke saw in Hastings the kind of profiteer who ripped a social fabric. Affecting aristocratic style, those expropriators were *homo economicus* hell-bent on breaking Brahminism. To those who worried that he might be overstating the case, Burke replied in 1786 "I know what I am doing, whether the white people like it or not".[15]

What Burke had to say against the "junto of robbers" in Dublin could have been said also of Hastings' men in India: they built no schools or public services, being motivated only by the love of quick profit; and so they had the boldness of obscure young men who "drink the intoxicating draughts of authority and dominion before their heads are able to bear it".[16] Burke was shocked by the complicity in all this of Indian middle-men, who prospered as stewards in much the same fashion as the bailiffs denounced so wearily by the Gaelic poets. But it was for the fallen nobles of India that Burke offered his plangent *caoineadh ar chéim síos na nuasal* (lament for fallen nobility). To the House of Lords in 1794 he declared: "I do not know a greater insult that can be offered to a man born to command than to find himself made a tool of a set of obscure men, come from an unknown country, without anything to distinguish them but an usurped power . . ."[17]

Whether the subject was England, India or France, the threat to traditional sanctity and loveliness was evoked by Burke in the image of a ravaged womanhood. In the *Reflections*, Marie Antoinette was described rather colourfully as fleeing from a royal palace in which no chivalric hand was raised to defend her:

> I thought ten thousand swords must have leaped from their scabbards to avenge even a look that threatened her with insult. But the age of chivalry is gone. That of sophisters, economists, and calculators has succeeded; and the glory of Europe is extinguished forever.[18]

The Gaelic poets usually imagined their monarch wedded to the land, which was emblematized by a beautiful woman: if she was happy and fertile, his rule was righteous, but if she grew sad and sorrowful, that must have been because of some unworthiness in the ruler. The artist was the fittest interpreter of the state of this relationship. So it was not hard for Burke to cast himself in the role made familiar by a hundred *aisling* (vision) poems, which evoked a willing, defenceless *spéirbhean* or "sky-woman", who would only recover her happiness when a young liberator would come to her defence. Where natural laws were transgressed, however, there could only be pain and strife. So it was, also, in Hastings' India, where Burke imagined that the Hindu womanhood stood defiled by an East India Company whose officials "ravage at pleasure".[19] Like Ireland, India appeared to him as a theatre of the unconscious, a place where unbridled instincts ran riot, while the constraints of civilization were abandoned by those very people who pretended to sponsor them.

In his later years, Burke chose to imagine the return of the repressed in the figure of an animal from the colonies now unleashed on the mother of parliaments:

I can contemplate without dread a royal or a national tiger on the borders of Pegu. I can look at him with an easy curiosity, as a prisoner within bars in the menagerie of the tower. But if, by habeas corpus or otherwise, he was to come into the lobby of the House of Commons while your door was open, any of you would be more stout than wise, who would not gladly make your escape out of the back windows. I certainly should dread more from a wild cat in my bed-chamber, than from all the lions in the desert behind Algiers. But in this parallel it is the cat that is at a distance, and the lions and tigers that are in our chambers and lobbies.[20]

His disillusionment with policies in Ireland and India led him to prophesy the end of empire (even before it had fully formed). That makes him the somewhat surprising precursor of today's "Third World" theorists, who offer critiques of cultural imperialism in the years of its slow decline. Ireland provided him, as it would provide many others, with a metaphor for the world beyond Dover, affording points of comparison which helped to explain events in places as far-flung as India or the Americas. The French terror, which he was quite sure no English audiences would willingly contemplate, he made available to his readers in a transposed account of life in post-Cromwellian Ireland, a hell in the grip of "demoniacs possessed with a spirit of fallen pride and inverted ambition".[21] The consequent suffering was as visible and tangible on the streets of rural Cork as in the suburbs of revolutionary Paris.

Burke was, of course, no Irish separatist. He believed that the link with England, though the cause of many woes, would be Ireland's only salvation. Nevertheless, as the product of an Irish hedge-school he had a natural sympathy, if not for revolution, then at least for those caught up in the stresses of a revolutionary situation. Conor Cruise O'Brien has inferred from this a conflict at the centre of Burke's writings between outer Whig and inner Jacobite: while the "English" Burke may on the surface be saying one thing, the "Irish" Burke may be implying quite another.[22] Thus, he questioned the common English view of the Irish as rebellious and emotional children, praising his people's self-restraint in the face of persecution. Taking up where Céitinn had left off, he attacked misrepresentations by more recent English historians: "But there is an interior History of Ireland – the genuine voice of its records and monuments – , which speaks a very different language from these histories from Temple and from Clarendon . . . [and says] that these rebellions were not produced by toleration but by persecution".[23] Burke contested English stereotypes of the Irish, because he saw in them projections onto a neighbouring people of those elements which the English denied or despised in themselves: but he believed that, taken together, the English and Irish had the makings of a whole person. This would prove an attractive proposition for many nineteenth-century theorists, and was the psychological rationale which underlay the Act of Union.

The Act of Union in 1800, which yoked the two countries together under the Parliament in London, represented a further integration of Ireland into English political life. It was the official response to the rebellion of 1798, a bloody uprising supported by radical Presbyterians, disgruntled Catholics and secular republicans, all of them inspired by recent developments in France. That insurrection had been crushed with matchless severity: the short-lived alliance between "Catholic, Protestant and Dissenter", decreed by its republican leader Wolfe Tone against the strength of England, would never be achieved again. The history of Ireland in the following century would be concerned more with sorting out the differences of the Protestant ascendancy and their multitudinous Catholic tenants and underlings: for, although the Union might be said to have secured Burke's dream of an Ireland taking its place in a developing British scheme of things, his calls for the amelioration of Catholic grievances went largely unanswered. A further uprising, led by Robert Emmet (another idealistic Jacobin of Protestant background) was easily put down in 1803 – though the image of Emmet as doomed young leader prompted many English artists, from Southey to Keats and Coleridge, to rebuke themselves for their own failure to live up to such high romantic ideals.

Only with the emergence of the great parliamentary agitator, Daniel O'Connell, was hope of a kind restored. Disparaged by his English enemies as "the King of the Beggars", he was perhaps the first mass-democratic politician of modern Europe in the sense that he built his power on the basis of an awesome popular movement. By 1829, this proudly Catholic leader had secured emancipation for his co-religionists: the Penal Laws against them were finally broken. He next set his sights on repeal of the Union, holding monster meetings at symbolic historical venues across the country. Tens of thousands of labourers, fisherfolk and farm workers walked to hear him: and his speeches, delivered in English by a man keen to prick the conscience of newspaper-readers in the centre of power in London, had a mesmeric effect. By his ringing eloquence, his parliamentary cunning and his back-slapping cajolery, O'Connell achieved an ideal *rapport* with the Irish peasantry, a rapport which would be the envy and aspiration of many writers of the Irish Renaissance. It was said that up to 100,000 flocked to O'Connell's last monster meeting at Clontarf in 1843, the site of a famous victory by which the Irish had terminated Viking power in Europe. The authorities, sooner than see such self-confidence grow, prorogued the meeting; and its organizer, who believed that the freedom of his country did not justify the shedding of a drop of blood, submitted. It was a fatal climb-down: O'Connell never reached the old heights again, and the movement for Repeal foundered. The lessons of a failed parliamentary and democratic system were not lost on O'Connell's more tough-minded critics in the national movement. Yet it would not be an exaggeration to call O'Connell one of the inventors of the modern Irish nation: for a heady period, he gave its members a corporate identity and a sense of their own massed power. The sense of disappointment when that power failed to register with the authorities was all the greater.

Disappointment gave way to desperation in the years of famine during the 1840s. Almost a million people died from starvation and associated disease: and, in the same decade, one and a half million emigrated. Irish-speaking areas were among the hardest hit, with the result that only a quarter of the population was recorded as speaking the language after 1851. Through the earlier years of hunger, the British held to their *laissez-faire* economic theories and ships carried large quantities of grain from the starving island. Arguments raged (and still do) as to the degree of British culpability, but Irish public opinion was inflamed. While some landlords behaved with great callousness towards their ruined tenantry, others were heroic in generosity and in organizing counter-measures: but pervading all was a sense that this was the final betrayal by England. As so often, the balance of the debate was well registered in the popular peasant saw: "God sent the potato-blight, but the English caused the Famine".

If Wolfe Tone and the United Irishmen had looked to revolutionary France for support in 1798, the post-Famine generation turned its eyes toward America. The Fenian Brotherhood stepped into the political vacuum, spurning O'Connellite agitation for the older, trusted methods of an oath-bound secret society which had been favoured by Tone. Ever afterward the cultural as well as political leaders would look to the new world for funds, for manpower, above all for a republican example. Hence the mandatory American tours not just by subsequent revolutionary leaders but also by intellectuals such as Oscar Wilde, W. B. Yeats and Douglas Hyde. Hence also the eventual adoption by Irish writers of Walt Whitman as the model of a national bard. The Fenian philosophy was summed up by one of the leaders, John O'Leary, who opined that it was useless for an Irishman to confront an Englishman without a gun in his hand. This was a view reflected in another popular proverb which warned children against three things: "the horns of a bull, the hoof of a horse, and the smile of an Englishman".

Through all these decades, Protestant Ireland continued to produce more than its share of idealists, who sought to hold a middle ground. The Young Ireland leader, Thomas Davis, had founded *The Nation* newspaper in 1842 with the help of Catholic friends. Sometimes described as naïve dreamers by caustic critics, the Young Irelanders included a few such among their numbers: one vowed to abstain from intoxicating liquor "until Ireland was free, from the centre to the sea", a rather self-denying prospect. But Davis had flint and iron in him as well. He viewed O'Connell's bluff, back-slapping politics with fastidious distaste, discerning in its lineaments an emerging Catholic sectarianism (in place of Tone's "common name of Irishmen"). A Catholic nation would have no place for a Davis, just as surely as the Protestant nation proclaimed in Dublin in the previous century had based itself on the assumption that Catholics simply did not exist. Davis bravely tackled O'Connell in public on the issue; and in forthright essays he identified cultural activity as the true course of a more ecumenical nationhood. "Educate that you may be free" was a favourite motto. He provided later leaders of the Irish Renaissance with many of their crucial ideas: he contrasted the philistinism and gradgrindery of England with the superior idealism and imagination of Ireland. He was not, however, anti-industrial, believing that it was as important to mine the ore at Arigna as to publish a patriotic poem: indeed, he saw these two actions as intimately linked, for his central thesis was that Ireland would never achieve its full industrial and entrepreneurial potential until it had first recovered its cultural self-confidence – and that would only be regained through political separation from England. The Union claimed to accord the Irish all the freedom of citizens of the most prosperous nation in the world; in practice, it simply provincialized them in the name of a facile cosmopolitanism.

These powerful and penetrating analyses were cut off by Davis's death in 1845 at the early age of thirty-one. It would be left to Yeats, Hyde and a later generation to restore to culture its central importance in the liberation of a people: and even if Davis had lived a longer life, the Famine and the Fenians would probably have obscured his contribution. The portents for a cultural alliance of Catholic and Protestant were never very encouraging: through much of the Famine decade stories circulated about Protestant preachers offering starving peasants soup and clothing in return for religious conversion. Across the north, especially, sectarian tensions continued to heighten, with Catholics supporting a separatist nationalism and Protestants the Orange Lodges. O'Connell might have failed as a political agitator, but his equation of Catholicism and nationhood was proving all too seductive to many desperate souls. Yet, when the Fenians rose in rebellion in 1867, many Catholic bishops denounced them, forbade them the sacraments and, in certain spectacular cases, excommunicated them. Republican separatism never enjoyed much clerical support. Rural communities could often identify the Fenian in their number by the fact that he did not go to mass or that, when he did, he took no communion. W. B. Yeats, who was himself for a brief period a member of the Irish Republican Brotherhood, would work mightily to keep open this gap between "Catholic" and "national" feeling. On it the very notion of a cultural renaissance depended.

One of his exemplars in this regard was the next great Irish leader, Charles Stewart Parnell, a Protestant landlord from County Wicklow who seemed in all things the antithesis of O'Connell – silent where he had been gregarious, aristocratic as opposed to populist in style, cold and disdainful whereas the predecessor had been warm and wheedling. To this complex man, whom they called the uncrowned king of Ireland, the emerging masses entrusted their fate and their party, which he led at Westminster through the 1880s. He displayed immense strategic guile in philibustering its sessions, using his numbers to tip the balance of power and, once or twice, immobilizing its political processes. The great issue of the decade was land, a debate initiated ten years earlier by Gladstone's first Land Act of 1870 which, following the disestablishment of the Church of Ireland in the previous year, had effectively put the Protestant ascendancy on notice that its end was near. By its famous no-rent policy of "boycott" – so named after Captain Boycott, one of its victims in Mayo – the Land League helped win many famous victories; and Parnell's shrewd obstructionist tactics did the rest.

Throughout the later nineteenth century, Ireland functioned as a sort of political and social laboratory in which, parabolically, the English could test their most new-fangled ideas – ideas about the proper relation between religion and the state, about the changing role of the aristocracy, above all about the holding and use of land. Indeed, experiments of this kind can be traced as far back as the 1830s, when Ireland was given a streamlined system of national education and a country-wide postal network years ahead of England, which only adopted the models after they were seen to thrive and prosper. All this may help to explain the seeming paradox of a modernist literature and cultural politics in a country too often noted for its apparent backwardness. In fact, by the 1880s and 1890s, Ireland was in certain respects clearly advanced by contrast with England. In politics, it was confronting its national question (something which, even today, the English have not done), dismantling church-state connections, and evolving a republican politics based on a theory of citizens' rights. A highly-educated younger generation, finding few positions available commensurate with its abilities or aspirations, was about to turn to writing as a means of seeking power: out of the strange mixture of backwardness and forwardness everywhere, it would forge one of the most formally daring and experimental literatures of the modern movement.

As a laboratory, of course, Ireland had also known some less pleasant experiments – *laissez-faire* economics, oscillations from conciliation to coercion, curfews and martial law – for it was a crucible in which Britain not only tested ideas for possible use back home, but also for likely implementation in other colonies. The process was reciprocal. Inevitably, the arriving Irish, in their tens of thousands, occupied and used England as a laboratory in which to solve many of their own domestic problems at a certain useful remove. The career of Parnell, no less than those of Wilde and Shaw, might be read as an instance of the theme.

The crisis which overtook the aristocracy under the challenge of Parnellism can be understood with reference to a quip of Oscar Wilde: property, he joked, gives people a position in society, but then it proves so expensive to maintain that it prevents them from keeping it up. In some ways, this had been a problem long before Gladstone devised his Land Acts, a problem which was traceable back to 1800. After the Act of Union, Dublin was a "deposed capital"; its season was no longer splendid; many landlords spent more and more time in England; and the self-confidence which had characterized the Anglo-Irish of the eighteenth century began rapidly to wane. One frustrated leader of this enfeebled aristocracy, Standish O'Grady, berated his peers in a pamphlet of 1886: "Christ save us! You read nothing, know nothing!"[24] Parnell, assisted by the Land League, was simply delivering the final blows which would complete the fall of feudalism in Ireland. He never overtly endorsed the violence deployed by agrarian insurgents, but he could not help being its beneficiary: in this, too, Parnell remained an enigmatic and ambivalent figure, despite repeated British attempts to discredit him with links to organized crime. In the end, just when

Home Rule seemed a real possibility, he was broken by his love for Kitty O'Shea, a woman married to a member of his parliamentary party. Cited as a co-respondent, he was abandoned by Gladstone (whose non-conformist conscience was outraged) and denounced as a public sinner unfit for leadership by the bishops and priests of the Catholic Church. His party split amid terrible rancour and he died in his beloved's arms at Brighton in 1891.

Parliamentary methods had once again revealed their limitations, and a younger generation of intellectuals turned from politics back to culture and to the teachings of Thomas Davis. The poet Yeats met the ship which bore Parnell's remains back to Dublin; and when the leader was buried at Glasnevin a meteor appeared to fall from the skies. The way was open for a literary movement to fill the political vacuum. Its writers would take Standish O'Grady's versions of the Cuchulain legend, and interpret the hero not as an exemplar for the Anglo-Irish overlords but as a model for those who were about to displace them. Cuchulain provided a symbol of masculinity for Celts, who had been written off as feminine by their masters. A surprising number of militant nationalists accepted that diagnosis and called on the youth of Ireland to purge themselves of their degrading femininity by a disciplined programme of physical-contact sports. The Gaelic Athletic Association had been founded in 1884 to counter such emasculation and to promote the game of camán (hurling) beloved of the young Cuchulain. If the British Empire was won on the playing fields of Rugby and Eton, then on the playing fields of Ireland was being perfected a new generation which might call the permanence of that victory into question.

IRELAND – ENGLAND'S UNCONSCIOUS?

IRELAND – ENGLAND'S UNCONSCIOUS?

The British professed themselves baffled by the twists and turns of Irish political history. They complained that whenever they seemed close to solving the Irish question, the Irish had a dreadful habit of changing the question – first Catholic emancipation, then the holding of land, then home rule and repeal. The manifestation of official bafflement had been a policy which oscillated crazily from coercion to conciliation. This was, in part, a mimicry of the Irish capacity to veer from insurrectionary to constitutional methods, from political excitement to sober cultural self-questioning; but the policy had even deeper psychological roots in the ambivalent feelings of English people about their Celtic "Other". The stereotypical Paddy could be charming or threatening by turns. The vast numbers of Irish immigrants who fetched up in England's cities and towns throughout the nineteenth century found that they were often expected to conform to the stereotype: and some, indeed, did so with alacrity. "The Irish are sensible of the character they hold in England and act accordingly to Englishmen", observed the poet John Keats as early as 1818.[1] Such tendencies had been in evidence for decades by the time he noted them. Coming from windswept, neolithic communities of the western Irish seaboard to the centres of industrial England, many found it easier to don the mask of the Paddy than reshape a complex urban identity of their own. Acting the buffoon, they often seemed harmless and even lovable characters to the many English workers who might otherwise have deeply resented their willingness to take jobs at very low rates of pay. Their English gaffers and fellow-workers would, for the most part, have found the traditional culture and ancient pieties of these immigrants baffling beyond belief. The stereotype had indeed certain short-term advantages. It permitted some form of elementary contact between the immigrant and the native English: but it necessitated only a circumscribed relationship, which the Irish could control

*and regulate at will. An art of fawning duplicity was perfected by many,
who acted the fool while making shrewd deals which often took their rivals
unawares. The Irish in England were compelled to "read" their host
country's codes in their attempt to study its defects, for it was from their
defects that the English derived their way of seeing, and not seeing, them.*

Through the centuries from Spenser's View *to Arnold's* Irish Essays, *most
English persons who visited Ireland did so as colonial administrators, war-
mongering soldiers, planters or tourists. Their contacts with the natives were
inevitably attenuated. What the real Ireland or Irish were like, few of them
could have known. Many experts, indeed, were able to set themselves up
without the indignity or inconvenience of first-hand experience, Matthew
Arnold being the outstanding example. As so often happens in such cases,
Irish Studies were pursued in England under pressure of a political crisis.
Just as Charlotte Brooke had published her* Reliques of Ancient Irish
Poetry *(1789) as an attempt to introduce the Irish to the English muse,
and thus to stave off an impending uprising, so Arnold's call for a chair of
Celtic Studies at Oxford and a "Union of Hearts" policy came on the verge
of the Fenian rebellion of the 1860s. Handwringing in the wings of
revolution has been perhaps the central pastime of experts in Irish Studies.*

*By Arnold's day, the image of Ireland as not-England had been well and
truly formed. Victorian imperialists attributed to the Irish all those emotions and impulses which a harsh mercantile code had led them to suppress
in themselves. Thus, if John Bull was industrious and reliable, Paddy was
held to be indolent and contrary; if the former was mature and rational,
the latter must be unstable and emotional; if the English were adult and
manly, the Irish must be childish and feminine. In this fashion, the Irish
were to read their fate in that of two other out-groups, women and
children; and at the root of many an Englishman's suspicion of the Irish
was an unease with the woman or child who lurked within himself. Oscar
Wilde's exploration of the inner world of childhood, no less than his
flaunted effeminacy, may well have been his sly commentary on these
hidden fears. The political implications were clear enough in that age of
severely limited suffrage: either as woman or as child, the Irishman was
incapable of self-government. Such a notion of the Anglo-Irish relationship
was nothing other than a neurosis, as grandly reactive as that which still
afflicts those men who define masculinity in purely negative terms as not-
feminine, and who fail therefore to construct themselves from within.
Victorian imperial theorists were especially prone to these drastic self-
repressions, using neighbouring peoples, notably the French in their sexual
habits, as equivalent versions of not-England.*

There was, inevitably, a more benign interpretation of these slot-rolling mechanisms, and it was offered by Matthew Arnold as a celebration of the Celtic personality which, he hoped, might yet save the Philistine English middle-class for poetry and high feeling. "The Celtic genius had sentiment as its main basis", he explained, "with love of beauty, charm and spirituality for its excellence, ineffectualness and self-will for its defect".[2] Such a genius flourished in short lyric bursts, but not in "the steady, deep-searching survey".[3] Arnold showed remarkably little patience for the steady, deep-searching survey himself, basing most of his ideas on the radical theories of Ernest Renan, who had contended that the Irish, quintessentially Celtic, had worn themselves out taking dreams for realities and were, in consequence, incapable of political progress. Of actual Irish-language texts themselves, which might or might not have borne out his notions, Arnold was almost entirely ignorant.

This did not prevent his generation of Celticists from asserting that Irish glories were all in the past, a past which invariably turned out on inspection to have been a disguised version of the contemporary British imperial present. So the ancient hero Cuchulain died strapped to a rock, single-handedly defending the gap of the north after a lifetime spent knocking the heads off his rivals' bodies; and as his life ebbed away, a raven alighted and drank his blood. This combination of pagan energy and Christ-like suffering was of just the kind recommended for the production of muscular Christians at Rugby, suggesting that the revivalist Cuchulain was little more than a British public-schoolboy in drag. In a famous poem of the period, it was said of the Celts that "they went forth to battle and they always fell"[4]: the lament is for an heroic distant past and for the sense of failure in every subsequent challenge to empire. These laments, and the allied myth of a golden age, were allowed by the imperialists, and sometimes even encouraged when, as in Shaemas O'Sheel's much-anthologized poem, they were uttered in the occupiers' language.

Matthew Arnold, like his exemplar Burke, was never an Irish nationalist: indeed, in 1886, during the Home Rule crisis he proclaimed himself a staunch critic of Gladstone's proposal, arguing that the "idle and imprudent" Irish could never properly govern themselves.[5] Scholars have demonstrated that even when his intention was to praise some positive qualities in the Celt, Arnold never ceded his authority: he was the consummate surveyor, the Celt the consummately surveyed. Those who came after him, and who actually studied Irish persons and places at closer quarters, often sought evidence to bear out his theories. Any recalcitrant complexities had to be converted back into a more familiar terminology in a tyranny of books over facts. And yet it was with the tyranny of facts that Arnold had proclaimed the Celt quite unable to cope!

Arnoldian ideas won support among bien-pensant *English liberals, who agreed that Celtic spirituality and poetry might repair many gaps in the English personality. If the Irish had failed to master pragmatic affairs, that was simply attributable to their superiority in matters of the imagination. "Saving England" became a perennial revivalist theme. It is remarkable, in retrospect, how durable such thinking proved, even among those Irish who fancied that they had exploded it. Many embraced the more insulting clichés of Anglo-Saxonist theory on condition that they could reinterpret each in a more positive light. The modern English, seeing themselves as secular, progressive and rational, had deemed the neighbouring islanders to be superstitious, backward and irrational. The strategy of the revivalists thus became clear: for bad words substitute good, for* superstitious *use* religious, *for* backward *say* traditional, *for* irrational *suggest* emotional. *The positive aspect of this manoeuvre was that it permitted Irish people to take many images which were rejected by English society, occupy them, reclaim them, and make them their own: but the negative aspect was painfully obvious, in that the process left the English with the power of description and the Irish succumbing to the pictures which they had constructed. The danger was that, under the guise of freedom, a racist slur might be sanitized and worn with pride by its very victims; and that the act of national revival might be taken away from a people even as they performed it. Sometimes in their progress the revivalists would seem to reinforce precisely those stereotypes which they had set out to dismantle: nevertheless, this was an inevitable, nationalist phase through which they and their country had to pass en route to liberation.*

The story of the Irish risorgimento *begins, perhaps surprisingly, with Oscar Wilde, a man who saw England as a holy place to be conquered by force of intellect and imagination. The problem never fully confronted by the English was that much of their history had happened overseas, and so they could easily deflect attempts to discuss its meaning. Céitinn had told them in uncompromising terms, but in an Irish-language narrative which they could safely ignore. Burke had, in turn, hinted at certain corruptions of empire which might, one day, come home to roost. Wilde, however, was perhaps the first intellectual from Ireland who proceeded to London with the aim of dismantling its imperial mythology from within its own structures. He saw that those who wished to invent Ireland might first have to reinvent England.*

Two

Oscar Wilde – The Artist as Irishman

"Was there ever an Irish man of genius who did not get himself turned into an Englishman as fast as he could?" asked Henry Craik in an immortal line;[1] and no better illustration could be found than the career of Oscar Wilde, which began with his arrival as a student in Oxford in the autumn of 1874. Having put the Irish Sea between himself and his parents, the young genius proceeded to reconstruct his image through the art of the pose. According to Yeats, Wilde in England "perpetually performed a play which was in all things the opposite of all that he had known in childhood and youth. [He] never put off completely his wonder at opening his eyes every morning on his own beautiful house and in remembering that he had dined yesterday with a Duchess . . ."[2]

The home which Wilde had left in Dublin was, on the other hand, "the sort that had fed the imagination of Charles Lever, dirty, untidy and daring",[3] and it was presided over by two eccentric parents who seemed to have stepped out of a bad stage-Irish melodrama. Sir William Wilde, although a most eminent surgeon and scholar, was reputed to be the dirtiest man in Dublin. "Why are Sir William's nails so black?" asked the mordant students who assisted at his operations, and the answer was "Because he has scratched himself".[4] The Lord Lieutenant's wife one evening refused the soup at the Wilde home, because she had spotted her host dipping his thumb into the tureen. That same hand, it was alleged, on one notorious occasion administered a whiff of chloroform to a female patient as a prelude to an amorous overture.[5] Lady Wilde turned a blind eye to the peccadilloes of her husband, just as he indulged the strident patriotism of his wife, who wrote under the pen-name "Speranza" for nationalist journals. His monumental studies of the antiquities and archaeology of Ireland were matched by her collections of folklore and outpourings of nationalist verse. To her second son, Lady Wilde bequeathed a love of the pose and a theatrical personality.

From the outset, her attitude to Oscar was ambivalent. She had longed for a girl and so, when the boy-child arrived like an uninvited guest, she was somewhat miffed. Thereafter, this ardent feminist and radical alternately pampered and neglected him. His love for her was melodramatic but genuine, as was his repeated espousal in later writings of her doctrines – especially her belief in a woman's right to work and to engage in political activity. Persistent rumours about his parents' sexual adventurism may, however, have given rise to doubts about his own legitimacy, which would ultimately be put in the mouth of Jack Worthing in *The Importance of Being Earnest*:

> I said I had lost my parents. It would be nearer the truth to say that my parents seem to have lost me . . . I don't actually know who I am by birth . . . I was . . . well, I was found.[6]

The mild fear of technical illegitimacy concealed in Wilde a far deeper concern to establish his true personal identity. His famous parents were probably too busy to offer the one commodity that is signally lacking in all his plays, that continuous tenderness and intimacy which might have given him a sense of himself.

The future master of paradox was already wavering between national extremes, emulating his mother's Irish patriotism in one poem, only to salute Keats as "poet-painter of our English land"[7] in the next. Already, he was evolving the doctrine of the androgyny of the integrated personality, which would find immortal expression in the wisecrack that "All women become like their mothers – that is their tragedy. No man does – and that is his".[8] The loutish sexism of the first half of the proposition is fully retrieved by the sharp intelligence of the conclusion.

The sexual uncertainty induced by a neglectful but dominant mother was heightened by the massive disappointment of Wilde's first love for Florence Balcombe, the beautiful daughter of a retired naval officer. Having met her in the summer of 1876, he wrote to a friend: "She is just seventeen with the most perfectly beautiful face I ever saw and not a sixpence of money".[9] That he was serious about her is confirmed by the characteristically flippant reference to cash: but she spurned the young dandy for the more Gothic thrills of life with a minor civil servant named Bram Stoker, thereby causing Wilde to fire off a letter in which he vowed to "leave Ireland" and live in England "probably for good".[10] Here was yet another nightmare from the Irish past to be suppressed by a famous career in England. Wilde easily cut the cord which bound him to the land of his parents, for Sir William died while he was at Oxford. The loss of one parent was a misfortune, but the loss of two might indicate carelessness, so Wilde installed his mother in proximity to himself in London after his graduation, but at a chaste distance from his own quarters. He announced to startled guests at their weekly *soirées* that mother and son had formed a society for the suppression of virtue. It was only later that they saw what he meant.

In the meantime, he busied himself with the task of arranging a pose based on the art of elegant inversion. All the norms of his childhood were to be reversed. His father had been laughed at by society, so he would mock society first. His father had been unkempt, so he would be fastidious. From his mother he had inherited a gigantic and ungainly body, which Lady Colin Campbell compared to "a great white caterpillar"[11] and which recalled all too poignantly the gorilla-like frame of the stage Irishman in Sir John Tenniel's cartoons. To disarm such critics, Wilde concealed his massive form with costly clothes and studied the art of elegant deportment. His mother had sought to reconquer Ireland, so he would surpass her by invading and conquering England. She had wished to repossess Irish folklore and the native language, but he would go one better and achieve a total mastery of English.

"I am Irish by race", he told Edmond de Goncourt, "but the English have condemned me to speak the language of Shakespeare".[12] It was not the most onerous of sentences and he admitted as much to an audience in San Francisco: "The Saxon took our lands from us and made them destitute . . . but we took their language and added new beauties to it".[13] Decades later, the same diagnosis would be offered by James Joyce: "In spite of everything Ireland remains the brain of the United Kingdom. The English, judiciously practical and ponderous, furnish the over-stuffed stomach of humanity with a perfect gadget – the water closet. The Irish, condemned to express themselves in a language not their own, have stamped on it the mark of their own genius and compete for glory with the civilized nations. The result is then called English literature".[14]

Wilde's entire literary career constituted an ironic comment on the tendency of Victorian Englishmen to attribute to the Irish those emotions which they had repressed within themselves. His essays on Ireland question the assumption that, just because the English are one thing, the Irish must be its opposite. The man who believed that a truth in art is that whose opposite is also true was quick to point out that every good man has an element of the woman in him, just as every sensitive Irishman must have a secret Englishman within himself – and *vice-versa*. With his sharp intelligence, Wilde saw that the image of the stage

Irishman tells far more about English fears than Irish realities, just as the "Irish joke" revealed less about Irishmen's innate foolishness than about Englishmen's persistent and poignant desire to say something funny. Wilde opted to say that something funny for them in a lifelong performance of "Englishness" which was really a parody of the very notion. The ease with which Wilde effected the transition from stage-Ireland to stage-England was his ultimate comment on the shallowness of such categories. Earnest intellectuals back in Dublin missed this element of parody and saw in Wilde's career an act of national apostasy: but he did not lack defenders. Yeats saw Wilde's snobbery not as such, but as the clever strategy of an Irishman marooned in London, whose only weapon against Anglo-Saxon prejudice was to become more English than the English themselves, thereby challenging many time-honoured myths about the Irish.[15]

The costs of such a gamble, however, might be too high, entailing a massive suppression of personality. In rejecting the stage-Irish mask, Wilde took a step towards selfhood, but in exchanging it for the pose of urbane Englishman, he seemed merely to have exchanged one mask for another, and to have given rise to the suspicion that what these masks hid was no face at all – that the exponent of "personality" was fatally lacking in "character". To his mortification and intermittent delight, Wilde found that his English mask was not by any means a perfect fit. The more he suppressed his inherited personality, the more it seemed to assert itself. "The two great turning-points of my life", he wrote in *De Profundis*, "were when my father sent me to Oxford and when society sent me to prison".[16] It was a revealing equation, for in both institutions he learned what it was to be an outsider, an uninvited guest, an Irishman in England.

To his friends in Oxford, he was not so much an Anglo-Irishman as a flashy and fastidious Paddy with "a suspicion of brogue" and "an unfamiliar turn to his phrasing". At the university's gate-lodges, he took to signing himself "Oscar Fingal O'Flahertie Wills Wilde", filling two lines of the roll-book with the indisputable proof of his Irish identity. His flirtation with Roman Catholicism at Magdalen College was rather more serious and much more costly than that of his English peers: for an Englishman the Catholic Church evoked incense and Mariolatry, but for an Irishman it was the historic faith of an oppressed people.[17] As a consequence of his devotion to the Scarlet Lady, Wilde was punished by exclusion from his half-brother's will at a time when he was sorely in need of funds. Yet he refused to deny his interest in Catholicism, which may have been enhanced by the dim recollection of having been brought as a child, at the whim of his mother, for a second baptism in the Catholic Church at Glencree. It is possible that the "desire for immediate baptism" expressed by the two leading men of his greatest play may arise from that experience: certainly, the playwright made sure to have a Dublin Passionist Father at his bedside just before he died.

At all events, Oxford strengthened in Wilde the conviction that an Irishman only discovers himself when he goes abroad, just as it reinforced his belief that "man is least himself when he talks in his own person" but "give him a mask and he will tell you the truth".[18] Years later, when Parnell was at the height of his power in 1889, Wilde wrote in celebration of *his* Celtic intellect which "at home . . . had but learnt the pathetic weakness of nationality, but in a strange land realized what indomitable forces nationality possesses".[19] Wilde saw his own career as running parallel to that of Parnell, another urbane Irishman who surprised the English by his self-control and cold exterior. Always a separatist, Wilde poured scorn on the latest English debate on "how best to misgovern Ireland" and wrote a mocking review of one of James Anthony Froude's books on the subject.

In his view, Froude on Ireland was a perfect example of all that was amiss with Britain's attitudes: "If in the last century she tried to govern Ireland with an insolence that was intensified by race hatred and religious prejudice, she has sought to rule her in this century with a stupidity that is aggravated by good intentions". The man who complained that the modern attempt to solve the problem of slavery took the form of devising amusements to distract the slaves saw the political version of such distraction in the endless rehearsals of the Irish Question at Westminster. He closed a review of Froude's *The Two Chiefs of Dunboy* with a straight-faced inversion of the author's purpose: "as a record of the incapacity of a Teutonic to rule a Celtic people against their own wishes his book is not without value". (West Indian islanders coined the term "Froudacity" to describe Froude's lofty condescension: in *The English in the West Indies* [1888] he had found it impossible to think that the former slaves of the area could ever hope to run their own government.) Wilde brilliantly glossed the latest Froudacity: "there are some who will welcome with delight the idea of solving the Irish question by doing away with the Irish people". His solution was more complex and daring: to become a very Irish kind of English man, just as in Ireland his had been a rather English kind of Irish family. The truth, in life as well as in art, was that whose opposite could also be true: every great power evolved its own opposite in order to achieve itself, as Giordano Bruno had written, but from such opposition might spring reunion.

Wilde's art, as well as his public persona, was founded on a critique of the manic Victorian urge to antithesis, an antithesis not only between all things English and Irish, but also between male and female, master and servant, good and evil, and so on. He inveighed against the specialization deemed essential in men fit to run an empire, and showed that no matter how manfully they tried to project qualities of softness, poetry and femininity onto their subject peoples, these repressed instincts would return to take a merry revenge. Arnold's theory had been that the Celts were doomed by a multiple selfhood, which allowed them to see so many options in a situation that they were immobilized, unlike the English specialist who might have simplified himself but who did not succumb to pitfalls which he had not the imagination to discern. Wilde knew that in such Celtic psychology was the shape of things to come.

Wilde was the first major artist to discredit the romantic ideal of sincerity and to replace it with the darker imperative of authenticity: he saw that in being true to a single self, a sincere man may be false to half a dozen other selves.[20] Those Victorians who saluted a man as having "character" were, in Wilde's judgement, simply indicating the predictability of his devotion to a single self-image. The Puritan distrust of play-acting and the rise of romantic poetry had simply augmented this commitment to the ideal of a unitary self. This, along with the scope for psychological exploration provided by the novel, may have been a further reason for the failure of nineteenth-century artists before Wilde to shape a genuinely theatrical play, Shelley's *The Cenci* being far better as poetry than as drama. Wilde argued that these prevailing cultural tendencies also led to some very poor poems written in the first person singular: all bad poetry, he bleakly quipped, sprang from genuine feeling. In the same way, he mocked the drab black suit worn by the Victorian male – Marx called it a social hieroglyphic – as a sign of the stable, imperial self. He, on the contrary, was interested in the subversive potential of a theatricality which caused people to forget their assigned place and to assert the plasticity of social conditions. Wilde wrote from the perspective of one who sees that the only real fool is the conventionally "sincere" man who fails to see that he, too, is wearing a mask, the mask of sincerity. If all art must contain the essential criticism of its prevailing codes, for Wilde an authentic life must recognize all that is most opposed to it.

In consequence, in *The Importance of Being Earnest*, each person turns out to be his own secret opposite: Algy becomes Bunbury, Jack Earnest, as in Wilde's career the Irelander turned Englander. Whatever seems like an opposite in the play materializes as a double. For example, many critics have found in it a traditional contrast between the brilliant cynicism of the town-dwellers and the tedious rectitude of the rural people; but that is not how things work out. Characters like Canon Chasuble and Miss Prism are revealed to have contained the seeds of corruption and knowingness all along, while Cecily has her most interesting (i.e., evil) inspirations in a garden (rather reminiscent of her biblical predecessor). So every dichotomy dichotomizes. Wilde's is an art of inversion and this applies to gender stereotypes above all: so the women in the play read heavy works of German philosophy and attend university courses, while the men lounge elegantly on sofas and eat dainty cucumber sandwiches.

Far from the men engaging in the traditional discussion of the finer points of the female form, it is the women who discuss the physical appeal of the men: when Algernon proposes to Cecily, it is *she* who runs her fingers through his hair and asks sternly: "I hope your hair curls naturally, does it?"[21] (The answer is "Yes, darling, with a little help from others".) When Algy rushes out, Cecily's instant response is: "What an impetuous boy he is! I like his hair so much". The last word on these inversions of gender roles is spoken by Gwendolen, when she praises her own father for conceding that a man's place is in the home and that public affairs may be safely entrusted to women:

Outside the family circle, papa, I am glad to say, is entirely unknown. I think that is quite as it should be. The home seems to me the proper sphere for the man. And certainly once a man begins to neglect his domestic duties he becomes painfully effeminate, does he not? And I don't like that. It makes men so very attractive.[22]

It would be possible to see this cult of inversion as Wilde's private little joke about his own homosexuality, but it is much more than that: at the root of these devices is his profound scorn for the extreme Victorian division between male and female, which he saw as an unhealthy attempt to foster an excessive sense of difference between the sexes. A recent historian of clothing has remarked that if a Martian had visited Victorian England and seen the clothes worn there, that Martian might have been forgiven for thinking that men and women belonged to different species.[23] In the history of men's fashions over the previous four centuries, it was only in the Victorian age that men presented themselves with no trace of the "feminine". The Elizabethan gallant had been admired for his shapely legs, starched ruff and earrings; the Restoration rake for his ribbons, muff and scent; the Romantics for their nipped-in waists, exotic perfumes and hourglass shapes. Such details indicate that the androgyny of the male and female had never been fully suppressed.

Wilde always liked to create manly women and womanly men, as a challenge to the stratified thinking of his day. He had seen in his mother a woman who could edit journals and organize political campaigns in an age when women had no right to vote; and it was from her that he inherited his lifelong commitment to feminism. "Why should there be one law for men, and another for women?" asks Jack of Miss Prism near the end of *Earnest*: [24] if the double standard is right for men, then it is right also for women; and if it is wrong for women, then it is wrong also for men. Wilde demonstrates that the gender-antitheses of the age were almost meaningless: in the play, it is the women who are businesslike in making shrewd calculations about the attractions of a proposed marriage, while it is the men who are sentimental, breathless and impractical.

By rejecting such antithetical thinking, Wilde was also repudiating the philosophy of determinism, that bleak late-nineteenth-century belief that lives are pre-ordained by the circumstances of birth, background and upbringing, a conviction shared by a surprising range of the age's thinkers. [25] The extreme sects of Protestantism had long believed in the notion of the elect and the damned, but radical critics such as Marx and Freud evolved secular versions of the theory, viewing the person as primarily the effect of childhood training and social conditioning. For these figures, environmental factors often overwhelmed the initiatives of the individual, a view summed up in the Marxian claim that consciousness did not determine social being but that social being determined consciousness. To Wilde, who believed in the radical autonomy of the self, this was hateful stuff. He saw the self as an artwork, to be made and remade: for him, it was society that was the dreary imposition. "The real life is the life we do not lead", [26] i.e., the one lived in pure imagination and in acts of playful dissent which deliver us from the earnestness of duty and destiny.

The Importance of Being Earnest challenges ideas of manifest destiny by the strategy of depicting characters reduced to automatons by their blind faith in the pre-ordained. Gwendolen idiotically accepts Jack in the mistaken belief that he is Earnest: "The moment Algernon first mentioned to me that he had a friend called Earnest, I knew I was destined to love you".[27] The whole plot machinery creaks with an intentional over-obviousness: Jack, for instance, says that the two girls will only call one another sister after they have called each other many worse things as well, and this is exactly what happens. The women, perhaps because they seem to have been more exposed to Victorian education than the men, show a touching faith in determinism: ever since Cecily heard of her wicked uncle, she talked of nothing else. Her faith, however, takes on a radical form, as she finds in it the courage to reject the tedious, all-female regime of Miss Prism and to bring her *animus* to full consciousness in the ideal Earnest with whom she conducts a wholly imaginary affair before Algy's actual arrival. In doing this, she was already rejecting the notion of an antithesis between herself and others, because she had already recognized the existence of that antithesis in herself. Just before meeting her wicked uncle, she denies the idea of a black-and-white world: "I have never met any really wicked person before. I feel rather frightened. I am afraid he will look just like everyone else".[28] Wilde insists that men and women know themselves in all their aspects and that they cease to repress in themselves whatever they find unflattering or painful. In abandoning this practice, people would also end the determinist tyranny which led them to impute all despised qualities to subject peoples. Anglo-Saxonist theory, as we have seen, insisted that the Irish were gushing and dirty by inexorable inheritance, and as unable to change any of that as they were unable to alter the colour of their eyes.[29] But Wilde showed otherwise.

The Wildean moment is that at which all polar oppositions are transcended. "One of the facts of physiology", he told the actress Marie Prescott, "is the desire of any very intensified emotion to be relieved by some emotion that is its opposite".[30] The trivial comedy turns out, upon inspection, to have a serious point; the audience itself is acting each night and must be congratulated or castigated for its performance; and the world will be an imitation of the play's utopia, rather than the play imitating an existing reality. That utopia is a place built out of those moments when all hierarchies are reversed as a prelude to revolution: so the butler begins the play with subversive witticisms which excel those of his master, and the master thereafter goes in search of his half-suppressed double.

The psychologist Otto Rank has argued that the Double, being a handy device for the off-loading of all that embarrasses, may epitomize one's noble soul or one's base guilts, or indeed both at the same time.[31] Which is to say that the Double is a close relation of the Englishman's

Celtic Other. Many characters in literature have sought to murder their double in order to do away with guilt (as England had tried to annihilate Irish culture), but have then found that it is not so easily repressed, since it may also contain man's utopian self (those redemptive qualities found by Arnold in Ireland). Bunbury is Algy's double, embodying in a single fiction all that is most creative and most corrupt in his creator. Bunbury is the shadow which symbolizes Algy's need for immortality, for an influential soul that survives death; and, at the same time, Bunbury is that ignoble being to whom the irresponsible Algy transfers all responsibility for his more questionable deeds. The service which the Irish performed for the English, Bunbury discharges for his creator: he epitomizes his master's need for a human likeness on the planet and, simultaneously, his desire to retain his own difference. Hence the play is one long debate about whether or not to do away with Bunbury. Lady Bracknell's complaints sound suspiciously like English claims that the Irish kept on changing their question:

> I think it is high time that Mr. Bunbury made up his mind whether he was going to live or to die. This shilly-shallying with the question is absurd. Nor do I in any way approve of the modern sympathy with invalids. I consider it morbid.[32]

Erich Stern has written that "in order to escape the fear of death, the person resorts to suicide which, however, he carries out on his double because he loves and esteems his ego so much".[33] Virtually all analysts agree that the double is the creation of a pathologically self-absorbed type, usually male, often chauvinistic, sometimes imperialist: only by this device of splitting can such a one live with himself. Rank actually contended that the double arose from a morbid self-love which prevented the development of a balanced personality.[34] If this is so, however, then killing or annihilating the double is no final solution, for his life and welfare are as closely linked to that of his author as are the Irish to the English, women to men, and so on. No sooner is the double denied than it becomes man's fate. Like the "Celtic feminine" in a culture of imperial *machismo*, it comes back to haunt its begetters, enacting what Wilde called the tyranny of the weak over the strong, the only kind of tyranny which lasts. So, in the play, whenever he is most stridently denied, the double always turns out to be closest at hand. When Jack says "My brother is in the drawing room. I don't know what it all means. I think it is perfectly absurd", Algy asks, perhaps on behalf of all uninvited Irish guests:

Why on earth don't you go up and change? It is perfectly childish to be in deep mourning for a man who is actually staying for a whole week with you in your house as a guest. I call it grotesque.[35]

The denied double thus ends up setting the agenda of its creator, who, being unaware of it, becomes its unconscious slave. The women in the play set the agenda for men, Bunbury for Algy, butlers for masters, and so on, even as the Irish Parnellites were setting the agenda for England, repeatedly paralyzing politics at Westminster.

Writers throughout history have found their version of the double in art, that diabolical enterprise which paradoxically guarantees immortality; and this is the one employment of the double which may not be a form of neurosis, since it is presented "in an acceptable form, justifying the survival of the irrational in our over-rational civilization".[36] But other uses are pathological and doomed, since the double is devised to cope with the fear of death but reappears as its very portent. That fear gives rise to an exaggerated attitude to one's own ego, leading to an inability to love and a wild longing to be loved. These, sure enough, are attributes of Algy and Jack before the women break up their self-enclosed rituals (and, it might be added, attributes of British policy in Ireland before independence).

There could hardly be a more convincing psychological explanation of the strange oscillation between conciliation and coercion in imperial policy towards Ireland than Rank's report on the tactics employed in the making of the double. The notion of the "innocent" and "spontaneous" Irish may have been an emotional convenience to those Victorians who were increasingly unable to find satisfaction for feelings of guilt in universally-accepted religious forms. The myth of an unspoilt peasantry, in Cumberland or Connemara, was, after all, a convenient means of emotional absolution from guilt in a society for which natural instinct was often tantamount to a vice. The sequence of coercion following upon conciliation could be explained in terms of outrage with the symbol when it failed to live up to these high expectations.

If this is so, then the play becomes (among other things, of course) a parable of Anglo-Irish relations and a pointer to their resolution. This should not seem surprising. Wilde, in London, offering witty critiques of imperial culture, was one of the first in a long line of native intellectuals who were equipped by an analytic education to pen the most thorough repudiation of their masters. The violent denunciation of Europe produced by Frantz Fanon would be written to a Hegelian method in the elegant style of a Sartre. In a somewhat similar fashion, the English didn't just create their own colonialism in Ireland; they also informed most hostile interpretations of it.

The Irish, by way of resistance, could go in either of two ways; and Wilde, being Wilde, went in both. On one side, he duplicated many of the attributes of the colonizer, becoming a sort of urbane, epigrammatic Englishman (just as militant nationalists, going even further, emulated the muscular imperial ethic with their own Gaelic games, Cuchulanoid models and local versions of the public schools). On another more subversive level, he pointed to a subterranean, radical tradition of English culture, which might form a useful alliance with Irish nationalism and thus remain true to its own deepest imperatives. Sensing that England might be the last, most completely occupied, of the British colonies, Wilde offered in saving Ireland to save the masters from themselves. For the Irish, of course, knew more than their island neighbours: their problem was that of a quick-witted people being governed by a dull one. As Hegel had observed, the losers of history, in learning what it is to lose, learn also what it must be like to win: they have no choice but to know their masters even better than the masters know themselves. To them, the masters (though tyrants) remain always human, but to the masters the subjects are not human, not persons, not really there at all. Hope therefore comes from the initiatives launched by the slaves.[37]

The psychologist Ashis Nandy observed these tendencies at work in occupied India, whose citizens often sought to become more like the British, either in friendship or in enmity. A martial ethos was cultivated, ostensibly to threaten the occupiers with violent insurrection; but this was really a subtler form of collaboration with the British culture. The new muscular Indians came, nevertheless, to view the feminized Indian male as one whose identity was nullified by these self-cancelling polarities, a victim of a pathology even more dangerous than that of femininity itself.[38] Hesitant European well-wishers like E. M. Forster would provide in a character like Dr. Aziz a portrayal of the Indian's lack of manly fibre, as if secretly willing the nationalists to open revolt. A liberationist reading followed, rejecting the either/or polarities of male and female, England and India, and embracing instead an alternative both/and mode of thought, which opposed male or female to the ideal of androgyny, English or Indian nationalism to the ideal of liberation.[39]

This was at once the occupiers' darkest fear and deepest need: that "instead of trying to redeem their masculinity by becoming counter-players of the rulers according to established rules, the colonized will discover an alternative frame of reference within which the oppressed do not seem weak, degraded . . ."[40] This led Indian subjects to see their rulers as morally inferior and, with their new-found confidence, to feed that information back to the British in devious ways. This was also Wilde's mission in London, a place (he said) of intellectual fog, where only thought was not catching. "Considered as an instrument of thought, the English mind is coarse and undeveloped", he wrote: "The only thing that can cure it is the growth of the critical instinct".[41] That instinct was not always welcomed: two weeks before Wilde's first trial, a versifier for *Punch* magazine called for the extradition of such colonial androgynes:

> If such be "Artists" then may Philistines
> Arise, plain sturdy Britons as of yore,
> And sweep them off and purge away the signs,
> That England e'er such noxious offspring bore.[42]

Indians like Nandy came to see Wilde as embarked on the attempt to save England from the deforming effects of industrial pollution. "I would give Manchester back to the shepherds and Leeds to the stock farmers",[43] Wilde proclaimed as a young student of Ruskin; but years later, he sensed that a psychological repair-job was called for as well. The colonial adventure had led not only to suffering and injustice overseas, but had corrupted domestic British society to the core. The projection of despised "feminine" qualities onto Celts or Indians had led, inexorably, to a diminishment of womanhood at home. Wilde's first act on taking up the editorship of the *Ladies' World* was to rename it *Woman's World*; and in his plays he argued for those feminine qualities deemed irrelevant to a thrusting industrial society.

The hierarchical view of humankind, on which imperialism justified itself, led to a purely instrumental view of the English working-class, but that class would never rise in revolt, since the empire also *reduced* class tensions by opening up careers overseas to talented members of the lower orders. Nandy held that Wilde's effeminacy thus threatened a fundamental postulate of the colonial mentality *in Britain itself.*[44] Certainly, Wilde seemed at all times anxious to feed back his most subversive ideas to the ruling class, as when he published his essay "The Soul of Man Under Socialism" in the upmarket *Fortnightly Review* (1891). In such feedback may be found the essence of that carnival-esque moment towards which each of his plays moves: when the wit and laughter of the low rejuvenate the jaded culture of the high, and when polyphonic voices override the monotones of perfunctory authority. "Rather more than a socialist", Wilde described himself with real accuracy as "something of an anarchist".[45]

What is canvassed throughout *The Importance of Being Earnest* is nothing less than the revolutionary ideal of the self-created man or woman. Even the odious Lady Bracknell finds herself inadvertently proposing a Nietzschean idea: that if nature hasn't equipped you with a good father, you had better go and manufacture one: "I would strongly advise you, Mr. Worthing, to try and acquire some relations as soon as possible".[46] Jack, therefore, has to create himself *ex nihilo*, inventing the tradition of himself. Born and first bred in a railway station, he appears to have defied all notions of paternity (or what Lady Bracknell calls "a recognized position in good society"). In Edward Said's terms he exemplifies *affiliation* (the radical creation of one's own world and contexts and versions of tradition) rather than conservative *filiation*. Lady Bracknell has no doubts as to where all this is leading: to the break-up of family life into its individual units and to "the worst excesses of the French Revolution".[47] Revolution is a spectre which she raises when the education of the lower classes is mentioned: if successful, it may lead to a home-grown uprising and acts of violence in Grosvenor Square.

The politics and psychology of the play are quintessentially republican: Bunbury must not be interred in England but in Paris, home of European radicals and Fenian exiles. All this is scarcely surprising from the pen of one whose mother had determined to "rear him a Hero perhaps and President of the future Irish Republic";[48] from one whose first play *Vera: Or The Nihilists* was deemed too republican for the London stage and performed instead in the United States; from one who told an American audience after the Phoenix Park killings in 1882 that England was "reaping the fruit of seven centuries of injustice"[49] and who said that England would only be fully saved when it too became a republic. Wilde's republicanism was a declared feature of his agenda in London from the outset. In 1881, he sent a political pamphlet by his mother to the editor of *Nineteenth Century*, adding "I don't think age has dimmed the fire and enthusiasm of that pen which set Young Irelanders in a blaze".[50] Contrary to many aesthetes who yearned for Renaissance-style patrons, he asserted that the republican form of government was the one most favourable to art.[51]

The debate about republicanism had been very much in the air during Wilde's teenage years. In 1871 a radical politician named Charles Dilke had called for the abolition of monarchy at a meeting of working men: for this he was ostracized and his subsequent gatherings broken up. The London *Times* editorialized: "these are evidently improper points, to be handled, and that with little candour or delicacy, before an assembly of working men".[52] Prime Minister Gladstone assured the queen on 21 December 1871 that "it could never be satisfactory that there should exist even a fraction of the nation republican in its views";[53] and together they both ran a nationwide campaign for royalism. So successful was this that the subject was not widely debated again until 1922–3, the years immediately following Irish independence, when the matter was raised at Labour Party meetings in the north-east of England.[54] This gives some sense of Wilde's daring as a thinker, as well as illustrating that the so-called Irish question was truly parabolic, a device by which British radicals could explore contentious topics at a somewhat safe remove. For example, some years after Wilde's fall from grace the question of homosexuality was raised, once again in a charged Irish context, by the allegations made at the trial of Sir Roger Casement in 1916. The Irish question was merely the sounding-board for unacknowledged English questions.

Certain questions recur in each of Wilde's plays, and so also do certain observations. *Lady Windermere's Fan*, for instance suggests that England has no room for the "heart", which it invariably breaks. The most vital character on stage, Mrs. Erlynne, chooses to emigrate, taking with her Lord Augustus Lorton; and he feels set free of his country rather than deprived of it. Imperialism has, apparently, sapped English society of two elements, the creative and the criminal, leaving only dull suburban types. What life there is in it comes from the outside, from the visiting Mr. Hopper of Australia, who takes the one unattached young woman in the play back with him. Wilde's implication is prophetic of the end of empire: for while Britain wins further victories overseas through such innovators, it will be in a state of terminal decay at home. A society which has no place for its dissidents, its creators or its youth is a society in trouble. Wilde knew this only too well, since he came from such a place: Ireland. And he said that the remedy was for England to adopt some Irish qualities while shedding Irish territories.

If the English used Ireland as a laboratory in which to test their society, Wilde was happy to use England as a testing-ground for Irish ideas and debates: for, in his mind, the two could not be separated. Though it was never viewed as such in Ireland, he saw his own art as part of the Irish Renaissance, jokingly telling Shaw that their mission was to dispel English fog so that it could make way for the "Celtic School".[55] What he meant by the latter phrase, he explained in "The

Critic as Artist": "it is the Celt who leads in art . . . there is no reason why in future years this strange Renaissance should not be almost as mighty in its way as that new birth of art that woke many centuries ago in the cities of Italy".[56]

But this did not mean that Wilde could write directly of the Ireland of his youth. That would have entailed him in the bad faith of reproducing an environment which he knew he should be contesting; and that is something which no radical author could countenance (unless, like Shaw, he wrote of the contrast between how the land was and how it should be). Ireland in the nineteenth century was a confused and devastated place, suspended between two languages; and Wilde was committed to sketching the lineaments of no-place, otherwise known as Utopia, something which Ireland or indeed England might yet become. Where Arnold had hoped to see the object in itself as it really was, Wilde wished to see it as it really was not. At a time when the Irish were often accused by the English of mischievously changing the question, Wilde was thinking farther ahead than either side in the debate. So far from responding to the questions posed by the epoch, art (for him) offered answers even before the questions had been asked.

There is a further reason why, in order to deal with Ireland, a play such as *The Importance of Being Earnest* had to be set in England. Wilde had discovered that an Irishman only came to consciousness of himself as such when he left his country. Wearing the mask of the English Oxonian, Wilde was paradoxically freed to become more "Irish" than he could ever have been back in Ireland. "It is only by contact with the art of foreign nations that the art of a country gains that individual and separate life that we call nationality . . ."[57] Identity was dialogic; the other was also the truest friend, since it was from that other that a sense of self was derived. A person went out to the other and returned with a self, getting to know others simply to find out what they think of him or herself. This seeing of the entire world through the other's eyes was an essential process in the formation of a balanced individual; and so Wilde loved England as genuinely as Goethe loved the French. He quoted Goethe on the point: "how could I, to whom culture and barbarism are alone of importance, hate a nation which is among the most cultivated of the earth, and to which I owe so great a part of my own cultivation?"[58]

That was a universal theme: the persons who gave its name to France were indeed Germanic Franks, for a culture could only be surveyed and known as such from the outside or, at least, the margins. Identity was predicated on difference, but the colonizers of the 1880s and 1890s were conveniently forgetting that fact in their anxiety to make over the world in their image; and they would have to be reminded. A some-what similar jolt must also be given to those national chauvinists who were too eager to deny any value to the occupier culture; and Wilde, by announcing the Irish renaissance with works which appeared to be set in England, administered that rebuke. One says "appeared to be set in England", of course, for a reason which must be finally explained.

English literature had a liberating effect on Wilde: it equipped him with a mask behind which he was able to compose the lineaments of his Irish face. This was to be a strategy followed by many decolonizing writers; and, as so often, it was the Argentinian, Jorge Luis Borges who gave the fullest account of the method. He described the insistence that Argentine artists deal with national traits and local colour as "arbitrary" and as a "European cult" which nationalists ought to reject as foreign. There were no camels in *The Koran*, he said, because only a falsifier, a tourist or a nationalist would have seen them; but Mohammed, happily unconcerned, knew that he could be an Arab without camels. Borges, indeed, confessed that for years he had tried and failed to capture Buenos Aires in his stories, but that it was only when he called Paseo Colon the rue de Toulon and only when he dubbed the country house of Adrogue Fiste-le-Roy that his readers found the true Argentine flavour. "Precisely because I did not set out to find that flavour, because I had abandoned myself to a dream, I was able to accomplish, after so many years, what I had previously sought in vain".[59] Wilde advanced the same argument when he said that the more imitative art is, the less it expresses its time and place: what compels belief in a portrait is not its fidelity to the subject so much as its embodiment of the spirit of the artist. Borges, for his part, found that being Argentine was either a fate or a mere affectation: if the former, then it was futile to try consciously for an Argentine subject or tone, and if the latter, then that was one mask better left unworn, for it could only be donned in the degrading pretense that the mask actually was the face.

In Ireland, writers soon found that it was – as George Russell said – foolish to try consciously for a Celtic feeling.[60] Wilde never made that elementary mistake. His few recorded comments on the "realistic" Anglo-Irish novelists of the nineteenth century are caustic. Croker and Lover did not really see Ireland so much as "a humorist's Arcadia": "they came from a class that did not – mainly for political reasons – take the populace seriously . . . of its passion, its gloom, its tragedy, they knew nothing".[61] Wilde charged them with making the error of magnifying the one sort they did encounter – affable carmen and feckless servants – into a type of the nation. They produced a literature of the "I-know-my-natives" kind, a set of texts purporting to record native psychology as quaint and reassuring to rulers who might otherwise have feared that, if the natives eluded knowledge and control, then anything was possible. Wilde wanted no truck with such representational fallacies. Implicit in his comments on these novelists was the recognition that one of the objects of colonial policy was to maintain conditions in which the production of serious works of literature describing a society in all its complexity was well-nigh impossible. In an address to an American audience, he linked artistic and national freedom, telling his listeners somewhat luridly that "with the coming of the English, art in Ireland came to an end . . . for art could not live and flourish under a tyrant".[62] This was, in any strict sense, untrue: what became problematic was not art, as such, but rather that form of art called literary realism.

Wilde refused to write realist accounts of that degraded Ireland which he only partly knew, and he took instead Utopia for theme, knowing that this would provide not only an image of revolutionary possibility for Ireland but also a rebuke to contemporary Britain. "England will never be civilized till she has added Utopia to her dominions", he concluded in "The Critic as Artist", adding the vital afterthought that "there is more than one of her colonies that she might with advantage surrender for so fair a land".[63]

Three

John Bull's Other Islander – Bernard Shaw

One of the first voices raised in defence of Wilde was that of his compatriot in London, George Bernard Shaw. His one full-length play set in Ireland, *John Bull's Other Island*, was written in 1904, which was also – as it happened – the year in which the veteran Land League radical Michael Davitt published *The Fall of Feudalism in Ireland.* By then, Wyndham's Land Act of the previous year had helped Irish farmers buy out more land from the aristocracy, but a sceptical Shaw was not convinced that the fall of feudalism was complete. With so many men and women of enterprise lost to the emigrant ship, the emerging breed of new peasant proprietors seemed anything but the dynamic class needed to revitalize a jaded society. Most of the new petty landlords were far more concerned with land ownership than with land use, as a suspect new pastoralism took hold on the popular mentality. Worse still, the cultural movement in which this pastoralism prevailed seemed devoted less to a *revival* of Irish culture than to its mummification. The social revolution, imagined by Davitt, was already being aborted by an *arriviste* rural Catholic middle class. That class found no great difficulty in playing up to the expectations of a romantic English liberal visitor, such as Tom Broadbent in Shaw's play. He was the dramatist's warning that the wrong kind of "revivalism" might produce exactly what the British now wanted, a tourist's landscape of colourful, non-threatening characters, who mark off their "interesting" cultural differences from the London visitor, even as they become ever more tractable to his economic designs.

Like Wilde, Shaw was another Irishman who used England as a laboratory in which he could redefine what it meant to be Irish. In *John Bull's Other Island*, the defrocked priest Peter Keegan finds wonders in Oxford that he had never seen at home, but on his return to Ireland he discovers that the wonders had been there all the time. "I did not know what my own house was like", he concludes, "because I had never been outside it".[1] In similar fashion, the mock-villain Broadbent only discovers what it means to be an Englishman when he pays a visit to Ireland. "Ireland", declared Shaw, "is the only spot on earth which still produces the ideal Englishman of history".[2] *John Bull's Other Island* is Shaw's attempt to show how the peoples of the two islands spend most of their time acting an approved part before their neighbours' eyes: and these assigned parts are seen as impositions by the other side rather than opportunities for true self-expression. In the play, stereotypes are exploded, for it is the Englishman Tom Broadbent who is a romantic duffer, while the Irishman Larry Doyle is a cynical realist. The underlying reasoning is sound, for the Irish have become fact-facers through harsh poverty, while the English have enjoyed a scale of wealth so great that it allows them to indulge their victims with expansively sentimental gestures.

On the one hand, Broadbent cynically plots the ruin of the village of Roscullen and packs a gun before his visit to the place; on the other, he fills his head with sentimental claptrap about the charms of rural Ireland. As his caustic Irish partner observes, he keeps these separate ideas in watertight compartments, each "warranted impervious to anything it doesn't suit you to understand".[3] The very ambivalence of Broadbent's gestures evokes the common English oscillation between coercion and conciliation, between contempt for and envy of all that the imperialist denies in himself. A similar ambiguity will mark the gestures of the Englishman Haines in the opening chapter of Joyce's *Ulysses*; he, also, will take refuge from bad dreams behind an imported gun, yet he also will have come over to Ireland to savour the wit and wordplay of the Celtic revival at first hand. So, too, in the opening act of Shaw's play, Broadbent is charmed by the antics of Tim Haffigan, a stage Irishman who wishes him the top-o-the-mornin', until Doyle exposes him as a fraud and an impostor, born not in Ireland but in the streets of Glasgow. Doyle insists that the stage Irishman is a creation of the British folk mind: "all Haffigan has to do is to sit there and drink your whiskey while you humbug yourself", he warns Broadbent, but to no avail, for his English partner attributes this anger to "the melancholy of the Celtic race".[4] Doyle remarks that sweeping generalizations about the Celtic race constitute the most insidiously aggressive of all the tactics used by Englishmen – because they imply that the English are invariably the surveyors and the Irish the surveyed (with the depressing inference that the Irish can neither analyze nor represent themselves). Such talk does more harm than ten coercion acts.

Froude's theory that Celts would thrive only under the benign guidance of Saxons, is voiced confidently by Broadbent, despite his pretensions to liberalism: "I saw at once that you are a thorough Irishman, with all the faults and all the qualities of your race: rash and improvident but brave and good natured: not likely to succeed in business on your own account perhaps, but eloquent, humorous, a lover of freedom . . ."[5] The fact that the reverse might actually be true – that the Englishman needs the Irish to help him determine his own identity, just as Broadbent relied heavily on Doyle for their joint business success – would not have struck many in Shaw's London audience. Yet the play is at pains to stress that all nationalisms rely for their construction on outsiders and others.

If the very notion of a centrally administered, united Ireland is an English invention, then many of the features of English nationalism are patented by German Jews, according to the anti-semitic Broadbent: "If my name was Breitstein, and I had a hooked nose and a house in Park Lane, I should carry a Union Jack handkerchief".[6] He goes on to refer to a nationalist English song as one written "by a German jew, like most English patriotic sentiment". The Germans thereby help to create the fiction, the "imagined community", that is England; and the English help to invent the idea of Ireland and, in return, are assisted by those Irish in sharpening the definition of themselves. This, indeed, is one of the services to his London audience offered by Shaw in the play.

As an empirical, fact-facing Irishman, Larry Doyle felt uneasy in his own country: his youthful desire was to learn how to do something and then to get out of Ireland in order to have the chance to do it. The plot itself seems to suggest that an Irishman will succeed far better in England than in Ireland, where the only successful men are all English. In Ireland, Broadbent plays the role of a lover of the Celts, the English liberal in search of round towers and fresh-faced colleens. So, by his outrageous antics in the role of English duffer, he manages to see only the Ireland he has come to see, a land of buffoons, derisive laughter and whimsy, where a pig can be taken for a ride in his car and an Englishman (i.e., himself) voted the fittest man to represent Roscullen in parliament. He adopts the protective coloration of the stage-English buffoon to the enormous entertainment of the natives, who reciprocate by adopting the protective coloration of the stage-Irish peasant, taking tea at the wrong time of the day and laughing hysterically at every event which ensues. Larry Doyle foresees that, for his antics, Broadbent will not be mocked out of town but will be rewarded with Larry's sweetheart and Larry's seat in Westminster: "He'll never know they're laughing at him – and while they're laughing, he'll win the seat".[7]

The driver who ferried Broadbent into Roscullen told him that the finest hotel in Ireland was there, but there is no hotel, just seventeen pubs. Aunt Jude excuses the driver: "sure he'd say whatever was the least trouble to himself and the pleasantest to you".[8] This is the psychology which underlies the acting of both sides, Irish and English. For the Irish, the callow labourer Patsy Farrell exudes an air of helpless silliness which, says a Shavian stage direction, "is not his real character, but a cunning developed by his constant dread of a hostile dominance, which he habitually tries to disarm by pretending to be a much greater fool than he really is. Englishmen think him half-witted, which is exactly what he wants them to think".[9] This, however, is precisely the strategy adopted by the conquering Englishman, who, according to Larry Doyle, "does what the caterpillar does. He instinctively makes himself look like a fool, and eats up all the real fools at his ease while his enemies let him alone and laugh at him for being a fool like the rest. Oh, nature is cunning, cunning".[10]

In other words, at root the English and Irish are rather similar peoples, who have nonetheless decided to perform versions of Englishness and Irishness to one another, in the attempt to wrest a material advantage from the unsuspecting audience of each performance. Each group projects onto the other many attributes which it has denied in itself, but at bottom both peoples are alike. This socialist perception is embodied in Hodson, the servant of Broadbent, who does indeed find in Ireland the flexibility of mind to disown his master and to point to the common cause of the dispossessed Irish labourer and the exploited English proletariat. He is, moreover, as impatient of Irish whining as of English repression, pointing to the fact that the bulk of the English work-force was exploited at even closer hand than the Irish peasantry by the imperial system. In all of this, he speaks for the Shaw who wrote: "The people of England have done the people of Ireland no wrong whatever . . . in factory, mine and sweatshop they had reason to envy the Irish peasant who at the worst starved on an open hillside . . . the most distressful country . . . has borne no more than her fair share of the growing pains of human society . . ."[11]

Shaw's play, like Wilde's career, is a radical critique of the Anglo-Irish antithesis so beloved of the Victorians and of many Irish revivalists. By the simple expedient of presenting a romantic Englishman and an empirical Irishman *John Bull's Other Island* mocks the ancient stereotype. Of course, that is not the end of the story, for, by his performance of absurd sentimentality, Broadbent effectively takes over the entire village on the terms most favourable to himself, while Larry Doyle loses his cynical self-composure in the face of the ruin of his people. Larry's sophisticated intellect paralyses him into inactivity, for he has grown too subtle and too cynical, foolish in his very cleverness, whereas Broadbent's blinkered vision is what allows him to be so efficient, so finally clever in his very foolishness. In the end, the Anglo-Irish antithesis has been questioned only to be reasserted in a slightly modified form.[12]

Doyle had suspected and predicted as much: to the claim that the Land Acts have abolished landlordism, he responds derisively that they have simply multiplied the number of petty landlords in every parish. The new proprietors, tuppence-ha'pennies looking down on tuppences, will be far more cruel to the landless labourers than ever the landlords were: Doyle accurately predicts the use to which patriotic rhetoric will be put by the emerging new rancher class, as it seeks to consolidate its selfish interests at the expense of the national economy. His prophecy uncannily anticipates Frantz Fanon's words, half a century later, in *The Wretched of the Earth*:

> . . . the landed proprietors will insist that the state should give them a hundred times more facilities and privileges than were enjoyed by the foreign settlers in former times. The exploitation of agricultural workers will be intensified and made legitimate. Using two or three slogans, these new colonists will demand an enormous amount of work from the agricultural labourers, in the name of the national effort of course. There will be no modernization of agriculture . . . the only efforts made to better things are due to the government . . . the landed bourgeoisie refuses to take the slightest risk . . . The enormous profits which it pockets, enormous if we take into account the national revenue, are never reinvested. The money-in-the-stocking mentality is dominant in the psychology of these landed proprietors . . .[13]

This is simply the theoretical version of what Larry Doyle phrases more colourfully in the play, when he foretells that his and Broadbent's syndicate "will use your patriotic blatherskite and balderdash to get parliamentary powers over you as cynically as it would bait a mousetrap with toasted cheese. It will plan, and organize, and find capital while you slave like bees for it".[14] Keegan foresees all this too, but without relish, telling the planners:

> . . . you will drive Haffigan to America very efficiently; you will find a use for Barney Doran's foul mouth and bullying temper by employing him to

slave-drive your labourers very efficiently; and [*low and bitter*] when at last this poor desolate countryside becomes a busy mint in which we shall all slave to make money for you, with our Polytechnic to teach us how to do it efficiently, and our library to fuddle the few imaginations your distilleries will spare, and our repaired Round Tower with admission sixpence, and refreshments and penny-in-the-slot mutoscopes to make it interesting, then no doubt your English and American shareholders will spend all the money we make for them very efficiently in shooting and hunting . . .[15]

It is, appropriately enough, left to Keegan to explain Broadbent's efficient victory: "let not the right side of your brain know what the left side doeth. I learnt at Oxford that this is the secret of the Englishman's power of making the best of both worlds".[16] By mastering the stereotype, by pretending to be a stage-fool, Broadbent has eaten up all the real fools, just as Larry predicted. Ireland has, on this occasion, been a profitable laboratory for another English experiment.

All of which raises a number of questions. Just how sincere were Broadbent's good intentions? Is he, in short, a conscious hypocrite or a woolly-minded liberal imperialist? His language in the play is couched in two tonalities, one sentimental and the other pragmatic, one idealistic and the other sinister, but both often deployed within a single sentence. He tells Larry Doyle, for instance, "Home Rule will work wonders *under English guidance*":[17] and then proceeds to offer a wholly cynical explanation: "We English must place our capacity for government at the service of nations less fortunately endowed; so as to allow them to develop in perfect freedom to the English level of self-government". It's not surprising that English audiences always assume that Broadbent's gun is only a paper-weight, while the Irish remain quite certain that it is loaded for potential use. It is possible, of course, to see Broadbent as one of nature's innocents, the sincere functionary who mistakes his own interest for the most selfless idealism: but the sheer sardonicism of some of his sentences would indicate that a shrewder brain is at work. Indeed, the opening stage directions warn that he can be "sometimes eager and credulous, sometimes shrewd and roguish".[18] Is he ever both at the same time? – as, for example, when he acquires Larry's former sweetheart Nora as a consummate political wife who will win him support among the Roscullen villagers of whom he says: "We must be thoroughly democratic and patronize everybody without distinction of class".[19] If that sounds, perhaps, like an unintended oxymoron, then the sentence which soon follows, concerning the canvassing of Keegan's vote, is all hypocrisy and guile: "What really flatters a man is that you think him worth flattering. Not that I would flatter any man . . . I'll just go and meet him".[20]

It would appear, therefore, that Broadbent is merely playing the stage Englishman in Ireland, the better to get the villagers off guard and into his pocket. Now and then, he lets his mask of joviality slip, as when he says that there are only two sorts in the world, the efficient and the inefficient, and that Matt Haffigan is worked out. To Keegan's protest at this ruthlessness, Larry Doyle says that Haffigan doesn't matter, at which point Broadbent replaces his mask of bonhomie by saying "O, it's hard on Haffigan".[21] When Keegan thereupon offers his devastating prophecy of what will happen to the landless labourers under the syndicate, Broadbent gives the hypocrite's tell-tale start of recognition. But is Keegan any less of a hypocrite? After all, he says at once that he may even vote for Broadbent and his plans.

Is Larry Doyle any better? He himself seems unsure as to whether his partner is a conscious or unconscious hypocrite. His accusation that Broadbent keeps conflicting ideas in sealed watertight compartments seems the sketch of a *conscious* rogue: but later he calls Broadbent a romantic duffer, who doesn't even realize when the Irish are mocking him. So he is not at all clear as to the nature of the man whom he knows best. Nonetheless, Larry is a rather impressive diagnostician with a keen analytic brain. At the level of instinct, however, Broadbent may be more assured, as when a sixth sense tells him that Larry's reluctance to return to Ireland may be connected with some unfinished business with a woman. Does Broadbent want Nora because he needs a political wife, or because he is genuinely moved by her Irish charm (as moved as Larry is by the "animated beefsteaks" whom he meets in London breadshops)? Or is Broadbent fascinated by Nora because he suspects, deep down, that Larry still loves her?

Larry remains a rather confusing guide on all these matters. The stage directions which introduce Nora describe her from the viewpoint of Larry in England. At the age of thirty-six, with a paltry income and no prospects, she is an eighteenth-century figure, a diluted version of the *aisling* heroine, a Cathleen ní Houlihan gone pallid and limp: "useless, sexless, an invalid without the excuse of a disease, an incarnation of everything in Ireland that drove him out".[22] Compared with Shaw's manly heroines, she seems vapid and weak; and non-existent compared with the Cathleen ní Houlihan, whom Yeats celebrated in an Abbey play of two years earlier. If she is Ireland, this woman has been awaiting the return of her lover, or the courtship of any man, for a long time. Yet no sooner does Larry set foot in Ireland than he is once again embroiled in all the old complexities of the courtship. He wants her, but something self-defeating in his temperament prevents him from having her. This is the Larry of whom his English partner has observed that he has no capacity for enjoyment and could never make any woman happy. In truth, the play seems to suggest that Larry Doyle cares more for Broadbent and owes more to him, than he cares for or owes to any Irish person:

> Don't you understand that I'm Irish, he's English. He wants you and he grabs you. I want you and I quarrel with you and have to go on wanting you.[23]

All this would seem to ratify the stereotype, of the ineffectual Celt, who shows a disinclination to submit to duty or (if Nora epitomizes Ireland) to the discipline of self-government, and who actually prefers to pass such disagreeable chores on to the more skilled English.

It would be possible to interpret the plot not only as a proof of English hypocrisy but also, more surprisingly, of Irish cunning. It can certainly be argued that it is the Irish who, at all key moments, are the true manipulators of the situation. They have a rooted disrespect for parliamentary democracy and don't wish to waste their money or their personnel on its empty rituals: and so it pleases their sense of irony to send an Englishman to represent them at so meaningless a convocation. All the better if he takes a local spinster with him, and reinvests some of his private means in the decaying village. Larry might even be seen as the arch-conspirator here – "allowing" his pal to win the woman and seat which he never really wanted anyway, and using Broadbent as the flak-catcher and front for an exploitative syndicate of which he himself is the evil genius. True enough, it is Broadbent who takes the brunt of Keegan's closing diatribe against industrial capitalism, while Doyle escapes relatively unscathed, even though he repeatedly uses the word "we" to describe the syndicate.

Whether the ultimate cynicism is imputed to Broadbent or to Doyle, the ending is pure Celticism, a ratification of the cliché of the efficient English administrator and the impractical Irish doomed by their complexity of mind to hopeless incompetence in the world of affairs. Both sides exemplify contradictory thinking, but the Englishman can keep the compartments of his thought separate in the manner of a professional specialist, while the Irish are victims of what Parnell once called "the cursed versatility of the Celt".

Such a surrender to the stereotype comes most strangely in a play which set itself to dismantle just that kind of thinking, and which has done so up to a point, poking bitter fun at the extent to which the Irish revival was really a farce got up for English tourists. That revivalist moment would, decades later, be described by Frantz Fanon as a classic ploy of the occupier, who decides to mummify and exhibit the colonial culture at just the moment when the natives have determined to modernize it. Shaw, in his essays, repeatedly warned English tourists that modern Ireland was "in full reaction against both servility and the stage Irishman", adding that so determined were the natives to resist English illusions of them that "it is a point of honour with the modern Irishman to have no sense of humour"[24] – but the play itself more despondently suggests that there will be no escape from mummification. Indeed, with his plans for golf clubs and polytechnic schools, the occupier can even cast this transformation of a native culture into tourist kitsch under the guise of modernization. Keegan concludes his bleak, almost Marxian diagnosis, with a demonstration that this "dream of efficiency" is no better than the futile dreaming derided by Larry Doyle early in the play. But then he, as we have seen, is coopted by Broadbent, who considers him a dead ringer for an Irish Ruskin. Clearly, Broadbent's greatest intellectual achievement is to have converted half the villagers into literary material.

Yet there is in Keegan's climactic speeches at least the makings of an alternative to the Anglo-Irish antithesis epitomized by Doyle and Broadbent. Keegan's dream is of a place or state of grace where such slot-rolling categories are transcended, a place where the state is the church because the church is the people, three in one and one in three, a utopia where work is play because play is life. His diagnosis is clearer than Doyle's: the Englishman is clever in his foolishness, the Irishman foolish in his cleverness. Liberation is possible only to those who surmount those categories and who reject that specialization of roles to be found wherever the left side of the brain doesn't know what the right side is doing. Shaw's repeated critiques of the professions – which he compared to prostitution in *Mrs. Warren's Profession* – are based on his conviction that the specialist is a mere barbarian and that only a fully integrated personality can restore a sane society. Keegan is a Blakean visionary who senses that, having lost contact with his feminine instincts, man has lost half his political wisdom and compassion: without these attributes, his own gifts are no longer a source of strength but a liability, since reason untouched by emotion tends to the vices of specialization and exploitation.

Again and again, Larry Doyle regrets the division of his Irish world into two halves: a world of brutal fact and unreal dream, the one never mitigating the other but both completely compartmentalized. However, he cannot move beyond this diagnosis. Alone among the characters on stage, Keegan can see that the perception of such a choice may itself be a product of the imperial mission. It was, after all, a contradiction within the English mind which led it to project inconsistent attributes onto the Irish, who were held to be at once dreamy and spiritual, scheming and sinister. Arnold, as has been shown, sought to combine Celtic dreaming and Saxon pragmatism in a single, renovated British personality – but the insistence that facts are always brutal and dreams invariably unreal is a very English mode of thought; and Shaw saw no reason why the Irish should accept it.

Many postcolonial writers have pursued in art a magic realism which reconciles poetry and fact in such a way that they become indistinguishable: and this, in the play, is Keegan's intent. He sees Ireland as holy ground, a blessed place where Utopia might yet be found, but he also fears that it may be turning into a little England. His loose, easygoing priesthood recalls the early Christian Ireland of wandering scholars, even as his three-in-one symbology recalls St. Patrick. Compared with all that richness, he finds the modern world a grim exercise in anglicization and gradgrindery:

> . . . a place where children are scourged and enslaved in the name of parental duty and education; where the weak in body are poisoned and mutilated in the name of healing, and the weak in character put to the horrible torture of imprisonment . . . It's a place where the hardest toil is a welcome refuge from the horror and tedium of pleasure, where charity and good works are done only for hire to ransom the souls of the spoiler and sybarite . . .[25]

– and the truly lost are those, like Broadbent and Doyle, who seem happy in such a hell. Keegan's mission is to save them, as Ireland must save England, not by repairing the flaws of an industrial civilization but by transcending it altogether. To Broadbent's promise that the tourists will bring money from England to Ireland, Keegan scoffs: "As they brought money from Ireland to England. Has that saved England from a poverty and degradation more horrible than we have ever dreamed of?"[26] In restoring Ireland, Keegan would hope to reinvent a better England for Broadbent to return to as well.

In the final analysis, however, for all his wonderful talk, Keegan is hard put to save himself. He must assume an antic disposition simply to survive as licensed jester and unofficial guru to the villagers: already, indeed, an Irish Ruskin. The price of his extensive knowledge and versatile intellect is incapacity. His diagnosis may be sharper than Doyle's and his vision more probing, but his plight is even more circumscribed. However bravely he may have tried to transcend the Celtic categories, his last state perfectly exemplifies the problem of one defeated by his very own superiority of spirit.

This was, of course, Shaw's problem too: his increasing tendency, after the turn of the century, to create in his plays a visionary figure whose insights, though always as practical as they were idealistic, were not negotiable in any currencies known to this world. The consequence is a repeated frustration among audiences at the apparent failure of his plays to match their devastating diagnoses with something approaching a workable prescription. Instead, they seem to veer off into inconclusive reverie and, in doing so, sometimes surrender to the already-discredited opening categories. So a play which begins as a plea for sexual freedom may end as a paean to monogamy; a call for a Superman may lapse into a programme for Emersonian self-help; a vindication of St. Joan may turn out to be a justification of her accusers; and a dismantling of the Anglo-Irish antithesis may conclude with an unexpected reassertion of its veracity.

It is no accident that the British Prime Minister Arthur Balfour should have attended *John Bull's Other Island* with cabinet colleagues on four separate occasions, or that King Edward VII should have broken his chair while laughing at the production. After all, the play gratified English vanity, by managing at once to criticize the old stereotype and at the same time to suggest that it was true in a deeper and subtler way than many suspected. English audiences not only found their ancient prejudices confirmed by a witty Irish playwright, but could leave the theatre with unexpected and sophisticated evidence in support of their ancient bias. It was all too fitting that Shaw should have described himself as a faithful servant of the English people. There is a real sense in which his own play is an artistic casualty of the vice of compartmentalization which he satirizes. The plot issues in an emphatic victory for the efficient and romantic Englishman, while all the subversive witticisms have been uttered by the cynical but inactive Irishman.

This was the selfsame dualism which Shaw detected in the plays of Wilde, each of which contains some scathing aphorisms at the expense of a classbound society, but whose power to disturb is disarmed by the reassuringly conventional nature of Wilde's plots. In such plots, the aristocratic society always seems to win out: in *The Importance of Being Earnest* Lady Bracknell can, finally, marry Gwendolen off to a young man of her own exalted class. Both Wilde and Shaw are ultimately English writers in the strict terms of Shaw's own definition of Englishness as a talent for keeping ideas separate in distinct zones. If the right side of the brain doesn't know what the left doeth, the plots of these plays are entirely at variance with the subversive one-liners and jokes. All of which is a measure of the artistic constraints on any radical dramatist who sought a career on the London stage at the time.

Shaw was, however, always able to justify his continuing residency in England. "I could have been a poet like Yeats and Synge", he boasted in the preface to *John Bull's Other Island*, "but I prided myself on thinking clearly and therefore could not stay . . . Whenever I took a problem, I always pursued it to its logical conclusion and inevitably it resolved itself into a comedy . . . England had conquered Ireland, so there was nothing for it but to come over and conquer England".[27] In casting himself as a faithful servant of his adopted country, Shaw did not mean to under-rate the subversive potential of all servant classes, that honourable Jeeves-like tradition of helping their masters out of the scrapes in which they have landed themselves. And not just the masters. Having studied Marx, Shaw knew that he was also honour-bound to emancipate the English proletariat, a group far more in need of leadership, he felt, than the Irish peasantry.

Although they numbered only one tenth of the population of Britain, the Irish held the balance of power in the House of Commons, whose business seemed dominated by Irish grievances and questions. Shaw, for his part, was perfectly convinced that Ireland was a far happier and freer country than England. He believed that Britain, too, had unresolved national questions: and Home Rule for England became one of his more lasting hobbies. With perfect consistency, however, he refused to take his hat off for the playing of the English national anthem until Ireland was recognized as a free state with its own house of parliament. He was terrified, nevertheless, that a separatist agitation might go the whole hog and completely sever the English connection. The Irish, through their political affiliation, wielded a considerable and benign influence over the English, but total separation would leave them with no hold at all, while the iron laws of economics would allow England to retain a great deal of power over Ireland without attendant responsibilities.

Shaw liked to joke that "when people ask me what *Sinn Féin* means, I say it is the Irish for *John Bull*".[28] He foresaw just how abjectly Irish nationalism would mimic its English model, and he feared that in that process the republican aspiration might die. That aspiration was to maximize national sovereignty, while cultivating beneficial links of trade and culture between peoples. "There are more republicans in England today than in Ireland", he wrote, "and a severance between them and the republicans of Ireland may or may not be expected on other grounds; but it is anti-republican".[29] Absolute independence was a delusion of the kind which had prevented the chauvinistic English from acknowledging their dependence on Ireland. It would be a disaster if Irish nationalists were to repeat this ancient English mistake. Shaw was absolute in his conviction of the need for a closer relationship, conducted on a voluntary basis, between the two island peoples.

ANGLO-IRELAND:
THE WOMAN'S PART

THE WOMAN'S PART

As offspring of Dublin's Protestant middle class, both Wilde and Shaw found it perfectly natural to seek a career in London which was, after all, the metropolitan centre of culture in the English-speaking world. Such a move was much less obvious for members of the Protestant aristocracy. England, by the final decades of the nineteenth century, was a very changed place, heavily industrialized and filled with a new élite, whose social standing derived more from money than from land. Many leaders of English society were now openly hostile to aristocrats: and even those who admired people of caste were by no means certain that the occupants of draughty, decaying mansions in windswept Irish landscapes really counted as "top drawer".

Ever since the time of Jonathan Swift, there had been a pressure on the Anglo-Irish to throw in their lot with the natives. Faced with an uncomprehending monarch and parliament, Swift had urged his compatriots, by way of surly revenge, to burn everything English except coal. Over the century and a half which followed, it became more and more clear that a strange reciprocity bound members of the ascendancy to those peasants with whom they shared the Irish predicament. Many decent landlords genuinely cared for their tenants and felt responsible for their fate: that care was often returned with a mixture of affection and awe. Others were negligent and some cruelly exploitative: but these attitudes served also to emphasize the kindness of the better sort. Ascendancy women, employing kitchen maids and domestic staff, often enjoyed rather developed relationships with a whole network of families in the wider community: they shared in the joy of christenings and weddings, the sadness at sickbeds and wakes. When the doom of the big houses was sealed by the Land Acts, Shaw was not the only commentator to wonder whether the lot of the landless labourer would prove happier under peasant proprietors than it had under paternalistic landlords. These fears were most often articulated by ascendancy women, among whom Edith Somerville, Violet Martin (whose pen-name was Martin Ross), and Augusta Gregory were the outstanding literary figures.

It was the new economic pressure which compelled both Somerville and Ross to turn to art for a living which the big house could no longer provide, but also for a fully comprehensive image of the crisis. Their profound Christian convictions led them to a tragic sense of the underlying injustice of their own privileged position, while their concern for family tradition led them to lament what seemed sadly like the end of the line. They preferred, however, to live out that process in Ireland than to seek refuge from it in an English villa. Perhaps at the back of minds well versed in Jane Austen's Mansfield Park *was a faint hope that, somehow or other, renewal might yet come from without.*

Augusta Gregory, for her part, was one of the first Irish aristocrats to make the link between the Irish case and the wider challenge posed by the anti-colonial world. At first she sympathized with distant rebels in Egypt and India, only later to make the scandalized discovery that the trouble-makers at her estate gates were hardly very different. That recognition led to her transformation from a colonial wife to an independent modern woman; and, in the course of that transformation, she emerged as a major artist.

Four

Somerville and Ross – Tragedies of Manners

Of all the major Irish writers, Edith Somerville and Martin Ross (whose real name was Violet Martin) are the most difficult to catch in the act of greatness. Some of their readers have struggled to reconcile the seemingly superficial nature of their subject-matter with the near absolute command of human experience evident in the success of their presentations. For decades, Irish Irelanders refused to read them at all, on the basis of a notorious review of *The Real Charlotte* which depicted its authors as finished *shoneens*, abject imitators of English ways. The fact that some of the sharpest satire in the novel is reserved for the absurd preconceptions of a visiting Englishwoman, Miss Evelyn Hope-Drummond, did not give such detractors pause. Nor did the stubborn choice of the authors to stay on and work in Ireland rather than marry and settle in England (as so many others were doing) cut any ice. "My family has eaten Irish food and shared Irish life for nearly three hundred years", wrote Edith Somerville, "and if that doesn't make me Irish I might as well say I was Scottish or Mormon or Pre-Diluvian!"[1]

Accused of creating stage-Irish rogues and buffoons for consumption in England, Somerville and Ross did something far more subtle – "they sold their intimate knowledge of Ireland in order to remain living in it".[2] Like most of their class, they had little love for England, feeling quite betrayed by its leaders. So far were they from stage Irishry that they noted with dismay the willingness of Irish country people to play Paddy or Biddy for the amusement of their social superiors. Charlotte Mullen is a dire example of the rising new breed:

> "Well, your ladyship", she said, in the bluff, hearty voice which she felt accorded best with the theory of herself that she had built up in Lady Dysart's mind, "I'll head a forlorn hope to the bottom of the lake for you, and welcome; but for the honour of the house, you might give me a cup o'tay first!"

Charlotte had many tones of voice, according with the many facets of her character, and when she wished to be playful she affected a vigorous brogue, not perhaps being aware that her own accent scarcely admitted of being strengthened.

This refinement of humour was probably wasted on Lady Dysart.[3]

The failure of this ploy anticipates the self-defeating nature of Charlotte Mullen's more grandiose plots in the book, illustrating just how alert Somerville and Ross were to the small details by which people give themselves and their destinies away. But it also proves just how deep was their understanding of rural Irish society, so deep, indeed, that it raised in them the severest reservations about the representation of the peasantry in the dramas of the Abbey Theatre. Courted by Lady Gregory to write a play for it, Violet Martin was given a sample copy of Synge's *The Well of the Saints* for her comments. She was not impressed and wrote a bracing and blunt reply:

> This is cast in a form so simple as to be at times too simple as far as mere reading goes. I suppose the dialect is of the nature of a literal translation of Irish, but it seems to me to lack fire and spontaneity – you know, and no one better, what the power of repartee and argument is among such as these. It is inimitable in my opinion, I mean that no one who is not one of them themselves can invent it – and it is so much a part of themselves that to present them without it makes an artificial and unreal picture . . .[4]

Edith Somerville also refused to be recruited to the movement, finding its plays a strange mix of Gaelic saga and modern French situations. Violet Martin was beguiled so far as to visit Coole Park, where she met W. B. Yeats: later, she sent her partner a wonderfully savage account of the outing on which she permitted him to carve her initials on the famous tree:

> WBY did the carving, I smoked, and high literary conversation raged and the cigarette went out and I couldn't make the matches light, and he held the little dingy lappets of his coat out and I lighted the match in his bosom. No one was there, and I trust no one saw, as it must have looked very funny.[5]

The Abbey directors said that they wanted a "Shoneen play": "I suppose that means middle class vulgarity", wrote a mordant Martin to her partner.

As always, Yeats's instincts were remarkably keen. Violet Martin did know almost as much about the middle class of Dublin as she did about the Anglo-Irish gentry in their country houses. When her brother Robert had abandoned the family seat at Ross as unviable in 1872, she had gone with her mother to live on Dublin's northside, a place evoked in all its scrupulous meanness in the opening pages of *The Real Charlotte*. The experience, though a social humiliation, was priceless to the artist. "She learned much of that middle sphere of human existence that has practically no normal points of contact with any other class, either above or below it",[6] recalled Somerville, who marvelled at how well her partner retained her poise and nobility of bearing. The cousins' portrayal of the northside is bleak in the extreme, catching nothing of its vivacity or scruffy charm (these would await Joyce and O'Casey), but it is bleak for a simple enough reason: the petty gradations of snobbery which characterized shabby-genteel city life were quite lacking in the countryside, where class differences existed on a much grander scale, but were negotiated by people in a mode of mutual courtesy. Or at least, thought the cousins, those small snobberies had been quite lacking until the confounded English liberals had contrived to unleash the forces which would destroy the old feudalism in Ireland.

The Martins of Galway had been among the most benign of landlords, bringing their estate to the verge of ruin by the generosity with which they provided for starving tenants during the famines of the 1840s; but in 1872, that *annus horribilis* in the family history, the old reciprocity was broken and the tenants, ungrateful and energized, voted for the Home Rule candidate against Violet's father. He died a broken man: "It was not the political defeat, severe as that was; it was the personal wound and it was incurable". Martin herself returned to Ross, years later, with her mother, in hopes of reopening the house: and she used her earnings as a writer to that end. But the old relationships would never be restored.

The resident magistrates, of whom the pair wrote in a mode of hilarious comedy, were henceforth as likely to be shot by defiant rebels as hoodwinked by fundamentally loyal but roguish retainers. Decades earlier, Maria Edgeworth in *Castle Rackrent* had imagined a trusting and easy commerce between landlord and tenant which, by the time she wrote the book in the aftermath of the Act of Union, was strictly historical; and so it was for the Irish cousins. An increasingly disconsolate Martin wrote to Somerville in 1894, marvelling at the popularity of Aylmer Somerville as master of the Rosscarbery hunt:

I really don't see or hear of any other part of Ireland where the farmers are so friendly and the rebel paper will back up the gentlemen in improvements and in sport. I see that one day the Skibbereen district will be a fifth province in Ireland – refusing to receive Home Rule, and governed by Aylmer, under a special warrant from the Queen.[7]

It was, of course, a fantasy. Even the more nationally-minded Somerville, who as a child had nursed a sneaking regard for Fenian rebels, could write with real bitterness of how "Parnell and his wolf-pack were out for blood, and the English government flung them, bit by bit, the property of the only men in Ireland who, faithful to the pitch of folly, had supported it since the days of the Union".

The bright, sparkling surfaces and fluent narrative method cannot conceal the dark undertow of *The Real Charlotte*, their greatest novel, published in 1894: while the form is jaunty with the ironies of good social comedy, the content is a tragic tale of the collapse of big house culture. This is what gives their writing its power to haunt the mind in ways that seem out of all proportion to its easy, middlebrow charm, for even as the style sings of hope the message is despair. The hope, always fragile, lay in the prospect that the declining aristocratic family of Bruff House would receive an injection of vitality in the form of Francie Fitzpatrick, a vivacious but uncultured young woman for whom the effête heir, Christopher Dysart, finally conceives a fondness. Though the traditional comic conclusion in a happy and sensible marriage is teasingly dangled before the reader, it is not to be.

Francie will commute between the squalor of lower-middle-class Dublin and the elegance of Bruff, much as Fanny Price commutes between her disorderly family home in Portsmouth and the splendour of Mansfield Park: but a Jane Austen-style ending is not possible, for Francie is too high-spirited to be amenable to Christopher's pallid pleas. The big house will not be renewed, as Charlotte Mullen, Francie's plotting cousin, had planned: instead of a purposeful fusion of classes, there is a noisy and pointless collision. Everyone's designs are thwarted, most of all those of the reader, whose sympathies are aroused and subsequently defeated by almost all the characters. The comic ending promised is delivered, with interesting reservations – Francie weds the shady but besotted land-agent Roddy Lambert – only to be taken away at the latest possible juncture and turned into absurdist terror, when the Dubliner falls fatally from her horse.

At this very moment, Charlotte Mullen, who has loved Roddy for two decades, is finally free to claim him, but before the news comes she avenges herself on him by revealing her own part in the exposure of his financial corruption to the Dysarts. Even she, the master-plotter all through, fails in the end to save either Bruff House or herself, and in her failure may be read the defeat of an entire society. The new peasant proprietors are depicted in *The Real Charlotte* as having nothing of lasting value to contribute, beyond a greedy materialism: and so Somerville and Ross are driven to dismiss their *dramatis personae* at the close with an amused but exasperated shrug. Their final wrench from desperate hilarity to blank terror has been criticized as melodramatic, but it perfectly captures the psychological dynamic of Anglo-Ireland in the nineteenth century, of a people who swung between disintegration and intermittent comedy. If the mere Irish often struck a happy-go-lucky pose in the face of dire poverty, the gentry found that it had no inner resources of a similar kind. In Charles Lever's novel *Tom Burke of Ours*, Darby-the-Blast shrewdly noted the reason why a whimsical mood or a vivid phrase could be an asset in dealing with the landowners:

> The quality has ne'er a bit of fun in them at all, but does be always coming to us to make them laugh.[8]

There is a real sense in which the literature of the Irish revival arose out of the ironies of such a master-servant relationship. Francie Fitzpatrick is simply the final consummation of this tradition, whereby an exhausted upper-class seeks not just humour, but also sexual release, in a vibrant under-class.

That such redemption might not only be possible but also reciprocal is made very clear early on, when Christopher saves Francie from drowning in the lake. She brings out in his personality something of the lost hero, convincing him in the process that he may yet confront "the mysteries of life into which he had thought himself too cheap and shallow to enter".[9] Equally, she learned at Bruff a sense of the value of social decorum and "some vision of the higher things". The suggestion is that Francie has real potential, beneath her rather gaudy surface, and that it takes a true lover to see it: "he had found out subtle depths of sweetness and sympathy that were, in their responsiveness, equivalent to intellect".[10] There is also, inevitably, the possibility that Christopher is fooling himself, a possibility to which he, as a natural sceptic, remains open. Yet the moments of shared intensity between the pair are as near as he comes to grace.

Before their meeting, his personality has already set in a pattern of self-negation: we meet him as a man without a role, happy to retrieve a

ball at a tennis-party, "an occupation that demanded neither interest
nor conversation". Though twenty-seven years of age, he is neither
aggressive enough to be a soldier, nor sporting enough for a gentleman,
being "'between the sizes', as shopmen say of gloves".[11] A dandy
without a court, he is immobilized by his very intelligence:

> He had the saving, or perhaps fatal power of seeing his own handiwork
> with as unflattering an eye as he saw other people's. He had no confidence
> in anything about himself except his critical ability, and as he did not satisfy
> that, his tentative essays in painting died an early death. It was the same
> with everything else. His fastidious dislike of doing a thing indifferently was
> probably a form of conceit: it brought about in him a kind of deadlock.[12]

The result is that, when Francie refuses his offer of marriage, he is easily
repulsed and does not press his suit. The servants at Bruff are amused at
her non-existent table-manners, but Gorman the butler, with a shrewd
instinct for the survival of his employers, "gave it as his opinion that
Miss Fitzpatrick was as fine a girl as you'll meet between this and
Dublin, and if he was Mr. Christopher, he'd prefer her to Miss Hope-
Drummond, even though the latter might be hung down with dia-
monds".[12] Francie has not only the glamour of youth but an energy
that brooks no compromise: and in this, at least, she is superior to the
Dysarts. Lacking follow-through, Christopher concludes that he is as
ineffectual in love as in other arts: he seems saddened by the fact that he
is saddened so little at its failure, and so he takes up another inconsequential diplomatic posting.

One of Christopher's first admissions in the book is that he does not
understand the recent Land Acts: neither does Roddy Lambert, his
agent, but he at least exploits the accompanying confusion in order to
embezzle his master's funds. Like George Eliot's Middlemarchers on the
eve of the Reform Bill, the citizens of Lismoyle show scant interest in
the politics of the outside world: this is more a judgement on them
than on the body politic. Charlotte Mullen is a type of the new
gombeen class, living on usurious earnings and on unscrupulous profit-
eering, but Somerville and Ross rather unusually make their gombeen-
woman a Protestant (perhaps to avoid accusations of sectarian bias).
With no representative of the rising Catholic middle class in the novel,
Somerville and Ross are enabled to imply, with a touch of ascendancy
arrogance, that the decline of Anglo-Ireland had nothing to do with
any social forces outside its own.

The problem of the Dysarts is that of so many of the big house families in the novels of Jane Austen: a stasis that amounts to torpor. Their denizens' every gesture seems self-cancelling, as when the mother of the house plants chickweeds in the mistaken belief that they are asters. (The visiting Englishwoman is, of course, amazed that such a lady should be doing the gardener's work at all.) Against that torpor, the impulse-ridden Francie has a certain jaunty nobility, the nobility of a beautiful wild thing rather than that of the domesticated and tamed. Somerville and Ross debated long the advisability of killing her off at the end: "It felt like killing a wild bird that had trusted itself to you. We have often been reviled for that, as for many other incidents in *The Real Charlotte*, but I think we were right".[14] Edith Somerville's mother was one of the many readers who could find no nobility, only vulgarity, in Francie. "She deserved to break her neck for her vulgarity", she wrote rather harshly, "the girls had to kill her to get the whole set of them out of the awful muddle they had got into".[15] "All here loathe Charlotte", she intoned, protesting against the general nastiness of the characters and the weakness of Christopher.

Like many early reviewers, Mrs. Somerville admired the brilliant writing and cordially despised the "disagreeable characters", ignoring the fact that the novel is at its best in recording the plight of females in a small-town culture, the impossibility of their being away for long from disagreeable people. Even in the writing of it, Somerville and Ross were repeatedly chided for their dereliction of social duty on tennis-court and lake: the former complained that her suitor Herbert Greene had a persistent habit of ignoring the fact that she had work to do.[16] A century earlier, Jane Austen had complained that women had "scarce a half-hour they can call their own": and Edith Somerville's reports to her partner suggest that in the interim little had changed:

> To attempt anything serious or demanding steady work is just simply impossible here, and I feel sickened of even trying – we are all so tied together – whatever is done must be done by everyone in the whole place and as the majority prefer wasting their time that is the prevalent amusement.[17]

Their problem was that of their characters: to learn how to keep on terms with an often disagreeable social world without too great a dishonesty to themselves. Their satire was a classic instance of Austen-esque "regulated hatred":[18] they sought by it to find a mode of existence within society for critical attitudes which, if taken any further, might destroy it altogether. As a duo they could form a sort of alternative society, offering one another mutual protection and support: only an *individual* as steely as Austen could hold out against the mindless sociable consensus. Edith Somerville saw in her mother's misreading of her greatest novel incontrovertible evidence of the collapse of cultural standards in Anglo-Ireland. "It shows a failure of understanding that is awful in the light it sheds on the gulf between our and their mental standpoints", she confided to Martin: "My feeling is that *any* character is interesting if treated realistically. They care for nothing but belted earls or romantic peasants".[19] Again, the contempt for conventional taste is Austenesque, recalling that artist's determination to create a heroine "whom nobody will like very much". Francie Fitzpatrick is no Emma Woodhouse, but she shares some of her qualities of self-deception, impulsiveness and, at times, heedlessness. Of her Violet Martin said, "I think she ought to be in some way striking or in some way typical of her type, but not necessarily with leanings towards perfection".[20]

For all her flaws, Francie is far more charming than Mrs. Somerville allowed, and that charm is repeatedly heightened by contrast with her cousin. Where Francie comes across as insouciant and guileless, Charlotte appears as painfully manipulative; the former is all feminine vivaciousness, while the latter, even if she is blessed with a colourful use of language and a taste for advanced novels, tends to employ her intellect mainly to sardonic effect. Though named for Charlotte, the book begins and ends with the Francie who fails hopelessly to read her cousin's real motives. "The central struggle of the novel", in the words of one commentator, "is a struggle in which Francie scarcely knows she is engaged".[21] The narrative cannot, therefore, be continuously centred in her consciousness, if only because she has so little inner life to report: but what fascinates in *The Real Charlotte* is the author's elegant refusal to privilege any one consciousness at all. If Francie's is too rudimentary for constant interest, Charlotte's is too malign for ongoing empathy, Christopher's too tentative in its movements, Roddy's too self-caressing; and Hawkins (for whom Francie falls) appears to have no spiritual life at all. The result is a decentred narrative, in the course of which even household animals – cats, dogs, cockatoos – have fleeting moments of dramatized awareness.

The social world of Lismoyle is the more fully rendered in consequence: we see the characters not only as they see themselves, but through all the fluctuations of public opinion. Because Francie can move so easily from place to place, or from one social setting to another, the reader builds up something approaching a total portrait of a society, observing the amusing differences between one code and another, as she moves through its different layers. The indeterminate status of Charlotte Mullen, equally, allows her to speak on self-confident terms with the lady of the manor or, conversely, employ the Irish language to intimidate her tailor, Danny Lydon, or her powers of English to frighten the washerwomen tenants of her cottages. The filth of these cottages she sees more as a rebuke to the occupants than to herself: it is clear that Somerville and Ross, raised on the notion of responsible landlordry, would not share the view. They have the moral courage in such a scene to raise problems for which they have no ready answer. *The Real Charlotte* thus becomes one of the very rare Irish narratives which is actually a novel in the comedy-of-manners mode, calibrating itself to the layers of a fairly complex (if restricted) society.

Intending to criticize a society which they yet wished to remain within, Somerville and Ross chose to express their ultimate values by technique, with irony as a prevailing narrative point of view. Like other novels of manners, this is designed not just to be read but re-read, and its art is a strategy of preparations. The authors have an overall design in mind; the characters may be seen to fight it as it slowly envelops them; but in the end that design wins out and is shown to have been unavoidable. Every seemingly casual conversation or minor epiphany points forward as well as back, gaining resonance and meaning. When Roddy Lambert uses too much topsail on his boat, thereby almost drowning himself and his crew, something permanent has been implied about the self-destructive showiness of a man living well beyond his means: and so we are not surprised, hundreds of pages later, when his new wife proves also unequal to her challenges, "like a little boat staggering under more sail than she can carry".[22] The novel begins with a moment when Roddy Lambert saved Francie from falling from a bolting horse-and-cart; it progresses to a scene in which he warns her that "someday you'll be breaking your neck"[23] and with warnings that Francie is no great shakes as a rider; it plays tragic variations on her early reluctance to have *him* for rescuer ("Botheration to him! Why couldn't he have been somebody else?"); and it ends with her terrible and final fall. This patterning, as subtle as it is pervasive, suggests a controlling intelligence which is not simply sceptical but also definitive of social value, and an intelligence, moreover, which is embodied in the overall design. Amidst all the off-key notes struck repeatedly by most of the characters, the authors now and then strike a clear and singular sound, against which all others are heard as wanting. This is what lifted their art above the provincial guffawing of which they were sometimes accused, for as C. S. Lewis has written: "Where there is no norm, nothing can be ridiculous, except for a brief moment of unbalanced provincialism in which we may laugh at the merely unfamiliar. Unless there is something about which the author is never ironical, there can be no true irony in the work".[24]

Much of the irony is at Charlotte Mullen's expense. Though she is the character left to pick up what pieces remain at the end, she is also a classic study of "the banality of evil". In another world, and blessed with better looks, she might have been a cigar-smoking Emma Bovary, as well as the reader of French fiction which she is: but in this one, her attempt to import her orphaned cousin to reanimate a big house proves wholly abortive. Indeed, when Francie quite coolly refuses the offer of marriage from Christopher Dysart, for which Charlotte so long had plotted, it is as if the Heathcliffean element in the story passes from Francie (in whom it was benign) to Charlotte (in whom it festers). Thwarted in her desire for Roddy Lambert by Francie's marriage to him, she is left with nothing to pursue but her revenge, and so "the real Charlotte's will and the terror of her personality"[25] are finally allowed to show through. That personality has always been "amphibious", in the sense that the surface bubbles betrayed the real creature beneath, whom few in Lismoyle had suspected of having anything to conceal: and the ease with which she effects this deception suggests that her inventors were, to some extent, gleefully complicit in her contempt for a society so easily misled. Yet, in the final analysis, even her attempts at vengeance peter out into triteness and insignificance, as when she "looses" the new Mrs. Lambert (in the absence of her husband) to the predatory Hawkins.

If *The Real Charlotte* dismisses its characters with a shrug that is more exasperated than amused, that is only because the writers have been unable to imagine anyone surviving long in this society with an intelligence similar to their own. In Lismoyle provincialism and ridicule remain the order of the day, and this cannot but disappoint in a book which sought to ask the question: who shall inherit Ireland? The answer appears to be: nobody in particular, except for a few, random profiteers, and certainly not the Francie Fitzpatricks. At the closing scene, the servant Norry carries the terrible news of her fall to the now hopelessly-divided Charlotte and Roddy:

Neither Charlotte nor Lambert heard clearly what she said, but the shape-less terror of calamity came about them like a vapour and blanched the hatred in their faces. In a moment they were together at the window, and at the same instant Norry burst out into the yard, with outflung arms and grey hair streaming. As she saw Lambert, her strength seemed to go from her. She staggered back, and, catching at the door for support, turned from him and hid her face in her cloak.[26]

This is an ominous image of a landless class left rudderless in a new Ireland, whose putative inheritors are quite unequal to the challenges with which they have confronted themselves. Yet – and this is strange – at various moments in the unfolding of the tale, it is such persons who act as a choric voice within the plot for the authors' overall design.

Julia Duffy, facing ruin and appearing quite drunk to Christopher and Francie, can nonetheless encapsulate the entire second half of the novel in her ranting complaints:

Where's Charlotte Mullen, till I tell her to her face that I know her plots and her thricks? 'Tis to say that to her I came here, and to tell her 'twas she lent money to Peter Joyce that was grazing my farm, and refused it to him secondly, the way he'd go bankrupt on me, and she's to have my farm and my house that my grandfather built, thinking to even herself with the rest of the gentry . . .[27]

That Miss Duffy should be at once a landless peasant and ruined aristocrat increases the suspicion that Somerville and Ross implied more here than they cared to say. In the fate of a demoralized peasantry, hiding its terrified face in its cloak, they read the failure and the destiny of their own class. Near the very end, another rudderless old retainer, Billy Grainy, repeats the warning first given to Francie by Julia Duffy: "Ah-ha! go home to himself and owld Charlotte, though it's little thim regards you".[28] Miss Duffy had earlier mocked Francie: "Lady Dysart of Bruff, one of these days, I suppose . . . That's what Miss Charlotte Mullen has laid out for ye . . .",[29] followed by a derisory laugh. Second time around, in the lamentations of Billy Grainy, Francie intuits some sense of her fate in the faces of peasants at a passing funeral. "The faces in the carts were all turned upon her, and she felt as if she were enduring, in a dream, the eyes of an implacable tribunal".[30] A moment later the keen has broken out and she is dead. Somerville and Ross, in that gesture, implicitly concede that theirs has been an unconscionably jaunty book about a hopeless situation.

The cousins' concern about the fate of women in society led them to a strict investigation of some of its most persistent codes: and they are unsparing in the attitude which they adopt towards those "turkey hens" among their female characters, who abjectly defer to husbandly ways. The first Mrs. Lambert is slaughtered thus casually in a passing parenthesis, for the crime of uttering the words "Mr. Lambert" in conversation:

> Mrs. Lambert belonged to that large class of women who are always particular to speak of their husbands by the full style and title.[31]

This woman, who will later mistake a Shakespearian quotation for a strange term in cookery, dies an early death; and it is not altogether clear that the authors dissent from Charlotte's accounting of her as "that contemptible, whining creature".[32] Indeed, Charlotte, precisely because as an unmarried forty-year-old she lives at a certain angle to Lismoyle society, becomes in the hands of Somerville and Ross an invaluable instrument for social satire, more often vehicle than target:

> Possibly, also, the fact that she had no children placed her at a disadvantage with the matrons of Lismoyle, all of whom could have spoken fearlessly with their enemies in the gate; it deprived conversation with her of the antiphonal quality, when mother answers unto mother of vaccination and teething-rash, and the sins of the nursery-maids are visited upon the company generally.[33]

None of the main characters in *The Real Charlotte* enjoys a fulfilled family life: and children play a far less important part than animals in the narrative. It would be naïve to deduce that the authors were anti-family propagandists: after all, they both spent a large portion of their earnings in the defence of ancestral family seats. Edith Somerville had been in love with a charming but penniless young engineer named Hewitt Poole: his poverty put marriage out of the question, and this devastating experience may have caused her "to develop her own resources and to support herself financially".[34] She tended, thereafter, to speak affectionately of her books as her children, and to seek fulfilment of her nurturing impulses in art. In the process, she became a type of the New Woman of the Nineties. Of her friendship with Violet Martin she would later write:

> The outstanding fact, as it seems to me, among women who live by their brains, is friendship. A profound friendship that extends through every phase and aspect of life, intellectual, social, pecuniary. Anyone who has experience of the life of independent and artistic women knows this.[35]

She became, in time, President of the Munster Women's Franchise League. The ways in which the police abused and manhandled work-ing-class suffragists convinced her that it was the duty of aristocratic women to put their bodies on the line at demonstrations. In notes for speeches given across Munster, she asserted that the taxation of women who earned money and upheld the law without reciprocal political representation was a scandal. She was critical not of the family institu-tion as such, so much as of the manner in which middle-class men, themselves active in the community through their professional work, nonetheless sought to isolate and maroon women in the home. Mock-ing the cultural corollary of this tendency, she found the women featured in the writings of Rossetti, Thackeray and Trollope quite unbelievable: less flesh-and-blood females than women as men would have them to be. Such figures in life were to be distinguished from servants, she somewhat snobbishly suggested, only by the fact that they did not wear a cap and apron.

Within the movement for women's suffrage, Edith Somerville came to know colleagues who were also ardent Irish nationalists: after the death of her partner, who was a unionist, she appears to have moved closer to the separatist cause. National self-determination was the logical political corollary of the doctrine of Protestant self-election, but the movement for independence, far from engaging the energies of many rural Protestants, coincided rather with the enfeeblement of the reform churches in much of Ireland. The authors of *The Real Charlotte* had foreseen as much. There they recorded the collapse of Irish Pro-testantism into social decorum (viewed through Christopher Dysart's sardonic eye as he sat to pray in Lismoyle church):

> There was nothing suggestive of ethereal devotion about Pamela's neigh-bours. Miss Mullen's heaving shoulders and extended jaw spoke of nothing but her determination to outscream everyone else. Miss Hope-Drummond and the curate, on the bench in front of him, were singing primly out of the same hymn-book, the curate obviously frightened. The Misses Beattie were furtively eyeing Miss Hope-Drummond's costume; Miss Kathleen Baker was openly eyeing the curate.[36]

Thus the situation in gentry Cork. In lower middle-class Dublin things were no better, for it was a city whose parents sent their children to Sunday school so that they themselves might be free to snooze untroubled and unmolested after an ample lunch. A great point is made of the fact that, although Francie Fitzpatrick is herself a Sunday-school teacher, her religion is neither a social nor a spiritual reserve, when her time of suffering comes:

> . . . her mind was too young and shapeless for anything but a healthy, negligent belief in what she had been taught, and it did not enter her head to use religion as a last resource, when everything else had turned out a failure. She regarded it with respect, and believed that most people grew good when they grew old, and the sense passed over her with a vaguely pleasing effect of music and light.[37]

These lines could only have been written by women who understood the full force of Oscar Wilde's jibes that to be an Irish Protestant was to have no religion at all, but who in their own lives, by their professions and by their actions, indicated that they would have wished the situation otherwise.

Five

Lady Gregory and the Empire Boys

From the beginning, Augusta Persse's experience of life among the aristocracy was negative. It began at midnight on 14 March 1852, when her exhausted mother laid the newborn child to one side and tried to reconcile herself to the fact that the new arrival was not a boy. Neglected and forgotten, the baby almost choked. Her mother coolly remarked that she "would have been sorry for such a loss, because the other children would have been disappointed at not having a new baby to play with".[1] The father of the household was scarcely less monstrous: he believed in the Protestant doctrine of "election" and, having convinced himself that he would be among the saved, gave free rein to self-indulgence. The observant young Augusta was quick to notice the implications for Victorian womanhood: her father was able to control her mother, "treating her as a spoiled child, doing as he liked in great things, giving her a dress or paying her compliments to pacify her".[2]

Like many another child of the nineteenth century, Augusta turned from these flawed exemplars to a more reliable set of parents, choosing nature for her mother and God for her father. Most of all, however, she began to read the songs of those Young Ireland poets who, a generation earlier, had rejected their Anglo-Irish lineage and thrown in their lot with the common people. As her biographer records it: "The literature of Young Ireland, like the literature of most subject peoples, is an attempt to make up for the huge injury of having had, in a national sense, bad parents".[3] Rewarded with sixpences for her proficiency in memorizing the Protestant bible, the child secretly spent the cash on rebel songbooks. These gestures were hardly, at this stage, political: rather they were a healthy defiance of a parental regime which banned dancing lessons and performances of *Cinderella*, because "you can't tell where it might lead to".[4]

Equally predictable was an adolescent crisis during which the high-spirited girl was filled with scruples and began to fear that her defiance would leave her among the damned: now the pocket-money was spent on helping the poor and the ill. So the patterns of her personality were set in the form of a strong woman whose self-sufficiency was mitigated by a social idealism. When George Moore eventually met her, he found himself imagining Augusta "without a mother, or father, or sisters, or brothers, *sans attaché*".[5] It was an astute description of a woman who fathered and mothered herself. In the decades to come, her closest collaborator, W. B. Yeats, would respond warmly to her androgynous style, singling out her "masculine imagination" for particular praise. This conceit pleased him, since it confirmed his theory that the Irish were a feminine race with masculine imaginations, and the English a masculine race with feminine imaginations.

It was not completely surprising, in such a context, that her first passionate affair should have been with Wilfrid Scawen Blunt, who also admired her "masculine intellect".[6] She met him in Egypt in the winter of 1881: by then, she was safely married in the Victorian fashion to a much older man, Sir William Gregory, a former governor of Ceylon and now a landlord at Coole. Their first child, Robert, had been born in the summer of that year, and Sir William, for all his gentle ways, had not proved the most supportive of husbands: during the difficult pregnancy, he spent a great deal of time in London, fussing over his own health while his young wife was seriously ill. Even after the birth, he made it clear that the boy was not going to spoil the couple's travel plans and "privately voiced the wish that the child be shut up at least until the age of seven".[7] By the time the couple reached Cairo, Lady Gregory was pining for her baby and ready to console herself with a little romance.

Blunt was a horseman, a poet, and an uncommonly dashing woman-izer: an English Tory landlord by background and conviction, he was none the less a supporter of independence for the colonies. Meeting him at Shepheard's Hotel in Cairo, Lady Gregory "first felt the real excitement of politics" and "tumbled into a revolution".[8] The Gregorys had arrived in November, shortly after the Revolt of the Colonels led by Arabi Bey. These men sought not only a constitutional bill of rights and an enquiry into the grievances within the army, but also a measure of Egyptian home rule. Arabi was one of the peasant *fellaheen* who had risen, by personal merit and magnetism, through the ranks. His shrewd leadership had helped to foil an attempt on the part of the authorities to kidnap him and his sympathizing generals. Summoned to the Khedive's palace, he simply told his soldiers, "if we are not back at sunset, come for us" – and they did. No accusation had been made against him, but he had been described as "a man with ideas" better removed from the centre of action. Fascinated by the story, the Gregorys went to see him: "Arabi did not deny that much good had been done by foreign officials, but he thought it unfair that his countrymen were kept out of any important office".[9]

Sir William wrote eloquent letters to *The Times* in defence of Arabi and of the Egyptian cause. So did Blunt, who went so far as to buy a compound in Heliopolis, at which he and his wife pitched a tent, burned incense, ate nougat, and put on Bedouin costume in which to receive visiting sheikhs. Arabi, amazed at the speed with which Blunt could go native, began to wonder whether he might not be a British spy: but he need not have worried. The Blunts had already convinced themselves that "Arabi was right, that it would lead to the Turks, as well as the Christians, being turned out from the control of Egypt. And beyond that they had the vision of an Arab Caliphate, an independent Arab race".[10]

They must have made a strange quartet, the Blunts and the Gregorys, as they moved among the close-knit British community in Cairo. Some of its members were not slow to point to the anomaly in their position, as landlords in Britain and Ireland calling none the less for the abolition of similar privilege in Egypt. One colonial official, a Galwayman named Gerald Fitzgerald, "would sometimes threaten to come in return and wave the green Land League flag at the gates of Coole".[11] Sir William, notwithstanding his concern for the Arab underdog, was not above removing two sculpted heads, of Pan and Serapis, from the treasure-trove at Karnak, doubtless at a knockdown price.

Back in England the authorities favoured intervention, to clip Arabi's wings. Blunt grew philosophical, predicting "bloody war" but adding that "liberty was never gained without blood". It was hard, however, to whip up much public interest in the case: all the talk was of Ireland, where the Invincibles had so recently killed Chief Secretary Burke and Under-Secretary Cavendish. Not for the first time would Ireland distract Westminster statesmen from equally pressing business in farther-flung places. As for the generality of politicians, they were bored by all such questions and more exercised by domestic issues. "But what do you think of the Hares and Rabbits Bill?" asked one of a returned Lady Gregory: "That is a really important question".[12] At the Queen's annual garden party on 13 July, the company heard that Alexandria had indeed been bombed by their forces: ignobly, Blunt suspected that this was why Victoria was "beaming".

The British propaganda machine began its predictable campaign to discredit Arabi, with fantastic accounts of the opulence in which he and his family lived. As British troops advanced in the summer of 1882 on Arabi's forces, Lady Gregory wrote up an account of a visit she and Lady Blunt had made on Arabi's wife and children, stressing the modesty of their quarters, their generosity to visitors, and the dignified warmth of their manners. She stayed with Blunt in Sussex and together the pair talked treason. He begged her to issue "Arabi and His Household" forthwith. Lady Gregory's first published work appeared in *The Times* on 23 September 1882 under her own name, though, inevitably, some unworthy souls suspected her husband's authorship. The underlying psychological tactic would prove of service in years to come and to more than Lady Gregory: "A lady may say what she likes, but a man is called unpatriotic who ventures to say a word that is good of the man England is determined to crush".[13] Chenery, editor of *The Times*, could not pay her for the work, but proved sympathetic to Arabi. Why then, she asked, did he continue to print hostile reports from his correspondent in Cairo calling for Arabi's punishment? "Because of the influence of the European bondholders over *The Times*", he confessed. "Don't tell that to Blunt", joked her husband, "or he'll have sandwich-men walking with it down Piccadilly tomorrow!"[14]

Tel-el-Kebir duly fell to the English, and then Cairo itself. Arabi was captured and put on trial. Gladstone, distracted by Ireland, knew little of Egypt and foolishly left the formulation of policy to Foreign Office administrators. At his own expense, Blunt sent lawyers to Egypt, but couldn't bear to go back to a place where all his friends were either in jail or in hiding. "As to Cairo, what I cared most for in it is gone beyond recovery", he said: "Egypt may get a certain share of financial ease, but she will not get liberty, at least not in our time, and the bloodless revolution, so nearly brought about, has been drowned in blood".[15] Arabi disappointed Blunt (though saving him a small fortune in cash) by pleading guilty and being banished to Ceylon, where Sir William Gregory did much to ease his condition.

As for Lady Gregory, the whole experience did a number of things. It launched her as a writer, and it opened her mind to the powers of cultural nationalism, which would blossom years later in her work for Ireland. It also left her with an abiding distrust of politicians and political methods:

> That was the end of my essay in politics, for though Ireland is always with me, and I first feared and then became reconciled to, and now hope to see an even greater independence than, Home Rule, my saying has been long,

"I am not fighting for it, but preparing for it". And that has been my purpose in my work for establishing a National Theatre, and for the revival of the language, and in making better known the heroic tales of Ireland. For whatever political inclination or energy was born with me may have run its course in that Egyptian year and worn itself out; or it may be that I saw too much of the inside, the tangled webs of diplomacy, the driving forces behind politicians.[16]

As the final phase of the Egyptian tragedy unfolded, Augusta Gregory finally yielded to Blunt's entreaties and they became lovers. After a visit to Madame Tussaud's to inspect a new wax model of Arabi, they returned to Sussex together and there she found "the joys I was so late to understand".[17] In a remarkable sequence of sonnets to Blunt, she recorded her feelings:

> I kiss the ground
> On which the feet of him I love have trod,
> And bow before his voice whose least sweet sound
> Speaks louder to me than the voice of God.[18]

For her the affair with Blunt could never be more than a lyric fling: by it she not only transgressed the social proprieties of her age, but the borders of the politically acceptable as well. She encouraged Blunt in the writing of poems which fiercely denounced the behaviour of Europeans in Africa and Asia: and, in later years, she circulated his book *Ideas on India* as widely as she could. She herself visited India in 1886 and was not surprised to find his indictment justified. After just a month there, she wrote, "I have not met one single English officer or official, with the sole exception of Cordery, who has the least idea or takes the smallest interest in the history of the country, in its races or religion . . ."[19]

Through all these years, the Land War in Ireland gathered momentum: some landlords were shot, others were boycotted, and across the countryside the air was thick with the cries of families who were evicted for non-payment of rents. Nothing less than Home Rule would now satisfy Parnell, the leader of the Irish nationalists who was himself from the Protestant gentry. Lady Gregory was quite unimpressed by it all. She believed her husband to be a model landlord and remained convinced that the tenants loved, as well as respected, good masters. Blunt, although he continued to enjoy the privileges of his own holdings in Sussex, became a rapid convert to Parnellism. She scolded her friend, telling him that it was a vulgar and violent movement, "so unlike the Irish people, the poor who are so courteous and full of tact even in their discontent". He, for his part, found it "curious that she, who could see so clearly in Egypt, when it was a case between the Circassian Pashas and the Arab *fellaheen*, should be blind now that the case is between English landlords and Irish tenants in Galway". But property blinds all eyes, he moralized with no trace of self-irony, and "it is easier for a camel to pass through the eye of a needle than for an Irish landlord to enter the kingdom of Home Rule".[20]

By the time he wrote this, Blunt had been sickened by an eviction he witnessed in Ireland: "a brutal and absurd spectacle, 250 armed men, soldiers in all but name, storming the cottages one after the other of half starved tenants, and faced by less than half their number of women and boys . . . The houses were ransacked, the furniture thrown out, the fires quenched, and a bit of thatch was taken possession of as a token in each case that the landlord had reentered his rights. Then the inhabitants were turned adrift in the world".[21] So moved was he that he agreed to address a Land League meeting to protest against the evictions carried out by Lord Clanrickarde, a neighbour of the Gregorys. The meeting was proscribed; Blunt broke the ban and was arrested; and he was sentenced to two months' hard labour in Galway jail (making him perhaps the first Englishman to go to prison for the Irish cause).

The gentry exulted and joked that a prison haircut would prevent his posing as an Oriental for some time to come: but Lady Gregory was deeply troubled. In a poem she wrote:

> My heart is in a prison cell,
> My own true love beside,
> Where more of worth and beauty dwell
> Than in the whole world wide.[22]

In between bouts of picking tar from old rope, Blunt wrote his book of prison poems *In Vinculis*, which she later saw through the presses for him in 1888. By then the physical affair between them was well and truly over, and Blunt had moved on to other conquests: but he would always claim, somewhat complacently, that whatever she achieved of value in her subsequent years, he had kindled into life. Recalling "the timid unambitious woman" whom he first met in Cairo, he marvelled that "she so long was content with an almost silent part in her own house",[23] leaving all the talking and acting to Sir William. Yet this was the woman who went on, after her husband's death, to become the inspirer of the Irish literary movement: "She is the only woman I have known of real intellectual power equal to men and that without having anything unnaturally masculine about her". It would be hard to find sentiments which so brazenly mixed astute analysis and appalling smugness.

In the end, Lady Gregory herself had mingled feelings about the affair, fondly recalling its passion and excitement, while despising herself for the deceit of her own husband:

> What have I lost? The faith I had that right
> Must surely prove itself than ill more strong.
> For all my prayers and efforts had no might
> To save me, when the trial came, from wrong.
> And lost the days when with untroubled eyes
> Scorning deceit, I could hold up my head.
> I lead a double life – myself despise
> And fear each day to have my secret read.
> No longer will the loved and lost I mourn
> Come in my sleep to breathe a blessed word.
> Tossing I lie, and restless and forlorn,
> And their dear memory pierces like a sword.
> In thy dear presence only have I rest,
> To thee alone naught needs to be confessed.[24]

A Woman's Sonnets were written as a farewell to their passion: she put them into Blunt's hand after their last night of love. The pain remained for years, and she was tortured by scruples long after Sir William's death in 1892. The gain was only "a little charity", a recognition that she must never be one of the smug who cast the first stone at a sinner.

By 1907 Lady Gregory was an ardent Home Ruler, a director of the Irish National Theatre Society, and an emerging dramatist. She was also a victim of her success: after the *Playboy* riots, nationalists on the council in Coole instructed local children to boycott her house and to refuse all gifts from her. In the Abbey Theatre, she had connived in the appointment of Ben Iden Payne as a director, an Englishman criticized as a rather incongruous addition to an Irish national theatre. In this charged context, Lady Gregory wrote *Dervorgilla*, one of her most complex plays, which deals with an unfaithful wife of O'Rourke, King of Breffny, who eloped with Dermot McMurrough, a king of Leinster. O'Rourke then waged war on McMurrough, who asked for help from

Henry the Second of England: thus began the occupation of Ireland by the Normans.

The play itself is set in Dervorgilla's declining years, which she spends doing good works and praying at the Abbey of Mellifont: she has the status of a saint among her people, and only her closest servants know the guilty secret from her past, which they can be relied upon to protect. The mood is festive and jovial, much to Dervorgilla's relief: "it seems as if those were wrong who said the English would always bring trouble on us; there may be a good end to the story after all".[25] This was still a tenable position when it was written in 1907, at a time when many still believed that England would keep faith – and such optimism is echoed by the serving-man Flann: "There will be a good end, to be sure. A bad-behaved race the people of this country are. It is the strong hand of the English is the best thing to be over them". The sentiments are impeccable Anglo-Saxonist theory, suitably placed on the lips of a self-hating underling. However, Lady Gregory is also making fun of the irony of a literary revival which, to some degree, arose out of a master–servant relationship.

What makes her play so spellbinding is its insistence on confronting not just that sordid history, but the very sources of the colonial wound. Nobody knew better than the unhappy young girl at Roxborough that the accusations of a guilty conscience can seem endless:

> Was it not I brought the curse upon O'Rourke, king of Breffny, the husband I left and betrayed? The head I made bow with shame was struck off and sent to the English King. The body I forsook was hung on the walls shamefully, by the feet, like a calf after slaughter. It is certain that there is a curse on all that have to do with me. What I have done can never be undone. How can I be certain of the forgiveness of God?[26]

By way of contrast, her servants enjoy the easy confidence of the Catholic – quite unhistorical, to be sure, in a pre-Reformation setting – that a good confession to the priest, with the blessed Virgin Mary acting as "attorney for souls" every Saturday, will wipe the moral slate clean: "why not, or who would people heaven?" The ghost of William Gregory and the shadow of Blunt lurk not far below the surface of the text, as Dervorgilla grows increasingly desperate: "But if that neighbour, that stranger, that race, should turn kind and honest, or could be sent back, and all be as before, would not forgiveness be gained by that?"[27] She puts that question to the songmaker, who, like all choruses, tends to be more objective, less compliant, than the servants: sooner a cat become a kitten again, he says. The song he sings seems an anticipatory conflation of images from Ó Rathaille and other Gaelic poets of the dispossessed:

> The wild white fawn has lost the shape was comely in the wood,
> Since the foreign crow came nesting in the yewtree overhead.[28]

> D'aistrigh fia an fhialchruth do chleachtadh sí ar dtúis
> Ó neadaigh an fiach iasachta i ndaingeanchoill Rúis . . .[29]

Even the songmaker concedes that excuses must be found for all who are dead, and for that Dervorgilla whom the world imagines to be long gone.

Her loyal retainers, Flann and Mona, advise her to return to the confines of the Abbey and abandon her acts of charity to the poor, acts which have their source in her futile attempt to allay her own sense of guilt. They even go so far as to invent excuses for her dereliction: "It was not you went to Diarmuid McMurrough. It was not you followed after him to Leinster. It was he came and brought you away. There are many say it was by force. There are many that are saying that. That is the way it will be written in the histories".[30] If those books will be written by winners, popular lore – what is remembered by singing beggars – may tell a different story; and so Dervorgilla thirsts for accusation, taking upon herself full responsibility for her actions:

> O'Rourke was a good man, and a brave man, and a kinder man than Diarmuid, but it was with Diarmuid my heart was. It is to him I was promised before ever I saw O'Rourke, and I loved him better than even my own lord, and he me also, and this was long . . . It was he cast down the great, it was the dumb poor he served . . .[31]

Here the author is still trying to explore the psychic effects of her infidelity with Blunt, who did in truth serve the inarticulate and the oppressed: but she is also asserting the stubborn power of tradition to outlast the falsehoods in the history-books, the persistence of oral tradition over the lies of obliging lackeys. Near the close, Dervorgilla's serving-man Flann tries faithfully to prevent a clown from singing for the men of England: first he speaks reproachfully in his ear, then he puts his hand over his mouth, but to no avail. The subversive power of the artist cannot be denied, even if it is the casual ferocity of the colonizer that makes it possible, when one of the English sends an arrow through Flann's body rather than brook further irritation.

At the end, Flann is slain and his wife, beside herself with grief, lets slip the name of Dervorgilla. The latter feels strangely relieved at the knowledge that some of her entourage now spurn her: "there is kindness in your unkindness, not leaving me to go and face Michael and the Scales of Judgement wrapped in comfortable words, and the praises of the poor, but from the swift, unflinching, terrible judgement of the young!"[32] This lucid passage seems almost to presage the Easter Rising (which came less than a decade after the play) as a sort of Last Judgement on the Anglo-Irish: the fact that the local children coldly return to Dervorgilla prizes which she so recently gave them has a chilling autobiographical ring to it.

Yet the tragedy is more complex still. Dervorgilla speaks nothing more than the truth when she says of Flann "that old man had forgiven me and he had suffered by the Gall. The old, old woman, even in her grief, she called out no word against me". There Lady Gregory, with almost unbearable foresight, fastened upon the saddest paradox of all: that the Anglo-Irish – or at least a good number of them – had actually begun to be *liked*, as well as respected, at just that moment when they were about to be extirpated. Out of such a painful discovery Yeats would create the final epiphany of "Leda and the Swan". Yeats, of course, was a songmaker: and in the play, too, it is Dervorgilla who sinks slowly to die and the songmaker who wins out, with the ferocious objectivity of the artist. Dervorgilla must accept her role as mythic villainess:

> The rat in the cupboard, the fire in the lap;
> The guest to be fattening, the children fretting;
> My curse upon all that brought in the Gall,
> Upon Diarmuid's call, and on Dervorgilla![33]

The entire play is no more than a dramatized ballad which, despite intermittent delays and postponements, insists on taking its final shape as the listeners recognize in it the words and music of necessity. The woman who wrote it had come a long way from her days as an apologist for empire: now she could surprise Yeats by joking that Tennyson had as his God the British Empire and Queen Victoria as his Virgin Mary.[34]

If in *Dervorgilla* Lady Gregory allowed events from her secret past to flash forth in a moment of danger, then her treatment of the legend of

Grania in 1908–9 was one intense attempt to confront the full implication of her affair with Blunt. She chose Grania because of her willpower; she was a woman who "for good or evil twice took the shaping of her life into her own hands".[35] In the legend Grania had been betrothed to the elderly chief of the Fianna named Finn, but had chosen to elope with Diarmuid, the most handsome man in the land. *A Woman's Sonnets* had made it clear that their author saw herself guilty of "the crime of having loved thee yet unwooed" (a debatable interpretation in any *amour* involving Blunt, who needed little prompting): and so Grania, like the strong Celtic women of the romances, is portrayed as the one who takes the initiative and who must, in consequence, take upon herself the guilt:

> It is not his fault! It is mine! It is on me the blame is entirely! It is best for me to go out a shamed woman.[36]

This might seem like a reprise of Dervorgilla's more charged confessions, but there has been a significant change of approach between the two plays. Here the guilt of the Anglo-Irish as invaders is not equated with the author's disloyalty to her husband, but with her betrayal of her deeper feelings for the nationalist Blunt. Grania begins the drama seeing in the wounded Diarmuid an image of the strong-man-in-pain: and this appeals both to her sensitivity and to her strength. Sensing a challenge, Finn threatens death to any rival who steals his beloved, and Diarmuid readily agrees that this would be only just. He has no wish to elope with Grania and solemnly promises Finn that theirs will be a chaste liaison.

This is reminiscent of a vow made in the summer of 1883 by Augusta Gregory and Wilfrid Blunt that their sexual relation "should be replaced by one of a saner and less passionate kind".[37] The repeated use of Christian symbolism in the play suggests that the violation of her own religious code haunted Lady Gregory most painfully. Looking at the moon, Finn tells the departing pair that "before its lessening you will have lied to me"[38]: but Diarmuid, still convinced that he can remain chaste, promises to send unbroken bread in token of his pledge.

The second act, set seven years later, shows that a life of rambling and hunting in natural settings may finally pall: those who should have lived in leisured ease have been reduced to wandering tramps. Grania fears that she will lose her looks under stress of the elements, youthful looks which are cannily conserved by the settled, pampered women of the aristocracy: and she also worries that Diarmuid may soon tire of hunting and wish to rejoin the warrior band of the Fianna. Above all, however, Grania yearns to find a social context for their love: "certain it is by the respect of others we partly judge even those we know through and through".[39] Finn arrives, in the disguise of a messenger, only to be told by Grania that "as the bread that is broken and torn, so is the promise given by the man that did right in breaking it". This audacious use of Christian symbolism to underwrite a necessary sacrifice seems subversive in the extreme. Some might see it as parodic of Christian imagery, but it is more likely part of Lady Gregory's attempt to Christianize a pagan tale of the Celtic Revival and to endow her own love affair with some of the qualities of a saintly martyrdom. Finn equates all too easily with Sir William, in his hypochondria and in his rationalizations of his own failure to take revenge: "Yet, in the end there are few do it, for the thought of men that have passed their midday is mixed with caution, and with wisdom, and the work they have in hand".[40] Indeed, Grania's failure to recognize Finn beneath his disguise is symbolic of her real attitude to him: but it would also be true to say that even her lover Diarmuid can relate to *her* only at the level of myth and image. In this he depressingly resembles the Blunt who rather complacently took unto himself the credit for Lady Gregory's own achievements. It is all too symptomatic that the woman in *Grania* is condemned to only a supporting role in a man's love-affair with his own image.

Finn begins the third and final act behaving like an ageing fetishist, kissing the print left by Grania's foot upon the fields of Ireland. His desire has grown mimetic, being no more than a lust for the Grania whom he knows to be already wanted by Diarmuid. To Grania his real sin is malice, "putting a hedge between myself and Diarmuid". She rails against the unnatural bond laid on Diarmuid by his leader, and "he was a fool to make it, and a worse fool to keep it".[41] The result is that a king's daughter is living like a wandering tramp, an image of the Anglo-Irish gentry fallen upon hard times, like the Gaelic nobility which preceded them. Throughout the play, indeed, there is much talk of nobles experimenting with a life of beggary, just as the language of the play itself represents, in its homely directness, a critical attempt by Lady Gregory to explore the relation between the noble tale and the peasant Ireland in which it lingered. Diarmuid, having been tricked by the disguised messenger into fighting the King of Foreign, returns badly wounded.

When he regains consciousness, he believes that he is already dead and asks Finn to pardon him for an ill-remembered offence committed in the past. All of his thoughts are about Finn, his former Comrade of the *blutbrüderschaft*, and not about Grania: "It would be a very foolish thing, any woman at all to have leave to come between yourself and myself. I cannot but laugh at that".[42] Because his desire is only mimetic, Finn loses his interest in Grania at that very moment when Diarmuid seems to abandon her himself. She will have none of this, however, and insists that she will return to Finn:

> He will think to come whispering to you, and you alone in the night time. But he will find me there before him![43]

In fact, her return is purely technical: at the close, she has so little respect for any of these pallid men that she is compelled *to crown herself* queen.

The mocking laugh at the conclusion, which may come from the dead Diarmuid, or even from his still-living comrades, is surely at the expense of Finn who says:

> I thought to leave you and to go from you, and I cannot do it. For we three have been these seven years as if alone in the world . . . And now there are but the two of us left, and whether we love or hate one another, it is certain that I can never feel love or hatred for any other woman from this out, or you yourself for any other man.[44]

Grania is beyond such care: "there is not since an hour ago any sound that would matter at all, or be more to me than the squeaking of bats in the rafters, or the screaming of wild geese overhead". As she walks royally out, the peal of laughter stops as suddenly as it started, for she has in that very gesture invented and given birth to herself. Abandoned by male suitors who love only their own reasons for "loving" her, she steps outside their discredited system altogether. A world filled with male fantasists leaves women no choice but to get real: "It is women are said to change, and they do not, but it is men that change and turn as often as the wheel of the moon. You filled all Ireland with your outcry wanting me, and now, when I am come into your hand, your love is rusted and worn out".[45] That could have been the voice of the child who arrived, an unwanted and unloved female, at Roxborough House in 1852.

Grania was never performed in Lady Gregory's lifetime. She said that a three-act play with only three characters would tax even the most indulgent audience: but it may well be that the public ventilation of its very private themes would have taxed the author most of all.

YEATS: LOOKING INTO THE LION'S FACE

YEATS: LOOKING INTO THE LION'S FACE

At the outset, the aspiring young poet W. B. Yeats was sure that a literary career of any worth would only be possible in London. Ireland, for him, would be an "imaginary homeland", the sort of place endlessly invented and reinvented by exiles who fear that, if they do not give it a local habitation in words, it may entirely disappear. There was some justification for that fear. Friedrich Engels in a letter to Marx had described post-Famine Ireland as "an utter desert which nobody wants", a place with a number of big houses "surrounded by enormous, wonderfully beautiful parks, but all around is waste land".[1] The exiled patriot John Mitchel concurred: "the very nation that I knew in Ireland is broken and destroyed; and the place that knew it shall know it no more".[2] Yeats may eventually have returned to Ireland, like so many exiles before and since, simply to make sure that it was still there.

But first in London he busied himself with the invention of a literary movement and the shaping of a post-Parnellite culture. He had his poems published by a prestigious house, in whose offices he wore the black cloak of a professional Celt. (Some said that this gave him a priestly appearance, appropriate to the leader of a new cult: but the satirist George Moore quipped that it made him look like an umbrella left behind after a picnic.) At all events, London was the crucible in which the elements to make a modern Ireland were distilled. On the streets of that city, diverse persons and types met and conspired. Their haunts were the Irish Literary Society (founded in 1891), the Gaelic League (1893), and of course the Gaelic Athletic Association (set up in 1884). The political activists of a later period, as well as creative artists, first formed an idea of Ireland at these meetings: the list would include Michael Collins, first a young post office clerk but subsequently to become one of the most lethal guerrilla commanders of the new century; Desmond FitzGerald, 1916 rebel and minister of

the first Free State Government; *Pádraic Ó Conaire, author of the first
novel in the Irish language;* W. P. Ryan, *one of the great crusading
journalists of his day and a constant orchestrator of significant meetings
and clubs.*

*This loose federation of personalities was one of the very first groups of
decolonizing intellectuals to formulate a vision of their native country
during a youthful sojourn in an imperial capital – and then return to
implement it. Many would follow their example in other parts of the world,
but the Irish had only one precedent to which to turn for inspiration: the
invention of the American republic by Washington and Jefferson, and of its
democratic culture by Whitman and Emerson.*

*Yeats was perhaps the most gifted and charismatic member of that group
of exiles. In the fate of Wilde and Shaw – great artists reduced to the status
of mere entertainers by a public too scared to confront their radical ideas
with full seriousness – he found a warning for himself and for his friends. If
they were to create an authentic movement, Irish writers must commune
above all with themselves and with their own people. They must go back to
Dublin and there found a national theatre and publishing houses, in the
attempt to gather around them a truly national audience.*

Six

Childhood and Ireland

Most writers of the Irish Revival identified their childhood with that of the Irish nation: those hopeful decades of slow growth before the fall into murderous violence and civil war. In their subsequent autobiographies, childhood was identified as a kind of privileged zone, peopled with engaging eccentrics, doting grandmothers and natural landscapes. What they were describing, of course, was childhood in a colony, and there could have been few experiences as intense as that of family life in such a setting. The subject people owed no allegiance to the state, its courts, its police, its festivals, and so all the energies which might in a normal society have been dispersed over such wide areas were instead invested in the rituals of family life. As G. K. Chesterton remarked "wherever there is Ireland there is the family, and it counts for a great deal".[1] That comment was made after a visit to the family of John Butler Yeats in London, proving that habits so deeply rooted survived the experience of emigration, even among those like the Yeatses whose background was in the minor landowning class. The neighbours of the Yeats family in London, hearing the raised voices of father and son, sometimes falsely concluded that the two were locked in a violent quarrel, when in fact they were engaged in animated discussion of the family's life. Their friends in Blenheim Road could not understand, in the words of Lily Yeats, that this was simply "the Irish way".[2]

Whenever sons revolted against fathers in a revival text, the confrontation was soon metaphorized as the story of Ireland. The writer, typically, began the autobiography as a subject in the colony, clashed with and surmounted a father, and ended as the citizen of a free state or of a state intent on freeing itself. Beginning as a nonentity, he or she grew into an Irish person. Like Americans of the same period, the Irish were not so much born as *made*, gathered around a few simple symbols, a flag, an anthem, a handful of evocative phrases. In the process, childhood – like Ireland itself – had to be reinvented as a zone of innocence, unsullied and intense, from which would emerge the free Irish protagonist.

The celebration of the peasant by artists like Yeats was intimately connected with these aspirations: one of his favourite rhymes was "wild" and "child". It was a legacy of the English Romantics, whose peasants achieved Coleridge's ideal of carrying the feelings of childhood into the powers of manhood. The unselfconsciousness of the country-man's sense of place, as in the poetry of William Allingham, permitted Yeats to question the more programmatic and "conscious patriotism" of Davis and Young Ireland. For Yeats, as for Synge, the child's earliest feelings were for the colour of a known and concrete locality, which even a baby could express in gibberish and syllables of no meaning. As a boy in Sligo, Yeats had often thought how terrible it would be to go away and live where nobody would know his story or the story of his family. "Years afterwards", he wrote, "when I was ten or twelve years old and in London, I would remember Sligo with tears, and when I began to write it was there I hoped to find my audience". From that moment on, Sligo became a place sacred to the youth who longed to hold a sod of earth in his hand. "It was some old race instinct", he recalled, "like that of a savage".[3]

At the Godolphin School in London, he felt himself a stranger among the other boys: "there was something in their way of saying the names of places that made me feel this".[4] The Sligo of his early childhood became a dream landscape, a never-never-land to which it was hopeless to expect to return, "for I have walked on Sinbad's yellow shore and never shall another's hit my fancy". For Yeats, that fall came early with the enforced emigration of his family to London, in order that his artist-father could pursue an already-flagging career. "Here you are somebody", said a Sligo aunt to the nine-year-old departee, "there you will be nobody at all".[5] It was a fall from a pastoral landscape into a world of urban blight, war and treachery, as he would recall in the later poem "Nineteen Hundred and Nineteen":

> We too had many pretty toys when young:
> A law indifferent to blame or praise,
> To bribe or threat . . .[6]

The deeper the world plunged into the chaos of imperial wars and freedom struggles, the more necessary did it become for the poet to secure the Sligo idyll against accusations of *naïveté*, and the harder. The more he sought to recapture the dream, the more it seemed to elude him. When the much older man finally brought his newly-wed English wife on a boat-trip across Lough Gill, he failed ignominiously to locate, much less land on, the lake isle of Innisfree: a sign, perhaps, that the past in that simple-minded version was not easily recoverable.

Some of the less sophisticated texts of the early Yeats were attempts to deny civilization and its discontents by escaping to the Happy Islands of Oisín and Tír na nÓg, the land of the forever young. Similarly, the short stories of Patrick Pearse often stressed the redemptive strangeness of the child, bearing to fallen adults messages from another world. The paradox was that these texts, which so nourished Irish national feeling, were often British in origin, and open to the charge of founding themselves on the imperial strategy of infantilizing the native culture. What was lacking in them was what Yeats would later call the vision of evil, without which art was merely superficial, unable to chronicle the tragedy of growth and change.

It was just such an unreal state of changlessness which the writer seemed to endorse in his 1894 play *The Land of Heart's Desire*. Here a young man still in his twenties used a fairy-child to voice his disenchantment with the ageing process:

> But I can lead you, newly-married bride,
> Where nobody gets old and crafty and wise,
> Where nobody gets old and godly and grave . . .[7]

It is significant that when the young wife dies in the play, the child leaves the stage: experience has not so much been confronted as denied in this Celtic version of *Peter Pan*. All this is in keeping with the tendency of British authors of the late nineteenth century to confuse innocence with inexperience, whereas the earlier romantics Blake and Wordsworth had taught that the root-meaning of innocence (*innocentes*) was openness to the injuries risked in a full life. In the judgement of one critic, after the novels of Charles Dickens in the mid-century, "children no longer grow up and develop into the maturities of Wordsworth's *Prelude* . . . The image is transfigured into the image of an innocence which dies . . . of life extinguished, of life that is better extinguished, of life, so to say, rejected, negated at its very root".[8]

This is a fair account also of the landscape of early Yeatsian desire, where childhood is surrounded by a *cordon sanitaire* of nostalgia and escape. It is a world neither of change nor of growth: intense, unpurged feelings for childhood are not submitted to the test of adult life or, for that matter, of childhood itself. What the child actually *is* or *wants* means nothing in such literature, for this is the landscape of the adult heart's desire. Just as a sexist portraiture depicted women not as they are but as men wish them to be, so here the child is reduced to an expendable cultural object. The inhabitants of Tír na nÓg do not grow up, and this is not because they don't want to but because their adult creator (for the time being, anyway) prefers to keep them and his readers ignorant of a world based on sexual suffering and social injustice. This early Yeatsian attitude is based on the widespread but false assumption that childhood exists outside the culture in which it is produced as a state of unspoilt nature, and on the related assumption that children's literature can preserve for all values which are constantly on the verge of collapse. So, as a result of Yeats's equation between child and unselfconscious peasant, childhood is recommended as the zone in which the older forms of culture now jeopardized by modernity are preserved in oral tradition.

This has the unintended but undeniable effect of infantilizing the native culture. Within British writing, there had long been a link between children's fiction and the colonial enterprise, which led to an identification of the new world with the infantile state of man. Captain Marryat, that ultimate purveyor of lands of heart's desire, had once exclaimed: "what a parallel there is between a colony and her mother country and a child and its parent!"[9] All through the nineteenth century, the Irish had been treated in the English media as childlike – "broths of boys" veering between tears and smiles, quick to anger and quick to forget – unlike the stable Anglo-Saxon. In the words of historian Perry Curtis: "Irishmen thus shared with virtually all the non-white peoples of the empire the label childish, and the remedy for unruly children in most Victorian households was a proper licking".

In an age when children had few legal rights, the Irish and the child were victims of a similar duplicity of official thought. Present-day readers are often amazed at the fact that those same Victorian adults who wept copiously for the innocent outraged children of Dickens belonged to a generation which still sent children up into chimneys and down into coal-mines. The powerful have an instinctive desire to be entertained, and even accused, by their subjects. How else to explain the preponderance of female forms in the art galleries of a world so clearly run in the interests of men? Or the continuing popularity of Irish writers and media-personalities in England? The manipulation of childhood by sentimental Victorians was just another example of such functional hypocrisy: and it was no accident that the *cul-de-sac* into which writers on childhood were led was blown open not in England but in Mark Twain's United States.

Such renewal could not come from nineteenth century Ireland, because to write book-length celebrations of an Irish childhood was to flirt dangerously with the stereotype of the childlike Hibernian peasant. A shrewd awareness of this probably accounts for Yeats's growing reluctance to exploit the image of the child after the comparative success in the London theatre of *The Land of Heart's Desire*. Revival writers were caught in a double bind. Disenchanted with the growing murderousness of their land, they sought relief amidst the scenes of childhood memory, only to discover that the very act of dreaming that dream was itself tainted with the politics of Anglo-Irish relations. The inspired solution turned out to be part of the underlying problem.

So Yeats, though he devotes more than seventy pages of autobiography to "Reveries Over Childhood and Youth", uses the space to challenge English preconceptions by depicting himself as a gifted, mature child among rather juvenile, derivative English boys. At school in London during election time, he was amused at the way in which classmates covered the walls with the opinions relayed by their fathers from newspapers, whereas he, an artist's son, thought things out for himself. One of his recurrent narrative strategies is to reverse many traditional manoeuvres. Where the English had used the Irish as a foil to set off John Bull's virtues, Yeats now deploys the English boys as a measure of Irish intellectual superiority. He marvels, for instance, at the contrast between his father's view that it was bad manners for a parent to speak crossly to a child and the widespread English belief in discipline, law and force. Yeats would later repent of his rather English-style sentimentalization of childhood in *The Land of Heart's Desire*, but the writer who turns on Christmas Day 1914 from a war-torn world to "Reveries Over Childhood and Youth" finds in the past only suffering of a kind that led him in the first place to evoke it. This may sharpen the focus on an apparent contradiction in the autobiography between his nostalgia for Sinbad's yellow shore and the following thoughts from the opening chapter: "Indeed, I remember little of childhood but its pain, I have grown happier with every year of life, as though gradually conquering something in myself, for certainly my miseries were not made by others but were a part of my own mind".[10] The poet may have been too forgiving in this instance, for some of his troubles were caused by the puritanical gloom and inconsiderate handling which he experienced among the Pollexfens, his mother's people in Sligo. Permanently afraid of both uncle and aunt, the young boy

confused grandfather William Pollexfen with God, praying that he
might punish him for his sins.

Pollexfen himself was something of an eccentric, who could not bear
to hear the tapping sound made by the children with spoons as they
removed the top from an egg. He chastened them with an alternative,
and of course superior, method:

> His way was to hold the egg-cup firmly on its plate with his left hand, then
> with a sharp knife in his right hand to behead the egg with one blow.
> Where the top of the egg went to was not his business. It might hit a
> grandchild or the ceiling. He never looked . . .[11]

The Pollexfens passed on their propensity for gloomy introspection to
Willie, who was sometimes so filled with "hobgoblin fancies" that his
aunts wondered whether the boy was in possession of all his faculties.
This judgement would be echoed years later by London neighbours
who wondered why the nice young Yeats girls used to walk down
Blenheim Road "with the mentally afflicted young gentleman".

Small wonder that the poet in middle age could write of:

> . . . that toil of growing up;
> The ignominy of boyhood; the distress
> Of boyhood changing into man . . .[12]

or that the old man could write (in an imitation from the Japanese):

> Seventy years have I lived,
> Seventy years man and boy,
> And never have I danced for joy . . .[13]

For one of his earliest recollections had been of his grateful surprise
when great-uncle William Middleton had said: "We should not make
light of the troubles of children. They are worse than ours, because we
can see the end of our trouble, and they can never see any end".[14] As a
boy, Yeats made a mental note never to talk as grown-up people do of
the happiness of childhood. This returns us to the question already
asked in another way: how can these childhood ignominies be reconciled with nostalgia for the Sligo of Yeats's youth?

The simple answer is that Yeats's longings were for locations, whereas
his pains were caused by people. It may well be that beautiful landscapes, which assuaged boyhood pain, were sanctified in the memory of
later years by their association with intense early epiphanies. In his

autobiographical writings, George Bernard Shaw registered a similar discrepancy between his "devil of a childhood, rich only in dreams, frightful and loveless in realities" and the serene settings in which some of his days were passed. He did, however, recall one moment of ecstatic happiness when his mother confided that they were to live in Dalkey. "Under its canopied skies", he recalled at the age of eighty, he learned "to love Nature and Ireland when I was a half-grown nobody".[15] The plaque which now stands on Shaw's cottage in Dalkey may well in its inscription speak also for Yeats: "The men of Ireland are mortal and temporal, but her hills are eternal". Behind such an aphorism lies a familiar strategy of the Irish Protestant imagination, estranged from the community, yet anxious to identify itself with the new national sentiment. While Roman Catholic writers of the revival period seemed obsessed with the history of their land, to Protestant artists that history could only be, as Lady Gregory insisted, a painful accusation against their own people; and so they turned to geography in the attempt at patriotization. At the Godolphin School in London, patriotic English boys in Yeats's class read of Cressy, Agincourt and Union Jacks, while he, "without those memories of Limerick and the Yellow Ford that would have strengthened an Irish Catholic, thought of mountain and lake, of my grandfather and of ships".[16]

In emphasizing locality, Yeats, Synge and Lady Gregory were deliberately aligning themselves with the Gaelic bardic tradition of *dinn-sheanchas* (knowledge of the lore of places). Yet there was undeniably something strained about their manoeuvre, as Synge conceded in describing himself as a mere "interloper" among the islanders of Aran. Unlike most of his Irish contemporaries, Yeats spent a good part of his boyhood in England, a fact which may have allowed him, even while rather young, to reinvent his Irish childhood in a more pleasing pattern. Cynical commentators have often marvelled at just how many years Ireland's national poet managed to spend outside his native land, in keeping with the theory which has it that those Irish who live outside the island are a lot more starry-eyed about the place than those still living within it. (Frank O'Connor remarked during an American exile that he returned at least once a year to remind himself what a terrible place it was.) So, Yeats, too, is inventing Ireland, as he employs his autobiographer's art to remake his life. He wrote in the Preface:

> I have changed nothing to my knowledge, and yet it must be that I have changed many things without my knowledge; for I am writing after many

years and have consulted neither friend, not letter, nor old newspaper, and describe what comes oftenest into my memory.[17]

Yet, no matter how much insurance he takes out against the law court, this most forgetful of autobiographers knows that the past is irrecoverable, that paradise is always by very definition lost. If each of the main characters in Yeats's book has been "reborn as an idea", then so too has the image of childhood as a sign of cultural despair.

There is so little reference to childhood in the poems themselves that a reader might be forgiven for wondering whether the poet had a youth at all. Childhood is invoked fleetingly in some lyrics, but only as a measure of the adult man's desperation. "Among School Children" is about the suffering of being a woman, the costs of art, the sources of aesthetic and organic beauty – everything, that is, except school-children, who stare in momentary wonder before disappearing out of the poem. And "momentary wonder" is all that the poet feels at the sight of them. Since communication with the children seems out of the question, the kind old nun does all the replying. The infant Yeats puts in a brief appearance in stanza five, solely as a "shape" upon his mother's lap. Similarly, in "To a Child Dancing Upon the Wind", Yeats evokes the symbol in the title and first line, only to veer away in the second to the adult cares, of which the child is so irritatingly innocent:

> Dance there upon the shore;
> What need have you to care
> For wind or ocean's roar?
> And tumble out your hair
> That the salt drops have wet.
> Being young you have not known
> The fool's triumph, nor yet
> Love lost as soon as won,
> Nor the best labourer dead
> And all the sheaves to bind.
> What need have you to dread
> The monstrous crying of wind?[18]

A more orthodox romantic poet might have marvelled at the adult's culpable ignorance of childish ways, but not this one. Yeats resists the temptation to attempt an exploration of the inner world of the child; and this may be to his credit, since many who expend great intensity on children do so because they feel themselves subtly unfitted for the demands of adult life. Yeats was usually shrewd enough to play within his limits, recalling that he wrote *The Land of Heart's Desire* "in some discomfort when the child was theme, for I knew nothing of children".[19]

With other people's children the poet was painfully inept. On one notorious occasion, he frightened Oscar Wilde's children out of the room with a ghost story, which got only as far as "once upon a time there was a ghost". In later years, when he had children of his own, he often gave his infant son a baffled look, as if to ask how he had got there: a curious reversal of the difficulty which some children have in believing that their parents actually went to bed and conceived them. In terms of Christian theology, Yeats's exploration of the symbolic meaning of childhood was utterly heretical. Whereas Christianity sees the child as the living embodiment of a love which unites the parents, Yeats saw the child as the necessary physical evidence of the fact that a man and woman had momentarily tried, and failed, to be one:

> And when at last that murder's over
> Maybe the bride bed brings despair,
> For each an imagined image brings
> And finds a real image there.[20]

That same imperfection was found by Yeats in the experience of the Christian God, whose unsatisfactory and inconclusive love-affair with the world gave rise to the need for the incarnation of Jesus in the womb of Mary, a mystery summed up in the peasant adage: "God possesses the heavens, but he covets the earth". So the infant Jesus, like the child of even the truest lovers, is born out of love's despairing search for a moment of ecstasy: and this may be one of the implications behind the strange phrase "beauty born out of its own despair" in "Among School Children".

Through every phase of the poetry, one finds Yeats's lines freighted with these darker intimations from an adult world. "A Prayer for My Daughter" is less about the child in the cradle than about the kind of grown-up she might become. In "Among School Children" Yeats wonders whether the pain of his mother in childbirth is justified by the scarecrow he now feels himself to be. In a late poem "What Then?" the self-questioning of the time-bound man is even more radical:

> His chosen comrades thought at school
> He must grow a famous man;

> He thought the same and lived by rule,
> All his twenties crammed with toil;
> "What then?" sang Plato's ghost. "What then?"[21]

In such a painful world, only a few like Helen of Troy retain the self-delight of the child into their adult years:

> That the topless towers be burnt
> And men recall that face,
> Move most gently if move you must
> In this lonely place.
> She thinks, part woman, three parts a child,
> That nobody looks; her feet
> Practise a tinker shuffle
> Picked up on a street.
>   *Like a long-legged fly upon the stream*
>   *Her mind moves upon silence.*[22]

The chorus makes it quite clear that the experience of being three-parts a child is unshareable, unknowable.

All of which illustrates the tragedy which Synge found in the literary vocation: youth knows how to feel but not how to express, and by the time it has learned to express itself, it has all too often forgotten how to feel. No writer likes to admit that the unexpressed part of the life is the happy part, for to an artist expression is the ultimate fulfilment: but if expression is frustrated, that adds yet another dimension to the pain of the unrecorded life. This may explain why Yeats balanced the pain of childhood against the assertion that he grew happier with every passing year. The later life is the life expressed.

The poet who had little good to say of his own childhood had much to remark about the prevailing systems of education. Perhaps the pain of the one was but a further proof of the need for reform of the other. Throughout the autobiography, he is at pains to stress the comparative unimportance to the literary artist of reading and of books. "I have remembered nothing that I read", he writes, somewhat paradoxically, "but only those things that I heard or saw".[23] His envy is of those, like his mother, who read no texts but whose recollection of oral narratives was flawless. John Butler Yeats had indeed praised his wife as one who pretended to nothing that she did not feel: and in this he saw her as utterly unlike the average modern reader, who derived second-hand opinions from books. "Neither Christ nor Buddha wrote a book", wrote their (somewhat hypocritical) son, "for to do that is to exchange life for a logical process".[24] Yet we must assume this statement to be sincere. From the Pollexfens, Yeats seems to have gathered the notion that books can erode the integrity of self: art, like sex, may be the activity of an aching, unfulfilled heart:

> Players and painted stage took all my love,
> And not those things that they were emblems of.[25]

The man who saw himself faced with the rather puritan choice between a perfect life and a perfect work often wondered whether he should have thrown poor words away and been content to live. Nearing his fiftieth year, he closed the first volume of his autobiography with a repudiation of "all the books I have read", which were now dismissed as "a preparation for something that never happens".[26] That something may well have been a child, to judge by the introductory poem of the collection called Responsibilities, where the lyrical process of a book is deemed a poor compensation for the lack of better offspring:

> *Pardon, that for a barren passion's sake,*
> *Although I have come close on forty-nine,*
> *I have no child; I have nothing but a book,*
> *Nothing but that to prove your blood and mine.*[27]

The book is seen as the rival and enemy of the child. No great wonder that John Butler Yeats exclaimed, on reading the son's autobiography: "Don't ever throw a book at your child. He might write his memoirs".[28]

The book had been thrown out of momentary frustration at the son's slow progress at learning to read. Even at the age of seven, he had yet to master the alphabet: and throughout his adult life he remained a poor speller, blighting his chances of the Chair of English at Trinity College, Dublin by mis-spelling the word "Professorship" in his letter of application. That reluctance to enter the world of book-learning might be construed as a kind of repudiation of the colonizing code. To the end, Yeats believed passionately in education, which valued a child for its intrinsic sake, and he despised mere schooling, which concerned itself more with producing the kind of adult the child must eventually become. In his estimate, a true culture consisted not in acquiring opinions but in getting rid of them. Life was a learning of how to shed "civilized" illusions and a coming to terms with the desolation of reality. Many of his most remarkable poems – "A Coat", "Easter 1916", "Meru", "The Circus Animals' Desertion" – document that process, but there is a sense in which each, especially "Easter 1916", is a rewritten version of his earliest lyric of fairyland and childhood, "The Stolen Child". It is there that he expresses most chillingly his reservations about the alleged happiness of childhood.

The notion that "innocence" is something lost in a careless half-hour of late adolescence is risible. People either are or are not innocent to begin with, and those natural tendencies are reinforced with the passing years. Innocence is not inexperience, but its opposite. This realization led Yeats to discount much of his early work as the cry of the heart against necessity. "It is not" he wrote, "the poetry of insight and knowledge, but of longing and complaint . . . I hope some day to alter that and write the poetry of insight and knowledge".[29] Critics, taking him at his word, tend to describe "reality" for Yeats as a delayed but invigorating discovery, as if the mature poet caught the last bus back from Tír na nÓg just in the nick of time. Yet the critique of his own longing and complaint was actually written with exemplary self-awareness by a poet still in his early twenties: and those same reservations were built into the best early poetry such as "The Stolen Child". These texts are poised tensely between the real and the ideal, as if (in Yeats's own words about a fellow-poet) "some half-conscious part of him desired the world he had renounced".[30]

"The Stolen Child" is not so much a plea for escape as an account of the claims of the real world and of the costs of any dream. The agony and strife of human hearts in a world full of weeping are cited as legitimate reasons for leaving the landscape of reality, but the child, being "human", cannot but feel the tug of that world. A tension is set up between fairyland and the warm humanity of the country kitchen, which the child must abandon in forsaking the weeping of the world. In avoiding those tears, the child may also lose the capacity to feel: innocence will indeed be blank inexperience. The vagueness of the drowsy water-rats, the waning moon, the ferns and streams, can be no match for the concrete homeliness of feeling with which the poet renders the details of a country kitchen: the kettle on the hob, the ready intimacy with calves, and the solid reality of the bobbing brown mice:

> Away with us he's going
> The solemn-eyed.

He'll hear no more the lowing
Of the calves on the warm hillside,
Or the kettle on the hob
Sing peace into his breast,
Or see the brown mice bob
Round and round the oatmeal chest.
For he comes, the human child,
To the waters and the wild,
With a faery, hand in hand,
From a world more full of weeping than he can understand.[31]

The world which the child is leaving is rendered with far greater precision than the zones for which he is heading, and the effect is complex: the reader is left to wonder whether a terrible mistake has not just been made. The sinister change from second to third person ("that *he* can understand") suggests that the fairies have landed their quarry, already a mere object to their eyes, and so they tip a knowing wink to the unnerved reader. The poem may indeed be a critique of the misuse of the child image in certain forms of Celticism and Peter Pannery.

"Easter 1916", a far greater poem, is nonetheless a rewritten version of those themes: for again, the poet is tugged in opposite directions as a result of an event, which leaves him wondering about the costs in human terms of an abstract ideal. The technique is similar as well: the recounting in vivid detail of those quotidian pleasures which must pull even idealists back from their dream of death. The stone, emblematic of extreme idealism, is unchanging but also the object of a deathlike enchantment. Against it, the poet pits the physical sensations of achieved life, the warm domesticity of the family farm and its easy familiarity with animals:

A shadow of cloud on the stream
Changes minute by minute;
A horse-hoof slides on the brim
And a horse plashes within it:
The long-legged moor-hens dive,
And hens to moorcocks call;
Minute by minute they live;
The stone's in the midst of all.[32]

The world which the rebels are leaving is, once again, rendered with more lucidity than the zones into which they are headed: and, as before, the fear is that an irretrievable error has been committed. The closing refrain, as in "The Stolen Child", uses almost identical words, but the slight shift allows it to mean something quite different from what it did at the beginning. The unanswerable questions cause the poet to suspend any final judgement:

> That is heaven's part.
> Our part to murmur name upon name
> As a mother names her child,
> When sleep at last has come
> On limbs that had run wild . . .[33]

That reference takes us back to the child stolen by fairies from its rightful human mother, a child who departed "solemn-eyed", like Pearse and MacDonagh. It can hardly be a coincidence that both lyrics chronicle the loss of young life and the distress of mourners left to carry on. In the intervening thirty years, Yeats's view of dreaming has not changed. The man who dreamed of fairyland found no comfort in the grave: and here in "Easter 1916" the poet stands appalled at what Ireland has lost, some of its most gifted thinkers. For him, the dead heroes were all stolen children.

However, in dignifying them at the close with that beautiful image, the poet may have unwittingly trivialized their gesture and have done this in a time-honoured colonialist way. The rebels, being children, were not full moral agents, he seems to say, and so, even when they seem to have done wrong, they can be forgiven. "Be nothing said", he wrote elsewhere, "that would be harsh for children that have strayed". Like the black man in the slave-holding American south, they can be adjudged to be beyond the purview of the moral law. The colony can forgive the rebellion of the colonized: the mother can soothe her child with the incantations of a poet. "Easter 1916" is, in truth, the foundational poem of the emerging Irish nation-state, but it is also, in a perhaps inevitable sub-text, an imperialist's elegy for a headstrong but contained foe. In it, the Irishman is still a child.

Seven

The National Longing for Form

Ireland after the famines of the mid-nineteenth century was a sort of nowhere, waiting for its appropriate images and symbols to be inscribed in it. Its authors had no clear idea of whom they were writing for. Many of the native Irish were caught between two languages, shame-facedly abandoning Irish and not yet mastering English. "I see, sir, how it is with you", groaned one enlightened judge who offered to try a defendant in Irish and was refused, even though the man in the dock spoke only broken English; "you are more ashamed of knowing your own language than of not knowing any other".[1] Those Irish who were literate in English were not great buyers of books and so Irish artists wrote with one eye cocked on the English audience. They were, for the most part, painfully imitative of English literary modes, which they practised with the kind of excess possible only to the insecure.

Cultural colonies are much more susceptible to the literature of the parent country than are the inhabitants of that country itself, since plays and novels of manners have always been exemplary instruments in the civilizing of the subject. A colonized people soon comes to believe that approved fictions are to be imitated in life, and this notion in due time proves vitally useful to the exponents of resistance literature. Merely to describe a colonial society mimicking an approved literature is, however, to repeat in a boringly predictable fashion the previous modes. The most inspiring lesson which the resistance writer learns from the occupier is that the society around him or her may be no more than the institutional inferences drawn from an approved set of texts.

The ideal of a national poet, whether a W. B. Yeats or a Walt Whitman, is to displace this constricting environment and its accompanying forms: since freedom cannot be won in them, it must be won from them. This is the overweening ambition of many great writers, to create a new genre in the act of destroying another, but it is almost unbearably intensified in a colony. Irish radicals in the nineteenth century had been gravely informed by the political theorist Mazzini that theirs was an economic problem requiring resolution rather than the question of an oppressed nation. Mazzini denied that they possessed the unique philosophy, language, literature, dances or games which together were the signs of authentic nationhood. This was a brutal version of the tragic paradox which confronts all subject peoples: political independence is deemed justifiable only by a distinctive national "idea", yet the very forms of colonialist discourse prevent its articulation. So the very *search* for a method must become the decolonizer's justification. As Patrick O'Farrell has observed:

> . . . in fact, the two searchings, the British for an answer, the Irish for a meaning to their question, intersected on each other to their mutual frustration. No proposed external solution could ever satisfy the Irish, calm their troubles, for they as a people neither knew who they were, nor what they wanted – these were problems they would have to solve for themselves, themselves alone.[2]

Yeats's search has long been recognized as a quest for a mode of expression, which would precede any truth which it might express; even in later poems he could write:

> A passion-driven exultant man sings out
> Sentences that he has he never thought . . .[3]

or:

> Where got I that truth?
> Out of a medium's mouth.
> Out of nothing it came . . .[4]

This was nothing other than the search for a national style and, as such, the purest Celticism. Matthew Arnold had suggested that in Celtic writing, expression seemed usually to precede conceptualization: "Celtic art seems to make up to itself for being unable to master the world and give an adequate interpretation of it, by throwing all its force into style . . ."[5]

Most nation-states existed, so to speak, before they were defined, and they were thus defined by their existence: but states emerging from occupation, dispossession or denial had a different form of growth. Some (like Israel) were fully defined before they existed and so fulfilled the criteria set down by Mazzini. These, however, were few, and there was (and is) a lot of strain attending this artificial process by which an abstraction is converted into reality. Most dispossessed peoples fought a different fight. Under occupation, they could never be their distinctive selves, but in answer to Mazzini's challenge they had to *seem* so by an adopted attitude, an assumed style. This they would later proceed to justify by a recovered or discovered content. Style was the thing to be seized, the zone in which the battle of two civilizations would be fought out; and Yeats hoped that from his style a full man might eventually be inferred and, in due course – such was the enormity of his ambition – a nation.

The attempt, at a purely personal level, is well familiar to students of the romantic lyric, which is predicted on three selves: a past self, a reporting self which writes, and the self which the author will become by the very act of writing. In such a transaction, the "I" is necessarily precarious or inchoate, disappearing or scarcely born; but it is the identity towards which the lyric moves that is its *raison d'être*, and this by definition cannot be established until expression has ceased. It was such a model which Gilles Deleuze and Felix Guattari had in mind when they defined a minor literature, which is to say, a literature written in a major language by a minority group in revolt against its oppressors:

> . . . A major or established (i.e., imperial) literature follows a vector that goes from content to expression. Since content is presented in a given form of content, one must find, or discover, or see the form of expression that goes with it. That which conceptualizes well expresses itself. But a minor, or revolutionary literature begins by expressing itself and doesn't conceptualize until afterward.[6]

This explains why in Ireland the cultural renaissance preceded by many years the declaration of political independence (unlike the United States, which waited for over sixty years for its literary revival). It would also account for the preponderance of creative over critical texts in every phase of modern Irish literature. "Expression must break forms, encourage ruptures and new sproutings", wrote Deleuze and Guattari: "When a form is broken, one must reconstruct the context that will necessarily be a part of the rupture in the order of things." Those national authors, like Yeats and Whitman, who effect such breakages thereby become the first artists of the decolonizing world, prime exponents of the emergent literatures of modernity, which are formed around a single question: how to express life which has never yet found full expression in written literature?

The pressures on such an author are immense. A writer in a free state works with the easy assurance that literature is but one of the social institutions to project the values which the nation admires, others being the law, the government, the army, and so on. A writer in a colony knows that these values can be fully embodied only in the written word: hence the daunting seriousness with which literature is taken by subject peoples. This almost prophetic role of the artist is often linked to "underdeveloped" societies, but the notion that a people's economic state defines their total cultural condition can lead to such absurdities, mocked by the Nigerian novelist Chinua Achebe, as "show me a people's plumbing, and I can tell you their art".[7] Nonetheless, the need to resort to non-representational art is obvious to those writers who seek to elaborate a landscape of internal consciousness rather than submit to a despised external setting.

The Dublin of *Ulysses*, an occupied city, exists only on the fringes of Stephen Dedalus's gorgeous consciousness, for much the same reason that Yeats found it hard to attend to anything less interesting than his own thoughts. Attention is given less to the concrete world – about which the writer cares too little even to spurn it – than to the fertile minds which repeatedly displace it with their own superior alternatives. Art in this context might be seen as man's constant effort to create for himself a different order of reality from that which is given to him: against the ability to imagine things as they are, it counterpoises the capacity to imagine things as they might be. Fictions, though they treat of the non-existent, by that very virtue help people to make sense of the world around them.

Hence the yearning among peoples for the freedom which a magical consciousness can always create for itself. The realists, complained Wilde, "have sold our birthright for a mess of facts".[8] To challenge English ideas is merely to treat symptoms; only by rejecting English forms could the mind be opened to the democratic muse. There are the hints of alternative forms in Gaelic poems and place names, whose recovered literal meanings allow the poet to see his native landscape anew. Whitman's admiration for the word *Mississippi* (which to his ear flowed and unwound like the river) is paralleled by Yeats's ritual invocation of places known and esteemed. The love of catalogue common to both national poets may have its roots in the epic poetry of the Gael and the native American; but the ecstatic lists of native placenames which result are the Adam-like incantations of writers, rediscovering the exhilaration with which the first persons in Ireland or America named their own place and, in that sense, shaped it.

The attempt is forever frustrated, of course, since so many of the names have been lost or over-ridden by Anglicized versions, it seems to the poet that the "Sacsa nua darb ainm Éire" must be contested by his own private world. In effect, the artist volunteers to fill the cultural vacuum, as promissory note for a yet-to-be-implemented nation. Stephen Daedalus says that Ireland must be important because it belongs to him: the artist immodestly equates self and nation, so that by the end of *A Portrait of the Artist as a Young Man* one youth claims to incarnate the uncreated conscience of the race. Yeats makes the same pact in "To Ireland in the Coming Times":

> *Nor may I less be counted one*
> *With Davis, Mangan, Ferguson,*
> *Because to him who ponders well,*
> *My rhymes more than their rhyming tell*
> *Of things discovered in the deep,*
> *Where only body's laid asleep.*[9]

Both men may have learned the basic manoeuvre from Whitman:

> One's self I sing, a simple, separate person,
> Yet utter the word Democratic, the word *En-Masse.*

In such a self-charged context, nation-building can be achieved by the simple expedient of writing one's autobiography: and autobiography in Ireland becomes, in effect, the autobiography of Ireland. To read the autobiographies of Yeats, George Moore or Frank O'Connor is an experience akin to the study of Whitman's "Song of Myself": it is to be constantly impressed and unnerved by the casual ease with which they substitute themselves as a shorthand for their country, writing an implicit and covert constitution for their republics in images of their very creation.

The republican ideal was the achieved individual, the person with the courage to become his or her full self. The imperialists were not to be thought of as different, so much as aborted or incomplete individuals. By a weird paradox, their incompleteness was evidenced by their polished surface, their premature self-closure which left them at once incomplete and *finished.* The glossy, confident surface indicated a person immune to self-doubt and therefore incapable of development.

The Irish self, by contrast, was a *project*: and its characteristic text was a process, unfinished, fragmenting. It invited the reader to become a co-creator with the author and it refused to exact a merely passive admiration for the completed work of art. Similarly, in the African context, Achebe has observed that "when the product is preserved or venerated, the impulse to repeat the process is compromised"[10]: his own Igpo people, knowing that no condition can be permanent, devoted themselves to a perpetual flux of forms and styles, to meet each new force which appeared on the scene. Such openness, such freedom is not nobly chosen by an artist who might otherwise have sought the cowardly safety of closure: it is, rather, the inevitable result of the pressure under which the artist places him- or herself. If people create a world which exists only by the grace of their style, then language is placed under severe stress, being asked in effect to do much of those people's living and thinking for them. This explains the tremendous emphasis on style in Irish writing from the time of Yeats onward.

Wilde had said that the only question about a work of art was whether it was well or badly written. Yeats concurred, contending that "books live almost entirely because of their style";[11] he argued that the part in men of action which corresponded to style was the moral element. He found, therefore, in style that middle term which reconciled the seemingly opposed worlds of action and interpretation:

> . . . Men are dominated by self-conquest; thought that is a little obvious or platitudinous if merely written, becomes persuasive, immortal even, if held to amid the sway of events. The self-conquest of the writer who is not a man of action is style . . .[12]

Self-conquest, as opposed to conquest by others: what was proposed here was not a self-cancellation, but a self so possessed that it could withstand the pressure of proffered, inappropriate forms. So "The Lake Isle of Innisfree" was praised by the artist as the first poem with his own music and rhythm about it.

What Yeats meant by style, therefore, was something much more expansive, muscular and demanding than the usual inferences drawn from the word. "Is not style not born out of the shock of new material?" Synge had asked him, on returning with his destined dialect from the Aran Islands.[13] The poet simply glossed that brilliant question with the observation that the new material was Ireland, awaiting its shaper like wax upon a table. On the islands, Synge had found in his objective surroundings a world which, until that moment, had been a subjective puzzle within his own unclear and disordered imagination. But his discovered style had freed Synge from the merely literary, said Yeats, enabling him "to take the first plunge into the world beyond himself, the first plunge away from himself that is always pure technique, the delight in doing not because one would or could, but merely because one *can* do".[14] Ideas were of strictly limited importance in a process which dictated that style anticipate subject matter, which in truth it helped to bring to birth; and self-conquest was redefined as the plunge away from self into pure technique.

Synge's life became in Yeats's interpretation a demonstration of the fact that confident self-possession was the polar opposite of self-assertion, which invariably arose from uneasiness. Thinking perhaps of the Negative Capability of Keats, of his ability to allow character to pass into intellectual production, Yeats submitted that the act of appreciation of any great thing was an act of self-conquest, such attention being very close to prayer. In that context, his famous injunction to Synge to express a life that has never found expression may be taken as referring to Synge's own experience rather than that of the islanders (whose lives, after all, had been most fully expressed in Gaelic literature and lore). *Style* in Yeats's system was the *antiself*, the opposite which turned out on inspection to be the secret double: Synge achieved on Aran what Wilde achieved in England, a language which was the opposite of all that he had known and heard in childhood and in youth.

The Wildean style had been adopted as a gross assumption, a mask. Yeats agreed: virtue, to be active, must be an endless theatrical playing with such masks, for the self evoked by style was external, something encountered as coming from without, which only later led the discovery of an answering self within. He castigated those rudimentary souls who lacked this sense of the theatrical. The provincial's inability to imagine a second self, to play instinctively before a mirror, to formulate an awareness of how he must appear to others, was a failure of the republican imagination, for which *style* was always a conscious relation between a past and a putative self. Edward Dowden, the Professor of English at Trinity College Dublin, was just such a provincial, unable to shape a metropolitan but none the less Irish style, for he employed on himself the received categories of English thought. Failing in self-conquest, he became an easy prey to cultural conquest by others and so he refused to trust his own nature while writing on Shakespeare. Contrasted with him, a true artist like Synge was uninfluenced by the opinion of inferiors, an authentic self-begetting Irishman.[15]

Whenever Yeats raised the question of style, it was as if he saw in it the promise of an antidote to Anglicization. "The difficulties of modern Irish literature from the loose, romantic legendary stories of Standish O'Grady to James Joyce and Synge had been in the formation of a style".[16] Douglas Hyde's ordinary English style was "without charm"; his Hiberno-English, on the other hand, was the coming of a new power into literature. "England had turned from style",[17] and it was style, therefore, which allowed one "to look into the lion's face (as it were) with unquivering eyelash".[18] But England once upon a time had known style, in the "heroic self-possession" of Hamlet, who could teach a nervous Irish youth how to play magnificently with hostile minds. In imitation of his hero, the young Yeats made model speeches as a training for the world rather than because he had anything to say: expression once again preceding concept in his development. It was his awareness of this rather strange sequencing which led to one of his autobiography's most famous aphorisms: "It is so many years before one can believe enough in what one feels even to know what the feeling is". First, there was a cadence, or perhaps an image; later, a sense of its inner content – and that became the trajectory of *Autobiographies*, the bringing into being of a real man who might finally be found to lie behind the style which evoked him: "I must go on that there may be a man behind the lines already written".[19]

This version of identity is a cornerstone of Protestantism. "The love of God for every human soul is infinite, for every human soul is unique",[20] wrote Yeats in *Anima Mundi*; and so the individual must justify God's love by perfecting its object. Near the close of his autobiography, he explained that style was the slayer of the old, derived self and the enabler of self-conquest. His authority for this was the Protestant service for the Burial of the Dead:

> A writer must die every day he lives, be reborn as it is said in the Burial Service, an incorruptible self, that self the opposite of all that he has named "himself".[21]

Polonius's ideal of truthfulness to oneself was cited by the poet as an example of bogus romantic sincerity: against it, he posited a Wildean notion of personality, intensified over many multiplications, until it achieved a fragmentary but real authenticity. "Men rise on stepping stones of their dead selves to higher things", the title of a youthful essay, turned out for all its didactic banality to be a truer Protestantism:[22] the Keatsian and Wildean self, though conceived as a theatrical search for an enabling style, became the surest basis for intelligent self-scrutiny. Style rather than sincerity was the important thing, since style bespoke authenticity. For Yeats, therefore, there was no final conflict between morality and style. In his view, the only morality was style, for in the crisis of creation it was this which caused a person to fuse with the opposite, buried self. A great writer would thus be one who became his own ideal reader, an effect increasingly achieved by Yeats within the major poems composed after he had begun to work on his autobiography.

Colonialism is rendered in that autobiography as a tyranny of books over life; and so the nervous youth begins with borrowed styles, in the manner of Hamlet or Byron or Shelley, and his father fears that he will turn into another Dowden. "You do not talk like a poet, but like a man of letters", he is told.[23] Yet when the son offers his elders a bookish idea – that you only know a landscape when you see it at night – he is warmly praised. It is all rather confusing – as confusing as the young woman who simulates an emotion most convincingly when she feels least implicated in it. The world seems subjugated by a literature which has preceded this young man to every experience of it: if he falls in love with Florence Farr, the actress, she disparages his courtship by saying that she had seen just his action in the theatre and so it must be "unreal". Realist art has corroded authentic life: so Yeats *pére* is forever scolding his son for talking for effect, for being theatrical, for sounding like a book. Yet the romanticism of John Butler Yeats is ultimately found to be inadequate, since it is based on the ideal of a unitary self.

The terror of a book-ridden culture is most present to him who would be the pioneer of a national poetic and not just an innovator. Whitman had tried in 1850s America to write as if he were Adam and there were no such a thing as a book, but his oppressive awareness of literary conventions was never more apparent than in his swaggering indifference to them. Yeats faced a similar problem:

> Lacking sufficient recognized precedent, I must needs find some reason for all that I did. I knew almost from the start that to overflow with reasons was to be not quite well-born; and when I could I hid them, as men hide a disagreeable ancestry; and that there was no help for it seeing that my country was not born at all.[24]

Here he is trying to invent Ireland *ex nihilo*, or at least to recreate a flawed ancestor along more reassuring lines. The nation will be defined by its assumed style, by its successful fusion with an Image which will be the opposite of what it has been deemed to be.

Such a struggle is tragic in its exactions, demanding that one daily recreate all that environment and circumstances snatch away: however, it enables Ireland to challenge England and to transcend the slot-rolling antithesis between the two peoples. Nationalism and Unionism are but one another's headache; those who insist that art must be either English or Irish are boring; but a nation having defined itself by passing through opposites, may see those opposites acquire sex and engender. When this happens, an end will come to that restless arraignment of the English Other and to the consequent purging of heresy within: instead there will emerge a self-creating Ireland produced by nothing but its own desire. Though offered primarily as the fusion of a great man with his Image, Yeats's account of this moment has implications for Anglo-Irish relations and for the liberated person who may yet be their outcome:

> The two halves of their nature are so completely joined that they seem to labour for their objects, and yet to desire whatever happens, being at the same time predestinate and free, creation's very self. We gaze at such men in awe, because we gaze not at a work of art, but at the recreation of the man through the art, the birth of a new species of man.[25]

The project of inventing a unitary Ireland is the attempt to achieve at a political level a reconciliation of opposed qualities which must first be fused in the self. In other words, personal liberation must precede national recovery, being in fact its very condition. His father's idea of uniting Catholic imagination with Protestant efficiency must have seemed to Yeats a wily appropriation *for Ireland alone* of the Arnoldian theory of Irish creativity "completing" English pragmatism in a unified British personality. Here, again, a potentially insulting cliché is retrieved by Yeats in a subtle and subversive fashion, to underwrite the very separatist claim which Arnold sought to deny.

Yeats's new species of Irishman is not so much the creator of the Image as its outcome: and the liberated people are not the inventors of personal style but its inferred content. That content is necessarily a throwback to a premodern culture common to England and Ireland before relations went sour, a people's culture in which "all, artist and poet, craftsman and day-labourer, would accept a common design", and in which literature "though made by many minds, would seem the work of one mind".[26] The paradox is again Whitmanian: perfect freedom of individual expression is possible in a code whose values are nonetheless communal. Deleuze and Guattari find such a paradox underlying all minor literatures:

> Because collective national consciousness is often inactive in external life and always in the process of breakdown, literature finds itself charged with the role of collective enunciation. Especially if a writer is on the margins, this allows him all the more scope to explore the community consciousness.[27]

The songs of Douglas Hyde were sung by the common people: Yeats was massively moved by this and desired to achieve a folkloristic impersonality in his ballads, an utterance which, though personal, would seem communal, possible only to one who thinks like a wise man but speaks like the common people. He would ultimately seek that utterance in Unity of Culture:

> Is there a nationwide multiform reverie, every mind passing through a stream of suggestion, and all streams acting and reacting on one another, no matter how distant the minds, how dumb the lips? A man walked, as it were, casting a shadow, and yet one could never say which was man and which was shadow, or how many the shadows that he cast. Was not a nation, as distinct from a crowd of chance-comers, bound together by this interchange among streams or shadows; that Unity of Image which I sought in national literature being but an originating symbol?[28]

Yet these speculations leave the poet repeatedly in intellectual solitude, with the realization that Unity of Culture might only be achieved by exceptionally gifted persons. Style, again, would be their redemption, that solitary self-absorbed consciousness, glimpsed in the late poem "Long-Legged Fly", which creates its own environment. Style so understood is a war on the chancy and casual, on mere character or circumstance, "as some Herodiade of our theatre, dancing seemingly alone in her narrow moving luminous circle".[29] As clothes express more of the self than a naked body, so the rearrangement of experience, in a style deliberately adopted, offers "escape from the hot-faced bargainers and the money-changers"[30] of a crass, commercial society. Style may be a mask but, because chosen, it is truer than any face. The flaw in a provincial Irish youth is his refusal of style, his disinclination to displace the given environment with something deliberated: "A young man in Ireland meets only crude, impersonal things, things that make him like others . . . He never seeks to make rooms charming, for instance . . ."[31]

What most moved Yeats about Wilde was the sense of his all-white rooms in London as the dramatized play of a consciousness, a style. This fascination persisted in subsequent Irish writers: Synge sought to be the first great artist of the bilingual style; Beckett insisted that it was the shape rather than the content of the sentence that counted; and Joyce left that traditional division open to question with his claim that in *Ulysses* the style was the subject. To all of them, style was potentially redemptive, charged with the power to lift the fallen material of the given world to a new place of consciousness. Yet there was a price to pay; and Yeats would wonder in more than one poem if this early elevation of form over matter had been advisable. Useful it had undeniably been as a ploy with which to kick-start a national poetic; but what if the style never found its subject, what if the singer born lacked a theme, what if it was only (as Beckett bitterly joked) a bow-tie worn over a throat-cancer? The price was discharged most painfully by Joyce, whose *Ulysses* is a compendium of styles no one of which seeds into flower. Whitman's own obsession with masturbation may be rooted in a similar desperation: the uncertainty behind the excessiveness of tone testified to a fear of unfruitfulness.

To write a deliberately new style, whether Hiberno-English or Whitmanian slang, was to seize power for new voices in literature: and the pretence of the national poet is that he or she is not constructed by previous literary modes. Synge wrote as if he were Adam and this the first day of creation: so did Whitman and so, at times, did Yeats. Their problem was that the worlds which they created existed only as linguistic constructs and solely for the duration of the text. Each artist had, strictly speaking, no subjective self preceding the book as predicate; and so the text had no time other than that of its enunciation. Yeats gave his own rueful account of how he could only set up a secondary or interior personality "created out of the tradition of myself" and "alas only possible to me in my writings".[32] Since there were no clear protocols for a national poet, Yeats and Whitman were compelled to charm an audience into being by the very tone of their own voices, assuming a people in order to prove that they were really there. It followed that the role which they imagined for themselves had to be announced and then demonstrated in the very act of writing.

In his attempt, Yeats was able to invoke the ancient Gaelic bards as he tried to educate an English-speaking audience; but even more stunning is his insistence on self-explanation and autocriticism within the poem itself. He shared with Whitman the lonely pioneer's need to talk to himself, to review his own work, to become his own first and ideal reader. Both men did not just say things: they also said why these things were appropriate to a national poet. They affected to discuss their own performances with the implied nation of readers in an unbuttoned fashion seldom possible within the English poetic tradition. The poets became their own critics, even as they urged their readers to become their own poets.

A consciousness which liberates a national idea by means of a renovated style lives in eternal peril: that, after humiliating failures to reproduce itself in the material world, it may become an end in itself. The beautiful soul, too good for this world, ends up experiencing society only as an irritant on the fringe of awareness, and those who began in hopes of recreating the conscience of a race may finally settle for defending a wearied sensibility. That is the progress of many a revivalist autobiography, not least that of Yeats. He started out in the conviction that texts by Synge, Lady Gregory and himself would provide the foundation for "the idea of a nation":[33] much later, he sadly concluded that he must settle for expressing "the individual". One consequence of this was that Yeats, like Whitman, could never write a satisfactory novel. Nor, truth to tell, could the great Irish or American novelists. Joyce and Beckett, like Melville and Hawthorne, so transformed the genre that the characteristic narrative in both cultures was asocial, the ongoing monologue. Such monologues originated in a puritan tradition of anxious self-scrutiny, of every person being his or her own priest.

The crucial passages in a book like *Moby Dick* or *Ulysses* are written as soliloquy: and the great poems by Whitman and Yeats are based on introspective self-analysis. The Yeats who saw poetry as a confession by one side of his personality to the other clearly operated in this way, much like the Protestant child who awakened to the accusing voice of conscience in the opening pages of his autobiography. In many late lyrics, Yeats sought to "cast out remorse" as a prelude to the moment when the body blazed and he could celebrate it. "I sing the body electric" proclaimed Whitman in launching an ecstatic catalogue of bodily parts: and Yeats praised "the thinking of the body" in a democratic equality of matter and mind. For each poet, the decolonization of the body was a task almost as important as the decolonization of the native culture: those two freedoms went together. If the body was a metaphor for the state, then its repossession in an epic mode meant as much to Whitman as to Yeats and Joyce: it was part of their attempt to construct themselves as national artists.

Nineteenth-century American literature was such a clear instance of a

decolonizing culture that it would have been amazing if its writers did
not exert a tremendous influence on the makers of the Irish revival. The
influence of Whitman on Yeats is perhaps the most striking of all. In
the 1904 issue of *Samhain*, the journal of his national theatre society,
Yeats remarked that a national literature "is the work of writers who are
moulded by the influences that are moulding their country, and who
write out of so deep a life that they are accepted there in the end".[34]
This seems a deliberate echo of Whitman's famous declaration that "the
proof of a poet is that his country absorbs him as affectionately as he
has absorbed it".[35] In the 1904 essay, Yeats went on to say that the
initial relationship may be adversarial, since whenever a country produces a man of genius he is never like that country's immediate idea of
itself: "When I was a boy, six persons who, alone out of the whole
world it may be, believed Walt Whitman a great writer, sent him a
message of admiration, and of those names four were English and two
were Irish, my father's and Professor Dowden's. It is only in our own
day that America has begun to prefer him to Lowell, who is not a poet
at all".[36] Though Yeats would later claim that Whitman, like Emerson,
lacked "the vision of evil", he never ceased to regard the American as a
test-case, devoting his analysis of Phase Six in *A Vision* to Whitman's
attempt to reconcile individualism with communal ideals: which is to
say that he used him as a sort of sounding-board in his own internal
struggle between "freedom" and "necessity", self and society.

Both Yeats and Whitman were initially more popular in England
than in their home countries. Amy Lowell accused Whitman of playing
the wild man or stage Yank and thus of appealing to recent immigrants
whose America is large, simple, and had to be remade from day to day,
i.e., those whose America had to be blatantly asserted rather than
effortlessly assumed. The same strictures against Yeats as professional
Celt were, of course, offered by Joyce and subsequent writers in Ireland.
Yet both poets were far more subtle than such a critique implied:
Whitman's theory of poetic "suggestiveness" is close to the Yeatsian
doctrine of "the half-said thing".[37] Their poems are founded on a
necessary contradiction: they celebrate a nation's soul, while at the same
time insisting that it has yet to be made. The tendency of many of
Yeats's poems to begin with an emphatic statement only to end in self-
questioning offers a variant on Whitman's theory that it is the reader,
rather than the poem, who needs to be complete.

Whitman mythologized himself, as Yeats later would, by pursuit of a
mask, realizing what his disciple would put into words: that the poet is
never the bundle of accident that sits down to breakfast, but one who

speaks through a phantasmagoria. Both described their ambitions in bardic terms, invoking the example of Homer and Shakespeare in their new national contexts: and both wrote their greatest texts out of the subsequent tragedy and disappointments of civil war. Whitman saw himself as counsellor of president and people: and so did Yeats. Both assumed intimacy with their personal lives on the part of their readers, expecting even such esoterica as Whitmanian phrenology or Yeatsian gyres to be indulged and understood. Both, experiencing themselves as media for unseen forces which spoke through them, staked their claim as "representative men", as types of a nation. Yet the traditions which they pioneered were also international, in the sense that they were certain that the conditions which produced them and their poems could be repeated in other places. Yeats was indeed an exemplar to Indian poets like Rabindranath Tagore, as was Whitman to many Latin Americans including Pablo Neruda. Thus was born "the international theme". The Irishman, no less than the American, was the heir of all the ages, creating not just a national poetic but also a new species of man.

RETURN TO THE SOURCE?

RETURN TO THE SOURCE?

There was no shortage of advice for Yeats as he embarked on his project. Many cautioned him that the national longing for form could be appeased only by a return to the native language. Irish, however, had been in decline for centuries. Ever since the 1650s, it had largely ceased to be a medium in which an intellectual life was possible, becoming the language of the poor and, in truth, a decisive mark of their poverty. The setting-up of the National Schools in the 1830s (schools in which English was both the main subject and the sole medium of instruction) dealt another grievous blow, as did O'Connell's insistence that children be taught English as a language more fitted to the modern world of business, professional activity and, of course, possible emigration. It was, however, the Famine which arguably did most damage of all.

No sooner did the demise of Irish seem likely than various antiquarian societies were founded, often by interested Protestant gentlemen who wished to assert the distinctiveness of Gaelic culture even as their own professional activities often served to integrate Ireland ever more fully with Britain. A remarkable number sprung up in the Famine decade, including the Archaeological Society (1840) and the Celtic Society (1845), yet none of them was committed to the preservation or revival of the Irish language. The interest was strictly antiquarian: manuscripts were collected, studied and translated, but that was all. Of the Gaelic Union, still active in the latter part of the nineteenth century, it was caustically observed that its discussions and publications were conducted in the English language. None of these considerations blunted the ardour of those who preached a "return to the source" available only in the energies and potentials of the ancestral language. On the opposing side were to be found those who argued for a further integration with Britain, then at the apex of the modern world system: these contended that only by cosmopolitanism of the kind which they professed could Ireland become a truly modern state. Put like this, the argument might seem to have been conducted in familiar terms of tradition versus modernity, but this was not quite so: at a deeper, more interesting, level, the debate was about how best to modernize.

Modernity, after all, was not a state which the Irish could choose or reject at will: to be Irish was to be modern in the sense that the Irish were seeking to find a home for themselves after a period of chaos and disruption. The crisis at the imperial centre had been transferred to the colonial periphery, where drastic juxtapositions of wealth and poverty, of the advanced and primitive, were the order of the day. England could insulate itself from many developing conflicts and then confront them at a safer remove in its colonies: the problem was that, all too often, the English would fail to understand the debates in the colonies in their own terms. English historians and commentators would translate the challenge posed by the Gaelic League back into the familiar binarism of tradition against modernity, rural versus urban, culture as opposed to industry. This, however, was not at all how the Irish Irelanders saw things: had this analysis been true, they would simply have been making common cause with the most backward and conservative elements in English aristocratic tradition. They, on the other hand, had learned from Thomas Davis of the vital link between culture and industry, and so they opted for a both/and philosophy rather than the either/or binarism of imperial theory. The Gaelic League did indeed wish to revive Irish as a prelude to a recovered national pride and economic prosperity, but its methods — mass democratic action, workers' education, mingling of the sexes on a basis of equality at free classes and summer schools — were anything but conservative. The League was in fact responsible for organizing the first great industrial parades held on St. Patrick's Day.

The cultural movements to which the League gave rise also refused to succumb to simplistic notions of tradition and innovation as opposed entities. Patrick Pearse's call for Gaelic artists to get in simultaneous touch with Old Irish literature and with the mind of contemporary Europe would be one instance,[1] and his conflation of ancient Gaelic systems of fosterage with the educational theories of Maria Montessori might be another. Even the aesthete and playwright J. M. Synge contributed to the new both/and thinking with a proposal that a complex system of railways be constructed across the island, which would convey workers from their homes in healthy country cottages to built-up factory sites for the day's labour and back home again in the evenings.[2] That blueprint seems to anticipate the idea of the "electronic cottage" which would be advanced many decades later by ecologically-minded socialists.

At the root of these proposals was a sense, common to their authors, of the

Irish movement as an alternative to the values epitomized by London. Regarding themselves as a new centre, they refused to cathect the margins so that the English could persist in seeing themselves as central. Instead, they insisted, like Buck Mulligan in Ulysses, *that Ireland could be the om-phalos, the navel-point. The centre of gravity in the artistic world was indeed passing from London to Dublin.*

Even more audacious was another related idea: that London was not just provincializing, but itself provincial. Power in the emerging world system was always elsewhere: London itself was filled with characters looking nervously over their shoulders to distant exemplars in Paris or New York. If there was no longer any absolute centre anywhere, there was clearly no point in remaining the province of a province. Better by far, for those who found themselves at a nodal point in a webbed network, to assert a proud centrality, at least for themselves. For most of the nineteenth century, and for some time before that, England and the English had been presented to Irish minds as the very epitome of the human norm. Now it began to be clear that, far from being normal, England's was an exceptionally stressed society, whose vast imperial responsibilities were discharged only at an immense psychological and social cost.

In some respects, the invention of modern Ireland had far more in common with the state-formation of other European countries such as Italy or France. In other ways, the analogies – especially in the domain of culture – would be with the emerging peoples of the decolonizing world. The debates about language revival, like the arguments about nationality and cosmopolitanism in literature, anticipated those which would later be conducted in Africa and Asia. One abiding difference, however, which left the Irish experience unique, was the sheer proximity of the imperial power, as a not-always-appreciated model, as a source of ideas, and as a market for surplus theories and labour.

Few of these comparisons and contrasts were available to Irish writers at the time. When some comparisons were finally made, they were mostly cast in terms of Britain and Europe: so it may be useful here, having considered the ways in which the Gaelic League was representative of the forces of state-formation in Western Europe, to widen the angle of vision and analyse the forces in Ireland which prefigured those in the "developing" world.

Eight

Deanglicization

The Irish writer has always been confronted with a choice. This is the dilemma of whether to write for the native audience – a risky, often thankless task – or to produce texts for consumption in Britain and North America. Through most of the nineteenth century, artists tended to exploit far more of Ireland than they expressed. Cruder performers resorted to stage-Irish effects, to the rollicking note and to "paddy-whackery", but even those who sought a subtler portraiture often failed, not so much through want of talent as through lack of a native audience. Most of these writers came, inevitably, from the upper classes and their commerce with the full range of Irish society was very limited.

The audience for most writing was primarily in England, and its expectations had to be satisfied. Occasionally, a writer like William Carleton might spring from the common people to real international success: but that success, in removing the artist from his own people into the ranks of the "classes", would often seem like a form of betrayal. This was why a group at the end of the century came to the conclusion that, if they were to create a truly national literature, they must also gather a national audience. If they were to invent Ireland, they must first invent the Irish. "Does not the greatest poetry always require a people to listen to it?" asked Yeats,[1] whose dream was to achieve with the Irish masses the sort of *rapport* enjoyed in the previous century only by the political leaders Daniel O'Connell and Charles Stewart Parnell.

The very success of both of these statesmen posed a problem, for neither had promoted the Irish language. O'Connell, though fluent in it, said that he could witness without a sigh the gradual disuse of Irish as it made way for the "superior utility" of English in matters of business and politics[2]: and Parnell, a Protestant gentleman educated at Cambridge, never had occasion to learn the language. O'Connell had chosen to use English at monster meetings attended by Irish speakers, on the shrewd understanding that his immediate audience was converted and that his need was to move English readers of his words in the next morning's newspaper. Almost inexorably, English had become *the* language in which the Irish nationalist case was made: a knowledge was essential for rebels who sought to defend themselves in court or for those agitators who wrote threatening letters to landlords.[3] The very notion of a modern nation is of a community, few of whose members can see or know one another, and who are thus bonded less by their massed bodies than by the abstract mechanism of print-technology. "Print language is what invents nationalism", observes Benedict Anderson, "and not a particular language *per se*":[4] and so Irish, being largely part of an oral culture, was supplanted by English, the logical medium of newspapers, and of those tracts and literary texts in which Ireland would be invented and imagined. If the colonial administration justified itself by waving pieces of paper bearing "titles" to occupied land, then the resistance movement would have to come up with its own set of documents to make its countervailing claim.

The literature so produced would base itself on a return to the people, the "hillside men" who were charmed by the *hauteur* of Parnell, a landlord who had gone against his own class. In this thrilling example, Yeats could find a model for the movement he hoped to lead: and so he wrote in October 1901:

> All Irish writers have to decide whether they will write as the upper classes have done, not to express but to exploit this country, or join the intellectual movement which has raised the cry that was heard in Russia in the seventies, the cry "to the people". Moses was little good to his people until he had killed an Egyptian; and for the most part a writer or public man of the upper classes is useless to this country till he has done something that separates him from his class.[5]

Accordingly, in the idealism of youth, Yeats had tried in *The Wanderings of Oisin* to recreate a Gaelic golden age, but working from "a version of a version" of the Gaelic original at his seat in the British Museum, he produced only the rather derivative "Celtic colourings" of a late-romantic English poem.[6] The problem was the same one that he had diagnosed in the patriotic ballads of Thomas Davis and Young Ireland: "they turned away from the unfolding of an Irish tradition, and borrowed the mature English methods of utterance and used them to sing of Irish wrongs or preach of Irish purposes. Their work was never wholly satisfactory, for what was Irish in it looked ungainly in an

English garb and what was English was never perfectly mastered, never wholly absorbed into their being".[7] The themes might have been patriotic, but the forms were borrowed sedulously from the English romantics: a complaint which would be repeated by J. M. Synge, when he castigated the "bad art" often favoured by the Irish Irelander, "imitations of fourth-rate English poetry and nineteenth-century Irish novels".[8]

In exalting the fight against England into a self-sustaining tradition, the leaders of the previous century had largely forgotten what it was that they were fighting for: a distinctive culture of folktales, dances, sports, costumes, all seamlessly bound by the Irish language. This grave error became clear to a young Protestant named Douglas Hyde, a rectory child at Frenchpark, County Roscommon, who learned from humble cottiers in the fields around his parents' home the idioms and lore of a culture quite different from that of the Anglo-Irish drawing-room. By the time he had entered Trinity College, Hyde was an enthusiast: asked by a bemused fellow-student if he could actually speak this exotic language of which he talked so movingly, he responded "I dream in Irish".[9] In 1892, his ideas came to fruition in a famous lecture which was to be Ireland's declaration of cultural independence, analogous to Ralph Waldo Emerson's epoch-making address on "The American Scholar".

Hyde's gospel was epitomized by one word: deanglicization. He argued that previous leaders had confused politics and nationality, and had abandoned Irish civilization while professing with utter sincerity to fight for Irish nationalism. He sought to restore self-respect to Irish people, based on a shared rediscovery of the national culture: far from being "the badge of a beaten race", as Matthew Arnold had called it, the Irish language should be spoken henceforth with pride. Hyde's suggestion met with much cynicism and much amusement. Society ladies on meeting Hyde would whisper to friends that "he cannot be a gentleman because he speaks Irish": and even those more sympathetic to the language were often irritated by Hyde's wide-eyed fervour.[10] George Moore wickedly remarked that whenever in his public speeches Hyde reverted to his incoherent brand of English, it was easy to see why his greatest desire was to make Irish the first official language.[11]

But the young Yeats was profoundly impressed, on hearing Hyde's songs sung by haymakers in Connacht fields who were quite unaware that their author was passing: in such a moment, Yeats saw the return of a learned art to people's craft. Hyde truly had the capacity to make Ireland once again interesting to the Irish. Fired by his example, Yeats hoped for "a way of life in which the common man has some share in imaginative art. That this is the decisive element in the attempt to revive the Irish language I am quite certain".[12] He dreamed of a literary form so pure that it had not been indentured to any cause, whether of nation or of art, a form so fitted to a people's expressive ensemble that it would seem but an aspect of daily life.

Yeats wrote: "In Ireland, where the Gaelic tongue is still spoken, and to some little extent where it is not, the people live according to a tradition of life that existed before commercialism, and the vulgarity founded upon it; and we who would keep the Gaelic tongue and Gaelic memories and Gaelic habits of mind would keep them, as I think, that we may some day spread a tradition of life that makes neither great wealth nor great poverty, that makes the arts a natural expression of life, that permits even common men to understand good art and high thinking, and to have the fine manners these things can give". He went on:

> Almost everyone in Ireland, on the other hand, who comes from what are called the educated and wealthy classes . . . seeks . . . to establish a tradition of life, perfected and in part discovered by the English-speaking peoples, that has made great wealth and great poverty, that would make the arts impossible were it not for the sacrifice of a few who spend their lives in the bitterest of protest . . .[13]

This line of approach impressed many readers in England, too, who saw in it an interesting development of Matthew Arnold's critique of the specialist barbarism of the commercially-minded middle class. In seeking to express Ireland, these writers also hoped to challenge the culture of commercial exploitation in England: rather than have the Irish imitate the worst of English ways, they hoped to bring around a time when the English could emulate the finest Irish customs.

The invention of their idea of Ireland by Hyde and his friends happened, it should be noted, at the same time as English leaders were redesigning the image of England, in the decades between the 1880s and the Great War. These were the years when Queen Victoria, recovering from the republican challenge of Dilke and from her own grief after bereavement, restored a dimension of public pageantry to the monarchy, with much ancient costumery, archaic carriages and historical symbolism. Her 1887 jubilee proved so successful that it was repeated ten years later in 1897, and this prompted Irish nationalists in the following year, under the guidance of Maud Gonne, W. B. Yeats

and James Connolly, to mount a similar counter-commemoration of
the rebellion of 1798. Yeats said in March of 1898: "This year the Irish
people will not celebrate, as England did last year, the establishment of
an empire that has been built on the rapine of the world".[14] The new
mania in England for erecting statues to historic figures was also
emulated by the Irish, who began at once to collect funds for a massive
monument to Wolfe Tone (as if a state which still did not exist were
already rehearsing its consolidation by ceremonial recollections of the
revolutionary struggle). Both the jubilee-cult and the statuary were
relatively new phenomena, and mocked for their sentimentality by the
young James Joyce in *Dubliners*, but it is easy to understand the
function which they served.

The world was changing more in those thirty years than it had since
the death of Christ. All over Europe leaders sought to reassure peoples,
gone giddy from the speed of the changes, with images of stability. Part
of the modernization process was the emergence of nation-states, which
often arose out of the collapse of the old ways of life and so were badly
in need of legitimation: this was afforded by the deliberate invention of
traditions, which allowed leaders to ransack the past for a serviceable
narrative.[15] In this way, by recourse to a few chosen symbols and simple
ideas, random peoples could be transformed into Italians or Irish, and
explain themselves by a highly-edited version of their history. Gaelic
Ireland had retained few institutions or records after 1601 to act as a
brake on these tendencies: all that remained were the notations of poets
and the memories of the people. These played a far greater part in
Hyde's remodelled Ireland than they did in many of the other emerging
European countries. His lecture, rather cumbersomely titled "The
Necessity for Deanglicizing Ireland", was delivered to the Irish Literary
Society in November 1892, and it led, within a year, to the foundation
of the Gaelic League, a movement for the preservation of Irish. The fall
of Parnell, and subsequent split in the Irish Parliamentary Party at
Westminster, may have left a number of unionists and landlords feeling
free to express a cultural (as distinct from political) nationalism. If so,
there was a real shrewdness in Hyde's strategy. He launched his appeal
for Gaelic civilization as one coming from a man who could still feel
the landlordly hankerings of a disappointed imperialist:

> . . . It is the curious certainty that come what may Ireland will continue to
> resist English rule, even though it should be for their good, which prevents
> many of our nation from becoming unionists on the spot . . . It is just
> because there appears no earthly chance of their becoming good members

of Empire that I argue that they should not remain in the anomalous position they are in, but since they absolutely refuse to become the one thing, that they become the other; cultivate what they have rejected, and build up an Irish nation on Irish lines.[16]

That subterranean pull back to all things English as touchstones of excellence is ironic in a text headed "deanglicization", but Hyde knew what he was about. He wanted to found Irish pride on something more positive and lasting than mere hatred of England. Yeats agreed: "I had dreamed of enlarging Irish hatred, till we had come to hate with a passion of patriotism what Morris and Ruskin hated".[17] The reactive patriotism which saw Ireland as not-England would have to give way to an identity which was self-constructed and existentially apt. Those peoples who *had* constructed themselves from within, the French for instance, never accused their bad citizens of being "unFrench": but throughout the nineteenth century delinquents were often called "un-Irish", because Irish nationalism too often defined itself by what it was against.

The Gaelic League might properly be seen as a response to the failure of a political attempt by nationalist leaders to shock English opinion by showing up the discrepancy between English order at home and misrule on the neighbouring island. The Irish resolved instead to instil in their people a self-belief which might in time lead to social and cultural prosperity. In its early years, the League received encourage-ment from the more enlightened colonial administrators like Augustine Birrell, who hoped that it might help to solve problems which the authorities had found intractable.

As a movement, the League was opposed to the antiquarianism of previous groups like the Gaelic Union, only six of whose members could speak Irish properly: it was, in fact, modern in its view of tradition as a yet-to-be-completed agenda, and in its insistence on combining ancient custom and contemporary method.

Some cynics accused Hyde of confusing Anglicization with modern-ization. Joyce's Stephen Hero, noting the willingness of the Catholic clergy to support the League, said that the priests hoped to find in Irish a bulwark against modern ideas, keeping "the wolves of unbelief" at bay and the people frozen in a past of "implicit faith".[18] This was a rather sour response from a Joyce whose experience of the League had been fatally narrowed by his attendance at the Irish classes of Patrick Pearse. (Pearse in his youthful days found it impossible to praise Irish without virulent denunciations of English, an approach much less ecumenical than Hyde's.) In the 1892 lecture, Hyde feared that people, ceasing to be Irish without becoming English, were falling into the vacuum between two admirable civilizations, as one nullified the other. His disgust was not caused by a baffling modernity or a difficult hybridity, so much as by the anomalous English element in every self-defeating document of Irish nationalism. He pointed to "the illogical position of men who drop their own language to speak English, of men who translate their euphonious Irish names into English monosyllables, of men who read English books and know nothing about Gaelic literature, nevertheless protesting as a matter of sentiment that they hate the country which at every hand's turn they rush to imitate".[19]

This was a subtle probing of Irish psychology: patriotic Anglophobia it attributed not to a troublesome difference with England so much as an abject similarity, leading like poles to repel one another with scientific predictability. Anglophobia seemed most extreme in those areas of maximum deference to English ways, while in the *Gaeltacht* itself physical-force nationalism made little headway. Hyde was merciless on the mentality which "continues to apparently hate the English, and at the same time continues to imitate them". Since people absolutely refused to become English, he concluded, they might as well resolve to be Irish.

This analysis had many salutary effects. Most important, it was the signal for a rebirth of cultural and literary criticism. Before the end of the decade, D. P. Moran could remark that "much the perpetual flow of ridicule and largely unreasonable denunciation of England was turned from its course and directed back – where it was badly wanted – upon Irishmen themselves".[20] Moran went on: "From the great error that nationality is politics, a sea of corruption has sprung. Ireland was practically left unsubjected to wholesome native criticism, without which any collection of humanity will corrupt . . . To find fault with your countryman was to play into the hands of England and act the traitor". For most of the previous century, a kind of national narcissism had pervaded debates: ever since O'Connell had told his followers that they were the finest peasantry in the world, even constructive criticism had been treated as sacrilege. Such a high-minded allergy to critique has been found in the early phases of most movements for cultural resistance – but this sentimentality had to be transcended. D. P. Moran suggested that an Ireland content to continue as a not-England would be indescribably boring: "Will a few soldiers dressed in green, and a republic, absolutely foreign to the genius of the Irish people, the humiliation of England, a hundred thousand English corpses with Irish bullets or pikes through them, satisfy the instinct within us that says 'Thou shalt be Irish'?"[21] It was Irish strength, rather than English weakness, which would count in the end.

What shocked Hyde about contemporary England was the apparent ease with which its people had endured the loss of so many of their traditions for the sake of material advancement. For English folk traditions he had, like Yeats, much respect and tenderness. When he spoke of "this awful idea of complete Anglicization", the phrase, if taken literally, could only offend unionists: if it were taken as a reference to the pollution and greyness of an environment despoiled by unplanned industrialism, it might win many over. Hyde insisted that the English would not finally be to blame if the Irish decided to abort their own traditions: "what the battleaxe of the Dane, the sword of the Norman, the wile of the Saxon were unable to perform, we have accomplished ourselves".[22] This was true in the sense that Irish declined in the nineteenth century only when large numbers of the people opted to learn English, as a prelude to emigration or to a more prosperous life at home. The tally-stick, later to be cited by chauvinist historians as a weapon of British cultural terror, had actually been devised for the schoolroom by Irish people themselves, as Sir William Wilde (father of Oscar) observed with dismay in a Galway schoolhouse of the mid-century:

> The man called the child to him, said nothing, but drawing forth from its dress a little stick, commonly called a scoreen or tally, which was suspended by a string round the neck, put an additional notch in it with his pen-knife. Upon our enquiring into the cause of their proceeding, we were told that it was done to prevent the child speaking Irish; for every time he attempted to do so a new nick was put in his tally, and, when these amounted to a certain number, summary punishment was inflicted on him by the schoolmaster.[23]

Hyde sensed that a purely economic or political freedom would be hollow, if the country was by the time of its attainment "despoiled of the bricks of nationality". The listless condition of dozens of post-colonies in the twentieth century was astutely anticipated by Hyde: "just at the moment when the Celtic race is presumably about to largely recover possession of its own country, it finds itself deprived and stript of its Celtic characteristics, cut off from its past, yet scarcely in touch with its present".[24] Equally familiar in the emergent states of Africa and Asia would be accounts of how young men and women were found to blush with shame when overheard speaking their own language. As would happen in some of these societies too, many children were not even aware of the existence in their culture of two languages: in the Connacht known to Hyde, parents often spoke Irish only to children who answered in English only, and when Hyde asked some children "Nach labhrann tú Gaeilge?" (Don't you speak Irish?), the answer was "And isn't it Irish that I'm speaking?" This domestic situation was repeated in *Gaeltacht* classrooms where schoolteachers spoke only English to children who spoke only Irish: Hyde wondered if there was any other country in the world where schoolteachers taught children who could not understand them, and children learned from instructors whose language they could not really follow.[25] There were many indeed.

His holistic method led Hyde to emphasize the intimate link between clothing and language. As Yeats could bewail the ways in which Irish sentiment looked ungainly in English garb, so Hyde regretted that men of the midland counties had grown "too proud" to wear homespun tweeds. The analysis anticipated by decades the strictures of Antonio Gramsci and John Berger on the crumpled, ill-fitting suits worn in photographs by peasants and labourers early this century: their vigorous actions simply spoiled the suits which were quite inappropriate to the lives they led, being designed for the sedentary administrators of the ruling class, but the suits signalled their acceptance of being "always, and recognizably to the classes above them, second-rate, clumsy, uncouth, defensive".[26]

The rhetorical guile of Hyde has been insufficiently recognized: the deanglicization lecture which began with an appeal to unionist-imperialists could nonetheless be brought to a climax with the Fenian trope of a call for a house-to-house visitation, "something – though with a very different purpose – analogous to the procedure that James Stephens adopted throughout Ireland when he found her like a corpse on a dissecting table".[27] Though he might steal some of these Phoenix fires and might use "west-Britonizing" as a term of jocular abuse, Hyde was no narrow-gauge nationalist: for he encouraged the "use of Anglo-Irish literature instead of English books, especially instead of English periodicals. We must set our face firmly against penny dreadfuls, shilling shockers, and, still more, the garbage of vulgar weeklies like *Bow Bells* and the *Police Intelligence*". This diagnosis has more in common with the future strictures of F. R. Leavis or, for that matter, Theodor Adorno, than might at first seem the case. The alleged anti-modern element in Irish revivalism, of which revisionist historians have made so much, turns out on inspection to be a prophetic critique of mass-culture and of the vulgarization of popular taste. The Gaelic League, acting on Hyde's precepts, became in effect one of the earliest examples of a Workers' Education Movement, at a time of limited opportunity for many. It was also, in some respects, a precursor of the movement for multiculturalism which, in later decades, would seek to revise and expand syllabi, with the introduction of subaltern cultures and oral literatures. In other respects, of course, its leaders were dismissive of many popular publications and magazines which current exponents of Cultural Studies find worthy of attention.

There were only six books in print in Irish at the founding of the League in 1893, and most Irish speakers in the countryside were still illiterate. Yet much was achieved very rapidly: in one year alone, according to Yeats, the League sold 50,000 textbooks.[28] Thousands registered in language classes, and, in a decade which saw Fabian cyclists and suffragists take to the countryside for summer schools, the League was an interesting Irish version of the phenomenon. A civil rights agitation was mounted. Letters and parcels were addressed in Irish, much to the confusion of the postal authorities; and when a Donegal trader was prosecuted for inscribing his name in Irish on his wagon, he was defended in court by the young Patrick Pearse (his only appearance as a barrister, in what he called the ignoblest of professions).

Questions were raised in the House of Commons about such issues, but the crucial controversy arose in 1899, when evidence was taken by the Committee of Intermediate Education on whether or not it should ratify Irish as a valid school subject. The professors of Trinity College Dublin had taken fright at the League's success and warned Dublin Castle that it was a movement infiltrated by "separatists". Now they made a massive effort to remove Irish altogether from the secondary school system. John Pentland Mahaffy, a former tutor of Oscar Wilde and a Professor of Ancient History at Trinity, told the committee that, although it was sometimes useful to a man fishing for salmon or shooting game, it would be an unconscionable waste of time to teach it in schools, since it was "almost impossible to get hold of a text in Irish which is not religious or that is not silly or indecent".[29] Quite reasonably, Hyde asked how Mahaffy, a man ignorant of the Irish language, could make such sweeping claims: and he adduced evidence from a range of Celtic scholars to establish the value and scope of ancient Irish literature. Citations came from Windisch in Leipzig, Zimmer in Greifswald, Stern in Berlin, Meyer in Liverpool, Pedersen in Copenhagen, Dottin in Rennes; and York Powell of Oxford, a historian, wrote of the advantages to children of bilingualism. At this point in the controversy, Mahaffy revealed the source of his claims: Robert Atkinson, the Professor of Old Irish at Trinity who – in a remarkable anticipation of the line taken by prosecuting counsel in the 1960 trial of *Lady Chatterley's Lover* – declared that many Irish-language texts were unfit to have in the house alongside his daughters: if perused, they might cause a shock from which the young ladies might not recover for the rest of their lives.

Atkinson testified that the study of *Diarmuid and Gráinne*, then on the Intermediate course, was quite unsuitable for children: and he attacked one of Hyde's published stories as the doings of a common lout who never washed. He went on – with a tactic which would also be used by conservative academics in many emerging states – to denounce the native language for its alleged lack of a standard grammar and spelling. All in all, his evidence was a graphic illustration of the covert hatred among many exponents of Celticism for the peoples whose study made their professional reputations. Stung by Atkinson's strictures on grammar and syntax, Fr. Peter O'Leary embarked, in the League's weekly paper *An Claidheamh Soluis* (The Sword of Light), on a detailed examination of Atkinson's own treatment of the copula *is* in his scholarly edition of *Trí Biorghaoithe an Bháis*, which he found so faulty that a couplet soon spread across the land:

> Atkinson of TCD
> Doesn't know the verb *to be*.

In later exposures, O'Leary showed that Atkinson's Irish was so shaky that "he had not the grasp of it that a gossoon in a Connemara bog has".[30]

For all its offence and inadvertent hilarity, this controversy was useful, for the battle with the Trinity dons brought public opinion solidly behind the Gaelic League. Yeats played a leading part in this: in February 1900, he called upon members of parliament to use the old Parnellite methods of obstruction to insert the teaching of Irish into the Education Bill. He condemned Trinity College as provincial, "which the Literary Society is not, and the Gaelic League is not; we must fight against provincialism and die fighting".[31] In *Beltaine*, the theoretical journal of the Irish Literary Theatre, the dramatist Edward Martyn wrote sardonically of "the efforts of certain persons and institutions whose aim seems to be to create in Ireland a sort of shabby England".[32] By 1906, the League had secured the use of Irish in Gaeltacht schools, as a subject in itself and, in addition, as the usual language of instruction, a campaign significantly assisted by the writings of J. M. Synge.[33] By 1909, Irish had been made compulsory for matriculation at the National University, just a year after Hyde's appointment to a professorship there.

In calling for a return to national traditions, Hyde had made a telling point: that far from being fixated on the past, the Irish were in danger of making an irreparable break with their inheritance. This blockage had its roots in the enforced migrations and interrupted family histories of the nineteenth century, which had disrupted the national archive. Hyde, by his promotion of Celtic scholarship and of Irish, was seeking to repair and restore it. He was dismayed by that weird blend of external deference and private rebellion which characterized the Irish relation to England. What remained of the Irish identity had been preserved through the spiritual leadership given to many people by the Catholic church, but that same church had also blocked the expression of that identity by the more militant nationalists and republicans.

Hyde, in unstopping the sentiment, was also careful to recognize the spiritual dimension in a collection like *Abhráin Diaga Chúige Chonnacht* (The Religious Songs of Connacht). He did indeed woo the Catholic clergy, though for subtler reasons than Joyce might have suspected: he needed their endorsement as an answer to those pious Catholics who condemned the mingling of sexes at League functions as "occasions of sin". Moreover, he was well aware that the careers of many Irish-language enthusiasts among the Catholic clergy had been stymied, in Maynooth and elsewhere, as a result of their high-profile activities. Men like Lorcán Ó Muireadhaigh, Dr. O'Hickey and Walter McDonald got into trouble with the ecclesiastical authorities for promoting Irish, for insisting on its central importance in the syllabus for matriculation, and so on. Far from abjectly toadying to such figures, Hyde may have been attempting to accord them a degree of respectability, by featuring them on platforms at successful mass-meetings. Those priests would undoubtedly have contained within their ranks a predictable proportion of conservative, anti-modern theologians, as Joyce alleged – but there were others, such as Walter McDonald, who were at the forefront of progressive movement, as well as being completely ecumenical.

Apart from being a great ecumenist and reconciler himself, Hyde was ever the cunning tactician – properly grateful to have the support of prestigious Catholic priests, whose presence could serve to glamorize the Irish language in the eyes of a peasantry for whom it had long been a token of shame. As the priests had once done, so now he – a Protestant gentleman-scholar – assumed leadership of a people whose traditions had been so disrupted that they were estranged from their very environment.

A major agent of that estrangement had been the Board of Education, which throughout the previous century, in Ireland as in India, had encouraged the materially ambitious natives to abandon their culture. These people had been encouraged to view their own great narratives as mere myths to be discarded (much as the Elizabethan historians like Stanyhurst had mocked the "unscientific" memorialists of Gaelic Ireland). If anything, the situation in Ireland was more extreme than that in India, for the Irish school texts were given to every child and brooked no nationalism, whereas the Indian books were intended only for the élites and *did* allow a modicum of national sentiment. The value of the new education, the British claimed, was that it would help the people to dismantle the myths which still bound them to their own culture, and instead, in the words of Lord Macaulay's minute on India, "make them look to this country with that veneration which the youthful student feels for the classical soul of Greece".[34] However, the pitched battle put up by Trinity College against the Gaelic League had precisely the reverse effect to that intended and had thrown this entire process into jeopardy. By 1903, the constitutional nationalist Stephen Gwynn, a member of parliament, could write that "I have heard the existence of an Irish literature denied by a roomful of professors, educated gentlemen, and, within a week, I have heard, in the same country, the classics of that literature recited by an Irish peasant who could neither write nor read. On which party should the stigma of illiteracy set the uglier brand?"[35]

The disarray of political nationalism in the 1890s had allowed some unionists to adopt a more relaxed attitude to the Gaelic tradition, and the League made an appeal to a much wider version of nationality. The movement was so powerful in Belfast by 1899 that it could cram a meeting-hall which called for the teaching of Irish in schools:

All classes and creeds were represented at the gathering. The first resolution was proposed by an MA of Trinity College. Nationalists and Unionists, Protestants and Catholics, were equally earnest in their advocacy of the language – the Protestant Bishop of Ossory wrote in open approval of "a platform on which all lovers of our dear native land could meet as nationalists in the truest sense of the word".[36]

By 1904, it was the strongest democratic organization in the country, wooed by the directors of the Abbey Theatre and by John Redmond's Parliamentary Party which offered Hyde a seat in Westminster. He refused, but only on being cautioned that such a gesture would reduce the inflow of funds from nationalist sympathizers in the United States. The long-term implications of Hyde's position were by then becoming clear, and they were spelt out vividly by the Protestant canon James Hannay (*alias* George Birmingham, novelist) in 1907:

> I take the Sinn Féin position to be the natural and inevitable development of the League principles. They couldn't lead to anything else . . . I do not myself believe that you will be able to straddle the fence for very much longer. You have, in my humble opinion, the chance of becoming a great Irish leader, with the alternative of relapsing into the position of a John Dillon. It will be intensely interesting to see which you choose. Either way, I think the movement you started will go on, whether you lead it or take the part of a poor Frankenstein who created a monster he could not control.[37]

Hyde did lose control. The Fenian sub-text of his own language impelled his more ardent supporters towards a brazenly political commitment: and Hyde, whose uninterest in politics helped to widen his initial support, now found that his political *naïveté* could lead to the League's decline or, at any rate, its co-option by other forces. Though thousands of students had enrolled in the League's classes, few ever got beyond the learning of a few token phrases. Without state support, there was a clear limit to what could be achieved. Equally, the *Gaeltacht*, the repository of unbroken traditions, could hardly be saved by a non-political organization which, by its own self-denying ordinance, could never expect to bring about industrial reform. The Gaelic League saw very clearly that if the *Gaeltacht* were left to survive on tourism, it would soon become a mere reservation, a museum: "the language, the industries, and the very existence of a people are all interdependent, and whoever has a living care for the one cannot be unmindful of the other".[38] So Patrick Pearse urged a programme of industrial development and called upon Leaguers to settle in the west, thereby making a real commitment over and above the use of ritual phrases. They did not go, preferring, as Sean O'Casey sarcastically noted, to stay in the more respectable Dublin suburbs of Donnybrook and Whitehall, "lisping Irish wrongly" and wincing at workmen like himself who frequented their meetings.[39]

O'Casey's portrait of Hyde in his autobiography is a vicious travesty of a kindly visionary, but there is truth in its retrospective suggestion that the League seemed at times to have confused "the fight for Irish" with "the fight for collars and ties". The lyrics studied in League classes often seemed to favour mental over physical labour:

> Aoibhinn beatha an scoláire
> bhíos ag deanamh léinn;
> is follas daoibh, a dhaoine,
> gur dó is aoibhne in Éirinn.
>
> Gan smacht rí air ná ruire
> ná tiarna dá threise,
> gan chuid cíosa ag caibidil,
> gan mochéirí, gan meirse.
>
> Mochéirí ná aoireacht
> ní thabhair uaidh choíche;
> is ní mó do-bheir dá aire
> fear na faire san oíche.[40]
>
> The life of a scholar is pleasant
> as he pursues his learning;
> it must be clear to you, O people,
> that his is the pleasantest life in Ireland.
>
> Neither king nor prince controls him,
> nor does any leader however strong,
> he does not have to pay dues to clergy,
> nor does he wake early or have to do hard labour.
>
> Early rising and animal-minding
> are things he never needs to do;
> and he never pays any heed
> to the watchman in the nights.

Many Gaelic texts revived in the period were out-and-out attacks in the name of the Gaelic bards on the brutish parliamentarians of an earlier century. *Pairlement Chloinne Tomáis* (The Parliament of Clan Thomas), republished in 1912, probably helped to feed the forces of extra-parliamentary nationalism which gathered momentum in that year.

Some Leaguers projected an ideal self-image of the Gael as a descendant of ancient chieftains and kings. Irish Ireland countered the petty *"seoinín"* or West Briton, who asserted his superiority by imitating English manners, with its own form of invented Gaelic snobbery. Ireland became not-England, an apophatic construct which was as teasing to the mind as the notion of a horse as a wheelless car. Anything English was *ipso facto* not for the Irish, as it might appear to weaken the claim to separate nationhood, but any valued cultural possessions of the English were shown to have their Gaelic equivalents. Thus was born what Seán de Fréine has acutely called an ingenious device of national parallelism:[41]

English language – Irish language
English law   – Brehon law
Parliament   – Dáil
Prime Minister – Taoiseach
Soccer   – Gaelic football
Hockey   – Hurling
Trousers   – Kilt

It mattered little whether those devices had a secure basis in Irish history, for if they had not previously existed they could be invented, Gaelic football being a classic case of instant archaeology but definitely not a game known to Cuchulain.

Equally, because Englishmen were sensible enough to wear trousers in their inclement climate, it followed that the romantic, impractical Irishman must have worn a kilt. This garment pleased the revivalists with its connotations of aristocracy, of Scottish chieftains and pipers marching into battle; but the garment never was Irish; and subsequent historians have shown that the Irish wore hip-hugging trousers long before the English (and were reviled for the barbarous fashion by the new invaders). The kilt wasn't properly Scottish either, having been devised by an English Quaker industrialist, seeking an outlet for unused tartan *after* the highland clearances: it was worn by Scottish workers in the new factories because it was cheaper than trousers.[42] None of these considerations, however, prevented a generation of enthusiasts from raising the cry "Down with trousers!" Some devious souls tried to have it both ways, as in George Moore's recommendation that tartan trousers be worn to his Gaelic lawn-party at Ely Place. *An Claidheamh Soluis* contributed to this pan-Celtic lunacy when it announced its own inspired compromise: "We condemn English-made evening dress, but evening dress of Irish manufacture is just as Irish as a

Donegal cycling suit. Some people think we cannot be Irish unless we always wear tweeds and only occasionally wear collars".[43]

One historian has marvelled at how heated these debates could become and has suggested that the success of the League can be explained by "the opportunity it extended to a snobbishly-afflicted middle and lower-middle class to assert a new social self-respect".[44] Sean O'Casey spoke corrosively of these pretensions to respectability, but it was left to James Joyce to write the most lethal account of the careerism of some Leaguers in his short story titled "A Mother". A respectable woman named Mrs. Kearney sees in the League a chance to promote not the cause of Irish but the musical prospects of her daughter:

> When the Irish Revival began to be appreciable, Mrs. Kearney determined to take advantage of her daughter's name and brought an Irish teacher to the house. Kathleen and her sister sent Irish picture postcards to their friends and those friends sent back other Irish picture postcards . . . People said that she was very clever at music and a very nice girl, and, moreover, that she was a believer in the language movement. Mrs. Kearney was well content with this.[45]

The daughter secures a position as accompanist at a series of concerts in aid of the Éire Abú Society, but when the functions are poorly attended and the society cannot afford to pay the fee, the mother creates a nasty scene and insists on every last penny. Joyce could see how, for some, the new social self-respect could verge on hard-nosed bourgeois materialism.

It was, however, the *unworldliness* of Hyde's analysis which led to the confrontation with radical Leaguers led by Pearse, who insisted that Ireland should not merely be free but Gaelic, not merely Gaelic but free, and that the two aspirations were inter-dependent. By its refusal to follow this logic, the League got left behind in the years leading up to the 1916 Rising. By 1913, Pearse was announcing that "the Gaelic League, as the Gaelic League, is a spent force", though he was careful to add in another speech of the following year that "what will be accomplished by the men of this generation, will be accomplished because the Gaelic League made it possible".[46] Hyde was disgusted by Pearse's support for James Larkin during the Lock-Out of 1913, though, in fairness, it should be said that he may have been motivated by concern f r the hungry families of workers rather than the welfare of the bosses: but his break from the League came only in 1915, at a Dundalk conference which adopted a clear nationalist stance. He resigned the presidency amid tears and regret. "My own ideas had been quite different", he explained: "My own ambition had always been the language as a neutral ground upon which all Irishmen might meet . . . We were doing the only business that really counted, we were keeping Ireland Irish, and that in a way that the Government and Unionists, though they hated it, were powerless to oppose. So long as we remained non-political, there was no end to what we could do".[47]

By a wonderful irony, Hyde ended his days as first president of the Irish Free State, a golf-playing, grouse-shooting Anglo-Irish gentleman, who had never in his long life uttered a word from a public platform in support of Home Rule. His glory days had been the 1890s and the first decade of the new century, the heyday of the League, a period during which he supplied Synge and Lady Gregory with their literary dialect. He was described, with no exaggeration, as scholar-in-waiting to the Irish renaissance, furnishing Yeats with the figure of Hanrahan and a host of other *personae*. Sean O'Casey's rather savage comments on Hyde's snobbism and his "Déanta in Éirinn Irish" were tinged with the bitterness of retrospect, though it was noticeable that after Hyde's elevation to a university chair in 1908 references to him by writers became faintly mocking. George Russell was convinced that Hyde actively discouraged "the vital element"[48] in the League which would have been willing to challenge the conservative Catholic clergy. The man's popularity with crowds remained as great as ever, but rendered him a dubious quantity in the eyes of fastidious intellectuals. Yeats's poem "At the Abbey Theatre" is condescending rather than envious of that appeal; and George Moore depicted Hyde as the invertebrate kind of Catholic Protestant, "cunning, subtle, cajoling, superficial and affable".[49] This was rather too cynical an interpretation. In a land fissured along sectarian fault-lines, a "Catholic Protestant" was by no means an ignoble thing to be: the inclusiveness and ecumenism of Hyde's position would be a source of inspiration to many subsequent writers of Protestant background in later decades.

The real weaknesses of Hyde's position were to be found elsewhere: in his blithe assumption that a movement as opposed to mainstream unionism as the Gaelic League could somehow be non-political. Just as the League was weakened by its reluctance to examine the economic realities which underlay cultural policies (including the materialist motivations of some of its fair-weather enthusiasts), it was also blinded by a failure to examine the *political* assumptions of the movement. It was captured, as James Hannay so acutely predicted, not by the parliamentarians but by Sinn Féin, whose leaders took up the running after Dundalk. Cultural nationalism was soon supplanted by a more openly political movement, which in turn issued in the militarism of Easter 1916. Like many who partook in that uprising, Michael Collins had no doubt as to its intellectual sources: "we only succeeded after we had begun to get back our Irish ways; after we had made a serious effort to speak our own language; after we had striven again to govern ourselves".[50] It was not, however, the Easter Rising which put paid to the League's major influence and power. Rather, it was the unexamined contradictions in its programme which prevented it from gaining more unionist adherents and from keeping the militant nationalists at arm's length before the Rising. Later still, it would become redundant in the judgement of many because of the apparent embrace of its programme by the founders of the Free State. Nonetheless, of Hyde it could justly be said that he rescued the Irish element from absorption and made it, for a brilliant generation from 1893 to 1921, conscious of itself.

Nine

Nationality or Cosmopolitanism?

Even before the League held its founding meeting, Yeats had deflected the challenge which it posed to creative writers. Though many in decades to come would scoff at the patent contradiction of an Irish National Theatre staging plays in the English language, Yeats had solved that problem to his own satisfaction as far back as 1892:

> Is there then no hope for the de-Anglicizing of our people? Can we not build a national tradition, a national literature which shall be none the less Irish in spirit from being English in language?[1]

He answered that it could be done "by translating and retelling in English, which shall have an indefinable Irish quality of rhythm and style, all that is best in the ancient literature". Though the success of the League in the following decade would cause many English-speaking writers to learn Irish, and some to flirt with the idea of writing in it, the die was cast. Hyde was himself unwittingly to provide a spectacular example of the shape which events were taking: in his most successful collection, *Abhráin Ghrá Chúige Chonnacht: Love Songs of Connacht*, published in his *annus mirabilis* of 1893, he printed the Irish text on one side of the page and his own translation into Hiberno-English dialect on the other. It soon became clear, however, that the main appeal of this book to Yeats and his young contemporaries lay in Hyde's own translations, and especially in those translations written in prose rather than verse. The very success of the book caused the defeat of its initial purpose, for, along with popularizing Irish literature, it made the creation of a national literature in English seem all the more feasible.

Hyde's position was ambiguous from the start: in one sense, he was the leader of the movement to save Irish, but in another, he was a founder of the Anglo-Irish literary revival. Subsequent literary history was to emphasize the cruelty of the paradox: it was desperately un-fortunate for him that his campaign to save Irish should have coincided with the emergence of a group of Irishmen destined to write master-pieces in English. The fact that, without the Gaelic *substratum*, few of them would have written so richly and some might not even have emerged, simply underlines the accuracy of Yeats's initial reading of the situation. George Moore might call for "a return to the language . . . a mysterious inheritance in which resides the soul of the Irish people";[2] he might even threaten to disinherit his nephews if they failed to learn the native tongue; but when his own Irish teacher called at the appointed hour to his house in Ely Place, he had the butler tell him he was out.

The old *canard* that "the Gael must be the element that absorbs" was never seriously entertained by the writers: indeed, those who actually wrote in Irish were often more open to foreign (especially continental) influences than some who worked in English. It must be remembered that when D. P. Moran coined that polemical aphorism (in *The Philosophy of Irish Ireland* in 1905), it was at a time when the prestige of the Gael was still being restored after centuries of denial and when Irish speakers did not even enjoy the rights to education in their own language. Anyway, the declaration came with a notable qualification: it was prefaced by the more telling observation that "no one wants to fall out with Davis's comprehensive idea of the Irish people as a composite race drawn from various sources".[3] The real debate of the revivalist generation was about whether the literature it created should be na-tional or cosmopolitan in tone.

At the outset, the options were not polarized in that rather simplified way. In 1893, Stopford Brooke said that a poetry which was national would "be able to become not only Irish, but also alive to the interests and passions of universal humanity".[4] The debate really took fire in 1899 with the publication of exchanges between John Eglinton, W. B. Yeats, George Russell and William Larminie in the *Dublin Daily Express*, a pro-union paper. Eglinton, a man of northern Protestant background and a humanist by inclination, questioned whether the use of Celtic heroic figures by dramatists could eventuate in anything more than *belles lettres*. He contended that Cuchulain or Deirdre would refuse to be translated out of their old environment into the world of modern sympathies, and such a use of "a subject outside experience" could produce only a mere exercise rather than "a strong interest in life itself".[5] Yeats countered with the claim that art is not an Arnoldian criticism of life so much as the sacred revelation of a hidden life. At this point, George Russell intervened with a characteristically ecumenical attempt to reconcile the national and the individual idea: the nation as a formation existed to enhance the expressive potential of the person, rather than the person existing as a mere illustration of some prior national essence. He offered a shrewd distinction between shallow cosmopolitanism and national individualism:

> . . . there is little to distinguish the work of the best English writers or artists from that of their continental contemporaries . . . If nationality is to justify itself in the face of all this, it must be because the country which preserves its individuality does so with the profound conviction that its peculiar ideal is nobler than that which the metropolitan spirit suggests.[6]

Russell acutely foresaw how mass communications would homogenize the whole of Europe into a dreary imitative provincialism. The imperial European powers had carved up Africa at the Congress of Berlin and he was not impressed by the results: "Empires do not permit the intensive cultivation of human life . . . they destroy the richness and variety of existence by the extinction of personal and unique gifts".[7] Epic archetypes, on the other hand, would offset this abjection, awakening each person to the heroism latent in the self: "it was this idea which led Whitman to 'exploit' himself as the typical American".[8] In all of his writings, Russell – most unusually, for the time – equated the cosmopolitan with the imperial.

In a rudimentary sense, the controversy established Yeats as the upholder of nationalism, Eglinton as the defender of cosmopolitanism, and Russell as the seeker of some vaguely-defined middle ground. But this is to underplay the interesting points of contact in their thought: all were agreed on the advisability of using the English language. Though Yeats pursued a diplomatic alliance with the Gaelic League, Russell complained of its "boyscoutish propaganda" and Eglinton contended that a "thought movement" rather than a "language movement" could provide a surer basis for a true Irish identity.[9] Eglinton misunderstood deanglicization when he argued that "there was something lacking in a mental and spiritual attitude so uncompromisingly negative".[10] Though he did not know Irish, he inferred with a strange confidence that as a language it lacked analytic power and "had never been to school". Fearing the division of Ireland into two armed camps, like the Jews and the Samaritans, he reminded the League that "it was among the lost sheep of the house of Israel – amongst those who had lost the use of the Hebrew tongue – that the Jewish Messiah ap-

peared".[11] He denied that the word *Irish* accurately designated the
language which "is no longer the language of Irish nationality" and
"never was so"; and he wickedly but effectively questioned the revivalist
use of the peasant for ulterior political purposes by those who "are for
the most part ignorant of the old man personally". He was, however,
notably vague in his definition of what his more ecumenical nationality
might be constituted, preferring to ask that writers work from a "human" rather than an "Irish" standpoint.

Eglinton had not only an independent stance but a lively way of
adopting it. Like many self-declared humanists and secularists, he was
more concerned with the future than the past, and quite convinced that
while most virtues are individual, most vices are national. He feared
that a successful restoration of the Irish language would cut people off
from the rest of Europe, condemning them to speak always in an Irish
rather than a human capacity (and he had no scruple about presenting
these as opposed concepts). Unable or unwilling to concede the modern element in the Gaelic League, he mockingly inverted Hyde's slogan
and programme: "Literature must be free as the elements; if that is to
be cosmopolitan, it must be cosmopolitan . . . and I should like to see
the day of what might be called . . . the de-Davisization of Irish
national literature, that is to say, the getting rid of the notion that in
Ireland a writer is to think first and foremost of interpreting the
nationality of his country, and not simply of the burden he is to
deliver".[12] Eglinton badly underestimated the European dimension of
Gaelic culture, past as well as present: after all, the *dánta grá* (love
poems) were resolutely in the *amour courtois* tradition, and the revival
in Irish-language writing led by Pearse had urged its followers to make
contact with the Gaelic past *and also* "with the mind of contemporary
Europe". Moreover, Eglinton seemed to have forgotten Mazzini's dictum that every people is bound to constitute itself a nation before it can
occupy itself with the question of humanity, but that it does this in
order to be free to move on to that question.

There are, nonetheless, wonderful moments in the writings of Eglinton when he exudes a real impatience with the nationalist process, an
impatience which comes, as it were, from one who has moved on to
better things and is impatient for companions to catch up and keep
company with him on his journey. His strictures on the need of art to
speak for the people of the present seem admirable: he was quite
convinced that Yeats "lived back" in a nostalgic land of his imagination,
a place unchastened by the real Ireland all around the living poet. This
led Eglinton to mount a devastating, and wonderfully dialectical,

critique of what he saw as the major contradiction of the Irish revival: "All the great literatures have seemed in retrospect to have risen like emanations from the life of a whole people, which has shared in a general exaltation: and this was not the case in Ireland. How could a literature movement be in any sense national when the interest of the whole nation lay in extirpating the conditions which produced it?"[13] Yet, somewhere along the line of his argument, Eglinton aborted the incipient dialectic: he failed to note that element in Irish nationalism which willed its own supersession by a humanism not unlike his, and he failed to recognize the genuine achievements of nationalism, albeit in sometimes outmoded forms.

That blind spot may have been caused by his refusal to adopt the Yeatsian strategy and to separate himself from his own class and background. He saw himself as opposed to those dogmatic patriots who were too ready to extinguish self in the service of a cause, but for all practical purposes this amounted to no more than the traditional Protestant aversion to the more demonstrative type of Catholic. If his understanding of the intricacies of Irish Ireland was limited, his grasp of the cultural effects of colonialism was non-existent. Many readers of the *United Irishman* of 1902 must have smiled at the simplicity of his analysis of the history of "The Island of Saints":

> Ireland will have to make up its mind that it is no longer the old Gaelic nation of the fifth or twelfth, or even of the eighteenth century, but one which has been in the making ever since these islands were drawn into the community of nations by the Normans.[14]

There is no recognition there of the European scope of Irish monasticism or of the commerce of scholars over many centuries: however, the marvellous euphemism for the Norman invasion tells all – what others might see as cultural conquest, Eglinton welcomes as a happy cosmopolitanism. A similar use of the word by Lord Cromer allowed him to describe Egypt as a land whose future lay not in narrow nationalism but in a more "cosmopolitan" mingling of identities, grounded not on race but on "the respect men have always accorded to superior talents and unselfish conduct".[15]

It was such thinking with allowed Eglinton to salute Edward Dowden (whom Yeats had judged the quintessential provincial) as the possessor of a cosmopolitan mind of the first rank, "probably the first point touched by anything new in the world of ideas outside Ireland".[16] Dowden, for his part, made no bones about the link between the imperial idea and literary cosmopolitanism. Long before African critics complained that "cosmopolitanism" was actually a code-word for the values of imperial Europe, he breezily conceded the point: "The direction of such work as I have done in literature has been (to give it a grand name) imperial or cosmopolitan, and though I think a literature ought to be rooted in the soil, I don't think a conscious effort to promote a provincial spirit tends in that direction".[17] The idea that the revival might be a revolt *against* imitative provincialism completely escaped Dowden, though it had been signalled by Thomas Davis in the refrain of his most famous song:

> And Ireland, long a province, be
> A nation once again.

Even less did it strike Dowden or Eglinton that this revolt was also a protest against *the provincialization of England* by the forces of industrial society. The leaders of that protest saw provincialism as taking one of two forms: the first and more obvious being found in people who looked to some faraway centre for approved patterns of cultural significance, the second and more insidious being found in those who were so smugly self-assured that they had lost all curiosity about any other forms of life beyond their own. The Irish in the previous century had suffered from the former provincialism, as had many parts of England; but it was the modern English who, even more than the nationalist Irish, were now suffering from the latter kind. While the former existed only as a comparison with a remote model, the latter refused any comparison at all. Neither Dowden nor Eglinton could concede what stared artists like Yeats and Joyce in the face: that England itself had grown smugly provincial in its imperial phase, because its citizens had lost the capacity to conceive of how they appeared in the eyes of others. They were psychologically driven to conquer largely because they had no sense of their own presence.

The English decline into the first form of deference had been diagnosed by George Eliot in the novel *Middlemarch* (1871–2), whose subtitle was "A study of provincial life". In it, the Middlemarchers all choose to define themselves in the distorting mirror of other people's opinions and this is the cause of their undoing: "Even Milton, looking for his portrait in a spoon, must submit to have the facial angle of a bumpkin".[18] By the new century, the decline into imperial smugness had fed massively off the earlier insecurity, but the underlying problem of provincialism remained to be documented by D. H. Lawrence: in

Women in Love he shows lovers leaving home because "in England you can't let go",[19] only for them to find that England is a state of mind which they bring with them wherever they travel. It was hardly a coincidence that, as English culture lapsed into this provincialism of spirit, Irish artists rediscovered their long-suppressed yearnings for the wider world. The moment might even be dated to 1892, when the Examiner of Plays in the Lord Chamberlain's office refused a licence for the performance of *Salomé*, a play in French by Oscar Wilde. The Examiner, E. F. Smyth Pigott, was called by Shaw "a walking compendium of vulgar, insular prejudice".[20] Wilde, for his part, responded with the assertion that Paris was now the true home of personal freedom. *Salomé* was published there in 1893 and performed in the city three years later.

From this point onwards, Irish thinkers turned to Europe, and beyond, as they had done so often in previous centuries, for ideas and audiences. The debate in Joyce's story "The Dead" is about whether the Irish person of the future will holiday for recreation on the Aran Islands or on continental Europe. All of a sudden, England was a bore: which was what George Moore meant by his famous telegram announcing that the centre of gravity in the literary world had shifted from London to Dublin. Certainly, the axis which had once run from Dublin to London now ran from Dublin to Paris instead.

Little of this seems to have borne in upon Dowden or Eglinton. As the years passed and the evidence mounted, Yeats made it perfectly clear that his Irish revival was a revolt against a provincialism of mind which can sometimes inhere in imitative nationalism, sometimes in complacent imperialism, but which always seeks to reproduce itself in facsimile wherever it is found. After the *Playboy* riots, Yeats discovered that, in order to protect his movement, he had to fight as hard against nationalist provincialism as he had once fought against the closed minds of Trinity College:

> Many are beginning to recognize the right of the individual mind to see the world in its own way, to cherish the thoughts which separate men from one another . . . instead of those thoughts that had made one man like another if they could, and have but succeeded in setting up hysteria and insincerity in place of confidence and self-possession.[21]

The Gaelic obscurantist, the anti-intellectual priest, and the propagandist politician were all as inimical to the revivalist ideal as were the empire men or the shallow cosmopolitans. Yeats had believed that the language movement and the thought movement could be reconciled; though remaining open to influences from Europe, Asia and beyond, he based his doctrines on the conviction that there is no great literature without nationality and no nationality without literature.

For all their blind spots, Eglinton's essays had a capital value: they alerted many to a xenophobic element within the national movement, which often threatened to negate its own better ideals. Synge became aware of certain insular Leaguers who, "with their eyes glued on John Bull's navel, fear to be Europeans for fear the huckster across the street will call them English".[22] For all the talk about deanglicization as a fantasy of purification, it was the allegedly *French* decadence of Synge's plays, when clothed in a rural Irish garb, which stung nationalist critics. These solemn commentators would object to a *boulevardier* element, while blithely ignoring the far more potent English influence in Irish culture, an influence which went largely unnoticed only because it was pervasive. The more probing Irish Ireland polemicists were somewhat quicker to detect the English sub-text of many plays: D. P. Moran complained, for example, that Yeats and Moore in their version of *Diarmuid and Gráinne* "have changed Diarmuid from a Fenian chief into a modern degenerate",[23] something, incidentally, which Eglinton had said could not be done; and Patrick Pearse even more acutely heard echoes of Hamlet on the lips of the Cuchulain of *On Baile's Strand.* To all of which the authors could say "but that effect was fully intended". In the adaptation of Gaelic elements to English forms, both elements were vastly changed, as Yeats had hoped, and changed also were the adaptors. The literature which he and his colleagues produced arose not among the Irish speakers of the west nor among the drawing-rooms of a self-enclosed gentry, but from the impact of one civilization (Gaelic) upon another (English).

Davis's description of the Irish as "a composite race" had been borne out yet again. What had been billed as the Battle of Two Civilizations was really, and more subtly, the interpenetration of each by the other: and this led to the generation of a new species of man and woman, who felt exalted by rather than ashamed of such hybridity.

The essays put out by Yeats in the theoretical journals of his theatre elaborated on this theme with a remarkable cogency and coherence of purpose. In October 1902, for instance, he urged formal recognition of "that English idiom of the Irish-thinking people of the west . . . the only good English spoken by any large numbers of Irish people to-day".[24] With his tongue only partly in his cheek, he urged on the Intermediate Board of Education ("a body that seems to benefit by advice") a novel scheme to improve the written English of school-children:

> Let every child in Ireland be set to turn first a leading article, then a piece of what is called excellent English, written perhaps by some distinguished member of the Board, into the idiom of his own countryside.

The mind of official Ireland was, however, so colonized that it could not recognize that the people themselves had created a new idiom, neither standard Irish nor standard English, but something that "at its best is more vigorous, fresh and simple than either of the two languages between which it stands"[25]. Had the argument been conceded, the dialect would have become the natural idiom of church sermons, newspaper editorials or university lectures, but these prestigious discourses remained unaffected by what Yeats mischievously called "the idiom of those who have rejected or of those who have never learned the base idiom of the newspapers".[26] He found in Hiberno-English that elusive style, that pressure of individual personality and that shared joy in free expression which was not available in official sources. Alert to the fact that writers of English faced more difficult problems than those which awaited artists in the Irish language, he pointed out that "English is the language in which the Irish cause has been debated and we have to struggle against traditional points of view",[27] in other words, the rollicking note thought peculiar to the stage Irishman. For that very reason, it was important to challenge these associations.

Over five decades later, but in an analogous situation, in French Algeria, Frantz Fanon, the revolutionary and psychiatrist, found that he too had to struggle against the "traditional points of view" embedded in French, "a language of occupation": this he did by broadcasting in French the programmes of Radio Fighting Algeria, "liberating the enemy language from its historic meanings".[28] It was doubtless a similar complex of feelings which, in more recent years still, led the Indian novelist Salman Rushdie to declare: "Those of us who use English do so in spite of our ambiguity towards it, or perhaps because of that, perhaps because we can find in that linguistic struggle a reflection of other struggles taking place in the real world". Like Yeats, Rushdie clung defiantly to the hope that something was gained rather than lost in the act of translation, one result of which might be "radically new types of human being".[29]

The deployment by postcolonial writers of historically-sanctioned English, and their speaking of it in a writerly, erudite fashion, have become much-remarked features of this process. Back in the 1890s, Walter Pater had said that he wished to write English as a learned language. This was precisely how the Irish actors of Yeats's theatre spoke it, as the London critic A. B. Walkley discovered on attending a performance: "The unexpected emphasis on the minor syllables has an air of not ungraceful pedantry, or, better still, of old world courtliness. We are listening to English spoken with a wonderful care and slightly timorous hesitation, as though it were a learned language".[30]

The decolonizing programme of the theatre was made very obvious in Yeats's repeated invocations of the writers of the American Renaissance as models for his own. His notions of a national literature were derived from Walt Whitman, but so also was his idea of the reception of such writers: "If one says a National Literature must be in the language of the country, there are many difficulties. Should it be written in the language that one's country does speak or the language it ought to speak? . . . Edgar Allan Poe and Walt Whitman are national writers of America, although the one had his first acceptance in France and the other in England and Ireland".[31] The man or woman of genius moulded the nation, rather than being made upon its mould: and because of their creative unpredictability, they encountered opposition, but they were embraced there "in the end". In the meantime, they might have to turn for protection to the despised police of the colonial power, as Yeats did during the *Playboy* riots and as Rushdie would decades later: expressing the people's life was far more dangerous than merely exploiting it.

Yet, though Yeats's *Samhain* articles and Rushdie's essays in *Imaginary Homelands* would be separated over time by eighty years, the experiences evoked in them did not markedly alter. Yeats's new species of man is recognizably one of Rushdie's hybrids, "people who root themselves in ideas rather than places, in memories as much as in material things; people who have been obliged to define themselves – because they are so defined by others – by their otherness; people in whose deepest selves strange fusions occur, unprecedented unions between what they were and where they find themselves". The experience recalled in the essays is one of *becoming*, identity being not so much a possession as a way of being in the world. For that reason, the image of the migrant or traveller features much in their work, not only because in his displacement he symbolizes the uprooted intellectual, but more especially because he is adaptive, one who moulds the new places that serve also to mould him. "The migrant is not simply transformed by his art; he also transforms his new world", writes Rushdie, who says that in consequence "migrants become mutants, but it is out of such hybridization that newness can emerge". The search is for a mode of expression, a fuller articulation, and this quest becomes its own point for the writer. It becomes clear that for such, reality is a mere artefact until it has been embodied in a style: what Rushdie calls "the sense of a writer feeling obliged to bring his new world into being by an act of pure will, the sense that if the world is not described into existence in the most minute detail, then it won't be there".[32]

Yeats, who had undergone these experiences so many years before Rushdie, was also led to the paradoxical conclusion that a nation could only achieve consciousness through exposure to others. Similarly, a self could only awaken by an act of hybridization: for nothing could create until first it was split in two:

> All literature in every country is derived from models, and as often as not these are foreign models, and it is the presence of a personal element alone that can give it nationality in a fine sense, the nationality of its maker. It is only before personality has been attained that a race struggling towards self-consciousness is the better for having, as in primitive times, nothing but native models, for before this has been attained, it can neither assimilate nor reject. It was precisely at this passive moment, attainment approaching but not yet come, that the Irish heart and mind surrendered to England, or rather to what is most temporary in England; and Irish patriotism, content that the names and opinions should be Irish, was deceived and satisfied. It is always necessary to affirm and reaffirm that nationality is in the things that escape analysis.[33]

This powerful and penetrating paragraph is one of the first Irish articulations of the dialectics of postcolonial liberation. It repeats the warnings of Hyde, Moran and others about a nationalism which would be no more than an imitation of its English begetter: but it transcends their diagnoses by offering a subtle account of *how* so many who dream of liberation become blocked at that mimic stage.

Ten

J. M. Synge – Remembering the Future

The society depicted in *The Playboy of the Western World* is a colony in the throes of a land war, as the last phase of the campaign against feudalism in Ireland is enacted. Pegeen Mike refers with excitement as well as fear to the thousand militia then crossing County Mayo, scene of so many evictions which have left so many vagrants in the streets. Synge did not suppress the ugliness of colonialism – "the loosed khaki cut-throats", "the broken harvest", or the rigged juries "selling judgements of the English law" are all mentioned[1] – but this is mere backdrop. Synge was less interested in the colonial present than in the future. Assuming the inevitability of Home Rule, he tried instead to see so profoundly into the Mayoites' culture that the shape of their future might become discernible.

So he took the violence of the colonizers as read: his deeper interest was in how the colonized cope with the violence in themselves, their situation and their daily life. There is no obvious outlet in the world of the play for these instincts. The Mayoites offer no allegiance to the hated English law, which might allow them to channel their violence into socially-sanctioned punishments like the hanging of a murderer. The allegiance to the Catholic church, which by its sacrifice of the Mass helps to appease the human taste for violence, is also very weak. Father Reilly is so peripheral a figure to these fundamentally pagan people that Synge does not allow him to appear on the stage at all: only Shawn Keogh speaks of the priest without irony. Yet the villagers are saturated in violence and its attendant imagery. Sarah Tansey is willing to travel miles to set eyes on the man who bit the yellow lady's nostril by the northern shore. Such a people desperately need a hero who can bring their instincts to violence into a single clear focus: a hero, moreover, whom they can then convert into a scapegoat, onto whom may be visited any troublesomely violent tendencies that are still unfulfilled.

This figure must come from outside the settled community, for otherwise he might exact a terrible revenge through the intervention of angry relations. So, Christy Mahon comes from "a windy corner of high distant hills".[2] This permits the community the luxury of believing that with him the cycle of incremental violence will come to a final halt. Hence the importance of reading into Christy all the ills and frustrations that flesh is heir to. As his father so vaguely yet so magnificently says: "Isn't it by the like of you the sins of the whole world are committed?"[3] This would also account for Christy's radical blankness as a personality on his arrival: he is the seductive male version of those female models into whose gorgeous but empty faces men can read their most vivid fantasies. In this case, however, the role of sex-object is played by the male lead. A person thus sacrificed drains off the evil in a village and, in the very act of being disposed of, becomes endowed with the glamour of a holy healer who has the power to bind the community back together.[4]

But the play, on the night of the riots in 1907, was not heard to a conclusion – so we must look to the earlier acts for a cause. The monstrous spectacle of a deformed colonial life may have defeated the very sympathies which it could have aroused among nationalists in the audience. The frustration of knowing that they were more nauseated than sympathetic may have led many spectators to insure themselves against ensuing guilt by converting the play, through vilification and hearsay, into a genuine "monster". The physical assaults on the actors would be of a piece with this, since their effect would be to enhance the deformation and monstrosity of the players. Synge's play, and by extension Synge himself, thus became – like Christy – a scapegoat for the violence visited upon one another by the colonized.

Not long after Synge had served this function and died an early death, Patrick Pearse, repenting of his earlier attacks on play and playwright, wrote of him as an authentic martyr and contrasted that martyrdom with the facile careerism of an imperial administrator:

Ireland, in our day as in the past, has excommunicated some of those who have served her best, and has canonized some of those who have served her worst . . . When a man like Synge, a man in whose sad heart there glowed a true love of Ireland, one of the two or three men who have in our time made Ireland considerable in the eyes of the world, uses strange symbols which we do not understand, we cry out that he has blasphemed and we proceed to crucify him. When a sleek lawyer, rising step by step through the most ignoble of all professions, attains to a Lord Chancellorship or an

Attorney Generalship, we confer upon him the freedom of our cities. This is really a very terrible symptom in contemporary Ireland.[5]

By 1913 Pearse had endowed Synge with the saintliness of his own putative sacrifice – to be made three years later-for the work of art called Ireland. This moment had been adumbrated at the end of Synge's play: for not long after the scapegoat Christy serves his function of uniting previously quarrelsome men so that they can enjoy "peace now for our drinks", he is invested with the insignia of a lost redeemer by the very woman who evicted him: "O my grief, I've lost him surely. I've lost the only Playboy of the Western World".[6]

_The stock explanation of the riots is that nationalists rejected a work which appeared to satirize a drunken, amoral peasantry at a time when all patriotic dramatists of the National Theatre were expected to celebrate a sturdy people ready for the responsibilities of self-government. It is also said that pious Roman Catholics resented the insulting use of sacred phrases in lines like "With the help of God, I killed him surely, and that the Holy Immaculate Mother may intercede for his soul".[7] There is some validity in these arguments, but not much, given that other plays by Synge, even more extreme in these respects, were presented without disorder. The situation was, of course, rich in ironies, the most obvious being that the protesters shouted "We Irish are not a violent people" and then sprang at the actors to prove their point – confirming Synge's conviction that *some* were.

One says *some*, for little credence should be given to the cliché of the fighting Irish. The Irish have a *reputation* for violence (due perhaps to the overcrowded conditions in which their emigrants lived in British and American cities) but also a shrewd distaste for it. Though some have professed to admire "mythic" violence, they have more often than not shied away as individuals from the thing itself; and Yeats was in this respect a representative case. He wrote:

> Even the wisest man grows tense
> With some sort of violence,
> Before he can accomplish fate,
> Do his work, or choose his mate.[8]

Violence to some past self, in his system, became the necessary precondition for the remaking of a new one: yet, when that violence ceased to be rhetorical or psychic and became real, Yeats was filled with scruple.

Synge's extraordinary influence on the middle period of Yeats's poetry was attributable to his insistence that violence and poetry went hand in hand. There was, most strikingly, his declaration in the Preface to his own *Collected Poems*, which he submitted for editing and publication to Yeats, that "before verse can be human again it must learn to be brutal".[9] That sentence voiced his revolt against the artificial poetic diction which had so emasculated English poetry in the later nineteenth century. He believed that "the strong things of life are needed in poetry, also, to show that what is exalted, or tender, is not made by feeble blood". The weakness of Swinburne and Rossetti lay in their cultivation of a tenderness that was cloying rather than tough, while the problem with realists like Ibsen and Zola could be found in their naturalist depiction of sordid urban conditions unmitigated by any sense of beauty. In the life and language of western Ireland, however, Synge found a world that managed to be both tough and tender. A visit to the Aran Islands liberated the frustrated artist in Synge, who thanked Yeats for sending him with the remark that style is "born out of the shock of new material"[10] (Hemingway, another lyricist of violence, once said "what amateurs call a style is usually only the unavoidable awkwardness of first trying to make something that has not before been made").[11] Accepting the romantic symbol of the poem as a tender flower, Synge added that there was no flower which had not strong roots among the clay and worms.

A major investigation is conducted in *The Playboy* of the relationship between the flower and the crude life at its roots, between style and shock, which is to say between poetry and violence. In a private letter to an admirer, written soon after the riots, Synge remarked that "the wildness and, if you will, vices of the Irish peasantry are due, like their extraordinary good points, to the *richness* of their nature, a thing that is priceless beyond words".[12] So if the violence and the poetry sprang from a common source, it would have been impossible to separate them without a diminution of both.

In the opening act of *The Playboy*, Synge describes a people who only rise to intensity of feeling when they are recounting deeds of violence. Folk who once sat spellbound at the stories about Cuchulain now regale one another with tales of a more tedious sadism: of Daneen Sullivan who "knocked the eye from a peeler" and "the mad Mulrannies were driven from California and they lost in their wits".[13]

So obsessively are poetry and violence interwoven in the mental fabric of the Mayoites that the women seem incapable of describing poetry except in terms of violence, and unable to imagine violence except as a kind of poetry. To the comparatively reticent Christy of Act One Pegeen exclaims:

> If you weren't destroyed travelling, you'd have as much talk and streeleen, I'm thinking, as Owen Roe O'Sullivan or the poets of the Dingle Bay . . .[14]

– and she mentions the eighteenth-century Gaelic poet Eoghan Rua Ó Súilleabháin specifically, because his hot temper led to a tavern brawl and death from injuries received:

> . . . I've heard all times it's the poets are your like – fine fiery fellows with great rages when their temper's roused.[15]

Later still, Pegeen returns to the equation of poetry with violence when she tells Christy that he is a grand fellow "with such poet's talking and such bravery of heart".[16] The two notions are likewise coupled in her rejection of Shawn Keogh as "a middling kind of scarecrow with no savagery or fine words at all".[17]

At the end Christy has tamed his resurrected (and delighted) 'da' with the twin boast that he is "master of all fights" and will "go romancing through a romping lifetime".[18] Like his creator, he still equates brutality and romance. It is left to Pegeen to dismantle the equation in the name of the Mayo villagers:

> I'll say a strange man's a marvel, with his mighty talk; but what's a squabble in your backyard, and the blow of a loy, have taught me that there's a great gap between a gallous story and a dirty deed.[19]

If barbarism and culture are intimately linked, then it is the poetry rather than the brutality which impresses the Mayoites in the end. Synge's implication is that the besetting vice of the Irish may not have been pugnacity but paralysis. Pegeen's separation of gallous stories and dirty deeds is excessive. The space opened by her at the end between poetry and violence is, if anything, even more sinister than her earlier, absolutist identification of both. So, at the close, Mayo suffers the extreme colonial torpor described by Shaw: the facts seem more brutal than ever, the dreams even more unreal. Instead of closing with one another in a dancing dialectic, they move farther apart, leaving society unredeemed and apparently unredeemable. A revolution occurs, but it is happening offstage.

"Deeds are masculine, words feminine" says a proverb, as if to ratify Pegeen's separation: but *The Playboy* tells a more complex truth about how these categories interpenetrate one another. Its men commit most of the verbal violence onstage and are actually less aggressive in action, whereas the women, schooled to repress their instincts, are consumed by unappeased pugnacious impulses. There is violence in Pegeen, as in many persons, and it has not been assuaged by the gallous story: this becomes clear when she lights a sod of turf to cripple her former lover. This brutal act, deemed to be beyond belief by many of the play's first critics, is entirely in keeping with her character as revealed from the start. Emphasizing this scene, the original production underscored Synge's brilliant insight: that those who make rhetorical denials of their own violence invariably end up committing even more. In that sense, at least, the 1907 rioters finished the play for Synge with a demonstration of its central point. In all likelihood, that audience thrilled to the poeticized accounts of a distant violence in the opening acts, only to be nauseated by the deglamorized onstage repetition in the flesh: their revolt against the second murder may have arisen from a sudden onset of shame at how easily they themselves had accepted the first "killing". Like future Abbey producers, indeed like the Mayo villagers themselves, they repressed the violence in the text and subordinated it to the poetry, only to find the energies which they denied unleashed in some other form. Theirs was the dilemma of Pegeen Mike, whose aggression turned out to be an inextricable part of her vitality. To reject the "dirty deed" of Christy, she must also deny that element within herself, and yet, in following the dictates of polite society, something has been lost.

Synge was amused by the fact that the great deeds of a Cuchulain were typically applauded by men too timid to think of emulating them. In the Irish Ireland movement of his time, there were basically two schools of writing: one devoted to the heroic legends of Cuchulain and ancient heroes, the other to a vision of the western peasant as a secular saint and Gaelic mystic. By recreating *some* of the traits of the ancient hero in a puny peasant playboy, Synge offered his own caustic comment on the similarities and dissimilarities between the Irish past and present. His was a challenge to both schools, to concede, if they would, the savagery as well as the glamour at the heart of their cultural enterprise.[20]

If Synge's art were simply an analysis of the *relation* between barbarism and culture in Ireland, it would merit our respect: but it gains an added depth by serving also as an *example* of that relation. All culture is parasitic: what lives feeds off what dies and feeds without scruple.

Synge's was in truth a carrion vision, but he was always critically aware of its costs: and this is what distinguishes him ultimately from a writer like Lady Gregory. She once remarked on the strange discrepancy between the poverty of peasant story-tellers and the splendour of their tales. She was beguiled and moved by the contrast, as are many people who note that the black man, in losing so many battles, was compensated by all the best songs: but she left her analysis in that unresolved state, too pleased with the paradox, perhaps, to explore it further.

Synge was quite different. In his writings, he worried constantly about the gap between a beautiful culture and the poverty that can underlie it. In *The Aran Islands*, for instance, he notes how every piece of furniture, every chair, every table, has a personality of its own, lovingly imparted to it by its maker, albeit at immense cost in terms of time, trouble, pain – so great a cost, indeed, that the maker often seems to have been robbed of his identity in the very making, as his self passed into his production. One critic has astutely observed that the islanders are depicted by Synge as persons obsessed with the price of everything.[21] This is because they are people who can scarcely afford an individuality. In *Riders to the Sea* a drowned man is identified not only by his bruised and broken body, which even his mother would be "hard put" to recognize, but by a dropped stitch in his stocking, a mere object. The few traces of personality shown by his mother, her self-absorption in grief, are massive liabilities, almost criminal acts of self-indulgence, within the subsistence economy of the islands. Her final speeches of compassion, spoken as "an old woman" on behalf of all mothers left living in the world, represent a triumph over that selfishness, a return to folkloristic impersonality. Synge records all this with a terrified and terrifying accuracy, because he knows that, however spare and beautiful such a culture may seem to the outsider, its costs in human terms are just too high.

So he checks his own tendency to be charmed by the well-wrought stool or the beautifully-hewn table. Turning his back on William Morris and the folk radicalism of his youth, he reminds himself of a harder socialist school, and honestly concedes that all these beautiful effects are bound up with a social condition near to penury. He knows that that condition cannot last and so it has, therefore, the added charm of an exquisite, dying thing: and he does not finally oppose the change. He is sufficiently self-aware to admit that his very presence on the islands is a portent of that change. Though beguiled by much of the backwardness, he is an agent of that change, bringing the first alarm-clock to the islands (with the attendant notion of clock-time, efficiency and measurement) as well as his camera (itself creating a new narcissism among the islanders, which he observes with some disgust, since the camera was a curiosity employed by him to win the confidence and respect of the people). Seeing his photographs of them, the islanders tell Synge that they are seeing themselves for the first time.

Synge knows that he is only an interloper on Aran, a tourist, one of the first and, perhaps one day, one of the most famous among many: and that the more successful is his book called *The Aran Islands*, the more extreme will be the consequent disruptions of tradition by the day-trippers who will come in his wake. Indeed he has – though he never quite says this – a vested interest in those disruptions, because after they have had their effect, his book will be even more evocative than ever. He himself will feed off the death of the old Gaelic culture, as do all coroners and morticians. The covert desire of his book, to *make the present past*, is something that Synge shares with all his major creations, whether Maurya looking forward to the relative serenity of the long nights after Samhain, or Deirdre imagining how the story of her current exploits will be told forever. *That* is the only actual control which these women achieve over their lives. Otherwise, Deirdre is at the mercy of events, and Old Maurya is unable to bless a departing son because "something choked the words in my throat".[22] Both are doomed to repeat lines already known by heart, so that the striking beauty of their language is in direct contrast with its ineffectuality. The so-called exoticism of Synge's language is related to the remoteness of his characters from the "big world" with its standardized versions of English. The greater that displacement, the more untamed the life and the more colourful its deviations from the linguistic norm. But the dislocation which makes these people colourful is also that which leaves them powerless.

The mortal charm of Synge's dialect is the beauty that inheres in all precarious or dying things. Much of it is traceable to the Gaelic *substratum*, those elements of syntax and imagery carried over from the native tradition by a people who continue to think in Irish even as they speak in English. The famous "jawbreakers" – words like "bedizened" or "potentate" – are in the tradition of hedge-schoolmasters nervously advertising their new mastery of English polysyllabic effects to impress the parents of their putative pupils, in the absence of a more formal diploma. The tradition was at least as old as Goldsmith's village schoolmaster:

> While words of learned length and thundering sound
> Amazed the gazing rustics ranged around;

And still they gazed and still the wonder grew,
That one small head could carry all he knew.[23]

The potency of Synge's idiom derived in great part from the reported death of Irish; and the deader (or, at least, the more doomed) that language, the more vital the semantic energies that passed into Hiberno-English and the more magnificent that language seemed.

Hiberno-English, like Christy Mahon, owes its force to the apparent murder of its parent: and *The Playboy of the Western World* may thus be read as a critical reflection upon its own linguistic parasitism. The bleak joke, of course, is that standard English was itself rather jaded by cliché-mongers when Synge began to write. Synge saw that a deterritorialized Irish might yet deterritorialize English, leading to a bilingual weave more vital than either of the standard languages between which it stood. Yeats's crusades for a formal recognition of that dialect have been already discussed: against a "schoolmaster's ideal of correctness", which led to such clichés as "flagrant violations" and "shining examples", he pitted the dialect of country people, which was "an imitation of nothing English".[24] The accusation against Synge's peasants came, he said, from those whose minds were full of sentimental Kickhamesque novels written to an English literary formula.

This demand for an official recognition of Hiberno-English went unanswered. Nationalist leaders could celebrate standard Irish as a countervailing discourse to standard English, but they could not embrace the new hybrid language, which Synge was magnifying in its carrier Christy. Most nationalist commentators preferred to treat Synge as an unapologetic ascendancy parasite, stocking up his tourist's notebook with self-serving studies in a dying culture. D. P. Moran dubbed the dialect a "hopeless half-way house", neither good Irish nor good English, but a sort of bastard lingo which grew in the no-man's land between two authentic cultures.[25] More recently, Seamus Deane has added a subtler inflection to that analysis, describing Synge as one who creamed off the Gaelic culture in the few remaining areas where his class had failed to exterminate it, but where he could now appropriate its energies on the eve of their extinction.[26]

Such an analysis ignores Synge's critical awareness of the points which might be made against his own cultural project; and it slights the skill with which he infuses that awareness into his writings in the ways just described. Far from being a secret snob, Synge was a radical who grew up in an oppressed society, impressed by its cultural richness but even more horrified by its costs. The contention that the rioters against *The Playboy* were outraged by his ascendancy attitudes to peasant religion or rural psychology is in some measure a *retrospective* fabrication by nationalists, who convinced themselves that their objection was to snobbism. In 1907, it was the radical ideas in the play, as well as the accompanying violence, which did most to upset the nationalists, including the pre-revolutionary Pearse. Seamus Deane's critique of Synge, though not penned as such, is probably the most eloquent defence yet written of the *Playboy* rioters; and the strength of its arguments should remind us that those who disrupted the performance were no random collection of hotheads, but some of the most sensitive and intelligent thinkers of the time, risking arrest and imprisonment for the stand which they took. Nevertheless, Deane's reading of the play is mistaken, because it is based on revivalist productions and on a scholarly tradition which claimed Synge as one of Anglo-Ireland's crowning glories. (The major exponent of this interpretative tradition was T. R. Henn, who liked to portray Synge as a martyr to the Irish mob, perhaps because this assuaged his own guilt about ascendancy mistreatment of the natives.)

Synge was, by his own say-so, a radical, whom he defined as "someone who wanted to change things root and branch". He was a student of such texts as Marx's *Das Kapital* and *Communist Manifesto*, the works of William Morris, *L'Anarchie, Problems of Poverty, Principes du Socialisme* and *Basic Socialism*. He went to Paris in 1896 with the intention of immersing himself in the radical movement: "he wants to do good", lamented his mother, "and for that possibility he is giving up everything".[27] This was no passing youthful fancy: for in the last days of his life, at the Elpis Nursing Home in Dublin, he repeatedly sought to engage the nurses on the topic of feminism. The protesters may have known exactly what they were doing. They were middle-class nationalists who did not want a revolution: and so they attacked and tried to stop his play as it moved into its liberationist third act. This process must now be explained.

When Christy leads his father out towards the end of that act, "like a gallant captain with his heathen slave",[28] the pair constitute the image of a revolutionary community, while the villagers lapse into revivalism. In such a revolutionary community, the old take their cue from the young (rather than the other way round): so the stage directions emphasize Old Mahon's delight at this new assertiveness in his offspring.

Earlier in the play, this positive revolutionary potential had been suggested by a masculinization of women and a corresponding feminization of men. These reversals constitute that political and sexual unconscious, systematically explored in the Irish writings of Wilde and Shaw, Joyce and Yeats: but it was Synge, more than any other, who dramatized that moment when "the person is born, assumes his autonomy, and becomes the creator of his own values".[29] He seems to have believed that such reversals had always been possible to artists: for example, in suggesting to Molly Allgood that they write a play together, he proposed that he write the female parts and she the male. A revolution, however, would open such possibilities to all, on the anarchist principle that every man and woman could be an artist.

In *The Playboy* the women take the initiative in wooing; they enjoy the experience of trying on the hero's mud-spattered boots; and, generally, they disport themselves with a sort of locker-room bravado. The foremost among them, Pegeen, "would knock the head of any two men in this place"[30]: while the men of the village do seem to score more modestly on any available virility-test. The women complain that the Widow Quin's "sneaky" murder of her husband won "small glory with the boys itself",[31] as if the boys are a lot more easily cowed than the girls. Moreover, the sexual chemistry of the play vindicates Freud's contention that manly women are attracted, and attractive, to womanly men. The phrase "female woman" is used by Old Mahon as if to indicate a pained, sexist awareness that there is another kind: the kind attracted by his son. It was the female women who, of course, made of Christy a "laughing joke", but what mesmerizes *all* of the women is his femininity. Pegeen praises his small aristocratic feet (as if he is a fetishized sex-object of her starved imagination); the village women enjoy his nuances of delicate phrasing ("That's a grand story . . . He tells it lovely")[32]; and the Widow Quin has fantasies of putting him into a woman's dress by way of securing his liberation from persecution.

Perhaps the most telling moment is that when the village women burst in upon the risen Christy of Act Two, only to find him preening himself in a mirror: "Didn't I know rightly, I was handsome, though it was the divil's own mirror we had beyond, would twist a squint across an angel's brow?"[33] That was the cracked looking-glass of a servant, in fact: but now he knows the heady delights of a Caliban seeing his own face in a flawless mirror. The ensuing scene is Synge's mischievous repudiation of that sexist tradition, which encouraged male artists to paint nude females, into whose hands they put mirrors. Such paintings, though composed by some men for the delectation of others, purported to be high-minded commentaries on female narcissism: and, accordingly, the woman was rendered holding the mirror up to her face, or her breast, and the painting duly entitled "Vanity".[34] In a boldly feminist reversal, Synge has an embarrassed Christy unwittingly mock the stereotype by hiding the mirror behind his back and holding it up against his bottom, to the vast amusement of village women who comment: "Them that kills their fathers is a vain lot surely".[35]

There was ample sanction for such reversals in the utopian plays of Wilde and Shaw, but Synge added a Gaelic resonance entirely absent from their writings, and based on his knowledge of poetry in the Irish language from the seventeenth and eighteenth centuries. There, in works like *Cúirt an Mheáin Oíche* (The Midnight Court) by Brian Merriman, the writers had denounced the new Anglicization of sexuality in rural Ireland. Merriman was especially scandalized by the high-heeled shoes, the artificial cosmetics (*púdar*) and the clothing (*húda*) which characterized the new fashions, and his use of the accompanying Anglicized slang-words in the poem indicated his deep contempt. Though revivalist critics preferred to read all this as a nationalist critique of English culture by a defender of Gaelic values, there is much more than that at stake. What is under attack in such texts is the reification of the female body to the point where it becomes a fetish of the puritan male's imagination. Merriman's poem contains many other elements which would have been congenial to Synge: it is based on the idea of a court of love ruled by women; these complain of enforced marriages to spent old dotards, very much as Nora Burke complains in *The Shadow of the Glen*; they are frank rather than genteel in asserting their sexual urges; and the male poet is mocked, as Synge was on Aran, for being over thirty years of age and still unmarried.

An even more explicit critique of the Anglicization of sexuality in eighteenth-century rural Ireland may be found in "Bodaigh na hEorna" (The Churls of the Barley) by Art Mac Cumhaigh. Here the poet denounces the vulgar fashions worn by the females of a south Ulster family, which has circumvented the Penal Laws against Roman Catholics by making a small fortune from distilling:

> Is tócuil an tseoid níon bhodaigh sa ród
> Is cha ghlacann sí cóirú Gaelach,
> Mur mbeadh hata uirthi ar dhóigh, is crios air den ór,
> Is cleite ag treabhadh na gaoithe.[36]

The daughter of a churl is a proud jewel on the road

And she does not wear Gaelic fashions,
But a hat in new style, with a golden braid,
And a feather ploughing the wind.

Prose texts from the same period such as *Parliament na mBan* (The Parliament of Women, 1703) were even more elaborate in their critiques of a male chauvinism which had relegated women from public life to the domestic periphery. One year after Daniel Defoe's *Good Advice to the Ladies* (1702) the male "author" of the *Parliament*, Dónal Ó Colmáin, complained that the female sex had lost much of its power through lack of education and through the accompanying fetishization of the woman's body. Doubtless, in Gaelic Ireland as elsewhere, there were those for whom imbecility in females represented a great enhancement of their charms, but Ó Colmáin captured the authentic anger of women who would not brook such marginalization:

Do chítear daoibh go léir go mbíd a gcomhairlí agus a gcomhthionóil ag na fearaibh go laethúil ag déanamh a ngnótha agus ag tabhairt aire do gach ní bhaineas riu féin, i gcás, an uair bhíd siad ag trácht orainne, gurb amhlaidh bhímid mar chaitheamh aimsire, mar chompáráid, nó mar stoc magaidh aca de ló agus d'oíche. Agus fós, ní admhaíd siad gur daoine sinn ar aon chor ar bith, ach gur créatúirí sinn do cruthaíodh in aghaidh nádúir, agus nach bhfuil ionainn ach *malum necessarium*, "drochní is riachtanas do bheith ann".[37]

It is evident to you all that the menfolk had their meetings and conferences on a daily basis, doing their business and taking care of all that pertained to themselves – so that, whenever they mentioned us, we were simply a pastime, a comparison, or a source of mockery to them by day and night. And even still, they will not admit that we are human at all, save only that we are creatures created against the forces of nature, and that we are nothing but a *malum necessarium*, a bad thing which is necessary.

Of course, as a male writer, Ó Colmáin was speaking on women's behalf, just as a male poet, Merriman, voiced the female protest against false gentility in the *Cúirt:* two facts which, in themselves, indicate just how far Gaelic women had fallen from earlier times. For it was well known that the ancient Irish laws were remarkably liberal in their attitude to women. A woman could divorce a sterile, impotent, or homosexual husband, could marry a priest, and could give honourable birth to a child outside of wedlock. Merriman's poem was not the foreign-inspired debauch complained of by some puritans of the national revival, but a dynamic plea for a return to more radical traditions: according to one historian, however, "the natural development of these liberal customs was ... cut off by the imposition of English law on Ireland in the seventeenth century".[38]

Synge was well aware of the loss of these liberal traditions, but he delighted in pointing to those areas, such as the Aran Islands, still largely unaffected by the changes. The women of Inishmaan were, he noted, "before conventionality" in their frank, easy manners, which left them untainted by the false Victorian gentility of the women in Dublin, Cork or Galway. Instead, they "share some of the liberal features that are thought peculiar to the women of Paris and New York". The latter, he added in a notebook, "have freed themselves by a desperate personal effort from the moral bondage of lady-like persons".[39] He was doubtless recalling the New Women whom he had known on the Left Bank of Paris in the 1890s, women who earned their own livings as dancers, writers, artists. At a time when the wild, passionate and masterful women of the ancient Celts were being rediscovered by scholars, Synge put the debate about rural womanhood back on the agenda in the persons of Nora Burke and Pegeen Mike. After all, *The Playboy* starts and ends with Pegeen's plight as a trapped rural woman in a landscape virtually bereft of enterprising men, most of whom have been lost to English jails or to the emigration ship. The girls are all agreed that theirs is a dull life, "going up summer and winter (to the priest) with nothing worthwhile to confess at all".[40] Mayo is a community of timid apple-lickers, people who if tempted in the Garden of Eden, would have licked rather than bitten the apple.

Into this mediocre zone comes Christy, to all intents a landless, propertyless Shawn Keogh, but to all purposes a pure invention of Pegeen Mike. He starts out as and strictly is a nonentity, until he discovers in himself an unexpected gift for mimicry. Noticing the propensity of the Mayo villagers to narrate deeds with reference to the points of the compass, he retells his own deed in these derived terms: "he gave a drive with the scythe, and I gave a lep to the east. Then I turned around with my back to the north, and I hit a blow on the ridge of his skull, laid him stretched out, and he split to the knob of his gullet".[41] In Act One, it is Pegeen and the villagers who speak poetically, telling Christy who he is: and in Act Two, he is saluted as a poet merely for returning to the community, lovingly distorted, a magnified version of its own language.

It is one thing to parody the speech-patterns of interlocutors: it is quite another to appropriate the images, ideas and intensities of an entire literary tradition, as Christy does in wooing Pegeen. The dozens of borrowed lines deployed from *Love Songs of Connacht* may testify to Synge's versatility as a new kind of writer,[42] but, within the play itself, they also expose Christy's initial hollowness as a person, especially when declaring his love in phrases looted blatantly from the songs of the folk. Most of these borrowings occur in Act Two and the earlier part of Act Three, when Christy's desire has abandoned the language of reality for a factitious and flowery dialect. Not everyone, of course, would find such behaviour contemptible: there is a sense in which Christy becomes a kind of hero in these moments by creating a tradition for himself out of nothing but folk culture, thereby restoring to people an image of themselves. This was, as has been shown, one of Yeats's highest aspirations, never fulfilled in his own person, but envied in the achievement of Hyde.

For Synge's own purposes, Christy *has* to be an empty man at the outset, so that he will carry no baggage from his degrading past into the future. He rejects a false image of self (in the broken mirror) and chooses instead *to be*, creating instant, improvised traditions of himself out of the shreds of popular culture. Denied identity and freedom by his father's misrule, he is living evidence of the nullity to which oppression may reduce a person or a community. Yet that very nullity is also the source of his charm, for it offers the Mayo villagers an empty space into which they can read from a safe distance their fondest dreams. In the first two acts, Christy is the locus of village desire, carrying himself like a revivalist leader on a rise to absolute power. That power is, of course, bogus, since it is a function of the community's mediocrity and since it prevents either the leader or the members of that community from constructing themselves from within. But it is the gift of all desperately oppressed peoples: witness the Irish search for a Messianic hero through the nineteenth century, from O'Connell to Parnell, a catalogue of revivalist icons made and then broken. As saviour and scapegoat, as poet and tramp, Christy is their logical embodiment at the level of artistic imagination. For, after the famines and emigrations of the 1840s, "Ireland" had almost ceased to exist in the old Gaelic way: what was left – the remaining voices confirmed this – was a terrifyingly open space, in places and in persons.

It is this very emptiness in his personality and in his contexts which has allowed generations of critics to read so many different meanings into the character of Christy, whether Parnell, Cuchulain, Christ,

Oedipus or artist. In doing this, critics simply repeated the actions of the Mayo villagers, using Christy as a mirror in which to read and explore themselves. Indeed, the recorded responses to the play are, undeniably, extensions and imitations of its innermost theme. The villagers onstage discover that the radically transformed society which they had "read into" Christy is not what they wanted at all: and so they go back to their farce of revivalism, of fireside tales told about past heroes. Similarly, Synge's audience decided that they could not brook such innovation and versatility in a text, so they attacked it on those very points of its strength, Synge's knowledge of Gaelic Ireland. Excessive rhetorical claims had been made for Synge by Yeats and others (he was "the chap who writes like Sophocles, Shakespeare, etc."), which helps to explain some of the vehemence of the reaction against his work. This recapitulates the progress of Christy who makes no stylized claims for himself – other than the parricide, which he genuinely believed himself to have committed. The case for his own heroism is not made by him, but for him.

Chief among the claimants is Pegeen, whose invention Christy really is, her *animus* returned after centuries of Anglicization to the level of female consciousness. Her lament in the play's final lines is less for the physical man just gone offstage than for lost possibilities of her own womanhood. Christy has liberated an unsuspected femininity in her ("to think it's me is talking sweetly, and I the fright of seven townlands for my biting tongue")[43] mainly because he was so at ease with the female qualities in himself: and the woman in him took an undisguised pleasure in the man in her. Pegeen, being more of a traditionalist, could not fully reciprocate in this androgynous fashion. Though prizing his femininity, she oppressed her man by compelling him to live up to an extreme of hypermasculinity. He did this to an extent by winning all before him at the sports, thereby establishing that men who consciously recognize their *anima* are less effeminate than the Shawn Keoghs who are unconsciously enthralled by the repressed female element: but this was not sufficient for Pegeen. She wanted her partner to exemplify a manliness which she could not fully confront or contain, so much was there of it in herself. Doubtless the woman in him, having established her right to exist, connived in all this by demanding the usual proofs that, despite the contrasexual admission, the partner is still reassuringly male.

Christy, revealed as having *not* killed his father, fails her test. It is a mark of her conventionality that such a test, at this late stage, should still seem necessary. No sooner does he attempt another killing on the spot than she denies the very violence she had courted. When she drives him out at the end, it is as if her *animus* has been repressed back into the unconscious and demonized accordingly. The revolution occurs, but offstage and in the black-out. She, for her part, surrenders to gentility, kills off her *animus,* and opts to become a "proper" country girl of the kind lampooned by the Gaelic poets. As such, she will be a fitting mate for the "puny weed" Shawn Keogh. He restores the old patriarchy in the village by *telling* Pegeen to burn Christy's leg; and she submits, doing something which, in all probability, Shawn would be afraid to do himself. This is no contradiction, however, since the weakness of the ineffectual male has traditionally masked itself behind a pose of patriarchy, issuing orders and striking postures but achieving little for itself. Repressing a female dimension which it would require courage to confront, such men are enslaved to the *anima* and enfeebled accordingly. Repressing a male dimension which she briefly flirted with, Pegeen becomes once again enslaved to her animus, which explains her reversion to the harsh, sharp-tongued exterior which she presented in the shebeen before the onset of Christy. Compared with Shawn's dithering, this may give her actions the appearance of decision and despatch, but in any comparison with Christy she emerges as a coward who could not live up to the image of freedom for which they both had reached. She lets Christy go at the end, not really because he is weak, but because he has grown too strong for her. From now on, her *animus* denied, she will continue to obey Shawn Keogh.

The radical implications of the manly woman of Gaelic tradition were deflected by the Mayo villagers, even as the sensuous images drawn from the love-songs of Connacht were denounced as titillating by some puritans of the Gaelic League. It is ironic to recall, in this context, that the League's own president had edited the book from which Synge looted some of the most disturbing lines. Synge shrewdly remarked, however, that a writer could get away with things in Irish which would not be tolerated in English: a point depressingly confirmed in the 1940s when the independent state banned an English-language version of *The Midnight Court,* though the far more ribald Irish-language version remained available. Revivalism was proving rigidly selective of that which was worthy to be revived and translated into popular versions. Sexuality, it seemed, was not to be deanglicized. The conclusion of Synge's play proved bitterly prophetic of the sexual politics of the new state, which would deny the manly woman epitomized by Constance Markievicz and Maud Gonne, opting instead for de Valera's maidens at the rural crossroads, themselves a pastoral figment of the late-Victorian imagination. And thus a people who, in the nineteenth century, had thought in Irish while speaking English, came in the twentieth to "think English" even while they were speaking Irish.

The spark that lit the *Playboy* riots is well known, recorded in the famous telegram sent by Lady Gregory summoning Yeats to return at once from Scotland: "Audience broke up in disorder at use of the word 'shift'".[44] The controversial lines represented a modest, if mocking, reworking by Synge of a scene in the national epic. In the play, Christy tells the Widow Quin "it's Pegeen I'm seeking only, and what'd I care if you brought me a drift of chosen females, standing in their shifts itself maybe, from this place to the eastern world".[45] In Lady Gregory's *Cuchulain of Muirthemne* the hero regularly returns from combat filled with a *battle-rage*, which leads the men of Ulster to forbid his entry to the city of Emhain Macha. They fear that his spasms might destroy peace and damage city buildings, and so they conduct earnest discussions of the ways in which his ardour might be cooled. This is finally achieved by sending thirty women, stark naked, across the plain of Macha in serried ranks: and when the hero sees them, he blushes to his roots, casts down his eyes, and with that (say the manuscripts) "the wildness went out of him".[46] In his typescript version, Synge had his maidens "stripped itself"[47] (rather than in "shifts itself") but was clearly advised by Yeats that the more puritanical members of the Abbey audience could not tolerate such candour. (With commendable innocence, Yeats appears not to have realized that a scantily-clad woman can be even more inflammatory than a naked woman to the puritanical male mind.) The word "shift" had been used without offence in Hyde's *Love Songs of Connacht* (in Irish, of course, as *léine*): but when Synge politely pointed this out in a newspaper interview, the point was left unexplored in the ensuing controversy.[48]

It is hard, at the same time, not to feel some sympathy for the protesting audiences in the play's first week. Most were nationalist males[49] who frequented the theatre for political reasons, since the Abbey was one of the few national institutions in occupied Ireland. Few men anywhere in the Europe of 1907 could have coped with Synge's subversive gender-benders, least of all a group committed to the social construction of precisely the kind of Cuchulanoid heroism which the playwright was so mischievously debunking. Irishmen had been told that when they protested their voices rose to an unflattering female screech: and so they were off loading the vestigial femininity of the Celtic male onto icons like Cathleen ní Houlihan or Mother Ireland.

These were the men who accused Synge of "betraying the forces of virile nationalism"[50] to a movement of decadence. They were hardening themselves into hypermasculinity, in preparation for an uprising, rather than adopting the more complex strategy of celebrating their own androgyny. That Synge preferred the latter option is clear from the tripartite structure of his play, which corresponds very neatly with Frantz Fanon's dialectic of decolonization, from occupation, though nationalism, to liberation.

In Act One, Christy finds a false image of himself in the cracked mirror of his father's cruel home, the very image of Irish self-disgust under colonial misrule. In Act Two, he then discovers an over-flattering image of himself in the perfect mirror of Pegeen's shebeen, the very acme of Irish pride under the conditions of a self-glorifying revival. But nationalism, as Fanon warned, is not liberation, since it still persists in defining itself in categories imposed by the colonizer. A revolution couched in such terms is taken away from a people even as they perform it: it is only by breaking out of the binaries, through to a third point of transcendence, that freedom can be won.[51] Only in Act Three can Christy forget about the good opinion of others, throw that mirror away and construct himself out of his own desire (as opposed to allowing himself to become the locus for the desire of others). Only then does he lose the marks of a provincial who is doomed to define himself through the distorting mirror of a public opinion shaped in some faraway centre of authority.

The Mayoites, on the other hand, never achieve a rudimentary self-awareness, but abjectly defer to a set of laws which they privately despise. Like hopeless provincials, they have no sense of their own presence. Christy's by-play with the mirror in the second act may be narcissistic, but it does serve to *frame* his face, raising it from a commonplace thing to the realms of self-reflexive art. The very *representation* of that face bestows on it an interest it would otherwise have lacked, the growth of consciousness in various characters being indicated in the repeated phrase of recognition "Is it me?" This is "the transformation which takes place in the subject when he assumes an image"[52] . . . like those Aran Islanders who, contemplating Synge's photographs, saw themselves as if for the first time.

The perfect mirror in *The Playboy* points forward to that moment when Christy will form a conception of himself, rather than existing as a conception of others. This is the first act in any revolutionary agenda, a moment reminiscent of that when an insurgent Mexican peasantry broke into the great houses of landowners to be stunned at the sight of their entire bodies in the vast mirrors.

Until this point, Christy has been repeatedly described as one who is afraid of his own shadow, that shadow which is emblematic of his hidden potential, the dark, repressed aspects of himself: but he proceeds from that fear to active self-reflection in the mirror during the second act. This is, as yet, a somewhat superficial activity, an adolescent contemplation of ego rather than of self, but it nonetheless provides the means from which the self may finally be inferred. It is the psychological version, within the individual, of that rather revivalist form of nationalism which is self-conscious but not self-aware. Knowledge of the self rather than mere ego would be the personal version of liberation: and even as nationalism is a phase which a community must pass through *en route* to liberation, so the ego is an essential precondition for the revelation of self. If whole peoples can mistake nationalism for liberation, so there are egos which demand to be identified totally with the self, such as the inflated ego of Christy in Act Two. Equally, there are others which identify solely with the shadow side, persistently asserting their unworthiness, the self-loathing Christy of Act One. Integration can finally be achieved only by those who admit both positive and negative sides as authentic elements.[53]

Those, like Christy, who start with the shadow-side, are more likely to reach this terminus than those who blissfully bask, without reflection, in the ego-image of the perfect mirror. Worshippers of ego, lacking the critical capacity, become prisoners of their own impulses, whereas those who reflect on ego attain objective insights into their dark side and that of others. They learn, as Christy does, that the shadow of which they are initially afraid, is the mirror of an opposite within, the Yeatsian *antiself,* a set of elements all the more powerful for having been repressed. The ego is the mirror of the superficial person. Christy as a mirror-self in the first half of the play was like all mirrors lacking any image of *himself,* with the consequence that when an image showed in his mirror, it was the image of another's desire. By degrees, however, he moves from that passive state to one of active self-reflection, and so his behaviour is progressively less impulse-ridden and more deliberated: by the end, indeed, he can proclaim himself master of those forces which have been mastering him.

In Act One, Christy speaks prose, a prose which befits the frightened boy he is. In the next act, he perfects a factitious lingo, too flowery and exotic to be true: "It's her like is fitted to be handling merchandise in the heavens above".[54] This is derided as "poetry talk" by the Widow

Quin, who sees in it a falsely idealized account of "a girl you'd see itching and scratching, and she with a stale stink of poteen on her from selling in the shop". Such poetry talk is the interesting equivalent of the black-is-beautiful poetry of *négritude*, cultivated among the writers of Martinique in the 1940s. Fanon and Césaire were later to conclude that such exotic nativism was no final solution: and, in like manner, at the close of Act Three, Christy repudiates his former lyricism for an altogether more terse and telling language. He turns to the woman who had so recently loved him, but who now lights the sod to burn his leg, and on this occasion he offers no flowery speeches: "That's your kind, is it?"[55] After early Yeatsian eloquence, late Yeatsian terseness. After revivalist baroque, Joyce's style of scrupulous meanness, his dignified assertion of a people's right to be colourless. After nationalism, liberation.

Synge is arguably the most gifted Irish exponent of the three phases of artistic decolonization later described by Fanon. He effortlessly assimilated the culture of the occupying English and then proceeded to immerse himself in the native culture. Fanon's warning about the pitfalls of national consciousness is worth quoting at this point:

> The native intellectual who comes back to his people by way of cultural achievements behaves in fact like a foreigner. Sometimes, he has no hesitation in using a dialect in order to show his will to be as near as possible to the people . . . The culture that the intellectual leans towards is often no more than a stock of particularisms. He wishes to attach himself to the people; but instead he only catches hold of their outer garments.[56]

This, or something very like it, has long been the nationalist description of Synge, to be found most recently in the account of Seamus Deane: but it is, of course, a description of the Christy of the second act. Unlike that Christy, however, Synge does catch hold of a great deal more than the outer garments of a folk culture: and he never behaves like a foreigner. In the history of Irish writing, he more than any other artist exposed the ways in which a torrent of "exotic" talk may be poor compensation for a failure to act. Denounced as a stage-Irish exaggeration, *The Playboy* actually offers a sharp critique of the verbal exaggeration associated with the stereotype. The play's counterpoising of fine words and failed action makes it a caustic study of the fatal Irish gift of the gab. It was a measure of Synge's own artistic maturity that he could satirize his own great gift even as he exploited it most fully. In *The Playboy* his art reached such a pitch of sophistication that it could even raise doubts about the medium through which those doubts were expressed.

The only stage-Irish scenes enacted on the night of the riots were performed by the protesters in the pit. Synge himself claimed in an essay that the Abbey Theatre had "contrived by its care and taste to put an end to the reaction against the careless Irish humour of which everyone has had too much".[57] That sentence broke out of the Anglo-Irish antithesis by shrewdly implying a criticism of both the colonialist stereotype and the nationalist reaction to it. In his own art, Synge wonderfully fused what was best in English and Gaelic tradition, often doing this within a single work, as in the short satire against the women who hated *The Playboy*:

> Lord, confound this surly sister,
> Blight her brow with blotch and blister;
> Cramp her larynx, lung, and liver,
> In her guts a galling give her.
> Let her live to earn her dinners
> In Mountjoy with seedy sinners.
> Lord, this judgement quickly bring,
> And I'm your servant, J. M. Synge.[58]

The poem is in octosyllabic couplets, which Swift said were most suited to pungent, alliterative satire: but the notion of raising blisters on the brow of one who has spurned the writer's art is taken from Gaelic bards, who resorted to alliteration in such performances. So blended, the two traditions amount to something more than the sum of their parts, constituting – like the bilingual weave of Hiberno-English – a third term.

Synge's *Playboy*, a product of similar blending, was a sort of blueprint for a new species of Irish artist. In his hands, the meaning of Gaelic tradition changed from something museumized to something modifiable, endlessly open. He sensed that the revivalists' worship of the past was based on their questionable desire to colonize and control it: but his deepest desire was to demonstrate the continuing power of the radical Gaelic past to disrupt the revivalist present. In the play, after all, Christy not only fails to kill his father but decides in the end that he doesn't even want to: it is enough to know that the old man is now happily tractable to the son's future designs. This play is the "seething pot", into which Synge cast the shards of threatened Irish traditions, out of which the learning of the future might emerge.[59] In that context, it is hardly surprising that, decades after its first production, it should have been almost effortlessly translated into a Trinidadian version by Mustafa Matura under the revised title *The Playboy of the West Indies*.

REVOLUTION AND WAR

REVOLUTION AND WAR

The Parnell tragedy of 1891 had not spelled the end of the Home Rule movement, nor the collapse of parliamentary agitation. The Irish Party was badly split, but its members limped on: another attempt by Gladstone to introduce a Home Rule Bill in 1893 was defeated. After 1895, the conservatives held power and unionists felt safe for the time being. A new leader, John Redmond, emerged to rebuild the Irish Party in 1900 and to regain its old following. Things seemed to progress smoothly enough, especially when the Liberals were returned in 1906 with a strong likelihood that they would reopen the Irish question.

Beneath the calm unruffled surface of Irish political life, however, things were changing. A gifted journalist named Arthur Griffith had become founder-editor of the United Irishman *in 1899, a fiercely separatist paper which, though anti-militarist in ethos, called for a withdrawal of all Irish MPs from Westminster. Arguing that the Act of Union in 1800 had been illegal – purchased by bribery and corruption – Griffith suggested that, instead of attending parliament, Irish representatives should join with local councillors in a native government. Power was not something to be given or withheld at the whim of the British: it was a force inherent in the community, a force which Irish leaders could take and use in its name.[1] In 1903 Griffith formed his National Council: and, along with groups such as the Gaelic League and Inghinidhe na hÉireann (Daughters of Erin), it provided the nucleus for Griffith's Sinn Féin launched in 1908 (the title means "ourselves", indicative of self-reliance). Many members of the Irish Republican Brotherhood cultivated close friendships with Gaelic Leaguers (the Keating branch in Dublin was a hotbed of political revolutionaries)[2] and with members of Sinn Féin. But the appeal of the latter was limited for a long time, despite its pacifist programme and its declared allegiance to the British monarch: in a 1908 election in North Leitrim, it was beaten by a two-to-one margin by the parliamentary party. As late as 1912, Patrick Pearse was still capable of supporting the Home Rule move-*

ment and its parliamentary party from a public platform. The House of Commons passed a Home Rule bill in that year, which the more conservative House of Lords could not delay for more than two years. It seemed that by 1914 the deposed capital of Dublin would regain its own parliament.

These tortuous manoeuvrings were soon to be overtaken by a more volatile series of events. In northern Ireland unionist opinion, outraged by the Home Rule bill, pledged itself to raise arms against its imposition. Guns were run into Larne and the Ulster Volunteer Force was founded, to set up a provisional government in Ulster if need be. Almost a quarter of a million people signed the oath. The movement's leader was a Dublin lawyer, Edward Carson, who had prosecuted Oscar Wilde (a fellow-graduate of Trinity College) at his trial. He was assured of the support of the Conservative Party in England. In these circumstances, the Liberal Prime Minister, Asquith, persuaded Redmond that it would be foolish to coerce the unionists and wiser to retreat from his demand for Home Rule for the whole island. Nationalists in the south viewed this development with dismay and, insisting that the northerners began what they would finish, they set up their own army called the Irish Volunteers.

Meanwhile, urban unrest was growing. The Land Acts had permitted tenants to buy out holdings and food prices were high, so that rural Ireland seemed well content. In the cities, on the other hand, things were bad: Dublin's poor were among the worst-fed and worst-housed in Ireland, and the death-rate was actually the worst of any major European city.

To challenge these inequities, two Labour leaders, Jim Larkin and James Connolly, founded the Irish Transport and General Workers' Union in 1908; and by 1913 its power had grown to such a degree that one of the city's foremost employers, William Martin Murphy, resolved to break it. He welded hundreds of employers into a federation which locked out 24,000 members of the union. Over the eight months that followed, families starved; other workers went on supportive strikes; there were mass-meetings, riots and deaths. An Irish Citizen Army was established under Connolly to protect the workers, whose insurrection was effectively crushed. The Catholic hierarchy, on hearing that the children of some Dublin dockers were to be shipped to sympathetic families in England, intervened to condemn the plan; and Larkin was widely denounced as a troublemaker. However, the new mood of agitation survived the Lock Out.[3]

The outbreak of war in Europe changed everything. Home Rule was put on hold for its duration: it was to be the post-war reward for Redmond's support for England and for "plucky Catholic Belgium". Tens of thousands of Irishmen volunteered to fight (as they saw it) for the rights of small nations; other members of the Irish Volunteers felt in all conscience that this was not their war. Among the IRB, members agreed that once again England's difficulty could be Ireland's opportunity: slowly but steadily it recruited more and more key members from Sinn Féin and the Gaelic League. It already exercised the decisive influence in the Irish Volunteers.

The Rising came eventually on Easter Monday 1916 and lasted less than a week. Patrick Pearse, appalled by the slaughter of civilians, surrendered on the Saturday after Easter: over three hundred citizens had been killed in bombardment and fighting, as well as over one hundred and thirty British soldiers and seventy rebels. Though dubbed a "Sinn Féin rebellion" in the British press, it was nothing of the kind. It involved sections of the Irish Volunteers (under Patrick Pearse) and of the Irish Citizen Army (under James Connolly). The Pearse who by 1914 had concluded that the Gaelic League, as the Gaelic League, was a spent force now wanted an Ireland not merely Gaelic, but free.

The Rising was probably doomed: but for Pearse and Connolly to strike was to win, since their gesture kept the spirit of nationhood alive. All the same, some of the rebels were jeered and spat upon by Dubliners irate at the ensuing wreckage. Many other Dubliners were reported in overseas papers, however, as warmly cheering rebel gallantry.[4] It was the over-reaction of the British authorities which gave the insurgents the retrospective status of people's heroes. Word leaked out about the murder of Francis Sheehy Skeffington, the pacifist and socialist, who had tried to prevent looting of bombed-out shops and who had been arrested and summarily shot. Even worse was the painfully protracted execution of fifteen rebel leaders between May 3 and 12, despite a strong consensus that they should have been treated as prisoners-of-war. Martial law was imposed and 3,500 people were arrested, more than twice the number which had actually taken part in the Rising. Those participants who were not shot were interned, along with other nationalists, in camps which became schools for the coming war.

By 1918 the war-weary British, whose military ranks had been depleted, were threatening conscription on a surly and mutinous Ireland. Redmond had badly lost the initiative and misread the public mood about the war. Running on an anti-conscription ticket, Sinn Féin candidates swept all before them in the December elections, capturing 73 seats to the parliamentary party's 6. Their members applied Griffith's policy, set up their own parliament (Dáil Éireann), proclaimed their allegiance to the republic of Pearse and Connolly, and began the programme of passive resistance decreed in the pages of the United Irishman. *Alternative courts were set up without the paraphernalia of English wigs and gowns. In backrooms of public houses and in kitchens on outlying farms, an entirely illegal set of judges created a system in opposition to that of the British courts. They helped restore self-esteem to a community anxious to curb the kind of violence which erupts in time of social disorder, and anxious also to project itself as ready for the responsibilities of self-government. Some of the punishments were rather unorthodox: banishment to another county, to an offshore island, even to England where one MP protested against the use of his country "as a sort of convict settlement for men deported by Sinn Féin".[5] By 1920 Under-Secretary Cope was admitting that these courts were doing far more to erode British rule than the assassination campaign spearheaded by Michael Collins.*

The war of independence in which Collins played a leading part from 1919 to 1921 was a brutal affair. The rebels shot civil servants and policemen, raided and bombed barracks, ambushed the British forces and ranged across the countryside in "flying columns". Their opponents executed suspects without trial, terrorized republican families and, on several occasions, burned out entire townships or communities by way of reprisal for alleged disloyalty. (The notorious Black-and-Tans were particularly guilty in this regard and are still hated in Irish folk memory.) World opinion, especially that of Americans, was brought to bear on the British and in December 1921, after prolonged negotiations, they signed a Treaty with the Irish. This offered dominion status, but only to twenty-six southern counties: the six northern counties of Ulster would remain in British hands. Michael Collins, in his more optimistic moments, called it "the freedom to achieve freedom". In a darker mood, he privately conceded that in signing it he had signed his own death warrant.[6]

One of the other signatories was Arthur Griffith: he persuaded a majority of the Dáil to ratify the Treaty by 14 votes to 57. Éamon de Valera, the sole surviving commander from the Rising, argued that the Dáil had no right to do wrong. He and his followers opposed the oath of loyalty to the British crown. (Though, subsequently, they would claim to have also opposed the Treaty on the basis of its partitioning of Ireland, this featured much more briefly in the Treaty debate.) Instead of dominion status, de Valera proposed that Ireland have an "external association" with the British Empire, thus being free to conduct itself as a republic in external affairs.

A bitter election was fought on the issue in June 1922, with 58 pro-Treatyites returned, 36 against, 17 for Labour, and 17 representing other groups including farmers. A civil war of unparalleled bitterness then ensued, in which brother fought brother and men who had recently been comrades against a foreign enemy now killed and executed former friends. Michael Collins died as he had predicted by an assassin's bullet, but not before he had laid the basis for a national army. By then Arthur Griffith was also dead from exhaustion and ill-health. The republican "die-hards" held out until May 1923, but were comprehensively defeated. Many escaped to the United States, where a remarkable number rapidly achieved great success in business: others, under their leader Éamon de Valera, bided their time at home, while the new Cumann na nGaedheal government wielded power.

The British, for their part, were quite convinced that Lloyd George, the "Welsh Wizard", had solved the Irish question: but this was not so. A six-county state had left the unionists with precisely what they had sought to avoid: a home-rule parliament in Belfast. They had taken just six counties in the shrewd belief that this was as much as they could reasonably hope to hold for a permanent, built-in Protestant majority. The result was a one-party state, structured upon religious apartheid: in the words of one of its leaders "a Protestant parliament and a Protestant state".[7] The freedom purchased by Griffith and Collins, though they might have been forgiven for not fully foreseeing the consequences, had been bought at the expense of the northern nationalist minority. Lloyd George, far from solving the Irish question, hadn't even managed to change it.[8]

Eleven

Uprising

One summer Sunday, late in the nineteenth century, the poet and mystic George Russell stood on the esplanade at Bray and preached about the return of ancient Irish heroes. As it happened, among his auditors was that Standish James O'Grady whose *History of Ireland: Heroic Period* (1878-80) had made the exploits of Cuchulain available in English to a national readership. His object had been to provide in the ancient heroes exemplars who might reanimate the declining Anglo-Irish aristocracy. "I desire", he wrote in his preface, "to make this heroic period once again a portion of the imagination of the country, and its chief characters as familiar in the minds of our people as they once were".[1] Watching Russell share this explosive information with a more downmarket audience of weekend holidaymakers, O'Grady felt a pang of dismay and foreboding: but there was nothing he could do to recall the genie back to the bottle.

It did not take him long to sense what would happen when Cuchulain was appropriated as a role-model by the clerks and schoolmasters massed before him. "We have now a literary movement, it is not very important", he declared: "it will be followed by a political movement, that will not be very important; then must come a military movement, that will be important indeed".[2] O'Grady was but the first among many writers to witness with amazement what might happen when images and ideas crafted with care in the study took fire in someone else's head, and did so with an intensity which could express itself only in direct action. Years later, W. B. Yeats would ask "Did that play of mine send out / Certain men the English shot?"[3] The conditions for theorizing a revolution were indeed no different from those for starting one. After it was over, Russell would gravely but proudly admit the link between the idea and the action: "What was in Patrick Pearse's soul when he fought in Easter Week but an imagination, and the chief imagination which inspired him was that of a hero who stood against a host . . . I who knew how deep was Pearse's love for the Cuchulain whom O'Grady discovered or invented, remembered after Easter Week that he had been solitary against a great host in imagination with Cuchulain, long before circumstance permitted him to stand for his nation with so few companions against so great a power".[4] And in lines from a late poem, Yeats asked a ringing question:

> When Pearse summoned Cuchulain to his side,
> What stalked through the Post Office? What intellect,
> What calculation, number, measurement replied?[5]

– and the answer was in due time: India, Egypt, Nigeria, and so on.

The rebels did indeed set headlines for men and women in those far-flung places: and the Soviet revolutionary V. I. Lenin had predicted as much when he wrote in 1914 that a blow against the British Empire in Ireland was of "a hundred times more significance than a blow of equal weight in Asia or in Africa".[6] English socialists were inclined to the rather patronizing belief that freedom could only be won by the colonies *after* they had gained power in the mother country. It never struck them that the fastest advances towards modernization might come from the periphery. But in 1916, along with the Irish insurrection, came attempts at rebellion in French Annam and the German Cameroons. The Irish were, if anything, ahead of their time, as Lenin later remarked: "The misfortune of the Irish is that they rose prematurely, when the European revolt of the proletariat had not yet matured". The world-historical events which might thereby have ensued have been spelled out by Conor Cruise O'Brien: had the rebels waited until 1918, when the country was united against the threat of conscription, a Rising then with mass support would have called forth a British reign of terror, with the inevitable consequence of mutinies by Irish troops on the western front. By then, as a matter of fact, mass mutiny had taken Russia right out of the war, and the morale of both British and French armies was very low: so it would at least have been a possibility that the European ruling order might have collapsed.[7] James Connolly had foretold that "a pin in the hands of a child could pierce the heart of a giant". In the event, though the European order remained intact, the global order of British imperialism did not: those members of the British cabinet who saw the long-term implications for places like India and Egypt had their fears confirmed.

With hindsight, it is easy to see the 1916 rebels as an early instance of a decolonizing élite, and to advance the now-familiar analysis of economic frustrations and curtailed career opportunities which made the colony a factory of grievances. Modern educational reforms had produced a *cadre* of native intellectuals, not all of whom, by any means, could be drawn into the work of empire: but they also threw up new kinds of official, half-ashamed of the force by which they ruled. These self-doubts were sometimes visible to their more astute and restive subjects, and this had the effect of encouraging rather than mollifying rebels, who won more and more influential converts like Roger Casement and Erskine Childers over from the imperial side.[8] On Easter Monday 1916, when the rebels struck, the highest-ranking British officer on duty was an adjutant and the routine guards at the General Post Office had rifles but no ammunition.

Critics of the "irrationalism" of the 1916 leaders point to the relative prosperity of Ireland during the years of the Great War, when high food prices caused large sections of the economy to boom. This is to forget, however, that revolution more often comes not in the darkest days of oppression so much as at a time when people have the luxury of being able to stand back a moment from their own condition and make a shrewd assessment of it. The leaders of the Easter Rebellion were many of them well-to-do: it would be hard to assign a strictly economic motive to the involvement of a headmaster such as Pearse, a university don like MacDonagh, or a son of Count Plunkett. Nonetheless, the ordinary Dubliners who marched behind them had known the consequences of dire recession in a city of chronic unemployment, and for them the high food prices were yet another outrage. The grievances of many rebels *were* economic and, as always, such men and women were glad to find leaders who could give them a spiritual and moral explanation. The frustrations of *all* the fighters were cultural: they wanted a land in which Gaelic traditions would be fully honoured. On that point, also, George Russell was an astute guide: just a year after the Rising, he accounted for its significance to still-baffled officials. Empires, he complained, destroy native culture, achieving "the substitution therefore of a culture which has its value mainly for the people who created it, but is as alien to our race as the mood of the scientist is to the artist or poet".[9]

Despite his cheerful pragmatism as a shaper of the agricultural cooperative movement, Russell could never cast the Rising in simply economistic terms: to him it was exactly the reverse, a plea for spirit as against dull matter, for imagination against empiricism (which to him seemed but a synonym for imperialism). The energy of life was its desire for expression: but the forms proffered by England, however well-intended, just did not fit. There is remarkably little anti-English sentiment in the writings of the Easter rebels for all that. Many of them revered particular English poets – Pearse admired and even imitated Wordsworth; MacDonagh wrote a fine thesis on Thomas Campion and devoted his very last class at University College Dublin to the virtues of Jane Austen, before marching out to prepare for insurrection; and Joseph Plunkett learned much from Francis Thompson. What they rejected was not England but the British imperial system, which denied expressive freedom to its colonial subjects. It was for this reason that Yeats said that "no Irish voice has been lifted up in praise of that Imperialism which is . . . but a more painted and flaunting materialism; because Ireland has taken sides for ever with the poor in spirit who shall inherit the earth".[10]

The 1916 leaders have often been accused of glorifying violence but, apart from one notorious speech by Pearse, they must have been the gentlest revolutionaries in modern history. They rose in the conviction that further involvement by Irish people in the Great War would lead to far more bloodshed than their Rising, which they hoped would take Ireland out of the war altogether. The British saw their action as treachery and shot its leaders as casually as they shot daily deserters on the western front. It took George Bernard Shaw to remind them that they should, under international law, have treated the men as prisoners-of-war: "An Irishman resorting to arms to achieve the independence of his country is doing only what Englishmen will do if it be their misfortune to be invaded and conquered by the Germans".[11] By the time he had written that, sixteen men were executed: and Yeats captured the new mood.

O but we talked at large before
The sixteen men were shot,
But who can talk of give and take,
What should be and what not
While those dead men are loitering there
To stir the boiling pot?

You say that we should still the land
Till Germany's overcome;
But who is there to argue that
Now Pearse is deaf and dumb?
And is their logic to outweigh
MacDonagh's bony thumb?[12]

To the British this Rising among a people who had not even experienced compulsory conscription seemed utterly inexplicable. To those Irish writers who sought to account for it in artistic terms, it appeared at first to be indescribable in any available language. This was initially a problem for the rebels themselves: how to express the unknown in terms of the known? MacDonagh and Plunkett's studies of mystic authors and poets take on an extra significance in this light, as if both men were hoping to find in the mystic's texts a solution to the technical problem. Indeed, MacDonagh wrote in *The Irish Review* of the challenge confronting "the mystic who has to express in terms of sense and wit the things of God that are made known to him in no language".[13] The rebels, likewise, sought a dream of which they could not directly speak: they could only speak of having sought it. The invention that was the Irish Republic was initially visible only to those who were the agents of freedom glimpsed as an abstract vision before it could be realized in history. In his poem "The Fool", Pearse contemplated a point from which all outlines of the republic would become visible:

O wise men, riddle me this: what if the dream come true?
What if the dream come true? and if millions unborn shall dwell
In the house that I shaped in my heart, the noble house of my thought?[14]

From that vantage-point, many texts by Wilde, Shaw, Yeats, Synge and dozens of others might be seen to have represented, years earlier, a complex of ideas which found their fullest expression in the Rising of 1916. Yeats was the first knowingly to divine that connection when he told the young George Russell "absorb Ireland and her tragedy and you will be the poet of the people, perhaps the poet of a new insurrection".[15] Ironically, in the event, Yeats himself filled the role which he had reserved for his friend. His play *Cathleen ní Houlihan* (1902) cast the beautiful nationalist Maud Gonne in the part of a withered hag who would only walk again like a radiant young queen if young men were willing to kill and die for her. To the republican insurrectionist P. S. O'Hegarty, the drama became at once "a sort of sacrament", to the rebel Countess Markievicz "a kind of gospel".[16] The Rising, when it came, was therefore seen by many as a foredoomed classical tragedy, whose *dénouement* was both inevitable and unpredictable, prophesied and yet surprising. Though it remained mysterious to many, the event was long in the gestation.

Year one of the revolutionists' calendar was 1893, because it marked the foundation of the Gaelic League. Even more striking than this, however, was the aura of the 1890s which clung to the characters caught up in the crisis, for many had been impressionable adolescents in the aesthetic decade. The rebels, Wilde-like, opted to invest their genius in their life and only their talent in their work, for they offered their lives to the public as works of art. Seeing themselves as martyrs for beauty, they aestheticized their sacrifice. Most of all, they followed the gospel which asserted "the triumph of failure", the notion that whoever lost his life would save it. This idea underlies Thomas Mac-Donagh's play *When the Dawn is Come* and Pearse's *The Singer*, whose hero says:

> One man can free a people as one man redeemed the world. I will take no pike. I will go into battle with bare hands. I will stand up before the Gall as Christ hung naked before men on a tree.[17]

Equally, Joseph Plunkett's poem "The Little Black Rose Shall be Red at Last" reworks the bardic image of Ireland as *róisín dubh* (dark róisín) into a nineties-ish mode:

> Because we share our sorrows and our joys
> And all your dear and intimate thoughts are mine
> We shall not fear the trumpets and the noise
> Of battle, for we know our dreams divine,
> And when my heart is pillowed on your heart
> And ebb and flowing of their passionate flood
> Shall beat in concord love through every part
> Of brain and body – when at last the blood
> O'er leaps the final barrier to find
> Only one source whereon to spend its strength,
> And we two lovers, long but one in mind
> And soul, are made one flesh at length;
> Praise God, if this my blood fulfils the doom
> When you, dark rose, shall redden into bloom.[18]

Here the Gaelic conceit of a ruler married to the land, whose relation is mediated by the poet, is replaced by the image of a poet whose body bleeds into the earth. This sexual congress will restore new life even though he dies, like the victim of a fertility rite, in the act. In his devotion to the Romantic Image which at once discloses and withholds its meanings, Plunkett provided yet another example of the age's penchant for the half-said thing, the symbol radiant with partially-articulated possibility.

The challenge of using the known to hint at the unknowable would eventually strike Yeats, the most articulate of all the poets of the nineties, as the artistic problem posed by revolution. It is the question broached in his play *The Resurrection*: "What if there is always something that lies outside knowledge, outside order? What if at the moment when knowledge and order seem complete that something appears?"[19] That question, or a version of it, is embedded in many of Yeats's most visionary poems and plays: he is at his bravest and most vulnerable whenever he seeks to welcome the "rough beast" of the unknowable future, without recourse to the props of the past for help or support.

The Easter rebels are sometimes depicted as martyrs to a text like *Cathleen ni' Houlihan*, but rather than reduce the living to a dead textuality, Yeats at his most daring asserts the power of texts to come to life. As a poet, he invents an ideal Ireland in his imagination, falls deeply in love with its form and proceeds to breathe it, Pygmalion-like, into being. It is hard, even now, to do full justice to the audacity of that enterprise.

The odds against it were massive. Karl Marx had complained of the lamentable tendency of persons on the brink of some innovation to reduce history to costume drama by modelling themselves on some ancient Roman or Greek analogy, with the result that ghosts invariably appeared and stole their revolution. This was the mistake of all previous uprisings: to have presented themselves as *revivals*, so that the gesture of revolt could not be seen as such. Oscar Wilde's theatre, as has been seen, had suggested that the self was plastic and that it could show a people how to refuse their assigned place and instead assume a better one. Its ultimate lesson, however, was that the imitation of any model, no matter how exalted, was slavery: the real challenge was to create a new, unprecedented self. One historian of culture has stated the problem very well:

> Rebellions in *moeurs*, in manners broadly conceived, fail because they are insufficiently radical in terms of culture. It is still the creation of a believable personality which is the object of a cultural revolt, and, as such, the revolt is still enchained to the bourgeois culture it seeks to overturn.[20]

The adoption of a pose was one step: what the second was might soon become more clear. The first stage demanded the violation of proprieties and the wearing of exotic clothes, but the second would move beyond that reactive affectation to an account of how a renovated consciousness might live. Such freedom had no precedent, except perhaps in the Thermidorean first years of revolutionary France, where the streets "were to be places without masks" and where "liberty was no longer expressed concretely in uniforms: now there appeared an idea of liberty in dress which would give the body free movement". In the century after Thermidor, that barely-glimpsed freedom had been lost, but the experimental theatre of the 1890s, led by Wilde and Yeats, "created an expression for the body that went beyond the terms of deviance and conformity" and which contrasted utterly with the restrictive costume of the streets. "People turned toward the theatre to solve the problematics of the street", writes Richard Sennett, "to find images of spontaneity".[21] Ordinary people, having lost belief in their own expressive powers, turned to artists and actors to do what they could not, and to teach them accordingly how to repossess their own emotions.

Whereas O'Connell's rapport with the people had offered a model for artists to emulate, now the artists were to be heroic exemplars for the politicians: but this was to involve no slavish imitation of external qualities. Yeats sought not to inspire imitation in others, preferring to teach them to become themselves: "we move others not because we have understood or thought about those others, but because all life has the same root".[22] He saw that every Irish life was a ruin among whose debris might be discovered what this or that person ought to have been. His plays do not tell onlookers to be like Cuchulain, but to invent themselves: "The greatest art symbolizes not those things that we have observed so much as those things that we have experienced, and when the imaginary saint or lover or hero moves us most deeply, it is the moment when he awakens within us for an instant our own heroism, our own sanctity, our own desire".[23]

This was exactly the achievement of the 1916 rebels, who staged the Rising as street theatre and were justly celebrated in metaphors of drama by Yeats. All the mirrors for magistrates of ancient England had taught that "to be fit to govern others we must be able to govern ourselves": and the rebels had done just that. During Easter Week's performance, they were enabled both to show feeling and to control it: and so, in the eyes of their audience, both Irish and international, they had literally governed themselves. This ultimately invested them with a power far greater than their power to shock. Yeats had always equated heroism with self-conquest, that ability of great ones under pressure to

express some emotions while battening down still others held in reserve. This was the same tragic dignity admired in the rebel leaders by
the English officer who presided over their execution. By such example,
these leaders and their men urged all Ireland to do likewise, to conquer
and so to express selves, to recover the literal meaning of the words *sinn
féin.*

If there was an element of play-acting involved in the Rising, then
that is best understood in existential terms. "As soon as man conceives
himself free, and determines to use that freedom", wrote Jean-Paul
Sartre decades later, "then his work takes on the character of play".[24]
The rebels' play was staged to gather an Irish audience and challenge an
English one. In that sense, the Rising was a continuation of what had
begun in the national theatre, which had among its audience "almost
everybody who was making opinion in Ireland".[25] The early plays of
the Abbey Theatre had taught that the conditions of life are open: the
theatre can indeed be a place frequented by the "low" as they study
alternative possibilities for themselves, including ways in which they
might usurp their masters. Though it seemed to conspire with carnivalesque disorder, the playhouse also provided the necessary antidote,
for it encouraged a randomly-gathered crowd to sense its growing,
cohesive power. Yeats often liked to quote Victor Hugo: "in the theatre
a mob becomes a people". Indeed, the theory of tragedy propounded
by Yeats – as the moment when casual differences between individuals
are put aside for a communal solidarity of feeling – well captures that
moment. So it was fitting that the printing press on which the Proclamation of the Republic was done should have been hidden in the
Abbey Theatre. Many of the Rising's leaders had been initiated in
theatrical methods by the Abbey: no previous Irish insurrection had
been mounted in such avowedly theatrical terms. One of the first to fall
was Seán Connolly, an actor with the company whom Yeats would
recall in a late poem:

> Come gather round me, players all:
> Come praise Nineteen-Sixteen,
> Those from the pit and gallery
> Or from the painted scene
> That fought in the Post Office
> Or round the City Hall,
> Praise every man that came again,
> Praise every man that fell.

From mountain to mountain ride the fierce horsemen.

Who was the first man shot that day?
The player Connolly.
Close to the City Hall he died;
Carriage and voice had he;
He lacked those years that go with skill,
But later might have been
A famous, a brilliant figure
Before the painted scene.

From mountain to mountain ride the fierce horsemen.[26]

Every man and woman had been assigned a part in life: for Yeats, the question was not whether it was a good or bad one – rather it was whether he or she played it well. The actor could choose to resign the part, or to improvise as best he could in the absence of a clear set of instructions: however creative that improvisation, it would be based on a life-script appropriate to the actor's time and condition. Yeats, like Pearse, believed that each generation was set its own task and that theirs must fulfil a mission to renovate Irish consciousness. This destiny weighed all the more heavily on men and women who were still young when the century turned. To have embarked on life as the twentieth century began must have filled them with a sense of a divinely-ordained task. Pearse's own philosophy of Irish history was cyclical: the 1916 Proclamation noted that six times in the previous three centuries national rights had been asserted in arms. Some generations had surpassed others and carried out their life-task, but a generation which shirked the task would condemn itself to a shameful old age.

This complex of ideas – close enough to those propagated by Ortega Y Gasset in Spain at that period[27] – reflected a sharpened notion of *generation*, which emerged among European intellectuals after the turn of the century. This was partly a result of Freud's influential Oedipal theories, and even more a consequence of the pace of social change which was leaving the old and young no common ground on which to meet. Writers no longer seemed to address society as a whole: instead they fastened onto immediate contemporaries. It would be hard to find a better explanation of the styles of address adopted by Pearse, who repeatedly spoke to and for "this generation", men and women in their twenties and thirties who had been to school in the Gaelic League. Left all but leaderless after the fall of Parnell, that generation had no choice but to father itself. It set out to define a new code, in the knowledge that if it did not achieve freedom, it would at least have provided its basis, and have left to successors a philosophy and a set of actions against which the next generation could define itself. Only if such were not done could the men and women of 1916 be deemed to have failed.

Such a view of history, though often denounced as fatalistic, has much in common with the Marxist definition of freedom as the conscious recognition of necessity, and it was dramatized, with his usual brilliance, by Yeats in *The Dreaming of the Bones*. Here, a rebel soldier escapes from the Post Office in 1916 and flees to the west, where he encounters the ghosts of Diarmuid and Dervorgilla who, it is alleged, brought the Norman occupiers to Ireland. They wish to consummate their illicit love in a kiss. Unfortunately, they cannot until they are forgiven by the soldier, and this is something which (despite the wishes of the audience) he cannot do. They are dead, of course, and he is living: though he might wish to set their troubled spirits free, he must accept his appointed part. There is no freedom but the freedom to weave the cloth of necessity unfolded by the musicians (the real protagonists) at the outset.[28]

Men may make their own histories, said Marx, but not under the circumstances which they might ideally have chosen: instead, they are confronted with the tradition of dead generations which weighs like a nightmare upon the brain of the living. How this works is interesting: when a crisis becomes absolute and a desperate man is compelled to choose the unknown, his act can never be his alone, for "it takes place in circumstances directly found, given and transmitted from the past".[29] The new act joins itself to the ghostly event: and the actors discover that their stage is filled with the spirits of buried men and dead heroes. These spectral appearances are conjured out of the anxieties which attend all acts of innovation: they offer themselves as known vessels into which the unknown quantities of the future may be poured. For it is a fact that every disruption of routine living for the sake of a new ideal is traumatic: "every definite break with the past at once invites others and increases the strain upon everybody".[30] To allay the fear of the unknown, even the most innovative may have to present it as the restoration of some past glory. As the French businessmen of 1789 portrayed themselves in the role of ancient Romans recovering democratic rights, so Pearse summoned Cuchulain to his side to validate his ideal of a welfare state which would, so said the Proclamation, "cherish all the children of the nation equally". In reading out the Proclamation, as he stood before the Ionic pillars of the Post Office, to "a few thin, perfunctory cheers",[31] Pearse was knowingly enforcing the classical analogies. He saw that in a traditionalist society, it is vitally necessary to gift-wrap the gospel of the future in the packaging of the past. This Connolly also did when he presented socialism as a return to the Celtic system whereby a chief held land in the common name of all the people. Joyce adopted a similar tactic when he concealed the subversive narrative of *Ulysses* beneath the cover of one of Europe's oldest stories, *The Odyssey.*

This is a further justification of the theatricality of the Easter rebellion: alas, it was ill-understood at the time, even by some of its more pragmatically-minded participants. Complaining that the events had "the air of a Greek tragedy", Michael Collins sourly added: "I do not think the Rising week was an appropriate time for the issue of memoranda couched in poetic phrases, nor of actions worked out in a similar fashion".[32] Doubtless, as a volunteer, he was unimpressed by the choice of the Post Office as a military centre, since it left soldiers like himself exposed on all sides. As an act of dramatic symbolism, however, it was an inspired choice, since it cut across the main street of the capital city, paralyzing communications and forcing everyone to take notice. The selection of Easter Monday – when most British soldiers were on furlough at Fairyhouse Races – was not just a sound tactic, but another brilliant symbolization, since it reinforced Pearse's idea of the cyclical nature of history. Easter brought renewal, spring-time, new life to a dead landscape: and so it helped to justify and explain all previous abortive uprisings, for it wove them into a wider narrative, a myth of fall, death and glorious redemption.

It has become fashionable to portray the rebels as Catholic militants, because of the use of Easter symbolism. However, this is to read into their texts and actions a sectarianism which emerged only some time later, after the foundation of the Free State. The poetic imagery employed by Pearse and Plunkett was that of a generalized mystical Christianity rather than something specifically Catholic in overtone. In many ways, it took its cue from the Protestant notion of the "life-task" which informed so much of the writing by soldiers of imperial Britain in the Great War. "We cannot but be thankful that we were chosen, and not another generation, to do this work and pay this price"[33] was a refrain on the lips of the young volunteers who stood in line at recruiting offices with all the innocence of youths awaiting a great cricket match: and it was also the dominant idea of the Easter rebels. Such an attitude was possible only to a generation which had no first-hand experience of modern warfare with its mass graves.

Though British soldier-poets would soon know the hard realities and write anthems for doomed youth led to slaughter by callous age, the Irish case was different: the rebellion was short, its leaders (apart from de Valera) were shot, and so there was time for them to be glamorized in the long lull before the guerrilla war of independence began. Instead of a fearful revolution linked in the popular mind to a terror that devoured the revolutionary children, the Irish case was invoked by Pearse as an example of children devouring their own mother:

> Mise Éire
> Sine mé ná an Cailleach Béarra.
>
> Mór mo ghlóire
> Is mé do rug Cuchulain cróga.
>
> Mór mo náire,
> Mo chlann féin do dhíol a máthair.
>
> Mise Éire
> Uaigní mé ná an Cailleach Béarra.
>
> I am Ireland
> I am older than the old Woman of Beare.
>
> Great my glory
> I that bore Cuchulain the valiant.
>
> Great my shame.
> My own children that sold their mother.
>
> I am Ireland.
> I am older than the Old Woman of Beare.[34]

It was the death of the rebels, rather than that of their enemies, which would make a right rose tree, as Yeats retold:

> "But where can we draw water",
> Said Pearse to Connolly,
> "When all the wells are parched away?
> O plain as plain can be
> There's nothing but our own red blood
> Can make a right Rose Tree".[35]

The imagery here is of the Liberty Tree, more Protestant than Catholic, with its roots in radical millenarian sects; and the notion that republican revolt is simply the political application of Protestant principles found sanction in the demeanour of the rebels. In the face of ecclesiastical condemnation, many simply bypassed the mandatory consultation with their confessors before rising: hence the prolonged sessions within the Post Office during which Pearse, Plunkett and Desmond FitzGerald filled lulls in combat with complex theological justifications of what they had done.[36] (The recital of rosaries might also be seen as a way of repudiating those ecclesiastics who said that the rebels were no longer Catholics.)

Pearse was a prototype of the revolutionary ascetic who renounces love, family ties and all sensual gratification: and it is this power over himself which gives the ascetic authority over others:

> Fornocht a chonac thú,
> a áille na háille,
> is dhallas mo shúil
> ar eagla go stánfainn.
>
> Chualas do cheol,
> a bhinne na binne,
> is dhúnas mo chluas
> ar eagla go gclisfinn.
>
> Bhlaiseas do bhéal,
> a mhilse na milse,
> is chruas mo chroí
> ar eagla mo mhillte.
>
> Dhallas mo shúil,
> is mo chluas do dhúnas;
> chruas mo chroí
> is mo mhian do mhúchas.
>
> Thugas mo chúl
> ar an aisling a chumas,
> is ar an ród seo romham
> m'aghaidh do thugas.
>
> Thugas mo ghnúis
> ar an ród seo romham,

ar an ngníomh a chím,
is ar an mbás a gheobhad.

Naked I saw thee,
O beauty of beauty,
And I blinded my eyes
For fear I should fail.

I heard thy music,
O melody of melody,
And I closed my ears
For fear I should falter.

I tasted thy mouth,
O sweetness of sweetness,
And I hardened my heart
And I smothered my desire.

I turned my back
On the vision I had shaped
And to this road before me
I turned my face.

I have turned my face
To this road before me,
To the deed that I see
And the death I shall die.[37]

In the *aisling* poems the gallant liberated the captive woman: in this instance, however, the hero-poet turns away from her. Like Plunkett, he will paradoxically liberate her only by dying, to prove his "excess of love" (a phrase Pearse actually used, and which was repeated with an implication of moral accusation against the rebels in "Easter 1916"). Such cold, marmoreal love is all that is possible to an ascetic who holds out to his followers something even better than victory – salvation. Pearse took Irish asceticism out of the monasteries and made it active in the political world: and his followers were repeatedly told that they were the elect, chosen for this redemptive task. The "unprecedented inner loneliness" which assails all who wait for signs of divine election was endured by the rebel leaders in their theological debates.[38] Pearse, Plunkett, FitzGerald (and countless others, no doubt) were fast becoming their own priests.

None of this should seem in the least surprising. Modern revolutions have often been carried out by intellectuals who transmute the images and ideas of Christianity into a secular code. Marxism, insofar as it was a state religion, achieved much: but as a scientific theory of society, it would never have gone far. When Pearse called the people "its own Messiah", he was simply repeating Rousseau's insistence that "the voice of the people is, in fact, the voice of God".[39] What made Pearse and his comrades rather different from other modern revolutionaries was that, in their utterances, the religious rhetoric was never occluded or buried, but remained visible and audible on the textual surface.

It will never be fully clear whether the resort to such language by insurrectionists is sincere or tactical: each case must be weighed on its merits. Christian imagery certainly helped to reassure hesitant well-wishers of the morality of the Irish rebels' actions: and, yet again, it allowed the materially-subordinate culture of Ireland to express its conviction of its spiritual superiority to England. Most of all, however, it permitted the rebels to embody the unknown in a language which had a high voltage for most Irish people, especially for the poor. Conservative clericalist intellectuals were not slow to denounce such usage as blasphemous and distressing to ordinary Christians. The lawyer J. J. Horgan bluntly declared that the Rising was a sin and Pearse a heretic.[40] Yet what Pearse did was no different from what had been done by men like Yeats and Synge: he moved from faith in "the kingdom of God" to faith in "the kingdom of Ireland", employing the language of the former to launch his crusade for the latter. In effect, he equated patriotism with holiness. The revisionist historian and Jesuit, Francis Shaw, chose the fiftieth anniversary of the Rising to remark that "objectively this equation of the patriot with Christ is in conflict with the whole Christian tradition, and, indeed, with the explicit teaching of Christ".[41] It may indeed conflict with orthodox Catholicism: that, however, is not to say that it conflicts with Christianity as such, and many Protestant sects would have perfectly understood Pearse's equation of "the people labouring, scourged, crowned with thorns, agonizing and dying, to rise again immortal and impassable"[42] with the mystical body of Christ. If there is any substantive difference between the English revolutionaries of 1640 and the Irish insurgents of 1916, it is merely this: the English relied mainly on the Old Testament for their language, and the Irish on the New.

What troubled Hogan and Father Shaw in the 1916 writings was their unapologetic invocation of Wolfe Tone and, by extension, the "godless" anti-Catholic rebels of the French Revolution. Father Shaw,

citing clerical law, objected to Pearse's description of the Jacobin Tone
as a prophet. There may indeed have been a calculated snub to
ecclesiastical authority when Pearse wrote of being "rebaptized in the
Fenian faith", an organization which was itself under interdiction by
the Catholic church. However, most modern movements rapidly develop what has been called "a secular equivalent of the church", often
the primary system of education in decolonizing states, "imbued with
revolutionary and republican principles and content, and conducted by
the secular equivalent of the priesthood",[43] i.e., teachers like Pearse.

Going even further back in history, a study of the art of the French
Revolution would demonstrate a set of effects similar to those achieved
by Pearse. David's famous painting of "Marat Murdered in his Bath"
explicitly linked the image to that of Christ in a *Pietà*, with the
implication that the new martyr could fittingly replace the old.[44] There
are two ways of viewing this manoeuvre. It might be seen as an attempt
to extend and update a vibrant Christian tradition, to take a somewhat
jaded form and animate it with real contemporary feeling; or it could
be viewed as a subversive tactic, which converted the preceding Christian cult into an echo or parody of the more urgent and authentic
contemporary image. With his synthesizing mind, Pearse saw an unbroken continuity from Cuchulain through Christ to Tone, and he
would surely have preferred the first explanation, but there may have
been among his comrades some – Connolly and MacDiarmada spring
to mind – who favoured the second. The former usage could have been
defended as retrieving Christian language from recent debased applica-
tions (as when English bishops blessed guns that went off to fight
imperial wars); the latter might be seen as discrediting it entirely, once
the latent content had emerged. The phase of self-invention followed
hard upon the antiquarian phase, as the latent content of the revolution
(a welfare state, a native republic) emerged from beneath its manifest
symbols (Cuchulain, Jesus Christ).

The Edmund Burke who regarded revolution as a "dramatic performance" and "stage effect"[45] would have had little difficulty in making
such a separation. Nor would he have been overly surprised at the
difficulty which many students of 1916 have in separating the event
from its mesh of defining texts. Many literary works, especially plays,
had far greater an influence on the Rising than the event itself had on
those like Sean O'Casey who came to write of it afterwards. There is a
real sense in which *The Plough and the Stars* (1926) derives more from
On Baile's Strand (1903, 1906) than from the Dublin streets: the
notorious scene where Pearse's speechifying is juxtaposed against the

prostitute Rosie Redmond plying her trade in a pub seems a deliberate reworking of Yeats's play, in which a posturing Cuchulain, at war with the waves, proves utterly irrelevant to the needs of a hungry fool and a blind beggar. But, no sooner has that been said than one is reminded that *On Baile's Strand* may have had far more effect on the Rising itself: after all, its scene where the proletarians mimic the antics of a self-defeating royalty seems an anticipatory version of the revolution (as well as a clear borrowing of the by-play of Hal and Falstaff in Shakespeare's *Henriad*). What is at issue here is a dialectical tension between an action and its representation, a tension most wittily captured in lines from a recent novel of the Northern Ireland conflict:

> "But it is not like 1916".
> "It wasn't like 1916 in 1916".
> There was a long silence.[46]

The whole event has been remorselessly textualized: for it – more than any of its individual protagonists – became an instantaneous martyr to literature.

That process was foretold by Yeats in his poem "Easter 1916", which brought his waverings in the role of national bard to crisis-point. It enacts the quarrel within his own mind between his public, textual duty (to name and praise the warrior dead) and his more personal urge (to question the wisdom of their sacrifice). The poem speaks, correspondingly, with two voices, and sometimes enacts in single phrases ("terrible beauty") their contestation. The sanction for the first voice from bardic tradition was strong: but the force of the second was becoming more apparent to Yeats who increasingly defined freedom in terms of self-expression. He was abandoning the rather programmatic nationalism of his youth for a more personal version of Irish identity.

Now young men had re-enacted Cuchulain's sacrifice in Dublin's streets and Yeats felt compelled to confront his growing scruples about such heroism. The power of his poem derives from the honesty with which he debates the issue, in the process postponing until the very last moment his dutiful naming of the dead warriors: this had been, of course, the practice of bards after a battle, in which they invariably claimed that the land had been redeemed by the sacrifice. Yeats's entire lyric is a sequence of strategies for delaying such naming: and the expectations deliberately aroused by the title, which suggests unqualified encomium, are sharply contested, and disappointed, and then finally honoured in the text.

The "them" of the opening line are not identified, being nameless butts of past Yeatsian jokes who inhabited with this poet a world of casual comedy, where motley was the sign of a hopeless national buffoonery. The constipated repetition of "polite meaningless words" evokes a place seemingly incapable of change, of comic characters who, in Aristotelian terms, must go on repeating the same mechanical errors. However, these unpromising souls do manage to rise to the mythical out of their matter-of-fact beginnings, achieving the tragic transformation of pity and terror:

> All changed, changed utterly:
> A terrible beauty is born.[47]

What is evoked is the moment when the fragmented comic world of individuals at cross purposes is replaced by a lyric solidarity of tragic oneness, and individual attributes are subsumed into myth. "The persons on the stage, let us say, greaten", observes Yeats in an essay on the tragic theatre, "till they are humanity itself".[48]

Yet still he names no names, perhaps out of tact, more likely because he wants to assume intimacy and to place himself at the centre of an event which happened during one of his absences from Ireland. "That woman" (Constance Markievicz), "this man" (Patrick Pearse), "the other" (Thomas MacDonagh) are all discussed, praised, and their lost beauty, learning and literary skill are pondered. Even the despised John MacBride (who married Maud Gonne and was deemed a drunken lout in the earlier dream) must now be numbered, however reluctantly, in the song. Despite most "bitter wrong" done to the poet's beloved, he also has been transformed.

The third stanza offers an accounting of the joys of life which might have made these idealists reconsider their "dream" of death. As in "The Stolen Child", the homely realities of farm life and household animals seem concrete and alluring against the stone-enchanted heart. The horse-hoof plashing in the real pool seems somehow preferable to the winged horse ridden by Pearse in the previous stanza. The changes of cloud, birds and riders seem more vital than the unchanging stone: yet they only "seem" so, for without that stone in its fixity no ripples could vibrate at all. So the poet, with scrupulous exactitude, claims only that sacrifice "can" make a stone of the heart. By refusing to change the rebels have, in fact, changed everything, yet even in that recognition the poet is still not convinced that they were right. For "Easter 1916" is a covert love-lyric, written to soften an unrelenting woman, and the poet wishes to ask Maud to forget the stone for the flashing joy of the fully lived life. His own fanatical devotion has left him childless at fifty, a man who in another poem of the period would contrast the passionate coupling of Coole's swans with his own lonely mortality: and here the swans become hens calling out to their moorcocks, while the poet feels himself the victim of a dilemma ("excess of love") no different from that posed by the rebels' reckless self-sacrifice:

> What if excess of love
> Bewildered them till they died?

The final stanza collapses into a series of terrified questions, none of them properly answered, but each suppressed by an even more pressing interrogation. The post-bardic desperation of a prayer to God:

> O when may it suffice?

is checked at once by a return to traditional duties:

> That is Heaven's part, our part
> To murmur name upon name . . .

However, other questions will not be denied, though none can be entertained for long:

> What is it but nightfall?
> No, no, not night but death;
> Was it needless death after all?
> For England may keep faith
> For all that is done and said.
> We know their dream: enough
> To know they dreamed and are dead.

Those questions are charged with personal passion, while the statements are a fulfilment of bardic duties, shot through with tones of increasing resignation. The demetaphorizing imagination which could reduce a Pegasus to a splashing horse now revokes all romantic he-is-not-dead-but-sleeping evasions. This movement is complex, for it countervails the attempt by the rebels to raise their mundane lives to the level of the mythical. The rebels dreamed – as the poet had earlier "dreamed" MacBride a mere lout – and the verb suggests that they may have all been mistaken in various ways: but the poet writes as one waking to a new reality.

The hardest question of all is the last: what if the rebels' love was converted by the magic stone to hatred of England? But the thought is insupportable: and so the personal interrogations of the poet, about the cost to human integrity of such drastic self-simplification, are drowned out by the somewhat perfunctory but conclusive intonations of the bard:

> I write it out in a verse –
> MacDonagh and MacBride
> And Connolly and Pearse
> Now and in time to be,
> Wherever green is worn,
> Are changed, changed utterly,
> A terrible beauty is born.

The very stridency of the triple negation back in "no, no, not night but death" indicates how much forcing is needed to suppress those questions, if the poet is to deliver the encomium promised in the title. Those questions prove so searing as to throw into doubt the self-assurance of the refrain, a doubt already voiced in terms of the costs to their sexuality of the political convictions of Maud Gonne and Constance Markievicz.

At the outset of the poem, the refrain was declamatory enough: by the end of the third stanza, however, it is omitted, as if the poet is no longer sure that he has anything to celebrate. When it returns at the close, it comes back shamefacedly, as an admittedly rhetorical device to suppress the terrifying interrogation. It would be voiced hesitantly by a skilled reader, with the terror rather than the beauty now uppermost. The public bard is still trying to complete a poem which will please Maud Gonne, while the private lover is still hoping to cure her of political rigidity, urging her to forget the stone for the call of the moorcock. And, since "Easter 1916" is a love poem, its final refrain must be interrogative more than assertive, ironic rather than literal. The very fact that it is based on Gonne's recorded response to the Rising ("tragic dignity has returned to Ireland") would suggest that the poet can endorse it only with severe qualification. That qualification may be read into the rather clichéd tones of the closing lines, which seem sometimes like fillers ("Now and in time to be") or like jaded formulae ("Wherever green is worn"), indicating Yeats's bitter awareness that this utterance, too, will become part of the inevitable simplification of a complex event. As a national (rather than nationalist) poet, he has tried to articulate the contesting feelings of rival Irish groups at the time – the feelings of the rebels' supporters after the executions; the sentiments of those still convinced of England's goodwill; the pacifists who saw violence in terms of human cost; the ascendancy mockers. However, he foresees that these strands will all be forgotten, as the rebels are converted into classroom clichés and his own poem quoted only for a refrain which will be ripped out of its wider context. The rebels are changed, but into the fixity of heroes in a museum.

The underlying strategy is a delayed delivery of the audience's expectation, whose compelled attention the poet holds while he lodges all the necessary reservations. This allows Yeats to explore his own deeper affinities with the ascetic revolutionary mentality, so that his questioning of the rebels is not ill-bred, since it is really his interrogation of himself. Phrases from the writings of the dead men haunt his lines: for example, Pearse's "excess of love" which allows his "fool" to die for the Gael, leaving a sorrowful "mother" naming her child. The poem is thus a disguised exercise in inter-textuality, with the words of dead men modified by those of a living poet, who has grown terrified of the coercive power of texts. He goes through the inevitable guilt-ridden feelings of a survivor who has seen others live out more fully the implications of his Cuchulain, his Cathleen, his world. This may hint at a further reason for his prolonged hesitation to name: if to name is to assert power over the rebels, then to refuse that option is to admit their power over him, an influence discernible in his complimentary use of quotations and metaphors from their writings.

Dining with society personages in England when news broke of the Rising, Yeats must have felt himself marginal to the event: and his poem becomes his subsequent attempt to insert himself back into history, to regain control and to earn the right to perform that final bardic naming. Ironically, by the time the poet has won himself that right, he can no longer enjoy it. History has taken fire as virtue, but it has taken fire in someone else's head.

Twelve

The Plebeians Revise the Uprising

Such was the interaction between street and stage in the years after 1916 that the following note appeared on the programme for Sean O'Casey's first successful play: "Any gunshots heard during the performance are part of the script. Members of the audience must at all times remain seated". *The Shadow of a Gunman* was produced at the Abbey Theatre on 23 April 1923, while the final gunfire of the Civil War erupted sporadically through the ensuing, uneasy week. The events treated in the play had taken place less than three years earlier, in May 1920, but Joseph Holloway could write in his diary, after returning home from the production, of "that stirring period in our history".[1] It was as if, saddened by the frustrations of the 1921 Treaty and by the fratricide of the Civil War, he was already investing the War of Independence with the aura of a golden age when all Irish people could agree on what they were fighting for. Such nostalgia overlooked the massive suffering endured by many townlands at the hands of the Black-and-Tans. Not the least of O'Casey's achievements in *The Shadow of a Gunman* was to remind sentimental nationalists of just how wasteful and unheroic any war – even a war of national liberation – can be.

O'Casey was a working-class realist who focused his Dublin plays not on the deeds of warriors but on the pangs of the poor. These people found their streets invaded by rival armies who used them as shooting-galleries for weeks on end. O'Casey's deepest indictment of the rebels was that he allowed them to appear so seldom on his stage, as if to suggest the irrelevance of their lofty ideals to the actual needs of the urban poor. As far back as 1914, he had decided that James Connolly had made a terrible mistake in bringing his Irish Citizen Army into a direct alliance with the nationalist forces of the Irish Volunteers. He reminded Connolly of his oft-repeated maxim that you could paint all the pillar-boxes green and hoist the tricolour over Dublin Castle, and yet achieve nothing, for unless there was a change in the distribution of wealth, you would simply be exchanging one set of exploiters for another. He resigned from the Citizen Army on this and a number of related principles.[2] Events thereafter in Irish public life unfolded very much as he had feared.

His fullest artistic expression of the ensuing disappointment is in *Juno and the Paycock*. There, the stock melodramatic device of a legacy which turns out to be false would be taken as his sarcastic metaphor for what he derided as the fake inheritance of Irish republicanism. Equally, the melodramatic device of the rapacious Englishman who leaves a decent Irish girl pregnant could be read as his indictment of a dishonest and over-hasty British withdrawal, which seemed to create far more problems than it solved. The execution of Johnny Boyle in the play by former comrades was an apt image of a land sundered by civil war: but for O'Casey the most depressing feature of all was the sudden pretensions to respectability among republican families, as yesterday's rebels rapidly became the new managers and exploiters of the infant state. The Boyle family, who had once encouraged their son's republican principles, end up mocking him as a "die-hard", leading to the erosion of his self-confidence which causes him to betray his principles. But, long years before he had written this script, O'Casey had foreseen it all.

It was, in a sense, inevitable that he would identify his cause as that of the Dublin poor. He was born in 1880, one of thirteen children, eight of whom died in childhood. Dublin in those years was a raw and desperate place: its death-rate (forty-four in every thousand of population) was worse than the slums of Calcutta. Almost one-third of its citizens lived in tenements (many officially listed as unfit for habitation), and over two-thirds of the tenement-dwellers lived in a single room. On average, over fifty people lived in each tenement. Such a setting dictated the controlling mood of the Dublin plays, each of which is a study in claustrophobia, in the helpless availability of persons, denied any right to privacy and doomed to live in one another's pockets. Many of O'Casey's poetic speeches are attempts by characters to create a more spacious world in the imagination than the drab, constricted place in which they are expected to live. In that respect, O'Casey is an heir to Synge, who had found in the rich idiom of the peasantry an implicit critique of a monochromatic world. Moreover, all the nervous joking by characters about money-lending and evictions was rooted in the social realities of the time. Almost one-third of tenement-dwellers were evicted annually for inability to pay rent: hardly surprising when the average wage for an adult male was fourteen shillings for a seventy-hour week. In evidence given to the official enquiry into the cause of the 1913 Lock-Out, the labour leader Jim Larkin told the commission what every worker in Dublin already knew: that the dire accommodation in Mountjoy prison was nonetheless far superior to that on offer in the Dublin slums.[3]

Though O'Casey's family was nothing like the poorest of the poor, this was a life which he knew fairly well. His father died when the boy was young, bequeathing to his son a love of books, especially the sentimental melodramas of Dion Boucicault, in which O'Casey delighted to act. Their robust juxtaposition of farce and tragedy was a lesson he would apply in his plays, despite the raised eyebrows of some fastidious critics. O'Casey's idea of a well-made play was only partly conditioned by Abbey precedent: indeed, his autobiography recalls how he stood in a milling crowd outside the theatre on the night of the *Playboy* riots, consumed with curiosity yet cursing his inability to afford the shilling admission fee.[4]

An even more potent influence were the conventional Victorian melodramas (which he saw regularly at the Queen's Theatre for six-pence) and the stock situations of the music-hall variety show. Hence his delight in the comic male pair, straight man and joker, Davoren and Shields, Joxer and the Paycock, Uncle Peter and the Covey, Simon and Sylvester, each duo traceable to the stock Irish types of English drama. Though accused by purists of perpetrating another stage-Irish fraud, O'Casey breathed life into a moribund tradition, so that it was later available to Samuel Beckett, in such couples as Didi and Gogo, or Hamm and Clov. Indeed, the younger Beckett would astutely link O'Casey's drama to the music-hall in a handsome tribute: "Mr. O'Casey is a master of knockabout in this very serious and honourable sense – that he discerns the principle of disintegration in even the most complacent solidities. This is the energy of his theatre, the triumph of the principle of knockabout in situation, in all its elements and on all its planes, from the furniture to the higher centres".[5] Despite their youthful pomposity, those sentences explain O'Casey's immediate acclaim from Dublin audiences, for he saved the Abbey from financial ruin by wooing large numbers of the Queen's audience to his plays.

Before his advent, cynics complained that Yeats and his co-directors had a machine which tested each play for a mystery ingredient dubbed PQ (peasant quality); but after *The Shadow of a Gunman* audiences could see new kinds of character in an urban setting. Whether they were actually witnessing a radically new form of drama is doubtful, but certainly they were seeing elements of the variety-show in the revised contours of the Abbey play. These successes permitted the short-sighted labourer (then in middle age) to escape from poverty and they gave him the chance to challenge some of the emerging orthodoxies of the new state. While he entertained audiences with a song and a joke, he could question some of their ingrained assumptions. This Shavian technique had its dangers, of course: people, confronted with a sweetened propaganda pill, might learn how to suck off the sugar coating and leave the pill behind.

Nonetheless, O'Casey asked vitally important questions at just the right time. Though an early enthusiast of the Gaelic League, he detected a fatal addiction to respectability among his cohorts, some of whom had "confused the fight for Irish with the fight for collars and ties".[6] These people, he sourly noted, despised the labourer whose Irish was in truth far better than theirs. At about the time of his breach with the Citizen Army, O'Casey initiated a caustic analysis of the Gaelic League: "the problem of havin' enough to eat was of more importance than of havin' a little Irish to speak". By 1919 he had extended his critique of idealism to the sacred entity of socialism itself: "Self-realization is more important than class-consciousness. Trade Unionism may give the worker a larger dinner-plate – which he badly needs – but it will never give him a broader mind, which he needs more badly still".[7]

Nevertheless, the playwright was marked forever by his early years as a loyal assistant and secretary to Connolly in the Irish Citizen Army. It was as a socialist orator that he had first developed his rhetorical skills, with the constant repetition of key words and sonorous phrases to create a rhythmical, rolling cadence, mounting towards a crescendo in the closing sentence. This is a technique to be found not only in purple passages of his *History of the Citizen Army*, but in many protracted speeches of the plays. There is one major difference, of course: the style used in the history to extol military action is later used, even more powerfully, to denounce it. As a style, it won worldwide acclaim in the 1920s and 1930s, especially among emerging black writers, for whom Langston Hughes spoke when he wrote: "The local and regional can become universal. Sean O'Casey's Irishmen are an example. So I would say to young Negro writers, do not be afraid of yourselves. You are the world".[8]

That style could produce remarkable effects, as in Seamas Shields's commonsensical outburst in *The Shadow of a Gunman*: "I believe in the freedom of Ireland and that England has no right to be here, but I draw the line when I hear the gunmen blowin' about dyin' for the people, when it's the people that are dyin' for the gunmen! With all due respects for the gunmen, I don't want them to die for me!"[9] Shields, a man who has repented of his former republican idealism, orates from his untidy bed and is closer to O'Casey's views than any other character in a powerful, if finally coarse, play. He has the sharpness of mind to expose the ways in which war can mask its hideousness in the symbols of Christian belief:

> The country is gone mad. Instead of countin' their beads now they're countin' bullets; their Hail Marys and Pater Nosters are burstin' bombs – petrol is their holy water; their Mass is a burnin' building; their "De Profundis" is "The Soldier's Song" and their creed is, I believe in the gun almighty, maker of heaven and earth . . . [10]

Despite this intensity, the character develops a shrewd line in self-deflation. Reminded of a time when he himself believed in nothing but the gun, he jocularly replies "Ay, when there wasn't a gun in the country". Shields may also speak for O'Casey in his assertion that his is not an attitude of cowardice so much as one of practicality:

> . . . you're not goin' to beat the British Empire by shootin' an occasional Tommy at the corner of an occasional street. Besides, when the Tommies have the wind up they let a bang at everything they see – they don't give a God's curse who they plug . . . It's the civilians that suffer, when there's an ambush, they don't know where to run. Shot in the back to save the British Empire, an' shot in the breast to save the soul of Ireland.[11]

For O'Casey the twin competing factions of Orange and Green had become dreadful images of one another. However, a vital question remained: was this diagnosis that of a cynical, sidelined nihilist, or did O'Casey offer it from some alternative point of vantage?

He had at least one thing in common with James Joyce: a conviction that the songs and stories of the past always celebrated the wrong people, the smiters rather than the smitten. For all his impatience with republican militants, he was deeply moved by the assertion of the hunger-striker Terence MacSwiney that it was not the people who could inflict the most but those who could suffer the most who would win in the end. Hence his insistence that real heroism often emerges wherever and whenever it is least expected, frequently in women like Juno or Mary Boyle. Yet this heroism, on inspection, is often no more than a sturdy refusal of all abstract ideals in the name of the suffering human body. Mrs. Boyle, for instance, may sound at times like a commonsensical socialist, when she tells her wounded nationalist son: "You lost your best principle when you lost your arm: them's the only sort o' principles that's any good to a workin' man".[12] But she uses the same cutting eloquence to deride the labourist politics of her daughter: "When the employers sacrifice wan victim, the Trade Unions go wan betther be sacrificin' a hundred".[13] To her daughter's insistence that a principle is still a principle, she corrosively responds that principles don't pay the shopkeeper. Yet she becomes the moral centre of O'Casey's play, which itself amounts to little more than an attack on all -isms and a celebration of those wives who pick up the pieces left in idealism's wake.

O'Casey's code scarcely moved beyond a sentimentalization of victims, and this in turn led him to a profound distrust of anyone who makes an idea the basis for an action. If this was radicalism, Irish-style, it was a bleak illustration of the old truism that in Ireland "socialism" never stood for much more than a fundamental goodness of heart. As a dramatist (if not as a prose-writer), O'Casey proved no more capable than any of his characters of developing or analyzing an idea. He was at his best in describing the horrors of war rather than its causes: and he could show, with poignant detail, the defeat of entire communities in the face of imperial coercion, nationalist *naïveté* and the blindness of ordinary people to their real self-interest. But he seemed unable in any work of art to raise questions about the quality of thinking which could give rise to such blindness. He did issue his stirring demand, through Juno Boyle, that people abandon idealist illusions: she tells her daughter that war and want have nothing to do with the will of God: "Ah, what can God do agen the stupidity o' men?"[14] In this fashion, he told people that they had the power to shape their own lives, to be the subjects as well as the objects of history: but he aborted the dialectic at that point in a play which resolutely mocks anyone who takes an idea seriously. Ideas in his *schema* are anti-life: those who spout aphorisms from texts, whether theosophical or socialist, all emerge in the end as blathering and blithering idiots. This is not just true of *Juno and the Paycock* but of *The Plough and the Stars* which, for all its flaws, remains a remarkable play. In it, O'Casey confronted himself with the greatest technical challenge of his career, the challenge also faced by Yeats: how to represent onstage a revolution in all its nobility, its baseness and its unprecedented turbulence.

On the surface at any rate, O'Casey had many advantages with this topic. The Rising hardly needed to be theatricalized; it simply needed to be transferred from street to stage. Despite the patent sincerity of its leader, Patrick Pearse was, in the words of one of his staunchest female admirers, "a bit of a poseur".[15] He wore an ancient sword through much of the urban guerrilla confrontation and insisted on handing it formally to the leader of the British forces at the moment of surrender. The theatricality implicit in the choice of date and location was evident also in the demeanour of the rebel leaders: MacDonagh carried a swordstick and cloak, Ceannt wore a kilt and played bagpipes in the lulls between fighting, Plunkett sported Celtic rings and bracelets and, having been condemned to death by the court-martial, married the beautiful Grace Gifford in a midnight ceremony before his execution at dawn. In casting themselves in these self-appointed roles as sacrificial heroes, they were conscious of re-enacting the Cuchulain myth. Even the Proclamation repeated the Gaelic conceit of Ireland as a woman summoning "her children to her flag".

Yeats's poem "Easter 1916" is happy to treat the rebels as they saw themselves, but O'Casey is resolute in his refusal of such artfulness. A paradox ensues. The national playwright spurns the theatricality of the rebels and searches instead for signs of a defiant poetry on the lips of the urban poor, whereas it is the national poet who celebrates the insurgents in terms drawn from tragedy. O'Casey despises such heroics as boyscoutish vanity and he mocks the obsession with swords and uniforms as the decadent vanity of self-deceiving men. While Yeats lists the names of the warrior dead, O'Casey worries about the nameless civilian casualties. Where Yeats salutes the heroism of the rebels – while, of course, questioning its necessity – O'Casey goes farther and questions the whole idea of a hero. The Cuchulain cult appears to the playwright less as a spur to battle than as a confession of impotence. It is only the timid and the weak, he implies, who desire the vicarious thrill afforded by the blood-sacrificing rhetoric of Pearse, the speaker at the window in the second act.

This treatment must have recalled for older members of the Abbey audience Synge's own mockery of the Mayo villagers in *The Playboy of the Western World*: it had been a mark of their emptiness that they should have made a nonentity like Christy Mahon into a celebrity. In both cases, it was probably the critique of heroism (rather than specific irritants such as Synge's use of the word "shift" or O'Casey's juxtaposition of the Citizen Army flag with a prostitute) which roused nationalists to protest. The 1926 audience was tolerant enough of Yeats's refrain "A terrible beauty is born", but O'Casey later savaged it in his autobiography by titling one of its chapters "A Terrible Beauty is Borneo" (source of the famous Wild Man).[16] The difference between

Yeats's and O'Casey's responses can best be explained with reference to another play, *The Life of Galileo* by Bertolt Brecht. There, a youthful radical had appealed to Galileo to defy the church inquisition and, having been rebuffed, lamented "Unhappy the land which has no heroes": and that is the voice of Yeats. After due reflection, however, Galileo responds with the sad wisdom of experience: "No, unhappy the land that is in need of heroes"[17]: and *that* is the voice of O'Casey.

Not everybody concurred with Yeats's vision of the Rising as a Greek tragedy. At the end of the episode, one British officer sarcastically quipped: "The Irish ought to be grateful to us. With a minimum of casualties to the civilian population, we have succeeded in removing some third-rate poets".[18] The remark, though flippant and insensitive, has a kind of honesty about it: the honesty of a man who is still too close to an event to grasp its long-term significance. It is useful in other ways, too, because it reminds us that for every person a great public event is, also, and finally, a private experience. For most Dubliners, the week was memorable because of the difficulty in finding bread and groceries. Such personal considerations might also explain the public activities of many leaders, if we could only know for sure: it has been suggested, for example, that Pearse's school was in debt by Easter 1916 and that a rebellion appeared to him to be as good a way as any of escaping pressing creditors.

Apart from his political reservations, O'Casey had a personal reason for staying out of the Rising: he had to nurse his ailing mother, of whom he was sole support. This explains that poignant scene of the play which has the future rebels declare that "Ireland is greater than a mother/wife"[19]: O'Casey did not agree and chose to spurn the abstract Mother Ireland for the flesh-and-blood woman who needed his support back in East Wall. For years, through his work in the Gaelic League and Citizen Army, he had helped to wind the revolutionary clock: now, as it started to strike, he stayed away. Much the same might be said of Yeats who, as a young man, had been a figure in the Irish Republican Brotherhood: but in later years the *Playboy* riots marked his irreparable break with militant nationalism. Yeats was reported to be rather insulted that the leaders had not informed him before taking action. His immediate response was coloured as much by private as by public considerations: the knowledge that young rebels had been excited by his plays; the involvement of Pearse with whom he had collaborated; and, of course, the death of MacBride who had been his rival for the hand of Maud Gonne. Looked at in this way, O'Casey and Yeats appear as figures complementary to the rebel leaders. Men like Pearse and

MacDonagh had begun as playwrights and poets but, having failed to satisfy their natures in art, turned to a life of action.[20] O'Casey and Yeats had been political activists but, growing weary of the rigidity of many nationalists, had turned for glory to a life of art. It can be argued that while the writers were frustrated revolutionaries, the rebels were frustrated poets. Presumably, this was what the British officer meant by his quip.

The power of "Easter 1916" arises from the balance maintained between Yeats's public and private responses: his bardic duty to celebrate the dead was countered, as has been shown, by a personal questioning of hearts which seemed to have enchanted themselves to a stone. The latter image was borrowed by O'Casey for *Juno and the Paycock*: "Sacred Heart of the Crucified Jesus, take away our hearts o' stone an' give us hearts o' flesh!".[21] The final effect of Yeats's poem is a balanced assessment of the event, implicit in his subtle use of the stone image: for its very fixity and immobility cause ripples in the stream, just as the rebels by their unchanging fidelity changed everything. The tribute to those rebels seems the richer for being able to survive hard questions: it is self-critical, unlike the "ignorant goodwill" of the fanatic. "We make of the quarrel with others, rhetoric", said Yeats, "but of the quarrel with ourselves, poetry".[22] "Easter 1916" enacts that truth in its poised debate between public and private voices. This is not consistently the case with O'Casey's play, which sometimes seems less a quarrel with himself than with others, a retrospective attempt to justify his absence from the Rising and to question the motives of those who fought. His political reasoning is stated by the Covey:

> When I think of all th' problems in front o' the workers, it makes me sick to be lookin' at oul codgers goin' about dhressed up like green-accoutred figures gone ashtray out of a toy shop![23]

Later, he will remind listeners that more die of consumption than are killed in the wars, "because of th' system we're livin' undher",[24] and the only war worth fighting is to improve the material well-being of workers. In all this, tainted witness though he be, the Covey speaks for O'Casey who attempts in *The Plough and the Stars* to compose a tragedy of irrelevance – on the irrelevance of the rebels to the needs of the people in whose name they act, or the irrelevance of the speechifying Pearse to the needs of a prostitute. The irrelevance declares itself most obviously for O'Casey at the level of language. Pearse is heard to use the resonant idiom of Christian religion to promote his military purpose ("without the shedding of blood there is no redemption") and this leads to a confusion of realms: the listeners think themselves excited by a political challenge, when actually they may be responding to the familiar imagery of the Mass. The Covey's materialist diagnosis is vindicated, even if his shying away from Rosie Redmond exposes him as a prude: the crowd thrills at first to the rhetoric of Pearse, and then discredits his cause by their looting. O'Casey, therefore, chooses to locate Pearse offstage, suggesting he is not really a force in their lives: but there may be other, technical reasons for this treatment. Just as Synge's marginalization of Catholic priests owed much to his ignorance of rural spirituality, so O'Casey faces a problem which confronts all artists of revolution: how to render a turbulence which has eluded all previous framing devices?

This was, of course, initially a problem for the rebels, who solved it by using religious and mystical imagery: but for O'Casey, this was just not good enough. Pearse achieved a partial solution of the crisis of representation by resort to a biblical language: O'Casey, faced with the same difficulty, refused to attempt a solution at all. This is scarcely the radical ploy it has sometimes been made to seem. Rather than admit the powerful disruption of both Christian and Celtic codes by their subversive combination in the rhetoric of Pearse, O'Casey opted for the much safer, traditional repetition of Christian moralism: his Bessie Burgess, the loyalist alcoholic, is centralized. While the rebels are portrayed as prating of blood-sacrifice, she is extolled as the one personality onstage who actually honours that code. The gunmen are depicted by O'Casey, and by later revisionist historians, as Catholic bigots rather than as men who by rising risked damnation by official Catholicism. The Pearse on O'Casey's stage does not die, but is a dealer in the deaths of others: the brute facts of history, however, show that the gunmen died for the people, just as the people also died for gunmen.

O'Casey does, of course, achieve some piercing insights. He is acute on the self-deception of some rebels, as they flee the war-zone. Clitheroe fires a warning-shot over the heads of looters: however, he refuses to fire directly at them because "bad as they are, they're Irish men and women". His companion, Captain Brennan, follows James Connolly in asserting that the looters should be shot: "If these slum lice gather at our heels again, plug one o' them or I'll soon shock them with a shot or two myself".[25] While his anger is understandable, the snobbish contempt with which it is stated is not. As a matter of record, looters took mainly food and clothing, risking death to do so.[26] The phrase "slum lice" indicates a gulf of misunderstanding between some insurgents and the people in whose name they rose, a misunderstanding which has dogged the efforts of many republican militants in the decades since. The respectability of some Gaelic Leaguers was coming home to roost.

All of this is based on socialist criteria which people may admire or not as they please, but the single-mindedness of the critique may reduce the stature of the play. Great literature always has a place for the essential criticism of the code to which it finally adheres, which means that the play, if it is to be truly artistic, should render the full pressure of the nationalist appeal, especially if the superior validity of socialism is to be established. In *The Plough and the Stars*, however, the nationalist case is never put, merely mocked. This has led Seamus Deane to complain that all of O'Casey's gunmen are shadows:[27] not for even twenty minutes of a two-and-a-half hour play are the rebels allowed to state their case. The extracts used from Pearse's speeches are highly selective, focusing on his blood-rhetoric at the grave of O'Donovan Rossa, but giving no indication of his support for Dublin workers during the Lock Out of 1913.

Pearse's recantation in that year of earlier attacks on Synge showed his identification with the playwright in a martyr's role, but also the progressive refinement of his literary sensibility under the influence of MacDonagh. Connolly was also a conditioning force in those years, leading Pearse to move beyond the notion of a single Christlike redeemer to the idea of a people as its own Messiah. This was of a piece with O'Casey's rejection of individualist heroism; and, indeed, as 1916 approached, Pearse often seemed to out-socialize Connolly, as when he wrote of the democratic effect on nationalism of "the more virile labour organizations", or when he declared that "no private right to property is good against the public right of the nation. But the nation is under a moral obligation so to exercise its public right as to secure strictly equal rights and liberties to every man and woman within the nation".[28]

An urge to self-justification mars the artistic balance of O'Casey's play, an urge which probably had roots in the survivor-guilt of a former Citizen Army man. He recoiled, for honourable reasons, from the carnage of 1916, but the natural aggression that remained unpurged in his personality was finally vented on the rebels in his text. He was rigidly selective in the motives attributed to them. Doubtless, there were vain men in the Rising such as Captain Clitheroe, men as interested in self-advancement as in serving a cause; and doubtless there were weak men, like Lieutenant Langon, whose courage failed them when they were wounded or fell. But there were others too, whom O'Casey does not depict but who evoked heartfelt tributes from their enemies. In shaping his myth of the Rising, O'Casey was capable of inaccuracy, as when he portrayed the rebels using dum-dum bullets: even the official British enquiry found no evidence of that. Disgusted by a violence he had once endorsed, O'Casey felt the need to distort the evidence, exaggerating the mendacity of some rebels and the virtues of their British opponents.

In general, his rebels are shown as vain, strutting fellows in gaudy uniforms at the start of the play, and as frightened cowards all too anxious to doff their green jackets for the safe anonymity of civilian clothing at the end. O'Casey achieves a typically piercing, but partial, insight on this point. One of his reasons for resigning from the Citizen Army was his opposition to the wearing of uniforms, which he felt would simply mark out volunteers more closely as targets for their military enemies.[29] This was no better than the costume drama to which Marx had said all previous revolutions had been reduced. All the Cuchulanoid rhetoric, all the revivalist archaisms, had been a story of mistaken identity in which the protagonists were never free to become themselves. In *The Eighteenth Brumaire of Louis Bonaparte* Marx had written:

> An entire people, which had imagined that by means of a revolution it had imparted to itself an accelerated power of motion suddenly finds itself set back into a defunct epoch and, in order that no doubt as to the relapse may be possible, the old dates rise again, the old chronology, the old names, the old edicts which had long become a subject of antiquarian erudition, and the old minions of the law, who had seemed long decayed.[30]

O'Casey, like Marx, had no doubt that when a real revolution finally happened, the people would not mistake themselves for historic actors, but would wear their own clothes.

This insight is wonderfully dramatized by O'Casey: moreover, the fact that the tenements were once the splendid town-houses of the Georgian gentry permits him to play off the irony of inappropriate garb against the irony of an inappropriate setting for such everyday squalor and sudden heroics. In such moments, however, he is too strict with others and not half strict enough with himself. After all, that crisis of representation which troubled the rebels also bedevils the artist, because of the inability of inherited forms to contain an unprecedented action: and there is no evidence that O'Casey addresses the problem with any rigour. His play offers no formal innovation of its own, resting content with familiar techniques, and it takes no account of the possibility that the rebels themselves resorted to traditional imagery as a camouflage for their radical innovations. When Cuchulain is used to underwrite a welfare state, or Christ to validate the process of decolonization, then the donning of historical garb may not be quite as conservative as O'Casey thought. Nietzsche had argued that even modern man "needs history because it is the storage closet in which all the costumes are kept": such a one notices that none really fits him, so he keeps trying on more and more, unable to accept the fact that he can never be really well-dressed "because no social role in modern times can ever be a perfect fit".[31] All one can do is wriggle about in the old forms and, in doing that, improvise something slightly new: but O'Casey despises even that strategy.

He is unable, therefore, to allow for any complexity of motive. There can be no suggestion that the Rising might have been Clitheroe's way of seeking to advance the fortunes of his family and install a government which would dismantle the tenements in an independent Ireland. O'Casey, instead, has him return to the Citizen Army because he is bored with his recently-married wife and anxious for the social acclaim that accompanies the new rank of captain. There can be no rendition, either onstage or off, of the hope generated by nationalism at the time in the hearts of many socialists. Both Marx and Engels had argued that the Irish had a duty to pursue national rights in order to promote international socialism: only if British rule in Ireland were broken could socialists in Europe expect the collapse of imperialism and with it of chauvinist attitudes in Britain itself. Connolly had contended that until the national question was solved, socialism would never blossom in Ireland, a belief vindicated in the decades since his death, when a social revolution was prevented by a fixation upon the politics of partition. O'Casey, however, does not embody those arguments at any phase of his play: nor does he make it apparent that the young rebels of 1916 were but part of a European movement.

Pearse's sanguinary rhetoric is divorced from its cultural context, in order to heighten its ferocity: but it was all too typical of its time. To say, in 1915, as Pearse did, that "the old heart of the earth needed to be warmed with the red wine of the battlefields. Such august homage was never offered to God as this, the homage of millions of lives gladly given for love of country"[32] was not so very different from the lines of Charles Péguy:

Happy are those who have died in a just war;
Happy the ripe stalks and the harvested grain.

Nor was it at variance with Sigmund Freud's declaration (also in 1915) that unless it is placed constantly in jeopardy, life becomes "as shallow as an American flirtation" and that only with the prospect of ten thousand deaths a day "has it recovered its full content and become interesting again".[33] To the contemporary mind, this is hateful claptrap, but it perfectly reflected the death-wish of many chivalric young men, who truly believed that *dulce et decorum est pro patria mori.* The suicidal assassin at Sarajevo epitomized the fashion; and Pearse was a very representative specimen of what the historian Robert Wohl has called "the generation of 1914". Wohl says that this generation was composed mainly of intellectuals living in large cities, who concerned themselves "with the decline of culture and the waning of vital energies": they were "exalted by the conviction that they represented the future in the present" and dismayed by "their problematic relationship to the masses they would have liked to lead".[34] Pearse spoke very deliberately as a member of that generation when he opened a passage in "Peace and the Gael" by saying that "the last sixteen months have been the most glorious in the history of Europe".[35] Like others of his generation, he clung to the hope that war would turn out to be a rite of purification, and he considered spiritual values more important than economic facts. He, too, was caught between "a desire to spring forward into the future and a longing to return to the hierarchies and faith of the past".[36]

If this detracts from Pearse's originality as a thinker, it serves also to defend him against attempts to portray him as a bloodthirsty fanatic. The "European" dimension of Easter 1916 is swiftly passed over in *The Plough and the Stars*, so that the playwright can present nationalism as a pathology. It is never examined or presented in all its mesmeric power: rather it is caricatured. The superior validity of socialism is not so much demonstrated as assumed. In consequence, the drama itself is by no means an example of The Playwright as Thinker. The bracing confrontation between nationalism and socialism was well known to O'Casey, if only through Francis Sheehy Skeffington's open letter to Thomas MacDonagh written and printed in the *Irish Citizen* of May 1915: in it the pacifist radical denied that the war proposed against England could be anything better than "organized militarism".[37] Yet, when the Rising came, Skeffington risked and lost his life in the attempt to prevent discreditable looting: though on principle he could not be a fighter, he became in O'Casey's own words "the ripest ear of corn that fell in Easter Week".[38] This did not impel the dramatist to include his viewpoint in a play which does not brook such subtle intellectual discriminations. It was hardly surprising that Skeffington's widow should have been among its foremost assailants.

The robust, rolling language of the characters in *The Plough* may be linked to the strident attitudinizing of the playwright, for his failure of political imagination leads to a dramatic weakness as well. There can be no inner conflict in a play filled with set-piece speeches rather than two-way conversations. And the refusal to present the nationalist case can have only one result: it leads O'Casey to conclude that those Dublin slum-dwellers who were fired by the nobility and pragmatism of the rebel leaders were fools. By denying these factors, O'Casey makes the people seem like dupes, with the paradoxical consequence that Ireland's "worker playwright" finds himself satirizing the common people for their blindness. If men like Clitheroe and Connolly have fallen for an abstraction without substance, then this deprives their death of much dignity.

This satirical treatment of the Dublin poor has further implications. Though it is often said that O'Casey's gift was characterization, there are in truth no characters in O'Casey's slum: rather it is populated with urban leprechauns and sloganeering caricatures, forever jabbering in a sub-language of their own which owes more to the texts of Synge than to the idiom of the Dublin tenements. Those individualizing phrases accorded to figures soon grow wearisome and repetitive. Fluther Good's love of alliteration is entertaining in its way ("It'll take more than that to flutther a feather o' Fluther"), but it is a contrived literary way, the very reverse of the hard-edged realism for which O'Casey is claimed to stand.[39] Fluther's repeated "derogatories" invite the literate, theatrical audience to patronize rather than understand this half-articulate work-man in a manner which is not all that different from the "superior" British indulgence of blarney in the nineteenth century. The lovable peasant has been thereby introjected into the native Irish psyche, to reappear as a twentieth-century slum-dweller. The rolling cadences of Synge and the forms of the traditional Abbey play are ill-suited to the rhythms of urban life: O'Casey repeated but did not remodel them. Unlike Pearse and the rebels, he failed to make the older forms vibrate with an authentic contemporary feeling.

His Synge-song is admittedly lovely, but well removed from the clipped, cutting edge of inner-city Dublinesque eloquence, which al-ways contains an implied rebuke to the poverty which has given rise to it. Fluther's eloquence, on the other hand, is poetry talk rather than poetry: its patent factitiousness permits the audience to find him charming rather than worrying. It is O'Casey's invitation to his knowing followers not to distress themselves unduly with the plight of a worker whose linguistic reach hilariously outstrips his educational grasp. If pastoral obfuscations of rural poverty were the work of an affluent urban middle class, then this inner-city pastoral was also its invention, proof positive that decades of rising food prices had left the poor citizens as outcasts of the new state, and outcasts who could now safely be sentimentalized by those who had helped to repress them. The old *canard* that O'Casey's plays attracted the poorer people of Dublin to the Abbey was exploded by C. S. Andrews, who described the actual audience for *The Plough* as the new Free State élite.[40] Though there was much in the play to make such people gasp, there was even more to soothe and to reassure. This was especially the case in the handling of dramatic form: the author was so incurious, so derivative in this that one can only wonder if he ever suspected that his art might be complicit with the counter-revolution.

In *The Plough and the Stars* the radical tradition of the strong woman and hesitant male, which lent so much excitement to the plays of Wilde, Synge, Shaw and Yeats, is degraded to the level of a dead formula. The critique of the subterranean English elements in Irish nationalism is prosecuted skilfully enough: the rebels and the British soldiers accuse one another of "not playing the game", and a prim Victorianism underlies Ginnie Gogan's protestations of Irish national chastity. As always, however, O'Casey is far more a prisoner of the prevailing English stereotypical forms than are any of his characters: in his use of music-hall routines and in his Arnoldian view of Irish eloquence. This man who had been scathing of the Abbey's charge of a shilling admission-fee nonetheless submitted his play to its directors. O'Casey gave the appearance of challenging a triumphalist nationalism in his audience: but the truth is that he outraged only the radical republicans in it. Covertly, his play exercised a powerful appeal over the new élite, a grouping which had already begun to deny the very processes which had led to its installation. There was, of course, an element of bravado in the prostitute/flag scene on its first staging in 1926, creating a tension between platform and audience which may have served to distract from the lack of inner tension in the text. But with every passing year, as the ruling élites grew less and less radical in thinking, the appeal of O'Casey's Dublin plays actually increased.[41] He could be touted as a plebeian genius, given a welcome which was a testimony to the wonderful tolerance of the ruling order: but that order was never likely to be disturbed by his aborted dialectic, his failure to carry through the implications of his more promising analyses.

The protests against *The Plough and the Stars* were led not by narrow-gauge nationalists but by socialist republicans like Liam O'Flaherty and Hanna Sheehy-Skeffington. Somewhere or other along the line, the young O'Casey's project had inverted itself: he who had glimpsed the future at a moment before it could be fully realized in history seemed to fall back, exhausted, upon the available forms. His failure was similar to that of the middle-class nationalists whom he despised: in decades to come they would ban republicans from their airwaves and demonize them in public debates, for much the same reasons that he kept them on the edge of his stage.

A case could be advanced for O'Casey as an experimentalist in the narrower sense that his play combats the Victorian ideal of a central character who gathers in a single focus a drama's disparate meanings. *The Plough* certainly resists such Bradleyesque analyses and insists on being treated as a matter of overall design. O'Casey's concern is the fate of an entire community, rather than of this or that individual. Not even Fluther could be held to embody the moral pattern: he is but one of a number of persons for whom the audience's sympathies are aroused only to be defeated by some later let-down. All this links up with O'Casey's equal distrust of military heroism and might be praised as a socialist stratagem were it not already a well-known caricaturist's technique. There are no heroes on O'Casey's stage for the same reason that there are no heroes in the world of the cartoon: instead, all are clowns or victims, whose unawareness of their own failure to measure up to their ideals leaves them reassuringly ridiculous where otherwise they might have been frightening. The transformation of the simianized Land League agitator into a lovable Irish peasant by cartoon artists in London returned the Irish to the realms of the reassuring in many a gentleman's magazine. It may well be that O'Casey's inner-city caricatures appealed equally to suburban audiences, disarming by comic mockery a potentially threatening group and consigning them to the official unconscious, where they could enact a role similar to that once played for English people by the Irish.

To O'Casey, mockery seemed a sort of perverse heroism: the Bessie Burgess who constantly jeers Nora becomes her unexpected saviour at the close, by which time the diagnoses of the jibing Covey have all been confirmed. O'Casey's was indeed a satiric vision, but it is hard to imagine any workman seeing much of himself in Fluther, or any Dublin housewife identifying with Mrs. Gogan. "Such writings as touch no man will mend no man", said Alexander Pope, who also remarked that satire is a glass wherein people discover everybody's face but their own.[42] O'Casey treats his protagonists with much condescension, revealing selfishness to be their predominant motive. Those who fleetingly help their neighbours do so in a tone of self-admiration, like that of Fluther as he mends Nora Clitheroe's lock or the Covey as he reels off Marxist clichés. Many of the main speeches have a self-caressing quality, as if the stage were inhabited by egotists who talk at rather than to one another.

So, a consistently socialist perspective is not maintained to the end. Instead, *The Plough and the Stars* is an intermittently sharp diagnosis of the pitfalls in the path of a people's revolution. Through his suffering females, O'Casey calls on men to abandon illusions about their situation, but he does not see that this can be nothing other than the demand to end a situation which can feed such illusions. Insofar as O'Casey raises the issue of socialist analysis, it is to mock the exponents of ideas: the Covey is a real martyr to textuality, eternally quoting Jenersky's thesis on the origin and consolidation of the evolutionary idea of the proletariat and then denouncing an unfortunate prostitute. Ideas are considered only to be deflected as impediments to life: idealists are put on stage only for purposes of mockery. It is, in some ways, excessive to call O'Casey a satirist, for satire presupposes some norm, by whose criteria other ways of living are found wanting: it only works if there is something about which the writer is not finally satirical. In *The Plough and the Stars*, O'Casey uses socialism to denounce nationalism, and then finds socialism inadequate anyway. For him, all -isms are wasms. He thus achieves the unusual feat of making politics one of his obsessive concerns, and yet emerging as a type of the apolitical artist. He is that strangest of modern phenomena: an autodidact who becomes fiercely anti-intellectual.

What saves O'Casey from some of his own sentimental excesses is the fact that his instincts are often more honest than his mind. The play is dedicated "to the gay laugh of my mother at the gate of the grave" and is at its strongest, like Yeats's 1916 poem, in identifying those moments when the private world of the women and the public zones of the men refuse to stay neatly distinct. Nora wishes to make her home a haven and so she buys a lock for her hall door: but to O'Casey this is a futile gesture. He cannot avoid showing the home as an intimate reflection of the corruptions of the outside political world. The basic situation of the Clitheroes tells all: the young husband's interest in his wife is fading after just a few weeks of marriage, mainly because it is impossible for the couple to snatch even a few minutes of privacy in the crowded tenement. Their brief romantic scene is cloying to the point of embarrassment, not because Clitheroe's love is false, but because, lacking a developed idiom of tenderness, he is doomed (like O'Casey himself, in fact) to express an authentic feeling in a derived "insincere" form. The lack of privacy, the helpless availability to tenants, is the direct result of a social system which gives the lady from Rathmines a houseful of rooms and the Clitheroes not even one.

Nora's solution to poverty and overcrowding is to fill her flat with two other tenants in hopes of some day saving her way to better accommodation: Jack's is to buy a gun and strike for a better social order. So, the precise details of the play are at variance with its overall moral pattern. Overall, it suggests that the rebellion is the enemy of family life. O'Casey is forced by the facts of history to show a husband and wife who, though seemingly at odds, may be working towards the same end. Even more astonishing than Clitheroe's seven-week itch, however, is the older people's acceptance that this is the natural order of things. Mrs. Gogan rather savagely remarks by way of consolation to a deserted Nora: "if you'd been a little longer together, th' wrench asundher wouldn't have been so sharp".[43] This speaks volumes of the quality of married life in such conditions: the home which Clitheroe has abandoned is not as enticing as some of O'Casey's interpreters would have us believe.

At the root of this play and of Yeats's 1916 poem lay a set of allegations about the failure of sexual relations in Ireland. In the poem, Yeats expressed his conviction that those who deny or repress their sexuality will become sloganeering caricatures: and the Covey is a further illustration of the theme. Yeats had applied the same criteria to the protesters against Synge's *Playboy*, likening them to eunuchs maddened by their own sterility in the face of the creativity of Synge. That unease with sexual repression was a common refrain among writers of the revival. In his foregrounding of Rosie Redmond, O'Casey touched a very raw nerve: "There are no prostitutes in Dublin" shouted a protester, to which a defender of the author responded "I was accosted by one last night". This led to the final put-down: "Well, there were none till the British soldiers brought them over".[44] The exchanges had an added piquancy given the fact, recorded elsewhere by O'Casey, that many Dublin prostitutes had sheltered republican gunmen on the run from the Black-and-Tans. The whole scene was reminiscent of that during the *Playboy* riots when a young doctor told Synge that he could hardly refrain from standing on a chair and pointing out those protesters whom he personally had treated for venereal disease. The protesters against Synge had been dissident nationalists in a British colony: O'Casey's audience was a new élite, invested with power. It was for that reason, perhaps, that he did not develop a fully worked-out sexual politics in his Dublin trilogy. However, in choosing as an unexpected heroine a loyalist alcoholic, he was brave enough to offer his own wry comment on the myth of female purity beloved of Irish nationalists. As his admirer Denis Johnston would joke, "the birth of a nation is never an Immaculate Conception".[45]

The artistic problem remains, however: can Bessie's bravery retrieve the play at this late point? Her action is not just surprising but strictly unintentional. She is shot in a window-frame by the British army (in which her son so proudly serves), as she tries to comfort the ambitious housewife whom she hated for her youth and her pretensions. While her life ebbs away, she unleashes all the old animosity: "I got this through you . . . you bitch".[46] It is a moving line, in its refusal to be heroic, one of the few occasions of maximum pressure in the play when O'Casey resists the temptation to compose a rolling speech. But it is actually a refusal of tragedy, a studied refusal to enlarge her listeners' sense of the dignity or the possibilities of life. In many ways, it is a wonderful dramatic moment – but it leaves the audience with nowhere to turn, unless it can take a bleak kind of pleasure in finding things as bad as the mockers always claim them to be.

Irish producers have responded to this bleakness in the usual way: by playing up the buffoonery, the comedy and the farce, and by greatly subordinating the pain. (In similar fashion, after Synge's death, they extracted the violence from *The Playboy*, leaving only the lyricism; and, after Beckett's, they removed the suffering silences from *Waiting for Godot*, leaving only the pacy one-liners.) This device, though it has kept O'Casey remarkably popular, hardly honours his original intention. Today, there is far too little tension between the play and its audience, too little recognition that O'Casey saw himself as writing out the tragedy of an entire social class. Today, audiences see both *Juno* and *The Plough* as portending the decay and death of Dublin's inner city: they read them as laments for a lost community, conveniently forgetting that this decay happened as a result of policies which those audiences still sponsor, and that O'Casey's people were actually victims of a British imperialism whose existence many of his current admirers completely deny. It is largely O'Casey's own fault if the sentimentality which he indulged has proved catching among his admirers: but they may nonetheless be finding his characters more admirable than he did.

If O'Casey is impressed by these characters' endurance, he is also deeply worried by it, for he knows that it is more often blindness and ignorance rather than understanding and insight which enable people to go on. Though impressed by the human capacity to persist, he was also sufficiently Protestant to be scandalized by people's willingness to accommodate themselves to catastrophe, to acquiesce in disasters precipitated by irresponsible leaders. The trouble is that O'Casey himself becomes a party to that acquiescence, in his political denial of all hopefulness and in his artistic acceptance of outmoded forms.

Thirteen

The Great War and Irish Memory

For decades after independence, the 150,000 Irish who fought in the Great War (for the rights of small nations and for Home Rule after the cessation of hostilities, as many of them believed) had been officially extirpated from the record. No government representative attended their annual commemoration ceremonies in Christ Church: and none publicly sported a poppy. Such amnesia was weird, given the large number of families whose men were involved, but also considering the manifest links of mood and mentality between the Easter rebels and the battlers at the Somme. Although many soldiers in the trenches would have supported the official line that the Rising was a stab in the back, many others would have shared in the confusion reported by Monk Gibbon in *Inglorious Soldier.* This tells of how the young man of the British forces, home on leave, wondered whether he was in the right army.

The rebels emulated the demeanour of the British Army and proved that, in an issue which truly engaged their sympathies, they could be as brave as any. Accordingly, the soldier-poet Francis Ledwidge found no great difficulty in writing a lament for his friend Thomas MacDonagh in the internal rhymes favoured by Gaelic bards on such occasions:

> He shall not hear the bittern cry
> In the wild sky, where he is lain,
> Nor voices of the sweeter birds
> Above the wailing of the rain.
>
> Nor shall he know when loud March blows
> Thro' slanting snows her fanfare shrill,
> Blowing to flame the golden cup
> Of many an upset daffodil.

> But when the Dark Cow leaves the moor,
> And pastures poor with greedy weeds,
> Perhaps he'll hear her low at morn
> Lifting her horn in pleasant meads.[1]

Only a state which was anxious to repudiate its own origins could have failed – after a predictable period of post-independence purism – to evolve a joint ceremony which celebrated the men who served in either army. It is worth recalling, in this context, that the policemen who surrendered to the Easter rebels after a fierce battle at Ashbourne, Co. Dublin, reminded their captors that they were proud to be Irishmen too. In the same spirit, George Russell wrote the only significant poem of the time to lament the Irishmen who died in both conflicts. "To the Memory of Some I Knew who are Dead and who Loved Ireland", published in *The Irish Times* in December 1917, was, among other things, probably a response to "Easter 1916" and certainly a celebration of two Thomases, MacDonagh and Kettle:

> I listened to high talk from you,
> Thomas MacDonagh, and it seemed,
> The words were idle, but they grew
> To nobleness by death redeemed.
> Life cannot utter words more great
> Than life may meet by sacrifice,
> High words were equalled by high fate,
> You paid the price: You paid the price.
>
> *You who have fought on fields afar,*
> *That other Ireland did you wrong*
> *Who said you shadowed Ireland's star,*
> *Nor gave you laurel wreath nor song.*
> *You proved by death as true as they,*
> *In mightier conflicts played your part,*
> *Equal your sacrifice may weigh*
> *Dear Kettle of the generous heart.*[2]

Sean O'Casey, for his part, never saw the battle-fields of Ypres, the Somme or the Dardanelles, and for that rather flimsy reason Yeats rejected *The Silver Tassie*, arguably the writer's most accomplished play. O'Casey responded with corrosive derision: "Was Shakespeare at Actium or Philippi? Was G. B. Shaw present when St. Joan made the attack that relieved Orléans? And someone, I think, wrote a poem about Tír na nÓg, who never took a header into the Land of Youth". Yeats's answer was to lament that this play lacked "some unique central character who dominated all about him and was himself a main impulse in some action that filled the play from beginning to end". This rather naïve nostalgia for an easy, Victorian methodology came strangely from a stage experimentalist like Yeats, who might not otherwise have deserved the ensuing lecture from O'Casey: "God forgive me, but it does sound as if you peeked and pined for a hero in the play. Now, is a dominating character more important than a play, or a play more important than a dominating character? In *The Silver Tassie* you have a unique work that dominates all the characters in the play".[3]

That work is the war itself, which O'Casey finally brings to the centre of his stage, examining not alone its effect on civilians but also on the men who fought it. Once again, he investigates its fall-out on those in whose name it is being waged; and his theme is that its canker infects trench and home-front in equal proportions. O'Casey had no need to visit battle-fields: the war was all around him, visible in the disintegration of social and domestic relations. He measures its moral virtue in terms of the life which the soldiers defend (seen in Act One) and the life that follows the cessation of hostilities (seen in Acts Three and Four). He finds the culture eroded rather than ratified by the battles to protect it, much in the manner of the young pacifist Bertrand Russell who, on being asked why he was not at the front defending civilization, returned the white feather to his matronly assailant with the words: "Madam, I *am* the civilization they are fighting to defend".[4]

Yeats complained that the dramatic action of *The Silver Tassie* did not "burn up the author's opinions". O'Casey rejoined by asking why, then, the Abbey had mounted the opinion-crammed plays of Shaw. When consulted on the controversy, Shaw actually absolved Yeats: "he is not a man of the world and when you hurl an enormous chunk of it at him, he dodges it, small blame to him". However, Shaw helped O'Casey mount a production of his work in London. Thereafter, O'Casey in self-exile in Devon, deprived of a known audience and players in the Abbey Theatre, never again knew anything like the intense success or controversy of his Dublin years. His later plays veer off into symbolism or expressionism, which has led many Irish critics to identify *The Silver Tassie* as the work in which this wrong turning, as they see it, was made.

It is no such thing, but a play in which O'Casey maintains a near-miraculous balance between the real and the symbolic. In so doing, he solves many of the formal problems which had bedevilled his Dublin plays. In them, it was as if some inner censor had prevented O'Casey from displacing, even for a visionary moment, the oppressed and oppressive environment which he so despised. Significantly, those censors are still active in the Dublin settings of *The Silver Tassie* (as if the playwright feared that carping critics might catch him out violating some tenet of photographic realism); but these acts are set in vibration with the choric expressionism of the continental scenes. Even more subtly, within the prosaic Dublin scenes, there are redemptive moments of poetic drama, which led Shaw to praise the opening act as "deliberately fantastic chanted poetry".

This opens with a celebration of Harry Heegan's exploits in helping the Avondale Football Club to win a cup: the festive occasion, as so often in O'Casey, being shadowed by deaths in war. Here the women, enjoying governmental "separation money", are anxious to get their menfolk back "safely" to the war. They cannot understand the soldiers' irritability: "you'd imagine now, the trenches would have given him some sense of the sacredness of life";[5] and they turn to religion to justify war, for "the men that go with the guns are going with God".[6] In creating a sporting hero, O'Casey deliberately establishes an ideal of physical excellence which will be shattered in the war; and he mocks by implication the link between sport and empire in the upbringing of youth. Sport in the English schools had been long regarded as a sound preparation for battle, for the empire was built "on the playing fields of Eton"; and one company at the Somme went over the top kicking four balls, produced by officers seeking to give courage to their men.[7] A stage-direction says that Harry Heegan "has gone to the trenches as unthinkingly as he would go to a polling-booth. He isn't naturally stupid; it is the stupidity of persons in high places that has stupefied him".[8] That stupidity, which leads to a false identification of the values of religion and war, also afflicts Harry who, in his moment of victory, hoists the silver casket "joyously, rather than reverentially, as a priest would elevate a chalice". He lacks a reverence for life.

It was the second act which, in its expressionism, outraged early critics. Apart from Barney, no other character in the war-zone is identified as an individual: to the generals they are mere numbers. This was a master-stroke by O'Casey: had the play been ritualized from the start, the audience would have had difficulty sensing the characters as suffering persons, but because these characters have been introduced in naturalistic detail in Act One, the audience can know something of the extinction of personality which they now endure.[9] Such an effect could not be achieved either by realism or expressionism alone: it was the combination which was O'Casey's brilliant innovation. The backdrop of a ruined monastery suggests that the war has left nothing but the shell of a religion which agreed to validate it: on the other side of the stage, against the crucifix, is pitted the figure of Barney, tied for a breach of discipline to a gunwheel:

> And we show man's wonderful work, well done,
> To the image God hath made.[10]

If the soldiers have displayed an irreverence for life in war, they are also its manifest victims. In the war-zone, the idiotic remark of Mrs. Heegan comes strangely true: they come (when it is very late) to sense the sacredness of life. O'Casey never wrote a more tender scene. (Had he managed to extend a similar imaginative sympathy to the rebels of 1916, *The Plough* would have been a far greater work.) At times, the men's chants attain an intensity reminiscent of Eliot's religious poetry: on other occasions, their homely, cockney diction recalls the voices of the pub at closing time in *The Waste Land*:

> The padre gives a fag and softly whispers;
> "Your king, your country, an' your muvver 'as you 'ere".
> And last time 'ome on leave I awsks the missus:
> "The good God up in heaven, Bill, 'e knows,
> An' I gets the seperytion money reg'lar".[11]

In place of a God who refuses to appear, the soldiers can only conjure up nostalgic images of domestic bliss, of a child with a balloon, of a lane in Cumberland. The scene is cast in poetry, because their confrontation with the realities of terror and doubt has made them unconscious poets. The irrelevance of an officialdom which offers improving lectures on "the habits of those living between the Frigid Zone and the Arctic Circle" is patent: but the real shame is that soldiers capable of such intense effects in their own language should fall for the feeble rhetoric of their commanders, and end up praying to a gun which will surely destroy them. The whole of Act Two is in that sense a reworking of the second act of *The Plough*, where O'Casey depicted a people unable to understand the events that were overtaking them.

This act echoes all the key phases of the sacrifice of the Mass – the Kyrie; prayers of the faithful; prayers for the dead. However, there is no consecration, no mention of the silver tassie. That moment had occurred, out of proper time, in Act One, when Harry hoisted the chalice, but it was a false consecration, a blasphemous parody of the Mass, courting punishment. In this act, "every feature of the scene seems a little distorted from its original appearance",[12] which is how the tassie will appear on its return in later acts. By then, it symbolizes suffering rather than victory, a casket-turned-chalice. Harry comes to learn this deeper meaning and to confess that "the Lord hath given and man hath taken away!".[13] The war may be over in those two closing acts, but its horrors continue: as Harry says of his unrequiting lover, "the shell that hit me bursts forever between Jessie and me".[14] The question put in *Juno* – how does a society which creates heroes with such relish actually treat them when they fall? – is raised again with more subtlety. O'Casey shows that society can never discharge its responsibilities to such figures, for to do so would be to admit the self-deception which is the basis of the communal fantasy. (It seems a loss, in this connection, that he could not have written a play on the Free State's similar treatment of defeated republicans after 1923.) O'Casey demonstrates, with rare empathy, how the demobbed soldiers hated returning home, because they were tortured by their inability to describe the war to relatives: a problem which he had faced (and dodged) in *The Plough*. In Act Three here, nobody can talk honestly to Harry: his isolation is an eerie continuation of his condition in the war-zone, where each soldier stood on a spookily silent set and "only flashes are seen. No noise is heard".[15]

Harry Heegan has to cure himself of his own bitterness, because the others have learned nothing from the war: even his best friend Barney comes home only to steal his lover. The metaphor of illness which had persisted like a stain through O'Casey's earlier plays (in such figures as Johnny Boyle and Mollser) is enriched here, as the victim somehow fights back and asserts a measure of self-knowledge and of dignity. The post-war world, with its studied effort to be trivial, is acutely rendered, and the mood is similar to that of D. H. Lawrence's *Kangaroo*:

> We hear so much of the bravery and horrors at the front. It was at home the war was lost . . . At home stayed all the jackals, middle-aged, male and female jackals. And they bit us all. And blood-poisoning and mortification set in . . . They were feeding on our death all the while.[16]

The energy of O'Casey's anger is tapped and disciplined by ritualized choruses, by symbol and silence, and by his subordination of character to symbolic pattern, as the phases of prosaic realism are punctuated by passages of austere poetry. All of these make *The Silver Tassie* the most Yeatsian of plays, which leads to the suspicion that Yeats may have banned it from the Abbey Theatre because of a subconscious resentment that O'Casey had invaded his staked-out territory and made it his own too.

In later work still, O'Casey would further explore the possibility that a man or woman can take control of destiny. This search for a sort of Protestant self-election explains the visionary quality of *Purple Dust* and *Red Roses For Me*, in which he develops a fully-fledged Christian socialism of a kind lacking in the Dublin trilogy. In *Red Roses For Me*, he finally summons the courage to imagine Dublin not as the city is but as he would want it to be: the inference is that man will only transform the world through socialism after he has been first transformed by religious belief. Neither religion nor socialism alone was enough for O'Casey: religion had shown him the hollowness of life, and then life went and spoiled everything by demonstrating the hollowness of religion. Only a vision encompassing both could satisfy him in the end, and that vision was achieved for the first time in his portrayal of the battle-fields of Europe in *The Silver Tassie*.

That achievement is of a rare order in modern European writing, and almost unexampled in the dramatic form. It may have seemed churlish to criticize him for evasions, when he also confronted so much that other artists swiftly pass by.

War, after all, is the ultimate desolation of reality, a fantastic intensification of all that is noble and base in civil society. Writers, by tradition, use art to intensify reality, but war does this for them, unasked. Instead of the more usual task of making the everyday seem exceptional, it demands that the artist make the exceptional available in terms of the familiar. War writing is traditionally imagined as coming from the front-line back to the society in whose name battles are waged. It is seldom, if ever, imagined as written by combatants for other combatants. It is, in fact, rarely written by combatants at all, for they are too busy fighting. Some exceptions there have been in the thick of battle – Owen, Sassoon and the poets of World War One – but the Georgian traditions which they inherited proved quite inadequate to meet the technical challenge posed by the trenches. Their attempt, though never likely to convince, seemed all the more necessary in the face of the cover-up by officialdom: throughout the hostilities in the Great War, not a single paper, British or German, published a photograph of a single maimed body. The myth of the individual was still too strong.

In consequence, soldiers home on leave could find no words for their experience, and some found it hard to believe that they had been caught up in the hostilities hours before. Even on the battle-fields a sense of unreality seemed to pervade. Unable to see the enemy whom they were killing for days on end, soldiers sometimes resorted to theatrical gestures: a famous German gunner would stand by his machine above the trenches, fire a round, step gravely back, doff his helmet, and with a ridiculously excessive gesture, bow to the enemy infantry. Perhaps he was hoping to prove that an audience was indeed out there, or maybe he was just hoping to be killed.[17] Those generals who would later use the term "theatre" for the zones of battle were merely ratifying a notion which had struck Yeats and others at the start of the century. There was indeed a sense in which the 1916 insurgents were as real a presence in the poetry of Yeats as they ever were in their uniforms in the Post Office. The crisis of representation which dogged the neo-Georgians in the trenches also afflicted them.

Faced with these difficulties, a poet like Wilfred Owen could only "warn", but the public proved unresponsive. Reared on fables of heroism, it thought the whole thing a bracing game. The poets were on a hiding to nothing. The Great War was, in Scott Fitzgerald's words, the last great love battle, fought for all the old, high abstractions:[18] and so was Easter 1916. In England, those few soldier-poets who demanded a more honest language were silenced or put in mental hospitals. Yeats, when he came to edit *The Oxford Book of Modern Verse*, notoriously excluded their work: Owen, he complained, was "all blood and dirt and sucked sugar-stick".[19] This was, of course, the same Yeats who had denied a high degree of reality to the Great War, and who refused to write a poem about it on request.

One major reason for the widespread reluctance of people to engage imaginatively with the war was the fact that its mass-graves so clearly discredited the meliorism of the late nineteenth century. In "Nineteen Hundred and Nineteen" Yeats could admit that the "pretty toys" of youth were gone, but it was hard to give them up completely, a prospect which Henry James found "too tragic for any words".[20] He predicted that literature would remain silent on the topic, chastened by its own inarticulacy: and so, largely, it turned out. It was as if an entire generation's energy had been used up in the fighting, with little left to depict it afterwards. Even to attempt this seemed, to some sensitive souls, a betrayal of dead comrades left on the battle-field, an outrageous pretence of being able to communicate the immensity of their suffering. Some things resisted even literature. The fact that O'Casey had not been in the trenches may thus be more easily forgiven: had he been there, he would never in all likelihood have attempted *The Silver Tassie*. He had, after all, walked across a real Dublin battle-field in 1916, and, perhaps as a result, it had never found direct representation in his plays.

From this distance in time, the myths surrounding 1916 and the Somme seem almost identical. In Ireland it was soon put about that the most creative and promising intellects had been lost in the Rising by a small country that could ill afford such a reckless expenditure of young talent. "Easter 1916" was a primary sponsor of this myth, since it mourned not just Pearse but MacDonagh, the "helper and friend" who "might have won fame in the end". That was the Irish version of the English tale of a lost generation of brilliant officers cut down in their prime at the Somme. Both narratives had equally little basis in fact. Though British losses in the officer corps were heavy, most who served came home to become political and social leaders. Similarly, most of the intellectuals of the Irish Renaissance survived the experience of war and counter-revolution. In the case of England, it has been argued that "the myth of the rising generation provided an important self-image for the survivors" and "a means of accounting for the disappointments of the present".[21] James Connolly's sad prediction came true: the worship of the past really was a way of reconciling people to the mediocrity of the present. Moreover, the myth reflected the survivors' guilt at being alive while so many comrades were dead, along with the conviction that it might still be possible to show that the sacrifices had not all been in vain.

WORLDS APART?

Fourteen

Ireland and the End of Empire

Yeats was simply the first major literary intellectual of the century to lead his followers in darkness down the now-familiar road of decolon-ization: many would be the writers of emergent nations across the world who would come after him . . . Amilcar Cabral, Aimé Césaire, Léopold Senghor, Frantz Fanon, Ashis Nandy and so on. Ireland differed from other countries in several important ways, some of which increased the difficulties facing Irish leaders, others of which assisted them in their efforts.

Most obvious, perhaps, was the sheer duration of the colonial occupation, which lasted more than seven centuries. Set against that, however, was the close proximity of Ireland to England: affinities of climate, temperament and culture made it hard for the English to treat the Irish consistently as their absolute Other and led to attempts, such as the Act of Union in 1800, to assimilate the occupied land into a united kingdom. To some this seemed a benign offer of membership in one of the greatest organizations in human history: to many others it was the most insidious of all oppressive tactics. However one looked at them, the enforced intimacies of Anglo-Irish relations "created both bitterness and tolerances of unusual refinement".[1] It was a measure of the challenge faced by Hyde and Yeats that the Anglicization which they countered had penetrated every layer of Irish life, a situation rather different from that to be encountered in Africa or Asia, whose emerging peoples were generally not so deeply permeated by the culture of the colonizer. Ireland was so thoroughly penetrated that, apart from a few scattered areas of the western seaboard, it had ceased to exist as an "elsewhere" to the English mind.

These differences apart, there were many striking analogies between the arguments and experiences of the leaders of the Irish Revival and those in the wider world who would eventually follow them. The analogies were unclear to many Irish at the start of this century, for the simple reason that what they were doing seemed almost without parallel: they were the first English-speaking people in this century to win political and cultural freedom from a power which had not been defeated in war. The more acute minds, of course, could make their own comparisons: Wilfrid Scawen Blunt, the lover of Lady Gregory, was struck by the similarities between the causes of Arab and Irish independence, for both of which he worked . . . and a few years before the Easter Rising, Joseph Plunkett visited Egypt. Yeats sensed acutely enough that just as he and Russell looked to Whitman and Poe as exemplars of the democratic muse, so future Indian and African writers might look to them.

So he provided the Abbey Theatre in 1913 as a venue for a production of Rabindranath Tagore's *The Post Office*, a popular Indian play which suggested that redemption would not come from any parliament but only from a supernatural king: the proceeds of the production were in aid of St. Enda's, the school run on Gaelic principles by Patrick Pearse. Throughout his life, Yeats was keen to maintain contacts with Indian writers and intellectuals, sometimes supporting agitations for their defence against British courts. Rabindranath Tagore, for his part, was a serious student not just of Yeats but of other Irish authors: when asked by English administrators if they had not secured his individual freedom, he reminded them that people who had political freedom were not necessarily free in the expressive sense, merely powerful in worldly terms – an argument gleaned from Shaw's criticisms of the English in *Man and Superman* (1903).

"Until the Battle of the Boyne", wrote Yeats, "Ireland belonged to Asia".[2] By this he meant to imply a common racial and linguistic link between Indo-European peoples: a theory which, however far-fetched, was widely endorsed by leading Indian writers such as Lokmanya Tilak. Undeniably, many of those Irish who went to India had seemed to strike a profound chord with its peoples: Margaret Noble from Dungannon arrived in 1902 and rapidly emerged as an inspiring spiritual teacher and nationalist leader, who at her early death just eight years later was hailed by Tagore as "Mother of the Indian People". Mrs. Annie Besant, whom Yeats had come to know in theosophical circles in London, had a lasting impact on both Irish and Indian cultures, and was elected president of the Indian National Congress in 1917: she is credited by many commentators with the successful application of Irish methods of political agitation in the campaigns waged by Indian separatists.[3]

If the political influences flowed mostly from west to east, the cultural and spiritual traffic was as likely to move in the opposite direction. Both W. B. Yeats and George Russell studied eastern wisdom: early and late, Yeats proclaimed himself a follower of such spiritual teachers as Mohini Chatterjee and Sri Purohit Swami, with whom he worked on the *Upanishads*. The poet had hoped to visit India and to meditate there on a holy mountain, emptying himself of all earthly desire. However, the Steinach operation, which seems to have reactivated his sexual urge, put paid to that: literary Dublin, on hearing that monkey glands had been implanted, scoffed that this was like equipping a worn-out Ford with the engine of a Rolls Royce. Yeats did, however, receive a deputation of Indian writers and intellectuals, who asked him why he did not write in Irish. "No man can think or write with music and vigour except in his mother tongue", he told them; "I could no more have written in Gaelic than can those Indians write in English; Gaelic is my native language, but it is not my mother tongue".[4]

His hybrid predicament was not at all untypical of persons in the English colonies: and the analogies between the Irish and Indians were explored in this context by such leading contemporary novelists as Rudyard Kipling, who created in *Kim* (1901) a hero who should have been Irish, but whose father abandoned him in India to a fate which leaves him neither English nor Indian. Kim becomes, in consequence, the cross-dresser *par excellence*, skilled at imitating everyone else whenever that is necessary, but unclear as to how he could play the part that is truly his own. His ambivalence leaves him in one sense a recognizably Irish figure, at once an exponent of imperialism *and* one of its victims. He has, however, the unqualified sympathy which Kipling reserved for those who served the British Empire but did not personally benefit from that service. Though Kipling could see the potential of the Irish-Indian analogy in the promotion of empire, it did not seem to strike him that this was also being invoked by militant opponents of the idea in both countries.

Those opponents often found themselves sharing common ground and platforms in the United States, where exiled Irish nationalists were heartened by the support of Indians who studied their methods. The Home Rule agitation mounted by Shyamaji in India in 1905 followed the Irish example, and from that year onwards the *Gaelic American* and *Clan na Gael* journals carried extensive coverage of India. In 1907, the Irish Parliamentary Party rejected a British offer of severely limited autonomy. Aurobindo Ghosh, a radical leader of the Indian National Congress and editor of *Bande Mataram*, praised the party's refusal to be bought: "Instead of a separate nationality with its own culture, language, government, the Irish would have ended up by becoming a big

English county governed by a magnified and glorified parish council".[5] He urged his fellow-Indians to follow this unappeasable policy. Some of those who took his advice journeyed to England, in order to organize Indian militants: when a number of these were jailed, Maud Gonne and Sinn Féin advised their comrades on the logistics of mounting a rescue operation. The coaching cannot have been very thorough, since the van attacked by the Indians proved quite empty.

These alliances grew even stronger in the heady years of 1919 and 1920. Irish and Indians shared platforms across the United States, protesting against the deportation of Indian nationalists. The Ghadar Party – an organization of Indian workers in the US which wished by armed force to destroy the British Raj – presented Éamon de Valera with an engraved sword and an Irish flag: and on 28 February 1920 de Valera delivered a trenchant speech in New York at a meeting of Friends of the Freedom of India. Taking courage from the American example, he reminded his audience of Washington's message to the patriots of Ireland: "your cause is identical with mine", adding the inflection "Patriots of India, your cause is identical with ours".[6] He hoped that the ties which by then bound Ireland and America would soon bind Ireland to India; and, though the different conditions might call forth a variation in tactics, he urged immediate revolt: "We in Ireland, comparatively small in numbers, close to the heart of Britain's imperial power, have never despaired. You, people of India, remote from her, a continent in yourselves, seventy times as numerous as we are, surely you will not despair!"

De Valera scoffed at arguments that England went to Ireland or India "to teach them the way of prosperity and civilization". "When or where", he asked, "has the British Empire shown such altruism?" Rather these colonies were drained of wealth and food: the famines which plagued India in consequence might be unimaginable to Americans but were well understood in Ireland; and the massacre of unarmed civilians by General Dyer at Amritsar in 1919 "is nothing new to us". No Irishman needed a book to tell him what went on in India: he had only to consider the history of his native land, he said, to know that famine was the weapon used to kill off a people whose burgeoning population struck fear into the hearts of imperial administrators. Those who attributed poverty to native laziness had tried the same device on Ireland and had fooled nobody. De Valera pronounced himself unimpressed by claims, such as those advanced by Bernard Shaw, that it was only the British upper-class which was to blame. "The common citizen's vote it is that maintains his government in power", he averred, and if they fail to change their rulers, "they are guilty with the others", whatever their protestations of democratic government.

Americans should put pressure on trade union leaders, for "the rule of the people by a foreign despot is a terrible thing, but the rule of a people by a foreign democracy is the worst of all, for it is the most irresponsible of all". He commended a study of the Irish revival to his Indian friends: the lesson was that moral force alone would never convince the British unless backed up by physical force. He ended ringingly: "we swear friendship tonight; and we send our common greetings and our pledges to our brothers in Egypt and in Persia, and tell them also that their cause is our cause".[7]

The following month, a large party of Indian Hindus in native dress walked in the St. Patrick's Day parades of New York: and Irish sailors on the high seas carried messages and intelligence between Indian nationalists at home and abroad.[8] In the years that followed, groups like the Women's Irish Education League of San Francisco, founded after a visit by Hanna Sheehy-Skeffington, led boycotts of British ships and organized meetings for Indian speakers. There was a mixture of idealism and pragmatism in these alliances: many Irish were still convinced that British rule in India was the obstacle to the freedom of other colonial peoples, including themselves. Not all Irish nationalists were happy with this: though radicals like Liam Mellows sought to develop contacts, others (according to a British intelligence report) had "a poor opinion of the Indian extremists and decline to work with them".[9]

If many – perhaps a majority of – Irish writers and nationalists were slow to identify with movements elsewhere, this was because their minds were unresponsive to the comparative method, having been attuned to the revivalist idea that the Irish were unique, "like no other race on earth". The British authorities, of course, were under no such illusions and cabinet minutes from 1919 onwards recorded fears that if the Irish case were conceded, the flames of revolt would be fanned in India and elsewhere. Moreover, certain members of the cabinet, notably H. A. L. Fisher, grew frustrated by Lloyd George's obsession with Ireland in 1921 and lamented that the Prime Minister was neglecting the case of Egypt, during the negotiations late in that year of the Anglo-Irish Treaty.[10] After the Treaty had been secured, *The Round Table* predicted that the Egyptians and Indians now had every excuse for thinking that the English would concede to persistent clamour; and it warned that unless the English closed their ears, they would lose the empire and deserve to lose it.[11] During the previous summer, in private

sessions of the Dáil debates in Dublin, Sean T. O'Kelly reported
messages of congratulation from Poland, Turkey, India and Egypt: the
Indians and Egyptians, in particular, accompanied their message with
requests for advice on methods.[12]

Those Indian overtures came hard upon the mutiny of a group of
Irish soldiers in the Connaught Rangers during June of the previous
year, 1920, at the Wellington Barracks, Jullundur. News of the burning
of rural Irish towns and proscription of hurling matches prompted one
soldier, Joe Hawes, to tell his comrades that "we were doing in India
what the British forces were doing in Ireland".[13] Refusing to parade,
about thirty members of "C" company shouted "up the rebels!" Their
tearful commanding officer reminded them in an eloquent speech of
their great reputation, won over thirty-three years; but Hawes stepped
forward to say that while those exploits had been done for England,
this latest one for Ireland would be counted the greatest honour of all.
They said they would soldier no more "until all British troops had been
removed from Ireland" and they flew a makeshift tricolour. The authorities were fearful that Indian nationalists, on hearing of this turn of
events, might be emboldened to attack the British.

The Punjab was then in a state of tension and the killings at Amritsar
were fresh in the popular memory. At the end of June, there were three
hundred and ninety Irish mutineers by official estimate, and though
they refused to file in on command from one of their British officers,
they responded with discipline to the instructions of James Daly, who
had stepped forward to assert that he was now in charge of the
detachment. They were subsequently removed, bedraggled but defiant,
in bullock carts, carrying with them all their possessions in boxes, on
which perched their pet monkey, cockatoos and parrots. Told that they
could have no effect on policy and that their persistence would ruin
their careers, they took pause, but Daly assured them that what they had
done would be reported in every newspaper and emulated by the other
Irish regiments in the army. An attempt to detach and execute the
ringleaders was prevented by an elderly Roman Catholic priest who
interposed himself, beseeching the general to hold fire. Later, however,
after a courtmartial, five were condemned to death, two to life and two
to twenty years' imprisonment, one for fifteen years, and so on. Some of
the death sentences were commuted, but Daly was shot. "What harm?"
he wrote home to his Westmeath mother in a last letter on 19 February
1921: "it is all for Ireland". He refused a morphine injection and an eye-
bandage, telling his firing-squad that "some day the men in the cells over
there may be free". Thirteen bullets cut him to bits, so that fragments of

his flesh and bone stuck into the wall behind; but Hawes and the others reassembled the body as best they could for burial.

It seems that none of these men had any contact with Indian nationalists, and the mutineers who survived said that they had never thought to make any: but word soon got through. A Poona journal, praising these patriotic soldiers, contrasted them with the Indian troops who had "shot down their innocent countrymen and children at the order of General Dyer". A Delhi paper commented approvingly that "the Irish people can preserve their honour, defy the orders of the Government, and defeat its unjust aims".[14] The British intelligence network thought it likely that de Valera's speech in New York urging Indian-Irish collaboration might have motivated the men, but it seems unlikely that newspapers carrying this speech could have come into their possession.

It must also be remembered that, as British soldiers who had taken an oath of allegiance to the crown, the mutineers were in the strange position of being seen as "legitimate targets" by Irish republican gunmen, who actually killed dozens of ex-servicemen in the year after the mutiny. Some of the convicted mutineers, from their prisons back in England, appealed for leniency and early release, so that they might join the Free State army and assist the fight against de Valera's republicans in the Civil War. Not all who returned joined the army, or were even asked to do so. Cynics wondered if these men were patriots at all or merely disorderly crown recruits, but their subsequent tales of the brutality which they endured in English jails confirmed their status as folk heroes.

After the Civil War of 1922–3, the republicans tried to organize further contacts with other nationalist movements. In 1924, Sean T. O'Kelly told the Friends of the Freedom of India in New York that if the great empires found it advantageous to keep in touch with one another, their victims should too. As a representative of the Irish Republic in Paris during the World Peace Conference, he had tried "to form some kind of association" involving Ireland, India, Egypt and others,[15] but had received little support from any but the Egyptians. One reason, O'Kelly added sarcastically, was that India was represented by British officials and "a tamed Indian Prince or two in their train just to add a little dash of appropriate colour to the delegation". He was equally scathing about English administrators, dressed in Mohammedan garments for the purpose of convincing a gullible public that they represented the Arab peoples: "it was most humiliating to any honest person to see how all these great peoples of the East were treated". Even more distressing to O'Kelly was the refusal of the tamed Indian delegation "to risk being tarnished by even momentary association with an Irish rebel".

In a tone of high irony, O'Kelly went on to praise England's self-sacrificing mission in Ireland and India, and to mock the claim of their poor benighted peoples that "they had a highly developed educational system of their own and a distinct culture with a written as well as an oral literature of their own, thousands of years before the English". With robust sarcasm, he parodied the official theory: "it was for our good that England decried our language and our ancient literature and Anglicized or banned our schools and our colleges and our universities". He hoped that it would not take the Indians or the Egyptians as long as it had taken the Irish to learn the necessary lessons of such treatment, and so he quoted Tagore:

> To hold India forever is an impossibility,
> It is against the law of the universe.
> Even the tree has to part with its fruits . . .

and again:

> Brother, do not be discouraged for God slumbers not nor sleeps.
> The tighter the knot the shorter will be your period of bondage . . .

O'Kelly apologized to Indians and Egyptians for those of Irish background who had assisted in their oppression and "formed the backbone of the invading and destroying armies".[16] He promised to make amends for wrongs done by English regiments bearing such names as Connaught Rangers, Munster Fuseliers, Dublin Fuseliers, Inniskillens and so on. He also regretted the collaboration in the British administration of India by Irishmen who lacked the excuse of most soldiers that "what they did they did in ignorance, not in malice". Many soldiers, he conceded, had joined up as an alternative to starvation, only to find themselves used against their fellow-countrymen. He asked why India, "with a cultural history second to that of no nation in the world", should submit to mere military might; and he recalled for them the words of Terence MacSwiney, whose message, he believed, was taken up by Tagore:

> If you expect to live and to command respect in this world,
> First be prepared to give your lives for your mother . . .

The notion was most famously developed by Mahatma Gandhi, who wrote of Ireland in 1921: "I would like the reader to believe with me that it is not the blood that the Irishmen have taken which has given them what appears to be their liberty. But it is the gallons of blood they have willingly given themselves. It is not the fear of losing more lives that has compelled a reluctant offer from England, but it is the shame of any further imposition of agony upon a people that loves its liberty above everything else. It is the magnitude of the Irish sacrifice which has been the deciding factor".[17]

In his concluding remarks to the Friends of the Freedom of India, O'Kelly warned that the British loved to foster internal divisions in order to weaken the emerging nation: so Mohammedan, Hindu and Christian must sink their differences in the common name of Indian (a deliberate echo, there, of Wolfe Tone). Even more important was the moral and spiritual revolution then being led by Gandhi, he averred: "the soldiers who are engaged in the intellectual battle must lead and mark out the way for the army engaged in the physical conflict with the enemy".[18] And he ended his address as de Valera had commenced his, by placing both movements under the auspices of the American Revolution: as Thomas Jefferson had invented America, they were now about the work of inventing India and Ireland.

Despite these manifold contacts with Indian nationalists, it would be unwise to infer that a united anti-imperial front was ever a serious possibility. The vast distance between Ireland and India militated against it – it is significant that many of the contacts were made on US soil and publicized before largely American audiences. The evidence all suggests that the Indians were far more likely to proclaim their solidarity with the Irish than *vice versa*. De Valera and O'Kelly were uncomfortably aware that within the tradition of Irish nationalism was a strain of white triumphalism, which ran from John Mitchel to Arthur Griffith and which would never countenance such a solidarity. Even more depressing was the fact that an otherwise advanced thinker such as James Connolly did not develop a generalized anti-racist or anti-imperialist philosophy. Immediate realities in Scotland and Ireland were just too pressing.

All of which may help to explain why many Irish leaders and artists, having glimpsed the potentials of a global alliance with other emerging peoples, could so easily forget them in the drive to Europeanize the emerging Irish state.[19]

INVENTING IRELANDS

INVENTING IRELANDS

Kevin O'Higgins, Minister for Justice in the first government of the Free State, described his colleagues as probably the most conservative revolutionaries in history. They were autocratic in the way that military men often are. They were anxious not only to secure the state against internal attack but also to demonstrate to the British and the wider world that they could govern with discipline and authority. Just how conservative they were may be seen in their suppression of the Dáil Courts which had been set up during the War of Independence in 1920. Though the work of the courts was dangerous, complex and ill-rewarded, the lawyers and clerks who risked all to do it were seldom thanked by the militarists. Even if the republican side had won the Civil War, there is reason to doubt whether they would have treated the courts more tenderly than did Cumann na nGaedheal. Well before the Treaty, Cathal Brugha, that most stern of republican leaders, had no doubt that through the medium of the courts power was passing into the hands of ordinary people from the military élite: and he thoroughly disapproved of the development. Here was a graphic example of the kind of distorted and undemocratic thinking possible only to those who had fetishized the use of arms and neglected to consider the important cultural aspects of the campaign for freedom.[1]

This neglect would in time permit the politicians of the Free State government to retain as much power as possible for themselves by winding up the Dáil Courts. The "retreat from revolution" had already begun. Soon judges and lawyers would once again be donning the gowns and wigs of the British system; and the newly-liberated people would be employing the unmodified devices of the old régime upon themselves. War and civil war appeared to have drained all energy and imagination away: there was precious little left with which to reimagine the national condition.

There was, if anything, less freedom in post-independence Ireland, for the reason that the previous attempt to arraign the enemy without gave way to a new campaign against the heretic within. The censorship of films

*(1923) and of publications (1929) was a symptom of a wider censorious-
ness, of a kind which would be found in many infant states as they sought
to outlaw the impure and to keep their culture unadulterated by "corrupt"
foreign influences.* Among the first books to appear on the lists under ban
were Aldous Huxley's Point Counter Point, Family Limitation *by Margaret Sanger,* Wise Parenthood *by Marie Stopes and* The Intimate
Journals of Paul Gauguin. *They would soon be joined by works from the
pens of the foremost contemporary Irish writers, for whom it became a
perverse badge of honour (as well as a guarantee of reduced income) to be
given a censorship number. The red-light districts of Dublin, so raucously
celebrated in the writings of James Joyce and Oliver St. John Gogarty, were
closed down by religious campaigners: at one of their final soirées, a famous
harlot whirled and danced before the company like a dervish, her skirts
rising higher and higher until they revealed a pair of knickers beneath, in
the defiant green-white-and-orange of the tricolour of the mythical Irish
republic.*

*By the end of the 1920s many artists and intellectuals had come to the
bleak conclusion that Ireland was no longer an interesting place in which to
live: now they left. Stephen MacKenna, the friend of Synge, sometime editor
of* An Claidheamh Soluis *and translator of Plotinus, was one lost in this
way; George Russell, collaborator with Yeats, mystic poet and inspirer of the
agricultural cooperative movement, was another. But there were dozens: in
the notorious opening chapter of his book on* Synge and Anglo-Irish
Literature *(1931), Daniel Corkery listed them all, as if their exile and
expatriation constituted some kind of dereliction of national duty; yet he
was also honest enough to admit that most had gone because they could not
earn a living wage by pursuing the life of the mind in Ireland. George
Russell had doubted "whether a single literary man in Ireland could make
the income of an agricultural labourer by royalties on sales of his books
among his own countrymen, however famous he may be".² Until he was
awarded the Nobel Prize in 1923, Yeats had never earned more than £200
a year: on hearing the great news from an editor of* The Irish Times, *he
could not restrain himself from brutally interrupting the long-winded
speech of tribute with a question: "How much is it, man, how much is it
worth?"³ When he and his wife decided to eat a celebratory meal, they
could find nothing better in their larder than sausages.⁴*

*All of which is not to say that writers went without honour in the new
Ireland. Indeed, some politicians paid writers the ultimate tribute of
persecuting them and calling for their heads; other more enlightened leaders
simply harnessed the international prestige of artists for good domestic
purposes. Thus Yeats soon found himself chairing the committee mandated*

to redesign the national coinage, a committee which came up with beautiful designs based on Irish animals: the Paudeens who now fumbled in greasy tills did so looking for coins that bore his seal of approval. However, the pillar-boxes in which Paudeen posted his letters still bore the insignia of the British monarch under a light coating of green paint and the state apparatus went largely unmodified. A few streets and stations were renamed for national heroes, mostly drawn from the safer, more remote past, since current politics had proved so divisive; and the teaching of Irish was made the major activity in the nation's schools.

By then the language had been standardized along the lines demanded by Professor Atkinson, and a new internal imperialism, Gaeilge Chaighdeánach *(Standard Irish), sought to erase dialectal differences. Children who failed Irish tests were deemed to have failed their entire state examinations. Whereas in the nineteenth century many had been caned for speaking Irish, many were now punished for not speaking it properly or for not speaking it at all. Generations of children came to see it not as a gift but as a threat, and were hardly consoled by the thought that if they wrote their algebraic symbols in Gaelic lettering, they could score ten per cent extra marks in the examinations. Families in the Gaeltacht areas who spoke Irish were rewarded with government grants, a policy which provoked Dublin Opinion to describe Ireland as "the land which lost the leprechaun but found the pot of gold".*

Irish was taught in schools as a dead language, like Latin, full of complex grammatical rules and irregular verbs. It was taken from its wider cultural context of dances, sports and folk ways. Moreover, the texts written in the period were too patently designed for the classroom, or for what one angry writer called an audience of credulous schoolchildren and pre-conciliar nuns.[5] The whole burden of language revival was placed on hard-pressed schoolteachers, in the innocent belief that the substitution of Irish for English in the youthful mind would be enough to deanglicize Ireland. The ingenious device of national parallelism did not work on this occasion. Meanwhile, the Gaeltacht continued on its drastic social decline, losing 50,000 speakers in the first two decades of the state's existence.

Observing all this from his fastness in Paris during the 1920s and 1930s, James Joyce pronounced himself disappointed. He told Arthur Power, a painter visiting from Dublin, that there had actually been more freedom when he was a youth in Ireland, because the English had been in governance then and the people, unfettered by any sense of social responsibility, said what they pleased: now that they were responsible for their own fate, they appeared to have gone all cautious and middle-aged. As one exile after another – from Tom MacGreevy to Arthur Power, from Mary Colum to Samuel Beckett – confirmed the rightness of that diagnosis, Joyce might have been forgiven for concluding that he had made the right option in choosing exile in 1904. Insofar as men and women of his generation were to renovate the Irish consciousness, this was being achieved in the free zones of art rather than in the far-from-free state.

Yet there was perhaps a sense in which the artists, with their acute antennae, had warned of and anticipated the problem of living in a post-heroic age. Yeats in On Baile's Strand *had shown how self-defeating a commodity heroism can be, and how absurd it can seem when it has outlived its usefulness. That lesson might have sunk in were it not for the Great War, which devalued the quotidian as the banal and which reas-serted the power of the exceptional in human experience. One way in which Irish modernism marked itself off as very different from the European modernism of Joseph Conrad and Thomas Mann was in its respect for the great middle range of human emotion and destiny. Gide spoke for most European modernists when he said "Familles, je vous haïes": but Joyce in* Ulysses *had no compunction about celebrating family values. The ordinary was the proper domain of the artist, he joked, and the extraordinary could safely be left to journalists. So his great book is not only a protest against the militarism of the war and a celebration of the human body which that war did much to humiliate; it is also an attempt to recapture for modern literature the middle range of human experience from artists who felt that no living was possible unless conducted in zones of high ecstasy or utter depravity.*

A further feature notable in Irish modernism was its rawness, its sense of formal immediacy, its refusal of a knowing self-consciousness. The hero and heroine of Robert Musil's The Man Without Qualities *knowingly re-enact the Isis and Osiris myth in their own lives, and this is very different from the case of Leopold Bloom, whose re-enactment of the wanderings of Odysseus is quite unconscious. Joyce may wish to indicate that a true heroism is never conscious of itself as such; but this adage may also be applied to the practice of his own art, where there is no illusion of easy control, no cool command of material. Rather the situation appears to be one in which the plot has the author well in hand. Hence the awesome jaggedness and seeming formlessness of so many masterpieces of Irish mod-ernism, whether* Ulysses, *the trilogy of Beckett, or Flann O'Brien's* At Swim-Two-Birds. *By contrast, the masterworks of European modernism, such as* Heart of Darkness, Women in Love *or* The Magic Mountain *appear strangely traditional in form, as if the anxieties of life in the twentieth century have been poured back into the vessels of the nineteenth.*

All of which is to say that Wilde was perfectly right when he said that it was the Celt who led in art. Joyce never forgot that challenge. He did not become modern to the extent that he ceased to be Irish; rather he began from the premise that to be Irish was to be modern anyway. Yet he saw his art as a patriotic contribution to "the moral history of my country"; and he believed that he had done more than any politician to liberate Irish consciousness into a profound freedom of form. In this, as in so much else, he was accurate. It was the politicians who, in cleaving to tired, inherited forms, failed to be modern and so ceased being Irish in any meaningful sense.

Fifteen

Writing Ireland, Reading England

In the week of the Easter Rising *The Irish Times*, then an ascendancy paper (known as *The Squireish Mimes* among disdainful nationalists) had carried little news of the cataclysmic events passing just a few hundred yards from its office door. Its editorial mind was on higher things. "How many citizens of Dublin have any real knowledge of the works of Shakespeare?", it enquired in its emergency edition of Wednesday 27 April 1916: "Could any better occasion for reading them be afforded than the coincidence of enforced domesticity with the poet's tercentenary?"[1] If the explorer Stanley had carried a copy of Shakespeare with him on his civilizing mission into central Africa in earlier decades, the Anglo-Irish ascendancy in its moment of crisis could urge loyal citizens to immerse themselves in the culture which their soldiers were fighting to defend.

There was only one problem with this. Irish young people who studied English literature at the end of the nineteenth or beginning of the twentieth century found themselves reading the story of how they had been banished from their own home. Until the Gaelic League's campaign bore fruit, the Irish language had been banned from schoolrooms, in which children recited at morning assembly:

> I thank the goodness and the grace
> That on my birth have smiled;
> And made me in these Christian days
> A happy English child.

Hidden in the classic writings of England, however, lay many subversive potentials, awaiting their moment like unexploded bombs. So the young Irish man and woman could use Shakespeare to explore, and explain, and even perhaps to justify, themselves. For Yeats, the failure of Richard the Second was due not to bumbling ineptitude but to a sensitivity and sophistication in the man far superior to the merely administrative efficiency of Bolingbroke. In his reading, *Richard the Second* was, with Arnoldian inflections, the story of England despoiling Ireland. His was a Celtic Shakespeare who loved Richard's doomed complexity and despised the usurper's basely political wiles.

Edward Dowden of Trinity College Dublin, as leader of the efficiency-worshipping literary critics of the Victorian age, had heroicized Bolingbroke and belittled Richard: so Yeats proposed to restore to Shakespeare's texts an openness which they had once had, but long since lost under the distortions of an imperial interpretative psychology. "The more I read the worse does the Shakespeare criticism become", he reported after a period of study, "and Dowden is about the climax of it".[2] Whereas the Celt was held to be unable to cope with the despotism of fact, the greatness of Shakespeare for Dowden lay in his vivid perception of "the chief facts of the world" and in his acceptance of "the logic of facts". Dowden's playwright was distinguished by his "capacity for perceiving, for enjoying, for reproducing facts, and facts of as great variety as possible".[3] In other words, the Trinity don converted Shakespeare into an eminent Victorian, one whose imagination could confront and master the entire material world. Against that backdrop of prevailing orthodoxy, Yeats's re-reading of Shakespeare seemed iconoclastic indeed.

"Professor Dowden", explained Yeats, "lived in Ireland where everything has failed, and he meditated frequently upon the perfection of character which had, he thought, made England successful".[4] This was a polite way of phrasing the matter, which Yeats put a little differently when he wrote at the start of a new century about the literary revival: "The popular poetry of England celebrates her victories, but the popular poetry of Ireland remembers only defeats and defeated persons".[5] Yeats's reinterpretation of Shakespeare's history plays was massively influential; and the reversal which he brought about in criticism had consequences for creative art too. For one thing, it emboldened Yeats himself to write that epic cycle of dramas in which he reimagined the contest between Richard and Bolingbroke as the clash between Cuchulain and Conchobar, "a wise man who was blind from very wisdom, and an empty man that thrust him from his place and saw all that could be seen from very emptiness".[6] Yeats's Richard was no peripheral victim, but the centre of meaning, moral and poetic, in Shakespeare's play: if Bolingbroke epitomized the failure of triumph, then Richard embodied the triumph of failure. It was that very paradox which informed the thinking of the 1916 rebels, so it would not be completely fanciful to list Shakespeare among the revolutionary weapons available to the insurgents. *The Irish Times* had got it wrong again. The attraction of Shakespeare for Yeats lay in the skill with which he tapped popular lore. "Every national movement", he wrote, "as in Elizabethan England, has arisen out of a study of the common people, who preserve national characteristics more than any other class".[7]

Edward Dowden's desperate attempt to recruit Shakespeare to the ranks of the efficient imperialists was doomed: even if there might be some sanction for the imperial theme in the plays themselves, the very *notion* of the theatrical was itself the antithesis of the imperial idea. Theatre, it has been shown, allowed a people to play with freedom and so to realize it. Stage plays were "the symbolic opposite of the lasting colony": as far back as 1610, William Crashaw in a sermon given to a group of planters embarking for Virginia, declared that "the enemies of the godly colony were the devil, the pope and the players".[8] Three hundred years later, the founders of the Irish National Theatre Society could only have agreed. It was hard, however, for English critics to live with the consequences. Even after Yeats's successful completion of a revolution in Shakespearian studies, there were some muscular minds left in England to complain that "there is something in Richard which calls out the latent homosexuality of critics".[9] The Celtic feminine, in its insurrectionary mode, was beginning to bring out the homophobe.

In the summer of 1900, the Chief Examiner of Secondary Schools in Ireland had written a querulous note: "the answering of a number of candidates showed that they had not used the edition of *The Tempest* prescribed in the programme".[10] Was the youthful James Joyce one of the dissidents, bent on producing a more Celtic Shakespeare too? For Joyce, the entire Shakespearian canon was an ongoing narrative of exile and of loss: he even took time off in the middle of *Ulysses* to set mock-questions for the revised Celtic school's syllabus:

> Why is the underplot of *King Lear* in which Edmund figures lifted out of Sidney's *Arcadia* and spatchcocked onto a Celtic legend older than history?

And, what was more, he answered them:

> Because the theme of the false or the usurping or the adulterous brother or all three in one is to Shakespeare what the poor are not, always with him. The note of banishment, banishment from the heart, banishment from home, sounds uninterruptedly from *The Two Gentlemen of Verona* onward

till Prospero breaks his staff, buries it certain fathoms in the earth and drowns his book.[11]

Friedrich Engels had complained that the object of British policy was to make the Irish feel like strangers in their own land;[12] but he seriously underestimated their capacity to reformulate the culture which had been used as an instrument to "civilize" them.

A rereading of English literature thus began. Newspapers began to complain about the insulting renditions by visiting English actors of Irish parts. Joseph Holloway noted in his diary that "a music-hall knockabout Irishman would appear a lifelike portrait of the genuine article beside the Captain MacMorris as he was presented, in speech, action and appearance".[13] Resentment was expressed – and not for the first time – against English texts which misrepresented Irish persons, or which treated them as if they would never be in a position to understand or to challenge such writings. The comedy which Wilde extracted from the spectacle of the upper classes conducting intimate conversations in the presence of servants who are assumed to hear nothing was his exposure of the point of crisis which had been reached. The idea that the lower orders might store and use this information in future attacks on their masters never seems to have greatly exercised the official mind, anymore than English educators expected Irish students of Shakespeare to treat his works like captured weapons which might one day be turned back upon the enemy.

The Irish could use Shakespeare to repudiate those critics who "produced" him in their classrooms and on their syllabi; and, more vitally, they could feed their subversive rereadings back to England. Yeats's insistence that the Abbey Theatre tour London, Oxford and Cambridge with its plays, though criticized by touchy nationalists as a provincial's abject plea for metropolitan blessing, was in fact a masterful attempt to unfreeze English theatre from its petrified condition and to restore to classic texts an openness to many interpretations. Previous attempts at such feedback – Charlotte Brooke's Preface to the *Reliques of Ancient Irish Poetry* in 1789, for example – had proved abortive and were limited, anyway, by the desire of the ascendancy class to clear its name. Now, however, for the first time in history, most sections of the Irish population had a mastery of English, and so the traffic could flow in both directions. The Irish, often mocked as brainless lyricists, could practise *criticism*, in both the essayistic and creative mode, and could set themselves up as the brains (as well as the poets) of the United

Kingdom. Wilde, for instance, took a perverse delight in proclaiming that his own republicanism derived from that of Milton, Blake and Shelley; and he was caustic about attempts by literary critics to write such embarrassing details out of their histories. In his Commonplace Book, kept while at Oxford, he wrote: "To Dissenters we owe in England *Robinson Crusoe*, *Pilgrim's Progress*, Milton: Matthew Arnold is unjust to them because not to conform to what is established is merely a synonym for progress".[14]

This rereading of English literature was accompanied by an initial investigation of much that the academic canon suppressed, including texts from the United States by writers such as Hawthorne and Whitman, both of whom were exercised by the search for a republican tradition. Yeats's "The Lake Isle of Innisfree", as an early example, took its long running line from Whitman, and its underlying idea from Thoreau's *Walden*. Irish writers became increasingly aware of how the fate of their own country and that of other colonies had been interwoven through many points in history: as an instance, the first attempt at "modernizing" the societies which lay beyond Europe was made in 1798, when Napoleon abandoned his plans for a further, comprehensive invasion of Ireland and instead set his sights on Egypt. Accordingly, Irish writers became interested in the books beginning to emerge from other colonial outposts of what would later be called the "Third World", from India, Africa and Latin America. There were far fewer of these at the start of the century, of course, so the Irish knew that they must lead the way; but men like Yeats and Pearse were pleased to use the Abbey Theatre as the place in which to produce a play like *The Post Office* by the Indian Tagore. "Yeats thinks *The Post Office* a masterpiece" confided his friend William Rothenstein in a letter to Tagore in 1912; and the Cuala Press published four hundred copies in a special edition in 1914. Two years later, Yeats crafted a glowing introduction to Tagore's book *Gitanjali*.[15]

Throughout this period, there was a developing affinity with other colonized peoples. An uncompromising person, such as Joyce, could regret the mindless complicity with empire of those examinees who studied approved versions of *The Tempest* as a prelude to taking on the white man's burden in some equatorial land:

They turned into Lower Mount Street. A few steps from the corner a fat young man, wearing a silk neckcloth, saluted them and stopped.

– Did you hear the results of the exams? he asked. Griffin was plucked. Halpin and O'Flynn are through the home civil. Moonan got fifth place in the Indian. O'Shaughnessy got fourteenth. The Irish fellows in Clarke's gave them a feed last night. They all ate curry.

His pallid bloated face expressed benevolent malice and, as he had advanced through his tidings of success, his small fat-encircled eyes vanished out of sight and his weak wheezing voice out of hearing.[16]

There was, necessarily, a thinly-veiled aggressiveness about such readings of the national condition, rooted in a pivotal sense of hurt and grievance. But that mood soon passed as intellectuals began to notice, with interest and surprise, the equally deforming effects of imperialism on the sponsors themselves. Edward Dowden had written that the pervasive idea of *The Tempest* was that "the true freedom of man consists in service" whereas to a lout like Caliban "service is slavery".[17] As a Victorian exponent of evolution, Dowden had pronounced himself a scientific gradualist and, therefore, an enemy of the French Revolution: "no true reformation was ever sudden",[18] he opined. There spoke a nervous Anglo-Irishman of the later nineteenth century, the offspring of a family of landlords in a nation convulsed by the Land War and by the rise of a native intelligentsia, who could only read such interpretations of *The Tempest* with amused contempt.

Yeats, as has been seen, launched many sallies against Trinity College in general and Dowden in particular, but by the time he came to write *Autobiographies* anger had given way to pity for a talented man who failed to trust his own nature. The hostility to books all through *Autobiographies* is not just based on a desire to defend oral traditions, but on Yeats's distrust of the use made of the approved colonizer's books to pass on second-hand opinions. In a similar trajectory through *A Portrait of the Artist as a Young Man*, Stephen Dedalus's initial feeling for the Englishman who is Dean of Studies at the National University is "a smart of dejection that the man to whom he was speaking was a countryman of Ben Jonson"; but, after the professor has failed to understand the old English word "tundish", his final attitude is "a desolating pity" for "this faithful serving-man of the knightly Loyola".[19] By the time he wrote *Ulysses*, Joyce's complex and rather fraught dealings with the representatives of Britain overseas had led him to conclude that many of these functionaries were verging on madness. A similar strain is apparent in Haines's insistence on keeping a loaded gun at his bedside in the chapter set in the tower at the start of *Ulysses*.

The "tundish" incident in *A Portrait* is a reminder that the colony retained many of the linguistic features of Shakespearian England, words and phrases which had long fallen into disuse in the parent country. This hints at a broader truth: everything in a colony petrifies, laws, fashions, customs too, so that a point is reached at which the planter may come to resent the parent country's failure to remain the model it once was. The colony may, in extreme cases, be all that remains of a once-vibrant Englishness: hence Shaw's joke that Ireland, like India, was one of the last spots on earth still producing the ideal Englishman of history. And still producing, according to Synge, Elizabethan English:

> . . . It is probable that when the Elizabethan dramatist took his ink-horn and sat down to his work, he used many phrases that he had just heard, as he sat at dinner, from his mother or his children. In Ireland those of us who know the people have the same privilege . . . In Ireland, for a few years more, we have a popular imagination that is fiery, magnificent, and tender; so that those of us who wish to write start with a chance that is not given to writers in places where the springtime of the local life has been forgotten, and the harvest is a memory only, and the straw has been turned into bricks.[20]

Seamus Deane has seen in such a moment a last-ditch attempt by the Anglo-Irish to hold the parent country true to that full-blooded culture which was invoked to justify the imperial enterprise.[21] However, all independence movements kick-start themselves into being by repeating elements of the colonial culture: but that in no way implies that their sponsors intend to repeat its mistakes.

It is one thing to imitate your Shakespearian father; it is quite another to take the approach of Yeats and turn him into a revised version of yourself. Moreover, both Yeats and Synge were reaching back beyond the imperial mission to a pre-modern, carnivalesque vitality, to those elements which peoples shared before the fall into imperialism and nationalism – elements which survived in Shakespeare's plays, and which seemed to intersect, in suggestive ways, with the folk life of rural Ireland. All that was salt in Shakespeare's mouth seemed to flavour the speech of those parts of Ireland untouched by Anglicization, a riddle certainly, but not insoluble, since these were the parts that the imperial administrator just could not reach. Like the surrealists who would later explore those rejected images and ideas which had been banished to the sub-conscious, Irish writers seized upon all that was denied in official culture – holy wells, pagan festivals, folk anecdotes, popular lore – and wrought these things into a high art. The threat to such richness came not so much from industrial England as from the respectability of the emerging Irish middle class. That was why Synge feared that Ireland would have this popular imagination only "for a few years more". Even as he wrote, the repository of that imagination – the Irish language – was being slowly overridden by a grim Victorian moralism; but still he and Yeats hoped to blend the best of Gaelic tradition with the vital energies from premodern England that remained.

Central to this agenda was a refusal to play the victim's part. All through the nineteenth century, the Irish had been the champion whiners of the western world, proclaiming their suffering at every hand's turn. What was attractive about the revival generation was its generous admission that the deformities visited by colonialism upon the Irish were as nothing compared with the repression endured by the English, rulers as well as ruled. That generation saw Ireland as a privileged if pressured place, in which a new kind of person could be invented and the problems of the modern world worked out. They also saw Ireland as having more to offer than to gain. To Yeats and Pearse, Ireland might be the saviour of spirituality and art in an increasingly materialistic era (though the more acerbic Synge likened this project to decorating the cabin of a ship that was sinking). For his part, Synge inclined to think that Ireland would gain freedom only after the spread of socialist ideas in Britain. Ramsay MacDonald led paternalistic English socialists in articulating the belief that Ireland and the other colonies could only be free *after* the English had first freed themselves. Few European socialists considered the possibility that the strongest impulses towards renovation might come from the periphery: but, because Ireland was far nearer to the centre of power than any other colony, they watched it with nervous interest.

Karl Marx, after all, had written that "the English working class will never accomplish anything before it has got rid of Ireland". The dominion of England over Ireland was, he charged, "the great means by which the English aristocracy maintains its domination in England itself", since the steady supply of Irish labourers forced down wages among a divided working-class. However abject he might be, the English labourer was taught to see himself as part of a ruling nation in relation to the Irish, and in this way he became a tool of the aristocrats and capitalists of his country against Ireland, allowing them to strengthen their control over him. For a real transformation to become possible, according to Marx, the aristocracy had to be over-thrown by force and *that* was more likely to be done in Ireland by landless labourers than by the relatively quiescent English worker. Ireland was imperial England's weakest point: "Ireland lost, the British 'Empire' is gone . . ."[22] So it was the duty of the Irish to be as national as need be to secure this devastating international effect. The *cultural* version of this argument was developed by Yeats and Pearse. Whether materialist or spiritual, the notion of Ireland as a lever of transformation in the wider world took a hold on intellectuals between the 1860s and the Great War.

It should not, therefore, seem surprising that they set themselves the task of dismantling the master narratives of the neighbouring island and, in truth, of imperial Europe. In this they had much in common with a West Indian thinker such as C. L. R. James, who reread Shakespeare's works as a demonstration that *outsiders* had always been the decisive agents in history and the holders of the keys to their changing worlds. Being on the edge of things, a Shylock or an Othello saw far deeper than those caught up in them at the centre, and from this knowledge they learned what man as a creature truly is.[23] Of no play were more rereadings offered than of *The Tempest*, for it was the one which allowed Caliban, whether he was Irish, Trinidadian, or, for that matter, proletarian, to see as if for the first time his face in a mirror.[24] The very uncertainty among critics as to what sort of a creature Caliban actually is may have been part of Shakespeare's intended point. His conflation of Brazilians, Bermudans and New Worlders, along with references to Tunis, Algiers and Egypt, reinforce the now-widespread assumption that this is one of the first writings of the "Third World".

As Fanon acidly recalled, the language of the enemy comes freighted with historic meaning, every sentence being either an order or a threat or an insult. Joyce captured, better than most, the sense in which *every* child feels colonized and used by language, by words which mean one thing and then another, by phrases which sometimes provoke laughter and at other times love, and so on. But before Joyce, there was Shakespeare's Caliban:

> You taught me language, and my profit on't
> Is, I know how to curse. The red plague rid you
> For learning me your language.[25]

And after Joyce, there would be Beckett's Clov:

> I use the words you taught me. If they don't mean anything any more, teach me others. Or let me be silent.[26]

Caliban, of course, had no other language and so, like Clov, he pined for a prelinguistic quiet; but the Irish had. The pastoralist, however, convinced that he is marrying culture to nature, "a gentler scion to the wildest stock", always discounts what culture is already on the island, preferring to see it under the guise of nature. The brave new world is only new to those who can effect this self-deception. Dozens of Gaelic texts attest the fact that savages only emerge when persons fall into the chasm that opens between two cultures which do not interlock. The satire in *Pairlement Chloinne Tomáis* or "Bodaigh na hEorna" is aimed at the churl who speaks in broken English, putting off the restraints of Gaelic culture without achieving self-mastery in another.

Otherwise, to the Irish mind *The Tempest* was what many nine-teenth-century patriotic melodramas were: A True Story of the People, driven to Hell or to Connacht:

> And here you sty me
> In this hard rock, whiles you do keep from me
> The rest o' the island.[27]

This happened in history only after the natives had been found guilty of making the early arrivals "more Irish than the Irish themselves" through intermarriage and thus threatening to people the isle with Calibans. Even the unreality of Caliban and Ariel, the sense of them as projections who appear or disappear at Prospero's will, is in keeping with the fact that the colonial subject is a fiction created by the colonizer. But fictions may, if given a chance, become living fact. Caliban, like the younger Yeats and Joyce, plots a slave's revolt, a seizure of those intellectual tools which gave the imperial imagination mastery of half the globe. In particular, Caliban urges Stephano and Trinculo:

> Remember
> First to possess his books, for without them
> He's but a sot.[28]

That crusade against the hated book, symbol of an invading Christian-ity and later of the invading English, could be continued by many an Irish rebel. Small wonder that Edward Dowden saw Caliban as a serf, incapable of ennobling service; but, many decades afterward, that great exponent of Shakespeare's imperial theme, G. Wilson Knight, could still insist that Caliban "symbolizes all brainless revolution".[29] As comic butt, Caliban was fair game for any indignity. In these conservative readings, even the profoundly Christian idea of redemption of the high by the lowly played no part.

So congealed did these interpretations become that Aimé Césaire felt it necessary not just to rewrite but also to remake Shakespeare's plot. In his version, Prospero's masque is interrupted by the manifestation of an African god, over whom the invading ruler has failed to achieve full control. But perhaps Shakespeare needed less to be remade than reread. *The Tempest* may celebrate the imperium of imagination, but it is scarcely the apology for empire assumed by Dowden and Knight: it is, if anything, a critique of its failure even in its own terms to master by intellectual power all that it represses or denies. Instead of an isle of the blest, the invaders find that they have simply jeopardized what little culture they had already sustained; and, rather than an expansion of personality, they endure its drastic simplification for the sake of their survival. The denial of the natives entails the repression within the imperial personality of all those elements with which the natives are identified. Such suffering is hardly to be sustained for long without exhaustion:

> Now my dreams are all o'erthrown
> And what strength I have's my own
> Which is most faint . . .[30]

Yet Prospero does achieve the rudimentary grace to acknowledge "this thing of darkness" as "mine", and to recognize that his Other is also his innermost self. He also foretells that moment when his knowledge will fail in the face of that otherness which it can never fully fathom, that moment when the book will surrender to the fact and the invader find in himself the goodness to go:

> But this rough magic
> I here abjure, and when I have required
> Some heavenly music – which even now I do . . .
>   I'll break my staff
> Bury it certain fathoms in the earth,
> And deeper than did ever plummet sound
> I'll drown my book.[31]

Prospero really has no choice, for he is caught in a paradox: Caliban represents the elements of his own repressed personality, and so if he kills him, he destroys himself. Since there is only one slave on the island, to do away with him would be to do away with mastery. Yet this, quite irrationally, is what the colonizer can never quite admit: that "England" is an invention too, created in the endless dialectic between rulers and ruled. If the English first learned of the Irish from plays and texts, mostly written at many removes, many Irish equally concocted a nation of Englishness without direct exposure to the people thus "known". The *idea* of England preceded, for most Irish, the experience of it; and that idea was derived mainly from plays, rumours and letters home, but most of all, as the centuries passed, from books in the classroom. So, even in their fictions of one another, a strange reciprocity bound colonizer to colonized. It might indeed be said that there were four persons involved in every Anglo-Irish relationship: the two actual persons, and the two fictions, each one a concoction of the other's imagination. Yet the concoction leaked into the true version, even as the truth modified the concoction. After a while, neither the colonizer nor the colonized stood on their original ground, for both – like Prospero and Caliban – had been *deterritorialized.*

"Prospero lives in the absolute certainty that Language, which is his gift to Caliban, is the very prison in which Caliban's achievements will be realized and restricted". So wrote the West Indian novelist, George Lamming, who went on to say: "Caliban's use of language is no more than his way of serving Prospero; and Prospero's instruction in this language is only his way of measuring the distance which separates him from Caliban".[32] Seamus Heaney has rephrased the same idea in an Irish context with his complaint in "The Ministry of Fear" that "Ulster was British but with no rights / On the English lyric".[33] Joyce, however, sensed that the Irish, unlike the West Indians, had a native language which could help them to remould standard English along their own lines. So did Yeats and Synge. George Moore went so far as to compare a standard English thus revitalized by the Gaelic *substratum* to a jaded townsman refreshed by a dip into a primal sea.

Caliban was indeed proposing to save Prospero, but only as an inevitable part of the programme for saving himself. Besides, if Prospero could now be exposed in all his vulnerability, that was because he himself had supplied, however unwittingly, the instruments which led to that exposure. Out in the colonies, natives were capturing his guns and turning his own children against him, while back in the imperial metropolis, more and more natives poured in like uninvited guests, annexing his ideas and turning them back on their very authors. The sons of empire, inheriting bad fathers, were reinventing these delinquent parents in their own more hopeful image: and Prospero, with the instinctive desire of the affluent to be arraigned, secretly thirsted for accusation, conviction and renewal. For otherwise, both he and Caliban were lost.

It was for this reason that Father Shakespeare was reinvented across the developing world; and in Ireland he became, through the good offices of Ernest Renan, a Celt. The Hamlet evoked in Joyce's *Ulysses* is a variant of the type, "the beautiful ineffectual dreamer who comes to grief against hard facts"; and sly jokes are made in the book about "Patsy Caliban, our American cousin",[34] hinting at the overlap between the Irish and the New World. In thus laying violent hands on Shakespeare, Wilde, Yeats, Joyce and many others offered the act of reading as a rehearsal for or version of revolution.

What most attracted them to the later Shakespeare was his blend of strange fairytale magic and rich social documentation. Both strands appeared to have been separated in the art of Britain, yet the artists of the emerging nations sought to reconcile them once again. Wilde attributed the growing dislike of the imagination of the romantics to "the rage of Caliban not seeing his face in a glass",[35] and in saying so, he spoke for all peoples who felt that they had been edited out of their masters' narrative. He was just as probing in his explanation of the dislike of the new realist modes among colonized peoples: "the rage of Caliban seeing his own face in a glass".

That mirror signalized for Irish authors a realist aesthetic which merely allowed for reproductions of an environment which they felt obliged to challenge. Wilde, in *Intentions*, had questioned the notion of art as a mirror held up to nature, complaining that it would "reduce genius to the condition of a cracked looking-glass".[36] Joyce elaborated the diagnosis in the opening pages of *Ulysses*, in which "the cracked looking-glass of a servant" becomes "a symbol of Irish art",[37] a representation, that is to say, of those realist writers who have only captured the surface effects of life under occupation. He concurred with Wilde's view that art was not just a matter of surface but also of symbol, attaining greatness in moments when the real took on the contours of the magical.

The Irish writers sought, therefore, to reconnect realism and romanticism in a single moment, whether in Joyce's symbolic epiphanies, Synge's fusion of reality and joy, Lady Gregory's theatre with a "base of realism and an apex of beauty", or Lennox Robinson's mixture of "poetry of speech" with "humdrum fact".[38] Those stubborn, recalcitrant facts, popularly held to defeat the Celt, were now to be assimilated, but at no cost to the imagination, which could raise them to a higher power. Art might indeed hold a mirror up to nature, but Shakespeare's later plays had gone further and endorsed art as a natural phenomenon:

> This is an art
> Which does mend Nature, change it rather, but
> The art itself is nature.[39]

If art was indeed man's nature, then there need be no antagonism between them. Wilde went even further, however, insisting that though nature had good intentions, it was not always able to carry them out: and this was where the artist came in, to improve on the natural.[40] Thus was born – or, more truly, reborn – that writing which now goes by the name of Magic Realism.

Rereading England, the artists learned to rewrite Ireland, and so enabled an Irish Renaissance. In its critical thinking, it was largely a product of artists rather than academics. Compared with movements such as Marxism or feminism, nationalism has been generally deficient in theoretical criticism and, in this rather confined area, the Irish have contributed even less than, say, the Indians or the Caribbean peoples. The radical criticism of Shakespeare composed by Irish minds in the period was often skilfully concealed within works of art, as if a more overt practice might bring down immeasurable wrath. Yeats was in no doubt as to the villain of the piece: the system of education for annual examination, which left thirsty minds parched, crammed full of "facts" but denied "imagination". Dowden worshipped intellect but repressed emotion in his criticism: and Yeats eventually counted himself lucky to have escaped a spell at Trinity College, Dublin. Trinity men, sniffed Shaw (another non-attender), were all alike, by which he meant all wrong: and Wilde, in his most famous play, wrote a not-very-disguised essay on the failures of modern education.

In his *Autobiographies*, Yeats gave much attention to the system of education under which he had suffered, reporting his contention that it managed to strengthen the will only by weakening the impulses: "Intermediate examinations, which I had always refused, meant money for pupil and for teacher, and that alone".[41] Patrick Pearse called the Board of Intermediate Education a gloomy limbo:

> The teacher who seeks to give his pupils a wider horizon in literature does so at his peril. He will, no doubt, benefit his pupils, but he will infallibly

reduce his results fees . . . "Stick to your programme" is the "strange device"
on the banner of the Irish Intermediate system; and the programme bulks
so large that there is no room for education.[42]

It was a familiar tale of gradgrindery, told a thousand times in later
autobiographies from many different international settings.

The school attended by C. L. R. James in Trinidad geared all its
rhythms to the annual examination administered by a white official,
who awarded extra pay and promotion to those teachers whose students
did best. Cricket and Shakespeare (both of them to be illuminated by
James's brilliant writing) were designed "to prove to the colonizer that
civilizing had been a successful mission; and to the colonized that
civilization was by no means the monopoly of the mother country but
a larger game that anybody could play".[43] That, at any rate, was the
pious hope. Another West Indian, George Lamming, found the actuality more acrid:

> . . . books, in that particular conception of literature, were not written by
> natives . . . So the examinations which would determine that Trinidadian's
> future in the Civil Service, imposed Shakespeare, and Wordsworth, and
> Jane Austen, and George Eliot, and the whole tabernacle of dead names,
> now come alive at the world's greatest summit of literary expression.[44]

A third West Indian, V. S. Naipaul, has recalled with wry irony his
desperate attempt to translate Dickens's London into Caribbean terms,
setting his faces in local streets, seeing his drizzles as tropical monsoons,
and never feeling quite convinced by the strained set of equations.

An Irish youth, of course, found such transactions a little easier, if
only because of similarities between the Irish and English climate,
topography and physiognomy: but strain there was, nonetheless.
Patrick Pearse's critique of *The Murder Machine* (his phrase for the
colonial system of education) is relevant here. He was appalled at the
unfreedom of teachers and students, all compelled, despite differences
of region, class and personal psychology, to study the same rigid
syllabus, calculated to produce a *type*:

> To the children of the free were taught all noble and goodly things, which
> would tend to make them strong, proud and valiant; from the children of
> slaves, all such dangerous knowledge was hidden . . . And so in Ireland.
> Our education system was designed by our masters in order to make us
> smooth and willing slaves. It has succeeded; succeeded so well that we no

longer realize that we *are* slaves. Some of us even think our chains orna-
mental . . .[45]

Pearse was surprised that, for the most part, only low-calibre minds
were attracted into the teaching profession, whose members were, he
sourly noted, paid less than the colonial police. Nevertheless, these
teachers operated as a sort of thought-police on behalf of a system
geared to the manufacture of things rather than the growth of persons.
Such an indictment anticipated by decades George Lamming's account
of the emergent West Indian middle class, which read only those books
on examination syllabi and which saw education as "something to *have*,
but not to *use*".[46] It was the philistinism of these new managerial élites,
even more than intellectual repression by the authorities, which would
drive so many writers of emerging nation-states into exile.

A free child, said Pearse, would not become a replica of his mass-
produced teacher, but would rather achieve his innermost self: the state
existed to fulfil the child rather than the child to fulfil the state. Praising
Maria Montessori's methods, Pearse saw these as a contrast to those
favoured by the Intermediate Board. It offered not education but
schooling, under an institution which liked to think of itself as a
government, while in reality it was no more than a police administration.

> . . . There is no education system in Ireland . . . Education should inspire;
> this education is meant to tame. Education should harden; this education is
> meant to enervate. The English are too wise a people to educate the Irish,
> in any worthy sense. As well expect them to arm us.[47]

This anticipates Aimé Césaire's *Discourse on Colonialism* which laments
"a parody of education, the hasty manufacture of a few thousand
subordinate functionaries, 'boys', artisans, office clerks, and interpreters
necessary for the smooth operation of business".[48] Pearse's analogy
between learning and ammunition may have been prompted by his
memory of how Lady Bracknell in *The Importance of Being Earnest* had
said that a true education would lead to acts of violence in Grosvenor
Square; or maybe he was thinking of the claim that every Gaelic League
speech was like a bullet fired against an enemy who failed to disarm his
antagonist.[49]

Pearse's remedy was interesting: more, not less, English literature, as
an instrument of liberation. What was lacking at present, he contended, was a respect for ideas in their own right, a love of beauty, a

spiritual inspiration. Yeats agreed. Visiting the United States in 1903, he made his own comparisons between "the great mill called examinations" and the liberal education offered by an independent republic. At Bryn Mawr college for women, an instructor told him: "We prepare our girls to live their lives, but in England they are making them all teachers".[50] Wilde had already complained that in England those who could did, and those who couldn't taught: an inability to learn appeared to be the main qualification for a career in teaching, or, as he quipped, "in examinations the foolish ask questions which the wise cannot answer".[51]

"The work of the first Minister for Education in a free Ireland will be a work of creation", wrote Pearse, "for into a dead mass he will have to breathe the breath of life". He believed Maria Montessori's methods invaluable, but he wished to see them combined with the ancient Gaelic system of *fosterage*, of sons sent for special training to distant families or centres of excellence. Whether Pearse's notions of fosterage were accurate is doubtful, but, as his literary contemporaries reinterpreted Shakespeare for their own strategic purposes, so Pearse discovered in the Gaelic past the lineaments of a modernized state, with careers open to talents. According to him, at Clonard monastery a carpenter's son named Kevin sat alongside Colmcille, the son of a king, both of them studying under a charismatic teacher: and "never the state usurping the place of father or fosterer, dispensing education like a universal provider of readymades".[52] Pearse's inspiring rhapsody may have owed more to John Ruskin and William Morris than to any Gaelic records:

> . . . In the Middle Ages there were everywhere little groups of persons clustering around some beloved teacher, and thus it was that men learned not only the humanities but all gracious and useful crafts. There were no State art schools, no State technical schools: as I have said, men became artists in the studio of some master artist . . .[53]

This ideal was to be reasserted by Yeats in *A Vision*. There he conjured up a Byzantine mosaic artist who could answer all philosophical questions. In *Autobiographies* he explained how such an education could lead to Unity of Being:

> Somewhere about 1450, though later in some parts of Europe by a hundred years or so, and in some earlier, men attained to personality in great numbers, "Unity of Being", and became like "a perfectly proportioned

human body", and as men so fashioned held places of power, their nations had it too, prince and ploughman sharing that thought and feeling.[54]

Yeats wrote *A Vision* as a sort of Celtic constitution for a free Ireland, in the belief that such a moment might come again. And he wrote his epic cycle of Cuchulain plays in the conviction that their performance before an Irish audience would actually bring that moment round.

Materialists might scoff at such ideals as pure self-delusion on the part of culturalists, but the British themselves never underestimated their power to sway public opinion. When the 1916 rebels struck, the authorities had no doubt that a "poets' insurrection" would have to be countered by something more than gunboats: it would require a programme of intellectual counter-revolution as well. Literature itself became a weapon in the ensuing struggle, invoked by *The Irish Times* in its appeal to the values which it associated with Shakespeare, but also by the architects of imperial policy in London. In the aftermath of the Rising, as the poetry and prose of the rebel leaders were widely circulated among a sympathetic American audience, H. G. Wells, John Galsworthy and Arnold Bennett published essays critical of them in the United States. The poets' crazy dream was to be countered by some of the leading practitioners of modern English prose.[55]

Sixteen

Inventing Irelands

In theory, two kinds of freedom were available to the Irish: the return to a past, pre-colonial Gaelic identity, still yearning for expression if long-denied, or the reconstruction of a national identity, beginning from first principles all over again. The first discounted much that had happened, for good as well as ill, during the centuries of occupation; the second was even more exacting, since it urged people to ignore other aspects of their past too. The first eventually took the form of nationalism, as sponsored by Michael Collins, Éamon de Valera and the political élites; the second offered liberation, and was largely the invention of writers and artists who attempted, in Santayana's phrase, "to make us citizens by anticipation in the world that we crave".[1] The nationalism of the politicians enjoyed intermittent support from a major artist such as W. B. Yeats, but eventually he grew tired of it; the liberation preached by the artists sometimes won the loyalty of the more imaginative political figures, such as Liam Mellows or Hanna Sheehy-Skeffington. Inevitably, neither model was sufficient unto itself: even its stoutest defenders were compelled by the brute facts of history to "borrow" some elements of the alternative version.

The problem with the "return to the source" model was clear enough: there was very little source left, just a scattered Irish-speaking community in the most westerly regions. Nor were members of that community especially impressed by the lure of nationalism: a group of Blasket islanders, gathered around a cottage hearth in Easter Week 1916, was brought the momentous news of the rebellion in Dublin. "Abair an focal *republic* i nGaoluinn" (Say the word *republic* in Irish), urged the mischievous Tomás Ó Criomhthainn; but the islanders had no word, only a local king known as *an rí*. "Agus is beag a chuir a soláthar imní ach oiread oraibh" (And it's little its attainment troubled ye, either), added the laconic Ó Criomhthainn.[2] In his autobiography *An tOileánach* (The Islandman), he described his feelings of dismay when first he stepped onto the Irish mainland, and felt himself in alien territory. One generation later, when Muiris Ó Súilleabhain stepped off the same boat onto the same quayside, his strange, island gait prompted the derisive question "Murab Éireannach thú, cad é thú?" (If you're not an Irishman, what are you?), to which he replied after some thought "Blascaodach" (A Blasketman).[3] *Gaelic* would not easily be made equivalent to *Irish*.

These islanders and Gaeltacht-dwellers truly were the last Europeans, perched precariously on those very fastnesses where a whole civilization ran out of continent; and so they might have been seen to epitomize Europe at that point where it bordered on the emerging post-colonial world. "These strange men with receding foreheads, high cheek-bones and ungovernable eyes seem to represent some old type found on these few acres at the extreme edge of Europe", wrote Synge while among them, "where it is only in wild jests and laughter that they can express their loneliness and desolation".[4] Synge's greatest play, even in its title, can be read as a mockery of the presiding myths of the western, Eurocentric world; and his thwarting of generic expectations, in a comedy which concludes without the predicted marriage, was certainly an attempt to plunge his audience through the same experience of "cognitive dissonance" which he went through after setting foot on the islands. Weldon Thornton has persuasively argued that each of Synge's plays somehow eludes the generic stereotypes of tragedy or comedy, "representing as they do received western categories of response". He observes very justly that Synge's aim was to give an honest reflection of "the complexity, perhaps even the incongruity and irrationality, of his characters' feelings or their milieu, without regard for whether the result fell into a recognizable genre".[5]

In *The Aran Islands*, Synge constructed a sort of pastoral, which had many of the classic features of earlier forays in Africanist or Orientalist mode: the reconstitution of the setting as a landscape of the individual consciousness; the recognition on the part of the visitor that he can understand more of the natives than they will ever know of him; a betrayed friendship with a sensitive local youth; a mandatory but largely wordless romantic infatuation with a native woman; a readiness to being mocked by the natives for being unmarried at such a ripe age; and, finally, a sad withdrawal from a world which increasingly takes on the contours of a dream.[6]

Synge's pastoralism, however, is not of the conventional western kind which is designed to occlude painful class differences: in his world, rather than have aristocrats play at being peasants, he effects a revolutionary reversal, which allows him to impute to the islanders an aristocratic mien and lightness of foot (just as, in *Deirdre of the Sorrows*, he can portray peasants in the garb of royalty). His island is a Kropotkinian commune, wherein every man and woman becomes a sort of artist. Their work changes with the seasons, creating a wonderful versatility of body and of mind: and most of them can speak different languages. Inishmaan, the nearest analogy in Europe to the undeveloped world, affords "something of the artistic beauty of medieval life", whose artefacts "seem to exist as a natural link between the people and the world that is about them". When the *meitheal oibre* (voluntary work party) comes to a house to do the shared labour, work ceases to be such, becoming "a sort of festival" and the cottager "a host instead of an employer". On the neighbouring island of Inishmore, however, he notices the creeping class-consciousness of an "advanced" society: "the families here are gradually forming into different ranks".

Worse still, they have been theatricalized and corrupted by tourism. On Inishmaan, there was no difference between a role and a self, despite the "penury"; on the larger island, the natives know more. One of the things they know is how to play the part expected of them by English tourists: "I noticed in the crowd several men of the ragged, humorous type that was once thought to represent the real peasant of Ireland . . . As we looked out through the fog, there was something nearly appalling in the shrieks of laughter kept up by one of these individuals, a man of extraordinary ugliness and wit".[7] In that strange moment, Synge identifies the problem of the Irish nationalist mind in its deep, almost erotic, attraction to the English. English typology has encouraged this stage Irishman to mimic a stock type – with no saving sense of irony – and to confuse this type with "personality". The Gaelic Irish of Inishmaan are not sufficiently conscious to be nationalist, while the man from Inishmore is too Irish to be Gaelic. Such an Irishman is, in classic existential terms, overdetermined; to him there is no Irish identity above and beyond the Irish predicament. Irishness is like Jewishness, whatever people say it is. To be Irish, in such a context, is simply to be called Irish, and to know what that means you have to ask the English.

Those Gaelic poets who, in their moment of estrangement from the ancient culture, warned that from now on their people would be like the children of Israel, knew exactly what they were saying; for, as Jean-Paul Sartre would much later observe of Jews locked into a similar process, "the root of Jewish disquietude is the necessity imposed on the Jew of subjecting himself to endless self-examination and finally assuming a phantom personality, at once strange and familiar, that haunts him and is nothing but himself – as others see him".[8] Irish is like English – "familiar and foreign" – but nonetheless Irish for all that. The universal modern disjunction between role and self is true, twice over, of the Irish nationalist who, knowing that at last he is tolerated, must keep on proving himself and his nation. For this is the great burden of post-colonial national élites: that, unlike the islanders of the Great Blasket or Inishmaan, they must have an *idea* of Ireland.

Nor is the problem solved by a reversion to West British modes, for they are characterized by what Yeats called "their would-be cosmopolitanism and their actual provincialism".[9] If the person were to deny with ferocious intensity the Irish element in himself, he would in that very vehemence mark himself off as Irish. There seems no way out of this mirror-chamber created by the colonialists, because the natives' opinions of themselves are greatly influenced by the low esteem which their rulers have for them. The nationalist rebel feeds the English stereotype with his martyrdom, becoming visibly more like what he should be to deserve the fate mapped out for him. Even the would-be liberationist, for whom it is a point of honour to have no poetic phrase or humorous mood, lives in such daily anxiety that he will correspond to the stereotype that his conduct, too, is patently determined from the outside: whoever makes it his destiny to prove that there are no Irish ends up establishing that there are.

The English built their new England called Ireland: the Irish then played at building a not-England, but now they were playing at being not-Irish. That is a measure of the dire difficulty of reaching Fanon's third, liberationist phase. The people of the second, nationalist phase – especially those who have progressed in their thinking – want to know the "Irish" element within them solely in order to deny it. What Sartre remarked of the Jews is again apposite: "with them it is not a question of recognizing certain faults and combating them, but of underlining by their conduct the fact that they do not have those faults".[10] Repeatedly estranged from their experiences, they not only act but watch themselves acting; and so Irish wit, when it expresses itself, does so most often at the expense of its own. Dr. Samuel Johnson once joked that the Irish, being a fair people, never spoke well of one another.

Yet among their own kind, in moments of privacy, all this falseness ceases, and there is no oppressive sense of a tradition weighing them down. Moreover, if in such a setting they criticize the Irish, it is understood that they are being critical of a submission to one or other of these stereotypes: nobody is more anti-Irish in this positive sense than the Irish themselves. The inauthentic Irish fled from the pressure of the stereotype and then the English made them Irish in spite of themselves: but the more thoughtful Irish sought to free Ireland in the only meaningful sense by freeing their expressive selves. They did this, like Christy Mahon at the end of *The Playboy*, by constructing themselves from within and throwing away the mirror. In making themselves Irish, they did what he did and eluded final description; for to be a new species of man or woman is to lack a *given* identity, to be not nobody but not somebody either.

How exactly does the whole process work? Yeats's observations on national culture are helpful here, for he sees in it a flowering which, of its very nature, must wither. "Is not all history but the coming of that conscious art which first makes articulate and then destroys the old wild energy?" Once a face is framed, once a form is adopted, a self-consciousness insinuates itself into an action with a concomitant sense of loss. The nationalist self destroys itself by the very energies which define its being, and so the mirror must be smashed before being discarded. The process, though it may be humiliating, must be gone through: all thoughts must be embodied in form, however fallen, and the problems of the decolonizing intellectual who works with the tainted terminology of the colonialist are seen by Yeats as no different in kind from those which confront the saviour-poet. As "Christ put on the temporal body, which is Satan . . . that it might be consumed, and the spiritual body revealed", so poetry "puts on nature that nature might be revealed as the great storehouse of symbolism, without which language is dumb".[11] The making conscious of the Irish element leads it to create a perfect mirror in which to view itself, a narcissism of self-love followed by self-loathing, like that which causes a parrot in one of Yeats's poems to rage at its own image and then to break it. The past has returned, but in the form of self-hatred. In the estrangement which follows, Yeats becomes an instance of the modern man, bleak and yet free. Only the sinful, broken, tainted medium allows progress: another example of *felix culpa*, of going wrong in order to go right.

So, self is denied, then defined, before being superseded in a moment of breakthrough, when all mirrors are thrown away. Up until this moment, history has been a mere chronicle of facts, but in the fifteenth phase of *A Vision*, when revolution comes, the artists take history and "do its personages the honour of naming after them their own thoughts",[12] which is to say that they find in the forms of past heroism the lineaments of their desires. When the mirror is shattered by the alchemist, what is left is the luminous drop of distilled gold, which provides the illumination.[13] When the ego is released from the mirror phase of a mimic nationalism, a deeper self is freed, a self which has no further need of irritable assertion, but is serene enough to allow the forces of creation to flow through it. It can contain the culture so fully as to embody both its "nay" and its "yea", without setting one above the other.

Before this breakthrough comes a period which has been called "a nationalism of mourning".[14] At this time, it becomes increasingly clear that the longing for form has not been appeased by any of the models on offer, either literary or political, but is still "a dumb, struggling thought seeking a mouth to utter it".[15] Its incarnation in the inappropriate body of the inherited state exemplifies the paradox of a world in which every act is a suffering and every statement a loss of vital energy. If the energy of life is the urge to find a satisfactory expression, then a nation is but a longing for a new form, a sign that all dreams end in a beautiful body:

> Birds sigh for the air,
> Thought for I know not where,
> For the womb the seed sighs.
> Sinks the same rest
> On intellect, on nest,
> On straining thighs.[16]

Yeats had concluded that, if incarnation and crucifixion were identical, then a god who took a flawed human form was already suffering the ravages of a tainted medium. Yet *every* artist must follow suit: by taking on the flawed world's body, they achieve self-conquest, are born again to a recovered innocence and help others to recover it too.

That recovery comes at the instant when the self resolves to reshape available forms to a personal standard of excellence, and to see in such nationalist icons as Swift, O'Connell or Parnell not models for slavish emulation (as in a mirror) but illuminations of the onlookers' real potential, "precisely that symbol he may require for the expression of himself".[17] The moment of liberation is thus achieved when the return to the source is also an opening onto a mysterious future: "this instinct for what is near and yet hidden is in reality a return to the sources of our power, and therefore a claim made upon the future. Thought seems more true, emotion more deep, spoken by someone who touches my pride, who seems to claim me of his kindred, who seems to make me a part of some national mythology".[18] This may explain one of the paradoxes of post-colonial culture: that it can seem, at one and the same time, extremely old and extremely young, of ancient lineage and in a sense yet unborn. The world of the self-invented man is "the tradition of myself", by which the founder is also the final consummation of a whole stream of thought: so Yeats, who helped to define Irish literary nationalism in his own writings, became in time the lyricist who, in alternately bitter and melancholic modes, sang the nationalism of mourning. But his account of the collapse of the nationalist project would itself become the master-narrative of its successor and a further proof that "tradition may live in the lament for its passing".[19]

In this dynamic, the very meaning of the word *tradition* changes, since it no longer implies a museum of nostalgias but a reopened future. Yet the past must be honoured, albeit subordinated. "We cannot kill the past in going forward", writes Carlos Fuentes, the Mexican novelist, "for the past is our identity and without our identity we are nothing".[20] One of the tactics of colonialism was to deprive a people of their past precisely in order to deny them their future. Though it was quite understandable that people, in their anxiety to modernize, should dream of creating themselves *ex nihilo*, free of degrading past links, this was not to be absolute: the task rather was to show the interdependence of past and future in attempting to restore history's openness.

The colonialist crime was the violation of the traditional community: the nationalist crime was often a denial of the autonomy of the individual. Liberation would come only with forms which stressed the interdependence of community and individual, rather than canvassing the claims of one at the expense of the other. The question which faced the decolonizing world, the question to which it might become the answer, was: how to build a future on the past without returning to it? The danger of nationalist culture was its tendency to petrification and its martyr cult, which created in many adherents an unhealthy obsession with their future demise: the Deirdre of Irish lore constantly foretasting her legendary status is one example, the monks in Joyce's *Dubliners* who sleep in their own coffins another. Joyce, by his satirical treatment of statuary in *Dubliners*, mocks the tendency of nationalists to embalm themselves alive: they fetishize and manipulate the past to the point where they irretrievably lose it. The English occupiers, having lost their own past in this way, tried similarly to dispossess others, which was why a return to some sort of source seemed necessary, if the future was to be more than a vanishing point. "The past is the only certifiable future we have", says Fuentes: "The past is the only proof that the future did, in effect, once exist".[21] Hence his motto: *remember the future, imagine the past.*

Imagine is the operative word for the liberationist who, far more than the nationalist, needs the sanction of previous authority if history is to be blown open. That sanction comes from history not as chronological narrative but as symbolic pattern, in which certain utopian moments are extracted from its flow. The 1916 Rising announced itself in this way, not only as the outcome of the previous thirty years, but also as a moment charged with the utopian energies of 1803, 1848 and 1867. As Walter Benjamin remarked: "to Robespierre ancient Rome was a past charged with the time of the now, which he blasted out of the continuum of history. The French revolution viewed itself as Rome incarnate".[22] This means also that the nationalist present which was 1916 must have construed itself under the aegis of the liberation which would finally replace it. The rebels had instinctively grasped the *constellation* which their era formed with those earlier ones, and with those "millions unborn" of whom Pearse dreamed in his poem. Accused by their critics and by future conservative historians of being fixated on the past, they were anything but: what they sensed was their power to redirect its latent energies into new constellations. They therefore reserved the right to reinterpret the past in the light of their desired future, which they recruited against a despised present. So they implemented Nietzsche's programme for all who have not been given a good father: they went out and invented a better one, a better past.

History thereby became a form of science fiction: in order to get a fair hearing in a conservative society, the exponents of revolution had to present their intentions under the guise of a return to the idealized patterns of the past. Connolly, dreaming of a classless communitarian society, must present it in *Labour in Irish History* as a restoration of a system akin to that of the ancient Celtic laws; and Pearse could present the theories of Montessori as but the fosterage practised by the Gaelic chief. Each man put on the mask of a historical actor to bring something new into being: each dropped into a familiar role in order to learn something new about himself. *The Odyssey* was no more intrinsic to Joyce's *Ulysses* than was the Cuchulain myth to the leaders of 1916: such narratives provided a respectable scaffolding behind which the rebels were free to improvise.

The most spectacular scaffolding of all was provided by nationalism and the nation-state: forms which might at any moment be kicked away to reveal the radical new structure which had been improvised beneath. Claiming to revere the scaffolding of the older forms, the Pearses, Connollys and Joyces were not-so-secret innovators. They understood that one must forget much of the past if anything is to be created in the present: or, at least, one must constantly re-edit that past in the light of current needs. The hope for progress, Nietzsche had said, was to "wipe away whatever came earlier in the prospect of reaching a true present . . . a new departure".[23] No wonder that Michael Davitt, the author of Ireland's new departure in land-holding, was one of those who gave rise to the radicals' creative misinterpretation of the Irish past. And no wonder that Nietzsche saw history and modernity as opposed ideas: what was modern about the 1916 thinkers was precisely their disruption of chronology, their insistence on the revolutionary idea of tradition.

This is all quite at variance with the common nationalist view of tradition as something which has come to a conclusion. Its exponents fancy that they are the final point of history and the past a foil to their narcissism. Such a past has in effect lost its future, its power to challenge and disrupt: it exists only as a commodity to be admired, consumed, reducing its adherents to the position of tourists in their own country, whose monuments and heritage centres can be visited or re-entered by an act of will. Its people are lulled by their leaders to "become drunk on remembrance",[24] to recover the past as fetish rather than to live in the flow of actual history. The fetishizing, once permitted, affects everything – even the landscape is treated like a reified woman's body – so that, after independence, the actual landscape is slowly transformed by the touristic industries until it conforms to the outlines of the original fantasy. In other words, the Cathleen ní Houlihan of real flesh and blood must impersonate for her lovers the sort of woman they want her to be, and she must leave her own desires unimplemented. In such a nationalism, the "lyrical stage"[25] completely overrides the historic concreteness of the revolution. It is made possible by an endless harping on an idealized past, which is used as a distraction from the mediocrity of the present. James Connolly foresaw this when he warned that a neglect of vital, living issues might "only succeed in stereotyping our historical studies with a worship of the past, or crystallizing nationalism into a tradition, glorious and heroic indeed, but still *only a tradition*".[26]

The penchant for commemoration is a tell-tale sign of a community which, pained by the process of unequal development, has difficulty in adjusting to modernity. Yet the nationalism to which it appeals *is* modern in the sense that it rejects a dynamic traditionalism and seeks to abort the historical process. The inappropriate forms left by the occupier lead the nationalist to violate the rights of minority groupings, and also the customs and familial structures of the people. By way of compensation, nationalism then learns how to mythologize the very values which it has been helping to destroy: it was 1930s Ireland, wrecked by emigration and the consequent break-up of families, which insisted on defining the family as the basic unit of society. But the reality did not measure up to the rhetoric. Each year, returning emigrants were invited to visit this petrified society, and to inspect it as once a colonial official might have reviewed a primitive tribe's progress on a special reservation. Of such a phenomenon, Sigmund Freud had written: "the reservation is to maintain the old condition of things which has been regretfully sacrificed to necessity everywhere else . . . The mental realm of fantasy is also such a reservation reclaimed from the encroaches of the reality principle".[27]

The goal of early national leaders was stasis, not growth – an economy which guaranteed a frugal sufficiency for all. De Valera's pastoral politics owed much to Thomas Jefferson, sharing his hope of having things both ways, of avoiding the savagery of absolute, untamed nature, and also the desiccation of great modern cities. In the ideal Ireland of the nationalists, there was to be no drab, workerist conformism: neither were there to be massive differences of wealth or status. This would be a world in which men could fertilize and farm the land with machines made, most conveniently, elsewhere. By no means ridiculous, this was the state sought by many other leaders, to solve the problem posed by modernity with *the right kind of modernity.* Recognizing the protest against a shallow cosmopolitanism latent in the national movements, its sponsors hoped for a new dispensation, under which the best of tradition might blend with the benefits of modernity. Such a radicalism was both modern and counter-modern. In that sense, it was a political version of literary modernism, which compensated for all that was lost in the consumer society by emphasizing the complexity, beauty and quality of many traditions. It was in this sense that the cultural values promoted by Yeats and Synge could be both very new and very old, evoking Adam and a perpetual Last Judgement.

The problem was that these ideals could never be expressed or embodied in the form of the inherited nation-state; and politicians who took over those forms, unmodified, effectively asked their people to live like an underground movement in a country under occupation. All the old apparatus was maintained: the ever-burgeoning capital city with its dominance over the rest of the country, even after its institutions were seized by people from the countryside; the planting of the tricolour on a state apparatus explicitly designed to disempower local communities; the emulation of the social hierarchies of imperial Britain at just that moment when they were falling to challenges in the parent country. The graft of Victorian-Edwardian values onto the emerging Ireland which they ill-fitted can be seen in the idiotic imposition of English lettering where once Gaelic characters had been used to write Irish (rather reminiscent of those educators in independent Algeria who preferred the Latin to the Arabic alphabet). Even more remarkable was the uneasy proliferation of names for the new state: the Irish Free State; Éire; Ireland; the Irish Republic – each one less satisfactory than the next, and each increasing that yearning for a true republic of the mind.

The people were so exhausted by the expenditure of energy in dislodging the occupier that they seemed to have little left with which to reimagine their condition; and the coarsening effects of all uprisings on those caught up in them took an inevitable toll as well. As George Russell wrote: "there is a danger in revolution if the revolutionary spirit is much more advanced than the intellectual and moral qualities which alone can secure the success of a revolt".[28] So, for all his lofty ideals, de Valera was compromised by the inherited forms. He was soon to be seen wearing a top hat, and a morning-suit to consultations with the Papal Nuncio. The less the forms fitted current experience, the more necessary it became to retreat for consolation and compensation into the myth of a pristine, innocent Gaelic past. A revolution which began by seeing liberation as choice had rapidly become a quest for *liberation from choice*, a quest for a few pious certainties. Those who had once fought alongside de Valera seeking revolution or death now faced in his period of rule the death of their revolution. Increasingly, he and his colleagues lapsed into nostalgia. The more the legitimacy of their state was challenged, the greater their appeals to the sanction of the past: it was now the "die-hard" republicans who, refusing all compromise, continued to dream of an open future. While de Valera sought legitimation in the backward look, they sought justification in the coming times.

What faced the politicians was a conundrum no different from that which confronted the writers: hard though it was to grapple with the social order left by the departed British, it was harder still to posit a social order that did not exist. Not only that, but the attempt was made in the 1920s and 1930s, that period during which intellectuals across the world began to despair of the political order as such and to retreat into a world of privacy in which each could make a separate peace. Excessive hopes had been nurtured by thinkers unused to the chastening experience of actual power: manic depression often resulted from the frustrations of freedom. Just as it had been the *independent* republics of Latin America which in the nineteenth century destroyed many native cultures, so now in the twentieth, it seemed that the Gaeltacht was dying faster than ever in an independent Irish state. Yeats, as so often, captured the new mood of disappointment, even before it had fully taken shape: in "Nineteen Hundred and Nineteen", he looks back with some bitterness to a time when "we pieced our thoughts into philosophy / And planned to bring the world under a rule / Who are but weasels fighting in a hole".[29] Whether he is referring to the imperial idea or to the nationalist hope is strictly immaterial: the lines remain deliberately vague, because in them the poet repudiates a programme for saving humanity which may have inscribed into it the anxious self-aggrandizement of the original imperial impulse. He is already suspecting that he may indeed be one of those modernists who set out to save the world, and ended defending a sensibility.

In "Ancestral Houses", he can even reread his beloved image of the sea-shell as epitomizing the crisis all around him, the incongruity of new matter ill-housed in an obsolete setting:

> . . . though now it seems
> As if some marvellous empty sea-shell flung
> Out of the obscure dark of the rich streams,
> And not a fountain, were the symbol which
> Shadows the inherited glory of the rich.[30]

The sea-shell, though precious and beautiful in its way, is also empty and dead. It has only the shape, the formal outline, of the life which it once contained . . . being now no more than a museum-piece ejected by the stream of life and removed from the source of its vitality.

In these recognitions, however, Yeats was moving away from a facile nationalism and returning to the ideal of unfettered self-expression which had, after all, been the rationale for the Irish revival. Confronted with the censorship of art and information by the new state, he said:

For the past hundred years Irish nationalism has had to fight against England, and that fight has helped fanaticism, for we had to welcome everything that gave Ireland emotional energy, and had little use for intelligence so far as the mass of people were concerned, for we had to hurl them against an alien power. The basis of Irish nationalism has now shifted, and much that once helped is now injurious.[31]

In truth, this had become clear to him as soon as Synge became the target of nationalist attack: when Synge began to create, Yeats suddenly realized that he must abandon the creation of a Holy City of the imagination and instead express the individual. If colonialism violated the community, then a nationalism which humiliated the individual could never be an adequate response. In his poem "The Fisherman", Yeats contrasted audiences: one, the face of "a man who does not exist" but who is associated with the passionate dawn and the dead Synge; the other, the actual national audience, craven, philistine, and as yet "un-reproved".[32] After *The Playboy*, Yeats noted how those extreme politics which once in Ireland had sought intellectual freedom now seemed to have united themselves to a hatred of ideas. The revolt against all forms of modernity latent in the more regressive types of nationalism had begun. Yet Yeats continued to will the new state into being, if only so that he could function as one of its foremost critics.

The difference between the two versions of Irish Renaissance might best be explained by invoking Lionel Trilling's brilliant distinction between *sincerity* and *authenticity*. Sincerity, a congruence between avowal and feeling, can be admired by those naive enough to believe that there is no problem of form: it is based, in part, on the Romantic ideal of a definite identity, which it becomes the labour of a lifetime to be true to. Authenticity is a more excruciatingly modern demand, which begins with the admission that there *is* a problem of form and that this makes the congruence between avowal and feeling all the more difficult. It makes the concession that a person, or indeed a nation, has a *plurality* of identities, constantly remaking themselves in perpetual renewals. Those writers who made the struggle with inherited structures their theme fell into this category, unlike most of the political leaders who never directly addressed the question.[33]

Those nationalist politicians, instead, followed the practices of the Romantic artists of the nineteenth century and said: there is an essential Ireland to be served, and a definitive all-Ireland mind to be described. However, the artists often rejoined: there is no single Ireland, but a field of varied forces, subject to constant negotiations, and there is no unitary Irish mind, but many Irish minds, shaped by a common predicament which sometimes produces the same characteristics in those caught up in it. The sincere nationalist asked writers to hold a mirror up to Cathleen ní Houlihan's face: the artist wistfully observed that the cracked looking-glass, which was all that remained after his anger had led him to smash it, rendered not a single but a multiple self.

The attempt to express an authentic set of feelings through a flawed medium runs like a leitmotif through Irish renaissance texts: it is to be found in the Wildean adoption of the mask (emulated by Yeats), in the borrowed clothes sported by Christy Mahon and Stephen Dedalus, in the anxiety of Beckett's characters to regret the cliché even as they submit to it. The attacks on literature as such in many works are made by artists who know the supreme importance of judging by appearances. The heroism of the dandy, who achieves a witty self-mastery in an adverse situation where there is no court for the free play of his talents, takes on in the colonial setting an altogether deeper poignancy: for he, too, is a prisoner of obsolete forms, he also has been instructed to blast his way into modernity with equipment more suited to a previous task. Caught between two worlds, one half-dead and the other still struggling to be born, the Irish writers sometimes had to pour their thoughts and feelings into incongruous containers. Hence the obsession with the encumbrances of costume in so many texts, prompting Yeats, for example, to resolve to abandon the coats of mythology and "walk naked". Inheriting the genres of made men, the Irish were somehow expected to use them to describe men in the making. Hence the recurrent obsession with the pseudo-couple: Jack/Algy, Doyle/Broadbent, Robartes/Aherne, Stephen/Bloom, Joxer/Boyle, Didi/Gogo; the writers were asking themselves on just what terms could men even begin to combine.

Many of the classic texts take as point of departure the splintering of a family, leading the characters to break out into a wider world: it was as if, in such narratives, writers were rehearsing the break-up of the imperial family. Irish family-life throughout the nineteenth century had been broken by emigration and uprooting, and it could not anyway have functioned as symbol of conservation or continuity; and so the family structures which persist in works like *The Playboy* or *Ulysses* often do so in a mode of parody. What is enacted in them is the moment when the family breaks up into its constituent parts and the individual recovers autonomy. This is an act of self-begetting, of a kind described by Jean-Paul Sartre when he said that "I always preferred to accuse myself rather than the universe, not out of simple good-heartedness, but in order to derive only from myself".[34] What was offered in such works was not a *revival* so much as a rebirth, a *renaissance* which assumed the inadequacy of fathers and which celebrated children who proceeded to act as parents to themselves. If the prospects for a full-blown Gaelic revival had been suffocated by those who wanted merely a Victorian gentility expressed in the Irish language, then there really was no choice but to encourage each individual to conceive, all over again, of his or her self.

The danger of national fanaticism was its tendency to politicize the private dimensions: and the weakness of liberation was its urge to privatize *all* experience. Taken to an extreme, liberation could be so relentlessly modernizing as to cut people off from the ways of their ancestors and to take away their reasons for living. The stand-off between both movements often expressed itself in the developing world in the disjunction between the state and the nation: within the state structures, people voted and behaved conservatively, but in reality they cared little for these structures and remained fundamentally anarchic in their everyday behaviour. Their real codes – tribal, familial or simply personal – seemed to exist beyond these other zones. In consequence, many people had a double consciousness, a sense in each person of living somebody's life other than one's own.

The contradiction within nationalism is obvious enough: its covert desire to mimic the extirpated power while disowning its overt influences. The rage which follows causes the native to break the mirror in which he cannot see himself. Caliban is indeed the New Man for whom the old way of life is rapidly losing its meaning, but who has not yet broken through to the new: his plotting of the murder of Prospero may be seen as the nationalist phase of the revolt. Yet the dream of *The Tempest* is of an end to coercion of all kinds. The tables of the new law must, however, be written in the language of the outlaw, in the bastard lingo that grows between two competing nationalisms. Since the old, inherited forms cannot be purified, they must be remodelled. "The one duty we owe to history", said Wilde, "is to rewrite it"[35] (just as the one duty he felt he owed to nature was to improve on it). If the ages were invariably the fleshed-out symbols of some earlier art-form, that was only because life ("poor human life", as Wilde called it, "terribly deficient in form")[36] was forever straggling in the wake of art, seizing upon its forms as soon as it caught up with them in order to express itself. So boys playing girls in Shakespeare's dramas helped to evolve a new, completely modern sense of girlhood and womanhood.

It is in this context that the forms evolved by Irish artists take on extra-literary importance. Such forms can be seen as answering questions which have not yet been fully asked in the more conventional political sphere. Rather than adapt themselves to the inherited genres, the writers tried to adapt the genres to themselves. Their texts thus became the signposts standing on a shattered road to a future, which would be admirable to precisely the extent that it did not as yet exist. It was something like this which Herder had in mind when he said that "a poet is a creator of a people: he gives it a world to contemplate, he holds its soul in his hands".[37] Again and again in their writings, Irish authors recur to the notion of art as providing the forms which will become the actual environment of the future.

At first, this form was nationalism. In 1888 Yeats wrote that "one can only reach out to the universe with a gloved hand – that glove is one's nation, the only thing one knows even a little of".[38] Then Yeats began to worry the glove, as all do only when it ceases to fit. By the time Synge was writing, Yeats could already hear "the wreck of the Ireland of my youth" in the *Playboy* row, even as Synge himself heard the "death-rattle" of a nation in the very moment of its apparent revival, during the singing of patriotic songs at the Irish Literary Theatre. Such a national culture must always be a nostalgia, visible only in an eternal retrospect as the after-image on a retina. Just as the Anglo-Irish began truly to see the Irish land when they ceased to own it – having for years owned a land they could not really see – so now the Irish nationalist phase of revival was over even as it announced itself, was only studied and known as such when it began to disintegrate.

Yet even in the move onward to the next stage, there would be temptations to regress, moments when Yeats would feel like choosing autocracy as a refuge from his insecurity. Each generation, asked to prise open the future with a technique derived from the past, could find itself slipping back: just as nationalism could take on many of the contours of colonialism, so liberation might sometimes look like a revamped nationalism. As Fred Jameson has written: "it is as though 'genuine' desire needed repression in order for us to come to consciousness of it as such . . . yet transgressions, presupposing the laws against which they function, thereby end up precisely reconfirming such laws".[39] Nonetheless, in a culture where expression often precedes conceptualization, form will determine eventual content, and life imitate art in the manner suggested in Yeats's play *The King's Threshold*:

> What bad poet did your mothers listen to
> That you were born so crooked?[40]

or again:

> I said the poets hung
> Images of the life that was in Eden
> About the child-bed of the world, that it,
> Looking upon those images, might bear
> Triumphant children.[41]

So, the shape taken by an experimental narrative may hint at the solution to the seemingly insoluble contradictions of a civil society, teaching it how to combine the benefits of modernity with the warmth of community. An art which deliberately opposes its own age is reflected in a notion of genius as never like the country's idea of itself: but from the contest with current codes a symbolic projection of the future community emerges. Kenneth Burke's model of language as symbolic action is helpful here, since "it begins by generating and producing its own context in the same moment of emergence in which it steps back from it, taking its measure with a view towards its own project of transformation",[42] an instance of art reminding us of the very contradiction of which it is itself the resolution. The sloughed-off earlier environment remains as an archaic scaffolding, once useful, now increasingly open to parody, yet somehow contained within the newer order, if only as a reminder that it needed to be created. Art comes not in that moment between the second and third phase, when the realist approaches the magical, but in that moment when the dreamer, installed in the third phase, reaches back to the cast-off reality. Those who persist in taking that discarded scaffolding for an actual living environment doom themselves to adolescence and eventual erasure – but the scaffolding had its undeniable uses in its day and can be preserved within the new dispensation. Such a utopia will deliver the self "from the anxieties of reality, but will still contain that reality".[43]

Synge's art is a telling example of all this. It is based on the notion that it is possible only to one person in one place at one time; and yet somehow it is a result of a collaboration, because "no personality is enough to make a rich work unique".[44] Such an individual expressed the entire generation in the act of expressing himself or herself. In Synge's world, there is no split between private and public, between urban and rural, between science and art. Instead, the dreamer Synge looks back from the zones of liberation on the reality of a nationalist phase, which he frames and critically evaluates. In *Deirdre of the Sorrows* this is done by exploring the relation between the heroic tales and the fallen Ireland in which they are still told: but between the heroic ideal and the reduced storyteller, Synge can open a space of freedom. This is the gesture rehearsed in his poem "Queens", which lists the ancient, magnificent queens of legend, but concludes:

> Yet these are rotten, I ask their pardon,
> For we've the sun on rock and garden:

For these are gone and you're the queen
Of all are living, or have been.[45]

That same gesture is repeated in his farewell to Celticist trappings in "The Passing of the Shee":

Adieu, sweet Angus, Maeve and Fand,
Ye plumed yet skinny Shee,
That poets played with hand in hand
To learn their ecstasy.

We'll stretch in Red Dan Sally's ditch,
And drink in Tubber fair,
Or poach with Red Dan Philly's bitch
The badger and the hare.[46]

Deirdre of the Sorrows is Synge's fullest exposure of the bankruptcy of the aristocratic code, which yearns for its own dissolution, but which hesitates to end. These telling moments indicate not just the hesitations of the colonizer before his final departure, but also the difficulty of extirpating the nationalism left in its stead. The play, however, enacts Synge's protest against those other, more nostalgic reinterpreters of the legend who recruit a past for the war against the future, rather than using it in that extirpation of the present which alone makes the future possible. For the nationalist, the sloughed-off is always at that moment constituted and frozen as a work of art to be admired, but, for the radical artist, form is the promise of an environment yet to be born.

Many of Synge's finest ideas – including the notion of the Hiberno-English dialect as "an art more beautiful than nature"[47] – have their origin in Wilde's dialectical aesthetics. The moral necessity of lying if something new is to be created; the failure of the mirror of realism; the desire for a form which is beautiful to the extent that it is unprecedented; the use of the iambic line to distinguish the poet-hero – all these derive from Wilde and are rooted in a single conviction: that the artist is one who proceeds not from feeling to form but from form to thought and passion, for "the mere form suggests what is to fill it and make it intellectually and emotionally complete".[48] The loveliness which has long faded from the world held scant interest for such a mind, which is more exercised by a loveliness yet to be made. The new man and woman of the emerging world must be, in the literal sense, barbarians, who no sooner know the forms of the past than they rid themselves of them. Beauty is, by definition, unprecedented; and to measure it by the past is to measure it by a standard on the rejection of which its real perfection depends. To realize the present, one must realize every century that preceded it and that went into its making. In the end, however, the dialectic must work through its human agents, in art as in politics: for as Wilde said:

> . . . the past is of no importance. The present is of no importance. It is with the future that we have to deal. For the past is what ought not to have been. The present is what man ought not to be. The future is what artists are.[49]

Seventeen

Revolt into Style – Yeatsian Poetics

Yeats's notion that *style* might be an agent of redemption is canvassed in the opening two lyrics of his *Collected Poems*. Both the Happy and Sad Shepherd tell the same sad story: but the former's glad heart ensures that it is finally given a melodious inflection, while the latter's gloom distorts the material to "inarticulate moan". *Le style, c'est l'homme*: content is again proven secondary, illustrative, pliable. Real joy derives less from right thinking than from achieved self-expression. Yeats has little to say and much to express: and what he expresses is the unimportance of ideas or content:

> Go gather by the humming sea
> Some twisted, echo-harbouring shell,
> And to its lips thy story tell,
> And they thy comforters will be,
> Recording in melodious guile
> Thy fretful words a little while,
> Till they shall singing fade in ruth
> And die a pearly brotherhood;
> For words alone are certain good:
> Sing, then, for this is also sooth.[1]

Art may soothe the pain it describes so well: to express an emotion may also be to purge oneself of it. If singing can be truth, then style itself may be the subject. Insofar as man pursues themes, he does not choose them: rather, they choose him:

> There was a man whom sorrow named his friend . . .[2]

The danger of a world constructed on a foundation of pure style is self-enclosure, a point illustrated by the imperviousness of the dewdrops to the Sad Shepherd's overture:

But naught they heard, for they are always listening,
The dewdrops, for the sound of their own dropping.

Self-delight has its narcissistic limits, and so the attempt to communicate with a shell proves circular. Again, in "The Indian on God",
creativity seems to betoken self-enclosure, each person seeing God as a
version of himself. Humans insist on seeing God as human, but Yeats
knows that the soul may exist in many other forms. The parrot in "The
Indian to His Love" rages at his own image in the enamelled sea,
fearing such self-enclosure but seeking the antiself. In the end, there is
but one consolation: if pain can be transmuted into art, and assuaged
by it, then something has been achieved.

Many of Yeats's early lyrics are written to a "traditional air", as if the
style preceded their content; or else they rework traditional themes and
images as if redeemed by Yeatsian style. In this manoeuvre, Yeats seems
to be hoping to add a little of his own art, just as folktale tellers do
before relaunching the story back into the impersonality of tradition:
once again, the implication is that he is a sort of "Homer", a name to
which such texts may in time be appended. The poet, in seeking to
dramatize himself, seems to become pure medium, the poetry evolving
more at the instigation of words and rhythms than from the pressure of
felt experience. The fear is that he may lose touch with the popular
mood "and learn to chaunt a tongue men do not know".[3] Style is, none
the less, prioritized, irresistible, a mode of action and power, as against
the antithetical world of thought, contemplation, knowledge. Love is
given to style, because all dreams yearn to take their appropriate form,
whether a man seeking a woman's or a God coveting the earthly.
However, the fusion with that form is ever imperfect and incomplete,
for, if it were fully achieved, the passionate emotion would be expressed
and thereby lost. Many of Yeats's single-sentence "breath-poems" deal,
indeed, with expiration, the dying fall into the moment of death.

Some attempt to conceptualize this method is offered in "The
Moods": bodiless souls descend into forms, and these constitute the
"moods" which impel actions in the world, but the style or mood
determines the content of an action. This allows Yeats to respond to the
puritan charge of the bad faith implicit in *mimesis* with the counter-
claim that art creates, rather than describes, emotions and moods:

Literature differs from explanatory or scientific writing in being wrought
about a mood . . . argument, theory, erudition, observation are merely what
Blake calls "little devils who fight for themselves", illusions of our visible

passing life, who must be made to serve the moods, or we have no part in eternity.[4]

A style, like a mood, goes fishing for a subject in the unconscious, but, once expressed in an embodied form, the subject – as in "The Song of Wandering Aengus" – may elude human control. The poet's attempt to recapture what he had created – a girl, a nation – is enacted by revision, by the attempt to see again and control all that floated free: but this proves impossible. The elevation of style over subject is possible only in that liminal, twilit world of wavering rhythms and half-said things, wherein the critical faculties are dulled but not annihilated. In these moments, the all-too-present danger is sentimentality.

"The Cap and Bells" is the fullest exploration in the early books of the process. It tells the story of a young queen who will only accept the jester's love (content) after first receiving quite separately its instruments, the cap and bells (form): yet another case of expression becoming the very condition of conceptualization. The jester must lose his powers of creativity, his expressive instruments, before he can be sure of her love. The woman who enables art thus becomes also its enemy, and so the female who castrates *is* art. *He* wants the woman, but she wants the desire of the man, an irreconcilable conflict. Like all pornographers, she substitutes a part for the whole, his instruments for his soul: but, of course, he has already done the same to her, in fetishizing her foot and her hair. While in the pornographic mode, she holds his cap and bells in triumph, and sings while he is castrated. His prophecy is thereby fulfilled: "I will send them to her and die".[5] Self-castrated, he can experience ultimately in death. Only after this death can his soul blend with her body and, at that moment, she also dies, reuniting with her beloved in song. In the hereafter alone are form and content perfectly at one.

It would be possible to read the poem in many other ways – the male, as slave to an unacknowledged *anima*, being compelled to risk all for a full encounter; the Irish artist in England abandoning the court jester's self-castrating role for a more authentic national art; the high price paid by the licensed fool for his plain speaking. But these are already obvious interpretations. The deeper life of the poem bespeaks a poet's ambivalence about his art and his subservience to image and symbol. Again and again, in early love poems, the poet encounters an exacting woman, whose cruelty makes necessary the very art which she then proceeds to jeopardize. No wonder that he may wish the beloved dead in those moments when she is not killing him. A volume like *The*

Wind Among the Reeds is deliberately organized around styles and moods which later, taken in consort, yield up a meaning. For style is here a mode of arrangement.

"Never Give All the Heart" might equally be read as a recommendation to throw energy into form rather than content: in other words, never to say it all in one poem, for, if one does, then *all* is lost in the act of expression. "The painter's brush consumes his dreams" will be one way of putting this; "our love letters wear out our love" another. The half-said thing is dearest, to lovers as well as to poets, since it still leaves them their role; and a passionate lover would, anyway, never wish to suspect that most of the passion was on the other side. Moreover, if one could seem to say it all in one poem, that could only be a dishonest appearance: recall the actress, described in *Autobiographies*, who could best mimic a feeling only after it was all but gone.

This raises the inevitable question about art as bad faith, but perhaps the notion of a false imitation of a true thing is more applicable to performers than to artists. The paradox in "Never Give All the Heart" is bitter and that bitterness is rendered in the jagged syntax and awkward repetitions. On the one hand, there is the need to "act", but on the other there is the impossibility of acting out of deep feeling. The answer is the Mask, a necessary fakery, which, if consciously and confessedly manipulated, is not vulnerable to the charge of bad faith. The Yeatsian/Wildean theory is uncompromising on this point: it is possible to fake a nation into existence via a style, and what is thus created need be no pale imitation but a radical creation. The exemplar for the nation is not to be slavishly imitated, but one who awakens each man and woman to the hero in themselves, "because all life has the same root".[6]

Hence the rigour brought to the discussion of style in "Adam's Curse", the point being that what seems a nonchalant aristocratic mode is actually hard, middle-class work:

> A line will take us hours maybe;
> Yet if it does not seem a moment's thought
> Our stitching and unstitching has been naught.[7]

The poem is itself an example of the method: a conversation-piece built out of the rhythms of an apparently effortless everyday speech. The styles of the outcast groups, of beggar and landless labourer, are recruited to redeem an altogether more sophisticated but threatened aristocratic wisdom, by a writer who wishes to think like a wise man but express himself like the common people. And the reward for such successful articulation is to be thought an idle trifler by the workaday bourgeoisie:

> Better go down upon your marrow-bones
> And scrub a kitchen pavement, or break stones
> Like an old pauper, in all kinds of weather;
> For to articulate sweet sounds together
> Is to work harder than all these, and yet
> Be thought an idler by the noisy set
> Of bankers, schoolmasters, and clergymen
> The martyrs call the world.[8]

Yet a shaped singing style is not just a basis for "self-conquest", but also an escape from the hot-faced bargainers and money-changers, indeed the only answer to the question which its own success raises. In the end, Yeats will conclude that only the styles of the outcast classes can redeem the language of the nation. So, in the poem, he attacks the middle class, bitterly describing poetry in their terms (of work, reward, trade). Even more, he attacks those (including himself) who succumbed to the bourgeois disease of seeking for precedents in books, of imitating approved models rather than looking inside themselves. Of course, it is a functional irony that "Adam's Curse" adds to that tradition of learned love, in which all books become an endless rehearsal for something which never happens, agents of that delayed gratification which is the essence of the Yeatsian life.

That irony underpins many of the poems in *In the Seven Woods*, which seem anxious to extirpate "literary" precedents from a tradition, but end by adding yet another. The rejection of literary models is based, in part, on the knowledge that sometimes even a style can go out of fashion "like an old song": the dire prophecy of the Sad Shepherd may be fulfilled. If "Adam's Curse" established the fundamental affinity between artist and women in their joint labour to be beautiful, "The Mask" echoes the idea in its call for a deliberate regulation of self-giving spontaneity. Masks, like assumed styles, are essential but problematic: they offer not the truth, but a way towards it. The poem suggests that women are seen as images more than as persons, and yet they must with labour maintain both of those aspects. The pretence involved in wearing masks may betoken a courtesy which hinders love, or it may make available the only viable form of expression. The tension between mask and face intrigues the man: however, the woman rightly refuses to remove the mask, for she senses that the truth lies at that unknown point where mask and face, antiself and self, are one.

Since style is the mask from which the whole person may be inferred, so the forms of an art may in time provide the synecdoche for a nation. This utopian idea explains Yeats's yearning for the success of the Dublin Municipal Gallery and for the return to it of the Lane Collection of paintings. If the arts lie dreaming of what is to come, then the renovated content of a free Ireland may emerge when least expected:

> And maybe I will take a trout
> If but I do not seem to care . . .[9]

The terrifying difficulties attendant upon such a creation are traced in "The Magi", whose lines reach forward only to fall back, and whose slow accretion of clauses conveys a rising sense of expectation, reinforced by the thrice-repeated "all", which is yet unfulfilled. Even the opening word "Now" is so qualified by the following phrase as to be annulled; and that technique of self-cancellation persists all through:

> Now as at all times I can see in the mind's eye,
> In their stiff, painted clothes, the pale unsatisfied ones
> Appear and disappear in the blue depth of the sky
> With all their ancient faces like rain-beaten stones,
> And all their helms of silver hovering side by side,
> And all their eyes still fixed, hoping to find once more,
> Being by Calvary's turbulence unsatisfied,
> The uncontrollable mystery on the bestial floor.[10]

"The Magi" is really an anticipatory style looking for an enabling content, a form without a finalizing substance; and this technique of anticlimax will be used with even greater subtlety in the elaborate stanzas of later poems like "In Memory of Robert Gregory" and "Among School Children".

An anticlimax is precisely what "The Magi" accuses Christianity of providing. The unsatisfactory incarnation of the divine in a fallen human body offers some hint of the sufferings implicit in submitting to a single form; and this comes the more appositely in a volume where Yeats deals, for the first time, with the chancy, sordid, reduced realities of an all-too-flawed Ireland. The assumption of form can be a severe experience of humiliation: the self-conquest of the stylist is won only out of an initial degradation. However, the poet, if he were to wait for knowledge, might never begin his quest: and so he must start with the search for a form. William Blake saw the body as satanic, but Christ took that form; likewise, the artist-martyr takes on the weaknesses of the flawed medium which he chooses, before casting it off again. "Incarnation and crucifixion are one",[11] declared Yeats, by which he meant that style and form, pursued outside the self by a poet, are fully known as one only at the moment of death.

By this logic, Synge could never have rested quiet in the tomb, until he had found his antiself on Aran. "In Memory of Major Robert Gregory" not only chronicles such exemplary moments in exemplary lives: it becomes also an instance of that enactment, eluding the artist's intended controls, as the deliberated poem gives way to the authentic one, the manifest to the latent content. The final stanza is an auto-critical explanation of the seeming formlessness of the poem:

> I had thought, seeing how bitter is that wind
> That shakes the shutter, to have brought to mind
> All those that manhood tried, or childhood loved
> Or boyish intellect approved,
> With some appropriate commentary on each;
> Until imagination brought
> A fitter welcome; but a thought
> Of that late death took all my heart for speech.[12]

The very difficulty of enunciating that final line is part of its meaning, for now the poet too endures "lack of breath", with his heart literally in his mouth, blocking utterance. Acknowledging its own redundancy, after a patently ludicrous attempt to tabulate and catalogue elements of a very casual build-up, the poem's baffled silence is in fact the greater tribute, rather like that offered at the end of "The Fisherman", which concludes that the audience for (as well as the content of) a national art has yet to be inferred.

In Yeats's middle period, the Dancer becomes an emblem of pure form, sheer contour, devoid of intellectual content ("opinion"), which is now subsumed by style. What Michael Robartes wishes to see is the supernatural element incarnated in bodily form; but the yearning for "thought" is not so easily denied:

> . . . it's plain
> The half-dead dragon was her thought,

> That every morning rose again
> And dug its claws and shrieked and fought.
> Could the impossible come to pass
> She would have time to turn her eyes,
> Her lover thought, upon the glass
> And on the instant could grow wise.[13]

This represents a phase of womanhood with which the poet fully identifies himself by now, that moment when every rational control is lost and a supernatural visitation becomes possible. It is the moment of second coming and, indeed, the moment of Leda.

The famous question which closes "Leda and the Swan" assumes that the price of full knowledge is indifference; and this is entirely in keeping with Yeats's long-standing conviction that to poets the half-said thing is most attractive. The point was, indeed, repeated at the end of "Meditations in Time of Civil War" where "the half-read wisdom of daimonic images" was to "suffice the ageing man as once the growing boy"[14] (though, of course, there is an element of resignation about the word "suffice"). While feminists have denounced the lyric as a glamor-ization of rape, it is possible to see that mythical rape as Yeats's metaphor for artistic creation and the poet as identifying with the put-upon woman.

As a mere medium for the awesome, impersonal power of super-natural forces, Yeats knew that he possessed massive gifts of technique (poetic "power") but that his intellectual control over such language (analytic "knowledge") lagged sadly behind. It is undeniable that his skill with words far outstripped his abilities as a thinker. His father had often joked: "You want to be a philosopher, Willie, and are only a poet", but the son was consistently aware of the dilemma. He refers to it in "Vacillation" ("What, be a singer born, and lack a theme?") and again in "The Circus Animals' Desertion" ("I sought a theme and sought for it in vain"). He was being no more than honest when he wrote:

> Those poets that in their writings are most wise
> Own nothing but their own blind stupefied hearts.[15]

The result is that many of Yeats's most memorable lines are striking without being lucid (like the end of "The Second Coming", where the rough beast may be a divine agent of inspiration, heralding not only a new era but also new subjects for poetry). This need not necessarily be a bad thing, for great poetry often has the capacity to communicate before it is fully understood; but that surrender of intellectual control did trouble Yeats, who sometimes felt more violated than illuminated by image and symbol.

A pervasive theme through *The Tower* is the cost of worshipping images. The bird in "Sailing to Byzantium" achieves a highly qualified triumph, permanence being won only at the cost of mobility and growth. The image of Hanrahan, recalled by the poet in "The Tower", threatens to unhinge his mind to such a degree that the poet must abort the sentence, crying out "enough": he fears that, instead of mastering the image, it will master him, in much the same way that the images of Mary Hynes in Raftery's poetry so inflamed Clare countrymen that they strayed into the bog of Cloone.

Often, when Yeats evokes an image, he feels threatened. This is especially true of the potent image of the swan, which in "Among School Children" causes him yet again to abandon a sentence with the cry "enough!". At these moments, he may feel unhinged and even tempted to abort not just the sentence but art itself – as in the third section of "Nineteen Hundred and Nineteen":

> The swan has leaped into the desolate heaven:
> That image can bring wildness, bring a rage
> To end all things, to end
> What my laborious life imagined, even
> The half-imagined, the half-written page . . .[16]

The swan promises an experience bestial as well as divine, and threatens the abolition of art as well as portending inspiration. The poet who has been seeking an impersonal style must, like Leda, surrender to the "indifferent" poetic beak,[17] being merely a passive agent of universal history.

Until recently, critics debated why the fingers in the poem were "vague" as they pushed the feathered glory from "loosening" thighs. Was Yeats describing the blurred effect in a painting of the scene? Or webbed feet? Or was he implying some sort of consent with the word "loosening"? The violence of "blow", so the argument ran, was mitigated by "caressed", though words like "caught", "staggering" and "helpless" suggested no acceptance whatever. Most readers, noting the ambiguity in lines 7 and 8 (ambiguous as to whether it is Leda or the swan feeling the strange heart beating) decided that consent, whether resigned or exacted, had been given at about that point. Perhaps the question asked simply whether the bird could put on her feeling with his knowledge; or perhaps it referred to Leda's experience of the strange, pulsating swan – it didn't seem to matter much in the end. There were even some highly traditionalist males who saw the poem's subject not as rape but as seduction.

All of this, however, misses the point that consent was assumed even before the start, by the swan with regard to Leda, and also by Yeats *vis-à-vis* the reader. The poet's technique of assumed intimacy – a polite phrase for a rape of readerly sensibility – is manifest in the emphatic opening "A sudden blow". A Yeatsian poem seldom follows nineteenth-century protocol in the sense of earning its terms or extending the traditional courtesies of literature to the reader; rather, it tends to assume absolute consent and in-feeling with its given world. ("Pythagoras planned it" – but what? "I have met them at close of day" – but whom?) So Leda becomes an emblem of the poet's violation by the Muse, and also of the poem's assault upon the sensibilities of the reader.

The trajectory of this lyric is in keeping with the strategies adopted in "The Magi", "The Second Coming" or the stanzas of "Among School Children": a rising tide of rhetorical expectation over a slow accretion of clauses, leading to a final line that is somehow disappointing or downbeat, expressive of frustration and puzzled into question. This is a technique not only for bathos – all of life again being a preparation for something that may never happen – but for post-coital indifference. If "consent", or at least "resignation" has been the mood after the opening resistance by Leda, then this makes the final indifference of the swan almost tragic.

The question in line 8 asked, apparently, whether the swan could combine the "feeling" of Leda with its own "knowledge"; the question at the end asks whether she put on his "knowledge": in other words, had she foreknowledge of her story, of how she would bear Clytemnestra who would kill Agamemnon after his return from the siege of Troy? If stanza one was centred on the swan, and stanza two queried Leda's response, then the rest of the poem centres on the puzzled poet with his final, rather voyeuristic, query. As always, there seem to be three people involved in this affair. Though the bird is at all times brutish and threatening, there is something finally concessive about that closing "let her drop", as if he were not in full control, perhaps even frightened by all this strangeness.

At the most obvious level, the poem identifies the swan with the supernatural authority and power of the creative imagination; and so the broken wall and burning roof are less significant as historic facts than as immortal elements of a poet's epic narrative. Art and image are "engendered" there. At a deeper level, however, these references to one war remind us that Yeats was writing in the year of another: 1923, italicized at the foot of the sonnet. This leads to the possibility of interpreting the swan as the invading English occupier and the girl as a ravished Ireland. The girl is more expert in "feeling", the swan in "knowledge". She is a mere mortal, whereas he comes from an imperial eternity. The debate about her alleged consent recalls vividly those common clichés to the effect that the Irish were colonizable because they secretly wished others to take command of their lives. The poem might then be read as a study of the calamitous effects of the original rape of Ireland and of the equally precipitate British withdrawal. The final question would then be asking: when the Irish took over power from the departing occupier, did they also assume the centuries-honed skills of self-government and control (or "knowledge")? The "indifferent beak" might then be Yeats's judgement on the callous and irresponsible suddenness of an unplanned and ill-prepared British withdrawal. The "Anglo" side of Yeats, a man now in mortal peril himself during the civil war, must have felt the precipitate nature of the withdrawal a hard betrayal, and a betrayal of possibly tragic dimensions, given that the two peoples had seemed in recent years to have come to a forced but real understanding, rather like the uneasy concord between woman and swan in the poem. The "Irish" side of Yeats was just plain angry, an anger palpable in the bitter, bleak monosyllables of the close.

The poem was to have been about one kind of politics, the Russian Revolution and its aftermath, but Yeats explained in a commentary that the lyric which he eventually wrote was different: bird and lady took possession of the scene, and he claimed that all politics went out of the poem. If politics went out, it returned again in the cited date and in the civil war imagery. The poem which Yeats delivers in his moments of greatness is invariably not the one which he sets out to write, nor even the one which he often thinks he is writing in the early lines. "Leda and the Swan" may indeed be another account of the artistic or even the readerly process: but in teasing out those themes, it has much besides to say on the crisis of a newly independent people.

Eighteen

The Last *Aisling* – *A Vision*

For Yeats, the rough beast slouching to Bethlehem recalled that incongruous couple of two thousand years earlier, who brought into the world a child destined to announce a new dispensation:

> The Roman Empire stood appalled,
> It dropped the reins of peace and war
> When that fierce virgin and her Star
> Out of the fabulous darkness called[1]

Now, in the years following Irish independence, Yeats struggled to define an alternative vision of society. *A Vision*, for all its arcane lore, was intended by him to provide a spiritual foundation for the new nation-state. The indefinite article of the title is unusually tentative for such an ambitious document. This would suggest that Yeats remained somewhat sceptical about the project. He had always encouraged his youthful friend, George Russell, to question his visions: and his relation with his own instructors was appropriately dialogic:

> Except at the start of a new topic, when they would speak or write a dozen sentences unquestioned, I had always to question, and every question to rise out of the previous answer, and to deal with their chosen topic.[2]

That interrogative case of mind had led, years earlier, to his expulsion from the esoteric section of the Theosophists for seeking, in a quasi-scientific fashion, to conjure up the spirits of dead flowers. Such a person was well capable of imagining the possible reservations which might assail readers of *A Vision*:

> Some will ask whether I believe in the actual existence of my circuits of sun and moon . . . To such a question I can but answer that if sometimes,

overwhelmed by miracle as all men must be when in the midst of it, I have taken such periods literally, my reason has soon recovered; and now that the system stands out clearly in my imagination, I regard them as stylistic arrangements of experience comparable to the cubes in the drawing of Wyndham Lewis and to the ovoids in the sculpture of Brancusi. They have helped me to hold in a single thought reality and justice.[3]

That is a recipe for perpetual scepticism: for Yeats would always seek to balance things as they are against things as they should be. He was keen to include those very "facts" in a system of binaries, which would ultimately be transcended by a third term, the unnameable "thought" which combines both reality and justice.

The son of a sardonic artist, Yeats was bound to be a sceptic. He despised the literature of the single point of view, the "single vision" of a mechanistic psychology which he equated with "Newton's sleep".[4] He would have endorsed Scott Fitzgerald's declaration that the mark of a first-rate mind is its ability to hold opposed ideas while yet retaining the capacity to function.[5] Such a liberal imagination, recognizing the best features of the opposing viewpoint, was a legacy of his father's upbringing, which taught that there was no cause so bad that it had not been defended by good men. The son's tolerant sense of the doubleness of all deep experience may also be attributable to the spiritual hyphenation of the Anglo-Irish, forever seen as English in Ireland, and always Irish in England.

This meant that Yeats could never sponsor one term of an antithesis for long without moving to embrace its opposite; and, even as he sidled away from the original term, he would cast longing glances back in its direction. Despite a reputation for dreaminess, he was as *"Anglo"* (cautious, analytic, even cunning) as he was *"Irish"* (passionate, careless, emotional). Ultimately, his guile led him to expose the limitations of either term by fusing both, and to do this in the conviction that while it takes talent to discern differences, only genius can establish the underlying unity. So, according to his developing system, the members of his pantheon of English literature, Shakespeare, Blake, Shelley, were honorary Celts by nature and temper; and Yeats himself could confess, near the close of his career, that he owed his Irish soul to England. By such devious routes, an Irish national poet emerged from English tradition, much as a rough beast transpired out of the stony sleep of Christendom.

One cone in the system of *A Vision* is, therefore, interpenetrated by its opposing cone, and one gyre by its antagonist. Those contrary gyres may well be a version, in world-historical terms, of the Anglo-Irish antithesis out of which Yeats and the Irish revival came, but, if so, they are also part of his attempt to transcend it:

ANGLO GYRE – PRIMARY: democratic, scientific, factual, objective, Christian, realistic, God over one soul.

CELTIC GYRE – ANTITHETICAL: hierarchical, aesthetic, visionary, subjective, pagan, idealistic, multiple self.[6]

Belonging to Phase 17, Yeats has elements of the Primary about him, and hints of the anglophone, but he is predominantly Antithetical or Celtic. The interpenetration of cones perfectly captures his dual inheritance.

The word *visionary* is included in the Antithetical Celtic gyre, and with justice. *A Vision,* however tentative a title, deliberately refers the Irish reader back to the *aisling* or vision-poem, practised by the fallen bards like Ó Rathaille to whom Yeats was increasingly attracted. The outlines of the *aisling* were rigidly formulaic:[7] it began with a poet, frustrated and weak, falling into a doze by river, lake or mountain-side; and thereafter, he was visited by a *spéirbhean* or sky-woman, who was in effect a medium for a supernatural power. The misfortunes of modern Ireland were next described, its weakness and diminished grandeur lamented: then, with occult symbolism and complex metaphor, the *spéirbhean* would foretell the return of Gaelic rulers and values, and the extirpation of the Saxon occupier and of his levelling administrative methods. It was from this convention that Yeats appears to have drawn his framework for *A Vision.* That the *spéirbhean* should in this particular instance have been his own English wife must have tickled his sceptical imagination: but Mrs. Yeats proved a wonderful medium.

In his essay on Matthew Arnold and the Celtic element in literature, Yeats had endorsed the basic outlines of the Celticist analysis, but for the word "Celtic" had repeatedly substituted the word "ancient". As early as 1897, he was expanding the meanings of "Celtic" to global dimensions, sensing that the ancient was due for a return. For that reason, as well as for its roots in *aisling* tradition, it makes some sense to read *A Vision* as a kind of Celtic constitution, first published in 1925, at a juncture when the new Irish state, of which Yeats was by then a senator, was seeking to codify its own laws and customs.

The reference in the introduction to a dispensation combining reality and justice is a throwback to the ancient Brehon system under which the functions of *file* and *breitheamh,* poet and judge, were one. "Thought is nothing without action" was Yeats's motto.[8]

Even at the level of elementary psychology, *A Vision* has much to teach Irish people concerning, for example, the need to internalize demons which were once external. The book therefore offers "a distinction between the perfection that is from a man's combat with himself and that which is from a combat with circumstance".[9] Now that the English have gone, the Irish may draw back from the prosaic quarrel with others to the more poetic quarrel with the self. Perhaps hoping for a softening of the physical-force elements in Irish nationalism, Yeats had asked: "Why should we honour those that die upon the field of battle? A man may show as reckless a courage in entering into the abyss of himself".[10]

A Vision's are mostly internal quarrels, struggles with the Daimon inside the person: but these are shadowed at a political level by the Irish Civil War which, in Yeatsian terms, was a regrettable but almost predictable phase in nation-building. A perpetual shying-away from the tensions of the old Civil War in England had led to effete manners and a drab caution in public debate. The Irish Civil War rehearsed within *A Vision*, on the other hand, was one conducted between Anglicized habits of compromise and the unappeasable Celtic hosts.

A Vision is a Celtic constitution not solely for Ireland but for all the world, after the rough beast has come again. Initiated in 1917 to help defeat the forces of materialism, it was aimed in particular at the Marxists, whom Yeats saw as sponsors of the hated industrial revolution. The book is his counter-Renaissance myth, launched at a time when Ireland was "living in the explosion" after 1916, a period which saw the decline of deference, the organization of urban labour and of rural soviets, and the spread of James Connolly's pamphlets among young activists. *The Irish Times* editorials of 1918–19 repeatedly stressed fears that the country was turning communist: and so did Yeats. The language in which he voiced this concern proved conclusively that, when the chips were down, he spoke neither for the noble nor the beggarman, but for the emergent middle class. He feared that the national coalition of "peasant proprietors and capitalists" would be split in two by the attempt "to create a dictatorship of labour". In April 1919, he wrote:

What I want is that Ireland be kept from giving itself (under the influence of its lunatic faculty of going against everything which it believes England to affirm) to Marxian revolution or to Marxian definitions of value in any form. I consider the Marxian criterion of values as in this age the spear-head of materialism and leading to inevitable murder. From that criterion follows the well-known phrase: "Can the bourgeois be innocent?"[11]

A Vision is not, thereby, an *encyclopedia fascista*, as certain radical poets of the 1930s would subsequently claim. A self-confessed fiction rather than a degenerate myth, it is saved by its own scepticism. Moreover, it is impeccably "liberal" in its anxiety to tackle its Marxist opponents on their stronger rather than weaker points: their roots in Bruno, Hegel and Kant. The notion behind the system of gyres – that every power necessarily creates its own opposition – comes from Bruno and Hegel, as well as sounding a somewhat bizarre echo of Marx's theory of class conflict. Bruno, of course, had added that such opposition was the prelude to a final reunion, which in the Marxist scheme took the form of a classless society. The latter idea Yeats could never endorse: but his view that "every movement in feeling or thought, prepares in the dark by its own increasing identity and confidence, its own execution", closely echoes Marx's description of a capitalism which nourishes the seeds of its own destruction. Indeed, Yeats's confidence in the human capacity to predict the shape of the future – a confidence shared with Marxists – might leave him open to the charge of sponsoring a dreary determinism. He saw history as endless repetition: Marxists saw it as a straight line.

Yeats also resembled the Marxists in his certainty that, although the basic plot of history had been written, a person was free to improvise what freedom and dignity he or she could. Engels, after all, had defined freedom as the *conscious* recognition of necessity; and so did Yeats. In *Explorations* he added: "History is necessity until it takes fire in someone's head and becomes freedom or virtue".[12] The fire is not Promethean or Marxian however: it does not remake the world so much as burn up the tragic protagonist's relation to it. The Yeatsian soul is free, but free only to disappear into a higher element: "I found myself upon the third antinomy of Immanuel Kant; thesis: freedom; antithesis: necessity; but I restate it. Every action of man declares the soul's ultimate, particular freedom, and the soul's disappearance in God; declares that reality is a congeries of beings and a single being . . ."[13] The marriage-bed is Yeats's symbol of the attempt at a solved antinomy, the epitome of the sexual near-miss: "it were more than the symbol could a man there lose and keep his identity, but he falls asleep".[14]

The freedom which *A Vision* allows is that offered by the Musicians to Deirdre in Yeats's play: the freedom to live out the fore-ordained plot on her own chosen terms with her own improvised lines, and to give that plot one or two forward shoves:

> . . . The stage-manager, or Daimon, offers his actor an inherited scenario, the *Body of Fate*, and a *Mask* or role as unlike as possible to his natural ego or *will*, and leaves him to improvise through his *Creative Mind* the dialogue and details of the plot. He must discover or reveal a being which only exists with extreme effort . . . But this is antithetical man.

> . . . For primary man I go to the *Commedia dell' Arte* in its decline. The *Will* is weak and cannot create a role, and so, if it transform itself, does so after an accepted pattern, traditional clown or pantaloon . . . and substitutes a motive of service for that of self-expression. Instead of the created *Mask* he has an imitative *Mask*; and when he recognizes this, his *Mask* may become the historical norm, or an image of mankind.[15]

The clown of "The Cap and Bells" had been castrated, because he was a mere entertainer rather than an exponent of self-expression: he was like Wilde or Shaw when at their weakest, embodying the norms of Primary England. Their masks were then external, worn as part of a game played with society, in the attempt to establish what others thought of their performance: but for Yeats the true mask was something internal, chosen in the deeps of the mind, a revelation to himself of his Antithetical Irish being far more than a manifestation of it to others.

The universal history of politics and art is rendered in *A Vision* in terms of the original Anglo-Irish antithesis, yet its paradoxical hope is to transcend those terms. It does this, in a partial and conditional way, by admitting the interpenetration of one by another in all vital natures. Without this interpenetration, the balance of forces known as *life* is impossible. It can be no coincidence that the heroism of Yeats's Anglo-Irish precursors is described, in the decade after *A Vision*, as the quest of those who sought to transcend those binaries and evolve a "Third Way".

Edmund Burke was a telling example, for he confronted Yeats with two irreconcilable theories – the absolute efficiency of the state versus the absolute freedom of the individual. The first, if taken to extreme, led to tyranny; and the second, likewise, to anarchy. Burke, therefore, refused to see politics solely in terms either of the state or the individual, and he attempted to reconcile the conflict by inventing the modern idea of the *nation*.[16] Yeats's essays invoke this tradition, insisting that the Irish nation must steer a middle course between drab statism and piratical individualism, aligning itself with neither. Such strictures would hardly feature in the encyclopaedia of a fascist.

Moreover, Burke believed that Locke and his theory of sense-perception ignored the *historical* dimension, the way in which communities were held together by tradition. By submitting all to the test of reason, Locke had ignored the play of historic forces which had helped to shape things. History was more than a succession of self-interested men; and so Yeats supplied a history of Man, viewed from a near-anthropological standpoint, as Swift, Goldsmith and Berkeley had seen him. These, said Yeats, "found in England the opposite that stung their thought into expression and made it lucid". Berkeley's famous claim that "we Irish do not hold with this" was a denial of the world of Locke and Newton. "That was the birth of the national intellect and it caused the defeat in Berkeley's secret society of English materialism, the Irish Salamis".[17]

What had outraged Berkeley was Locke's repudiation of the primary qualities of weight, mass and so on, as properties objectively belonging to things. Locke held that they were mere sensations produced in us by the physical characteristics of things. His assertion that there was "nothing like" the ideas of secondary qualities (colour, taste and so on) "existing in the bodies themselves" dismayed Berkeley, since it seemed to exclude any room for poetry. Berkeley believed that things exist only in so far as we perceive them. Yeats went further to assert that each man or woman creates a purely personal world, as against Locke who claimed that, under standard conditions, each person would see "the same thing".[18] To Yeats, Blake's well-publicized attacks on the empirical Locke set the republican poet in well-chosen Celtic company, along with Scotland's David Hume. Yeats was delighted to endorse this revolt by the Celtic fringe. His Berkeley was the man who argued against Locke in his *Treatise on Human Knowledge* (1710) that communication was not the only object of language, but also "the raising of some passion . . . the putting of the mind in some particular disposition". Burke in his *Enquiry* also suggested that poetry "does not depend for its effect on the raising of sensible images", for its habit is "to affect by sympathy rather than by imitation".[19]

In the decade following Irish independence, Yeats in his writings aligns himself with these thinkers and argues for innate ideas (birds nesting; girls looking in a certain way at passing boys) rather than the *tabula rasa*. As far as he is concerned, Locke's distinction between primary and secondary ideas took away the world and gave people excrement instead. Berkeley, on the other hand, restored the world, with his demonstration that all qualities of shape, as well as of colour, depend on the perceiver:

Fragments

I.
Locke sank into a swoon;
The Garden died;
God took the spinning jenny
Out of his side.

II.
Where got I that truth?
Out of a medium's mouth,
Out of nothing it came,
Out of the forest loam,
Out of the dark night where lay
The crowns of Nineveh.[20]

If expression precedes conceptualization, that is because Nineveh did not exist until the poets first created it with their sighing. Yeats had written in "The Symbolism of Poetry": "I doubt indeed if the crude circumstance of the world, which seems to create all our emotions, does more than reflect, as in multiplying mirrors, the emotions that have come to solitary men in moments of poetical contemplation".[21] The fear voiced in the poem is of the uniformity and massification of English society, whose members were all (according to Blake) "inter-measurable", or (in Yeats's elaboration) "chopped and measured like a piece of cheese".

To these members of his eighteenth-century pantheon, Yeats added Goldsmith (for his delight in the concrete details of everyday life), Swift (for his love of the Hounynhyms and his hatred of machines), and Burke (for his image of the state as a slow-maturing tree). He was particularly struck by Burke's idea that the radical Jacobins, lacking a vision of evil, oppressed mankind by their excessively high expectations which left "little mercy for the imperfect". No matter how great the energy of the reformer, opined Yeats, a still greater was required to face with equanimity the unreformed and irresponsible elements of life. Deriding communism as just the latest "Santa Claus" of the radical movement, he asserted a preference for a politics of tragic resignation, which meant resignation to all that was flawed and finally unreformable in the human psyche. "We begin to live when we conceive of life as a tragedy".[22]

Yeats's rather Augustan desire to balance the claims of individual and state, of freedom and necessity, led him to embrace Walt Whitman, the great reconciler of self and mass. Accordingly, he placed this poetic founder in Phase 6 of *A Vision*:

> . . . he used his *Body of Fate* (his interest in crowds, in casual loves and affections, in all summary human experience) to clear intellect of antithetical emotions (always insincere from Phase 1 to Phase 8), and haunted and hunted by the now involuntary *Mask*, created an image of vague, half-civilized man, all his thought and impulse a product of democratic bonhomie, of schools, of colleges, of public discussion. Abstraction had been born, but it remained the abstraction of a community, of a tradition, a synthesis starting, not as with Phase 19, 20 and 21 with logical deduction from an observed fact, but from the whole experience of the individual or of the community: "I have such and such a feeling. I have such and such a belief" . . .[23]

A question remains about all this: how convincing is Yeats's Third Way? How real is his transcendence of the binaries of freedom and necessity at that weird moment when the latter takes fire as the former in the human head? Yeats did not see the world as a thing to be remade, but as an object of contemplation, conceived not for the purpose of reformation so much as revelation. Since that revelation could hardly be enacted socially, it must first of all be internalized within the self.

Mechanistic philosophy had reduced the mind to the quicksilver at the back of the mirror: however, said Yeats, the internalizer of the quest-romance must turn lamp, becoming in this contemplative moment "predestinate and free, creation's very self". The critic T. R. Whitaker has construed this phase of Yeats's thought: "in such phrases, he reformulated that alchemical shattering of the objective mirror and distilling of the luminous drop of gold which had concerned him since the time of his apocalyptic romances, and which properly symbolized both the artist's transcendence of the cyclical world and his imaginative growth within the world".[24] A parallel enactment in Act Three of Synge's *The Playboy of the Western World* has Christy Mahon abandoning the mirror of realism as the sign of human vanity and learning to illuminate his roadway by a self-generated inner light. Public opinion of what a man is will never disclose the true self, being rather a distorting mirror. Yeats finds this out for himself in "A Dialogue of Self and Soul" when, speaking of "the finished man among his enemies", he asks

> How in the name of Heaven can he escape
> That defiling and disfigured shape
> The mirror of malicious eyes
> Casts upon his eyes until at last
> He thinks that shape must be his shape?[25]

The only answer known to Yeats was that of Mohini Chatterjee, who "taught that all we perceive exists in the external world – this is a stream which is out of human control, and we but a mirror, and our deliverance consists in turning the mirror away so that it reflects nothing".[26] Mirror-historians can only chronicle a world of accumulated facts; but in "Dove or Swan?" Yeats reanimates history as a force taking fire as symbolic pattern in the human head. Such a moment follows an act of attention or contemplation elsewhere described by Yeats as a form of self-conquest: his stylistic version of revolution. *Style* was his Third Way beyond action and contemplation; artistic living his Third Way transcending freedom and necessity; metaphor his way of holding in a single moment reality and justice. If Part One of *A Vision* – like the opening half of "Easter 1916" – devoted itself to an account of the metaphorizing imagination, then Part Two, like the second half of the poem, represented a relentless demetaphorization.

This answers one of the stock objections to *A Vision*: how can such an abstract system come from so noted a hater of abstraction? But there is a still further complaint that is often made: if each value is cancelled by a counter-value, are we not left with a self-destructive, nugatory scepticism? In actual practice, the opposed values are not *exactly* balanced, since the system is so manipulated as to favour the antithetical Celtic over the primary English elements:

> A *primary* dispensation looking beyond itself towards a transcendent power is dogmatic, levelling, unifying, feminine, humane, peace its means and end; an *antithetical* dispensation obeys imminent power, is expressive, hierarchical, multiple, masculine, harsh, surgical. The approaching *antithetical* influx and that particular *antithetical* dispensation for which the intellectual has begun will reach its complete systematization at that moment when, as I have already shown, the Great Year comes to its intellectual climax.[27]

Nor do the opposed values cancel one another out, since they remain vibrating in a sort of dynamic equilibrium, which itself constitutes a Third Way, more vital for the nonce than either between which it arises. The history of the Anglo-Irish is telescoped into these following sentences from *A Vision*:

> When I look in history for the conflict or union of *antithetical* and *primary,* I seem to discover that conflict or union of races stated by Petrie and Schneider as universal law. A people who have lived apart and so acquired unity of custom and purity of breed unite with some other people through migration, immigration or conquest. A race (the new *antithetical*) emerges that is neither the one nor the other, and often after somewhere about 500 years it produces, or so it seems, its particular culture or civilization. This culture lives only in certain victorious classes; then comes a period of revolution (phase 22) terminated by a civilization of policemen, school-masters, manufacturers, philanthropists, a second soon exhausted blossoming of the race . . .[28]

Far from offering a deconstructive nihilism, *A Vision* envisages Ireland as an imagined community. It also allows that the fiction is forever self-interrogating, a capacity all the more crucial at a time when many apologists for the Irish Free State suffer from single vision and from Newton's sleep.

Nineteen

James Joyce and Mythic Realism

Joyce's *Ulysses* is often treated as a definitive account of the mind of modern Europe in 1922, the year of its publication: but, for that very reason, it is also a recognition that Europe of itself was nothing without its colonial holdings. *Ulysses* is one of the first major literary utterances in the modern period by an artist who spoke for a newly-liberated people. The former provost of Trinity College Dublin, J. P. Mahaffy, clearly sensed Joyce's disruptive power when he lamented that his publications proved beyond doubt that "it was a mistake to establish a separate university for the aborigines of the island, for the corner-boys who spit into the Liffey".[1] That use of the word *aborigines* captures a central truth about James Joyce: outcast from Ireland, scornful of Britain, and uneasy about the humanism of a Europe to which he could never fully surrender, he became instead a nomad, a world author.

Virtually alone among the great post-colonial writers, he did not head for the imperial city or for the lush landscapes of the parent country: for him, there would be no Naipaulian "enigma of arrival", no pained discovery that the culture to which he had been assimilated lacked, after all, a centre. He took this as understood from the start and cut himself adrift from all cosy moorings: it was his strange destiny to be a central figure in world literature, and yet somehow tangential to the cultural life of both Ireland and England. Though he jokingly saw himself as the most recent of the *Wild Geese* – those Irish rebels who sought training in the armies of Catholic Europe after 1691 in hopes of returning to expel the occupier – he was, in truth, a sort of migratory *gastarbeiter* from a peripheral country with a chronically depressed economy.

Like many migrants in the decades since, Joyce performed in central Europe his own research and field work, his own reverse anthropology,[2] while perpetually fretting that the homeland he had abandoned was about to disappear. "If she is truly capable of reviving, let her awake", he wrote in 1907, "or let her cover up her head and lie down decently in her grave forever".[3] The migrant intellectual is forever assailed by the feeling that he or she is speaking before a tribunal, and so it was with Joyce. He tried in journalistic articles to convey to the developed world something of his people's desolation. He had no great faith that his meaning would be understood. Adopting, for strategic purposes, the urbane tone of a central European, he described a bizarre and unjust murder-trial of a speechless defendant back in Ireland. "The figure of this dumbfounded old man, a remnant of a civilization not ours, deaf and dumb before his judge", he told his Triestine readers, "is a symbol of the Irish nation at the bar of public opinion".[4]

That old prisoner's problem was a version of his own: how to express the sheer fluidity and instability of Irish experience in a form which would be nonetheless comprehensible to the arbiters of international order. Ireland was indeed a precarious invention, a fiction which might yet be sufficiently imagined to become a fact: but in 1907 its people were estranged from the past, a nation of exiles and migrants, caught on the cusp between tradition and innovation. They were in but not of any situation in which they might find themselves, their reality the experience of perpetually crossing over from one code to another. The shortest way to Tara, the ancient centre of Celtic civilization, was indeed through Holyhead, that clearing-house for exiles *en route* to the cities of England and continental Europe. Yet into his own exile Joyce took with him the ancient Gaelic notion that only in literature can the consciousness of a people be glimpsed.

There were so many different levels of national experience to comprehend: and yet there was available to Joyce no overarching central image, no single explanatory category, no internal source of authority. Too mobile, too adaptable, the Irish were everywhere and nowhere, scattered across the earth and yet feeling like strangers in their own land. The fear which gripped Pearse, MacDonagh and Desmond FitzGerald in 1914 – that a great historic nation was about to disappear as tens of thousands of its men went willingly to the slaughter of another country's war – had also assailed Joyce. He began *Ulysses* in the hope of discovering through it a form adequate to this strange experience, one which might allow him eventually to proclaim the tables of a new law in the language of the outlaw, to burrow down into his own "Third World" of the mind. For an audience in the made world, he wished to evoke a world still in the making.

He was, in that sense, one of those migrants who create newness out of the mutations of the old. The novel in the hands of a Rushdie or a Naipaul has come to be seen as a form through which the members of an educated native élite address their former masters: but, decades before they wrote, Joyce had used prose narrative to capture the jokes, oral traditions and oratory of a people, who might never have committed these to print themselves, unless they had been part of a more achieved, self-confident culture. Though *Ulysses* is indeed the collective utterance of a community, it is hard to imagine anyone within the world of the book (except possibly Stephen) actually writing it all down. "I have put the great talkers of Dublin into my book", boasted Joyce, "they – and the things that they forgot".[5] For all that, there will be few to imagine either a Leopold or Molly Bloom *reading* it, which makes it in this respect too a supreme instance of the post-colonial text.

Yet these characters are in no way unmodern or unsophisticated. Joyce set his book in the "centre of paralysis" that was Dublin in 1904, in the conviction that if he could get to the dead heart of that city, he could render the discontents and estrangements of the modern world. As an Irishman, he could never condone the glib assumption that "undeveloped" countries like his own were like the developed ones at an earlier stage of their growth: not for him the easy evolutionism of Darwin or Marx. Joyce was radical enough in *Ulysses* to present Mr. Deasy's optimistic Christianity and the socialist's vision of a classless society as two sides of the same oppressive coin. He knew better than that. He knew from personal experience that to be modern is to experience perpetual disintegration and renewal, and yet somehow to make a home in that disorder. The Irish, through the later nineteenth century, had become one of the most deracinated of peoples; robbed of belief in their own future, losing their native language, overcome by feelings of *anomie* and indifference, they seemed rudderless and doomed. Though *Ulysses* is set on a day in 1904, it is necessarily a portrait of the late-Victorian Ireland which went into its making and, as such, a remarkable outline of colonial torpor.

What had happened in Ireland was what would happen across the world in the later nineteenth and early twentieth century: traditional patterns of living had been gravely disrupted, but without the material compensations which elsewhere helped to make such losses tolerable. The people were suffering from that most modern of ailments: a homeless mind. Their small but persistent hope was that somehow they might yet manage to modernize in a human mode and put an end to the loss of meaning which was all they knew. Very few of them nursed regressive dreams of a return to the past, but they did yearn for a more bearable version of modernity. Against that backdrop, both the 1916 Rising and *Ulysses* can be interpreted in rather similar ways: as attempts to achieve, in the areas of politics and literature, the blessings of modernity *and* the liquidation of its costs. In other words, the Irish wished to be modern and counter-modern in one and the same gesture.

By the time that Joyce began writing *Ulysses* in 1914, most of the industrial world, and not just its colonial outposts, was overcome by a sense of *anomie*: indeed, the Great War was proposed by many as a heroic alternative to such meaninglessness. Joyce's project of recounting "the dailiest day possible" takes on a radical significance in that context: he wished to reassert the dignity of the quotidian round, to reclaim the everyday as a primary aspect of experience. But this was in no way intended as a surrender to that colonial life which had been evoked so unerringly in *Dubliners*. There Joyce had described an Ireland filled with echoes and shadows, a place of copied and derived gestures, whose denizens were turned outward to serve a distant source of authority in London. Such a collection of prentice stories would be written in later decades by many another member of an emerging national élite ashamed of his or her colonial setting, and taking bitter consolation in an ability to render all the futility with a wicked precision. Writing it all down may well have been Joyce's personal alternative to acts of political violence, his way of seizing power.

Each of the stories in *Dubliners* chronicles an abortive attempt at freedom, an attempt which is doomed precisely because it couches itself in the forms and languages of the enemy; and this becomes a prophecy of the failure of a nationalism which would insist on confining its definitions to the categories designed by the colonizer.

Each narrative in *Dubliners* tells a similar tale, of an impulse arrested or else enacted to a point where it becomes self-negating: in either case, the gesture of revolt is fated always to have the old, familiar tyranny inscribed in it.

The short-story genre promised Joyce an escape, a line of flight from the formal inappropriateness of the novel, which was calibrated to a settled society rather than one still in the settling. But the escape-route which it offered Joyce proved just as illusory, just as self-defeating as that which beckoned and then frustrated his characters. When he had finished the stories, he was rewarded by no sense of difficulties overcome: though they are bound together by themes, symbols, even characters, the collection does not quite become a novel. Each story moves to an epiphanic revelation of an impasse, a paralysis which marks its termination, because if it were to proceed any further it would exfoliate into a much more extensive and unlimited type of narrative: the process which was allowed to happen just once when "Mr. Hunter's Day" became *Ulysses*. Latent in *Ulysses* was this vast and multi-faceted assemblage: as Yeats shrewdly observed, the stories contained the promise of a novelist of a new kind.[6] However, their author was at that early stage no more able than his characters to fit that narrative together. All he could work with were shreds and patches, assembled to no clear overall purpose other than the revelation of such fragmentation to its victims. As Deleuze and Guattari were to write in a somewhat similar context of Kafka's stories: "never has so complete an *oeuvre* been made from movements that are always aborted, yet always in communication with each other".[7]

The style in which the stories of *Dubliners* was written was one of famished banality, whereby Joyce found his own appropriate level of linguistic under-development, taking Hiberno-English in its post-famine, post-Gaelic disorder to a degree of "scrupulous meanness".[8] Irish was for him no longer a feasible literary medium, but a means whereby his people had managed to reshape English, to a point where their artists could know the exhilaration of feeling estranged from *all* official languages. Joyce never felt tempted to try to write in Irish, and he affected to scorn its senile folk narratives on which no individual mind had ever been able to draw out a line of personal beauty: but deeper than the disdain went a kind of fear, a sense of shared trauma at the loss, in most parts of Ireland through the nineteenth century, of the native language.

The fate of a sullen peasantry left floundering between two official languages, Irish and English, haunts the diary entries by Stephen Daedalus in *A Portrait of the Artist as a Young Man*:

> John Alphonsus Mulrennan has just returned from the west of Ireland. European and Asiatic papers please copy. He told us he met an old man there in a mountain cabin. Old man had red eyes and short pipe. Old man spoke Irish. Mulrennan spoke Irish. Then old man and Mulrennan spoke English.[9]

Joyce there mocks the widespread hopes of a language revival, of opening the lines of communication to a Gaelic past: but it is obvious from *A Portrait* that neither was he fully happy with the English-speaking Ireland of the present. Though the old peasant might struggle to recall a few phrases of Irish for the Gaelic Leaguer's notebook, the truth (as Joyce saw it) was that English did not provide a comprehensive expressive medium for Irish people either. That is part of the tragicomedy of non-communication pondered by Stephen Daedalus during a conversation with the Englishman who is dean of studies at his university:

> The language in which we are speaking is his before it is mine. How different are the words *home, Christ, ale, master,* on his lips and on mine! I cannot speak or write these words without unrest of spirit. His language, so familiar and so foreign, will always be for me an acquired speech. I have not made or accepted its words. My voice holds them at bay. My soul frets in the shadow of his language.[10]

The death of language takes many forms besides fatigued cliché, and one of them – in Ireland, at any rate – was the loss of the native tongue.

The moment when Joyce wrote in English, he felt himself performing a humiliating translation of a split linguistic choice. In his writings, he seeks to express that sundering; and, eventually, in *Finnegans Wake* he would weave the absent texts in the space between standard Irish and standard English. But in the passage just quoted, he posits a harassment of the Irish student's emotional nature by the Englishman's intellectual culture. On such a subject, Joyce was resolutely conservative. He knew that the colonial education system offered Irish children an alien medium through which to view their native realities. To interpret those realities through literary forms which were alien to them would serve only to make the people seem even more unknown and unknowable. Hence Stephen's unrest of spirit.

No matter how brilliant Joyce's use of English, it would always run the risk of being seen as his way of serving his colonial master: English would be the perceptual prison in which he realized his genius, and the greater his achievements, the greater the glory reflected on the master language. In *A Portrait*, Stephen goes on to complain to a Gaelic Leaguer: "My ancestors threw off their language and took another . . . They allowed a handful of foreigners to subject them. Do you fancy I am going to pay in my own life and person debts they made".[11] The hatred in that sentence is not so much for the Irish language as for the fact of its humiliation and repression: but pay the debt Joyce does. Shreds of Irish would turn up repeatedly in *Ulysses*: and by the time he wrote *Finnegans Wake*, Joyce had learned to emphasize the ways in which Irish caused its speakers to rework English, so that the book's underlying idiom is his own idiolect of Hiberno-English. But his treatment of the language and its speakers is never confident or final:

beneath the pose of disdain lies a real fascination and an even deeper fear.

In the treatment of Mulrennan's peasant in Stephen's diary at the close of *A Portrait*, split-mindedness has grown to near-hysteria:

> I fear him. I fear his red-rimmed horny eyes. It is with him I must struggle all through the night till day come, till he or I lie dead, gripping him by the sinewy throat till . . . Till what? Till he yield to me? No. I mean no harm.

Joyce turned his back on Gaelic Ireland with mixed feelings, and no final certainty that silence, exile and cunning were answers to the challenge posed by the native tradition. And well might he have been afraid:

> Mulrennan spoke to him about universe and stars. Old man sat, listened, smoked, spat. Then said:
> – Ah, there must be terrible queer creatures at the latter end of the world.[12]

This is not just a caustic parody of Synge's peasants, but a terrified recognition that Joyce's liberation from Ireland was more apparent than real: it haunted him forever in the form of his wife. He knew in his heart that the writing of a post-colonial exile is a satanic pact, a guilty compromise, a refusal of a more direct engagement. As he wrote in near-confessional mode much later in *Finnegans Wake*: "he even ran away with hunself and became a farsoonerite, saying he would far sooner muddle through a hash of lentils in Europe than meddle with Irrland's split little pea".[13]

Joyce may well have left Ireland because he sensed that it was a country intent on using all the old imperialist mechanisms in the name of a national revival. In *Dubliners* he offered the people a look at themselves in his nicely-polished looking-glass: but his enraged audiences broke the mirror, only to find their rage fruitless, since they were left with a fragmented mirror and a broken image of themselves. The gesture of revolt merely deepened the crisis of representation. Salman Rushdie has said that the exiled writer is "obliged to deal in broken mirrors, some of whose fragments have been irretrievably lost".[14] For Joyce, writing was a measure of his own exile from Ireland, but also of that Ireland from its past, of Hiberno-English from standard languages, and of writing itself as a fall from oral culture – emigration simply emblematized these denials. Yet Joyce struggled hard with censorious printers in order to publish *Dubliners* in Ireland, because he was convinced that it represented a necessary first step "in the spiritual liberation of my country".[15] He was well aware of what happens when a colonial writer loses contact with his native audience and writes only for an international élite: he wanted to mediate between Ireland and the world, but most of all to explain Ireland to itself.

If *Dubliners* was Joyce's *exposé* of an Ireland frozen in servitude, *A Portrait* was his exploration of the revivalist illusion. It offers one of the first major accounts in modern English literature of the emergence of a post-colonial élite. The fat young man in the final chapter who rapidly listed off the results of the examinations for "the home civil" and "the Indian" was for Joyce the living incarnation of those forces which made it imperative for him to emigrate.[16] The emerging middle class did not see literature as something which might be made an element of daily vision: for them an education was a means to an administrative post. In this, too, Ireland had much in common with the experience of other emerging nations, where traditional codes often accommodated themselves happily enough to administrative mechanisms. In his 1907 essay titled "Home Rule Comes of Age", Joyce painted a devastating picture of the new comprador middle class, the constitutional nationalists whom he portrayed as working hand-in-glove with the imperial exploiters:

> . . . the Irish parliamentary party has gone bankrupt. For twenty-seven years it has talked and agitated. In that time it has collected 35 million francs from its supporters, and the fruit of its agitation is that Irish taxes have gone up 88 million francs and the Irish population has decreased a million. The representatives have improved their own lot, aside from small discomforts like a few months in prison and some lengthy sittings. From the sons of ordinary citizens, peddlers, and lawyers without clients they have become well-paid syndics, directors of factories and commercial houses, newspaper owners, and large landowners. They have given proof of their altruism only in 1891, when they sold their leader, Parnell, to the pharisaical conscience of the English Dissenters without extracting the thirty pieces of silver.[17]

Joyce was scathing about the kind of revival which would be possible under such leadership at home: more torpor, more betrayal, more unconfessed self-loathing. He foresaw the plight of an "independent" state under the constraints of neo-colonial economics: "the Irish government about to be born will have to cover a deficit ably created by the British treasury". Nobody should be fooled or persuaded by "the fact that Ireland now wishes to make common cause with British democracy".[18]

In essay after essay written in the first decade of the century, Joyce asserted his conviction that the Irish were understandably disloyal to the British monarch because they were the victims of misrule. "When a victorious country tyrannizes over another, it cannot logically be considered wrong for that other to rebel",[19] he told Triestine readers, adding that nobody could any longer believe in purely Christian motives for such policies. "A conqueror cannot be casual, and for so many centuries the Englishman has done in Ireland only what the Belgian is doing today in the Congo Free State . . ." Joyce astutely predicted that the same divide-and-rule policy which had carved up Africa would lead British conservatives to incite Ulster Unionists to rebel against any settlement with the leadership in Dublin (this was one of the most accurate predictions of partition). Ireland remained poor, he averred, because English laws were designed systematically to ruin the country's industries. The Irish Parliamentary Party might pursue reconciliation with unionists for its own Home Rule purposes, but ordinary Irish men and women could never forget the centuries of broken treaties and industrial sabotage: "can the back of a slave forget the rod?"[20] Nor was Joyce at all convinced by the good intentions of enlightened British liberals: in an essay called "Fenianism" in 1907 he brutally declared: "any concessions that have been granted to Ireland, England has granted unwillingly, and, as it is usually put, at the point of a bayonet".[21]

All this is worth reviewing, because Joyce has too often been portrayed as a cosmopolitan humanist with an aversion to militant Irish nationalism. However, when it came to prescriptions, he parted with the irreconcilables, seeing in their ideals nothing but a point-for-point contradiction of English Tory thinking.[22] If the constitutional nationalists were in danger of being co-opted by empire, the militants were at grave risk of embracing the imperial psychology in a reworked form. Joyce heaped repeated mockery on the imitation of English models by Irish revivalists.

The closing sections of *A Portrait* raise sharp, difficult questions about the meaning of a Gaelic culture which had been "lost", a loss which can be established by the revivalists only in terms of a valued English scheme of things. What the revivalists sought to rediscover was merely a projection of imperial fantasy, eventually embodied in the person of Haines in *Ulysses*. The mistake of the revivalists would be repeated in Africa and India in later decades: too often an "African" or

an "Indian" culture would simply be one which could be easily translated into forms comprehensible to European imperial minds. The
revivalists failed to recognize that tradition in that sense is always
syncretic: only a "tradition" which was the invention of the colonizers
could so facilely disintegrate to be supplanted by a ready-made modern
equivalent.[23] The question put by Mazzini to the Irish – what distinctive civilization justifies your separatist claim? – would be raised again
and again. Joyce had his own reply and it was not the expected one: "if
an appeal to the past in this manner were valid, the *fellahin* of Cairo
would have all the right in the world to disdain to act as porters for
English tourists".[24] His claim would base itself not on the past but on
the future: Ireland's conscience was yet "uncreated". Stephen Daedalus
in *A Portrait* rejects all calls to a loveliness which has long faded from
the world and prefers to seek a loveliness which has not yet come into
the world. In Joyce's hands, the *bildungsroman* was an instrument with
which to investigate the Irish experience, and the ensuing self-under-
standing was a discovery of the real Ireland of the present. After the
famines and the decline of the Irish language, the autobiographical
narrative became doubly important in explaining to a baffled people
who they were.

What Mulrennan's encounter with the peasant told them was not
comforting: it would be impossible to reclaim whatever had been lost.
The very construction of a *Gaeltacht*, a zone of pristine nativism, might
itself be an effect of colonialism rather than an obvious answer to it. In
Joyce's texts, there is a double exposure: he indicts colonialism, as do
the revivalists themselves, but then he proceeds to indict the native
culture for not living up to expectations of it, for not being an
authentic *elsewhere*. The revivalists feel this lack, too, but they respond
by making the peasant the embodiment of sacred values which the
peasant himself would never claim to uphold, converting him into a
fetish of unsatisfiable desire.[25] The revivalist thus comes to know the
"melancholy of the collector", the tantalizing hope that the next sal-
vaged lyric, the next native speaker, will perhaps reveal the holy grails
that he seeks. Yet these cultural trophies can offer no more than a
fleeting charm, for to linger over any for too long would be to confront
in them the selfsame emptiness which led the revivalist, in desperation,
to evoke them. The tragic knowledge which awaits the revivalist is that
also which attends the imperialist, who comes to the native quarter in
search of the authenticity of the exotic. Desiring a pristine experience,
Mulrennan is thwarted: hoping to recover the scope of an ancient
culture from which he was cruelly separated, he finds instead a peasant

whose inheritance is as broken as his own. There is no absolute *else-where* to be found, not even a final frontier where the theory of Irish innocence and the discontents of English civilization could come to a competitive point.

This was Joyce's perception: that Ireland is just another of those modern places, where there is no *there* any more. The nationalists who denounced England were, more often than not, denouncing an England inside each one of themselves. Their search for a pristine "Ireland" was a quintessentially English search, because it involved them in the search for a corresponding "England" as well, if only so that they might repudiate it. Since "Ireland" in such a construction was largely an English invention, those who took upon themselves the burden of having an idea of Ireland were often the most Anglicized of the natives. The devising of the ludicrous category *un-Irish* was among their weird achievements, though, in actual practice, nothing could have been less typical of the Irish than the attempt to make an ideology out of Irishness.

The problem of the Irish was not so much rootlessness as the fact that they had roots in too many different places at once – Scandinavia, Normandy, Spain, England and so on. "To tell the truth, to exclude from the present nation all who are descended from foreign families would be impossible", Joyce wrote. In the face of such variousness, a unitary racial nationality could never be more than "a convenient fiction", and that fiction would only be convenient if it could evolve a form hospitable to the many strands that made up Irish experience.[26]

Mulrennan's encounter had shown that the architects of Ireland could not know it except as a possibility, glimpsed from the perceptual prison of imperial fantasy, whose ideal peasant was indeed "a man who does not exist, a man who is but a dream".[27] This representational debacle arose from the impossibility of rendering a consciousness which, being uncreated, did not exist as such. Yet Joyce knew that the men most ignorant of a country were invariably the ones to believe that they could represent it. Even the leaders of political nationalism early this century had, in effect, to bluff the new state into being, proclaiming unification in the name of an Ireland or an India yet to follow. The more scrupulous among them, like Mahatma Gandhi, realizing that the unity which had proved invaluable in the struggle against empire might become a denial of difference after liberation, urged that the national congress should liquidate itself after independence.

Neither in Ireland nor in India were internal minorities much regarded, and so movement was frozen in its nationalist stage. Joyce, foreseeing what was to come, attempted in *Ulysses* to unleash a plurality of voices which would together sound the notes that moved beyond nationalism to liberation. After Mulrennan, there was no choice but to put oneself in the place of that absent Other that was the peasant, to take as one's own responsibility that emptiness and to fill it with the sound of voices. *Ulysses* would, like Joyce's earlier books, hold a mirror up to the colonial capital that was Dublin in 1904: but, unlike them, it would also be a book of utopian epiphanies, hinting at a golden future which might be made over in terms of those utopian moments.

Benedict Anderson has observed that the problem which besets many a partitioned state is of having been "insufficiently imagined".[28] That is hardly surprising, for the builders of modern nation-states were expected to dismantle the master's house and replace it with a better one, using only what tools the master cared to leave behind. A similar issue is raised in the opening chapters of *Ulysses*, where Stephen's problem is a version of Joyce's: he wears the second-hand trousers cast off by Mulligan, and yet somehow in them he must learn to cut a dash. The search for a true home is conducted in inappropriate, inherited forms. The first chapter of *Ulysses* is set in the Martello Tower in Sandycove, built by the British authorities to forestall a possible French invasion in support of Irish republicans. A colonial structure, it none-theless allows the youths to improvise what freedoms they can. If Joyce adopts a somewhat incongruous scaffolding of Homer's *Odyssey* for a subversive narrative, then Stephen and Mulligan attempt a similar transformation of the tower, which they plan to make the centre of a modern Irish culture. All are compelled to reshape past forms in keeping with the needs of the present. Joyce's initial chapter is named for Telemachus, the embittered son in *The Odyssey* who was angry because the land of his father was occupied by foreign warriors: in the story, false suitors of his mother shamelessly waste his patrimony, while the goddess Athene (disguised in *Ulysses* as an old milkwoman) advises him to leave his mother and seek the absent father.

Even at this early stage, Joyce employs the technique of mythical realism, juxtaposing Odyssean marvels against the Irish quotidian. This method has been shown to have been implicit in many texts of the Irish revival, especially the early plays of the Abbey Theatre, whose writers were among the first to grasp that fantasy, untouched by any sense of reality, is only a decadent escapism, while reality, unchallenged by any element of fantasy, is a merely squalid literalism. Joyce's early books, with their unusual blend of symbolism and naturalism, added much to this method: but it was in *Ulysses* that it reached its apogee. Henceforth,

Joyce would equate realism with the imperial/nationalist narrative: it was the favoured mode for chronicling the fate of the European bourgeoisie. The Irish experience, however, was not fully comparable with the European in this respect, because the Irish middle class was not yet fully formed. The split between modernity and undevelopment was obvious to Joyce within Ireland itself in the almost surreal juxtapositions of affluence and dire poverty, of ancient superstition and contemporary *anomie*. No merely realist method could do full justice to that. A form had to be created which would, in the words of Salman Rushdie "allow the miraculous and the mundane to coexist at the same level – as the same order of event".[29] That form was adumbrated in *Ulysses*.

The modernism of Joyce was not only that of Mann, Proust or Eliot: even more it anticipated that of Rushdie, Marquez and the post-colonial artists. For them, modernism did not signalize a move from univocal realism to multivocal hyperreality, but from a realism which never seemed real at all to a pluralism which did try to honour the many voices raised after independence.[30] European radicals still followed Rousseau in asking how it was that, born originals, people still died as copies. However, the post-colonial artists, born as copies, were determined to die originals. The modernizers from Europe sought to expose the myths of traditional societies to the scrutiny of analytic reason, but they never dismantled the myths which bound them to their own culture. Joyce's canny blend of myth and realism did just that, using each term as a critique of the other, so that neither could achieve its goals. Rather than levelling all differences, however, he produced in *Ulysses* a genuinely multicultural text, which didn't just redraw the boundaries between discourses at some other point. And he provided a model for the magic realists in the refusal of *Ulysses* to ground itself in a narrating subject or an identifiable author: instead he offered a text without any final authority.

The risks of such a venture are still huge, and must have been all but unimaginable when Joyce wrote. Joyce's answer was to seek a tradition and, in that very act of seeking, to invent it.[31] Such a tradition exists more in its absence than in its presence: it is its very lack which constitutes an artist's truest freedom, for nothing could be more deadening than the pull of the past. Yet the very denial of tradition can become the most potent tradition of all, the tradition of inherited dissent, which is all the more powerful for being paradoxical. Borges denounced the conceit of his fellow-Argentinian writers that they were creating *ex nihilo* as reminiscent of that moment in history when the Emperor of China ordered the Great Wall to be built and all books written before its commencement to be burnt.[32] Joyce was quite open in his admiration for, and rapturous devotion to, the European classics. "Apart from a few professors of philology, who receive a salary for it", writes Roberto Retamar, "there is only one type of person who really knows in its entirety the literature of Europe: the colonial".[33] These elements are present also in Joyce, but with a difference: he mocked them to perdition in the bookishness of Stephen and, again, in the writerly exchanges of the men in the National Library. In that scene, most of them speak in dead quotations and citations, as they are surrounded by the "coffined thoughts" of a cultural cemetery.[34]

Joyce, therefore, adopted an attitude of lofty condescension to the European realist novel. He sought a method which could treat of the superstitions of a pre-modern community, which existed alongside and within a society already developed beyond the confining outlines of the nation-state. He did this in the conviction that the religious sensibility can sometimes survive more honestly outside of church structures and official dogma: for him art could be the third principle which, mediating between the material and sacred worlds, offered that new thing, "a secular definition of transcendence".[35]

By setting the past and present into dialectical tension, the mythic method undermined the European enlightenment's notions of time and linear progress. Instead, it evoked a world of cycles and spirals, which mocked the view of history as a straight line and they set in its place another, very different model. Separate chapters of *Ulysses* overlap in chronology, and even separate sections of the "Wandering Rocks" chapter narrate the same events in time as seen from different perspectives, rendering by this means a most varied set of voices and experiences. The linear time of the realist novel denied all this and sought to dispose of time in neat parcels, but Joyce, in restoring a sense of an Eternal Now, also restored time's mystery.

One explanation of this return to the mythical is the conviction that the enlightenment project in its merely European form was incomplete. Yeats, complaining that nineteenth-century meliorists lacked the vision of evil, prayed for delivery from a mechanistic rationalism. The darker forces thus excluded were bound to reassert themselves on the peripheries: Ireland – like Africa, India or Latin America – was bound to become a sort of fantasy-land, as a result of psychological self-repression at the imperial centre, a repression crucial to the imperial enterprise. In Yeats and Joyce, and in many writers of the developing world, certain themes and images seem to recur, as if inevitably: the self as labyrinth, the notion of the environment as a place calibrated to solitude, the sense that all texts are psychological rather than social explanations.

The critique of imperial educational methods in the chapter known as "Proteus" perfectly accords with Yeats's attack on rote memory-work and on that compilation of facts which excluded all feeling and emotion. In later sections of *Ulysses*, especially "Circe", Joyce would explore the forbidden night-world of the dreamer whose censors have been freed. In a more general way, his book deliberately utilized all the discredited materials and despised potentials banished from the European mind-set, in a manner similar to the Abbey playwright's adoption of the superstitions and folk beliefs of a derided native culture. Clearly, a realist text, with its narrative stability and its depiction of intense personal relations in an ordered society, would have been inadequate to Joyce's needs: what he faced was an under-developed country under the yoke of empire and a people's culture which was oral rather than written in its predominant forms.

To understand the evolution of mythical realism, it must be seen as the outcome of a desperate refusal by native artists of the recommended European novel. In eighteenth-century Ireland, for instance, the tellers of romantic tales responded to the challenge in predictable ways. The anti-hero made his first appearance in Gaelic Ireland in *Stair Éamuinn Uí Chléire* (The Story of Eamonn O'Clery, 1710), a parodic reworking by Seán Ó Neachtain of medieval texts. The author, dissatisfied with the two-dimensional characters of the romances, seemed caught between the desire to mock them in a hilarious send-up and the wish to supply a more realistic motivation for the virtues and weaknesses of the central character.

Modern Gaelic scholars tend to see in the emergence of such an anti-hero "a noteworthy phenomenon which suggests a decline in cultural standards",[36] but it really represents the attempt by artists in the Irish language to marry their oral narratives to the forms of Cervantes and Fielding. The attempt failed mainly because there were few Gaelic printing-presses in eighteenth-century Ireland. England was undergoing an industrial revolution and a massive growth in towns, as Fielding produced his masterpieces for the expanding middle class. In Ireland, speakers of the native language still told the old romantic tales, which were filled with supernatural wonders and were recited in public to a credulous audience. The European novel, on the other hand, was a realistic account of everyday life, to be read in silence and in private by the sceptical, solitary reader. It dealt in private emotions and psychological analyses which were lacking in the world of most storytellers.

Ó Neachtain and his contemporaries did their best to conflate the two modes, but without a printing-press could go no further;[37] and nineteenth-century Irish novelists in English simply repeated the prevailing English methods, in a tradition which stretched from Edgeworth to Griffin, from Carleton to Moore. Only Joyce in *Ulysses* managed to take the form out of that rational, middle-class world and to restore some of the magical elements of the romances – as when Mr. Bloom ascends into heaven, at the close of "Cyclops", "like a shot off a shovel", thereby escaping his pursuers.[38] The deadpan narration of the attendant factual details ("at an angle of forty five degrees over Donohoes' in Little Green street") anticipate by some decades the somewhat similar ascension of Remedios the Beauty in *One Hundred Years of Solitude*. In both cases, the writers achieve their characteristic effect by a subversive *combination* of the mythical and the real.

Whether the results of their labours should be called "novels" is a highly debatable point: it is more likely that they are written in new forms for which there is, as yet, no agreed generic name. There is a strongly parodic element at work in *Ulysses*, mocking the heroic militarism of epic, the supernatural wonders of folk-tale, the psychological verisimilitude of the novel, but the form which results is in no way confined by these targets. Due homage is paid to those targets: their working conventions are laid bare, in an active exploration of each mode which is also an exercise in literary criticism: however, the parody is no merely temporary transgression, but a gesture which precedes a radical break. *Ulysses* illustrates the dictum that every great work of literature not only destroys one genre but helps to create another. Radical parody of this kind has the effect of speeding up this natural development of literary form: its ensuing narrative frees itself sufficiently from the targeted texts to constitute a fresh and autonomous form,[39] a further proof that (in literature, as in politics) the urge to destroy may also be a creative urge.

What is enacted is an energetic protest against those who would convert a once-enabling form into a life-denying formula: and that protest is based on the conviction that all genres – not just the epic basis of *Ulysses* – are mere scaffoldings, which may permit a new text to be created, but which should be unsentimentally dismantled when the work is well done. On this marvellous mutation, Fredric Jameson has a pertinent comment:

> The failure of a generic structure, such as epic, to reproduce itself not only encourages a search for those substitute textual functions that appear in its

wake, but more particularly alerts us to the historical ground, now no longer existent, in which the original structure was meaningful.[40]

Yet even this statement is scarcely enough for, despite all the mockery of those militarist elements of *The Odyssey* which have been superannuated, there is also in *Ulysses* a genuine refunctionalization of other, less disposable aspects. If classical epic depicted an individual risking all for the birth of a nation, *Ulysses* will instead present a hero living as the embodiment of community values. If bodies were pulverized in ancient epic to support its ideals, *Ulysses* will, chapter by chapter, celebrate each distinctive organ, offering an "epic of the body" as an image of the restored human community.

A *part* of each earlier form survives in the assemblage that is *Ulysses*, but it would be foolish to name the book for one or other of these genres. Insofar as it is susceptible of generic analysis, it might dynamically interelate not just with Homer or Rabelais but also with Borges or Rushdie, serving as a rallying-point for the emergence of a new narrative mode. For Joyce, the shattering of older forms permitted the breakthrough of a new content, a post-imperial writing. The danger, as always, is that conventional critics will seek to recolonize that writing, or any other baffling text by an Irish artist or a Latino or an Indian, translating its polyvocal tones back into the too-familiar, too-reassuring terms of the day-before-yesterday.

Another, even greater, danger in interpreting *Ulysses* would be to treat it as a "Third World" text which is, in *all* aspects, the very antithesis of a "First World" narrative.[41] Yet the Ireland which Joyce chronicled had its share in the making of empire, as well as of its victims. It was, in that respect, a vivid reminder of the relentless reciprocity by which one set of experiences is bound to the other. If Europe scarcely has any meaning without the suffering of the native peoples who contributed to its opulence, and if the "Third World" is but an effect of European desires, then Ireland affords a field of force in which the relation between the two is enacted within the community.

Europe, after all, was the creator of both the dialectics of liberation *and* the ethic of slave-holding: what characterizes Joycean modernism is its awareness of the need to write both of these narratives *simultaneously*. Each situation has its unique aspects and to construct the "Third World" exclusively as a manageable other of the "First" is, at a certain point, to submit to the very tyranny the phrase was designed to deplore. There is, however, a linked and even greater danger: that of conceiving the encounter as of two *distinct* worlds facing each other, rather than as social worlds which are part of one another, though differently constituted. Ireland's historical disadvantage, being a European people who were nonetheless colonized, afforded it a remarkable *artistic* advantage. The country was, and still is, one of those areas where two codes most vividly meet: and, as such, its culture offers itself as an analytical tool at the very twilight of European artistic history. It, too, was asked to remain marginal, so that other peoples could feel themselves central. Now in a position to negotiate between colonizer and colonized, it could be forgiven for strategically seeing itself as a centre. If the "west" turns to the exploited peripheries in the desire for a return of all that it has repressed in itself, the post-colonies turn to the west as to yet another command.[42] Ireland, in between, provided Joyce with a more visibly open site of contest, and a reminder that each side in that contest needed the other for a completed account of its own meanings.

The great absences in the texts of European modernism are those native peoples whose exploitation made the representations of European magnificence possible. Even writers such as Conrad or Forster who showed some awareness of the issue were unable to render with comprehensive conviction the lives of Africans or Indians.

Irish writers of the time gave English readers some inkling of the life behind that blankness: and they could do this because they wrote in the language of the imperialist, about what it was like to grow to maturity in an occupied country. Radical modernism, as practised by a Joyce or a Rushdie, has been a prolonged attempt to render this accounting, to write a narrative of the colonizers and colonized, in which the symbiotic relation between the two becomes manifest. This is usually based on a recognition by the members of a nomadic native intelligentsia of all that has been repressed in the imperial texts and all that has gone uncomprehended in the native fables. The two orders of reality, when taken together onto a third plane, make for a new level of meaning.

Ireland, in Joyce's schema, was one of those liminal zones, between old and new, where all binary thinking was nullified, and where there could be a celebration of manly women and of womanly men. He recognized the extent to which nationalism was a necessary phase to restore to an occupied people a sense of purpose: and he distinguished sharply between the xenophobic nationalism of the imperial powers and the strategic resort to nationalism by the forces of resistance. The men in the pub in "Cyclops" are a case in point. They mimic English Francophobia ("set of dancing masters"), but they are not anti-foreign, evincing a real sympathy for people of colour living under the lash in other corners of empire. Humanist critics like Richard Ellmann who castigate their chauvinism have failed to note that their range of reference is not Eurocentric, but far wider than that of most humanists themselves.[43] The law, which seems established to many Anglo-American readers of *Ulysses*, did not appear as such to Joyce, being merely a tyranny based on official terror.

Nevertheless, Joyce in *Ulysses* never fell into the trap of equating nationalism with modernization: indeed, his spiritual project was to attempt to imagine a meaningful modernity which was more open to the full range of voices in Ireland than any nationalism which founded itself on the restrictive apparatus of the colonial state. If the patriots cloaked the fundamental conservatism of their movement in a rhetoric of radicalism, Joyce more cannily chose to dress his utterly innovative narrative in the conservative garb of a classical narrative. This led many critics to the mistaken view that he offered his critique of nationalism from the vantage-point of a European humanist. A close reading of *Ulysses* will, however, throw up far more evidence of its anti-colonial themes.

As one of a subject people, Stephen can empathize fully with the Jews, whose behaviour he recalls from his time in Paris: "Not theirs: these clothes, this speech, these gestures".[44] Here is another oppressed, landless people, whose gestures, clothing and inherited structures are not their own, but the cast-offs of overlords. One of these overlords, Mr. Deasy, repeats Haines's view of history as a perpetual search for scapegoats, and he too blames various women (McMurrough's wife, and Kitty O'Shea) for Irish wrongs. The repeated offloading of blame emphasizes the need for one who will incorporate all the despised elements in himself: Leopold Bloom.

Before his advent, however, Stephen takes his walk along Sandymount Strand, dragging up ideas and images from his unconscious as he looks out over the sea. Rejecting the ideal of a restored Gaelic culture, he prefers creation *ex nihilo*. Tramping on the dead shells of the past, he intuits a radically different future, and so he rejects Mr. Deasy's stasis for a world of flux. At present, he seems able to play every part except his own, but the attempt to seize power by the act of writing has begun. Stephen's weighty self-consciousness has often intimidated readers, who may not appreciate that the portraiture is largely satiric. Joyce is dramatizing a consciousness suffering the over-effects of a recent university education, and immobilized accordingly.

Stephen's style of interior monologue is "writerly", developing at the instigation of words, unlike that of Bloom which will respond to the pressure of actual experience. Stephen's rejection of the quotidian ("Houses of decay . . .")[45] is most unJoycean, and will not be ratified by Bloom. A painfully provincial intellectual, Stephen strikes aesthetic poses in hopes of investing himself with an innate authority, but he has been slighted even by a serving-woman. He is shrewd enough in his impersonations, however, to sense an echoing falseness in the bravado of his English rulers, all mimicking the ideal type (which they are not) in a "paradise of pretenders".[46] Mulligan, a degraded instance, has seized the key to the tower, whose rent Stephen nevertheless pays, while the Englishman goes free of charge. This overlord and his Irish toady strike Stephen as a neo-colonial act, "the panthersahib and his pointer".[47]

At this stage, after just three chapters, Stephen disappears into the book, which becomes thereafter an account of why his consciousness cannot be further elaborated in that society. The consciousness of Stephen certainly exceeds all available literary styles, which it wears with a richly ironic sense of their formal inappropriateness. Where a youth in an English novel would probably quantify and test the solidity of the landscape, Stephen sees it as a mere theatre for the improvisation of a free consciousness, a summons to reverie. He is the first instance in *Ulysses* of a succession of characters – Bloom, Gerty MacDowell, various unnamed narrators, Molly – all of whom will be doomed to express real enough feeling in inauthentic form.

Finding himself nowhere, Stephen attempts to fabricate an environment: "signatures of all things I am here to read".[48] But the problem is that his learning is more dense than his setting. He is a dire example of the provincial intellectual weighed down by the learning of the European literary tradition. His world, like that of his colleagues later in the National Library, is a parade of second-hand quotations, of gestures copied from books, of life usurped by art. Joyce may have used English with a lethal precision impossible to most of his English rivals, but he was well aware of the humiliation felt by the *assimilé* who speaks the language with a degrading, learned correctness: and he had a corresponding sense of the ways in which such persons softened raw realities by the euphemisms of art. Here he mocks the manner in which Stephen's consciousness is at the mercy of literature. Joyce was himself often accused of developing his narrative at the instigation of words rather than felt experience, but this is true strictly and only of Stephen. Joyce's own texts are profoundly dissatisfied with available forms and words, and they refuse any final homage to art, celebrating instead those aspects of life which generally elude literature.

Far from being an autistic surrealist, as early detractors complained, Joyce felt that he struggled under far too many controls. Like Stephen, he tried in his art to reconstruct a world out of barbarism, to begin again with Finn again. His problem in handling Stephen was that faced before him by Synge with Christy Mahon, by Shaw with Keegan, by Yeats with his *personae*: to return a figure of such renovated consciousness back into an unredeemed community would be tantamount to humiliating that figure and destroying that consciousness. Previous writers had solved that problem by refusing the return: the sensibility of their heroes became an end in itself rather than a way of reshaping a world, and their final glamour resided in the audience's awareness that no form could be found commensurate with their own capacity for wonder, that no words could represent their heightened inner state. Joyce, however, came to this point relatively early in *Ulysses*, and so, in the fourth chapter, with the onset of Bloom, he shifted his investigation from the mind of Stephen Dedalus to the setting which thwarts its articulation.

Yet what he finds, almost at once, is that there is no "society" to report, even within Bloom's own household in Eccles Street. A few pages of interior monologue are sufficient to make clear that the Blooms can never know one another as the reader will come to know each of them. Indeed, the tragedy of the interior monologue will be revealed to lie in the counterpoint between the richness of a person's thoughts and the slender opportunities for sharing those thoughts with others in conversation. What is depicted in the ensuing chapters could hardly be called a society in the conventional sense, being rather a gathering of fugitives, of submerged groups, of clamorous competing voices and of speakers who do not often listen to one another. If the traditional European novel has a plot which hinges on a number of crucial dialogues, then this is not such a narrative at all, being constructed more around monologues, soliloquies and reveries.

What is evoked in "Calypso" is the world of the outsider Bloom, who registers his distance from the social consensus by use of the word "they" to describe his fellow humans. His Jewishness, like his Irishness and his femininity, resides in the experience of being perpetually defined and described by others, as whatever at any given moment they wish him to be. In part, this is because he remains an enigmatic open space. There is no initial physical description of him and, over the hundreds of pages to follow, scant details are let slip, beyond the fact that he has a gentle voice, sad eyes, and is of medium height and weight. If acquaintances are more readily classifiable than intimates, he retains some of the mystery and indescribability of a close friend.

Something similar might also be said of the Dublin through which he moves: its settings are only shadowily evoked, and a knowledge of them is assumed. This was a recognized feature of epic narrative, whose environments were well-known to auditors in no need of predictable descriptions. The assumed intimacy of oral narration is even more blatantly a feature of a printed text like *Ulysses*. To address *anyone*, a person must presume to be already inside another mind even before conversation begins, and so Joyce must fictionalize his reader. Yet, though he knows the traditional protocols which permit entry, his whole enterprise is to subvert them: for he wants not only to enter his reader's consciousness, but to *alter* it.

Bloom is rather wary of literature and of its tendency to soften hard realities. No sooner does he enjoy a vision of an eastern girl playing a dulcimer, as in Coleridge's "Kubla Khan", than he applies the brakes to that vision. Yet, although he refuses to use books to "read" life, he is quite keen to convert experience into metaphor, likening a poster on a nearby window to a patch over an eye. He thinks of jotting his wife's sayings onto his shirt cuff, as a prelude to including them in a story: but Joyce's own reservations about written literature beautifully negate all this, when he ends the chapter with Bloom wiping his bottom clean in the toilet with a page from *Titbits*. Writing is deathly, and in this book, the letter kills; while it is speech, especially the silent speech of thought, which seems to issue from the uncensored depths of the unconscious. Bloom's language is as oral as Stephen's writerly: like all adepts of an oral culture, he uses balanced, rhythmic language and cites proverbs and old saws as an aid to memory and adjudication.

Perhaps the most significant oral narrative cited in *Ulysses* is John F. Taylor's speech on imperialism and dispossession, a speech which described Moses bringing "the tables of the law in the language of the outlaw"[49] – and the phrase might be taken to indicate a new dispensation for literature, written, however, in the experimental language of the rebel. Yet the speech is couched in pure Victorianese, scarcely an assured basis for its own separatist argument, and admired more for its style than its content. Joyce may imply that the Celtic love of style for its own sake is masturbatory. He makes equally clear that the fragments of endless quotation ("Lay on Macduff") bespeak a nervous provincialism and the pedantry practised by a repressed people who fear that they may be second-rate. Stephen, of course, is affected by the same virus, but at least his quotations generally occur in internal monologue. Vast learning in the newspaper office is put in the service of futility, in a world where conversations lack a central set of overarching themes.

In the National Library scene of "Scylla and Charybdis", the narrator manages to mangle the names of the protagonists and to mock the widespread fashion for pseudonyms among men who fear to become themselves. The conversation, accordingly, is smothered by quotations. The Quaker librarian Lyster is treated as a man more concerned to drop names than advance arguments. He talks in essayistic clichés which show how writing can corrupt speech. In his library, as in so many others, little reading but much talking ensues. Joyce presents its "coffined thoughts" in "mummycases"[50] as deathly (in keeping with the earlier link made between printed sheets and defecation). Stephen complained in "Proteus" of having to breathe "dead breaths", which might now in the library be seen as the endless quotations from the dead authors that swirl all around him. His own refusal to publish his theory of *Hamlet* is his way of refusing to embalm his idea. The library in this chapter parallels the graveyard in "Hades", with the librarian in the role of the gate-keeper and Stephen's review of the coffined thoughts recalling Bloom's musings over the dead.

The librarian echoes Goethe's view of Hamlet: "the beautiful ineffectual dreamer who comes to grief against hard facts"[51]; but this is the purest Celticism. Stephen – and, we may assume, Joyce – is not convinced at all, pitting the brute realities of Shakespeare's actual history ("he drew a salary equal to that of the lord chancellor of Ireland")[52] against all Yeatsian attempts to Celticize a poet, whose most famous creation he sees in a more imperialist light:

> Not for nothing was he a butcher's son, wielding the sledded poleaxe and spitting in his palms. Nine lives are taken off for his father's one. Our Father who art in purgatory. Khaki Hamlets don't hesitate to shoot. The bloodboltered shambles in act five is a forecast of the concentration camp sung by Mr. Swinburne.[53]

In open revolt against that Celticism which was patented by Matthew Arnold out of the pages of Ernest Renan, Stephen sarcastically notes the latter's relish of the later writings of Shakespeare: but he proceeds to reinvent a bard more serviceable to himself, one in whom the "note of banishment" can be heard from start to finish.[54]

The trouble to which Joyce went in "Wandering Rocks" to invent a vice-regal cavalcade (which never actually happened) suggests his continuing anxiety to emphasize the colonial theme. The other procession recorded is that of Father Conmee, whose identification with members of the declining aristocracy is as notable as his relationship with the rising nationalists. The atmosphere of toadying and deference, which surrounds both figures, had dissolved by the end of the Great War and the victory of Sinn Féin in 1918. Joyce must have known that the manners, which he correctly attributed to 1904, were largely historical by the time he published *Ulysses*.[55] The respective paths of church and state do not cross at any point in the chapter, as if to suggest the tacit truce which has permitted them to carve up Ireland between them; but Joyce is also at pains to suggest that neither Stephen nor Bloom pays homage to the colonial power. Whereas others "smiled with unseen coldness", or provocatively stroked a nose, the two men are neither insolent nor craven (the usual polarity of reactions as reported, for instance, by Forster in *A Passage to India*, 1924). Already acting with an unconscious affinity, they have embarked on the mission set down by Stephen: to kill, not in bloody battle but in the depths of the mind, the twin tyrannies of priest and king.

Half-way through *Ulysses*, in a chapter of fragments, each of which represents *in parvo* a chapter of the book, Joyce adopts a god's eye view of Dublin, from which distance both men appear (like everyone else) as mere specks on the landscape. This serves to remind us that thousands of other lives and monologues had been proceeding as we read the earlier chapters; and that any might have been centralized in the book. Joyce's assumption of intimacy with the streetlife of Dublin now grows a mite treacherous, as the reader is fed a series of false leads. For example, the Viceroy who passes in cavalcade is given many titles, but never the correct one: Gerty MacDowell thinks him the Lord Lieutenant, two old ladies fancy he is Lord Mayor, and Mr. Kernan is convinced that he has just seen Long John Fanning. Though the king's man scrupulously acknowledges the salutes (which come, absurdly, even from the singers of rebel ballads), he remains as unknown to any of his subjects as they to him.

The "Cyclops" chapter, set in a pub rather symbolically sited in Little Britain Street, is Joyce's most trenchant exposure of the psychology of narrow-gauge nationalism, though it would be foolish to ignore its equal critique of imperialism. The patriotic Citizen (loosely modelled on Michael Cusack, founder of the Gaelic Athletic Association in 1884) possesses a one-track mind, which leaves him intolerant of all foreigners among whom, of course, he includes the Jews. Bloom, as an internationalist, profoundly tests the Citizen's tolerance, enabling Joyce to do two things with their scenes – to distinguish Bloom's liberationism from the Citizen's nationalism, and to show how closely the latter's ideas were based on English models which he claimed to contest. Against that backdrop, Bloom emerges as much "more Irish" than the Citizen.

The Citizen denounces British violence, but re-enacts it in his own brutality towards Bloom. He was once a Fenian, until he violated those principles by grabbing the land of an evicted tenant. His cronies, though scornful of the British parliamentary system, mimic its procedures, preferring not to call one another by name and often referring to Bloom as "him". The boxing-match between Myler and Percy is a comment on the vicarious taste for violence among Dubliners, who can nonetheless appear genuinely appalled by British military cruelty. Bloom alone is upset by these tastes, and upset in a way which links him back to Stephen, who saw the school playing-field as the source of history's nightmare. Bloom (though he rather inconsistently favours capital punishment for certain crimes) can see nothing superior in employing Irish violence against its colonial counterpart: "Isn't discipline the same everywhere? I *mean*, wouldn't it be the same *here* if you put force against force?"[56] (These views, which link him to the anarchists, will be fleshed out by later revelations that he went even further than Michael Davitt, favouring the expropriation of private property.) It is at this point that he asserts that love is the very opposite of "force, hatred, history, all that".[57] The price of uttering such a truism is eviction, as Bloom hurriedly adds: "I must go now", in the manner of a departing Christ. Later, the Citizen will threaten to "crucify him"[58] and Bloom will indeed ascend into the skies, like Christ from Mount Olivet. This man, who will finally be embraced at their meeting by Stephen as "Christus, or Bloom his name is, or after all any other" has many analogies with Jesus, a figure born in a colony to a marginal family and destined to be a scapegoat for communal violence.

Linked to this in Joyce's mind was the masochistic element in the Irish character, whether reliving the legend of the Croppy Boy (betrayed by a soldier dressed in the garb of a bogus priest) or of Robert Emmet's execution. At the climax of the hanging of the rebel, a "handsome young Oxford graduate"[59] offers his hand to the condemned man's lover: clearly, he is a version of Haines, and the epitome of the English forces now taking over the Irish Revival on their own terms. In the figure of the woman who willingly hands herself over to the Oxonian, Joyce indicates a sell-out of national interests in a moment of apparent patriotism, to the English scheme of things. He seems to have been troubled by the frequent assertion that Ireland was subdued only because the Irish were inherently subduable.

This might, by extension, be a way of suggesting that the Jews were used as a scapegoat for Ireland's problems, just as they were used by Haines and Deasy to account for England's economic woes. In this, too, Irish nationalism could be a depressing image of its English parent. Joyce might, therefore, be implying that the real problem is the failure of timid men (like the Citizen or the singers in the Ormonde bar) to tackle the British, and that they have failed in this because they are secretly in awe of them. It thus becomes easier to create a knock-on Jewish victim from within their own ranks than to face the full implications of their own victimage. So the Citizen ends up persecuting the man who gave the idea for Sinn Féin to its founder.

This is not as paradoxical as it seems, for the nationalists appear to Joyce as analogous to the leaders of African tribes who manage, in the end, to co-operate with the imperial mission. The passage read out from a newspaper by the Citizen reflects – though this would never strike him – very badly on himself:

> – The delegation partook of luncheon at the conclusion of which the dusky potentate, in the course of a happy speech, freely translated by the British chaplain, the reverend Ananias Praisegod Barebones, tendered his best thanks to Massa Walkup and emphasized the cordial relations existing between Abeakuta and the British Empire, stating that he treasured as one of his dearest possessions an illuminated bible, the volume of the word of God and the secret of England's greatness, graciously presented to him by the white chief woman, the great squaw Victoria, with a personal dedication from the august hand of the Royal Donor.[60]

The mockery of the willingness of a Protestant clergy to legitimize British imperialism is put to double-edged use by Joyce, given his caustic treatment earlier in the chapter of the Catholic clergy's endorsement of the Gaelic League: the priests listed at its meeting were, variously, academics, leaders of religious orders, parish controllers and so on. In this, as in much else, one tyranny is seen to duplicate another, though the fellow-feeling of the drinkers in the pub with the victims of imperialism in the Belgian Congo seems real enough:

> Did you read that report by a man what's this his name is?
> – Casement, says the citizen. He's an Irishman.

– Yes, that's the man, says J. J. Raping the women and girls and flogging the natives on the belly to squeeze all the red rubber they can out of them.

However, the drinkers bring an equal moral outrage to bear on the holders of petty official jobs, always a source of resentment in a city of high unemployment:

> Sure enough the castle car drove up with Martin on it and Jack Power with him and a fellow named Crofter or Crofton, pensioner out of the collector general's, an orangman Blackburn does have on the registration and he drawing his pay or Crawford gallivanting around the country at the king's expense.[61]

Though the Homeric parallel is manipulated with great deftness in every chapter, Bloom remains quite unaware of it. Joyce, committed to the ordinary, finds him admirable in his refusal to mythologize either himself or others. In a book where both Stephen and Gerty try unsuccessfully to emulate approved patterns, Bloom unknowingly achieves their desire. Refusing to conform to the prescriptions of a text, he reserves his small measure of freedom, and through his unconscious deviations, he establishes the lineaments of an individual personality. He creatively misinterprets past moments, in keeping with his current needs. Moreover, his is a "repetition with difference" and out of those differences he constructs a system of resistance to literature. This becomes the basis for a new kind of hope in an Ireland too rich in examples of characters who make themselves willing martyrs to ancient texts. Though repetition is a crucial theme throughout the book, what saves Bloom is his conviction that things can be different, while somehow remaining the same. In a somewhat similar way, what animates Joyce is his conviction that Homer can be rewritten. It would not be excessive to read *Ulysses* as a deliberate attack on *The Odyssey*, which it divests of its ancient authority by converting it into a botched-up version of *Ulysses*. The audacious assumption is that *The Odyssey* will henceforth be read mostly by those who have first learned of its importance through a reading of Joyce's book.

Accordingly, later chapters like "Oxen of the Sun" find in the rise and fall of the Irish nation echoes of a more general decline of European civilization. In a voice parodic of Haines, an Englander confesses his imperial crimes. Joyce plays with the notion that the self-discipline needed to run an empire finally drove many of its rulers mad, or into drug-dependency:

– My hell, and Ireland's, is in this life. It is what I tried to obliterate my crime. Distractions, rookshooting, the Erse language (he recited some), laudanum (he raised the phial to his lips), camping out. In vain! His spectre stalks me. Dope is my only hope . . . Ah! Destruction! The black panther![62]

Within the chapter is enacted the rise and decline of English literary tradition also.

The shipwreck in Homer's Book Twelve is re-enacted in the disintegration of all major literary styles of English literature, from Anglo-Saxon to the present. But the mockery of the Holy Family myth of Christendom extends the attack to western civilization as a whole: *everything* is negated. Early critics, in their terror at this, devoted themselves to the analytical pleasures of hidden symmetry in order to absolve themselves of the search for meaning, perhaps because they suspected in their hearts that there might be no meaning at all. *Ulysses*, therefore, offers a challenge more difficult than that held out by any sacred text, yet it refuses to become a sacred text itself.

To confront the void within the self is the awesome task addressed in the final chapters. Their schematizing of experience is intentionally excessive on Joyce's part – for example, the catechism form of "Ithaca" parodies the attempt by the Catholic Church to ravish the ineffable and to submit the mystery of life to a form imposed from without. Society is increasingly experienced by Bloom and Stephen as an autonomous, external force; and though both men meet, they feel less in direct relation to one another than they feel towards the force which oppresses them and prevents them from becoming themselves. Joyce concludes that there can be no freedom for his characters within that society: they exist in their interior monologues with a kind of spacious amplitude which proves impossible in the community itself. So his refusal to provide a "satisfactory" climax in their final meeting is his rejection of the obligation felt by realists to present a coherent, stable, socialized self.

In the macrocosm of Joyce's world is a "principle of uncertainty" which leads him and his characters to attempt an almost manic precision in the microcosm. The attempt at rigid control of the empty space which mocks all human life is a colonization by the masculine principle which loves to order, to tabulate, to map and to judge – the tradition represented by the written book. "Oxen of the Sun" had thrown that tradition into deep question: now the large full-stop at the close of "Ithaca" may signalize the cessation of the written word, the better to make way for the oral, feminine narrative of Molly Bloom and Anna Livia Plurabelle.

What Yeats wrote in another context in 1906 might be apposite here: "In Ireland today, the old world that sang and listened is, it may be for the last time in Europe, face to face with the world that reads and writes, and their antagonism is always present under some name or another in Irish imagination and intellect . . . The world soon tires of its toys, and our exaggerated love of print and paper seems to me to come out of passing conditions".[63] Joyce concurred: his own texts increasingly substituted a sentient ear for an imperial eye, and, like his disciple Beckett, he trained himself to process the voices which came, as if unbidden, from his unconscious. *Ulysses*, judged in retrospect, is a prolonged farewell to written literature and a rejection of its attempts to colonize speech and thought. Its mockery of the hyper-literary Stephen, of the writerly talk of librarians, of the excremental nature of printed magazines, is a preparation for its restoration of the human voice of Molly Bloom; and, in a book where each chapter is named for a bodily organ, the restoration of her voice becomes a synecdoche for the recovery into art of the whole human body, that body which always in epic underwrites the given word. A restored body becomes an image of the recovered community, since the protection of a body from outside contact has often been the mark of a repressive society.

Like Yeats, Joyce presented himself as a modern Homer, a type of the epic narrator even in his reluctance to begin ("Who ever anywhere will read these written words?").[64] He knew that his national culture, in which a centuries-old oral tradition was challenged by the onset of print, must take due account of both processes. *Ulysses* paid a proper homage to its own bookishness, but, caught on the cusp between the world that spoke and the world that read, Joyce tilted finally towards the older tradition. Like all epics, his would only be given its full expression in the act of being read aloud.

SEXUAL POLITICS

SEXUAL POLITICS

In the 1920s James Joyce liked to joke that his country was entering "the devil's era"; and historians now tend to agree that the next three decades were indeed "the age of de Valera". More had died in the Civil War than in the War of Independence, but once again out of the ashes of defeat the republican phoenix arose.

The new government was conservative in social policy, impartial in its handling of the civil service (most of those servants who had been trained under the British scheme happily worked on in unchanged structures), and had a proper arm's-length relationship with the army and police. The country was slowly recovering from the devastation of war and poverty was still widespread, made worse by the international economic recession of the late twenties and thirties. In 1926 de Valera and his followers left Sinn Féin and founded Fianna Fáil, which its members liked to call "a slightly constitutional party".[1] They took their seats in the Dáil as the largest opposition party (it was rumoured that some of them carried small firearms in their pockets, should any difficulty arise). As the economy worsened and the government cut old-age pensions, it became clear that Fianna Fáil would win the election of 1932. Mr. Cosgrave's government quietly and smoothly passed the seals of state office to men who just a decade earlier had denied the state's right to exist and sought to kill its representatives. A crucial test of the stability of a young democracy had been passed.[2]

De Valera was something of a world figure, well known to Irish Americans and also to the leaders of decolonizing movements overseas. He was made president of the council of the League of Nations in the year of his election. At home he announced a programme of industrialization and further deanglicization (he would remove the oath of allegiance to the British Crown from the 1922 Constitution). He also refused to pay land annuities of £5 million per year to the British, in defrayment of a loan advanced years earlier to farmers wishing to buy out landlords. Britain retaliated by taxing Irish cattle on point of entry, and the Irish duly riposted with a surcharge on British imports. A so-called Economic War lasted until 1938, further depressing the economy.

De Valera's main achievement in this decade was the legitimation of state institutions: those IRA veterans who protected his early election rallies from enemy attack in 1932 soon found themselves at odds with the disciplined new régime, but there were fewer and fewer dissidents as erstwhile republicans were drawn into the mechanisms and lured by the rewards of government. De Valera himself soon began to appear at ceremonial occasions sporting a top hat. A neo-fascist organization called the Blueshirts (after their Continental counterparts the Brownshirts) had formed itself as a private army to meet the threat of "Dev's Bolsheviks", but (despite having some marching songs written for it by W. B. Yeats)[3] enthusiasm and membership soon evaporated. After decades of high theory and violent practice, Ireland was in no mood for ideological fanaticism: a pragmatic government which could knock down some Dublin slums and build housing estates in their stead seemed a preferable option.

The year 1932 marked one thousand five hundred years of Christianity in Ireland (at least if you were taught, as most were, that St. Patrick had come in 432). A large Eucharistic Congress was held by the Catholic Church in the Phoenix Park, and both major party leaders, de Valera and Cosgrave, were permitted the honour of bearing the papal legate's canopy. As leader of Cumann na nGaedheal, Cosgrave had always submitted legislation with moral content for approval to bishops as a prelude to laying it before the Dáil; but de Valera, after the formal excommunication of republican troops by Catholic bishops in 1922 and despite his own extraordinary personal piety, had been rather slower to come onside. When he did, however, he came with a vengeance.

His 1937 Constitution was vetted by senior Catholic clergy before being unveiled to the public. Though Collins was now a part of history, for de Valera politics often seemed no more than the prosecution of their personal feud by other means. In theory, de Valera's Constitution was designed to replace that which had been framed by his rival under duress in the aftermath of the Treaty. So the new document declared Ireland "a sovereign, independent, democratic state" in the abstract: that mystical republic for which so many had longed. But there was nothing very republican about the "special position" accorded to the Catholic Church in Ireland as "the guardian of the Faith professed by the great majority of its citizens".[4] If northern unionists were offering a Protestant parliament to a Protestant people, ninety miles down a poorly-surfaced interconnecting road Mr. de Valera was offering a Catholic people a theocratic state, whose Constitution began with the preamble "In the Name of the Most Holy Trinity . . ."

Despite all this, the Protestant Douglas Hyde found no difficulty in accepting a unanimous nomination to become president and guarantor of a Constitution which many felt was less than generous to his co-religionists. Collins's 1922 model had sedulously avoided any special reference to the Catholic Church and had provided for a Senate chamber (Seanad) to represent minority interests, one of the government nominees being W. B. Yeats.

Though Yeats (like other modern writers) was to flirt with fascism in the foolish conviction that life for artists might be better under cultured despots, his fundamental political instincts remained those of a liberal republican.[5] He opposed the ban on divorce in 1925, arguing that "the price you pay for an indissoluble marriage is a public opinion that will tolerate cynical and illegal relations between the sexes".[6] He applied similar logic in arguing that to refuse married women the right to remain in the civil service would be to rob it of many gifted women and to encourage a more contemptuous attitude to the marriage vow.

On the censorship of art, he was never less than scathing. The government had defined the word "indecent" as meaning (among other things) "calculated to excite sexual passion".[7] Such a definition, while merely ridiculous to a man of letters, constituted a sacrilege to a Thomist. Whereas Plato had separated soul and body, St. Thomas had rightly laid down that on the contrary the soul is wholly present in the body and all its parts. This being so, it was unChristian as well as unkind to condemn sexual passion, a return to the dark ages when Platonic thought dominated the painters of Europe, who depicted Christ with a head of pitless intellect and a pinched flat-chested Virgin holding a stiff doll-like child. Such an art arose from a contempt for the God-given body, and therefore for the Creator who had assumed human form. Yet, within fifty years of the death of Thomas Aquinas, that art had been transformed to a celebration of the body so liberal that nobody complained when Raphael chose his mistress as a model for the Virgin — "and represented her", said Yeats, "with all the patience of his sexual passion as an entirely voluptuous body".[8] It was for similar reasons that Yeats praised Aubrey Beardsley for painting St. Rose of Lima ascending into heaven on the bosom of the Madonna, her face enraptured with love, but (he coyly added) "with that form of it which is least associated with sanctity".[9]

As the protégés of the Irish system of education sought to legislate such art out of existence, it was no wonder that Yeats could complain that Catholic schools tended to destroy the great mysteries, symbologies and mythologies which the Catholic faith, more than most other versions of Christianity, can give. He never tired of reminding Irish readers that God had taken on the indignity of bodily human form. When the Christian Brothers publicly burned a magazine containing the beautiful "Cherry Tree Carol" – in which the infant Jesus speaks from his mother's womb – Yeats mischievously accused them of not really believing in the Incarnation: "They think they believe in it, but they do not, and its sudden presentation fills them with fear, and to hide that horror they turn on the poem".[10] For his own part, Yeats never lost his humour. During one debate, he informed his fellow-senators that the three monuments in Dublin's main thoroughfare were all encouraging: the epic lecher Daniel O'Connell, Admiral Nelson (whom Joyce had dubbed "the one-handled adulterer"), and finally Parnell, the Galahad in extremis, *proclaiming that no man had the right to set the boundary to the march of a nation and pointing towards the nearest maternity hospital.*

However, by the time that Éamon de Valera came to frame his 1937 Constitution, Yeats was in poor health, the leading artists were either in exile or on the margins of Irish society, and the opposition to it was spearheaded by a group of remarkable women, many of them veterans of the old republican movement. Having caught a whiff of freedom in the revolutionary decades, they were not now willing to become second-class citizens for any man, even one widely believed by his followers to possess semi-divine attributes. They deeply resented a constitution which told them that their sole place was in the home.

The problem for these radical women lay deep in the psyche of Irish nationalism. The aisling *poets of the eighteenth century had always imagined woman not as an autonomous person but as a site of contest: the wilting* spéirbhean *or skywoman lay back and languished until deliverance came from abroad in the person of a gallant national saviour. In vain did feminists point out that her original problems were due to a similar sort of English gallant: men were the smiters in this monodrama, women the smitten. Even the age-old notion of the land as female and the ruler as her lawful bridegroom conspired in the creation of this myth; and twentieth-century British propaganda posters, depicting Hibernia as a beautiful maiden torn between the demands of thuggish republicans and solid Saxons, did nothing to dispel it.[11] There were dozens of masterful women in the national movement who had challenged these stereotypes, in the home and outside it, providing leadership, ideas, art and military force: but whatever chance they might have had of forging a state which truly reflected their interests was lost.*

There were many who argued that the chances of such liberation had never been great. In the years leading up to the Easter Rising, Francis Sheehy-Skeffington – who became well-known as a socialist and pacifist –

*had developed a comprehensive critique of nationalist hypermasculinity.
His letter to Thomas MacDonagh praised the rebels' ideals, but denied that
the war which they proposed to wage could ever be "manly". The questions
which he put were terse: why were arms so glorified? will not those who
rejoice in barbarous warfare inevitably come to control such an organization? why were women not more centrally involved? "When you have found
and clearly expressed the reason", he told MacDonagh, "you will be close to
the reactionary element in the movement itself".[12] Skeffington, who was
murdered by a British officer in the course of his attempts to prevent looting
during the uprising, became thereafter an inspirational figure for non-
violent Irish republicanism: but the misogynistic streak which he had
detected in the national movement was not so easily purged. Despite the
involvement of many strong-minded women – such as Maud Gonne,
Constance Markievicz, Louise Gavan Duffy and, indeed, Hanna Sheehy-
Skeffington – the Irish political movement remained largely a men's club.*

*Anglo-Ireland watched all these developments with a mixture of fascina-
tion and horror, but it did not go untouched by them. Writers such as
Elizabeth Bowen maintained the tradition of Somerville and Ross, leaving
a priceless artistic account of events as viewed through Big House windows.
Among the women of the Catholic middle classes, Kate O'Brien and Mary
Lavin faithfully recorded the small triumphs and quiet desperations of lives
which might otherwise have gone completely unremembered and unre-
marked.*

Twenty

Elizabeth Bowen – The Dandy in Revolt

During the Easter Rebellion of 1916, while gunfire raked across St. Stephen's Green as Countess Markievicz and her force engaged the British army, afternoon tea was served at the usual time in the lounge of the Shelbourne Hotel. We know this because Elizabeth Bowen records it in her elegant history of that ascendancy institution. She was well aware from personal experience of the uses of such nonchalance: to her, polite behaviour was something which "does really help to jack up morale".[1] When the Rising broke out, she was away at school in England. News of it was her first indication that something like a national revival had been afoot. Like many of the heroines of her books, she found herself away from the scene of the action when something decisive was happening: the national revival had been judged far too inconsequential a thing for her own Anglo-Irish family to form any clear opinion of it. "Who would ever have thought the Irish would turn out so disloyal?"[2] might well be taken as typical of their reaction.

The Rising was, among other things, a systematic attempt to restore Dublin's metropolitan status, lost since the Act of Union: the Anglo-Irish gentry were by 1916 hopeless provincials, if by provincial one means to indicate people who have no sense of their own presence. Their world, as depicted by Bowen, is one whose members are constantly isolated from the wider society around them by the great walls encircling their demesnes: major events unfold on the other side of those walls, events which the aristocrats within make a point of not noticing. Unlike Edith Somerville, who studied the Irish language and kept abreast of the progress of the Gaelic League, the occupants of Bowen's Court in County Cork built their lives on "the negation of mystical Ireland".[3] Her ancestors, she freely conceded, had driven Gaelic culture "underground, with its ceaseless poetry of lament";[4] now, though a revival was in full swing, she showed no great curiosity about it. This was a mark of baffled incomprehension rather than ill-will: in her early years, she had been so sheltered that she had no idea that Protestants did not make up the majority religion in Ireland. An only child, she was shunted between Ireland and England, away from an ailing father and into the care of a mother who died suddenly when Elizabeth was only thirteen. If she grew up "*farouche*, haughty, quite ignorant of the outside world", the sort of self-invention in such a condition was perfectly typical of her class:

> It is possible that Anglo-Irish people, like only children, do not know how much they miss. Their existences, like those of only children, are singular, independent, secretive.[5]

The Anglo-Irish curbed their feeling, because their prosperity was erected on "a situation that shows an inherent wrong", the expropriation of the native Irish. Most relationships with the natives could only have issued in unpleasant accusation: it was better, therefore, to confine them to a few loyal cooks and retainers. For the rest, "the new ascendancy lacked feeling, in fact feeling would have been fatal to it". No wonder that Elizabeth Bowen became an expert analyst of the death of the heart. She saw hers as a class which, unlike its English counterpart, achieved its position through injustice – "the structure of the great Anglo-Irish society was raised over a country in martyrdom"[6] – and subsequently failed to justify its privilege by service. It enjoyed power without taking responsibility for the wider countryside over which it ruled: instead, it simply pulled up the drawbridge. That this suited the more lethargic and unambitious commoners as well as overlords was among the least of its recommendations:

> The Irish landowner, partly from laziness, but also from an indifferent delicacy, does not interfere in the lives of the people round . . . The greater part of them being Catholics, and he in most cases a Protestant, they are kept from him by the barrier of a different faith . . . (and) a good-mannered, faintly cynical tolerance, largely founded on classes letting each other alone.[7]

This stand-off may have been less pleasant for both parties than she implies. *The Last September,* set in Cork during the War of Independence, tells of a big house whose younger members yearn for some intrusion from the world of actual rebels; and a former insurgent himself, Seán Ó Faoláin, in reading the book could not help wishing for one of a different kind, a truly contrapuntal narrative about a Danielstown House "that was at least aware of the Ireland outside . . . that, perhaps, regretted the division enough to admit it was there".[8] Protesting against the elegant self-enclosure of the novel, he asked for Irish books which were not water-tight compartments: Gogol in *Dead Souls* had linked divided worlds, and Chekhov had many stories about doctors who climbed walls. Bowen knew exactly what he meant, remarking in a subsequent interview in *The Bell* that when the Great Irish Novel would finally be written "I fancy you'll find that it has been written by a Protestant who understands Catholicism and who, very probably, has made a mixed marriage".[9] For her own part, it was scarcely her fault that she had found such knowledge unavailable, encountering in her earlier years "an almost sexual shyness on the subject of Roman Catholics".

It might be added that what gives *The Last September* much of its bittersweet poignancy is the innocence of the Anglo-Irish as they go to meet their doom:

> If Ireland did not accept them, they did not know it – and it is in that unawareness of final rejection, unawareness of being looked at from some secretive, opposed life, that the Anglo-Irish naive dignity and, even, tragedy, seem to me to stand. Themselves, they felt Irish and acted as Irishmen.[10]

This poignancy rises to a genuinely tragic resonance in the fact that, having blocked off feeling, these people now seem as admirably unaware of their own suffering as they once were so scandalously unaware of the pain which they inflicted on the dispossessed. A similar imperviousness, if not to feeling then at least to its overt expression, was noted in Elizabeth Bowen by friends and contemporaries. Like others of her kind, she lived at a certain remove from her own emotions, some part of her always held in reserve and able to monitor an experience, even as she submitted to it, with a cold, clinical precision. This observant detachment had long been a feature of Anglo-Irish writing, which achieved an almost anthropological status, seeking to view man as if he were a foreign, even non-human, witness of himself: but, in the writings of Bowen, existence takes on "the trance-like quality of a spectacle",[11] not only for the author who anatomizes it but for those caught up in it as well.

The English planters who had occupied Ireland were, in a sense, the first Provisionals, by no means certain of their tenure in a land where they would always be outnumbered by those whom they had extirpated. They knocked down the woods which had sheltered recalcitrant rebels, and huckstered off the leavings at sixpence a tree. If their grander houses seemed built for eternity, that was largely to allay the fear that they might be going home on the next boat: the exterior show of spaciousness and command was intended to mask an inner uncertainty. All they had to protect themselves against the avenging masses was an attitude, an assumed style. Elizabeth Bowen wrote that the big house of rural Ireland was "like Flaubert's ideal book, about nothing",[12] something which constructed itself around a lack, sustaining itself by the inner force of its style. This style, like the Yeatsian antiself, represented an ideal of courtly behaviour and *sprezzatura* to which the new ascendancy might aspire: it helped the founders of the line cope with the thought that their tenure might only be provisional, and it enabled the final descendants to maintain a semblance of defiant decorum long after the tradition had started to collapse. The training of the Anglo-Irish turned out to be an arduous preparation for the moment when style was all that they had left . . . for those takers of the toast and tea at the Shelbourne Hotel. The manner remained intact long after the men and women themselves had snapped.

For Bowen herself, all of this made a perfect sense in terms of her art. If the Anglo-Irish were a hyphenated people, forever English in Ireland, forever Irish in England, then she knew that better than most. At school in England, she played up her wild Irish side, yet she also tried to make herself more English than the English by her perfect decorum and style. Her truest sense of herself may have come when she was in motion, crossing from one country to another, in the manner of her heroine Lois in *The Last September*:

> She shut her eyes and tried – as sometimes when she was seasick, locked in misery between Holyhead and Kingstown – to be enclosed in a nonentity, in some ideal no-place, perfect and clear as a bubble.[13]

There is a real desperation here, for the bubble which she creates is grimly like the self-enclosed estate at Danielstown: and if you start out building a Utopia, you may indeed end up nowhere.

Bowen's own style, mannered but functional, was formed (like that of the big house) as a mode in which a desperate soul sought an assured sense of identity: she turned to art for a stability which was unobtainable in the world. That style prefigured an ideal version of herself which she might yet live up to. It had the additional advantage of offering the marooned daughter an attitude with which to address a society: "My

writing, I am prepared to think, may be a substitute for something I
have been born without – a so-called normal relation to society. My
books *are* my relation to society".[14] Nothing made full sense to her that
was not in print. She wrote not so much to record as to invent a self, a
self which lived on the hyphen between "Anglo" and "Irish". And she
explored that moment when the self peeps out of its cocoon in *The Last
September*, the novel for which she always confessed a special feeling of
tenderness.

Set in the Troubles of 1920, the story centres on Lois Farquar, the
orphaned niece of Sir Richard and Lady Naylor, owners of the Danielstown estate. Outside rebel soldiers engage in the final phase of a war of
liberation against the British, one of whose soldiers, Gerald Lesworth,
falls in love with Lois: inside, the Naylors and their visitors concentrate
on tennis parties and dances. The house epitomizes order and continuity, the values on which it is assumed that Lois will pattern her life;
but it exacts a huge tribute from its occupiers, condemning them to
cold nights and claustrophobic days. Lois feels haunted by the house,
because its lack of an inner dynamic seems a reflection of her own:

> And she could not try to explain . . . how after every return – awakening,
> even, from sleep or preoccupation – she and those home surroundings
> further penetrated each other mutually in the discovery of a lack.[15]

She is, therefore, immobilized by the very traditions which, in theory,
should uplift her.

It would be facile to present her life as a stalemate between self-
expression in Gerald's arms and doing the right thing by the Naylors,
who disapprove of such an attachment. In truth, she trusts her own
feelings too little to know whether what she experiences with the
English soldier is love. The forms of good behaviour have preceded
her to every experience. In the company of a world-weary older man,
whom she rather fancies, a Mr. Montmorency, she wonders how her
carefree dancing up the estate avenue must appear in his eyes:

> He had seemed amazed at her being young when he wasn't. She could not
> hope to explain that her youth seemed to her also rather theatrical and that
> she was only young in that way because people expected it. She had never
> refused a role . . . She could not hope to assure him she was enjoying
> anything he had missed, that she was now unconvinced and anxious but

intended to be quite certain, by the time she was his age, that she had once been happy. For to explain this – were explanation possible to so courteous, ironical and unfriendly a listener – would, she felt, be disloyal to herself, to Gerald, to an illusion both were called upon to maintain.[16]

For Bowen, there is not necessarily anything ignoble about this willingness of Lois to impersonate the kind of woman others may want her to be: after all this was the author who insisted that it is by illusions that people live. But in playing a role, Lois becomes dimly aware of a buried life within her which seems humiliated by such gestures. Like Christopher Dysart, similarly situated in *The Real Charlotte*, she feels enough to know that she should feel more, knows enough to sense how little she really knows. She, also, is effete, with the added hopelessness that she recognizes such effeteness in herself. Caught in the open spaces between a role and a self, she finds a strange attraction in a house whose very architecture and furniture provides her with those stage directions which tell an actor how to perform: "I like to be in a pattern . . . I like to be related; to have to be what I am. Just to *be* is so intransitive, so lonely".[17]

Yet, there is in Lois a real scruple about such pattern and relation: her mind is too fine to be violated by a single idea. She may envy those who know exactly who they are, but she also fears such certainty. When she finds her path on the estate crossed by a rebel Irishman in a trenchcoat, she feels a weird mixture of envy and terror:

> It must be because of Ireland he was in such a hurry . . . She could not conceive of her country emotionally . . . His intentions burned on the dark an almost invisible trail; he might well have been a murderer he seemed so inspired.[18]

The "lack" around which the house is structured is of a basic, animating principle: its members nervously rely on the mercy of rebels and on the efficiency of British soldiers to guarantee their own safety, yet they stand for nothing themselves. Lois is a good deal more compliant in these evasions than she would care to admit. When she overhears Mrs. Montmorency speaking of her in an adjoining room, she panics and rattles the bedroom utensils, so as not to hear the rest: "She didn't want to know what she was, she couldn't bear to: knowledge of this would stop, seal, finish one. Was she now to be clapped down under an adjective, to crawl round lifelong inside some quality like a fly in a tumbler".[19] All she hears, therefore, is "Lois is very – "; but what she *is*, she will never know.

The contemplation of the daily round at least allows for the post-ponement of such ultimate questions: in these matters Lois at times appears to be little better than the other occupants of Danielstown. Sir Richard retreats into worries about dinner etiquette in order to spare himself thinking of the dire destiny of his estate; and Lois, finding in Gerald's kiss "an impact, with inside blankness", effectively cocoons herself inside the house which wants no truck with him. Identity is more to be feared than desired: that kiss is, in its way, as invasive and categorical as the prowler in the trenchcoat, promising this woman only "a merciless penetration".

Yet Lois is as much a victim of Danielstown values as the Irish rebel who crosses her path: for the Anglo-Irish are as guilty of ignoring the needs of the heirs within as of the dependents without. In return for nothing, the young are compelled to adopt a time-honoured set of manners and attitudes, to be "sealed" and "finished", so that the social forms may survive the death of their contents. Living in a period house, they are effectively told to embalm themselves alive, perform approved routines, and deny all feeling. Gerald Lesworth may talk at times like a set of press cuttings, but he is infinitely more modern a personality than anyone at Danielstown, precisely because he can talk about his feelings. He is only an anachronism in the sense that he is fighting in Cork for an England of the mind, which still means something in gentry Ireland, but which his own country has long ceased to be. War has modernized the national manners: where once the English re-pressed feeling, now they express it.

A minor character in the novel, Mrs. Carey, speaking to the wife of a British soldier, "feared she detected in her a tendency, common to most English people, to talk about her inside. She often wondered if the War had not made everyone from England a little commoner".[20] Lady Naylor, for her part, is quite dismayed by the new English propensity to "tell one the most extraordinary things, about their husbands, their money affairs, their insides. They don't seem discouraged by not being asked. And they seem so intimate with each other: I suppose it comes from living so close together".[21] She regards Gerald as a most improper suitor for Lois, since he comes from a lower social class, but most of all because he is modern, i.e., English. ("They tell me there's a great deal of socialism now in the British Army", muses her distraught husband.) Gerald represents what England is becoming, and the planters believe instead in a pre-war England, which has changed beyond all recogni-tion, but whose lineaments they can still vaguely discern in the ascen-dancy holdings of west Cork. So he must die for an ideal which in his own country has long been disposed of, offering protection to a people who do not even care for him. Elizabeth Bowen was all too aware of the accompanying ironies: by the time she wrote *The Last September*, her theme was historical ("in those days" is the phrase which opens the second paragraph), and she had seen the great life's work of her lawyer father on *Statutory Purchase in Ireland* outdated even before its day of publication by the Anglo-Irish Treaty of 1921.

This tragedy of irrelevance is made possible only by the unawareness of what is at stake among the rulers of Danielstown. Whether that ignorance is willed or deliberate depends very much on the individual. Sir Richard seems genuinely distracted by household affairs; his more practical wife, however, says "I make a point of not noticing". This becomes the prevailing attitude adopted by occupants of the house not alone to outsiders but to one another. Lois turns away from Lady Montmorency's definition of her, and not merely through politeness, but as a protest against a world in which one is more likely to be talked at than talked to. She knows that if she overhears it all she will be even less free to invent herself, and more likely to be shaped by an implied pressure of social expectation. What is said in Danielstown is less often heard than overheard, as an unwelcome insight into what others may think of the overhearer.

Ideally, the young should have their part in shaping the house, in bringing in new blood; but, instead, sex seems "irrelevant" and the house asserts its absolute right to shape them. In his anger and frustration, its heir Laurence yearns for "some crude intrusion of the actual",[22] adding that "I should like to be here when this house burns". Lois also launches a covert counter-appeal to the values of the insurgents in an early conversation with Gerald, in which she marvels that, while nearby soldiers were dying, she was cutting out a dress that she didn't even need:

> How is it that in this country that ought to be full of such violent realness, there seems nothing for me but clothes and what people say? I might just as well be in some cocoon.[23]

What she wants Gerald to do is to agree, and to admit that this is hardly a state of things worth fighting for.

Anglo-Irish self-control in such circumstances is patently ridiculous but so also is the "moral" English pretence that it would be ignoble to abandon such people. In a sharp outburst, Lois voices her rejection of the role of besieged maiden, and devastatingly links her repudiation to the revivalist image of Cathleen ní Houlihan:

Can you wonder this country gets irritated? It's as bad for it as being a
woman. I never can see why women shouldn't be hit, or should be saved
from wrecks when everybody complains they're superfluous.[24]

This appeal to Gerald, early on in the book, to come out in his true
modern colours and stop playing the Galahad, is matched at a much
later stage by the moment when Lois and her friend Marda, having
stumbled upon a sleeping rebel in a mill, refuse to betray him to the
authorities. Enraged by a society in which the true expression of feeling
is inadmissible, Lois smoulders with much the same kind of resentment
as the rebels: it is, of course, a kindness to Danielstown, as much as to
the surprised rebel, that nothing is to be said.

During the encounter, the insurgent's gun had fired quite by accident
(like the balloons which seemed to burst, spontaneously and point-
lessly, at the British army dance). This evocation of a violence without
agency conveys the sense of powerlessness of all individuals, nationalists, imperialists and gentry, in the vacuum of authority left by the
Naylors. It also suggests that the big house children are subconsciously
willing the final conflagration. The rebels, like Lois and Marda, are
simply marginal witnesses and participants in a history which eludes
any final control by individuals: "not noticing" is part of their ethic
too. And yet somehow that rebellion frees both parties, returning
Ireland to the Irish, and freeing Lois and her cousin Laurence to
become themselves.

As always, Lois is somewhere else when the great events happen. By
the time Gerald dies, they are no longer lovers, so she denies herself any
false romantic gesture over him, unlike the hypocritical Lady Naylor,
who writes a letter to his mother praising the dead man's heroism and
happy life. By the time that Danielstown burns, Lois is too far away for
her response to be worthy of report. Yet there can be no doubt that the
end of the house means that at long last she can escape the cocoon: she
is free now to enter a world of risk and growth rather than languish in
one of fear and inexperience. The next tragedy in which she participates
will at least have the merit of being her own.

Bowen's Court, of which Elizabeth was sole female heir, did not
burn: instead, she maintained it, at large expense and emotional stress,
until the burden became too great, and it was sold and razed in 1960.
Many of her friends, Seán Ó Faoláin included, considered her foolish
to keep up the struggle for so long, but she felt the obligation very

deeply, even though she betrayed characteristically little emotion on the day when she finally drove away from it.[25] If the artist had shown a secret complicity with Irish insurgents in causing Danielstown to burn, then it must be said that the same artist had created the estate out of nothing: the rebel who smouldered within her was more than counter-balanced by the lady of the manor, who presided like a goddess over a world of her own creation. After Bowen's Court was gone, she began to look back with increasing tenderness on her own race and class: and the virtues of nonchalance replaced the imbecilities of "not noticing" in her assessment of the Anglo-Irish:

> If they formed a too-proud idea of themselves, they did at least exert themselves to live up to this: even vanity involves one kind of discipline . . . To live as though living gave them no trouble has been the first imperative of their make-up; to do this has taken a virtuosity into which courage enters more than has been allowed. In the last issue, they have lived at their own expense.[26]

However, this willingness to see such people even more tenderly than they saw themselves had been evident in *The Last September*. When Laurence announces that he wishes to be around when Danielstown burns, Mr. Montmorency is outraged not just by the expression of such sentiments, but by the young man's insistence that they would all be so careful not to notice. To Mr. Montmorency, life was "an affair of discomfort, but that discomfort should be made articulate seemed to him shocking".[27] To the cynicism of the modern undergraduate, he would infinitely prefer the desperate composure of the dandy: and, if *The Last September* retains the power to move readers, that is, at least in part, because it is one of the very few works of literature to consider the dandy as a fit subject for tragedy.

Traditionally, the dandy has been the stuff of comedy, especially in the brilliant Anglo-Irish example of Oscar Wilde. There are, in truth, many lines and passages in *The Last September* to which he would happily have laid claim, as when Lady Naylor voices her derisive opinion of a young suitor from a villa in Surrey, that bastion of transient modernity:

> His mother, he says, lives in Surrey, and of course you do know, don't you, what Surrey *is*. It says nothing, absolutely; part of it is opposite the Thames Embankment. Practically nobody who lives in Surrey ever seems to have been heard of, and if one does hear of them they have never heard of

anybody else who lives in Surrey. Really, altogether, I think all English people very difficult to trace. They are so pleasant and civil, but I do often wonder if they are not a little shallow: for no reason at all they will pack up everything and move across six counties.[28]

This neatly sums up the dandy's perennial problem: how to maintain an aristocratic hauteur and decorum in the absence of any available court at which to rehearse and play out such gestures. Self-conquest and self-discipline were the answers, according to Yeats, who said that there is always something of heroism in being sufficiently master of oneself to be witty. In Wilde's personal confession that he had to strain every muscle in his body to achieve mastery of a London dinner-table, Yeats found his pattern of such self-conquest: what seemed spontaneous and stylish was in fact the outcome of rigorous rehearsal.

This is why it "takes a heroic constitution to live modernism",[29] because the resistance offered by the modern world to the *élan* of a person is out of all proportion to his or her strength: hence the dandy's intermittent desire for the relief of death. Mr. Montmorency is not the only inhabitant of Danielstown who grows tired from the strain of maintaining a jaunty front: even Laurence and Lois in their more typical moments might be seen as types of the dandy-in-revolt:

> Lois thought how in Marda's bedroom, when she was married, there might be a dark blue carpet with a bloom on it like a grape, and how this room, this hair, would be forgotten. Already the room seemed full of the dusk of oblivion. And she hoped that instead of fading to dusk in summers of empty sunshine, the carpet would burn with the house in a scarlet night to make one flaming call upon Marda's memory.[30]

The dandy's craving for oblivion is "not a resignation but a heroic passion",[31] in fact the only form of heroism still practicable in the absence of a courtly backdrop. A hero thus becomes someone who knows, and says, and lives the truth that traditional heroism is no longer possible. Against the platitudinous salute to Gerald's death which causes Lady Naylor and her friends to say "It was heroic", before looking down at their gloves and dogs, Lois sums up the dandy's crisis in conversation with a female friend:

> "I wouldn't mind being properly tragic . . ."
> "If one's not quite certain, one never knows where one is".
> "– It's just that I feel so humiliated the whole time".[32]

The problem is that there is nothing for such a one to do, as she tells Laurence: "But I want to begin on something . . . There must be some way for me to begin . . . what do you think I am for?"[33]

Nobody at Danielstown, least of all Mr. Montmorency, is capable of answering that. When asked what the British soldiers are dying for, he insists that "our side is no side" – "rather scared, rather isolated, not expressing anything except tenacity to something that isn't there – that never was there. And deprived of heroism by this wet kind of smother of commiseration".[34] Nothing is left to such a man but beautiful manners and a perfect stylization of every gesture, for here indeed is Walter Benjamin's essential dandy, "a Hercules with no work". Mr. Montmorency, who had great plans for a new life in Canada, is left to attend to nothing more portentous than the folding of his wife's dresses. Of such a man might Benjamin have been thinking, when he wrote his account of the dandy's tragedy in which

> . . . nonchalance is combined with the utmost exertion of energy . . . There is a special constellation in which greatness and indolence meet in human beings too . . . But the high seas beckon to him in vain, for his life is under an ill star. Modernism turns out to be his doom. The hero was not provided for in it; it has no use for his type. It makes him fast in the secure harbour forever and abandons him to everlasting idleness. In this, his last embodiment, the hero appears as a dandy . . .[35]

The point about such a one is that he is a descendant of noble ancestors, who must now live with the seismic tremors of the bourgeois market, learning how to conceal his horror at these shocking fluctuations and deteriorations with a pose of imperturbability. The dandies, who are the final, decadent flowering of their tribes, were expected to project an illusion of control in a changing, disintegrating society: to combine astute reaction with a relaxed demeanour and facial expression. All at Danielstown are in that sense dandies, operating under a dire stress which can never be shown. Lois and Laurence are simply the ultimate versions, who sense that being a dandy is yet another role, and who protect themselves against this humiliation by so distancing themselves from their relations that even their existence takes on the quality of a performance. Finding all about them strange on principle, they are doomed to isolation.

Lois and Laurence know that it is the dandy's tragedy to be able to play every part except his or her own, to become a martyr to performance. The available forms always seem to be appropriate to a prior experience, and never to this one. Their styles end up overriding the very experiences they should embody. Elizabeth Bowen noted how this decadence had manifested itself in Anglo-Irish writing, leading real people to make over their lives in terms of available literary images, whether ascendancy Gothic or peasant buffoon:

> Propaganda was probably at its most powerful before there was a name for it. Both classes in Ireland saw themselves in this mirror: the gentry became more dashing, the lower classes more comic. We are, or can become at any moment, the most undignified race on earth – while there is a gallery, we must play to it.[36]

The relation between the Irish and English has been endlessly complicated by such play-acting, "a mixture of showing off and suspicion, nearly as bad as sex".[37] The ambivalence felt by Bowen towards the English is, in the end, based on an outraged conviction that only the Anglo-Irish had, in the twentieth century, the courage still to live the myth of a traditional England. The property which had given them their high social position was, however, now preventing them from keeping it up, a bitter dandiacal paradox first recorded by Oscar Wilde, and crystallized by Bowen when she defined an Irish estate as "something between a *raison d'être* and a predicament".[38]

Like all dandies, the Anglo-Irish were reluctant occupiers of the role, but once committed to it, they discharged it with verve:

> Husbands and wives struggled, shoulder to shoulder, to keep the estate anything like solvent . . . The big house people were handicapped . . . by their pride, by their indignation at their decline and by their divorce from the countryside in whose heart their struggle was carried on. They would have been surprised to receive pity. I doubt, as a matter of fact, that they ever pitied themselves . . . It is, I think, to the credit of the big house people that they concealed their struggles with such nonchalance.[39]

This is, of course, an implied rebuke to those natives who put on the *poor mouth* as a means of coping with impoverishment: but Bowen is also making the point that property, like an assumed style, helps to uplift morale and behaviour. A house for her is never a mere setting, but a coded set of instructions as to how its occupants should behave. The whining of the mendicant peasant, like the destructive rage of the rebel, might be traced to their lack of such a civilizing influence: "I submit that the power-loving temperament is more dangerous when it either prefers or is forced to operate in what is materially a void. We have everything to dread from the dispossessed".[40] That sentiment is wonderfully multivalent, since it also anticipates the autocratic madness of certain Anglo-Irish dispossessed, barking, like Beckett's Pozzo, their orders into an empty, contextless space.

The problem for those who choose to live only by style is that their performance is always liable to breakdown: the refusal to register suffering can all too easily shade into a reluctance to feel anything at all. It is summarized in the title of another of Elizabeth Bowen's novels: the death of the heart. Often this refusal of feeling, strangely compounded of inexperience and disillusion, is set against a background of social disintegration. Like Beckett's clowns, Bowen's ladies and gentlemen find themselves caught in a crisis of perpetual anticipation followed by inevitable disappointment, with all their days an expensive preparation for some splendid epiphany which never transpires. The dandy who begins with a taste for the heroic soon finds that there is no theatre in which to enact heroism, and so he or she is driven back into the studio and drawing-room, there to bemoan such frustration. Perhaps the most finished example of the type in nineteenth-century literature is Flaubert's Frederic Moreau, a figure who arises in the interregnum between a lost *ancien régime* and its replacement by a clear new code. Still touched by romantic theory, Moreau can nonetheless feel the emptiness within: his plight is to be sure that society is a fraud, and yet to be unsure whether the self that makes this diagnosis is any better. Refusing all risk, he permits the world to overwhelm him. "What have I to do with the world?", he asks in the manner of Lois Farquar: "Others struggle after riches, fame, power – I have no occupation".

Each self with which Frederic Moreau experiments is not sustainable for long: for the intelligence which tells him that the world is corrupt is used finally and most formidably against himself. What makes him a poignant figure is also what makes Lois and Laurence so moving. If Laurence is a reminder that the dandy is forever in danger of falling into cynicism, Lois is a warning that the dandy must cultivate illusions, even after the chance to entertain any illusions has been lost. "Illusions are art, and it is by art that we live, if we do",[41] wrote Bowen. This is the option taken up by Lois. On one side of her is the cynic Laurence; on the other is the sentimental Livvy, who thinks *Melisande* a beautiful poem and marries the first soldier who crosses her path. Apart from the temptation to lapse into cynicism, the dandy may also be beguiled into indulging rather than transcending the self: if feeling can be denied by

an assumed imperturbability, it can also be dissipated into easy sentiment by a realist, whose very nose seems already too "experienced".
Lois, a true dandy, remains suspended between codes and worlds.

As did her creator, who remained a wanderer to the end. Elizabeth
Bowen saw herself as a being without final context, and she understood
the desperation behind the attempt to build a world on nothing but an
illusion of style. This had been the complex fate of the Anglo-Irish
from the outset, but it was the last ones like herself who lived it most
fully:

> Tradition is broken. Temperament, occupation, success or failure, marriage,
> or active nervous hostility to an original *milieu* have made nomads of us.
> The rules we learnt in childhood are as useless, as impossible to take with
> us, as the immutable furniture of the family home.[42]

Yet, in that very disavowal of a native background or identity, she
becomes a voice for all those uprooted, dispossessed Irish, from the
Gaelic earls who fled in 1607, through the rapparees and exiled Fenians
of later centuries, down to the Joyce and Beckett who had to put
themselves at a distance from Ireland in order to convince themselves
that the place had ever existed.

For the dandy's tragedy turns out to have been the story of the bards
who woke up to find themselves wandering *spailpíní*, and of gentry
who were reborn as tramps. All such nomads know the truth of Wilde's
aphorism: that the first duty in life was to adopt a pose, a style, a way of
being in the world, and what the second was nobody had yet found
out. Erecting a fragile world of words in the midst of the surrounding
disorder, these artists were all hybrids, with that raffishness which is
always the other side of the dandy's elegance. Bowen saw such complex
persons as "never being certain that they are not crooks, never certain
that their passports are quite in order",[43] and above all, like those
dandies who were prone to facial twitches, "unnerved by the slightest
thing". That such a description applies as much to Gaelic as to Anglo-
Irish writers and leaders may well be what makes Bowen the Aogán Ó
Rathaille of her time and class. The great Gaelic poet who refused to
call abjectly for help had his counterpart in the woman who, when she
drove from Bowen's Court for the last time, refused to look back. The
old order left her as stranded as any of her characters, and the new
offered no place, so she was left with no choice but to invent herself:

> I think we are curiously self-made creatures, carrying our personal worlds

around with us like snails their shells, and at the same time adapting to wherever we are . . . cagey, recalcitrant, on the run, bristling with reservations and arrogances that one doesn't show.[44]

Twenty-One

Fathers and Sons

In societies on the brink of revolution, the relation between fathers and sons is reversed. The Irish *risorgimento* was, among other things, a revolt by angry sons against discredited fathers. The fathers had lost face, either because they had compromised with the occupying English in return for safe positions as policemen or petty clerks, or because they had retreated into a demeaning cycle of alcoholism and unemployment. The Irish father was often a defeated man, whose wife frequently won the bread and usurped his domestic power, while the priest usurped his spiritual authority. Most fathers accepted the English occupiers as part of the "given" and warned their sons against revolt. This did not prevent the fathers from being enthusiastic revivalists; on the contrary, their very caution made revivalism all the more necessary as a form of cultural compensation. In *A Portrait of the Artist as a Young Man* Simon Dedalus recalls the athletic feats of his youth and asks whether his son can vault a five-barred gate. Wherever one looks in the literature of the Irish renaissance, one finds fathers lamenting the red-blooded heroes now gone and evoking the conquests achieved in their own pasts. Joxer and Boyle, Michael James and Philly Cullen, these are all debased versions of the revivalist search for a hero, who can, of course, only be a hero if his deed has been done in the past.

In a colony the revolt by a son against a father is a meaningless gesture, because it can have no social effect. Since the natives do not have their hands on the levers of power, such a revolt can neither refurbish nor renew social institutions. To be effective it must be extended to outright revolution, or else sink back into the curtailed squabbles of family life.[1] The pressure and intensity of family life in such a setting is due to the fact that the family is the one social institution with which the people can fully identify. The law, the state apparatus, the civil service, and even the official churches are in some sense alien. Albert Memmi noted disconsolately how few of his fellow-

Tunisians under occupation showed any awareness of, much less aptitude for, government: they were simply subjects rather than citizens. This lack of civic commitment he adduced as the major reason why colonized peoples are usually among the last to awaken to national consciousness. When the sons of each generation rebelled, they soon saw the meaninglessness of their gesture and lapsed back into family life, as into "a haven in a heartless world": yet it was a haven that, in every respect, reflected the disorder of the outside colonial dispensation. The compromised or broken father could provide no convincing image of authority. In Memmi's words: "It is the impossibility of enjoying a complete social life which maintains vigour in the family and pulls the individual back to that more restricted cell which saves and smothers him".[2] All that remains is for the son, thus emasculated, to take the place of the weak and ineffectual father.

The classic texts of the Irish renaissance read like oblique meditations on this theme. Many secondary artists, such as Patrick Pearse and Patrick Kavanagh, wrote about the over-intense, clutching relationship between mother and son without displaying any awareness of the underlying implication that the very intensity of the mother-son relationship suggests something sinister about the Irish man, both as husband and father. Women sought from their sons an emotional fulfilment denied them by their men, which suggests that the husbands had often failed as lovers: but the women could not have achieved such dominance if many husbands had not also abdicated the role of father. The space vacated by the ineffectual father was occupied by the all-powerful woman, who became not just "wife and mother in one"[3] but surrogate father as well. Many primary writers – Joyce, Synge and O'Casey among them – therefore sidestepped the cliché and resolved to examine the deeper problem of the inadequate Irish male.

O'Casey is famous for his juxtapositions of industrious mothers and layabout fathers, of wronged girls and unscrupulous, sweet-talking men. In *Juno and the Paycock* Mary Boyle is left pregnant by a rascally schoolmaster and then disowned by her boyfriend of long standing. All this she can take. It is only when her father disowns her and her child that she breaks down: "My poor little child that'll have no father". Mrs. Boyle's rejoinder is O'Casey's terse epitaph on the Irish male: "It'll have what's far better. It'll have two mothers".[4]

That same indictment of Irish fatherhood echoes through the work of Joyce, who chronicles a whole series of unreliable, inadequate or absent fathers, priests and authority figures. The Stephen who at the beginning of *A Portrait* proclaimed his father "a gentleman" ends by scoffing at him as "a praiser of his own past".[5] By the start of *Ulysses* he has fled the father in search of an alternative image of authority and self-respect: "Why did you leave your father's house?" asks his saviour, only to be told "To seek misfortune".[6] At the core of Joyce's art is the belief that fathers and sons are brought together more by genetic accident than by mutual understanding, and that most sons are compelled to rebel. "Who is the father of any son that any son should love him or he any son?"[7] asks Stephen. Pondering his dead mother's love, he wonders "Was that then real? The only true thing in life?"[8] So the basic groundwork of *Ulysses* is identical to that of *Juno* – the truth of maternity interrogates the myth of paternity.

Similarly, Synge's plays depict a rural Ireland whose enterprising males are either in jail, the grave or America, leaving such "puny weeds" as Shawn Keogh to inherit the land. In this kind of place, father-killing may be a moral necessity as well as a dire compulsion. In Synge's *Playboy*, frustrated young women lament the banality of their confessions to Father Reilly, "going up summer and winter with nothing worthwhile to confess at all";[9] and Pegeen condemns a father who believes so little in protecting his daughter that he abandons her for the flows of drink at Kate Cassidy's wake – an all-male affair that ends with "six men stretched out retching speechless on the holy stones".[10] What brings Pegeen and Christy together is their shared belief that fathers are intolerable, since Christy was driven to "kill" his father, who tried to earn extra drinking money by marrying off his hapless son to the horrendous Widow Casey. It is no surprise to learn that, although Mahon's other children have abandoned him, they are still haunted by his ghost: "and not a one of them, to this day, but would say their seven curses on him, and they rousing up to let a cough or sneeze, maybe, in the deadness of the night".[11] Both Synge and Joyce depicted motherless sons in their masterpieces, the better to dramatize the real roots of the problem of the Irish male as inadequate father.

Although Joyce, Synge and O'Casey all vividly describe the widespread disenchantment with the Irish male as father, none of them offers a convincing analysis of the causes of parental failure. And this despite the fact that a remarkable number of the foremost writers of the period either lost their fathers at an early age (Synge, O'Casey), had ineffectual fathers (Joyce, Shaw, O'Connor), or had fathers who might be described as gifted failures (Yeats, Wilde). The tortuous attempts by certain non-Irish critics to account for the recurring theme of weak paternity may make us glad that the artists did not similarly seek to explain away the phenomenon. One reason for the obsession is hinted at in the opening story of *Dubliners*, where Joyce depicts an orphaned boy fighting free of the oppressive aura that surrounds a dead and discredited priest. In Synge's *Playboy* the priest never appears onstage, as if to suggest that he is no longer an authoritative force in the people's lives. The orphaned youth and discredited priest seem paradigms of a late-Victorian culture deprived both of God and of the consolations of a received code. "If there is no God", cries out a baffled soldier in a novel of Dostoevsky, "then how can I be a captain?" Many a Victorian father may have asked the same question about his own fatherhood, just as many a Victorian son may have decided, with another of Dostoevsky's characters, that after the death of God anything – even father-murder – was possible. It is no accident that the self-invented Christy Mahon promises Pegeen Mike the illicit delights of poaching fish in Erris "when Good Friday's by".[12] Henceforth, the day on which God died will be the day on which man learns to live.

This revolt of an artistic son against an unsatisfactory father was, of course, a leitmotif that spanned the literature of Europe from D. H. Lawrence to Thomas Mann in the early years of the twentieth century. The breakneck speed of change in society gave added force to the concept of "generation", and the gap which had always separated fathers from sons grew so wide as to suggest that the young and old inhabited totally different countries. For the first time in history, perhaps, writers found themselves forced to write solely for their own immediate generation – as F. Scott Fitzgerald joked, an artist speaks to "the youth of today, the critics of tomorrow and the schoolmasters of ever afterward".[13] To a modernist generation intent on making things new, the fact of fatherhood was an encumbrance and an embarrassment. The emerging hero was self-created like Jay Gatsby, who sprang from some Platonic conception of himself, or an orphan of indeterminate background, or a slayer of fathers.

There were, however, particular pressures in Ireland which gave that revolt an added urgency. The fathers were often broken men, and emigration had robbed the community of potential innovators. In such a context, the revivalist search for heroic models could take on a negative overtone: in a land peopled by Michael Jameses and Simon Dedaluses, the cult of heroism might as easily be a confession of impotence as a spur to battle.

Whenever a social order starts to crumble, these dramas are enacted in a reversal of the relations between fathers and sons. Frantz Fanon observes that, as families break up into their separate elements under the new stress, the true meaning of a national revival emerges: "Each member in this family had gained in individuality what it had lost in belonging to a world of more or less confused values".[14] Women assert their independence of fathers and husbands, often appearing more manly than their partners: this masculinization of Irish women may be found in many classic works of the Irish revival. Equally telling is Fanon's account of the men. At first, he says, the father gives the impression of indecision and evasiveness, while even those sons who have adopted nationalist positions remain deferential in the home. With the coming of revolution, "the person is born, assumes his autonomy and becomes the creator of his own values". The father still recommends prudence but the son, in rejecting that counsel, does not reject the father. "What he would try to do on the contrary", writes Fanon, "would be to convert the family. The militant would replace the son and undertake to indoctrinate the father".[15]

Thus, Christy Mahon walks off the stage in control of his delighted parent in a situation which has been captured by Fanon: "At no time do we find a really painful clash. The father stood back before the new world and followed in his son's footsteps".[16] The old-fashioned respect for the young, which Wilde had jocosely suggested might be dying out at the start of the 1890s, would be evident again for three decades, even in the poetry of Yeats, whose denunciations of old age are a pervasive theme. Common to many great authors of the Irish *risorgimento* is the notion of self-begetting. Wilde's enactment of this myth has been fully described: but Shaw's career was predicated even more self-consciously on the glories of the man who fathers and authorizes himself. His father was wholly inadequate, in both the breadwinner's and the paternal role. George Carr Shaw took his young bride Lucinda to that unlikeliest of honeymoon spots, Liverpool, and got so drunk on the first night that he was incapable of sexual activity and had to be undressed by his frustrated partner. When she opened his wardrobe and a shower of bottles cascaded out, she knew that she was doomed. In later years, young Bernard would ask "Mother, is papa drunk?", only to receive the bitter reply "Is he ever anything else?"[17]

Shaw grew so ashamed of his connection to this inadequate father that he suppressed the very names which linked them, recreating himself as "GBS", "the self-invented child of his own writings".[18] When the public records office in Dublin was burned years later during the Civil War, the playwright announced a further breach with his ancestry by boasting to journalists: "I am an Irishman without a birth certificate".[19] The genteel poverty induced by the father's drunkenness meant that Shaw escaped university and the generally desultory attempts by headmasters to educate him in received ideas. His mother was so busy pursuing her musical career that she neglected him, with the consequence that "all the work of disciplining and educating myself, which should have been done for me as a child, I had to do for myself".[20] Indeed, Lucinda Shaw was so distracted by her music-teacher Vandaleur Lee that her son sometimes wondered whether this man, and not George Carr Shaw, might not be his actual father. He was happy, at all events, to appoint Lee as a sort of surrogate father, along with his uncle Walter:

> This widened my outlook very considerably. Natural parents should bear in mind that the more supplementaries their children find, the better they will know that it takes all sorts to make a world. Also, that though there is always the risk of being corrupted by bad parents, the natural ones may be – probably ten per cent of them actually are – the worst of the lot.[21]

Here, as in the cases of Yeats, Joyce and many others, the revolt of the son is not the usual cliché of rebellion against a tyrannical parent, but the subtler instance of a protest against a colourful but self-divided father's inability to offer any clear lead at all.

All children in colonies, writes Salman Rushdie in *Midnight's Children*, possess this power to reinvent their parents and to multiply their fathers as the need arises. Saleem Sinai, the protagonist of Rushdie's novel, has "the gift of inventing new parents for myself whenever necessary":[22] since he was born at the founding moment of the new state, this is appropriate, because India too is trying to father itself. A land which was an imperialist fiction attempts to constitute itself an irrefutable fact, with "a new myth to celebrate, because a nation which had never previously existed was about to win its freedom . . . catapulting us into a country which would never exist, except by the efforts of a phenomenal collective will".[23] Androgyny becomes in that book the prerequisite of the person who would become his own father, and mother too.

In Joyce's *Ulysses*, likewise, Stephen Dedalus becomes "himself his own father", "made not begotten", on the selfsame principle which leads Christy Mahon to liquidate his own father in order to be free to conceive of himself. This repudiation of the biological parent in a colonial situation takes on a revolutionary character, since it involves not just a rejection of authority but of all official versions of the past; and it proclaims a determination to reinvent not only the self but the very conditions which help to shape it. Inventing a better father necessarily demanded that Irish writers invent an alternative version of the past. Fathers, in such a situation, often give children "the impression of being undecided, of avoiding the taking of sides, even of adopting an irresponsible and evasive attitude".[24] If the child were to confine his points of reference to the family unit, the ensuing frustrations could prove "traumatic": but, under stress of events, a younger generation which had previously looked to the father to determine its values now discovers that each must seek them for him- or herself.[25]

Of no spiritual progress are these remarks more true than of the life of W. B. Yeats as traced in *Autobiographies*, which he had intended to call *Father and Son* until his discovery that Edmund Gosse had already used the title.[26] Yeats's was the story of a father who had made "being undecided" a vocation, reworking and revising his paintings to such a degree that the man ruined his own career.[27] John Butler Yeats praised the myopic sincerity of Polonius – "to thine own self be true" – perhaps because his own personality was so irresolute and indeterminate. Looking back over many years, the son wrote: "it seems to me that I saw his mind in fragments, which had always hidden connections I only now begin to discover".[28] It was left to the son to articulate a holistic vision which was implicit but unexpressed in the father's life. John Butler Yeats had, indeed, held up Edward Dowden as a perpetual warning of what happens to gifted men who refuse to trust their own natures and so cannot become themselves, lapsing into provincialism. In other words, he read his own fate in Dowden's, as surely as William Butler Yeats read his own possible destiny in his father's.

The autobiography thus becomes a sustained and strenuous attempt to vindicate the father's insistence that "some actual man" be felt behind a poem, "with a speech so natural and dramatic that the hearer would feel the pressure of a man thinking and feeling".[29] In short, it will in its final moments bring into being – rather than simply report – the self which lay in fragments behind all of it until that point; and so Yeats also will be reborn as the self-invented child of his own writings. The Prodigal Father was delighted rather than dismayed by this implementation of his secret desire. The son, rejecting the father's prudent counsel, did not reject the father, recruiting his experience in the creation of a new set of values. Indeed, so "reinvented" did John Butler Yeats feel by his more famous offspring that he chose to end his days in New York, as far as seemed decent from the son's pervasive influence.

The self thus created becomes thereby the ideal reader of the text, of which it is the son and creation. But the process is nothing like as easy as that glib formulation makes it seem. For one thing, there is the problem of inappropriate form; for another, there is the impeding culture of censorship. The opening pages of Joyce's *Portrait* encapsulate the problem, in the story told about a moocow by Stephen's father and in Stephen's song:

> O, the wild rose blossoms
> On the little green place.

"That was his song" – but, of course, it wasn't since it was derived; and, furthermore, it was liable to mistaken, childish recitations:

> O, the green wothe botheth . . .[30]

The language which so enmeshes the child is the language of the father. The hand lifted by Christy Mahon against Father Time Bearing his Scythe, the hand raised against the wielder of the *logos*, is the same hand which arrogates to itself the right to reshape the given lines into the contours of art, symbolized by a green rose. Synge and Joyce, after all, tell versions of the same story. At the start of *The Playboy*, Christy Mahon is given a narrative by the villagers, effectively telling him who he is, but he ends by writing his own script: "I'll go romancing . . ." Similarly, at the outset of *A Portrait*, Stephen hears the father's tale of a moocow, but concludes the book writing a poem and a diary.

Yet Stephen's final mastery is of a limited kind, involving many humiliating compromises with a received language. He recognizes, as he performs in the school play, that his script has been written by others: "the thought of the part he had to play humiliated him".[31] Even his own poem seems derivative, nineties-ish pastiche. Yet underlying the book is the desire to find an enabling narrative, which would permit a person to represent the self: as Hannah Arendt has written in another context –

> The principle of explanation consists in getting the story told – somehow, anyhow – in order to discover how it begins . . . The basic assumption is that the telling of the tale will itself yield good counsel. This second look at his own history can transform a man from a creature trapped in his own past to one who is freed of it.[32]

The older generation in a colony on the eve of revolution behaves with irresolution: suspicious of occupier values, it finds, nonetheless, that it cannot break through to a newer system. The young write narratives attacking the old in hopes of forcing their parents into a declaration of their "true" underlying feelings. All of this serves merely to erode even further the self-confidence of the elderly, to a point where their influence virtually ceases to exist. The result is a fatherless society, in effect a society on a semi-permanent war footing; and so it is no surprise when the vacuum thus created is filled by the self-created codes of the young.

The Freudian theory of patricide is but an extreme version of this story: for "it is not Oedipus which produces neurosis; it is neurosis – a desire that is already submissive and searching to communicate its own submission – that produces Oedipus".[33] What was written, again and again through the Irish revival, was an *Anti-Oedipus*, which saw the ancient tale not as awful tragedy but as happy comedy. True, the children of Oedipus felt the pangs of fear and guilt which assailed the scattered offspring of Old Mahon – but Christy's comic patricide becomes the basis of a true morality, and it is his insurgency which makes History possible. The ensuing search for a father-surrogate may be rooted in a desire to erase the memory of the necessary patricide . . . but no surrogate and no actual father can suffice for the child who must invent a self. For, as Nietzsche wrote:

> With what water could we cleanse ourselves? . . . Shall we ourselves not have to become Gods, merely to seem worthy of it? There never was a greater event and on account of it, all who are born after us belong to a higher history than any history hitherto.[34]

The fathers in *A Portrait* and *The Playboy* are so unvital that they can scarcely *see* their sons at all. Having told Stephen the moocow story, "his father looked at him through a glass".[35] Old Mahon, on reaching the Mayo village, fails utterly to recognize his son in other people's descriptions of him. But it is the fathers who are crucially absent from their own lives: in any but the biological sense, they are scarcely fathers at all. Hence the repeated use of the forename "Stephen" in *A Portrait* rather than the ridiculed surname of the father ("What kind of a name is that?").[36] The progress of Stephen is registered through the book, despite the inevitable humiliations and compromises, in his increasing control over the language which repeatedly threatened to control him. In its phases, it uncannily recapitulates the growth of Christy Mahon through three distinct zones of discourse: from the discourse imposed by others at the outset, through the excessively flowery idiom of the adolescent period, to the terseness of the diary.

That said, it should be added that this constant preoccupation with father-figures in revival texts is the tell-tale sign of a society which is unsure of itself and of its ultimate destiny. Its rebellions are conducted not so much against authority figures as against their palpable absence. These gestures rehearse not the erosion of power so much as the search for a true authority, and in them will lurk the danger of re-Oedipalization. The revolutionary slaying-of-the-father most often ends simply by instituting some new father or authority-figure. The very notion of a self-inventing, fatherless being is rooted in the actual experience of a real father; and re-Oedipalization proves difficult to avoid. Freud himself was a case in point. In his Viennese years, he had developed the theory that all politics are reducible to the primal conflict between father and son. As a boy, he had been reprimanded by his father for urinating in his trousers: "The boy will come to nothing!" This was, he suspected, the source of his subsequent ambition: at that moment he decided to show his father that he *could* amount to something. Years later, as a successful adult, he had what he called, significantly, his "revolutionary dream", in which a strong son reprimanded a guilty father for the same offence.[37] Though this was a revenge of sorts, it did not trouble the inherited Oedipal categories: Freud, as is well known, was at pains to proclaim his "fatherhood" of psychoanalysis, and it was precisely in that role that he was rejected by Jung and Rank.

In Irish political and social life, matters did not unfold as in the texts of Wilde, Synge and Joyce, or as in the theories of Fanon and Memmi. Instead, the fathers had their revenge on the sons for daring to dream at all. What was conceived as a journey to an open future became instead a nostalgic regression into a protected past. Such an apostasy was possible once the leaders of the emerging nation-state decided to make adolescence itself into an ideology. In other words, the state was to be frozen in Synge's mirror-gazing second phase, and revivalism was made into an end in itself rather than a means by which to prise open the future. Those who had begun with the claim to have invented new forms of politics almost all ended as conservatives; and it was the military heroism, rather than the creative and critical thought, of the 1916 rebels which they celebrated.

In retrospect, it became clear that in many nationalist treatments of the father-son theme, there had been confusion over who might win the trial of strength, and also over *who was really who*. The nationalists seemed young, but their muse was old . . . as Yeats had warned in a bitter poem:

ON HEARING THAT THE STUDENTS OF OUR NEW
UNIVERSITY HAVE JOINED THE AGITATION AGAINST
IMMORAL LITERATURE

Where, where but here have Pride and Truth,
That long to give themselves for wage,
To shake their wicked sides at youth
Restraining reckless middle age?[38]

The tight-lipped young idealists were easy prey for those who asked
them to harness their talents to an unmodified colonial administrative
machine; and in so doing they betrayed whatever youthfulness they
had. Rebels against an authority which failed to be authoritative, they
turned out to be in many cases arch-conservatives. The rhetoric of
youth was widely used in the new state, but often to occlude the fact
that many (including many young dissidents) were being barred from
their rightful share in the determination of national policy.

In that context, the passivity of males and the assertiveness of females
in many texts of the revival may be judged to have carried with it a
conservative undertow. The historian Peter Gay noted a similar con-
junction in the art of Weimar Germany; "again and again there are
scenes in which the man puts his head, helpless, on the woman's
bosom".[39] In a culture of chronic male unemployment, such moments
seem explicable as male self-hatred. If so, the "truth of maternity" and
"myth of paternity" may have indicated an element of self-laceration in
the art of some Irish males. Gay's comment on the Weimar scene can
be translated, with only a little strain, into terms appropriate to life in
the new Irish state: "the revenge of the father and the omnipotence of
the mother . . . were both equally destructive to the youth".[40]

Critics of such an analogy, and of the preceding analysis, might argue
that a fiercely patriarchal system, such as colonialism, could hardly have
left men feeling useless in their domestic spheres; and there is ample
evidence to show that the head of the Irish household was often just as
autocratic as his British counterpart. It can, indeed, be argued that the
patriarchal society of which he was a part would lead the Irish male to
strive all the more for control within his own family, if only because of
his political and social impotence outside it. But the evidence of Irish
texts and case-histories would confirm the suspicion that the autocratic
father is often the weakest male of all, concealing that weakness under
the protective coverage of the prevailing system. The fathers in Joyce's
Dubliners come home to beat their sons, in part as a response to the

fact that they are tyrannized in the office. Patriarchal values exist in societies where men, lacking true authority, settle for mere power.

Recent refinements in psychiatric theory may help to explain the psychological process at work. Children with problems have traditionally been described as mother-dominated, but such problems may often be attributed to the *father's* refusal to assume full responsibility. It is argued that the father's role is central in the second year of a child's life: the toddler needs space in which to achieve the beginnings of independence, but the mother feels a natural sadness at the prospect of a less intimate bond. The father at this point must try to compensate for this loss by reclaiming his place as partner, as well as by fulfilling the duties of father. If he fails to do so, he makes it harder for the mother and child to take the necessary steps back from one another. Many fathers in societies may lack the self-confidence, or hope for the future, that such a deed demands; and by failing to intervene at the right moment they launch another generation into a further hopeless cycle.

On the other hand, those fathers who *can* demonstrate that they are not under the mother's control help to cure the child of absolute dependency. By asserting his due authority over his children, the father allows them to explore their own anger until they can control it at will and learn to stand up for themselves. Even more importantly, the father teaches the child that other people have needs too, and that everyone functions as a member of wider and wider groups.[41] When such fatherly authority is not asserted, the child may become a self-indulgent subversive with no respect for the configurations of the larger community . . . in other words, a rebel.

Modern Ireland appears to have produced many such, according to a clear-cut formula which illustrates the foregoing analysis: weak fathers make way for clutching mothers to raise rebel sons. If the father does learn to assert himself, on the other hand, the child can begin the task of achieving a vision of society as a whole and the even more exhilarating challenge of framing an alternative. Such reassertion of himself by the father is *not* a return to patriarchal values: it is no more than a proper manliness. Patriarchy is, rather, the tyranny wrought by weak men, the protective shell which guards and nurtures their weakness.

Ireland produced more than its fair share of conservative rebels, and very few revolutionaries imbued with a vision of an alternative society. After independence, a fear of the bleakness of freedom had so gripped the people that autocracy and censorship were the order of the day. Re-Oedipalization became manifest in all walks of life, brought on by sheer exhaustion: the energy consumed in expelling the British had been so great that there was little left with which to reimagine Ireland. Virginia Woolf convinced herself that she could detect signs of the same fatigue in *Ulysses*, which she explained as follows: "Where so much strength is spent in finding a new way of telling the truth, the truth itself is bound to reach us in rather an exhausted and chaotic condition".[42] Her remark applies more to the Ireland abandoned by Joyce than to the liberationist poetics of his wonderful book.

Against the polyvocal pluralism of *Ulysses*, the new state rapidly proved itself rigid and autocratic in character. In *The Fear of Freedom*, Erich Fromm showed how such a character worships the past, believing that what has been will eternally be: "To wish or work for something that has not yet been before is crime or madness. The miracle of creation – and creation is always a miracle – is outside his range of emotional experience".[43] Creative attention would mean giving one's attention not to the injured Samaritan, so much as to the full person whom this act of imaginative kindness will bring into being. What is true of individuals may also be true of nations, so that a real patriotism would base itself not on the broken bones and accumulated grudges of the national past, but on an utterly open future. Unhappily, this was not to be in Ireland, and for an entirely predictable reason. The Irish language and culture were in decline, with the result that those who suffered from a tenuous sense of selfhood tended to prostrate themselves before apparently charismatic leaders. Incapable of self-sufficiency, many people nursed feelings of hatred for the authority which had so humiliated them. The way out of this crisis was to idealize some ordinary mortal – Parnell, Collins, de Valera – as the super-epitome of the history that was overtaking them. This idealization harmlessly drained off the accumulated feelings of hatred, while the glamour surrounding the "uncrowned king" or "chief" converted the humiliation into intelligent obedience.[44] The accompanying pathology might be described as "revivalist".

The paralysis that Fanon detected in certain newly-independent African states also gripped independent Ireland:

> The leader pacifies the people . . . unable really to open the future . . . We see him endlessly reassessing the history of the struggle for liberation. The leader, because he refuses to break up the national bourgeoisie, asks the people to fall back into the past – and to become drunk on remembrance.[45]

Such a leader has no comprehensive programme: he desires not so much to lead as to occupy the position of leader. So, in the Irish case,

Éamon de Valera, the "boy from Bruree" must be the subject of endless radio broadcasts to remind listeners of his rise from humble country cottage dweller to shaper of a nation. That the nation is *not* being shaped is what this self-mythologizing is designed to occlude: this type of hero, confronted with each crisis of statecraft, can do little more than repeat the tale of his own apotheosis. History, under such a dispensation, ceases to be progressive, becoming instead an endless repetition of familiar crises, with no hope of resolution. The fight becomes more important than the thing fought for, and "history" is deemed history only if it exactly repeats itself.

In *Life Against Death*, the psychoanalyst Norman O. Brown points out that "under the condition of repression, the repetition-compulsion establishes a fixation to the past, which alienates the neurotic from the present and commits him to the unconscious quest for the past in the future. Thus neurosis exhibits the quest for novelty, but underlying it, at the level of the instincts, is the compulsion to repeat".[46] This is doubtless the sort of revivalism which Conor Cruise O'Brien had in mind when he accused his countrymen of seeming determined to commemorate themselves to death. It is instructive, in that context, to contrast the behaviour of the Irish electorate in the 1930s and 1940s – which consistently re-elected ex-gunmen who talked repeatedly of past gunplay – with that of their counterparts in Britain, who unsentimentally disposed of Winston Churchill after World War Two lest his once-valued martial rhetoric come between them and a welfare state.

In Ireland, following a limited form of independence in 1922, the shutters came down on the liberationist project and the emigrant ships were filled not just with intellectuals but with thousands of young men and women. People began to emigrate not only from poverty or the hated law, but also because the life facing them was tedious and mediocre. The revivalists had won: the fathers with their heroes and ghosts from the past. The revolutionaries were snuffed out: the sons with their hopes of self-creation in the image of an uncertain future. Yet the revenge of the fathers was barren in almost every respect, since it represented a final surrender to received modes of thought. A renaissance, which should have extended personal freedoms, served only to confirm the pathology of dependency.

One final explanation for this failure may lie in the fact that the father/son dichotomy was, if anything, too sharp in the Ireland of the time. Late marriage among adults had led to huge gaps of age between parents and children; and the constant emigration of people in their thirties and forties often left towns and villages without an "intermediary generation" to help the old and young adjust to one another:

In ordinary times, younger generations must adjust to the way of their
elders; in times of rapid change, elders were more open to the wisdom of
youth. If there were no generations, there would be no way for new
knowledge – that is, knowledge that comes from fresh experience – to be
transmitted and to be assimilated by older age-groups; and, at the same
time, if it were not for the existence of intermediary generations, cultural
transmission could never be accomplished without conflict.[47]

Antonio Gramsci added subtle modulations to this analysis, arguing
that a generational conflict occurs when an older generation fails to
educate the young to meet the tasks set by their time. Often the young
wish to transfer their allegiance from the retrogressive class to a more
progressive one, but this attempt may be blocked by the emerging
élites. The "old" order loses its power to attract the young, but the
"new" order is prevented from winning power. "An old generation with
antiquated ideas may be followed by a young generation with infantile
ideas, if the intermediary generation that should correct the old or
educate the new is missing or quantitatively weak".[48]

Yeats inclined to the opinion that Gaelic Ireland lost its natural
leaders and traditions of leadership with the flight of the Wild Geese,
and to that he attributed the infantile formations of public opinion
among the nationalist clubs of young men and women. Gramsci – an
unlikely bedfellow of the poet – would probably have agreed. He
argued that this pattern is more likely and of graver consequence
among the subordinate classes, because their intellectual élites lack a
cultural tradition, and because the few individuals in these groups who
are at the height of their historical epoch have a difficult time organizing an intellectual centre that can effectively counter the hegemony of
the dominant social coalition.[49]

Modern Irish history bears out that analysis. The decades in which
significant social and political progress was made tended to be the ones
which saw a palpable drop in emigration by adults. During the 1870s
and 1880s, with the United States in the grip of a prolonged recession,
many potential emigrants opted to stay in Ireland and make a stand:
the result was the successful land agitation. Again, during the uncertain
years of World War One, the outflow of population was much reduced,
and the frustrations of those caught at home helped to fan the flames of
the Easter Rising.[50]

Twenty-Two

Mothers and Daughters

The ritual killing or replacement of fathers by sons is the stuff of legend as well as of social progress: though it may have begun in the tragic mode, it is by now a tradition so extensive that there is a place within it for comedy, such as the masterpiece by Synge. The son must challenge the father to become a man. What daughters must do in order to become women is more problematic: killing the mother could hardly be enacted in any recognizably comic mode. Even the more radical thinkers of the modern age defined the revolt of women in terms of the attempt by wives and daughters to break free of the constricting images of the female devised by men, and devised as often by men of national resistance movements as by men of the occupying power.

A common claim by imperial administrators was that women, so often repressed by traditional native cultures, would fare better under the *Pax Britannica*. In an age when the women of Britain lacked the citizen's elementary right to vote, this argument seemed hollow indeed. Across the globe, those women who committed themselves to the programme for decolonization found in the very conditions of that struggle the lineaments of their own freedom. The constant risk of arrest and incarceration run by nationalist males made it imperative that their partners could earn a living or support a family. Their families took on the contours of resistance, becoming in effect "alternative models of human organization":[1] the one free zone in which people could be themselves, the one space in which the occupier could not enter; and many of the women in such families assumed equality with men as a natural right.

When Parnell and the leaders of the Land League were arrested in 1882, the Ladies' Land League, under his sister Anna, took over the campaign, as would the women of India in later decades after the arrest of Nehru. Parnell was unnerved by the militancy of the women and feared that he might be mocked for "sheltering" behind them. His sister encouraged her followers to become self-sufficient, to develop their powers of organization and oratory; and she was soon being denounced as a "fanatic" and "harridan", by dismayed nationalists as well as by enemy imperialists. Her movement ignored her brother's command to drop its no-rent policy and was consequently dissolved: but many of her followers, having sensed their political power, went on to use it in challenging new ways. They felt that they had every right to disobey laws which they had no part in framing.[2]

The odds against the crusaders for women's rights were formidable. By the second half of the nineteenth century, the number of women workers in industry had dropped substantially; their contribution to agriculture seemed less important as farmers switched from tillage to livestock; and daughters came to rely more and more on dowries offered by elderly fathers. Ireland became, in consequence, a society pervaded by male values. The historian Joseph Lee has lamented that the Catholic Church's achievement of spiritual hegemony, through its control of the educational system and its regular religious crusades, should have coincided with the era of Victorian propriety. The passion and realism of the old Gaelic love poetry were replaced by a coy sentimentality. He finds it ironic "that at a moment when educational opportunities increased for Irish women, the educational system began to be more systematically used to indoctrinate them into adopting as self-images the prevailing male view of women". The very spread of literacy became, in these circumstances, "another instrument for stifling independent thought".[3]

Literacy, of course, would always be a two-edged sword: and the extension of access to education was bound over time to produce a new, more independent type of woman. In 1904 Trinity College Dublin was opened to women: that same year, Francis Sheehy Skeffington resigned as registrar of the Royal University over the non-recognition of women graduates. By 1909 the National University of Ireland had placed women on an equal footing with men, following a wily and resourceful campaign by Mary Hayden, who would become a professor of history in the institution.[4] To some extent, the colleges may have been shamed into making these concessions by the example of the Gaelic League, an organization which had always recruited women as well as men, being indeed the victim of priestly censure for its mingling of the sexes at classes and summer camps. Agnes O'Farrelly, one of the first women to take an external degree in Celtic Studies, gave lectures in League classes in the years before 1909, when it was still not possible for her to teach

at the National University: later she, too, was a professor there. Queen
Victoria had lamented the "horrors" of the new feminists, and in this
she was supported by the more conservative Catholic clergy. One parish
priest in Kerry opined that "it was a sure sign of the break-up of the
planet when women took to leaving their homes and talking in public".[5]

The initial response of many Irish women to such strictures was to
link the call for female and for national rights. "I had read all the books
about the position of women", wrote the literary critic Mary Colum,
"which corresponded in a way to that of the oppressed races".[6] Her
friend, the suffragist Hanna Sheehy-Skeffington, agreed, but warned
against the danger that a narrow nationalism might simply use women
in a subordinate capacity. She cited Mary Wollstonecraft in support of
her case: "To fight men's battles for them and to neglect those of
women has always been regarded as true womanly, though when men
fight for their rights on the broad basis of humanity they are not
accused of selfishness. The cause of an oppressed group is fully as great
as that of an oppressed nation and deserves no taunt of narrowness".[7]
Nevertheless, the suffragists learned useful lessons from their male
counterparts, emulating the Parnellite policy of "marking" government
candidates at election time. The women, in turn, devised many tactics
which would be imitated by the men: the 1912 hunger-strike by four
women, among them Hanna Sheehy-Skeffington, would be repeated by
male nationalists not only in Ireland, but also by Gandhi and his
disciples, who found further sanction for it in Indian tradition.[8] It was
supported by a wide range of Irish opinion from Tom Kettle to Patrick
Pearse: though Mrs. Skeffington found that some of her choices of
nineteenth-century novels for prison reading proved unwise: "One
instinctively skips in books the descriptions of food; I never realized
before how much both Scott and Dickens *gloat*, and how abstemious
are the Brontës and Jane Austen".[9] No doubt, the story of Catherine
Earnshaw had a certain grim appeal.

Countess Constance Markievicz emerged as perhaps the most force-
ful proponent of the link between national and female self-sufficiency.
Against the glamour and egalitarianism of the revived national movement, she held that the imperialists could offer women only a genteel
bondage:

> The feminist cause in Ireland is best served by ignoring England and
> English politicians . . . The United Irish League (with the exception of one
> branch, we believe), the Loyal Orange Association, the Liberal Home Rule

Association are exclusively masculine bodies. The Gaelic League and the
Sinn Féin organization are the only ones in existence at present where
women are on an equal footing with men. For that reason they are worthy
of the support of every Irish suffragist.[10]

Many nationalists were emboldened by this analysis to question the
logic of Irish women seeking the franchise from an oppressive *foreign*
power. Celtic scholars buttressed such arguments by outlining the
superior rights enjoyed by women – in fact, upper-class women –
under the ancient Brehon laws; but Hanna Sheehy-Skeffington insisted
that the English were only partly to blame, a contention which she
proved (to her own satisfaction, at any rate) by demonstrating that
contemporary Irish women had fewer rights in law than their English
counterparts.[11] She was, of course, in favour of a universal adult
suffrage, not merely "votes for ladies". Just how convoluted these
debates could become was evident in the strictures of D. P. Moran's
Leader to the effect that Irish suffragism was an abject example of West
Britonism: "the movement in Ireland smacks rather of imitation of the
English, and we do not regard it as a native and spontaneous growth".[12]
This was raising Ireland-as-not-England to the power of a pathology.

   Most radical women of the time believed in an Ireland not merely
free but feminist, not merely feminist but free: "so therefore", wrote
Constance Markievicz, "the first step on the road to freedom is to
realize ourselves as Irishwomen – not as Irish or merely as women, but
as Irishwomen doubly enslaved and with a double battle to fight".[13]
Even the Skeffingtons, in the years of rising national militancy before
the rebellion, came to accept this view: "There can be no free nation
without free women; neither can there be free women in an enslaved
nation".[14] Yet they were both constantly troubled by the instrumental
view of women adopted by many of the Irish Volunteers (founded in
1914). This group's rhetoric stressed "manly" and "martial" qualities
and its leaders seemed distressingly prone to patronize the female
professors and suffragists of Cumann na mBan (The Society of Women), its sister organization.

   The writer and critic Mary Colum acidly noted that Volunteer
references to women were made "as obliquely as possible, in order not
to alienate any potential supporters".[15] Hanna Sheehy-Skeffington was
appropriately underwhelmed. Nor was she particularly impressed by
the theory that misogyny in Ireland was entirely due to the British
presence: she knew Irishmen too well to fall for so naïve a diagnosis.
The Irish Citizen voiced her doubts:

Cumann na mBan . . . continues to work for the Irish volunteers in a purely subordinate capacity, without any voice in the control of the organization, without any official declaration from the Irish Volunteers that the "rights and liberties" for which they stand include the rights and liberties of women.[16]

By then, however, the suffragist movement had been fatally split over whether or not to support war efforts; and Cumann na mBan was seizing the hour. Mrs. Skeffington was soon making regular appearances on its platforms, encouraged by Thomas MacDonagh, who had debated the treatment of women with her husband and who proved more sympathetic than some of his comrades. Countess Markievicz served as president of Cumann na mBan for nearly seven years. Its annual convention reported over eight hundred branches active in the country.[17] Some had joined in response to James Connolly's warning that the vote would not heal all women's disabilities: it was indeed possible, he said, that most women might exercise it in favour of the forces of reaction (which, he added, they had a perfect right to do).[18] He urged suffragists to follow the example of the independent group Inghinidhe na hÉireann (Daughters of Erin) and to commit themselves to programmes for the alleviation of childhood poverty, poor housing and the problems of working mothers. The journal of the Inghinidhe was *Bean na hÉireann* (Irish Woman) and it often contained columns by Maud Gonne and Constance Markievicz. The latter's gardening feature became a *cause célèbre* for its rather strained conflation of violent nationalism with pouting feminine gentility:

A good nationalist should look upon slugs in a garden much in the same way as she looks upon the English in Ireland, and only regret that she cannot crush the Nation's enemies as she can the garden's, with one tread of her dainty foot.[19]

When the rebellion came in 1916, over ninety women took part. The largest contingent, about sixty, came from Cumann na mBan, whose members took no direct part in the fighting, but performed assigned tasks as nurses, cooks and dispatch-carriers (probably the most dangerous activity in Easter Week).[20] Not all were pleased with the way in which they were treated. At Boland's Mills, Commandant Éamon de Valera turned down their offer of help, saying that he did not wish to add to his problems by employing unproven women warriors: much later, he would rather indiscreetly confess to Hanna Sheehy-Skeffington that this had been a bad move, since it meant that he had to release some of his best men for "womanly" chores such as cooking and catering.[21] The ambiguous position of women in the emerging republic was summed up by Mrs. Skeffington's own predicament: she had been named as one of the five members of the provisional government which would come into being if the Rising were successful, but she had been named without her knowledge or consent.[22] Nonetheless, the Proclamation was, for her and for many others, an inspiringly radical document: it addressed itself equally to women as well as to men, it guaranteed equal rights to all, and it announced the welfare state of which so many, all over Europe, had dreamed. It implicitly recognized that the risks which women were taking for the republic were the same as those being run by men.

The women of the Citizen Army adopted an even higher profile.[23] Countess Markievicz commanded a battalion of troops in St. Stephen's Green; Dr. Kathleen Lynn acted as chief medical officer; and Margaret Skinnider led a squad of men against a British machine-gun post, being severely wounded in the attack. She had already acted as a roof-top sniper and, to the dismay of male comrades concerned for her safety, tried to organize a bombing of the Shelbourne Hotel. In all, fifteen women fought at St. Stephen's Green. After the hostilities had ceased, about eighty were arrested, among them Helena Molony, the Abbey actress, trade unionist and suffragist. The countess was held at Kilmainham Jail, where she underwent the bitter experience of having to listen daily for the gunshots which executed a succession of her male comrades. She, too, was sentenced to death, but the verdict was commuted, and she was transferred to Holloway Prison in England, along with Kathleen Clarke. The latter had been designated to take charge of the entire Irish Republican Brotherhood in the event of its Supreme Council being arrested:[24] clearly, the British took a somewhat less gallant view of the rebel women than did some of their Irish opponents.

Hanna Sheehy-Skeffington, newly widowed, visited the women in Holloway and stepped up her own nationalist activities. The Irish Parliamentary Party MP John Dillon wrote to warn her that the British were now in an ugly mood: "if you are imprisoned again, it may very well be your last adventure". She met this kindly warning with a withering scorn: "I wonder what you would have thought in the old days, when prison was still an 'adventure' to you, if a friend suggested that you retire into private life to save Britain the trouble of assassinating you".[25] Zeal such as this was what Cathal Brugha had in mind when, years later, he recalled that it was the women, in the depressing aftermath of 1916, "who kept the spirit alive, who kept the flame alive and the flag flying".[26]

Not all of Mrs. Skeffington's witticisms were premeditated. With the threat by the British to conscript Irishmen into the war effort, she went into overdrive. Her ringing declaration that "the women of Ireland will not tolerate the taking-away by force of their men-kind",[27] though it carried a personal poignance, must have occasioned some guffaws among radical feminists who might have been forgiven for seeing in such a policy the chance of a restored Celtic matriarchy. The vote had finally been given to women over thirty in February of that year, and, despite the fears that it would be used to buttress the *status quo*, the reverse happened. Women voters, united against conscription, helped Sinn Féin to a famous victory; and Constance Markievicz became the first female MP elected to the House of Commons. She would soon become the first Irishwoman in government, as Minister for Labour of Dáil Éireann in 1919.

Throughout 1919 and 1920, women served as Sinn Féin magistrates, shunning the wigs and gowns of the British dispensation. They also spoke out strongly against the constant raids by British forces on republican homes, almost fifty thousand in 1920 alone. Traditional rhetoric concerning "the sanctity of the family" proved a potent resource in such resistance: and some women, moving beyond mere rhetoric to active involvement with the military campaign, were described by one republican ironist as "able to work from the home".[28] In this way, few were traced or arrested. Hanna Sheehy-Skeffington toured England, explaining to meetings that the Black-and-Tan campaign was a direct consequence of World War One: "men with shattered nerves" had been sent "to create terror".[29] This was a somewhat more charitable construction than other Irish nationalists were putting on events. Speaking at the Oxford Union, W. B. Yeats said that "not law, but English law, had broken down in Ireland".[30] Like Mrs. Skeffington, he supported the Democratic Programme of the 1919 Dáil, arguing that "Sinn Féin brought justice into his part of Ireland for the first time in centuries". She would probably have endorsed his further comment that "the only complaint against Sinn Féin was that it protected property a little too rigorously". She warned her English audiences, composed mainly of Labourites and feminists, that forces like the Tans might be used in time against their own people, if unemployment and discontent increased.[31]

When the Anglo-Irish Treaty of 1921 was put to Dáil Éireann for ratification, all six women deputies spoke trenchantly against it. During the long and heart-rending debate, Cumann na mBan attempted to hoist a Union Jack over the building, as a mordant commentary on what was being proposed. The unbending stance of many of the women delegates was put down to the fact that, as bereaved relatives of national martyrs, they were allowing their hearts to rule their heads: but they indignantly denied this, arguing the case on its merits. Speaking in all for more than four and a half hours, Mary MacSwiney, widow of the hunger-striking lord mayor of Cork, said she would "have neither hand, act nor part in helping the Irish Free State to carry this nation of ours, this glorious nation that has been betrayed here tonight, into the British Empire". Her performances lived long in the memory of those who witnessed them: one of her interventions took more than two hours. "If England exterminates the men, the women will take their places . . . and if she exterminates the men, women and children of this generation, the blades of grass, dyed with their blood, will rise, like the dragon's teeth of old, into armed men and the fight will begin in the next generation". She spoke with unconcealed contempt for what she saw as a compromise: "I ask the Minister of Defence, if that is the type of soldier he has, in heaven's name send the women as your officers next time".[32]

The suggestion that the Treatyites were unmanned touched a raw nerve: one outraged soldier derided Mrs. MacSwiney and her five sister republicans as "women in men's clothing". This was in truth a "dastardly remark", as Constance Markievicz averred in demanding its retraction; but it was one that signalled the end, in practical politics at any rate, of the dream of an androgynous sexuality. Her response was to appeal for justice "to these young women and young girls who took a man's part in the terror".[33] Cumann na mBan in a formal statement insisted that its members had "regained for the women of Ireland the rights that belonged to them under the old Gaelic civilization, where sex was no bar to citizenship, and where women were free to devote to the service of their country any talent and capacity with which they were endowed; which rights were stolen from them under English rule, but were guaranteed to them in the Republican Proclamation of Easter Week".[34]

It was a forlorn hope. At a vast meeting in Cork in 1922, Michael Collins, leader of the pro-Treaty forces, thanked the women for their work, but offered no clear vision of their part in shaping the new Ireland. When Hanna Sheehy-Skeffington went to meet him, she found a man with "a touch of the dictator", whose ideal Ireland was "a middle-class replica of the English state (certainly not an ancient Gaelic Ireland)". She detected in him "the usual soldier's contempt for civilians, particularly for women, though these had often risked their lives to help him".[35] Her campaign to have the franchise extended to women over twenty-one was beaten in the Dáil, in her opinion because the Treatyites feared that most younger women would follow the female deputies in opposing the settlement. During the following year, that decision was reversed and the 1922 Constitution gave women full voting rights, seven years before their sisters in Britain and Northern Ireland: but the inveterate opposition of women deputies to the Treaty had deeper long-term consequences. It prompted the government's propagandists to caricature political women as "hysterical", a term used by W. B. Yeats as well as by P. S. O'Hegarty: the latter said that "they busied themselves with nothing but the things of death".[36]

Yet, by a paradox which seems to have escaped O'Hegarty's notice, it was those same republican women – "republicans without malice" as Lady Gregory inventively dubbed them – who made a last-ditch attempt to broker a peace between the two sides as they slipped into a futile Civil War.[37] They were not thanked for their efforts. In the hostilities that followed, most of them, perhaps predictably, took the republican side and many found themselves summarily imprisoned by the military courts, which took an even less sentimental line on the incarceration of women than the British had done during the War of Independence. When they protested against the humiliating conditions in which they were held, they were condemned by the Catholic clergy: more than one, in going against the bishops, cited the example of Joan of Arc.[38] The young Minister for Justice, Kevin O'Higgins, sounded the familiar notes of male resentment when he derided "hysterical young women who ought to be playing five-fingered exercises or help-ing their mother with the brasses".[39] Joan of Arc was not to be mistaken for Cathleen ní Houlihan.

Through the decades after the Civil War, woman's role was redefined in purely maternal and domestic terms. Though republicans like Kath-leen Clarke and Hanna Sheehy-Skeffington opposed this tendency, they were now portrayed as cranks in the popular press. The exodus of talented writers and radical intellectuals from the state left them no more than a peripheral force. Remarkably few women spoke out against the repressive laws introduced in respect of deserted wives, widows' allowances or the rights of unmarried mothers. For a full half-century after political independence in the twenty-six county state, only three women actually served on a jury, so that – in the words of

Mary Robinson – "the assessment of criminality has been an entirely male assessment".[40] Hanna Sheehy-Skeffington mocked the underlying thinking: that women should not serve on juries, lest they be compelled to hear evidence that would most definitely not be "nice". She opposed the ban on married women in the professions on the same grounds advanced by W. B. Yeats: that it would discredit the institution of marriage. And, like Yeats, she rather mischievously pointed out that classics of literature, such as the Bible or *Romeo and Juliet*, might have to be banned under censorship legislation against texts "which excite sexual passion".[41] Throughout the 1920s and 1930s, the numbers of women at work or active in public life continued to drop sharply.

The rise to power of Fianna Fáil in the early 1930s did little to change things. Some more innovative branches of the party fielded female candidates in elections, but all did badly at the polls. "If they are not supported by their own sex", said one politician, "it is difficult to see what we can do".[42] When Éamon de Valera came to write his Constitution of 1937, his former comrades of a feminist disposition were outraged at its treatment of women: the man who had rebuffed Cumann na mBan in 1916 had learned nothing in the meantime. In theory, his new Constitution was designed to sever all remaining, degrading connections with the British Empire; in practice, it served to copper-fasten partition and to secure the allegiance to the new state of many whose support, up until that moment, had been conditional. The problem of legitimating the uncertain state structures overrode the concerns of women, and also those of Protestants, intellectuals, artists, northern nationalists and republicans, all of whose rights were either curtailed or excluded. If the partition of 1921 had ensured a Protestant parliament for a Protestant people in Belfast, its logical corollary was a Catholic Dáil for a Catholic people in Dublin. The very existence of the twenty-six county state suited the conservative elements of the Catholic Church very well, since it permitted the passing of clericalist legislation without a significant debate such as might have been expected in a pluralist republic.

Hanna Sheehy Skeffington, true to form, accosted de Valera. So did the veteran Protestant republican, Dorothy Macardle. So did the Association of Women Graduates, led by three professors: Mary Hayden, Agnes O'Farrelly and Mary Macken. Pointing out that his own Constitution was markedly less liberal in its attitude to women than the Collins Constitution of 1922, they demanded the retention of articles from the earlier document: otherwise women would be treated as "half-wits".[43] Even this rather cautious request was refused. Dorothy Macardle wrote in a letter to de Valera on 21 May 1937: "The real crux is the question of employment. The language of certain clauses suggests that the state may interfere to a great extent in determining what opportunities should be open or closed to women; there is no chance whatever to counterbalance that suggestion or to safeguard women's rights in that respect".[44]

A "feeble" attempt during the constitutional debate, to challenge that part of Article 41 which stated that "woman by her life within the home gives the State a support without which the common good cannot be achieved" to include also "women outside the home", was easily deflected.[45] Dorothy Macardle was uncompromising in outlining the implications: "I do not see how anyone holding advanced views on the rights of women can support it, and that is a tragic dilemma for those who have been loyal and ardent workers in the national cause".[46] De Valera was immovable. Securing the state and its borders was now the major concern of a man who had once fought for a poets' republic but who, in more recent times, had come to regard poets with almost as much distrust as he displayed towards women.

The worst fears of Hanna Sheehy-Skeffington had been realized: what was on offer in the new state was – according to her friend, Helena Molony – "a sorry travesty of emancipation".[47] The histories of that new state purported to explain how it came into being and, in the process, they omitted anything like a full account of the central part played by women up until the liquidation of the revolution in 1921. The cautious, clericalist nationalism which these histories promoted was "a carefully constructed bulwark against a resurgence of a radical anti-imperialism, that, drawing on the grievances of the artificially-created minority of the north, might fuse with the disappointment of small farmers, women, workers and intellectuals in the south",[48] in order to reopen the possibilities of liberation.

Those who continued to raise the unresolved national question, although they were accused by some feminists of distracting attention from bread-and-butter issues, had a point: there may have been a link between the partitioning of Ireland and the curtailment of women's rights as citizens. Had Ireland remained a single political entity, including almost a million and a half Protestants, it would scarcely have been possible for de Valera to take the following sentiments, expressed in a letter from the President of Blackrock College, John Charles McQuaid, as a basis for his legislation and for his answers to the republican women: "These feminists are very confused. Both *Casti Connubi* and *Quadragesimo Anno* answer them". Men and women had not equal rights to work of the same kind, said the cleric, but "equal rights to *appropriate* work".[49] What was seemly for women was to be found in the home.

The curtailment of the rights of women and of Protestants manifested itself in a return to a more traditional portraiture of masculinity and femininity in creative literature. In the vigorous obscenities of Crazy Jane, Yeats might ventriloquize a voice which challenged the new priestly censoriousness, but even he went on to confess that he felt the need to "exorcize" the figure, whose language had grown "unendurable".[50] If, in the revival period, Catholic writers had "exalted Irishwomen as emblematic mothers and desexualized spiritual maidens, the Anglo-Irish writers of Protestant background often acknowledged sexual desire and power as significant elements in the characters and roles of their heroines"[51]; but now, the conservative tradition had won. The androgynous vision of a world whose gender boundaries were endlessly open turned out to have had a wider political, as distinct from a merely personal, meaning: the manly women and womanly men of the Irish renaissance had positioned themselves on the cusp between worlds – between the colonizer and the colonized, between west and east, between having (a phallus) and being (a woman). Now, such a confusion of gender boundaries could stand only for "the fragile status of nationality", and so it was ruthlessly disallowed. The ideologues of independent Ireland reverted to the old, neurotic philosophy which saw the male as in all things the opposite of the female. In doing so, they succumbed to a classic nationalist delusion, which would soon become evident in other emerging nation-states:

> As *man* and *woman* define themselves reciprocally, so national identity is determined not on the basis of its own intrinsic properties but as a function of what it (presumably) is not . . . Nations are forever haunted by their various definitional others. Hence, on the one hand, the nation's insatiable need to administer difference through violent acts of segregation, censorship, economic coercion, physical torture, police brutality. And hence, on the other, the nation's insatiable need for representational labour to supplement its founding ambivalence, the lack of self-presence at its origin . . .[52]

In simpler terms, the leaders of the new state remained painfully uncertain of its legitimacy. This was a condition calculated to generate endless crises of self-legitimation, and with them a nervously patriarchal psychology. In the literature of the emerging nation, woman reverted to being a site of contest rather than an agent of her own desire. "No nationalism in the world has ever granted women and men the same privileged resources of the nation-state": the claim of women to nation-hood frequently depends on marriage to a male citizen, and almost always women are "subsumed only symbolically into the body politic", representing not themselves but "the limits of national difference between men".[53] This captures precisely the kind of double colonialism under which James Connolly had said Irishwomen were compelled to live: and the new Ireland rapidly revealed itself to constitute the problem rather than the solution.

The unmodified state apparatus proved itself to have been the last, most lethal, gift of the departing imperialists: and the obsession with the father-son relationship, as a crisis of legitimation, seemed to deepen with each succeeding generation of male authors. A student of modern African or Caribbean writing would find no surprise in this: and the explanation has been given in a recent book on *Nationalisms and Sexualities*:

> Post-colonial governments are inclined, with some predictability, to gen-
> erate narratives of national crisis, driven perhaps – the generous explanation
> – to re-enact periodically the state's traumatic if also liberating separation
> from colonial authority . . . Typically, however, such narratives of crisis serve
> more than one category of reassurance: by repeatedly focusing anxiety on
> the fragility of the new nation, its ostensible vulnerability to every kind of
> exigency, the state's originating agency is periodically reinvoked and rati-
> fied.[54]

The writers go on to remark that those "who successfully define and superintend a crisis, furnishing its lexicon and discursive parameters, successfully confirm themselves as the owners of power".[55] Such super-intendents in Ireland were almost invariably male, or, in rare cases, females who had made a betraying compromise with the new élites. These became obsessed with defending borders and achieving a separa-tion of realms: for it was on such borders, on such separations, that their privilege and power depended. Yet, among ordinary people and among those intellectuals who dissented, could be found many who preferred still to leave the borders porous and ambiguous: when the official armies cratered a road, people could always be found to fill the hole in.

Basil Davidson has described the nation-state as "the black man's burden" in contemporary Africa, and has made his own observations of these developments:

What the peoples think upon this subject is shown by their incessant emigration across these lines on the map, as well as by their smuggling enterprises. So that even while a "bourgeois Africa" hardens its frontiers, multiplies its border controls, a people's Africa works in quite another way.[56]

The aesthetic implications of this popular dissent were, of course, a return to a philosophy of hybridity and androgyny, of the kind which informed the *risorgimento*. The truest reality of a people would always be experienced in those moments when they crossed from one code to another.

Such "cross-dressers" have never been completely absent from post-revival Irish writing: but the price of crossing the border for literary women was that few of them could ever hope to return. Kate O'Brien, for instance, found her best novels banned by the national censorship board and ended her days living in Kent, from which she sent columns to *The Irish Times*, whose very title "Long Distance" rendered "her need to remain apart and her wish to stay in touch".[57] *The Land of Spices* (1941) is a protest against Irish insularity and a complex study of the ways in which Catholicism and nationalism were elided, to the exclusion of a more "European" awareness, in the minds of those who would inherit the new state. Its rather sympathetic portrayal of a strong and sophisticated nun at the outset of World War One, and its counter-pointing of her life of discipline with the vocation of a young apprentice artist, indicate the author's conviction that the family in Ireland had become a trap which many spirited women would want to avoid. A once-jailed suffragist, introduced late in the book, awakens the young heroine to an artistic calling which seems at odds with the prevailing ideals of femininity in her convent school. Yet the fact that its mother superior should, like the feminist, find herself at frequent odds with the local bishop suggests that the nuns may have found a kind of self-sufficiency within their own considerable estates. That power was, of course, jealously monitored by the bishops, but it could never be completely contained, as the protagonist shows in making her break into the world. Many of O'Brien's other females are not so lucky: most are caught, sooner or later, in the introverted routines of family life, whose very insularity has been read as indicating Ireland's self-estrangement from Europe during the years of World War Two.[58]

If for some women writers the family was a trap, for others it remained what it had been during the time of the British occupation: a zone of resistance in which intense love and small kindnesses were still possible against the wider backdrop of a heartless political world. Mary Lavin, opting for a separate peace, refused the grand themes of nation and female destiny, which exist beneath the surfaces of her work only as modes of implication and irony. A sceptical romantic, she insisted that love has a perpetual power to redeem and surprise: and if, in pursuing this theme, she tended to restrict her female characters to the domestic round, she did the same with her men. The public world was to her a world well lost for such moments. Insofar as Lavin protested against religious oppression, she offered the principled dissent of a true believer who detected that spirituality might, in a conformist community, move from living form to dead formula. Her fear appeared to be that the Catholic religion, even in Ireland, was collapsing into a matter of mere social decorum: so she was appropriately sardonic about those who treated their own celibacy as a heroic denial of appetite rather than a positive expression of spiritual value. At moments, she could be quite scathing about the degradation of ritual to routine.

But her touch was ever light and easy. She had no desire to dig society up by its roots: rather she worked to hold it true to its own nobler imperatives. Her stories and novellas offered, nonetheless, the fullest and most sympathetic account of the lives of Irish women in the early decades of the independent state: they centred on structures of feeling more than on the revelation of character in unfolding plot, and were based on the understanding that the family is not only a key to identity, but the proper referee of generational conflict and even, when necessary, the subverter of unpleasant social tyrannies. Precisely because so much was repressed, or existed only at the level of form or decorum in the wider society, the family for her became a mysterious register of all that was elsewhere denied. It could sometimes bend and break under the pressure of those who asked it to do their living for them, but it also showed itself surprisingly resilient and able to afford fulfilment to many intense emotions. Such passions might express themselves only as symbolic implication or gentle understatement: but they were no less real for that.[59]

Lavin's methods, as well as her characters, were a perfect illustration of the contention that only those who know deep feelings experience the need to displace them in symbol and metaphor. Her quiet style seldom drew attention to itself, working more by innuendo than by statement. Though her focus was on individuals, often caught in autumnal solitude after a fulfilled passion, her values were those of her community. She thus became that most rare thing in Ireland: a writer who found expressive freedom in rather than from the available community; and one who somehow managed, as did hundreds of thousands of unsung women who were not artists, to find within those constrictions a way of mapping the contours of the human heart.

PROTESTANT REVIVALS

PROTESTANT REVIVALS

In May 1922 the situation of Protestants had appeared to change after independence, and their synod had accordingly directed the archbishop of Dublin to ask Michael Collins "if they were permitted to live in Ireland or if it was desired that they should leave the country".[1] Some had indeed been burnt out. The new state, therefore, bent over backwards to assuage their fears by rather paradoxically appointing sixteen Protestant unionists to the first Seanad; but within two decades the number of Protestants at primary schools in the state was halved from 28,000 to 14,000. Yeats's speeches to the senate have to be read against that depressing backdrop. Opposing the proposed censorship of films, he said on 7 June 1923 that "you can leave the arts, superior or inferior, to the general conscience of mankind". In the debate on legislation which sought to outlaw divorce, he told the senators on 11 June 1925, "if you show that this country, Southern Ireland [sic], is going to be governed by Catholic ideas and by Catholic ideas alone, you will never get the North . . . Once you attempt legislation on religious grounds you open the way for every kind of intolerance and for every kind of religious persecution". Far from preserving sexual morality in the countries which adopted it, the law of indissoluble marriage encouraged a cynical tolerance of dishonesty and irresponsibility in sexual relations. Moreover, to impose separation without the prospect of remarriage on couples whose relationship had irretrievably broken down was to force "the law of the cloisters" upon all. He recalled Parnell's vow to Kitty O'Shea: "in the opinion of every Irish Protestant gentleman in this country he did what was essential as a man of honour. Now you are going to make that essential act impossible and thereby affront an important minority of your countrymen".

As so often, Yeats saw in the liberal attitudes of Protestantism a more authentic version of the codes of Gaelic Ireland. To the complaint by Colonel Moore that young people were now wedding in the knowledge that their marriage might last only a year, Yeats jocularly replied "an ancient

Irish form of marriage". In a second, undelivered draught of his speech, Yeats asserted that he was one of those who "believe as little in an infallible book as an infallible church". Here, he distinguished that lobby of sceptics (of which he named himself a member) from "men who follow the teachings of some Church that is not under Rome". In other words, he conceded that in certain moments his Protestantism was strategic, a useful stick with which to beat the Catholic philistines of the Free State Senate, just as it had served the same purpose for Synge, enabling him to extol the nation of Grattan, Emmet and Parnell against the narrow-gauge nationalists. Yet, both men showed cunning in these controversies: and so Yeats's more trenchant critique of the anti-divorce law was never delivered, and undelivered also was Synge's Open Letter to the Gaelic League. The fact that Yeats was not recalled for a further term in the Senate after 1928 indicates just how well-judged his caution was: the token Protestant senators had now served their purpose and could be quietly dismissed by the theocrats of the new state.

One day after his "retirement" from the Senate, Yeats predicted that the proposed Censorship of Publications Bill, through the use of the phrase "subversive of public morality", could in time permit a government minister to exclude books like Marx's Kapital, *Darwin's* The Origin of Species, *or the novels of Flaubert, Balzac or Proust, "all great love poetry", "half the Greek and Roman classics", and everything on the Roman Catholic Index. The rigid fighting spirit which had proved invaluable in the struggle to free Ireland of English rule was now becoming a damned liability. It was creating intolerance in a state which now, more than ever, needed to redefine itself as "a modern, tolerant, liberal nation".[2] In* Pages From A Diary *written in 1930, Yeats defined his own understanding of the unfinished business of Irish republicanism: "Preserve that which is living and help the two Irelands, Gaelic and Anglo-Ireland, so to unite that neither shall shed its pride".[3]*

It was a noble aspiration, but it flew in the face of realities. In Northern Ireland, sectarian hatreds had been sharpened ever since 1916. The Easter Rising was portrayed by Ulster unionists as a stab in the back of those committed to the war effort. By 1920 there were riots and pogroms in Belfast, as chronic unemployment led Protestant workers to drive Catholics out of their jobs in factory and shipyard. Southern unionists in the main opposed the partitionist settlement: even Carson wished to keep Ireland united, but with dominion status as part of the British Empire. However, a unionist state was what emerged in 1921: the anger of the Catholic minority at this arrangement simply redoubled northern Protestant enthusiasm for it.[4] Though there is evidence that Collins worried for northern nationalists, and may even have planned attacks on the state, most southern politicians were surprisingly indifferent to the plight of the Catholic minority. The unspoken consensus appeared to be that eventually Northern Ireland would sue for terms of unification, being unable to survive as such a tiny economic entity. Meanwhile, those in Dublin who felt that they had a full-time job securing their own state were, in all likelihood, secretly relieved to be spared the task of quelling that sizeable loyalist army which, in a thirty-two county Ireland, could only have compounded their problems.

The Orange state which emerged was sectarian to an astonishing degree. Constituencies were gerrymandered to copper-fasten Protestant supremacy; discrimination in the allocation of jobs and homes kept Catholics in the position of second-class citizens; and even the more ambitious members of the minority were thus loath to apply for posts in the police and civil service to which, at least in theory, they were entitled. The Royal Ulster Constabulary was a paramilitary force equipped with guns and armoured cars, unlike the Gardai Siochána of the Free State. The "B-Special" police force played an ignominious role, its interpretation of peace-keeping being the administration of regular beatings to members of the Catholic population (this work often done in collusion with the UVF). The authorities soon had at their disposal a raft of measures, including internment and extradition. The "Special Powers Act" of 1922 remained on the statute-book for fifty years, becoming the envy of the uncivilized world.[5] When Justice Minister Vorster introduced his notorious Coercion Bill at the South African parliament in 1963, he quelled all protest with the remarkable observation that he would be "willing to exchange all the legislation of that sort for one clause of the Northern Ireland Special Powers Act".[6]

Life for northern nationalists was hard. Some of their elected leaders boycotted the Stormont parliament in Belfast; and those who took part in it were never embraced. In all the years of Stormont's existence until it was prorogued in 1972, the Unionist Party voted in only one amendment proposed by nationalists and that was to a wildlife bill! High unemployment rates and poverty seemed endemic in Catholic ghettos: the young socialist republican Paddy Devlin recalled sitting at his parents' kitchen table while a single boiled egg was split three ways.[7] Thus emerged one of the great puzzles of modern European political life: that as Britain led the war against fascism and pioneered the welfare state, its leaders nonetheless maintained and bankrolled on their very doorstep a one-party system characterized by religious bigotry and political repression. Again and again the rulers of Britain were warned of festering discontents, while the leaders in Dublin regularly heard horrifying testimonies from northern Catholics driven south from pogroms.

In the uncertain summer of 1936, the British Council for Civil Liberties complained in a report that Ulster unionists had been allowed to create "under the shadow of the British constitution a permanent machine of dictatorship".[8] The report made an explicit comparison with fascist régimes in Europe, where there was a total identification of party and state. British public opinion remained indifferent. In Dublin, de Valera's 1937 Constitution was scarcely an adequate answer. It asserted that the national territory was the whole island of Ireland, but such verbal republicanism was of scant consolation to the stateless minority of Northern Ireland, and could only inflame the sectarian bitterness of their oppressors. Anyway, the Constitution went on to exclude the six northern counties from de facto jurisdiction, "pending the reintegration of the national territory". While seeming to make a territorial claim, it actually gave the first formal recognition to partition: the more eagle-eyed northern nationalists correctly deduced from it that they were on their own.

By comparison with all this, life for the Protestant minority in the twenty-six counties was comfortable. Though civil rights to divorce and contraception were denied in law, it was possible for many to circumvent these disabilities by a trip outside the jurisdiction. Because they were such a small minority, they posed no threat to the new order and, provided that they remained reasonably quiet and contented with their lot, they were untroubled. Even at the height of the War of Independence, there had been few personal attacks on Protestants, the insurgents confining themselves to the burning of ascendancy houses. The legacy of history meant that, though the Free State had its share of poor Protestants, they were generally well protected by their charitable societies, and most Protestants enjoyed an affluence well in advance of the average.[9] They tended, however, to have an arm's-length relationship with the institutions of the new state and with its parties, though there were always exceptions like Douglas Hyde. A significant number, especially in the earlier years, simply preferred to leave. Few enough of them would have cited theological hatred as a cause of their going, for even amidst the passions of Northern Ireland the verbal attacks on Protestants had rarely been religious, more often taking a political form.

In the south, such anti-partitionism as was voiced was feeble in the extreme: the factors which caused Protestants to leave were often the same considerations that impelled Catholics to take the boat as well – economic stagnation, boredom, a search for a more sexually liberal society, resentment against a culture of censorship. Mr. de Valera was as careful to befriend the professors of Trinity College as his predecessors had been to create Protestant senators: nevertheless, when he unambiguously announced in a broadcast to the United States two years after the passing of his Constitution by popular vote that "we are a Catholic nation",[10] the members of the religious minority who had been reassured by the elevation of a co-religionist to presidential office might have been forgiven for wondering which of the gestures to take the more seriously.

Twenty-Three

Protholics and Cathestants

In *Saint Joan* Shaw causes the heroine to say that, although the English soldiers may become devils incarnate when they touch French soil, in England – the place made for them by God – they behave honourably enough. She endorses national pride, while repudiating a chauvinism which can develop into imperialism. The English chaplain in the play is the most strident imperialist onstage: he believes that English nationalism is so perfect a code that it entitles its sponsors to impose themselves on other peoples as well.

In previous plays, Shaw had offered similar portraits of a self-assured imperial psychology. Tom Broadbent in *John Bull's Other Island* had proclaimed it the mission of the English to place their capacity for government at the service of nations less fortunately endowed. How one nation could progress *in freedom* to become the facsimile of another is not a question which detains Broadbent. What was good for England is – must be – good for the world.

The self-deceiving mentality which permitted a junta of robbers to live at peace with their consciences always fascinated Shaw, who was acutely alert to the part played by religious convictions in the process. It was, after all, in the name of *religion* that English armies made so many political conquests, afterward taking the markets as a reward from heaven.

Shaw was well aware that the British monarchy was a Protestant institution. On coins the monarch was named defender of the faith (*defensor fidei*) and, therefore, the proper ruler of empire. As the product of a Protestant schooling in Ireland, however, Shaw must have wondered at the contradiction underlying a religion which sought to evangelize that empire with a faith whose first principle was the right to democratic individualism and private judgement. This was a paradox as glaring as Broadbent's enforced freedom. At the core of Shaw's thinking is the conviction that well-intentioned English duffers have managed to construct a world out of such unexamined contradictions, but that the edifice will crumble once the inconsistencies are exposed.

The brand of Christianity brought by the British to places like Ireland or India could, in the right hands, become a powerful weapon of insurgent nationalism. "I am violently and arrogantly Protestant by family tradition", he boasted, "but let no English government count on my allegiance. I am English enough to be an inveterate Republican and Home Ruler".[1]

On another occasion, he said he was "proud of being a Protestant, though Protestantism is to me a great historic movement of Reformation, Aspiration and self-Assertion against spiritual tyranny rather than that organization of false gentility which so often takes its name in vain in Ireland".[2] The bogus gentility of Dublin Protestants had led them to empty their religion of much of its spiritual content, making the Church of Ireland more a social club than a community of true believers. This thinning may have been attributable, at least in part, to a shrewd intuition by the ascendancy class that a politicized version of self-election could issue only in one slogan: Sinn Féin.

That theological timidity troubled Shaw, who understood that it might eventually lead to the marginalization of the Protestant community in an Irish Free State which would badly need such people, if it were to become a pluralist democracy. He also foresaw how it could leave the way open for extremists of Northern Ireland to assume the leadership of Irish Protestantism, a development which proved even more disastrous than he had feared.

The false gentility of southern Protestants had roots that went back to the eighteenth century. In the 1790s, Edmund Burke had written that the clashes in Ireland had less to do with popes than with potatoes. The Irish problem, as he understood it, was the resolution of a Protestant minority to reduce a Catholic majority to slavery under a military power, and thereafter to divide the public revenues, the result of general taxation, as a military booty solely among themselves:

> By the use that is frequently made of the term . . . the name Protestant becomes nothing more or better than the name of a persecuting faction, with a relation of some sort of theological hostility to others, but without any sort of ascertained tenets of its own, upon the ground of which it persecutes other men; for the patrons of this Protestant Ascendancy neither do, nor can by anything positive, define or describe what they mean by the word Protestant.[3]

Shaw was simply rephrasing that idea, when he wrote that Irish Protestantism was "not then a religion but a side in a political faction; actuated less by theological principle than by class prejudice".[4]

His remedy for this state of affairs might have surprised many socialists, who would have expected him to call on the Protestants to abandon their spiritual posturing and to admit the material nature of their interest in Ireland. Instead, in 1912 – the year which marked the foundation of the paramilitary Ulster Volunteer Force – Shaw called upon them to recover the lost contents of their faith and become again fully-fledged protesters. "What is wanted on both sides of the Irish Sea", he wrote in that year, "is a little real Protestantism".[5] He saw the need for Protestant values, and not just token Protestants, at the centre of the Irish national and literary revival. Self-assertion against tyranny became, in Shaw's mind, the enabling principle of the modern nation-state. The education given the natives brought them to a point at which they could demonstrate how, even within its own set terms, the imperial code flagrantly contradicted itself.

Shaw's *Saint Joan* is, therefore, not just a feminist play: it is also a sharp dismissal of one of the earliest exercises in English expansionism. The Maid's claim that the English are fine at home and awful overseas anticipates a famous assertion in Forster's *A Passage to India* (1924): "the original sound may be harmless, but the echo is always evil".[6] In other words, the English in England behave with decency, but out in the colonies the rejects of that parent country offer only botched impersonations of the very people they have never managed to be. The result was what Burke and Shaw both described as a materialistic middle class posing as an aristocracy, falsifying themselves and inducing an echoing falseness in others. Forster showed in his novel how that echo could have lethal effects on those who heard it but could not identify it for what it was. Shaw's Joan has no such difficulty, and fights honourably to repulse the English to their own soil, on which they could be free to resume their true selves again.

By casting his Joan as a Catholic, who just happens to be a sort of Protestant saint, Shaw rebuked not just British imperialism, but those of his compatriots foolish enough to equate "Catholic" with "nationalist", or to see in the national revival the promise of a final triumph for Catholic Ireland. Exposing imperial mindsets, the play also repudiates the answering narrowness of a certain kind of Catholic nationalism.

The Palestinian writer Edward Said has complained that the study of imperialism as an issue was until quite recent times declared off-limits by most twentieth-century Anglo-American critics.[7] English and

American scholars worked in institutions often founded or funded with spoils of empire: and they were unlikely to bite the hand that feeds them.

If imperialism has been little considered in Anglo-American scholarship, the study of cultural Protestantism has been treated as off-limits in modern Ireland. There are many reasons for this. For one thing, at a time when murder-gangs prowled the streets of Belfast and Derry, genteel people shied away from any debate that savoured of the sectarian. Another explanation may lie in the fact that southern Protestantism puts a premium on private judgement and is correspondingly wary of making grandiose general statements about itself.[8] In the infant state, Protestants were reticent in the assertion of their civil rights, adopting a live-and-let-live policy, and acting with such self-effacement that they have been all but effaced. This near-erasure was effected partly by the Catholic Church's *Ne Temere* decree, which forbids the children of mixed marriages to be raised as Protestants; by the collapse of many rural parishes; by migrations to England; and so forth.

One consequence of this effacement may be the unspoken assumption by most literary critics that the Protestantism of leading Irish writers was only superficial, that it did not deeply colour their writings, and that, therefore, those who abandoned it could do so without the trauma registered by Joyce in the account of his own apostasy in *A Portrait of the Artist as a Young Man*. If Joyce can be credited with annexing, for his own artistic purposes, the notion of *epiphany* or the Catholic theory of *transubstantiation*, then it is no great surprise that libraries are full of books with titles like *Joyce Among the Jesuits* or *Joyce's Pauline Vision*. These studies are all written in the conviction that Joyce remained obsessed by the religion which he professed to reject, but there is not a single full-length book yet written on the Protestant elements in the art of Shaw. The same might be said of each of the following: O'Casey, Beckett, Synge, Yeats. This state of things is profoundly if quite unintentionally insulting to these artists, since it implies that their religious experiences were as shallow as those of the timid fellow-Protestants whom they criticized so fiercely in their writings.

A cursory inspection of their texts would reveal just how deeply they were imbued with Protestant values. Even the alleged thinness of southern Protestantism had a saving grace, for it threw its writers back upon their own resources. This may explain why Protestant Ireland continued to produce far more spiritually audacious artists than did Catholic Ireland, even – perhaps *especially* – after entering its slow decline in the latter half of the nineteenth century. The failure of Maynooth College, the national seminary founded in 1795, to produce a single theologian of international stature in its first century of existence was attributed by George Moore to the fact that "the Roman Catholic Church relies on its converts, for after two or three generations of Catholicism the intelligence dies".[9] The Protestant intellectual, by contrast, lived in a state of perpetual anxiety and self-questioning, as one of the few remaining leaders of a pressured minority whose clergy had ceded control, but it was a state conducive to the creation of literature.

In a mainly Catholic island, where the *nostra* of that faith were part of the air everyone breathed, few writers of Catholic background have cared to discuss the spiritual content of religion, preferring to focus (as Joyce did) on its social effects or its personal consequences. There is, of course, much writing about religion in Ireland, but, for all that, remarkably little religious writing, little spiritual probing in the literary form. What there is comes not so much from the Catholic side, as from Protestant-trained minds such as Shaw, Yeats, Beckett or O'Casey. The latter, for instance, always insists in his plays on self-responsibility as a Protestant virtue: in *The Plough and the Stars*, it is the drunken loyalist who finally sacrifices her life for Nora Clitheroe, while all around her Catholic neighbours speechify about Christian giving. The theatricalization of the nationalists evokes only O'Casey's distrust. In *Juno and the Paycock* his desire to strip away such symbolic artifice is implemented in the final removal from the stage of the few poor sticks of furniture which remain. The false consecration of the chalice by Harry Heegan at the central moments of *The Silver Tassie* may also arise from O'Casey's scepticism about a religious cult of blood-sacrifice, which can so easily be invoked by war-mongers. In *Red Roses For Me* a countervailing form of responsible Christianity is sponsored by the Protestant clergyman, who endorses a socialist strike against exploitative factory-owners.

Equally, Synge invented an Ireland which was a zone of displaced Protestantism. Finding his mother's evangelical fervour too great a burden to be borne, he propounded his own aesthetic version: "Soon after I had relinquished the Kingdom of God I began to take a real interest in the Kingdom of Ireland".[10] In *The Playboy of the Western World* may be found a series of reworked biblical themes – as, for example, when Shawn Keogh leaves his coat in the hands of the men in the shebeen: "Well, there's the coat of a Christian man!"[11] Christy, the Christ-like scapegoat, being presented with gifts by three village girls is a clear parody of the infant adored by the Magi . . . and so it is predictable that he should later ride an ass in triumphant entry after the sports, like Jesus on Palm Sunday, and that he should more generally take upon himself the "sins of the world". There is undeniable mockery in these manoeuvres, as if Synge were avenging himself on the rigid religion of his mother by having such unabashed pagans rehearse its themes: but that mockery is relatively light and gentle, compared to the savage handling of sacred Catholic references ("With the help of God, I did surely, and that the Holy Immaculate Mother may intercede for his soul").[12]

That anti-clerical strand in Synge's thought erupts spectacularly in *The Tinker's Wedding*, where the tying-up of a priest in a sack was deemed too unholy a gesture for early Abbey audiences: but it is never far from the surface of each of his plays, which delight in putting sacred formulae to frankly secular uses. *The Shadow of the Glen*, in its very title, recalls the biblical valley of darkness, with its intimations of dreadful evil and good shepherds. *The Well of the Saints* was originally called *When the Blind See*, but that underlying idea yields some very unholy conclusions: "The Lord protect us from the saints of God".[13] *Deirdre of the Sorrows*, set in an undeniably pre-Christian world, makes much of those motifs which the later churches never fully Christianized: "by the sun and the moon and the stars, I thee wed".[14] Synge remained obsessed by the Bible. There is a strongly biblical rhythm, tone and imagery to his language, and he was at all times fascinated by the idea of the Word.

Little wonder, then, that his characters are often so anxious to bring their lives into conformity with a revered text ("and a story will be told forever"),[15] though Synge was also aware, from his painful arguments with his mother, of the suffering to which this could give rise.

There was nothing triumphalist about the cultural Protestantism of such writers. Far from it. As in the case of Joyce, their conscious use of religious terminology was often subversive of the codes from which they had ripped it. They were exemplary instances of the mind "employing the energy imparted by evangelical convictions to rid itself of the restraint which Evangelicalism had laid on the senses and intellect; on amusement, enjoyment, art; on curiosity, on criticism, on science".[16] What distinguished them from Joyce, however, was the fact that so many of them came from families with ecclesiastical or rectory backgrounds – so many, indeed, that Vivian Mercier once joked that "the true purpose of the Irish Literary Revival was to provide alternative employment for the sons of clergymen after disestablishment had reduced the number of livings provided by the Church of Ireland".[17]

In fact, it was the convulsions wrought by Darwinism and the Higher Criticism which left these intellectuals unable to embrace the faith of their ancestors along traditional lines. (Had Catholic priests and nuns been allowed to marry, it is arguable that the intellectual life of Catholic Ireland might have been enriched by their offspring: but, under the rules of the Catholic Church, this was impossible.) Refusing to follow the clergyman's calling, the scions of the rectory sought to aestheticize elements of Protestant belief, in the conviction that the place once held by the priest would now be taken by the *literatus*. As soon as the Bible had been reduced to mere literature, it was inevitable that writers would assume burdens once thought more appropriate to the leaders of religion. With the waning of Christian belief came a crisis in the spiritual leadership of the Protestant community, which passed from clerical to lay intellectuals. The latter confidently expected to be held in the same esteem as the clergy had once been, and were often dismayed when their reluctance to preach the old beliefs led to their being disowned by family and by Anglo-Irish kindred.

Caught in the no-man's-land between the two main island traditions, they attempted to "theorize" their position, and to construct utopian schemes. The absence of a truly metropolitan culture in Dublin in the later nineteenth century, along with a centuries-old feeling of exclusion from real political influence over their land, was all the more conducive to such idealistic thinking. Standish O'Grady said "I have not come out from my own camp to join any other. I stand between the camps and call".[18] One of the attractions of the ancient Gaelic world lay in the fact that such people could identify with it as they could never have identified with post-Reformation Gaelic Ireland. It was sufficiently remote and vague to be malleable to their current purposes, but it also provided – pagan rituals and all – the bedrock on which a common Irish culture had been built before later divisions. Yeats, deprived by Huxley and Tyndall of "the simple-minded religion of my childhood", made a new religion, "almost an infallible Church of poetic tradition", of a fardel of Celtic stories.[19]

Nor was this enough. All of these writers wished for a fusion of two traditions, not just Gaelic with Anglo-Irish, but Catholic with Protestant as well. Their dream was of a wonderful new hybrid, nicknamed a *Protholic* or a *Cathestant*.[20] George Moore's threat to convert from Catholicism to Protestantism in the letters column of *The Irish Times* was a jocular expression of this *weltanschauung*: but the life and writings of Oscar Wilde provide a more contemplative example.

Wilde, though born and baptized a Protestant, died attended by a

Dublin Passionist. His art oscillates between a puritan distrust of art (*Dorian Gray* is a highly moral critique of the Paterian cult of intensified experience) and a luxurious surrender to the idea of the *felix culpa* or educative effects of sin ("Experience is the name that Tuppy gives to his mistakes").

The thesis of the Catholicized Protestant and the Protestantized Catholic had been implicit in the Irish Revival from the outset. It was hugely ironical that while Protestants like Hyde, Lady Gregory and Yeats went about collecting legends of healing wells and peasant miracles, the Catholic clergy was resolutely attempting to extirpate these beliefs, or at least, to subordinate them to a more rationalized theology. Each side appeared to be taking on some protective coloration from the other, in keeping with Yeats's declaration in his essays of the need to "bring the two halves together". His father, John Butler Yeats, had taught that the Catholic Church was "good for the heart but bad for the brain", adding that "had the Irish been Protestants they would long ago have thrown off the English tyranny".[21] This fully anticipated Shaw's statement that a true Protestant was *ipso facto* an Irish Republican.

All this did not mean that John Butler Yeats or George Bernard Shaw despised Catholicism: they simply felt that a fusion of both traditions would produce a new Ireland greater than the sum of its parts. If Matthew Arnold had hoped that Irish imagination could raise and ennoble English pragmatism and that both could couple in a complete British person, John Butler Yeats deftly repeated this manoeuvre, but in the opposite direction, recruiting the pragmatism of the English Protestant for an expanded and enhanced Irish personality. This appropriation was but another example of a "Celticist" idea reinterpreted by a Yeats in subtle and unexpected ways: for, while Arnold had proposed his fusion of Celtic and Saxon elements in order to deny the separatist claims of the Irish, John Butler Yeats mischievously modified it, with the strategic purpose of *asserting* that very claim. "Given the Protestant's natural efficiency", he told John Quinn, "the Catholic Irishman would leap to far higher altitudes than the Protestant will ever attain – because of his imagination and traditions".[22] The implication was inescapable: a true Irish intellectual would be a spiritually-hyphenated being, a well-balanced person with a chip on each shoulder. Every honest Catholic could henceforth become his or her own best priest; and, equally, all Protestants should be able to confess their sins, once in a while, not just to their God but to someone else.

It was Shaw, more than any other writer, who argued that without strong doses of Protestant self-reliance, the Irish Catholic mind would never free itself of imperial occupation. If Joyce could refer to

> O Ireland, my first and only love
> Where Christ and Caesar are hand in glove . . .[23]

Shaw contended that the unquestioning obedience given by Catholics to a priest whom they called "father" (rather than "brother") merely fostered in them a submissiveness which had proved invaluable to the English too. Shaw's own career, which he obliquely recounted in his version of *Saint Joan*, blasted a way out of that colonial impasse in its rejection of *all* fathers, paternal, ecclesiastical or imperial. Instead, he asserted the glory of the self-invented person, who fathers him- or herself. This attack on father-figures eventually led Shaw into a crusade against "bardolatry" or the worship of Shakespeare as the father of English literature. Set free of his birth certificate, which was burned during the shelling of government offices, Shaw managed to escape all the constraints of family, class and, indeed, nation. Though born into a family which had pretensions to wealth and position, he soon became what he jocosely termed a "downstart": he lost one class, but he entered no other.[24] Similarly, by emigrating to London, he lost a country, but embraced no other, for he was never accepted nor did he seek acceptance as an Englishman. Bohemia would henceforth be his native country: and in its open spaces he was free to create GBS *ex nihilo* (virtually), and to write plays which explored Protestant ideas of self-invention or self-determination.

In England, he discovered that he was apparently Irish, and also what this might be made to mean. He came to associate Dublin with poverty, failure and begrudgery, and London with ideas of self-help, will-power and energetic reform. Success came neither quickly nor easily, but by a disciplined programme of hard work, wide reading and relentless self-promotion, he achieved his goals, becoming in the process more and more enamoured of the puritan virtues which he found in a sub-stream of English authors from Milton and Bunyan down to Blake and beyond. It was this which convinced him of the need for real Protestantism back in Ireland. Ireland had been kept apart from the mighty stream of European Protestantism by its preoccupation with its own unnatural condition. A fixation on articulating grievances had kept the country light years behind others in social and industrial development. The remedy, however, was not to ignore the colonial wound, but to clean and cure it. Despite his internationalism, Shaw did not scruple to use a phrase like "this open wound of the denial of our national rights", asserting the entitlement of a people to be misgoverned (if need be) by themselves rather than efficiently repressed by others. "I would rather be burned at the stake by Irish Catholics", he announced, in yet another half-identification with Joan of Arc, "than be protected by an Englishman".[25]

Twenty-Four

Saint Joan – Fabian Feminist, Protestant Mystic

"A man always describes himself unconsciously whenever he describes anyone else", wrote Shaw. On another occasion, he phrased the same idea slightly differently by saying: "The best autobiographies are confessions, but if a man is a deep writer all his works are confessions".[1] The relationship between Protestantism and autobiography is well documented and is based on the fact that the Protestant confession is made to the self. In seeking a narrative of expiation, such a mind produces autobiography, sometimes taking the form of poetry as in the case of Wordsworth's *The Prelude* or of drama in the writings of Shaw.

Saint Joan, as depicted by the playwright, is, without ever knowing it, one of the earliest exponents of Protestant self-interrogation. She listens to her inner voices and follows their dictates, in the conviction that no mere priest or bishop should come between herself and her god. She upholds that right to private judgement which would, in later centuries, become a cornerstone of Protestantism. So Shaw, brought up as an Irish Protestant, came to interpret the career of this French Catholic peasant girl as a parable of emerging Protestantism in a Catholic-dominated society. In other words, he read her life in France as an allegory of his own youth in Ireland. As a boy he had believed that every Catholic, including famous ones such as Pope Pius IX or even Joan of Arc, would burn in the flames of hell:

Then when I was seven years old, Pope Pius IX ruled that I, though a little Protestant, might go to heaven in spite of my invincible ignorance. But I made no reciprocal concessions at the time. I hope this service of mine to the Church (the play *Saint Joan*) may be accepted as a small set-off against the abominable bigotry of my Irish Protestant childhood, which I renounced so ingloriously when I grew to some sort of discretion and decency that I emptied the baby out with the bath, and left myself for a while with no religion at all.[2]

This is tongue-in-cheek stuff, for it is as a nascent Protestant that Joan is celebrated by Shaw.

In his later years, the playwright did come to see himself as a versatile religious man, a kind of Catholic-Protestant. "My own faith is clear", he wrote somewhat jauntily, "I am a resolute Protestant, I believe in the Holy Catholic Church, the Holy Trinity of Father, Son (or Mother, Daughter) and Spirit, in the Communion of Saints, the life to come, the Immaculate Conception . . ."[3] Perhaps it is wisest, therefore, to see his Joan as an equivalent kind of Protestantized Catholic, a "Cathestant" imagined by a "Protholic".

If Shaw's childhood in Ireland may have helped him to feel his way into the situation of Joan, how truer still must this have been of his experience as a tongue-tied and timid young Irishman among the self-confident lions of literary London. His story, after all, was remarkably similar to Joan's: the youth from the provinces who comes to a big city, renounces a former role as one of life's losers, and proves twice as capable as any of his former masters. Moreover, the resolute feminism which caused Shaw to wonder whether God might not be a woman and Jesus his daughter would also have increased his identification with Joan, for she made herself manly, even as he sought to become womanly.

Shaw was himself convinced that, if Joan had been less manly and more womanly, she would probably have been canonized a saint long before the year 1920, when the honour was finally bestowed. Her emphasis on private judgement was, of course, a massive threat to the order of the medieval church and state, but so also was her sexual ambiguity construed as a challenge to the hierarchical relationship of male and female. She demanded the right to wear a soldier's clothes, and to have her hair bobbed in the manner of a young buck. This causes titters among the court ladies at the start of Shaw's play; but it was also one of the reasons for which she was eventually burnt at the stake as a witch. "I am a soldier", says Joan to her French comrade Dunois in the middle of the play, "I do not want to be thought of as a woman".[4]

The teaching of the Catholic Church on the issue of women in men's clothing was clear enough. The Book of Deuteronomy had taught that all who put on the garments of the opposite sex were "an abomination unto the Lord thy God". The historical Joan not only failed to relent, but – unlike Shaw's character – steadfastly refused to give any explanation of her behaviour, such as the preservation of her chastity among an army of uncouth and lewd men. One of her most recent biographers, Marina Warner, has accounted for that obstinacy in the following way:

> Through her transvestism she abrogated the destiny of womankind. She could thereby transcend her sex; she could set herself apart and usurp the privileges of the male and his claims to superiority. At the same time, by never pretending to be other than a woman and a maid, she was not only usurping a man's function but shaking off the trammels of sex altogether to occupy a different, third order, neither male nor female, but unearthly, like the angels whose company she loved.[5]

So Marina Warner contends that Joan's transvestism unsexed her, but that it did not confer manhood, leaving her instead an "ideal androgyne", to be known not as a woman but as a person. She goes on:

> There is no mode of being peculiar to the third sex, or to androgyny. But as the rejection of femininity is associated with positive action, it assumes the garb of virtue in the classical sense VIRTUS; and so she borrowed the apparel of men, who held, at least in theory, a monopoly on virtue, on reason and on courage, while eschewing the weakness of women, who were allotted to the negative pole, where virtue meant weakness and humility, and nature meant carnality.[6]

So the historical Joan saw herself not as male, but as "not-female", an epicene being who, in cutting her hair, renounced and transcended sexuality. The paradox was that, in the eyes of her inquisitors, this transvestism constituted an abomination, whereas under the eye of eternity that sexlessness gave her the appearance of saintliness, on the Pauline principle that after baptism "there is neither male nor female, for ye are all one in Christ Jesus". Marina Warner contends that such transcendence can never be complete, because the imitation of Christ is still the imitation of a man, and a man, moreover, who is taken as the human touchstone. "Ironically", she concludes, "Joan's life, probably one of the most heroic a woman has ever lived, is nevertheless a tribute to the male principle".[7]

This final judgement might be qualified. The *overt* appeal of a woman in man's clothing may well be to some vestigial concept of male superiority: but this would only be so if that clothing were obviously *borrowed* from a man, as in Shakespearian comedy. This is not at all the impression conveyed by Shaw's Joan. She does not seem enamoured of manliness: rather, she is embarrassed by the constrictions of gender. She is shown as one committed to breaking through the superficial trappings of personality to authentic selfhood, as in the early scene where she cleverly punctures the disguises of the Dauphin and Gilles de Rais, who have swapped robes in order to test her clairvoyant powers. Joan has, of course, no difficulty in doing this, even though the Dauphin is a stammering neurotic and Gilles de Rais has a naturally magnificent bearing. She drags out the retiring Dauphin by the arm, saying tenderly: "Gentle little Dauphin, I am sent to you to drive the English army from Orléans and from France, and to crown you king . . ."[8]

That feat of identification seems supernaturally sanctioned: and so the timid Dauphin is moved to a new self-confidence by her daring: "You see, all of you; she knew the blood royal. Who dare say now that I am not my father's son?" One of the most touching features of the ensuing play is the tender, yet probing, badinage between these two, as if Shaw had set out to illustrate Freud's contention that manly women are attractive to, and attracted by, womanly men. Just as the powerless peasant Joan donned male clothes to achieve saintly as well as military standing, so also as a political activist she worked through a male, this pliable Dauphin, in order to shape the destiny of France. Through him she put on male political clothing as well.

At many different points during Shaw's play, Joan's selflessness seems manifest – when she beseeches Captain Robert de Baudricourt at the start to permit her to go as a soldier in company to the Dauphin; or again before her interrogators; or, ironically this time, at the end in the face of her admirers. Deeper still, however, is the audience's awareness that only a woman of massive independence of mind would dare to expose herself to such risk. So she never seems more strong than when she seems most weak. No man in the world of the play ever conceives of her as a sexual object: and it is said by herself that she is not even good-looking. She appears to some, therefore, not so much as the virgin as a prototype of the witch; and it was doubtless as such that she was burned. This dimension makes her a logical precursor of today's feminists, and Shaw is at pains to exploit the connection between the historical figure and the liberated women of the 1920s in which the play was written. He particularly recreates her in the image of the Fabian woman of the Bloomsbury set, the kind of woman with whom Shaw mixed in London's intellectual circles.

This requires some explanation. All through the nineteenth century, men had put women on a pedestal of purity: by very definition, women were holier, purer, and more refined than men. The reasoning behind the ploy was clear enough: if women were refined, their delicacy must not be corrupted by the workaday world. The woman's place was in the home, as an angel of the house, preserving the values of civilization. Traditionalists argued that because she was refined, she was excused the burden of labour; but suffragists began to claim that because she was acquiescent, woman was denied the right to work and to vote in public affairs. The suffragists were right. Superior in theory, woman was deemed inferior in practice. What was fascinating, however, was the selective nature of the argument as advanced by many subsequent feminists. Although they rejected the notion of the woman's place being in the home, they never rejected the theory of woman's superior refinement and sensitivity. On the contrary, they used that as an argument for female independence and, in some extreme cases, for female dominance over men. In the Bloomsbury years, the 1910s and 1920s, this movement reached its flowering in a spectacular range of non-sexual relationships between androgynous women and passive men, the assumption being that woman, by her fastidiousness and grace, might civilize and ennoble her comrade.

Joan is a precursor of that tradition. In her relation with the Dauphin, she casts herself in the part of feminist civilizer. It is, of course, the woman in the Dauphin who is responding to the man in Joan, the woman who by tradition longs to have the world explained to her by a resourceful and canny man. However, in this case the explainer is the manly woman Joan. She contains both masculine and feminine attributes, as do many adolescents in whom gender orientations are as yet unresolved. In this also lies a clue to her stature as a comprehensive and universal heroine: the fact that, as a seventeen-year-old, she is in some ways still a child. Her final victory is the triumph of youth over age: she compels the old to adjust to the standards of the young, and the result is human progress. Even more subtly, in the part of a guileless child, she is able to confront the moral theologians with peasant proverbs and country wisdom, attempting – like a dynamic conserva-tive – to hold them true to the deepest implications of their own Christian tradition, a tradition which had been occluded and almost lost amid the rationalizations of priests.

This cuts to the core-value of the play: Shaw's Protestant distrust of a separate, self-appointed priesthood and his alternative view that every person should be his or her own priest. The deepest drama of the Protestant tradition is the one enacted between the individual soul and its God. To come between a sinner and his God is a terrible deed, for

Protestantism has a rooted distrust of the Catholic confessional (and what are the central inquisition scenes of Shaw's play but an obscenely protracted confession?). The Protestant confession tends to be a non-specific admission of guilt, but in the play the inquisition is cruelly pedantic in its pursuit of every possible detail of Joan's behaviour. For Shaw, a true confession is made to oneself and not to another person, much less an assembled gallery. This insistence was not just theological. He applied it also to doctors, dentists, lawyers, and all professions which claimed mastery of an arcane and learned discipline. He accused each profession of being "a conspiracy against the laity".

So, what better way to depict the obfuscations of the professional than by confronting the learned theologians with a child-mystic, by confronting the scholars of books with the listener to voices? As H. L. Mencken wrote in his book *The Nature and Origin of Religion*:

> The business of wrestling with omnipotence tends to fall into the hands of specialists, which is to say, into the hands of men who by habit and training are sub-normally god-shy and have a natural talent for remonstrance and persuasion. These specialists, by trial and error, develop a professional technique, and presently it is so complicated and highly formalized that the layman can scarcely comprehend it.[9]

Joan does not think of herself as a theologian, rather as a plain country girl caught in an unfamiliarly magnificent room with princes of the church whose words she cannot understand. She says what she thinks, because she is honest by nature and also because she is blissfully unaware of what she is supposed to think. Other Shavian heroines – such as Mrs. Warren or Raina – were painfully aware of how they appeared to others, and constantly viewed themselves through the eyes of an implied male. Joan, by contrast, is unaware of the courtly art of self-presentation. For Shaw she was just a paragon of ferocious simplicity: a country girl, rough-hewn and unadorned, and *not* a stained-glass saint. The play stresses the *accidental* nature of sainthood – given or withheld at the whim of vain professionals – and the intrinsic nature of a saintliness which is never conscious of itself as such. Since saintliness is innate rather than learned, Shaw slyly implies that it is impossible for the learned to be saintly. In this way, he dismantles the age-old association in the Catholic Church of learning and piety.

H. L. Mencken also contended that "within all the great religions there arise, from time to time, cults, which seek to rid worship of its formalization and artificiality. One of the most familiar of them is called mysticism". Joan is such a mystic, one of the elect who hears voices and deals directly with God. She therefore finds God wholly real and assumes neither a different voice nor an alternative vocabulary when speaking either to or about him. She bypasses all forms of liturgy and all human mediators with the divine. She experiences religion in its pristine mystical form. Of mysticism Mencken has written:

> The priests of all faiths naturally view such practices with suspicion, for they tend to discount the value of dogma and to make the devotee self-reliant and intractable. Open any treatise on pastoral theology and you will find the author warning his sacerdotal readers against old women who pray too much and are otherwise too intimate with God. If all the faithful inclined to mysticism, there would be empty pews in the churches and the whole ecclesiastical structure would begin to rock.[10]

For a brief period, at the end of the middle ages, Protestantism offered a return to the mystical experience, by curtailing the self-importance of priests and by leaving the faithful soul alone in the presence of the word of God. Joan is the creature of just such a moment in the history of religion; but, as a moment, it could not last for long. By the year 1522 Luther was already excommunicating the Anabaptists with all the intolerant certainty of a medieval pope, and his followers were docilely accepting his teaching, which had already erected itself as a scaffolding of rational analysis around the mystical moment.

As an exponent of late Catholicism, however, Shaw's Joan can be presented as an authentic precursor of true Protestantism, whose childishness takes an appropriate form. This, also, needs some explanation. Catholicism had tended to pursue sanctity within the quarantine of the monastery, a holy place set apart from the hubbub of life; but Protestantism was to reject such a self-conscious form of saintliness and to insist that virtue could only be virtue if tested out in the world. The puritan John Milton wrote, for instance, that he could never praise "a fugitive and cloistered virtue".[11] This Renaissance debate anticipates a nineteenth-century dispute as to whether childhood innocence should be quarantined or tested out in the world. Shaw took the latter view – Blake had always been a major influence on his thinking – and he saw Joan as an innocent abroad rather than enclosed.

As child, as woman, as manly soldier, as saint, as foremother of Protestantism and of French nationalism, Joan is one of the most versatile and composite heroines in the history of literature. The actress Judi Dench has said that, technically, the role is one of the most difficult in the theatre, since "when you're old enough to play it, you're too old".[12] Another difficulty is that Joan falls into none of the obvious categories of female heroism. There is a traditional way for an actress to play a queen, or a mother, or a romantic beauty, or even a saint; but Joan, in her day, was none of these things. She became, therefore, an open space into which any age or author could read a preferred meaning – to the feminist, a liberated woman; to the religious, a saint; to the French, a patriot; and so on.

Since Catholics are encouraged to believe unreservedly or not at all, so Joan's canonization implied a complete repudiation of those who tried and sentenced her.[13] Shaw rejected such Manichean analysis and in his play depicted no clash of good against evil, preferring to see the conflict as one of consensus against conviction. This allowed him to create complex characters who are a credible blend of idealism and cynicism, of fervour and pragmatism.

Like a latter-day Marxist, Joan speaks as if history had a necessary shape and the whole duty of the individual were to recognize that necessity. For now, according to her, nothing should come between king and people, just as no priests should come between the soul and its god. Joan's idea is rather similar to the argument by James Connolly in *Labour in Irish History* that a Gaelic ruler held land in trust to God on behalf of an entire people.[14] Warwick knows that if the people look to the king rather than their immediate feudal lord, then aristocracy is lost. And he fears that the Church might work willingly with the centralized power of the king: which is to say that he predicts what eventually happened. His enemy is two-pronged: Protestant private judgement in theology, the national separatist idea in politics.

This is a reminder that in his writings on Ireland Shaw consistently equated these two forces, on the basis that a truly Protestant Ireland would necessarily throw off English misrule. He was well aware that the whole idea of a united Ireland under a central administration was a largely Protestant invention: and that the corollary was obvious – the words "Catholic" and "nationalist" did not so easily go together as some glib Irish persons hoped. Nationalism, says Cauchon in the play, "is essentially anti-Catholic . . . for the Catholic Church knows only one realm, Christ's Kingdom".[15] The Archbishop points out caustically that, though the mob may love Joan, it cannot save her from the stake: only the church can do that. She replies in the tones of mystics from Eckhardt to Simone Weil: "What is my loneliness before the loneliness of my country and my God?"[16] The voices have never played her false.

The Inquisition is thereby divided. The Dominican Ladvenu hears echoes of the saints in her voice, while the Inquisitor hears only a diabolical pride alongside natural humility within the same soul. He reminds Joan of the fickleness of the common people as contrasted with the stability of the Church. Yet the Church itself has *not* been consistent, having surrendered her to a merely *political* force, her English enemies. Like those critics who read into Joan's life whatever meanings they wish, her inquisitors are wayward and shifting in their accusations – of flying like a witch, of wearing men's clothes, of theological disobedience. Shaw himself believes in the need for order: but he knows also that progress depends on disobedience. Hence the paradox finally conceded by Cauchon: that the heretic is always better dead, for mortal eyes cannot distinguish saint from heretic.

Her answers to cross-questioning show Joan possessed of a clear mind. She dressed as a soldier to avoid sexual impropriety. Asked if she is in a state of grace, she says "If not, may God bring me to it; if I am, may he keep me in it".[17] She turns the allegation of heresy skilfully back into the faces of her accusers, but is condemned anyway to solitary confinement to the end of her days in order to protect her soul. And all this after repenting! This is an interesting moment, for it allows Shaw to relaunch his old critique of jails as effective centres of penal correction. Far from shielding her, prison is more likely to expose her to the vices of the assembled criminals. Shaw's case against prisons is much the same as the puritan case against monasteries: both are unnatural communities, where people of a similar disposition are artificially banded together in an over-intense fashion, rather than being distributed evenly across a community on which they can act, if they are holy, or which can act upon them for their correction, if they are not. In effect, what the Inquisitor sentences Joan to is the life of a nun, eating simple food in solitary contemplation. She cannot accept this: the palpable injustice of the verdict convinces her once again that her accusers are idiots and it seems to her that they must be wrong about her voices too. So she goes to the stake.

The Epilogue simply establishes the further folly of all consensus viewpoints, by depicting the men who, a generation after her death, found it safe to declare her accusers not only mistaken but corrupt. Shaw has been at pains to show them as humane, if intellectually limited, men. Thus he rejects moral absolutism and prefers to focus instead on the appalling ordinariness of persecution: the worst tyrannies are the ones never noticed, because based on accepted everyday criteria. The road to hell is truly paved with the good intentions of sincere functionaries: as Joan says on her reappearance "They were as honest a lot of poor fools as ever burned their betters". Or, as the still-living Charles says to the now-dead Cauchon: "It is always you good men that do the big mischiefs".[18] The English chaplain de Stogumber appears, to confess that he connived in the cruelty to Joan simply because he had no idea from his own experience of what it would entail. "Must then a Christ perish in torment in every age to save those who have no imagination?"[19] and the answer is "Yes". The Catholic Church had to wait four hundred years before it found it safe to canonize its first Protestant!

And no sooner is she canonized than Joan fears that this may be a way of neutralizing her subversive powers. Canonized, and therefore forgotten. And so she returns insistently, forgotten but not gone, to say "Woe unto me when all men praise me!" and to ask when will the world be ready to receive its saints: "How long, Oh Lord, how long?"[20] For she is burned at the stake every day: and she will burn again.

Twenty-Five

The Winding Stair

Shaw wrote most of *Saint Joan* while sojourning in Glengariff and Parknasilla, County Kerry, in the summer of 1923: and he took the opportunity to test his "trial scene" by reading it aloud to two Catholic priests, Fathers Leonard and Sheehy.[1] Writing in the heart of republican Kerry, the backdrop of so many recent battles, Shaw must have sensed many local resonances in the theme of a nation fighting free of the shackles of foreign ownership. Like many of the Irish rebels, Joan was not a landless peasant but the offspring of strong farmer stock: "I come from the land . . ." The strange alliance of noblemen and clergy against the Maid would have been instantly decoded by Fathers Leonard and Sheehy as symbolic of those Catholic bishops who defended Anglo-Irish privilege and who excommunicated members of the Irish Republican Army. Even more challenging to them would have been Shaw's implication that nationalism was not necessarily to be equated with Catholicism, despite their imminent elision in the infant state. Throughout the play, Joan displays a subversive and enigmatic character, which refuses to reduce itself to a formula, a strangely open space which disrupts all complacent codes with which she comes into contact, as their sponsors wander in bafflement around her apparent irresolution. She refuses to become predictable or categorizable, even though she stays always simple.

Rejecting the idea of a national heroine as a "little old woman" or restored Cathleen-ní-Houlihan-style queen, Shaw celebrated instead an ideal androgyne. Deriding the masculinist values so often linked to notions of nationhood in the rhetoric which had been generated by the Great War and the Easter Rising, he explored the "flapper" psychology of the postwar period, including the new fashionability of the manly woman. Dismissing the sectarianism of both the north of Ireland and the south, he proposed his Joan as a Protestantized Catholic. Thus, he broke free of imperialist thinking; but he insisted, nonetheless, that the presence of the invading English had been a constructive element in the shaping of a French – or, by implication, an Irish – identity. Joan's self is wonderfully multiple: while others wish to simplify it for the sake of control, she refuses to surrender any of her identities, whether as soldier, woman, saint or mystic.

It can hardly have been a coincidence that, at that moment when Catholic triumphalists were seeking to make the independent Irish state an instrument of their theology, Shaw should have asserted that the woman canonized by the Vatican in 1920 was really an honorary Protestant. Nor can it have been an accident that the Protestant characters who began as peripheral figures on O'Casey's stage should so often have ended as the moral centres of the dramatic action. Repeatedly, in such writings of the 1920s and 1930s, the Protestant ethic emerges in sharp focus against a general Roman Catholic back-drop, as if to suggest that the artists were keenly alert to the dangers of a narrowly Catholic definition of Irish identity. A strange paradox emerged from all this: the mission to Protestantize Irish culture was only achieved to a significant degree *after* its sponsors had effectively conceded defeat in the political sphere. The ulterior motive of political oppression finally failed: the declared, "insincere" motive was honoured in the end, but in a highly occluded way within the zones of art. Of no set of texts is this more true than of the poems collected by W. B. Yeats in his 1933 volume entitled *The Winding Stair*.

If the lyrics of *The Tower* had been bound by a unifying theme, that must have been a Protestant scepticism about the worship of ideals or images: and, for Yeats, an ideal was invariably crystallized in an image. There was great danger in such raids on the ineffable, and the greatest danger of all lay in the indifference which might be the price of full knowledge: a discovery rendered in the bleak, bitter monosyllables at the end of "Leda and the Swan". If the half-said thing remained a mystery, the fully-rendered thing was by that very virtue lost – an idea which appears, slightly rephrased, in his autobiography: "Now that I have written it out, I may even begin to forget it".[2] This, under one aspect, is an idea of ritual purgation, but it has its liabilities as well. Even in the very exigencies of expression Yeats found a necessary and prior indifference, as in his account – in *Autobiographies* – of the actress who could mimic religious fervour and repentance only after their abatement, because by then they left her lukewarm enough to regard them from a dispassionate distance. Art itself might therefore be often no more than a successful faking of feelings which are all-but-dead to the artist. In conception and in execution, therefore, it might indeed be a scandal to the puritan conscience, a style bereft of honest content, a play-acting by the insincere.

Many of Yeats's essays on the folk poetry of the peasantry mix such a puritan distrust of "imitation" *per se* with a specifically national suspicion of the emulation of English forms which do not fit Irish experience. "If we busy ourselves with poetry and the countryman, two things which have always mixed with one another in life as on the stage", he wrote in 1902, "we may recover, in the course of years, a lost art which, being an imitation of nothing English, may bring our actors a secure fame and a sufficient livelihood".[3] In later decades, as a mature playwright, Yeats grew ever more scornful of the modes of "English" realism in an art which all too obviously sought to imitate, and in that sense compete with, life. Yeats's love of anti-representational theatre, a theatre which presents a truth of internal coherence rather than exterior correspondence to a known world, may have unexpected roots in his puritan unease at a too-easy confusion of art and life. The older, more primitive but more honestly conventional art forms are praised as being also much more beautiful, as opening up a magnificently alternative world rather than a badly-faked version of this one: "We have to prepare a stage for the whole wealth of modern lyricism, for an art that is close to pure music, for those energies that would free the arts from imitation, that would ally acting to decoration and to the dance".[4]

To answer the gnawing fear that art may, nonetheless, be an act in bad faith, it became necessary for the older Yeats to strive to bring into being a man who could decently lie behind his own artist's utterances. The worry which shadows the later poems of Yeats is that his youthful elevation of style over content was morally culpable, an exercise of "power" without appropriate "knowledge". He had seen the rape of Leda as a version of artistic inspiration, but a scandal as well; and so he identified more with the put-upon woman than the supernatural assailant. The fear that people are violated rather than illuminated by image-worship is repeated in "The Mother of God" in the 1933 volume; the subject is, of course, the Virgin Mary, a figure who traditionally raises the issue for Irish Protestants:

> What is this flesh I purchased with my pains,
> This fallen star my milk sustains,
> This love that makes my heart's blood stop,
> Or strikes a sudden chill into my bones
> And bids my hair stand up?[5]

Again, the experience is ambiguous. In directly adopting the female voice, the poet seems more unnerved than illuminated, as he assumes Mary's ignorance under visitation by the image. He, too, is a vehicle for such visitors of power, but one lacking in philosophic knowledge of what it may all portend. So in "Vacillation", he feels obliged to ask "What, be a singer born, and lack a theme?"[6] Like Samuel Beckett who made destitution sumptuous with possibility, Yeats could indeed proclaim that failure as a new theme in itself; and contend that *style* in such an art was no mere decoration, but a code-word for puritan self-conquest, for the perpetual struggle that is the pilgrim's progress. This would be the element in Beckett's writings saluted with the immortal quip "Themes, madame, I know not themes"; or, as Yeats was wont to ask, "What theme had Homer but original sin?"[7]

So Yeats's autobiography became the account of a man with a very few poses labouring to give birth to a self which might turn them into themes. R. P. Blackmur phrased the matter even more subtly when he proclaimed that Yeats's search was for a mode of expression rather than for a dogma to express.[8] This idea – of the limited importance of having ideas – is canvassed repeatedly in *Autobiographies*, where each truly great character is praised for choosing only one pose and holding to it: Raphael and Titian for constantly striking one note, and Homer for relentlessly pursuing "original sin".

Yeats's is a poetry which would, in all probability, cease to communicate if it were ever fully known, because its images would retain no power in reserve. Such reserves could, however, frighten a poet who, like Beckett, could break off the illusion created by his own writings, sometimes in mid-sentence. On the other hand, he must have wondered whether the poetry that ensued was not a surrender to stereotypes of the non-analytic, impulse-driven Celt, whose verbal skill outstripped his intellectual control; and he must have been even more perturbed by a too-easy mastery, by the trite or facile triumph of a kind represented by the golden bird in "Sailing to Byzantium". That figure achieved its qualified triumph as a subordinate image, but only at the cost of mobility and growth.

In "Sailing to Byzantium" the golden bird was "set upon" a golden bough to sing to lords and ladies and a drowsy Emperor. Now, in "Byzantium", art is no longer a mere servant of the Emperor, but has been elevated to the status of the imperial itself. Is the poem, thereby, a celebration of imperialism? Hardly, for it is the dangers, violence, even deadliness of image-making and of artistic triumph which are uppermost here. The twilight days of empire are dismissed at the opening with contempt, as are the unredeemed images:

> The unpurged images of day recede;
> The Emperor's drunken soldiery are abed;
> Night resonance recedes, night-walker's song
> After great cathedral gong;
> A starlit and a moonlit dome disdains
> All that man is,
> All mere complexities,
> The fury and the mire of human veins.[9]

The scene sketched is one of late-imperial, O'Caseyesque disorder, as prostitutes live off the remaining drunks of a bedraggled imperial army; and the attempt is to convert that tainted place into another Byzantium, a holy city where art and religion meet, as in the cathedral dome. This will be achieved by the poet's capacity to summon and then to purge a satisfactory image, to use art as a means of reaching God. To Sturge Moore's famous criticism that the golden bird of the earlier poem was as much of nature as of man's body, there will now be an answering supernatural affirmation. Yet, for all its rhetorical brilliance and technical power, the poem itself seems quite unsatisfied with its own resolution. The miraculous bird in stanza three is described as "embittered by the moon", by the world of time, seasons and human generation. The technical problem posed for the poet in "The Second Coming" is faced yet again: how to employ merely earthly images to conjure an unearthly condition, which will be free of all images and image-making? How can *images* be used meaningfully to describe a state in which all earthly symbolic codes have been cut free of their moorings? It can only be done by negatives:

> At midnight on the Emperor's pavement flit
> Flames that no faggot feeds, nor steel has lit . . .[10]

– and *that* to evoke flames at street-corners where soul is purified by an act of imagination! The technique is doomed to fail and the poem itself concedes it: "an agony of flame that cannot singe a sleeve" is Yeats's evocation of the unpurged guilt of dead souls arriving in heaven. In fact, the final stanza, though continuing to assert the imperial imagination's power to break up the bitter furies of our complex world into the eternal shapes of art, ends by returning us to the opening stanza and to its mire, fury and late-imperial squalor:

Those images that yet
Fresh images beget . . .

Here was enacted yet another failed attempt to escape from art to the
higher zones of the soul. Yeats believed that martyr and saint must first
show a capacity for all those worldly things that they subsequently
renounce; and so must the artist show a capacity to experience the
religious vision. This explains why Yeats, in the words of a brilliant
critic, saw art not as something you escaped to so much as something
you escaped from.[11] Yet he remained haunted by the mystery of art
which he flouted. Since it was apparently futile to use art in the attempt
to transcend art, the planned escape could never be fully achieved.
Hence the rising curve of rhetorical expectation in each stanza's deliberated syntax, followed by the inexorable "downer" of final lines such as

An agony of flame that cannot singe a sleeve . . .

or

I call it death-in-life or life-in-death[12]

That last line is self-lacerating, being a patently poor approximation for
the "superhuman" and a borrowing from Coleridge to boot. These last-
line exercises in bathos enact the same trajectory of anticlimax, which
may be found in the closing lines of the stanzas of "Among School
Children", where again the poet is distraught by the way in which
images live on to tease most cruelly their authors with a mockery of
their initial high intentions.

The poems of *The Winding Stair* offer some kind of answer to the
bleak pessimism of *The Tower*. As Yeats in ill-health turns into a
character out of Beckett, he flirts ever more closely with the possibility
of his own death; and, with each flirtation, feels himself summoned
back to life, if only for one more celebration of the colossal vitality
displayed by friends like Hugh Lane and Lady Gregory in the face of
their own mortality. In "Coole Park and Ballylee 1931", Yeats again
evokes the swan as an emblem of Anglo-Irish power and pride; but,
linked to the ailing Lady Gregory in this way, the image is no longer
threatening. Rather, its very strength and careless pride leave it precarious and vulnerable to bestial instincts of a lesser kind:

Another emblem there! That stormy white
But seems a concentration of the sky;

> And, like the soul, it sails into the night
> And in the morning's gone, no man knows why;
> And it is so lovely that it sets to right
> What knowledge or its lack had set awry,
> So arrogantly pure, a child might think
> It can be murdered by a spot of ink.[13]

Here the suggestion is of a superb animal destroyed by a stroke of a pen, a pen wielded by that very poet who earlier felt threatened with madness by the selfsame image. This is not just a wonderful example of Yeats as deconstructor, but a characteristic warning, repeated through many works, of the corrupting effects of the written word. The "spot of ink" spells the death of "life" and its replacement by "a logical process".

This recurring debate between faith and good works had been initiated decades earlier by Wilde, who said that he had put his genius into his life and only his talent into his work. Because *he* opted for art, Yeats cannot help looking over his shoulder at the road not taken and wondering whether it might not have been better to throw "poor words" away and start "to live". Hence, his view of art as something he might yet escape from. The argument between faith and good works comes to a head in the short poem called "The Choice":

> The intellect of man is forced to choose
> Perfection of the life, or of the work,
> And if it take the second must refuse
> A heavenly mansion, raging in the dark.
> When all that story's finished, what's the news?
> In luck or out the toil has left its mark:
> That old perplexity, an empty purse,
> Or the day's vanity, the night's remorse.[14]

Because art is unthinkable in heaven, where all perfectly-attuned beings are (we may assume) silent, the poet must risk damnation and repudiate the heavenly mansion. Only in suffering here on earth are images endowed with the redemptive strangeness of art: "Only an aching heart / Conceives a changeless work of art".[15] Such an art may soothe the pain it describes so well, but it changes or improves nothing: "what's the news?" All that can be said with certainty is that, like the Dancer in "Among School Children" who bruised body to pleasure soul, like the woman of "Adam's Curse" who laboured to be beautiful, like the poet who found fascination in what's difficult, so here, whether he had chosen life or art, the speaker would anyway have found himself choosing pain, difficulty, sweat: "In luck or out the toil has left its mark". If this option for self-improvement sounds like hard work and Samuel Beckett, then so it should: though both writers enjoy their cavalier moments of nonchalance and unalloyed ease, each is also humiliated by the curse of that rather Protestant Adam who learned that we pay for our pleasures.

This element in Yeats's thought had never been wholly dormant. The opening passage of *Autobiographies* describes how the young boy in Sligo had heard an inner voice of accusation at a remarkably early age:

> One day someone spoke to me of the voice of conscience, and as I brooded over the phrase, I came to think that my soul, because I did not hear an articulate voice, was lost. I had some wretched days until, being alone with one of my aunts, I heard a whisper in my ear, "What a tease you are". At first I thought my aunt must have spoken, but when I found she had not, I concluded it was the voice of my conscience and was happy again. From that day the voice has come to me at moments of crisis, but now it is a voice in my head that is sudden and startling. It does not tell me what to do, but often reproves me.[16]

From such beginnings, it is hardly surprising that Yeats should have come to define poetry as coming from the quarrel with oneself, a sort of secular application of the notion of "every man his own priest". He found that certain movements of the Protestant spirit might actually be conducive to, rather than inimical to, the creation of art: for, as he often observed, a mind cannot create until it is split in two. The puritan campaign against theatricality was, in fact, a self-defeating enterprise, since its call to introspection actually encouraged a man to play before himself, to stand back from himself and to try to imagine how the varied aspects of his own personality might appear to others.

Yeats's criticism of the provincial was that he lacked this spiritual discipline and so had no sense of his own presence, being doomed to define himself in terms set by a distant metropolis. Dowden was his tell-tale specimen: having failed to trust his own nature,[17] he wrote as would any Englishman of Shakespeare and of Shelley. This was, at root, a refusal of self-election by a provincial mind, which is contrasted, at the end of *Autobiographies*, with Synge's sturdily independent sensibility, that of an authentic national artist, who is depicted as reading only the classics and never bothering with newspapers or with the views of his inferiors.[18] So, by somewhat devious routes, Yeats came to endorse

Shaw's thesis of a connection between Protestantism and nationalism. His instancing of Dowden as a provincial was not only a way of hinting at what an alternative metropolitan selfhood might be, but also an exposure of one who was deficient in the true puritan techniques of self-scrutiny. A failure of the religious imagination militates against the creation of an autonomous national identity, which in turn accounts for an apostasy in the zones of art. If there is no nationality without literature, there is no great literature without nationality.

Many poems of Yeats achieve their electric power from the tension in them between two rival voices. Often, the overt structure of entire poems is based on such a debate, between He and She, or Hic and Ille (or, as Ezra Pound mocked, Hic and Willie). This was a characteristic strategy of the post-Protestant imagination at the end of the nineteenth century: in *The Autobiography of Mark Rutherford*, for example, William Hale White introduced "characters whose function is to speak for another side of his own mind and test ironically the strength of his developing convictions".[19] Another of White's tactics – to set his mature ideas alongside those of his troubled, younger self – will be equally familiar to readers of Yeats. But it is in *The Winding Stair* collection that these elements of split and secularized Protestantism, implicit in earlier work, are brought to the surface in a deliberate and explicit fashion, and this most clearly in "A Dialogue of Self and Soul".

In seeking literary sources for the poem, it is usual to mention Andrew Marvell's "Dialogue Between Soul and Body", but an equally valid source might well be Samuel Ferguson's prose work, *A Dialogue Between the Head and Heart of an Irish Protestant*. On the surface, the poet appears to choose Self, rebirth and the impure satisfactions of image-making over Soul, heaven and that stonelike silence which seems to pervade it. A closer reading reveals a Beckettian encounter, not a dialogue at all so much as a set of non-intersecting monologues, contributed by two speakers who can bear any ignominy, stress or toil, except that of listening to one another.

Soul summons Self to climb the stair to the top and thence to heaven, where all thought is concluded; he proposes escape from the "crime" of birth (another Beckettian twist); and he offers forgiveness on condition that art is abandoned ("man is stricken deaf and dumb and blind") and silence supervenes ("when I think of that my tongue's a stone"). Self cannot accept. The sword in his hand, though a consecrated holy object with its place in sacred ritual, is also a work of art and of war. The entire second half of the poem is Self's attempt not just to embrace the world of pain, toil and image-making, but in doing so to appropriate most of the vocabulary and insights of the now-silent Soul. Soul had asserted that "only the dead can be forgiven", but Self manages to sacralize art and, after confessing in classic Protestant fashion to himself, he is ready to "forgive myself the lot". Consequently, in the final lines, he is not just artistically creative, laughing and singing, not just "blessed", but also – like Coleridge's Mariner – redeemed by being once again able *to bless*:

> We are blest by everything,
> Everything we look upon is blest.[20]

The appropriation of Soul's terms and gestures may legitimize that closing use of the plural "we". Soul, though the initial summons to the stair was intransitive, did once refer to the emblem discussed by Self; it was Self who remained absolutely averse to interaction, lest he lose in heaven his capacity for art. A living man, though blind and drunk, can make images (however repetitive his diction) out of human suffering; a soul in pure darkness of ancestral night would find the tongue a stone. As if to bear this out, there is something strangely moribund about the smooth surfaces of Soul's diction. Self is not just a more moving poet, but his lines have a deliberate awkwardness and cultivated jaggedness which anticipate Beckett's own use of repetition and his own cultivation of linguistic clumsiness:

> . . . The mirror of malicious eyes
> Casts upon his eyes until at last
> He thinks that shape must be his shape.[21]

All those repetitions of "man", "faces", "What matter?", "I am content" are hardly suggestive of a careless cavalier ease. The final resolution, though real enough, has an element of strain and forcing about it – "I am content . . . I am content" – as if the anxious, conscience-stricken poet were not really certain that his sins were shriven at all. "We *must* laugh" precedes "We are blest".

In his magisterial book *The Protestant Ethic and the Spirit of Capitalism*, Max Weber addresses this very point: the awful uncertainty and loneliness of a religion which, having done away with person-to-person confession, found it had also abolished "the means to a periodical discharge of the emotional sense of sin".[22] The hardest person of all to forgive turns out to be oneself; and so the sinner is doomed to seemingly endless repetitions of the same narrative in hope of some

eventual expiation. Hence, Beckettian monologue and Yeatsian autobiography. Hence, also, the obsession with the word "remorse"
throughout *The Winding Stair*, whether the "night's remorse" of "The
Choice", the "cast out" remorse of "A Dialogue of Self and Soul", or
the plainly confessed "Remorse for Intemperate Speech".

The Self which forgives at the close of "A Dialogue of Self and Soul"
is, by definition, a deeper, more comprehensive self than the past
person who committed the crime and is now forgiven. Yeats's poetry
places itself within the tradition of a "search for evidences", which
encouraged a self-absorbed spirituality always keen to deduce symbolic
meanings for the self from any minor mutation of weather or landscape. The old puritan demand for "justification" is now applied to
nature, which is asked to provide a measure of the continuity and the
distance between past and present selves. The idealized landscapes of
childhood may evoke in Yeats a strong sense of national feeling (akin,
perhaps, to that felt by a soldier dying for his country on foreign
battlefields), but they are also the locales which evoke memories of
unconfessed, hard-to-admit guilts, as in "Vacillation":

> Things said or done long years ago,
> Or things I did not do or say
> But thought that I might say or do,
> Weigh me down, and not a day
> But something is recalled,
> My conscience or my vanity appalled.[23]

In that poem, Soul canvasses the claims of an artless heaven; the Heart
worries about its lack of philosophic theme, but decides that the fallen
world of Homer, its images constantly awaiting transformation, is
sufficient. However, the title makes it abundantly clear that this conclusion is reached only with much vacillation.

The remorseful failure to obey the Protestant ethic of getting gold is
brought about in "Vacillation" by the poet's submission to a deeper
puritan imperative – his need to unlock, study and know his inner self.
Like the subject of Beckett's 1938 novel *Murphy*, Yeats is caught
between the desire for workaday success ("perfection of the life") and
self-interrogation ("perfection of the work"). Reflecting this, there is a
tension throughout *The Winding Stair* between the attempted *sprezzatura* of "what matter?" and the ignominy and pain known in the
process of making a self. One part of Yeats, the idle, reckless, would-
be-aristocrat, does indeed say "what matter?"; but another aspect, his

middle-class and rather puritanical conscience, stands "appalled".

That conflict, common to more than Yeats and Beckett among modern Irish writers, had its roots in eighteenth-century Ireland, where a severe restriction of Catholic opportunity and a high degree of social mobility in the Church of Ireland community made for careers open to Protestant talents. The result was what the historian J. C. Beckett has called "a kind of aristocratic egalitarianism – since it was generally safe to assume that an Irish gentleman was a Protestant, there was a temptation to reverse the order and to assume that an Irish Protestant was a gentleman".[24] Even in that witty formulation, however, may be noted a fatal discrepancy which troubled John Butler Yeats between hard work and gentlemanly leisure: he complained that most Protestants could not really be gentlemen, because a gentleman by very definition was not preoccupied with getting on in the world and yet Protestant Ireland seemed to think of little else.[25]

The theoretical self-image of the Anglo-Irish was aristocratic and gentlemanly, but in practice, as Edmund Burke sarcastically noted, they were a middle class masquerading as an aristocracy. Though Goldsmith, Swift, Sheridan and Berkeley were all recruited by Yeats in *The Winding Stair* for his pantheon of ascendancy intellects, they were each of them impeccable representatives of the Irish Protestant middle class: hard-working men who lived by the pen and who felt, if anything, a very unYeatsian contempt for the idleness and mendacity of the rural ascendancy. Two centuries after Goldsmith's strictures, one of them, Louis MacNeice, remarked that (with the exception of Lady Gregory's and one or two others) the Big Houses contained no culture worth speaking of, "nothing but an obsolete bravado, an insidious bonhomie and a way with horses".[26] They were brought down less by IRA fire-bombs than by a combination of fast women and slow horses – in other words, by a decay that came mainly from within. This was recognized by Synge when he wrote that they were neither much pitied nor much deserving of pity.[27]

Yet, even if Yeats's overt attempt to concoct an Anglo-Irish pantheon in *The Winding Stair* is almost wholly factitious, his *covert* appeal to Protestant themes and spiritual techniques in the book is exemplary. How, then, to explain his youthful interest in Roman Catholicism?

As in Latin America today, the Catholic Church was splitting into two factions, a popular church filled with native folk inflections of Catholic lore and an insurrectionary politics on one side, and, on the other, an ecclesiocracy which collaborated with repressive government, while seeking at a spiritual level a more rationalized theology. When still a young writer, Yeats had seen in such Protestantization of rural life only a form of creeping Anglicization.

As he grew older, Yeats's view of Protestantism changed greatly. He became far more positive in his treatment of it, though, in truth, elements of that change are present as early as 1899 in "The Valley of the Black Pig". This poem links the fundamentalist's calamitarian idea of apocalypse with the end of empire:

> The dews drop slowly and dreams gather: unknown spears
> Suddenly hurtle before my dream-awakened eyes,
> And then the clash of fallen horsemen and the cries
> Of unknown perishing armies bent about my ears.
> We who still labour by the cromlech on the shore,
> The grey cairn on the hill, when day sinks drowned in dew,
> Being weary of the world's empires, bow down to you,
> Master of the still stars and of the flaming door.[28]

Years later, in "The Cold Heaven", he evokes the Lutheran image of a naked soul under "the injustice of the skies for punishment".[29] Protestant biblical phrasing would increasingly inform his celebration of writers like Synge, whose art allowed people to see "as we were Adam, and this the first morning".[30] The terms in which he cast Synge's art in "J. M. Synge and the Ireland of His Time" were those of the self-election of a proud, Protestant soul:

> . . . To speak of one's emotions without fear or moral ambition, to come out from under the shadow of other men's minds, to forget their needs, to be utterly oneself, that is all the Muses care for . . . All art is the disengaging of the soul from place and history, its suspension in a beautiful or terrible light to await the Judgement, though it must be, seeing that all its days were a Last Day, judged already.[31]

Synge's Ireland, like the biblical Israel, was a land at once very old and strikingly new. Its Hiberno-English was a "language as much alive as if it were new come out of Eden"[32] and so ancient too that it befitted a land verging on some apocalypse.

From the writings of Shaw, Yeats learned that the ideal of self-election was intimately linked to the crusade for Irish self-determination; and, in the Free State as one of its first senators, Yeats spoke up repeatedly for the civil rights and values of the Protestant community. In each case, Yeats sided with the underdog, initially with the Catholic peasantry in an English-occupied Ireland, and later with the minority in a new state already enacting legislation to outlaw liberties of the individual conscience. Like his father before him, Yeats continued to believe in a fusion of the two island traditions, but he found this quite consistent with the principle that both sides could "glory in our difference" at a personal level. Ordinary people could and should pay full respect to their inherited traditions, while offering tender care also to rival codes; it was up to the "saving remnant" of the nation's intellectual leaders to exemplify in their writings and in their lives that fusion of values which should be enshrined in the state's eventual constitution.

This would seem to be the central, if unexpressed, thesis which lies behind the poetry in *The Winding Stair* and the poetic thinking of *A Vision*. Through the 1920s and early 1930s, Yeats attempted to dissolve the antinomies of his thought with a Third or Middle Way. The major task facing his newly-independent nation was the reconciliation of disparate, once warring, factions, and the assignment of a new, expanded meaning to the phrase "Anglo-Irish". In similar fashion, Yeats tried to solve the gap in modern democracies between the One and the Many by the redeeming remnant of the Few; and, in personal psychology, to reconcile male and female in the ideal of androgyny. The poems of *The Winding Stair* show a writer resolving the clash of action and contemplation by the middle term of *art*. Of nothing was this search for a third term of synthesis more notable than of Yeats's view of the two major religious traditions of the island. Even the primary gyre in *A Vision* might loosely be termed Protestant, in its sponsorship of democratic, rational, Anglicized thought, as against the antithetical or Catholic gyre, which is hierarchical, aesthetic, visionary and subjective. The underlying desire of the book, of course, is to render those labels meaningless by reaching that point at which each gyre is interpenetrated by its own opposite; and so to write a kind of constitution for the infant state.

Yeats's project, in short, was to Catholicize the all-too-Protestant Ireland of his youth, and then to Protestantize the all-too-Catholic Ireland of his age. Perhaps inevitably, this programme was of limited use to those northern poets of Protestant heritage who succeeded him. W. R. Rodgers, a clergyman-turned-bohemian, was an exception to that rule, however. He was inspired not only by Yeats's millennarian vision of things, but also by his view of poetry as something born out of a man's struggle against himself. He also emulated the pursuit of erotic excitement in the later poems: but there was sometimes an excessive swagger about the gesture, as there was a kind of forced exuberance about the wordplay and the punning. Rodgers was working through a long-delayed reaction against the puritanism of a Presbyterian home in which mirrors and alcohol were banned and in which "Sunday dinner was cooked on Saturday night".[33] Small wonder that his verses became tipsy when he voiced his almost illicit celebration of the idea of "Ireland":

> O these lakes and all gulls that live in them,
> These acres and all legs that walk on them,
> These tall winds and all wings that cling to them,
> Are part and parcel of me, bit and bundle,
> Thumb and thimble.[34]

By contrast, John Hewitt's Methodist background was implicit in the caution with which he embraced the same notion:

> This is my home and country. Later on
> perhaps I'll find this nation is my own.[35]

Hewitt's lines are, accordingly, sober, straight and neat, his virtues those of the Roman legionary doing his duty to reclaim the wild soil of "The Colony". Though he is British as well as Irish, he knows that his people may have to come down on the side of one or the other term:

> we would be strangers in the Capitol;
> this is our country also, no-where else;
> and we shall not be outcast in the world.[36]

But, coming from the north where he had many brushes with the intransigence of the unionist establishment, he felt it enough to be the critic of his own people's rigidity, to be the dissident among dissenters. Not for him the dazzling dialectics of a Yeats, forever crossing and recrossing the sectarian divide.

There were those on both sides of the religious divide who knew what Yeats's project implied and did not like it one bit. The leading philosopher at Trinity College, A. A. Luce – who was a tutor to the young Samuel Beckett – issued dire warnings that if the Irish language were to be made a compulsory study for Protestants in schools, within a century half the Protestants of Ireland would have turned Catholic.[37] If the corollary of Luce's First Law is that the systematic study of Swift,

Berkeley and Goldsmith would in time make many Catholics turn Protestant, then that did not come to pass either! Professor Luce, though a gifted scholar, proved somewhat lacking in prophetic power. Nor was this his only mistaken prediction. The same man, in his report on his tutee Samuel Beckett at the end of his second college year, pronounced that the undergraduate's prospects were "quite dismal".[38]

Twenty-Six

Religious Writing: Beckett and Others

Three hundred years from now, Beckett will be remembered more for his prose than his plays, and not only because he wrote some of the most beautiful prose of the twentieth century but also because he was in such texts a supremely religious artist. In an Ireland whose institutional churches had for centuries policed spirituality, he confronted some of the great themes of the puritan conscience: work, effort, reward, anxious self-scrutiny, the need for self-responsibility, and the distrust of artifice and even of art. His work seems like an answer to Shaw's prayer for a writer who would redefine Protestantism. Beckett always wrote out of the conviction that theology was too important to be left to theologians.

His pilgrim's progress – which might better be called a *via dolorosa* – begins with the story "Dante and the Lobster", a meditation on the problem of pain. The informing idea is that although humans may be improved by suffering, which they can locate in a wider pattern of moral significance, a lobster boiled while "lepping fresh" can hardly be so improved. Luther's thoughts on a merciful god are replicated and the possibility of a piety which nonetheless has room for pity is mooted. Still, doubts nag. "It's a quick death", concludes the narrator with jesting desperation, only to be undercut by a more subversive and authoritative voice: "It is not".[1]

With the sudden death of his own father – a man seemingly in the prime of a successful life as a quantity-surveyor – Beckett had to confront the meaning of human suffering even more starkly in the mid-1930s. Most of his finest poems date from this period. They have sometimes been misread as simple love-lyrics, when they are in fact elegies mourning a man snatched from his family.[2] The arbitrary, undeserved nature of suffering is something on which Beckett meditates in all his writings: and this becomes the attempt to scrutinize and fathom the mind of a God who does not feel obliged to make any clarifying appearances of explanations. "Do you believe in the life to come?" asks a character in *Endgame*, only to be told "Mine was always that".[3] (This joke reappeared on a wall in Ballymurphy during the current Northern Irish war as "is there a life before death?") Or consider the following exchange between the tramps in *Waiting for Godot*:

Vladimir: You're not going to compare yourself to Christ!
Estragon: All my life I've compared myself to him.
Vladimir: But where he lived it was warm, it was dry!
Estragon: Yes. And they crucified quick.[4]

Kenneth Tynan once quipped that Beckett had a very Irish grudge against God, which the merely godless would never feel – a line which may indeed derive from the famous moment in *Endgame* when Hamm and Clov curse their creator: "The bastard! He doesn't exist!"[5]

If the godhead must assume a callous and indifferent front, so that faith may be a meritorious leap in the dark, then Beckett takes on some of these attributes as a creator. For one thing, his narratives often seem clinically unconcerned with the sufferings which they evoke, but this cruelty – like that of the theologians' god – is *assumed*, so that the reader may supply the missing flood of tenderness and emotion. The narrative is cruel only to be kind: and the mask of callousness is worn only as a test. For Beckett, as for the Old Testament God, every act of creation is a drastic exercise in self-limitation, a deliberate courting of failure. Since God was a perfect being, the creation of a flawed universe could only be a sacrifice of this perfection: and, in an equivalent way, for Beckett every created text is "a stain upon the silence", a silence which might have been the more admirable without it. In the familiar romantic equation of artist with godhead, Beckett discovered a most unfamiliar notion of art as self-impoverishment.

In his first collection of stories *More Pricks Than Kicks*, the protagonist Belacqua Shuah aspires to nothingness, quite literally: "What I am on the lookout for is nowhere, so far as I can see".[6] He wishes to live his life in a "Beethoven pause". Named after a character in Dante who lazily deferred his repentance until the last possible moment, and was therefore condemned to wait at the foot of Mount Purgatory enduring the same span of time in waiting as he had once passed in indolence, he embraces this idleness not as a punishment but as a liberation. He is "a dirty low-down Low Church Protestant high-brow"[7] in flight from the world of work, like the young Beckett who resigned his lectureship in

French at Trinity College and confessed to bemused friends that he preferred to lie on his back and fart and think about Dante. So Belacqua chooses to stay in bed, curled up in the foetal position adopted by his Danteesque model.

Yet Belacqua's declaration of war upon the work ethic is couched in decidedly Protestant terms, as the inevitable outcome of his desire for self-sufficiency in the world of pure mind. "The mind at last its own asylum" he muses longingly, in a parody of the famous passage in the great Protestant epic of Milton:

> A mind not to be chang'd by place or time.
> The mind is its own place, and in itself
> Can make a Heav'n of Hell, a Hell of Heav'n.[8]

(That Satan should have spoken these deathless lines merely shows that Milton's devil is a Protestant.) Yet Belacqua fails to achieve this self-responsibility, for "his anxiety to explain himself constituted a breakdown in the self-sufficiency which he never wearied of arrogating to himself".[9] He fondly imagines himself an indolent Bohemian, but at heart he is a puritan, seeking to replace the smooth Catholic rituals of the aesthetic adventure with a more literal-minded low-church honesty. He is, in fact, an anti-Bohemian, and so the narrative deliberately trips over itself, with jagged phraseology, intrusive footnotes, and authorial interruptions. That awkward style embodies a classic puritan theme: that only by our sufferings do we achieve any importance or convince ourselves that we exist. So Belacqua crawls cruciform along the ground beside Trinity College, strangely enjoying the pain of the rain beating against his exposed body, just as he likes to squeeze a boil on the back of his neck, because the ensuing pain is a "guarantee of identity".

For Beckett's early heroes (if that is the word), the most prolonged crucifixion of all is the necessity to earn a living by the sweat of their brows. They may be in reaction against the indolent, elegant nineties, but not entirely. So the novel *Murphy* was well described as a compound of Sodom and Begorrah. There is indeed a Wildean touch about many of its one-liners: "You saved my life. Now palliate it".[10] To Murphy the raising of Lazarus "seemed perhaps the one occasion on which the Messiah had overstepped the mark"[11]; and this *fin-de-siècle* languor is a pervasive element of Murphy's accidie.

An even deeper explanation of his indolence lies in his conviction that everyday work would prevent him from coming alive in his mind. His girlfriend Celia begins to understand that "a merely indolent man would not be so affected by the prospect of employment", that at the root of Murphy's refusal of the shallow Protestant ethic is a deeply puritan desire to unlock and occupy his own mind. This tragic conflict, also of concern to Yeats, will lead the later Beckett to create a near-monastic cellular set of structures for the protagonists of the trilogy and of the subsequent prose; but in *Murphy,* Celia persists for a time in insisting on a virtue that, far from being cloistered, is active in the world. Eventually, however, even she "cannot go where livings are made without feeling they were being made away".[12] So she stops pacing her beat as a prostitute in the market, "where the frenzied justification of life as an end to means threw light on Murphy's prediction, that livelihood would destroy life's goods".[13] Murphy, of course, has come to see the limits of a work ethic, which is indifferent to means and obsessed with ends.

Faced with this crisis Murphy – like Beckett – does not turn to Roman Catholicism, but to the religions of the east. In this respect, Beckett was not only following the example of George Russell and W. B. Yeats; he was also anticipating the movements of the 1960s which saw many "turn east". The theologian Harvey Cox has pointed out that these east-turners tended to come from similar backgrounds: they were usually white, upper-middle-class intellectuals, trained in Protestant spirituality, now grown increasingly dissatisfied with its over-rationalization.[14] Murphy certainly conforms to the prototype: he has a swami in Berwick Market cast his horoscope, which urges him to avoid exhaustion by speech, since silence is his fourth-highest attribute. A quietist to the last, he rejects the die-fighting ethic and speaks only when spoken to, and not always even then. His meal is "vitiated by no base thoughts of nutrition",[15] being more in the nature of a Zen tea-ceremony, whereby the mind can contemplate the permutation of five simple biscuits laid out. Most of all, whenever Murphy sinks into the unconscious and then returns, the narrative makes clear that he has not so much "come to" as "from". In other words, his birthmark truly is his "death-mark", since it records the precise moment when he lost his immortality in a merely corporeal form. Confronted with this loss, Murphy can only invent a set of koans and desperate uninterpretable puns, in the hope that when exhaustion supervenes, then wisdom will supervene too.

Though Beckett might be said to have moved beyond the formal Protestantism of his upbringing in that book, it stayed with him to the end, its trace-elements enriched and complicated by elements of eastern philosophy. In one sense, it might be possible to see the stark decontextualized tree on the stage of *Waiting for Godot* as just the sort of solitary, arbitrary image which summons the Zen meditator to the pleasures of contemplating a symmetry *without* any burden of attendant meaning. It is, however, also possible to see Beckett's stages, so stripped of unnecessary artifice or ornament, as low-church altars. The fact that they contain few props – which might indicate to actors how to move and behave – may indeed be a coded version of the puritan scepticism about images and image-making, and a statement of the need of the soul to go naked and unmediated before the godhead. "No symbols where none intended".[16] There is even a tendency in Beckett's writings to take a metaphor and strip it down to literal realities, as when Nagg and Nell spend their time in *Endgame* caught in dustbins, emphasizing the meaning of the modern phrase about "treating old people like garbage".[17] This relentless demetaphorization is part of Beckett's attempt to take as complete a responsibility as possible for his language and to avoid over-poetic or histrionic effects.

A deep reservation about play-acting is manifest in the implied condemnation of hypertheatricality of characters like Pozzo and Hamm in the famous plays. These reservations arise from a traditional puritan scruple about the ethics of impersonation, the fear being that in impersonating someone else the actor violates the person's integrity as well as his or her own. Unlike the London puritans of the 1640s, who merely closed down theatres as a way of condemning such places as dens of iniquity, Beckett uniquely carries that scruple into the heart of the theatrical activity, and so is constantly caught in the act of breaking the illusion which he has only just created. An actor can suddenly walk off-stage after a long scene for a lavatory-visit, while another may start to discuss the "performance" of that night's audience, in a mode which combines Wildean witticism with an unconcealed aggressive intent towards the whole notion of *mimesis*.

It is generally agreed that the technical challenges posed by the plays are awesome to the point of tears: the actress Billie Whitelaw cried under Beckett's exacting direction in rehearsals, and the actor Peter O'Toole recalled similar "bloodings" with a sense of near-outrage.[18] In *Waiting for Godot*, for instance, it is almost impossible for the actor playing each tramp to keep a clear memory of the sequence of his own lines as distinct from the other's, because their speeches criss-cross so confusingly throughout the play. The highly coercive stage-directions compound the audience's sense of how hard it is for each actor to hold down a role, how each actor onstage is caught painfully between a half-clear role and a half-constructed self, in that no-man's-land where the soul experiences raw exposure to what Beckett elsewhere called "the suffering of being".[19] In the performance of a Beckett play a very real revenge is being taken upon actors for the crime of being actors at all: the puritan war against theatricality is being carried right into the heart of the theatrical activity itself. This is made brutally apparent in *Waiting for Godot* at the level of plot, when Pozzo is "punished" for an insincere evocation of nightfall by the permanent fall of night over eyes henceforth blinded.

Beckett is, of course, modern in his scepticism about art and in his exploration of its limits, but there is also a more traditionally puritan element in his view of art as "ballsaching poppycock" and "a stain upon the silence". If there has to be a stain, he seems to urge, let it be as brief and confined as possible, on the route back to pure silence. Hence the increasing minimalism of his pieces. The monologues which result in such sumptuous minimalism may, however, have had their origins in the author's Protestantism, or what Hugh Kenner has called "the issueless Protestant confrontation with conscience".[20] If Joyce remained obsessed by the Roman Catholic faith which he rejected, then Yeats and Beckett both aestheticized elements of their childhood belief. Both men turned east, if not for an explanation, then at least for a moving expression of human bafflement in the face of creation. Many of Yeats's later poems emphasize the word "nothing" as a positive value, just like the Beckettian protagonist who rejoices in the fact that there is "nothing" to be done.

It is in the trilogy that Beckett evolves the most beautiful forms, as the linear plot of the western novel makes way for a structure which is the artistic equivalent of meditation and for a narrative which is the artistic equivalent of confession. Beckett reported that he conceived its first volume *Molloy* on the day he became aware of his past stupidity in not writing out of personal experience, in his refusal to accept the dark side as the "commanding side of my personality".[21] That phrase might be an inadvertent summary of the "plot" of *Molloy*, which chronicles the attempt by the prim, bourgeois Catholic Moran to confront the primeval Molloy within, to locate the panting antiself that struggles to emerge, divesting Moran of his illusions of property, industry, purpose, and, above all, traditional religious belief. Where the uncovering of this antiself was for Yeats a finally artistic imperative, it had for Beckett all the confessional qualities of a religious testimony, a point made when the author insists that he has no intention to "give way to literature".[22]

The first book of the trilogy contains a parody of the Roman Catholic confession and substitutes for its perceived formal insincerities

the muscular summons to a confessional testimony: by the end, however, even such Protestant testifying is exposed as self-defeating, since
the self-reliance preached by the Protestant can result only in the death
of the Old Testament God, as man listens instead to those inner voices
which require "no vengeful deity" to make themselves heard. That voice
can liberate Molloy, unchain his innermost self – the needle-point of
the mystic – and allow him to expiate by confessing the sins of the past.
Moreover, the man who once "found it painful to not understand" can
now accept the incomprehensible pattern of dancing bees. Part of his
comfort is the knowledge that the bees are an impermeable closed
system of their own and that he will, therefore, never be tempted to
offload responsibility for himself onto them: "And I would never do my
bees the wrong I had done my God to whom I had been taught to
ascribe my angers, fears, desires, and even my body".[23]

All forms of authority throughout the trilogy induce irresponsibility:
for instance, Moran's son always loses his way when accompanied by
his father, who keeps him rope-bound, but he survives handsomely on
his own. Like Murphy, each protagonist of the trilogy discovers that he
cannot resign his fate to an exterior godhead or cosmology, since in
every case the individual is "the prior system". Instead, as in Buddhist
practice, the godhead is increasingly ironized by multiple jocularities
and courted in expectant silences; and, while all this is going on, the
protagonists try to sink into that needle-point where the mystic
achieves both darkness and illumination. There is an undeniable "eastern" element in this progress, as is clear in the Buddha-like postures
adopted by protagonists in the knees-and-elbow position, in the desire
of the adept to please the master with a wisdom which nonetheless can
never be verbalized, in the attempt to cure all desire by ablating it. But
– though Beckett clearly learned much eastern wisdom from his reading of Schopenhauer – there is no necessity to posit an eastern influence
in a more direct sense. After all, the mystic moments thus attained were
central to the Protestantism of Luther in its pristine phase: what is
enacted is nothing other than the search embarked upon by countless
mystics. Even the noted prayer-meetings of Quakers were characterized
by long silences designed for just the kind of meditation during which
the godhead might be wooed to announce itself.[24]

It may be that the voice which speaks in the last fifty pages of *The
Unnamable* is the voice of God, insofar as that word has meaning in
this century: not any reassuringly traditional godhead, rather a core of
selfhood towards which all of Beckett's mystics move. He was interested
in studying the mind of God, which is perhaps why he once said that

poetry is prayer. He is one of those very rare writers who have captured the mystery of being in the world. He did this in religious language which was completely devoid of pretence or the accretions of institutional discourse.

But he was not utterly alone in this: for his example and endorsement inspired a group of young Catholic modernists to use poetry as a method of metaphysical exploration. In a famous review of 1934 Beckett praised Thomas MacGreevy for his recognition that "it is the act and not the object of perception that matters",[25] since self-perception was the primary theme. MacGreevy grew up in Tarbert, County Kerry, and had his cruel introduction to the wider world in the trenches of the Somme, where he was wounded twice. Out of that experience came "De Civitate Hominum", a war poem which runs well beyond an outraged Georgianism and whose fragmentary method was far more adequate to the dislocations it reported:

> I cannot tell which flower he has accepted
> But suddenly there is a tremor,
> A zigzag of lines against the blue
> And he streams down
> Into the white,
> A delicate flame,
>
> A stroke of orange in the morning's dress.
>
> My sergeant says, very low, "Holy God!
> 'Tis a fearful death."
>
> Holy God makes no reply
> Yet.[26]

MacGreevy's brilliant deployment of *vers libre* was his way of retaining some kind of hold on a world no longer felt to be regular:

> My rose of Tralee turned gray in its life,
> A tombstone gray,
> Unimpearled
> But a moment, now, I suppose,
> For a moment I may suppose,
> Gleaming blue,
> Silver blue,

> Gold,
> Rose,
> And the light of the world.[27]

That devotion to an epiphanic moment in the midst of a fallen universe had, of course, another sponsor in Joyce, whose rejection of all narrowing national traditions inspired MacGreevy, as it had impressed Beckett. The two young men came to know and esteem one another on the boulevards of Paris after 1928: but very different fates lay in store for them. MacGreevy returned to an Ireland which had little use for his brand of Catholic modernism: his poetic output all but ceased and after 1950 he was known only as the Director of the National Gallery in Dublin. It was a measure of the cultural introversion of post-war Ireland that, when he died on St. Patrick's Day 1967, there were few references in the obituaries to his achievement as a poet.[28]

Had MacGreevy remained in exile, he might have found for his mystic muse an environment more conducive to its kind of poetry: but he was nationally-minded and wished to live in Ireland. His contemporaries, Denis Devlin and Brian Coffey, perhaps by dint of embracing exile as their natural condition, managed to sustain longer poetic careers, although their work went uncelebrated in Ireland, except by the discerning few. Coffey studied in Paris with the Catholic writer Jacques Maritain, and subsequently worked as a professor of philosophy in St. Louis, Missouri, from where in 1962 he composed a free verse-letter, teasing out his divided feeling about Ireland and addressed to MacGreevy:

> Midnight now.
> Deepest winter perfect now.
> Tomorrow early we shall make the lunches
> for the children to take to school,
> forgetting while working out the week
> our wrestling with the sad flesh
> and the only Ireland we love
> where in Achill still
> the poor praise Christ aloud
> when the priest elevates
> the Saviour of the world.[29]

Coffey in many respects provided a comprehensive answer to Beckett's summons to self-perception as the central challenge of the age. His is not a God who on the last day will ask the sinner why he was not more like Jesus; rather he is one who will enquire just how fully he managed to become himself.

The struggle for saintliness in a world apparently abandoned by God engrossed Denis Devlin; but his vision is somewhat more optimistic, for he senses in the poetic act the power to heal the split between body and soul, between sexual and religious identity. Whereas Beckett's sexual partners remain eternally "twain", observing the workings of one another's bodies with mounting incredulity, Devlin's do know a moment of healing oneness. This he elevated into an aesthetic principle which annihilated the distance between subject and object, achieving that very fusion which Beckett had pronounced impossible in his early book on Proust. Inspired by French poets who had preached the marriage of Catholic art and symbolism, Devlin countered the provincializing tendencies of his native religion. "Lough Derg", his marvellous poem of 1946, locates the Irish penitential rites against the backdrop of a shattered Europe:

> We pray to ourself. The metal moon, unspent
> Virgin eternity sleeping in the mind,
> Excites the form of prayer without content;
> White thorn lightens, delicate and bland,
> The negro mountain, and so, knelt on her sod,
> This woman beside me murmuring *My God! My God!* [30]

This was yet another split to be healed: again and again Devlin's poetry insists that Ireland and Europe are not opposed complexes of meaning, and so he dedicates his elegy for Michael Collins to the anti-fascist novelist Ignazio Silone.

As a diplomat who knew the great cities of Catholic Europe in all their sensuous beauty, Devlin challenged the puritanical excesses of Irish Catholicism in lines of unambiguous eroticism, lines which may also owe something to the *Dánta Grá*, those *amour courtois* lyrics by Gaelic poets who saw in man's love for woman an image of a divine love for the human soul:

> Women that are loved are more than lovable,
>   Their beauty absolute blows:
> But little, like the urgent, carnal soul,
>   More than its leaves so mortal in the rose.
>
> O rose! O more than red mortality!
>   What can my love have said

That made me her imagine more than be?
Her mind more than mind, blood more than red?[31]

In the 1934 essay Beckett praised MacGreevy for "probably the most important contribution" to Irish poetry since the Great War; and he identified Devlin and Coffey as affording "the nucleus of a living poetic in Ireland". These he cast under the modernist aegis of Laforgue, the surrealists, Eluard, Eliot and Pound, contrasting them with the "Gossoons wunderhorn" of Irish revivalism, those antiquarian imitators of Gaelic prosody who were "delivering with the altitudinous complacency of the Victorian Gael the Ossianic goods".[32] Their flight from self-perception he considered to be the ultimate cowardice.

Chief among the offenders was Austin Clarke, whom Beckett went on to satirize mercilessly in *Murphy* as "Austin Ticklepenny". The libel was not only ill-judged but undeserved, for Clarke in truth used Gaelic tradition to confront rather than evade his own inner demons. A free version of the Middle Irish romance "The Frenzy of Sweeney" enabled him to explore the mental breakdown which resulted from his own youthful clash with a censorious Catholicism: and his employment of the Gaelic past was often deeply subversive of present rigidity. As early as 1929, in *Pilgrimage and Other Poems*, he invoked the Celtic-Romanesque world of medieval Irish Christianity as a place or state of grace in which rigour was qualified by imagination, duty chastened by a sense of beauty, and Gaelic values harmonized with libertarian visions. If this was a method which owed something to the example of Synge, it was also by no means opposed to the codes by which Denis Devlin reconstructed his world. The later, wonderfully erotic, works of Clarke were as calculated an assault on narrow-gauge Catholicism as anything penned by Devlin. Like his critiques, they had the additional merit of coming from within the communion.

For Clarke was a truly religious writer, yet another who yearned for the condition of the Protholic or Cathestant. He wanted a return to the loose, local structure of medieval monasticism, seeing in the hegemony of priests and bishops evidence that "the imperial and evangelical spirit of the British race"[33] had, since independence, been appropriated by Irish Catholicism. A poem like "Tenebrae", taking for theme the draping of all statues during Holy Week, asks whether the crucifixion may not carry within its imagery a dreadful negativity and masochism; and yet the artist knows that enlightenment models of reason, which cause his doubts, cannot fully account for the darker sense of life. There is no easy resolution of these dilemmas. "The Straying Student", who turns his back on the priestly vocation for fulfilment in a woman's arms, is left unsatisfied in old age:

> Awake or in my sleep, I have no peace now.
> Before the ball is struck, my breath has gone.
> And yet I trouble lest she may deceive me
> And leave me in this land, where every woman's son
> Must carry his own coffin and believe,
> In dread, all that the clergy teach the young.[34]

Confronted by the increasing intolerance and inflexibility of the official church, Clarke astutely suggested that the large numbers of vibrant young men and women who left Ireland for missionary work in Africa were a serious loss to the emerging Irish state, which stood badly in need of their flair:

> Too many are professed –
> He argued – boys, girls, all in black,
> Brown, white. The Church unbeds the State:
> Charity taught to emigrate.
> Farmyard and scythe gone. Grain unsacked . . .[35]

The imperial pretensions of the bishops were leading to a dreary repetition of all the old colonial mechanisms: the "Flight to Africa" resulted in an aged and repressive church, the sponsor of a new penal age which might set the educational ideals of Pearse at nought:

> Pearse founded St. Enda's, forbad
> All punishment: pupils were happy
>   At task and play.
> Our celibates raise cane and strap,
>   Smiling at May
> Processions that hide their cruel slapping.
>   Children obey
> In dread.[36]

Clarke's answer to all this had been implicit in his first play, *The Son of Learning.* MacConglinne, the wandering medieval student, gives free rein to his senses in it, even to the point of blasphemy: yet his is a challenge offered secure in the knowledge that his church and his God are strong enough to survive all assaults. A major figure in Gaelic literature, his spirit had been revived by Synge who prefaced *The Tinker's Wedding* with the hope that country clergy could tolerate non-malicious mockery, "as the clergy in every Roman Catholic country were laughed at through the ages that had real religion".[37] Clarke *is* MacConglinne, presenting himself as one who is just what the latter-day Irish church needs, a member of a loyal but strictly internal opposition.

All of the foregoing writers were incorporated, only with immense difficulty and after decades of delay, into the Irish literary tradition. Interest in Clarke and Devlin revived with the liberalization of the 1960s, but MacGreevy and Coffey were not rediscovered for another decade. Clarke lived long enough as a grand old man of letters in Dublin to witness, and in some measure to sponsor, his own revival: but the growth of interest in the others may have been connected with the elevation to international status of their promoter, Beckett. Yet the refusal of Irish criticism to engage with them in their heyday is sadly symptomatic of two underlying failures of imagination, one obvious, the other more obscure.

MacGreevy and Coffey and Devlin were deemed marginal because they embraced a modern European poetic at a time when inward-looking Irish intellectuals sought singularity and continuity with a simplified version of the Gaelic past. There was, in addition, no firm intellectual tradition of Irish Catholicism within whose framework the texts of these poets might have been more easily understood. Yet that explanation does not fully account for the case of Clarke: and it is based, moreover, on the questionable assumption that Irish *intellectuals* were as provincial in outlook as the political leaders. The less obvious factor may have been the inability of so many liberal intellectuals to respond with warmth to religious writing. The critic I. A. Richards had announced the severance of poetry from belief back in the 1920s when these artists began their work. The radical intellects of Ireland in the following decades were so busy seeking a separation of church and state that they were in no mood to sponsor a reconnection of religion and art. The paradoxical consequence must now be more clear: those forces which have worked against an understanding of the mystical element in the writings of Samuel Beckett are the same ones which denied recognition to the achievement of MacGreevy, Coffey and Devlin. Though nominally opposed to one another, the secular liberals and Catholic conservatives conspired to prevent a sympathetic hearing for these artists. No wonder that the young Beckett felt moved to open the one really positive review of MacGreevy's *Poems* with the insistence that "All poetry, as discriminated from the various paradigms of prosody, is prayer".[38]

UNDERDEVELOPMENT

UNDERDEVELOPMENT

Samuel Beckett may have preferred to live in a France at war rather than an Ireland at peace, but most of his compatriots were relieved to be out of World War II. Throughout the hostilities Ireland remained officially neutral (although pundits, aware that many thousands of Irish had voluntarily enlisted in the British war effort, used to ask "who are we neutral against?"). The general consensus supported Mr. de Valera's view that Ireland, still trying to rebuild itself after so much destruction, could ill-afford to expend its slender resources in a global confrontation.

Domestic opinion, blissfully unaware of much that the Nazis were doing, was anyway divided: while a majority probably sympathized with the British, many could be found to speak up for the Germans, on the age-old principle that "my enemy's enemy is my friend". Even the IRA members interned in the Curragh military camp on suspicion that they might seek an alliance with the Germans were badly split on the issue. The ancient adage that England's difficulty was Ireland's opportunity now took on a somewhat modified meaning, as Mr. de Valera began to put his theories of a self-sufficient Ireland, living on frugal comforts, to the test.[1]

During the war years petrol and food were rationed, and economic activity slowed down. Life in Ireland became even more inward-looking. The introspection of the twenties and thirties might have been explained as an attempt by disappointed idealists to find out where their revolution had gone wrong; the introversion of the forties was more provincial in tone, as the whole nation conspired in the fiction that Europe and the wider world did not exist. For all its suspicion of foreign ideas, the new state had played a proud part in international affairs. The Cumann na nGaedheal ministers had worked closely with Canadian leaders in the 1920s to remodel the British Empire into a looser commonwealth of self-governing states. In the 1930s Mr. de Valera had presided over sessions of the League of Nations. This was also the period when thousands of idealistic young priests, nuns and lay persons had travelled to preach the Christian gospel in the devel-

*oping world. Ever since the Famine, emigration had perforce made inter-
nationalists of the Irish, for there were few families without a son or
daughter or cousin writing letters home from some distant land.*

*In one sense neutrality was simply a telling demonstration of Irish
sovereignty, for it allowed Mr. de Valera to formulate a foreign policy quite
independent of Britain yet perfectly in keeping with the anti-conscription
ethic which had been the making of Sinn Féin in 1918. A Britain which
still bankrolled a corrupt one-party state on a partitioned island was hardly
owed any special favours. Though President Roosevelt of the United States
was also recruited to invoke Irish-American feeling in hopes of persuading
the Irish to join the allied forces, Mr. de Valera held firm. Only when Belfast
was bombed did he relent, to the extent of sending the Dublin and Dún
Laoghaire fire-brigades north to help douse the flames. Even at the war's
end, when Winston Churchill sneered in a notorious speech at Irish non-
involvement, Mr. de Valera waited for days before making a grave but
moving reply which perfectly captured the feelings of his people.²*

*Yet, in a more cultural sense, the policy of neutrality was also very
damaging, for it cut Irish intellectuals off from the wider world. A sense
of unreality pervaded cultural life. Nowhere was that more manifest than
in the colloquial term used to describe the period from 1939 to 1945: "the
Emergency". As a phrase it proves that the Irish can outstrip the English at
understatement any day of the week. In the dumb-show which unfolded,
Mr. de Valera felt obliged to make an annual exchange of birthday
greetings with the Spanish dictator General Franco and, eventually, to pay
a formal call of sympathy at the German embassy on the death of Adolf
Hitler.*

*Censoriousness prevailed in such a climate. A reproduction of Manet's
Olympus was denounced when it went on display in a Dublin gallery;
jazz music was banned for a time on Radio Éireann; and a number of
priests denounced young women who played camogie (the women's version
of hurling) or, in one ludicrous case, who rode bicycles. Books by Seán Ó
Faoláin, Kate O'Brien and dozens of Irish artists were banned, as was
Frank O'Connor's translation of Merriman's great Gaelic poem* Cúirt an
Mheáin Oíche *(The Midnight Court). Dublin Corporation voted to refuse
a gift of Rouault's painting "Christ Crowned with Thorns"; and, perhaps
most ridiculously of all, the Irish secret police (having locked up most
republicans) found nothing better to do with their time than to pay a call
on the poet Patrick Kavanagh. They seized a copy of his poem* The Great
Hunger *on suspicion that passages in it might be obscene. With a strong
relish for the absurd, Kavanagh invited his assailants into his apartment,
told them that they were probably right, and promptly served them tea.³*

Not all Irish artists found neutrality quite so amusing. Beckett's caustic opinion of it, even after the end of the war, was deemed improper for broadcasting on Radio Éireann; and the northern Protestant, Louis Mac-Neice, castigated the policy as one rooted in sheer selfish opportunism:

> But then, look eastward from your heart, there bulks
> A continent, close, dark as archetypal sin,
> While to the west off your own shores the mackerel
> Are fat — on the flesh of your kin.[4]

As events transpired after the war, the Irish did little enough to secure for themselves any benefits of the ensuing peace. Perhaps the most debilitating long-term effect of the neutralist policy was the way in which the introversion which accompanied it lasted well into the 1950s. Initially a defence mechanism, it acquired the force of a habit long after the original causes had been removed.

MacNeice himself opted for a different form of neutrality, calling down a plague on both houses in the internal conflict of Northern Ireland, which he sought to escape by means of a literary career in England. A pose of sardonic detachment made it possible for him to mock the revivalist pretensions of the southern state:

> Let the school-children fumble their sums
> in a half-dead language . . .

and to castigate the Sinn Féin ideal in a Europe at war:

> Ourselves alone! Let the round tower stand aloof
> in a world of bursting mortar.

Yet he was far too sophisticated a self-critic to rest easy in such postures. For one thing, he shared with Yeats an envy of the man-of-action for whom everything is more clear-cut, an envy

> of my own
> Countrymen who shoot to kill and never
> See the victim's face become their own.[5]

He was keenly aware of how quickly men can turn into what they despise: yet this, with unusually subtle modulations, was what happened to him, for as he grew older he achieved a rapprochement of sorts with "the south".

The Poetry of W. B. Yeats (1941) chronicles MacNeice's return to a poetic admiration of Yeats, a swerve which would in time be repeated by Auden and Spender; and the "nomad who has lost his tent" [6] *found himself increasingly attracted by the indeterminacy of a Dublin whose many masks seemed to hide no face at all:*

> She is not an Irish town
> And she is not English. [7]

The capital epitomized the identity crisis of a man who expressed the wish that "one could either live *in Ireland or* feel oneself *in England".* [8] *Estranged as the son of a Church of Ireland bishop from southern Catholics and northern Presbyterians, MacNeice cannily blocked the retreat to all commitments, not even managing a brief membership of the Communist Party during the 1930s. His dread of fixed positions allowed him instead to become a poet of the plural, to celebrate "the drunkenness of things being various": and there is about his performance a touch of the* flâneur, *who savours the sights and sounds of the urban setting, but with a sense that it is a setting in which he himself will never be able to settle on a role other than that of elegist to a more courtly time. MacNeice's "time" was war-challenged London, but somehow the aftermath never quite lived up to his expectations:*

> And nobody rose, only some meaningless
> Buildings and the people once more were strangers
> At home with no one, sibling or friend.
>   Which is why now the petals fall
>   Fast from the flower of cities all. [9]

In writing those lines MacNeice spoke also for the tens of thousands of other Irish exiles who had lived out the war years in England, fully convinced that theirs was a community which had been fighting for something worth having.

If Irish neutrality acquired the force of a prevailing habit, the same might be said of Irish emigration. Most who left did so for economic reasons, but some who followed them did so because so many of their friends and families were elsewhere. In brutal statistical terms the figures are an indictment of successive Irish governments and of their failure to achieve the Sinn Féin ideal of self-sufficiency. Since 1921 one out of every two persons born in the twenty-six county state failed to secure permanent employment there: the rest either emigrated or endured chronic idleness at home.[10] *But beneath the bare statistics lurk many diverse personal histories and social implications, which have rarely been confronted by those who remain on the island. To put the matter bluntly, those who left solved at once a personal and a national problem. By going most of them secured a better material life than would have been their lot had they stayed as a drain on an under-endowed public purse. By leaving they helped ensure a higher standard of living for those who remained. They were able to leave in hopes of good employment elsewhere because they were well educated, English-speaking, Caucasian in appearance and so able to integrate with ease into many developed economies.*

In these respects they were far more fortunate than the poor and unemployed of the emerging post-colonies of the equatorial world and of the southern hemisphere: for these, emigration was a much more traumatic, often less feasible option. Yet, had most of the emigrants stayed at home, Ireland would in fact have looked far more like a "Third World" country under the ensuing stresses. It might also have been a more volatile and interesting place.

The patterns of Irish emigration were persistent and deep, but they did not mean that the national experience was an anomaly in the histories of modern Europe. Far from it: they were yet another example of just how much the state-formation of Ireland had in common with that of other European peoples. Ever since the seventeenth century there had been massive migrations from Europe to the Americas and beyond. Without them European peoples would have been compelled to launch their industrial and agricultural revolutions against just the kind of demographic backdrop which has retarded such transformations in the "Third World" this century. A stark but much-neglected fact is that "the number of people of European ancestry living outside of Europe is currently twice the size of the population of the migrants' countries of origin".[11] Had they also remained, Europe today would surely look very different, and so might the "Third World" whose difficulties have been due more to external exploitation by such migrants than to internal factors.

These considerations help to convey something of the complex fate of the Irish, a people once colonized and compelled, by that very fact, to do some of their own colonizing in the wider world. If in certain cultural respects the Irish experience had much in common with that of other emerging states in Asia and Africa, in more directly political terms it was a very representative European democracy. By the time Mr. de Valera was established in power it was clear that many of the tell-tale symptoms of more fragile post-colonial societies were happily lacking: for example, the land question had been resolved; the military were quite free of autocratic tendencies, remaining obedient to elected politicians and president; and a reasonable degree of social consensus (some might call it torpor) prevailed. Within Europe itself a country such as Greece (the other former colony) betrayed far more of the classic symptoms of underdevelopment.

Nevertheless, all through the 1940s and 1950s the government in Dublin persisted with its policy of decolonization: Ireland was formally declared a republic in 1949, as the last legal links with the British commonwealth were purged. Fine Gael (the renamed Cumann na nGaed-heal party) under John A. Costello had managed to dislodge Fianna Fáil and lead the replacement coalition government in the election of the previous year: now it was seeking to out-de-Valera de Valera. A large statue of Queen Victoria was removed from a courtyard in front of the Dáil. Rival parties vied with one another in paying lip service (usually in English) to the ancestral language, which still dominated the timetable in schools, where its compulsory study yielded less than impressive results; and there was a general consensus that the "fourth green field" of Northern Ireland must be returned. However, those young men and women of the IRA who acted to bring this about soon found themselves behind bars, and some were even executed in the south as well as the north. The republic which Pearse and Connolly had sought to establish was looking increasingly verbal and fictional, as an IRA campaign initiated along the border in 1956 slowly fizzled out. The disappointments of republicans, as well as the increasing fanaticism of their postures, were well captured for audiences in London and in Dublin by Brendan Behan. He was simply updating a critique which had been initiated for the previous generation by Liam O'Flaherty, the Aran islander whose novelistic autopsies on Irish history (Famine) *and revolution* (The Informer, Insurrection) *were written with a melodramatic and elemental power. It was, however, in his depictions of the peasantry, notably in* Skerrett *and the marvellous Irish-language short stories of* Dúil, *that O'Flaherty achieved his greatest artistic success. There are many who consider* Dúil, *with its rural epiphanies in field or on water, the most poetic and satisfying collection of stories published by any Irish author since Joyce's* Dubliners.

Ireland remained a predominantly agricultural economy, but life on the land was Spartan. Few farms had been truly mechanized and the exploitation of the soil for cash crops remained lethargic. The revivalist obsession with ownership rather than use of land had given rise to many a bitter family feud, of a kind chronicled in the plays of John B. Keane or the poems of Patrick Kavanagh. Rural Ireland remained a deeply conservative patriarchal society, protective in its embrace of its children but harshly impatient with those who stepped out of line, especially if embroiled in a sexual

misadventure. The habit of late marriage was widespread: the accompany-
ing ethic of sexual continence was rooted less in the puritanism of
the Catholic Church than in the need to avoid further subdivision of
family farms to the point where they might be unviable. Accordingly,
older inheriting sons remained "boys" until their ageing parents agreed
to make way for a young bride who might start a new family with
them on the homestead. Many such "boys" were still waiting in their late
forties.

   Younger sons had no option but to pursue an emigrant career elsewhere.
They were regularly joined in their exile by small farmers whose units were
no longer economical. For many rural women the prospect of an arranged
marriage to an elderly, impoverished farmer was past all bearing, and they
voted with their feet by taking the emigrant ship to the fleshpots of "pagan
England", where many worked as nurses, teachers and governesses. Rural
Ireland was filled with broken families, whose fate seemed quite at variance
with the official ideology enshrined in de Valera's 1937 Constitution, of a
society which constructed itself on the sacredness of family life. Yet somehow
the myth of the Holy Family seemed to grow ever more glamorous and
wholesome the more the facts told against it. Far from feeling valued or
ratified by it, some women felt themselves demeaned. On the other hand,
many families, though separated by emigration, maintained an astonishing
degree of solidarity and mutual support. It is at least arguable that, but for
their strong family ties, many more Irish persons living in conditions of
underdevelopment and poverty might have gone to the wall.[12]

   It was just such a statement of underdevelopment that Patrick Kavanagh
explored in The Great Hunger, *his long poem of 1942 which he later*
dismissed as "the tragic thing". Using the word tragic *in this pejorative way,*
he suggested that in tragedy there is always something of a lie, a refusal to
believe in the benevolence of an over-watching God, who will set the
human comedy to rights in the end. Yet the world of subsistence farming
which he evoked in The Great Hunger *was a place of dire underdevelop-*
ment, economic, religious and intellectual; and the poem itself was a fierce
anti-pastoral, which won the admiration of Cyril Connolly, Stephen Spen-
der and W. H. Auden for its cultivated, banal repetitions and its slack line-
endings:

> *Maguire was faithful to death:*
> *He stayed with his mother till she died*
> *At the age of ninety-one.*
> *She stayed too long,*
> *Wife and mother in one.*

When she died
The knuckle-bones were cutting the skin of her son's backside
And he was sixty-five.[13]

The title seemed to promise a study of heroic peasants in the nineteenth century, but the text actually delivers a near-nihilist account of unheroic subsistence farmers in the twentieth. All of this is framed sarcastically in the cinematic techniques of a curious "First World" anatomizing the "Third".

The camera pans in the potato-gatherers at the start, creating a kind of anti-travelogue: but the Kavanagh voice grows more and more caustic in its anti-pastoralism, as it mocks revivalist versions of the peasant:

There *is the source from which all cultures rise,*
And all religions,
There is the pool in which the poet dips
And the musician.
Without the peasant base civilization must die,
Unless the clay is in the mouth the singer's singing is useless.
The travellers touch the roots of the grass and feel renewed
When they grasp the steering-wheels again.[14]

The portrait offered is of a Joycean rather than Yeatsian peasant, waking to consciousness in dark loneliness:

Although the literal idea of a peasant is of a farm-labouring person, in fact a peasant is all that mass of mankind which lives below a certain level of consciousness. They live in the dark cave of the unconscious and they scream when they see the light.[15]

The Great Hunger *repeats Samuel Beckett's thesis of 1934: that the failure of the revivalist poets to explore self was, among other things, a consequence of their resort for subject-matter to an uncritical celebration of peasant life. The subject of the poem, Patrick Maguire, fails to become himself because he cares too much for the dictates of mother, church and society. He is a proof of Kavanagh's contention that "tragedy is under-developed comedy, not fully born"*[16] *– for, if it were born, the sufferer could find the healing relief of laughter, emitted by one who can afford to take long views. Maguire, by contrast, is a victim of the tragedy that is underdevelopment and of the underdevelopment that is tragedy.*

The 1950s began with the collapse of the coalition government, when a proposal by the young minister Dr. Noel Browne to socialize maternal health care was denounced by the Catholic hierarchy and by the Irish Medical Organization of professional doctors. The so-called Mother and Child Scheme would long be cited by disappointed radicals (and by caustic unionists) as further proof of the contention that "Home Rule is Rome Rule". In point of fact, legislation very similar to that stymied in 1951 was passed just a few years later by a more adroit Fianna Fáil administration, back in power under Éamon de Valera as Taoiseach (Prime Minister). However, the economic undevelopment consequent upon the war years and upon the earlier "Troubles" was making governments less popular. Fianna Fáil lost power to another inter-party government led by Fine Gael in 1954. By the mid-1950s unemployment and emigration levels were again soaring, and de Valera was returned to office by a moody and fickle electorate.

One thing was very clear by now. The death of Arthur Griffith in the first year of the Free State had deprived the country of a man who might arguably have come up with a clear-sighted economic vision to set before the people, drawing on the both/and philosophy of national renaissance which had laid equal stress on industrial and rural development. De Valera, for all his talk of frugal self-sufficiency and his success in clearing some of the slums, had no macroeconomic strategy to meet the needs of a new age. He was by nature a cautious politician, ever ready to agree with the guarded advice of a British-trained Department of Finance whose addiction to economic orthodoxies was at least as great as the Department of Education's commitment to the curricular study of the Edwardian literary canon. Only when de Valera retired to become president in 1959 was the way open for the entrepreneurial and meritocratic successor Sean Lemass.

A pragmatist with leftward leanings, Lemass soon teamed up with an innovative civil servant named T. K. Whitaker and between them both men committed themselves to long-term economic planning for an industrialized Ireland. Time magazine captured the mood with a cover portrait of Lemass: behind his face perched a lucky leprechaun and the legend "New Spirit in the Oul Sod". It was a reasonably fair if kitschy impression.[17] The 1960s would be years of relative prosperity, when multinationals finally invested in Ireland; when children at last knew the benefits of free secondary education; when holidays in European resorts became possible for many; and when the long introversion of Irish intellectual life came to an end.[18]

As if to symbolize this opening out, Ireland had been admitted to the United Nations in 1955 and, from the very outset, played an influential role. The policy of neutrality and non-alignment impressed many leaders of the emerging new states in Africa and Asia, as well as the social democratic governments of Europe. In consequence the Irish were asked to act as honest brokers and to provide soldiers for peace-keeping duties in the former Belgian Congo and in Cyprus. They rose magnificently to the task. When in 1965 Sean Lemass paid a courtesy call on the Prime Minister of Northern Ireland, Terence O'Neill, and when later in that year he signed a Free Trade Agreement with the British, it seemed that a whole cycle of historical difficulties might be coming to a happy resolution. Ireland – or at least the southern part of it – no longer seemed haunted by the past. At the fiftieth anniversary celebrations of the Easter Rising in 1966, President de Valera looked a strangely forlorn and fragile figure as he took the salute from those of his old comrades who remained alive. Behind him on the dignitaries' platform sat "the youngest cabinet in Europe", bristling in mohair suits and ready to build if not the land of saints and scholars then at least an island of silos and silicon. Mr. de Valera might have considered the occasion a proud post-colonial moment: but the ambitious politicians behind him shifted uneasily in their seats as he reviewed the decades of progress and frustration. They were interested in the future. To them the best nations, like the best women, were the ones with no history. Ireland, for so long cut off from the outside world, was about to re-enter it fully.

They were right, of course – but so, in his way, was the old man who bored them under the pale Dublin sun. They would finally enter the European Economic Community amid much fanfare seven years later, but by then the old man, still presiding in the Phoenix Park, would learn just how much unfinished business he was leaving behind. Men and women make history, but never in conditions of their own choosing; and now the nightmare of history, as Joyce had feared it might, was to give them all a ferocious back kick.

Twenty-Seven

The Periphery and the Centre

The "national movement" for Irish political and cultural freedom has often been described as more a rural than an urban phenomenon. The fact that some of the fiercest fighting between the rebels and the forces of occupation took place in cities has never much dented the notion of rural Ireland as real Ireland. Like other forms of pastoral, this complex of ideas was a wholly urban creation, produced by artists like W. B. Yeats and George Russell and by political thinkers such as Éamon de Valera and Michael Collins. They were to a man the urbanized descendants of country people, and they helped to create the myth of a rural nation.

Those who protested by riot against *The Playboy of the Western World* in 1907 were not country people themselves, but their citified children and grandchildren.[1] The rioters accused Synge of misrepresenting the life of western Ireland, but what really galled them was the remorseless realism of his portrayal of that harsh life, which his detractors chose to view in softer focus, through a haze of sentiment and nostalgia. Like Patrick Kavanagh's *The Great Hunger* thirty-five years later, *The Playboy* was an uncompromising exercise in antipastoral, offered at a period when some nationalists in Dublin were concocting a highly conservative version of pastoral: the timeless Irish peasant noted for his stoicism and Christian piety. Country people who read books had long been aware that the bleaker aspects of their lives had gone unrecorded by the sentimental writers of the nineteenth century. A Sligo shoemaker had once confided in the young W. B. Yeats that for him the charms of Kickham's *Knocknagow* had begun to pall. "I want", he said, "to see the people shown up in their naked hideousness".[2] Synge's plays went some way to answering that need: when *The Playboy* was finally shown in the west, audiences found it unremarkable. Kavanagh's long poem of 1942 added a new realism to writing about rural Ireland, as had Myles na gCopaleen's *An Béal Bocht* of the previous year; but it was not until

Máirtín Ó Cadhain's *Cré na Cille* (1949) that the revivalist myth of the saintly western peasantry was exploded by a challenge from within that community.

The object of this myth had been to soften and even obscure the very real class differences emerging in rural communities after the Land Acts of the 1880s. Yeats gave the game away in a striking couplet:

> Parnell came down the road, he said to a cheering man,
> "Ireland shall get her freedom and you still break stone".[3]

However, his more usual strategy was to emphasize, rather than ironize, the vision of an ahistorical peasantry, unaffected by social change. He did this most succinctly in adopting the authoritative tones of the aristocratic war-hero Major Robert Gregory in "An Irish Airman Foresees His Death":

> I know that I shall meet my fate
> Somewhere among the clouds above.
> Those that I kill I do not hate,
> Those that I guard I do not love.

That much, at least, was an honest account of the difficulties faced by one Irish gentleman in working up enthusiasm for a British imperial war. But consider the lines which follow:

> My country is Kiltartan Cross,
> My countrymen Kiltartan's poor.
> No likely end could bring them loss,
> Nor leave them happier than before.[4]

Here the soft-focus lens is used to dissolve many class antagonisms just then emerging across the countryside. These differences had been faced without compromise as early as 1904 by George Bernard Shaw, whose play *John Bull's Other Island* dramatized the painful plight of the landless labourers faced with a new set of peasant proprietors intent on writing them out of history. Needless to add, these proprietors were the same *arrivistes* who were also determined to extirpate their old Anglo-Irish landlords.

Against that backdrop, the true poignancy of Yeats's lyric lines becomes apparent. In the fate of Kiltartan's landless poor, he has the doomed nobleman read his own: for both will be victims of the pushy new élite, the Catholic farming middle class. The landless labourer, like the ruined landlord, is mythologized by the artists of that class, at just that moment in history when it has effectively put both groups out of business. The Irish Paddy of the nineteenth-century British music hall had been an eloquent demonstration of the fact that every repressive regime, having fully crushed its victims, can then afford to sentimental-ize them as literary material; but that manoeuvre was now internalized and a new audience – the emerging Irish middle class – installed the landless peasant, the superannuated aristocrat and the urban poor as the bearers of an updated mythology. The notion of a timeless peasantry, like the dream of an ahistorical nobility, was a fantasy purveyed by the new élites who had seized the positions of power in cities and towns. W. B. Yeats, who liked to think of himself as the scourge of this philistine group, actually stood sponsor for their fondest myth when he celebrated his "dream of the noble and the beggar man".[5]

Hence, too, the rather paradoxical celebration of aristocratic values by some leaders of cultural nationalism. Many texts republished during the Gaelic revival, such as *Pairlement Chloinne Tomáis*, had been vicious satires by the dying Gaelic aristocracy of the seventeenth century against the parliamentarianism and levelling vulgarity of the Cromwel-lian planters. These texts were now used, with no sense of irony, by the new middle class of nationalist Ireland. In their anxiety to secure their own "aristocratic" credentials, its members blinded themselves to the fact that they represented a group exactly equivalent to those lam-pooned in their chosen texts. They were all "descended from kings", of course; and that self-image blinded them, as it blinded many others, to the real interests which they represented. Their dream-life expressed itself in the images and symbols of an immediately superior social caste – and their self-delusion was mocked by more radical Irish speakers who recalled the old sarcastic phrase, *ag sodar i ndiaidh na nuasal* (trotting after the nobility), once used to describe those who aped English upper-class ways. Many proud nationalists could counter this jeer with the claim that the traditions which they invoked were those of a *lost* Gaelic nobility, such as had been celebrated in the bardic and *spailpín* poetry of earlier centuries. This faking of an aristocratic lineage allowed the rising native élite to assert a new self-respect, but soon the fight for Irish had given way to the fight for collars and ties, as the latent motivations of many nationalists became more painfully apparent.

The aristocratic fetishism led to other, equally unfortunate, results. For one thing, it was yet another abject surrender to prevailing English

categories of thought. Such conformism to norms which arose neither
from their immediate inheritance nor from their daily experience left
the people vulnerable, within the prevailing imperial code, to the
charge of being second-rate, and recognizably uncouth in the eyes of
the declining Anglo-Irish ascendancy. Sensing that the English aristocracy saw itself standing at the apex of imperial culture, some nationalists played up the "noble" strain which was an undeniably potent
element of Irish literary tradition: so Cuchulain was recruited as a
role-model for the boys of St. Enda's College, Pearse's Scoil Éanna,
which served as an Irish version of the English public school.

The underlying psychology of this section of the national movement
was summed up, with his usual cryptic brilliance, by Samuel Beckett in
the phrase "the Victorian Gael". The political manifestations of such
thinking were soon evident in the infant state. A new use was found for
the Irish language as a kind of green spray-paint, useful in concealing
the embarrassing similarity of Irish ideas, as well as Irish post-boxes, to
their English models. It became all the more necessary to call the native
parliament the *Dáil*, in order to conceal its depressing similarity to the
hated Westminster model. A new word was needed, a word from the
Irish language, because for decades the revivalists had poured scorn on
all parliamentary procedures. The Parliament of Clan Thomas had
been ruled by churls and called *Pairlement* in Gaelic texts, as if the
botched version of the true English term were a sign that the new men
of the 1650s could never hope to achieve anything more than a pitiful
parody of English ways. However, the new men of the 1920s insured
against such mockery by changing the word to *Dáil*, a more aristocratic
concept indeed. It goes without saying that the constant vilification of
parliament in such works had its political side-effects: it strengthened
the hand of republicans who contested the legitimacy of the new
parliament in the emergent state.

What was clear, from the pages of Shaw and Joyce, was a picture of
the new peasant proprietors in the countryside and of an emerging
middle class in the cities and towns, which tended to be dominated by
first- or second-generation immigrants from rural areas. The interests
of both groups often overlapped, as Joyce acidly noted in *Ulysses*, where
the ad-canvasser Bloom tries to design a more efficient system for
transporting livestock to and from the city markets, and where a
headmaster, Mr. Deasy, pens a solemn letter to the newspapers on the
best methods of eradicating foot-and-mouth disease in cattle. Dublin
was in 1904 a classic example of a periphery-dominated-centre, that is
to say, a conurbation dominated by the values and mores of the

surrounding countryside. A photograph taken in the 1880s shows a flock of sheep being herded across the Carlisle Bridge into Sackville Street, *en route* to the docks. Exactly a century later, in a story called "Parachutes" by John McGahern, a character thinks of Ireland that "even its principal city had one foot in the manure heap". Seeing thistledown blowing like delicate parachutes across the fashionable arcade of Grafton Street, he recalls that behind the shopfronts are "backyards and dumps . . . and yards and gardens".[6] This is a bleak *leitmotif* in a story whose central point is the *anomie* endured on housing estates by school-teachers imported to the city from rural Ireland. They attribute to the city an experience of numbing anonymity, but McGahern's subtle perception is that this has less to do with urban life than with the squinting-window mentality which rural people have brought with them. They falsely vilify the rhythms of a city life which they have never entirely mastered, and correspondingly sentimentalize the rhythms of a country life which they have not yet, in their minds, completely abandoned.

That sentimentalization had only been made possible by a safe distance. It was never endorsed by those actually living on the land, whose few playwrights saw more brutality than lyricism in rural life. In this, they corroborated the findings of those radical writers like Synge who, at the turn of the century, reversed the more common revivalist trajectory and went from the city to the country, there to discover a bleak and bitter story. As if to vindicate Shaw's diagnosis, Synge also found a landscape riven with growing class tensions and a crass bourgeois moralism. *The Shadow of the Glen* offered an astringent critique of the new respectability among country people, which could cause a young man to marry for money rather than love (even though he was not poor), and to count out his coins onto a kitchen-table while his wife-to-be talks most plaintively of her lonely mountain-side life. Synge was astonishingly subtle in his delineations of the class configuration of the countryside. He was, in the words of Jack Yeats, who accompanied him on his trip through the congested districts, a keen observer of political conditions; and from his plays and prose there emerges a social spectrum ranging from stout farmers and their expectant sons, through landless labourers and tramps (who were offered casual work in certain seasons), to the outcast tinkers. Even among the tinkers, however, he noted a new drive towards respectability and settlement, as documented in *The Tinker's Wedding*, in which a young woman seeks to have her marriage-vow solemnized by a money-grabbing priest. The small-town morality was slowly penetrating even the wildest communities of the remote countryside.

Few of these variations or tensions found representation in the writings of the more conservative nationalists. Their desire was to fudge all painful differences, in the interests of a spurious national unity and to present the rural scene with one self-confident and unambiguous voice. The comments of Michael Collins have provoked more than one socialist critic to scornful commentary in this context. An arch-pragmatist in affairs of a military or political nature, he let his guard against sentiment drop when the subject was cultural identity. Whenever the talk turned to culture, he reached not for his gun, but for the soft-focus lens:

> . . . impoverished as the people are . . . the outward aspect is a pageant. One may see processions of young women riding down on island ponies to collect sand from the seashore, or gathering turf, dressed in their shawls and in their brilliantly-coloured skirts made of material spun, woven and dyed by themselves . . . Their cottages also are little changed. They remain simple and picturesque. It is only in such places that one gets a glimpse of what Ireland *may become again* [italics mine].[7]

It is all too easy by half, Synge without tears, or at any rate, *The Aran Islands* without the accompanying commentary which led Synge to remind himself that the most seductive features of island life were all bound up with a social condition indistinguishable from "penury".[8] Though beguiled, Synge found the costs of such beauty too high. Collins did not even raise the issue, opting for the escape-hatch of a subordinate clause, "impoverished as the people are . . ." Such a clause might have been more predictably found in a blue book report on the congested districts by a British civil servant. That such an elision could be effected by an Irish rebel leader suggests that his movement could offer only a very limited kind of freedom to his people.

The pastoralism of Collins, like his nationalist politics, was largely an English creation, with its roots in the Romantic movement of Wordsworth and the Lake Poets: yet the paradox, noted by Yeats, was that forms newly-invented by Irish artists ran the risk of being denounced as un-Irish:

> . . . Forms of emotion and thought which the future will recognize as peculiarly Irish, for no other country has had the like, are looked upon as un-Irish because of their novelty in a land that is so nearly conquered that it has all but nothing of its own. English provincialism shouts through the lips of Irish patriots . . .[9]

Yeats cannot have intended it so, but the statements of Michael Collins offer graphic illustrations of that final, brilliant aphorism. Again and again, Collins returned to his beloved rural images, but his preference was, typically, to evoke them in a fallen urban setting. So, in a very famous passage, he described how he felt like cheering at a sudden sighting of a donkey and cart in one of the suburbs of London. "I", he proclaimed, "stand for that".[10] This was classic pastoral – an imagined setting that was, to all intents and purposes, English, and a setting, moreover, in which the city was the zone for an unexpected surrender to the values of the rural pastoral. Collins in that statement has given the pastoralist's game away without so much as a wink: he was, in more ways than one, an innocent abroad in England.

To project oneself back into the revivalists' world is to come upon a situation which was more open and more complex than many cared to concede. The very texts which were seized upon to purvey in school classrooms the image of a generic ahistorical peasantry – the autobiographies of the Blasket islanders – fairly vibrate with class tensions. It has been jocularly suggested that the English have a class system and talk of little else; that the Americans have a class system, but pretend that it doesn't exist; and that the Irish are the worst offenders of all, since they operate a class system, but won't tell anyone what it is. A close reading of Blasket literature might provide some clues. For both Tomás Ó Criomhthainn and Muiris Ó Súilleabháin, to leave the island and set foot on the Kerry mainland for the first time was to experience all over again the fall of man, from a kind of anarchist commune into a world of snobbish differences. Island life had bred a tribe of communitarians, who shared a subsistence economy and the dangers of storm and sea. This made for a kind of instinctive egalitarianism, but what Ó Criomhthainn actually saw on the Dingle quayside was rather unsettling:

Chonnac daoine uaisle ina seasamh ann agus slabhraí timpeall a mbuilg, daoine bochta agus gan a leath-cheart d'éadach orthu . . .[11]

(I saw noble people standing there, with decorative chains around their waists, and poor people without their sufficiency of clothing.)

Mainland Ireland had been Anglicized and, in that process, filled with a soul-destroying class feeling. In *Cré na Cille*, a book set in the Connemara Gaeltacht, Máirtín Ó Cadhain built a dead woman's monologue around her complaint that her relations above the ground should have had the audacity to bury her in a fifteen-shilling grave rather than one of the guinea plots.

The absence of such divisions on the islands of Aran or the Blaskets was profoundly attractive to radical thinkers from J. M. Synge to George Thomson. The self-confident women of Aran in their flowing red dresses seemed free of Victorian restraint. Similarly, the refusal of a division of labour, Synge judged, had left each island man with a versatile character, as his work changed with the seasons, but demanded a constant vigilance, so that it was impossible for timid or foolhardy persons to survive long on the islands. He also noted how the recent introduction of a police force was slowly corrupting social morals on the islands, but he remarked on the fact that, despite this modernization, the islanders persisted in their age-old belief that imprisonment had no corrective effect on criminals.[12]

The mainland had been heavily infected with a mode of thinking which favoured the privatization of property and the provision of punitive state institutions. Engels's grim prediction was coming true: the Irish were beginning to act like strangers in their own country. The western islands, however, still subscribed to certain codes which might be restored; and they were visited and studied by English, as well as Irish, radicals. The Blasket islands offered George Thomson, a Cambridge don in flight from one of the most class-ridden societies in Europe, the prospect of an alternative community, and, even more than that, liberation from the very idea of the state as such. Devotees of the imagined community that calls itself a nation, the Irish had historically shown a marked aversion to the idea of the state; but, on the islands, that aversion had scarcely been felt, for the people treated the state in the same way that they treated notions of social class, with sublime indifference.

If the fundamental tensions created on the mainland by class feeling and by statist politics were visible to visiting islanders and to visiting writers from Dublin, how much more painfully obvious must they have been to the *victims* of such policies themselves. Synge referred to the rising rural middle class as "an ungodly ruck of fat-faced, sweaty-headed swine" and he went on:

> ... There are sides to all that western life, the groggy-patriot-publican-general-shop-man who is married to the priest's half-sister and is second cousin once-removed of the dispensary doctor that are horrible and awful ... In a way, it is all heart-rending; in one place, the people are starving, but wonderfully

attractive and charming, and in another place, where things are going well, one has a rampant double-chinned vulgarity I haven't seen the like of.[13]

In the decade-and-a-half after Synge made his observations, these latent tensions came to a head. The Co-Operative Movement made ground among dairy-farmers; and workers in a number of rural creameries had set up soviets by April 1920.

The rural community in the previous few years had witnessed an astounding decline in deference to all forms of authority. It has been justly pointed out that "the post-Rising labour movement was radical because, far from begging government or men of property to raise the labourer's status in traditional fashion by granting him land, it arrogantly asserted that the landless worker, as chief producer of the nation's wealth, was a superior person in his own right".[14] This is an image quite at variance with that of a stoic, unchanging peasantry. No doubt, the Great War and the waves of revolution which passed over Europe in its wake, as now-defiant soldiers returned home impatient with the discredited rhetoric of the upper-classes, had served further to erode all forms of authority.

If conservative politicians like Michael Collins produced a version of pastoral, so also did radical artists like Synge, for antipastoral is, for all its nay-saying, still a version of the mode.

Synge's reading of Marx's *Kapital* – especially of its famous sections on the division of labour and on the working day – is manifest in many pages of *The Aran Islands*, for example, the following:

. . . it is likely that much of the intelligence and charm of these people is due to the absence of any division of labour, and to the correspondingly wide development of each individual, whose varied knowledge and skill necessitates a considerable activity of mind. Each man can speak two languages. He is a skilled fisherman, and can manage a curragh with extraordinary nerve and dexterity. He can farm simply, burn kelp, cut out pampooties, mend nets, build and thatch a house, and make a candle or a coffin. His work changes with the seasons in a way that keeps him free from the dullness that comes to people who have always the same occupation. The danger of his life on the sea gives him the alertness of a primitive hunter, and the long nights he spends fishing in his curragh bring him some of the emotions that are thought peculiar to men who have lived with the arts.[15]

In Synge's eyes, the islanders constituted a sort of anarchist commune, composed of frank women and courageous men. He repeatedly made strategic contrasts between their integrity and the vulgar materialism then overtaking those mainland communities, which Yeats still idealized.

Two generations later, a working-class Dubliner, Brendan Behan, would find on the Blasket islands a community living a kind of life that was recognizable to someone from another peripheral social grouping, the inner city poor. The story of how, in these decades, the major record of Blasket life *An tOileánach* was censored by schoolteachers, in the process of being made safe for mainland classrooms, was yet another example of how a revolutionary text might be converted to revivalist purposes. Ó Criomhthainn's innocent accounts of adolescent sexuality on the islands, of how the local boys were delighted when a gust of wind raised the skirts of the girls ("D'fhéachas isteach in áit nár shaighneáil an ghrian ariamh"; I looked into a place where the sun never shone before) were pruriently excised.[16] It is even possible that the author anticipated this gelding of his text in the famous, closing statement that he and his sort would not be found again. A commune was dying on its feet, and even those few faithful representations of it in literature would be subject to revision, as personal freedoms came under the scrutiny of the nationalist censors.

How did so much radical energy get deflected from its original purpose? One answer is that the mainland rural community, after its emancipation in the late 1880s and 1890s, came to dominate the national agenda, marginalizing both the western islanders, the *Gaeltacht* and the inner-city poor. As Shaw feared, the Land Acts spelled a new lease for landlordism of a more petty variety. For a brief, glorious period, it did indeed seem as though feudalism might be about to fall in Ireland, as Michael Davitt reported in a hopeful book of 1904. Even Yeats could recall being exalted by this new mood:

> . . . after the agrarian passion we began to value truth . . . free discussion appeared among us for the first time, bringing the passion for reality, the satiric genius that informs *Ulysses, The Playboy of the Western World, The Informer, The Puritan* and other books and plays; the accumulated hatred of the years was suddenly transferred from England to Ireland.[17]

It is significant that Yeats locates this freedom of thought not in 1922, but two decades earlier, in the environment that shaped the genius of Synge and Joyce.

The "hatred of Ireland" recalled by Yeats was actually a repudiation of the backwardness and undevelopment of a neglected colony; but the agrarian question, which opened this self-critical debate, also by its very resolution ensured its premature closure. The ultimate victims of the Land Acts were the gentry and labourers, swept aside by the new proprietors, who made certain that the land agitation did not develop into a return to communal tenure. By 1916 a further group could have been added to the list of their victims, the urban poor, afflicted horribly by rising food prices and contracting job opportunities. The interests of the rural periphery were already coming to dominate those of the urban centre. Yeats, though he continued to fulminate against the philistinism of the Catholic middle class, was never more bourgeois than in his attacks on the bourgeoisie: and he assuaged their guilt about their victims by texts which reduced them to literary material. The new élites, in turn, paid Yeats the ultimate compliment which any post-colonial middle class can bestow, when they asked him to head the committee to redesign a national coinage. In later decades, it would be his proud image which would adorn the Irish twenty-pound note.

This domination of the rural over the urban led to some curious paradoxes. Taking their cue from Wordsworth, Coleridge and, most of all, from Matthew Arnold, the revivalists attacked the complacency and philistinism of the middle class, despite the fact that in Ireland a native middle class had not yet fully emerged as a social formation. Concomitant with this went an attack on the belching factory-chimneys and common corner-boys of city culture, despite the fact that no Irish conurbation, other than Belfast, had been significantly industrialized. And over and above those themes was laid an idealization of a peasantry which was itself already convulsed by internal tensions and material acquisitiveness.

This elevation of the peripheral over the central was an internalization of a model which, in the later nineteenth century, had characterized the politics of Great Britain and Ireland. When Parnell and his parliamentary party had held the balance of power at Westminster, they provided an object-lesson in how the Celtic periphery could paralyze the London centre. As Shaw remarked, in "How to Settle the Irish Question":

> . . . the Irish, though representing only one-tenth of the population of the whole and less than a third of the area, has more than a sixth of the membership, holds the balance of power, and occupies so much of the time of the House that its business seems to consist mainly of the discussion of

Irish grievances, though Ireland is in every way a happier and freer country to live in than England . . .[18]

In an essay called "Brogue-Shock", Shaw phrased the idea even more trenchantly:

> . . . Beyond a doubt, we Irish are the governing race in these islands; and I am not sure that the transfer of the seat of government from Westminster to Belfast or Dublin would not be the most natural solution of the problem. There never would be a Home Rule movement in England . . .[19]

This became the model which was internalized in subsequent Irish politics: rural Ireland was real Ireland, the farmer the moral and economic backbone of the country. That myth was given a further lease of life in each generation, by the urbanized descendants of landless labourers or by failed small farmers keen to create a compensatory fable of rare old times. Marooned in an unplanned city of tenements and housing estates, many people experienced real guilt-feelings for the "crime" of being new Dubliners at all.[20]

Even Brendan Behan in his autobiography conceded how hard it was for him to admit that the borstal boys from Liverpool and Manchester whom he met in jail seemed to know the same cultural parameters as himself: the weekly visit to the pawnshop, the fish-and-chipper, and so on. In the familiar manner of other post-colonial capitals, Dublin was overrun by unplanned migrations of rural folk, who had no sooner settled than they were consumed by a fake nostalgia for a pastoral Ireland they had "lost".

Patrick Kavanagh was the test-case here: at first, when he was still close to his Monaghan roots, he denounced the false consciousness of the peasant periphery, but after a decade or more in Dublin, he fell back into line with it, going to extraordinary lengths to recreate Baggot Street as an urban pastoral, "my Pembrokeshire". And *that* invented Ireland proved far more attractive to poetry-readers among the New Dubliners than had Kavanagh's bitter indictment of rural torpor in *The Great Hunger*. The conversion of Baggot Street into a rural idyll proved palatable to those politicians and architects intent on effecting somewhat similar transformations themselves, imposing a ruralist grid of community onto an urban setting.

The city planners were, in the words of a leading architect, "road engineers who are all first generation country people, who have no idea how cities should be developed".[21] For years, the police in Dublin were invariably of rural origin, as were most of its schoolteachers and civil servants; it was a rural Minister who designed the infamous tower blocks of Ballymun in 1966 in memory of the signatories of the Easter proclamation, and it was rural Ministers who held the Justice portfolio year after year, showing scant understanding of the problems of urban youth. Most of the political activists in the city had also cut their teeth in the countryside, from which they brought the clientelist traditions of brokerage politics, which prevented the emergence of a left-right ideological debate.[22]

The literary implications of all this are not far to seek, and have in fact already been considered. Fintan O'Toole has shown how the forms of drama inherited by Sean O'Casey from Abbey playwrights, while fitted admirably to describe a rural community, were quite inadequate to deal with the layers of urban life.[23] Every time O'Casey's characters try to seize the streets as their own, they are driven back to tenements which, with their multiple families in one building, operate like a rural community. O'Casey was doomed to describe the urban in constricting ruralist forms, perhaps because Dublin was intent on so conceiving of itself. The urbanized Synge-song of his characters appealed not to inner-city Dubliners themselves, but to the new élite of civil servants, town-planners, and teachers, living in the city's plushier outer ring. These people sentimentalized O'Casey's lovable proletarians who were, in fact, rapidly becoming the most spectacular victims of the new state policies.

As if in defiance, each of O'Casey's plays moves to a moment when a previously peripheral character becomes central, just as his location of the main action in the tenements is a desperate attempt to centralize communities deemed peripheral in the nationalist mythology. The city itself, with its rotting slums at the centre and its salubrious suburbs housing a rural-educated, ruling élite, seemed, even in physical terms, a periphery-dominated centre. The warders of its main jail spoke mostly in country accents, but the inmates seemed disproportionately drawn from the local hinterland. So, also, at the unemployment exchanges, the civil servants who distributed the benefit-money were often of rural origin, while the chronic unemployed were mainly Dubliners.

Few enough of those unemployed ever crossed the threshold of the Abbey Theatre which, located in the heart of Dublin's north inner city, continued all too often to play the rural classics for tourists and (increasingly) for the natives. The Abbey for long periods functioned more as an artistic museum than as an experimental or a people's theatre. On radio and in print media, the short story continued to enjoy a vogue as the quintessential Irish genre, purveyed with commercial success in foreign outlets such as *The New Yorker* by artists willing enough to play up local colour for an international readership. It is only fair to add, however, that the fixation on the short story may be discerned not far below the surface of such modernist masterpieces as *Ulysses*, *At Swim-Two-Birds* and Beckett's trilogy as well. Each of these is a thinly-disguised collection of short stories fretted into a form suggestive of the experimental novel. Nor should this seem surprising, given that the short story is the form which renders the lives of the marginal and the isolated, whereas the traditional novel tends to feature the urbane and complex relationships of a fully "made", calibrated society.

As a mainly ruralist genre, however, the Irish short story was as ill-suited as the traditional Abbey play to render the complex gradations of city life. The young James Joyce tried as best he could to press it into the service of that life, on the invitation of the editor of *The Irish Homestead* for "something simple, rural?, live-making? pathos? which would not shock its readers".[24] Sensing that Joyce might be chagrined to see his name alongside the week's cattle prices, he suggested that he use a pseudonym. Joyce despised "The Pig's Paper", as he called it, but pocketed the sovereign in payment and signed "The Sisters" *Stephen Daedalus*, thus giving birth to that famous *nom-de-plume* and fictive character.[25] Yet, on finishing *Dubliners* he felt frustrated by a book which seemed to want to be a novel, but couldn't quite move itself into that category.

Each character in the stories seems a sort of periphery-dominated centre him- or herself, a super-sensitive soul on whom other persons and forces wreak a terrible impact. In "The Sisters", for example, a boy is frightened that the noise he makes eating crackers may disturb the repose of others; and in "The Dead", Gabriel Conroy is more aware of how he appears to others than of how he is to himself. To most of the figures in these stories, power and authority lie "elsewhere". In the writings of a French artist such as Balzac, the movement towards selfhood is charted, as it were, by a movement from the provinces to the metropolis, that city of Paris which evokes notions glittering with human possibility. The citizen of a meritocracy can rise through the classes, learning as he goes, until finally he leans out over the rooftops of Paris and says: "Here I am at last at the centre of things, arrived". In the colonial Ireland of Joyce, however, things are not so cut and dried: the capital is, in fact, the centre of paralysis and the only freedom is the freedom to move out, a motion that is endlessly thwarted, just as the

attempts by Joyce's introspective characters to transcend interior monologue in acts of real communication with others are often stymied.

The sanctification of rural Ireland as real Ireland by those who
actually abandoned it to live in Dublin as members of the ruling élites
led to some interesting cultural effects. A pervasive theme in the
literature of the mid-century was the question: "can I live in my own
place?" The answer was usually "no" and for a variety of reasons: the
plum jobs were generally in Dublin, while rural communities seemed
to be in terminal economic decline. Independence brought its attendant paradoxes: although the Irish were now, at least in theory, possessed of cultural freedom, in practice they were still prisoners of the
iron laws of economics. Those who were not forced to migrate to
Britain or North America found, in many cases, that they had to go
to Dublin. The result was a capital city which, in classic post-colonial
mode, swelled vastly beyond its natural capacity, even as the rural towns
seemed, in many cases, to get smaller and smaller. This development
was as bad for Dublin and its citizens as it was for the communities of
the rural towns. While many Dubliners complained of having to live a
sort of underground life in a city which seemed to be under semi-
permanent occupation by outside forces, people in rural areas felt
oppressed and ignored by the burgeoning bureaucracy in the distant
capital. The old British policy of ruling the masses from the major
colonial seaport remained a central feature of the national life. There
was no attempt to reimagine Ireland along decentralized lines: although
some idealistic souls talked occasionally of the need to relocate government departments and semi-state offices in regional cities and towns,
civil servants proved often resistant to the few changes actually proposed. As Dublin and its hinterland began to hold one million people,
one in every three citizens, a common joke was that the entire island
would tip over as a result of the imbalance into the Irish Sea.

Those who left the land grew ever more sentimental about the world
which they had lost, and the effects of their pastoralism could be
discerned in state policy. The brothers and sisters, mothers and fathers
who remained on the land were spared heavy taxation, supported by
government subvention, and some of them would eventually enjoy an
affluence that was in excess of that known by most of the inhabitants of
Dublin. With that affluence came the motor-car, the television set, the
golf club and the deep-freeze: in other words, rural Ireland slowly
acquired many of the trappings of a sophisticated urban lifestyle, even
as the capital continued for a long time to be conditioned by the values
carried into it by new arrivals from the countryside. When the strain of

all this first began to show, it was in the institutions of the capital. Charged with the task of representing "the nation" rather than its own city hinterland, the National Theatre at the Abbey became somewhat moribund, failing to nurture new writing talent from Dublin or to function as a civic theatre. When revitalization came, it would come from the provinces, in the shape of writers like Brian Friel of Donegal or Tom Murphy of Galway, and of actors from the regional companies which seemed to thrive in proportion to the waning of the Abbey. It was as if the old nationalist narrative was beginning to break down, and "Ireland" once again became a problematic notion, as its people renewed their interest in its constituent parts. The novelist John McGahern was only slightly exaggerating when he described it as an island containing thirty-two independent republics.[26]

Twenty-Eight

Flann O'Brien, Myles, and The Poor Mouth

An Béal Bocht (The Poor Mouth, 1941) was the only book which Brian O'Nolan, alias Flann O'Brien, alias Myles na gCopaleen, wrote in his native language. Why only one, and this in particular? The answer may lie in the identity of the persona to whom the narrative was entrusted, Myles na gCopaleen.

Myles had been the comic hero of Dion Boucicault's play *The Colleen Bawn* (1860). Blundering but intermittently wily, he shot a murderer and accidentally saved the heroine's life. Liar, convict, horse-thief and poteen-distiller, he was the living antithesis of Victorian respectability, and so was hugely successful on the stage, offering audiences "a vicarious release from the solemn and righteous standards by which they tried to live".[1] At the same time as English onlookers continued to shower affection on this brainless but loyal fictional character (whose name means Myles of the Ponies), the real Irish were suffering famine at home and economic exploitation in the ghettos of British cities and towns. All too often, competition for work led to riots between Irish and English labourers; and the newspapers were filled with cartoons of the sinister, simianized Fenian agitator. When Irish bombs began to bedevil the domestic peace of England, and when Darwin challenged its spiritual composure, caricaturists had little compunction in depicting the Irish as monkeys or gorillas. Myles was simply the reverse-side of this coin – a victim of Victorian sentimentality, as his real-life counterpart was a target of Victorian bile. A stage-Irish buffoon, blundering his way through bulls and malapropisms in the foreignness of the English language, he was denied even the dignity of the sufferings of his flesh-and-blood cousin.

The strategy of *An Béal Bocht* now becomes clear. In the character of Myles na gCopaleen, O'Nolan rescues the buffoon from the Victorian stage and makes him articulate. The feckless clown who had once stuttered in broken English is now permitted to speak in his native language, and so he is shown not as the English wish to visualize him, but as he sees himself. The eclipsing "g", which had been omitted from the final word of his name in *The Colleen Bawn*, is now restored, so Myles na Coppaleen may resume the fuller status of Myles na gCopaleen. That jocular and exaggerated language, which was once the object of the dramatist's satire, has now become a *method*, by which other more fitting targets are attacked. Among the new targets are Irishmen (such as Boucicault) who abjectly conform to English stereotypes of the neighbouring island. Hence the mockery of Boucicault's fabricated brogue, of words like "diversions" and "adventures", which may mean something to amused English onlookers, but have to be pedantically explained to bemused Irish people in footnotes (as *scléip* and *eachtraí*), since the Irish may be encountering them for the first time.

Myles, therefore, attacks more recent writers who have replaced the stage Irishman with a stage Gael, or, as he dubbed them in a letter to Sean O'Casey, "the Gaelic morons here with their bicycle clips and handball medals".[2] In depicting the realities of poverty in the west of Ireland, *An Béal Bocht* is not only a send-up of the scenic landscape, Gothic ruins and romantic music of Boucicault's glamorized countryside; it is, even more urgently, an attack on the Dublin revivalists of the twentieth century, who could idealize the saintly simplicity of western life, only by ignoring the awful poverty on which it was based. With *The Great Hunger* and, later, *Cré na Cille*, O'Nolan's novel is a subversive anti-pastoral, a characteristic nineteen-forties reaction against some pious evasions of the revivalists. Through the use of his once-despised but now-functional language, Myles succeeds in depicting a world where all men, and not solely the Irish-speaking peasant, are seen for the buffoons that they are. The difference between Myles na gCopaleen and Myles na Coppaleen is the difference between a vehicle and a target.

The project of transforming a fictional character into the controlling author of a book is wholly consistent with the democratic programme mapped out for the modern novel in *At Swim-Two-Birds* (1939), which argued that each character should be allowed "a private life, self-determination and a decent standard of living". The borrowing of Myles from a previous work had also been sanctioned there: "The entire corpus of existing literature should be regarded as a limbo from which discerning authors could draw their characters as required".[3] Hence, also, the parodies of thinly-disguised refugees from the writings of Tomás Ó Criomhthainn and "Máire".

At the root of his interest in the name and nature of Myles na gCopaleen lay O'Nolan's obsession with the problem of establishing his own literary identity. Apart from its use in *An Béal Bocht*, the persona was used only in the regular columns of *The Irish Times* as the *nom-de-plume* of the anonymous author, who was precluded from signing contributions by his status as a civil servant. When the column began in 1939, it was intended that there should be three articles a week, all in Irish, but soon the versatile author turned to English as well. The latter articles appealed greatly to the upper-class readers, and inexorably their proportion and reputation grew. O'Nolan was well aware of the risk of "Paddywhackery" in the face of such an audience. He had read Yeats's warning that every writer must express or exploit Ireland; and for him that choice lay between expressing the nation to itself (mainly in Irish) or exploiting it for the amusement of a "superior" foreign audience (mainly in English). As if to register the costs to self-expression of reverting wholly to English in his newspaper-column, O'Nolan tampered with the spelling of Myles na gCopaleen yet again. A colleague at *The Irish Times* later recalled: "The change to Myles na Gopaleen was made, I think, after he had begun to gain some celebrity outside Ireland, in deference to the Anglo-Saxon epiglottis. We in *The Irish Times* cherished the pedantry of the eclipsis in the genitive, but he had his way".[4] It was as if, by this alteration, O'Nolan wished to indicate a loss of authenticity, a regression to the botched identity of Boucicault's clown. Only in *An Béal Bocht* did he stake out the secret territory of a separate novel in which he could carry out his original assignment under his honest pseudonym of Myles na gCopaleen.

In saving a part of himself for that great satiric work, he mocked by implication the newspaper editor who had initially commissioned all this stage-Irish folly. For the greatest single irony of *An Béal Bocht* lies in its dedication to R. M. Smyllie, the magisterial editor of *The Irish Times* and official mouthpiece of the ascendancy. In the dedication, his name is tampered with, in just the same way that his Victorian compatriots had mangled the spelling of Myles: thus R. M. Smyllie is transformed to "R. M. Ó Smaoille", and thence to the clan-leader "An Smaolach". The only Irish known to Smyllie was whiskey, which he drank from a hand covered in a white glove, a consequence of a promise to his mother on her death-bed that he would "never touch a drop again". Of the native language he knew not a word. Despite repeated entreaties to the uncharacteristically tight-lipped author, Smyllie never managed to ascertain the nature of the book, nor the reason for its dedication. He must, on occasion, have suspected that, despite the elaborate leg-pull, the author was in earnest. For, in dedicating his study of Irish identity to an Anglo-Irishman who could never hope to read it, O'Nolan had pointed to a central theme of his book – the tragicomedy of mistaken identity that lay behind the manufacture in Britain of the stage Irishman.

A corresponding anxiety about his own identity as an Irish writer haunted O'Nolan to the end, and was manifest in his restless adoption of varying pseudonyms. He once remarked that a writer needs "an equable yet versatile temperament, and the compartmentation of personality for the purpose of literary utterance".[5] Accordingly, he had resorted as a newspaper columnist to Myles na Gopaleen, as a novelist to Flann O'Brien, as an undergraduate wit to Brother Barnabas, and as a Gaelic satirist to Myles na gCopaleen. Amidst all this chopping and changing, one thing is clear: he never had the gall to sail under the colours of Brian O'Nolan. As Anne Clissman has noted: "it was almost as if, by putting Myles na gCopaleen forward, prepared to take on and conquer the world, Brian O'Nolan could retire to an impregnable and safe position".[6]

All this play-acting with proper names provides a clue to *An Béal Bocht*'s comic theme. If the triumph of Myles na gCopaleen is the recovery of his true identity, then the tragicomedy of the characters is that grinding poverty has left them with no identity whatever, not even the sense of a lost one which they might hope some day to recover. Nevertheless, these faceless peasants have aspirations to grandeur, as is clear from their chosen names – Bonaparte, Sitric, Maximilian, Ferdinand, etc. They aspire not towards the emulation of Cuchulain and the ancient Gael, but towards imitation of the great foreign commanders of military history, including Sitric, a Viking who waged unholy war on their ancestors. On his first day at school, Bonaparte O'Coonassa is asked to repeat his name for the roll-call. The litany which follows is a long-winded tribute to ten generations of noble aspiration, which have resulted in a total erosion of Gaelic identity:

> Bonaparte, son of Michelangelo, son of Peter, son of Owen, son of Thomas's Sarah, grand-daughter of John's Mary, grand-daughter of James, son of Dermot . . .

> Bonapairt Michaelangelo Pheadair Eoghain Shorcha Thomáis Mháire Sheán Shéamais Dhiarmada . . .[7]

At this point, the hopeful litany is cruelly interrupted by a blow from the English-speaking master and the terse announcement in a foreign language that "Yer name is Jams O'Donnell", a sentence which is uttered to every single child in Corcha Dorcha on arrival at school. In such ways is the identity of the eager youth eroded by the master. Bonaparte himself notes the loss of self consequent upon the teacher's interruption of the genealogical tree with a clout:

> James O'Donnell? These two words were singing in my ears when feeling returned to me. I found that I was lying on my side on the floor, my breeches, hair, and all my person saturated with the streams of blood which flowed from the split caused by the oar in my skull.

> Jams O'Donnell? Bhí an dá bhriathar seo ag gliogaireacht im cheann nuair tháinic mothú arís ann. Fuaireas mé féin sínte ar leataoibh ar an urlár, mo bhríste, mo ghruaig agus mo phearsa uile ar maothas ó slaoda fola a bhí ag stealladh ón scoilt bhí fágtha ag an mhaide ar mo chloigean.[8]

Bonaparte remarks acidly to his mother that, if every child in the district is Jams O'Donnell, then "isn't O'Donnell the wonderful man and the number of children he has?" ("feach gur fónta an fear é O'Donnell agus an líon sin clainne aige"). His mother tells him that the Old-Grey-Fellow, his grandfather, was also beaten on his first day at school and called Jams O'Donnell. At this revelation, Bonaparte decides that one day's education is enough and resolves never to return:

> – Woman, said I, what you say is amazing and I don't think I'll ever go back to that school but it's now the end of my learning.
> – You're shrewd, said she, in your early youth.

> "A bhean", arsa mise, "is iontach a n-abair agus ní dói liom go bhfillimse ar an scoil sin go deo acht deire an léinn anois déanta agam".
> "Táir críonna", arsa mo mháthair, "id mhion-óige dhuit".[9]

If the fawning peasantry betray a pathetic snobbery in baptizing their children with the names of illustrious foreigners, they also show a great distaste for the names of their own tradition: names such as Seán and Séamas have not been found in the area for generations. Conversely, the affluent Gaelic revivalists from Dublin, who visit the district every summer to learn Irish, are equally anxious to conceal their own inherited names. Here, O'Nolan mocks the subterfuge of the founder of the Gaelic League, Douglas Hyde, who employed the pseudonym *An*

Craoibhín Aoibhinn (The Pleasant Little Branch), in order to hide a
surname which pointed clearly back to invading English soldiery. In a
somewhat hysterical attempt to deanglicize themselves, city revivalists
adopt a strategy which is the reverse of that employed by the peasantry:
they discard their foreign surnames and adopt Gaelic titles such as *An
Nóinín Gaelach, Goll Mac Mórna* and *An Tuiseal Tabharthach* (respec-
tively, the Gaelic Daisy, Goll MacMórna and the Dative Case). They
also turn their backs on their actual heritage, in an attempt to acquire a
spurious identity. By such subtle satire, O'Nolan emphasizes that
affluence is no guarantee of a sure identity and that poverty is the
inevitable condition of those who have had their past identity taken
away. Affluence, at least, has the merit of leaving a person with a choice
in the matter, but it does not ensure that he will have the courage to be
himself.

O'Nolan was all too well aware that many colourless and weak-
kneed people had joined the language movement, in the hope that it
would give them a social identity, since they lacked the capacity to
mould their own. They adopted the kilt as their public costume, in
blissful unawareness that it was a foreign importation. The misconcep-
tion was so prevalent that even Gaeltacht dwellers were taken in.
Bonaparte O'Coonassa believes that the kilt signifies competence in
Irish and the Gaelic integrity of the wearer:

> There were men present wearing a simple unornamented dress – these, I
> thought, had little Gaelic; others had such nobility, style and elegance in
> their feminine attire that it was evident that their Gaelic was fluent. I felt
> quite ashamed that there was not even one true Gael among us in Corcha
> Dorcha.

> Bhí fir ann agus gúna simplí nea-ornáideach ortha – iad sin, dar liom, ar
> bheagán Gaeilge; fir eile ann le hoiread uaisleachta, shlachtmharachta, agus
> ghalántachta ina mban-chultacha gur léir go raibh an Ghaeilg go líofa acu.
> Bhí árd-náire orm nach raibh éinne fíor-Ghaelach inar measc i gCorcha
> Dorcha.[10]

An Béal Bocht fulfils the promise of its title, for it is a study of the
effects on Irish identity of generations of dire poverty. This is not
simply a matter of the material poverty of the western peasant, but
also of the spiritual emptiness of the town-dweller who cannot feel
himself a true Irishman until he has donned a kilt. In Ireland the phrase
béal bocht or "poor mouth" is used to describe the slavish tactic of the

person who makes a great show of poverty. This is done in order to wring sympathy and support from onlookers, a tactic which had become traditional in a region laid waste by deprivation. This theme is developed in the novel's sub-title *droch-scéal ar an droch-shaol*, "a bad story about the hard life". That last phrase became the eventual title of O'Nolan's next book, which was itself sub-titled "An Exegesis of Squalor", a perfect description of what had been already achieved in *An Béal Bocht*.

Anti-pastoralists like O'Nolan and Kavanagh were, of course, following a lead which had been given by James Joyce, whose own views on the peasantry became even clearer with the publication in the 1940s of *Stephen Hero*, in which the main protagonist says: "The glorified peasantry all seem to me as like one another as a peascod is to another peascod. They can spot a false coin, but they represent no very admirable type of culture. They live a life of dull routine, the calculation of coppers, the weekly debauch and the weekly piety".[11] This might have been an account of a townland where every man has the interchangeable name of Jams O'Donnell. For *An Béal Bocht* truly is the Irish version of *One Hundred Years of Solitude*, a book in which identities are fluid and interchangeable, as characters are trapped in repetitive cycles of time and rains that pelt down without mercy. It takes us beyond the stage-Irish thief who robs the rich for kicks or for revenge to a study of robbers so poor that they filch from one another.

Behind this desperate hilarity lies a real desolation: as Brendan Kennelly has observed, "this black vision sometimes transcends the satirical purpose it so brilliantly serves, and achieves at certain moments a real tragic intensity".[12] The satire and the tragedy are finally one, for in mocking the official clichés of previous Irish writers, O'Nolan is emphasizing the plight of a peasantry which has had foisted on it a falsely romanticized ethos . . . from stage Irish in the nineteenth century to stage Gael in the twentieth, one mask has simply been exchanged for another. For O'Nolan the most distressing aspect of this was the alarming number of Irishmen, in the last century and in the present, who were willing to conform to these stereotypes.

In the figure of the Old Grey Fellow (An Seanduine Liath) may be found the stage Gael, abjectly conforming to the fatuous clichés laid down in the classic Gaelic novels of "Máire" – to the effect that toddlers should be put to play for hours each day in fireside ashes, that girls in Donegal may be courted only in the middle of the night by two men who come match-making with a five-noggin bottle, and so on. He has no theory of his own to pass on to Bonaparte, other than clichés borrowed from Gaelic texts, and from his literary ancestor, the stage Irishman. Even the credulous Bonaparte soon discerns the lineaments of the time-honoured buffoon:

> . . . bedad, it was an incredible thing the amount of potatoes he consumed, the volume of speech which issued from him and what little work he performed around the house.

> . . . by dad, ba dhochreidte an oiread prátaí a d'itheadh sé, an oiread cainte bheireadh sé uaidh, agus a laighead oibre dhéanadh sé fá'n dtigh.[13]

His braggadocio is wholly within the tradition, as the maturing grandson notes:

> According to what I had heard, he was the best man in the Rosses during his youth. There was no one in the countryside comparable to him where jumping, ransacking, fishing, love-making, drinking, thieving, fighting, ham-stringing, cattle-running, swearing, gambling, night-walking, hunting, dancing, boasting, and stick-fighting were concerned.

> Do réir mar bhí closta agam uaidh, eisean an fear ab fhearr ins na Rosa le linn a óige. Maidir le léimní, polltóireacht, iascaireacht, suirghe, ól, gadaíocht, troid, leonadh-eallaí, rith, eascainí, cearúthas, siúl-oiche, seilg, damhsa, maíomh agus tarraingt-a'-bhata, ní raibh éinne sa dúthaí ionchurtha leis.[14]

He is, in short, a man whose whole life has been an epic campaign for the rehabilitation of the cliché.

The tragedy of rural Ireland is enacted in moments of high farce. That poverty which causes humans to cohabit with pigs and cows and hens may be tragic in cause but it is comic in effect – as when the O'Coonassa family are advised to build an outhouse, but mistakenly conclude that nature has ordained that they, rather than the animals, should go to live in it. After two nights of cold and rain, they entreat to be restored to their rightful abode, back with the beasts. For more than two hundred years, the stage Irishman had been associated in the English folk mind with animals, especially with pigs. According to one historian, the popular notion of the swinish mob helps to account for the porcine features assigned by cartoonists to agitators: "Because pigs played such a vital part in the Irish peasant economy, it was all too easy for comic artists to endow United Irishmen with snouts instead of noses".[15] Such visual metaphors persisted into the present century, when Bernard Partridge, the chief cartoonist of the magazine *Punch*, used the pig to denote the Irish people throughout the war of independence.[16] In *An Béal Bocht*, O'Nolan simply took the Englishman's metaphor for the Irishman's literal truth, effectively throwing the cartoons back in English faces with the suggestion that people, if treated for a time as animals in fiction, may begin to behave like animals in fact.

The comedy is never more bitter than when it is most funny. A whole chapter is devoted to the tribulations of living in the same house with Ambrose, a foul-smelling pig; and the Old Grey Fellow actually turns the family out onto the street rather than evict Ambrose. Later, when the government offers a grant for each child in the household who can speak English, he issues a number of piglets with jackets and trousers for the occasion. He stills the doubts of the lady of the house with the following speech extolling Sarah, the family's sow:

> She has a great crowd of family at present and they have vigorous voices, even though their dialect is unintelligible to us. How do we know but that their conversation isn't in English? Of course, youngsters and piglets have the same habits and take notice that there's a close likeness between their skins.

> Tá fuirean mhór clainne fá lathair aici agus tá bíogadh breá gutha ionnta má's do-thuigthe féin a gcanúin againn. Cá bhfios dúinn nach i mBéarla a bhíonn a gcóluadar le chéile acu? Dar ndói, cleachtaíonn daoine óga agus muca óga na nósanna céanna agus féach go bhfuil géar-chosúlacht idir a gcroicean.[17]

The inspector, when he comes, is given the benign assurance that "All speak English, Sor", including Jams O'Donnell (whoever he might be). The official departs happy with a job well done.

The Old Grey Fellow's judgement that there is little difference between a piglet and a youngster is vindicated by a curious event in the following chapter. One of the subsidized piglets strays from the farm and is lost, but returns in triumph a month later with not only its jacket and trousers intact, but also its pockets filled with a pipe, tobacco, whiskey and a shilling for good measure. These are the classic props of the Stage Irishman,[18] but in this case they constitute the unlikely reward for an evening's work with a professional linguist who tape-recorded the animal's grunts in the belief that they represented a particularly erudite form of Irish. That the collector should later have gained an honorary distinction from a German university for this work adds to the magnificence of the jest. Towards the end of the book, Bonaparte O'Coonassa is himself lost for a time in the mountains, before he manages to stumble back, naked and hungry, to his native parish. The lesson is not lost on the Old Grey Fellow, who lectures his feckless grandson:

— There's no understanding the world that's there today at all, said he, and especially in Corcha Dorcha. A pig rambled off on us a little while ago and when he returned, he had a worthwhile suit of clothes on him. You went off from us fully-dressed and you're back again as stark-naked as the day you were born!

"Níl míniú ar an saol atá iniú ann", ar seisean, "i gCorcha Dorcha go háirithe. Tamall ó shoin d'imigh muc ar seachrán uainn agus nuair d'fhill sé bhí culaith fhiúntach éadaigh uime. D'imigh tusa uainn lán-ghléasta, agus táir tagaithe arais anois, tú có lomnocht is bhí tú an chéad lá".[19]

It is in the same chapter that Bonaparte is prompted to put to the Old Grey Fellow the overwhelming question which is implicit in every page of the book:

— Are you certain that the Gaels are people? said I.
— They've that reputation anyway, little noble, said he, but no confirmation of it has ever been received. We're not horses nor hens; seals nor ghosts; and, in spite of all that, it's unbelievable that we're humans — but all that is only an opinion.

"An bhfuilir cinnte", arsa mise, "gur daoine na Gaeil?"
"Tá an t-ainm sin amuí ortha, a uaislín", ar seisean, "acht ní frith deimhniú riamh air. Ní capaill ná cearca sinn, ní róintí ná taibhsí, agus, ar a shon san, is inchreidte gur daoine sinn; acht níl sa mhéid sin acht tuairim".[20]

On the opening page of the book, Bonaparte had acknowledged that a person's name and his memory are the twin keys to his identity. Having been robbed of his name by the schoolmaster and having lost the memory of his father in early youth, he is well entitled to ask whether he has any human personality or is merely interchangeable with dumb animals. Certainly, he has no understanding of sex and no idea of where he came from:

I was born in the middle of the night in the end of the house. My father never expected me because he was a quiet fellow and did not understand very accurately the ways of life.

I lár na hoíche sin sea rugadh mise i dtóin an tighe. Ní raibh aon choinne ag m'athair liom óir duine cneasta a bhí ann agus ní go róchruinn a thuig seisean cúrsaí an tsaoil.[21]

Such ignorance seems widespread in Corcha Dorcha. Later, when the Old Grey Fellow decides to dress the piglets as English-speaking children, he tells Bonaparte's mother with cryptic cynicism that she will have a large household by the next morning. Even this woman seems baffled at such rapid procreativity for she says: "It's a wonderful world, but I'm not expecting anything of that kind and neither did I hear that a house could be filled in one night" ("is íontach an saol atá inniu ann – ach níl aon choinne agamsa lena leithéid agus ní clos riamh go raibh líonadh tí ann in aon oíche"). When Bonaparte attains his majority, he remains woefully ignorant of the facts of life:

I thought that babies fell out of the skies and that those who desired them needed only to have good luck and a spacious field.

Cheapas gur as na spéarthaí a thuit na leanaí agus nach raibh de dhíobháil ar éinne a bhí ag duil leo acht an t-á agus páirc bhreá fhairsing.[22]

Inevitably, when his own first son is born, he thinks that his household has been blessed with nothing more portentous than the arrival of another piglet – he cannot recognize his son for what he is, just as he has earlier failed to recall the memory of his own father. All continuity of identity from one generation to the next has been shattered by this elementary ignorance, just as the schoolboy's recital of his genealogical tree was rudely interrupted by the master.

Bonaparte is not the only character in Corcha Dorcha who has difficulty in distinguishing the human from the animal – nor are pigs the only beasts with whom humans are compared. In Victorian physiognomy the Irish were often represented as dogs, just as the English were likened to bulls, the Americans to bears, the Chinese to hogs, and so on. In *Comparative Physiognomies* (1852), James W. Redfield wrote: "Compare the Irishman and the dog in respect to barking, snarling, howling, begging, fawning, flattering, backbiting, quarreling, blustering, scenting, seizing, hanging on, teasing, rollicking . . . you will be convinced that there is a wonderful resemblance". Redfield went on to make a distinction between the aristocratic Irishman, represented by the noble wolfhound, and the base-born "scavenger-dog".[23] It was such lore that O'Nolan satirized in his depiction of Sitric O'Sanasa, the impoverished Stage Irishman *in extremis*, a man so poor that he has to fight with dogs for a dry bone. In competing with dogs for survival he becomes one in fact, as the Irish had already grown canine in Victorian fiction. Bonaparte reports:

> I often saw him on the hillside fighting and competing with a stray dog, both contending for a narrow hard bone and the same snorting and angry barking issuing from them both.

> Is minic a chonnac é sa dubh-luachair amuí ar thaebh an chnuic ag troid agus ag córaíocht le mada fánach, cnámh caol eatartha mar dhuais san iomathóireacht, an sranfach agus an tafan conafach céanna ag teacht uatha araon.[24]

Through the character of Sitric, O'Nolan mocks all those writers who would sentimentalize the holy poverty and sacred simplicity of the Gaelic peasant – "it had always been said that accuracy of Gaelic (as well as holiness of spirit) grew in proportion to one's lack of worldly goods" ("bhí sé riamh ráite go mbíonn cruinneas Gaeilge (maraon le naofacht anama) ag daoine do réir mar bhíd gan aon mhaoin shaolta"). One sentimental visitor, who spies Sitric deriving heady pleasure from a bottle of water, dashes the vessel to earth on the grounds that it "spiled the effect". Sitric cannot afford even that most stage-Irish nourishment, the humble spud. One of his neighbours, Máirtín Ó Bánasa, remarks tersely that "Whoever is without a spud for long is unhealthy" ("an té bhíonn gan phráta, ní bhíonn sé folláin") – a bow to Adam Smith who had written of the "nourishing quality" of the Irish potato, as evidenced by the strength of London Irish porters and the beauty of London Irish whores.[25] Verging on collapse from hunger, Sitric is saved by Máirtín who offers him the boiled potatoes which he had intended as a feed for his own pigs. In the process Sitric has become the *reductio ad absurdum* of the stage Irishman – with his fang-like teeth and protruding upper lip, he comes to share bones with howling dogs, spuds with squealing pigs, and is even driven on one occasion to swallow that most hackneyed of props, a piece of turf from the bog. The basic features of Boucicault's character are still retained – like Myles-na-Coppaleen, Sitric lives in a bare den by a rock-pool on a hill. However, through living in such proximity to animals and sharing their food, it is no surprise that Sitric finally opts for animality, preferring an underwater life as a seal to the frugal possibilities for humanity in Corcha Dorcha. The land-dog whom we met at the start of Chapter Eight soon degenerates into a badger, but his future and final status is anticipated when he starts to drink rain for nourishment. By the end of the section Bonaparte reports a sighting of a group of seals with Sitric among their number:

> At times since then he has been seen at high tide, wild and hirsute as a seal, vigorously hunting fish in the company of that community with whom he had decided to stay. I have often heard the neighbours say it would be a good idea to hunt down O'Sanasa, because by then he would have grown into a tasty trout-fish and might have a winter's oil in him. I do not think, of course, that anyone has had the courage to chase him.

> Chonnacthas ar bharra taoide corr-uair ó shin é, féachaint mhongach air ar nós na rón féin, agus é ag soláthar iasc go rabach i gcóluadar na muintire ar ghlac sé lóistín leo. Is minic a chuala-sa na cóursain a rá gur mhaith an bheart an Sánasach do sheilg, mar go mbeadh sé fán tráth sin fásta 'na bhreac bhlasta agus go mbeadh solus geimhrí ann. Ní dói liom, áfach, go raibh sé de mhisneach ag éinne dul sa tóir air.[26]

In this chapter on Sitric O'Sanasa, O'Nolan takes with myopic literalism some of the racist metaphors prevalent among the Victorian English and among the ascendancy in Ireland. Such metaphors had gained a particular currency in the 1860s, when Fenian outrages antagonized the British populace and theories of evolution disturbed the traditional folk mind. "Just as Darwinism appeared to lay bare the ugly realities of the struggle for survival, so Fenianism appeared to reveal the elemental beast in the Irish character".[27] Those respectable folk who resented having their bodies compared to those of black troglodytes could now make their own comparisons. It was scarcely surprising that they should have found closer resemblances between the apes and those races whom they feared or exploited, the Irish and the Negroes.

This is the burden of tragic knowledge in *An Béal Bocht*. O'Coonassa's demand to know if the Gaels are in fact human is also the question put by O'Nolan, a writer who was as agitated as any Victorian by what he called "the incompatibility of the flesh and the spirit". Benjamin Disraeli once remarked that the Victorian English wanted to be angels, but feared that they might be apes. That same neurotic dichotomy lies behind O'Nolan's blackest humours, with one crucial difference. He inverts the priorities of the Victorians, yearning not for the sanctity of the angelic but for the bliss of the primitive. He said that "imbedded in the flesh (and by no means in the spirit) is this disastrous faculty of reason. It has ruined many a man, the same reason". His elaboration of that idea went as follows:

> To sensible, thoughtful people, the thought of life, as life goes, must be something of a nightmare. It begins to look as if we humans were right until we developed consciousness with its two children, Memory and Imagination. If man was not "blessed" with consciousness or cursed with Memory, he could not look back. And if he were not "blessed" or cursed with Imagination, he would think nothing about the future.[28]

In *An Béal Bocht*, O'Nolan has taken the insulting metaphors surrounding the stage Irishman and explained that they are literally true, not just of the Irish but of the "awful human condition".[29] Behind the comical conventions, he has discerned the truth which neither the English caricaturists nor their Irish victims could face. In attacking these conventions with their own evasions, he has also provided his own deeply comic answer. Though that answer inverts that of the Victorian theorists, it arises from an equally agonized awareness of the contesting forces of spirit and flesh in humankind. *An Béal Bocht* may be one of the first parodies in modern Irish, but it is also one of the last Victorian melodramas.

Many other assumptions concerning the Irish in the nineteenth century receive mocking treatment in *An Béal Bocht*. The idea that the race was inherently lazy and incapable of being taught anything gained wide support, as did the conviction that "Irish Celts could no more change their temperaments than they could change the colours of their eyes".[30] Among the Irish in England, crime was believed to be inevitable and newspapers were studded with reports of the fighting Irish. In 1861, for example, though only one quarter of the population of Liverpool was Irish-born, the Irish accounted for over half the defendants appearing in city courts on charges of assault, drunkenness and breach of the peace.[31] By the later 1880s, almost one half of all Irish news items reported in *The Times* of London concerned political and agrarian crime, giving further credence to the idea that crime was endemic in the land. Needless to add, many native Irishmen were themselves convinced that this was indeed the truth.

The inevitable outcome of these policies is enacted in the classrooms of Corcha Dorcha, where every child is told that it is his destiny to be guilty of misdeeds, to be beaten and forced to answer to the name "Jams O'Donnell". The concept of the Irishman as an irredeemable and unchangeable idiot is itself not far removed from Aristotle's classic definition of comedy: "the comic character is static and goes on revealing itself". That sense of predestined failure communicated itself to many impressionable Irish people and was, no doubt, heightened by what O'Nolan called "the sense of doom that is the heritage of the Irish Catholic".[32] Those older characters in *An Béal Bocht* such as Bonaparte's mother or the Old Grey Fellow repeatedly tell the lad that he must play in fireside ashes and accept the grinding poverty and inevitable sense of failure. They are the unwitting accomplices of a tradition which deprived the Irish of identity. It is fitting, therefore, that when Bonaparte comes face to face with his father in the final chapter, he should be on his way to the same jail in which the father has already served a sentence of twenty-nine years – the exact span of the sentence on which he now embarks, in keeping with the inexorable logic of idiotic predestination which has propelled the book. It is even more brutally appropriate that he should have been sentenced after a trial in English, which he could not understand, for a crime which he did not commit. He is the peasant equivalent of Kafka's nameless citizen, a Joseph K. of the western world.

He who could not distinguish his first-born son from an outhouse pig now fails to identify his own father, until the broken old jailbird hoarsely mutters that his name is "Jams O'Donnell". At this point, only, does Bonaparte see the truth: that his identity is that of the thieving, drunken, vagrant that was once his father and will soon be his son. Like every other character in the novel, his features are never described, for, like the stage Irishman, he is more caricature than character, relying for his effect more on props than on the self-constructed personality. How could Myles na gCopaleen – who had just recovered his identity after more than a century of frustration – describe such a man? For Bonaparte, like all his stage-Irish predecessors, has no face.

The final paradox in this story of Mylesian identities lies in the fate of Brian O'Nolan. Having put an end to the role of Myles na gCopaleen as perpetual victim of English ridicule, the author himself became the ultimate victim of his newly-acquired persona. So successful was the column conducted thrice-weekly by Myles na Gopaleen in *The Irish Times* that it lasted for over twenty-five years, "on a level of wit, invention and intellectual virtuosity without parallel".[33] The cost was massive. Throughout the period, O'Nolan produced no works to equal the brilliance of his three early and major novels, *At Swim-Two-Birds*, *The Third Policeman*, and *An Béal Bocht*. More than one of his friends asked a difficult question: "had Myles na gCopaleen never existed, would the genius of Flann O'Brien have flowered in other unpredictable masterpieces?"[34] The answer must be a tentative "yes", with the *caveat* that the persona to blame was not Myles na gCopaleen but Myles na Gopaleen. For he was the fatal clown, the licensed jester, who lurked within O'Nolan, whom he roundly despised but whom he could never fully suppress. He offered his author the quick success and easy laughs which hold a deadly attraction for the Irish artist who knows he should express, but fears he may have to exploit, his material.

If O'Nolan succumbed early to that temptation to placate his newspaper audience, he did not do so before he had written three comic masterpieces. That is the measure of the immense talent wasted in the service of R. M. Smyllie. It was a common temptation in the period, identified by Patrick Kavanagh as the call to play the fool, to be another "gas bloody man", to enact in public the role of writer rather than to confront in private the anguish of real writing. In the case of Brian O'Nolan, the wonder was that he had endured as an artist for so long, for according to R. N. Cooke, he had already donned, with only some pangs of conscience, the jester's mask even before he graduated from university. Cooke's assessment of the brilliant student debater is a fitting epitaph of the real achievement and actual waste of one of Ireland's major writers: "Unfortunately, his fame as a funny-man was such that he was typed as a debater. The Society expected it from him and he seldom disappointed . . ."[35] But his real potential, as thinker and as artist, may have never been suspected, and was surely not realized.

Twenty-Nine

The Empire Writes Back – Brendan Behan

Brendan Behan first saw his father through prison-bars. Not long after his birth in 1923, the infant was taken to the jail in which Stephen Behan, even then a veteran republican, was held as a consequence of the Civil War.[1] Two decades later, the son himself would be in prison as a republican prisoner.[2] It was said that, in all political debates among detainees at the Curragh Camp, there were three factions – those who were pro-Hitler, those who were against him, and Brendan Behan.[3] The effect of prison on most of the republicans, including Máirtín Ó Cadhain, was to redouble their political fervour: the effect on Behan, however, was to leave him with an abiding distrust of all commitments. His plays are O'Caseyesque in their sharp critique of idealism, so sharp that they come perilously close to downright nihilism. Ultimately, they owe more to the absurdist theatre of Ionesco, Genet and Beckett than to their forerunners in the Irish dramatic movement.

This was, of course, the real reason why *The Quare Fellow* was rejected by the Abbey and by each of the larger Dublin theatres. Eventually, it was accepted by Alan Simpson for the miniature Pike Theatre, whose maximum capacity was fifty-five seats. On the opening night, Behan announced to the audience: "I didn't write this play: the lags wrote it".[4] Apart from first-night critics, that audience was composed mainly of ex-convicts, many of whom felt that they were "inside" again, such was the claustrophobic experience in the Pike. Using a method of lighting derived from ballet (overhead and lateral, but no frontal light), Simpson achieved a "three-dimensional emphasis on the actors, which made the stage look bigger than it really was".[5] This helped to bring out one of the play's themes: the attempt by prisoners to create in words a sense of spaciousness and open possibility denied them in their daily routines. That this attempt was also made by each warder was part of Behan's exposure of the corrupting effects on the human spirit of prison life.

Some of the actors in the cash-poor company played warder and prisoner alike, which further served to emphasize Behan's conviction that, under such stressful conditions, the opposite might easily become the double. Neither the warders nor the prisoners (with just one exception on each side) question the wisdom of the authorities who sentence one killer to death and reprieve another: they accept that the logic of such authorities is absurd and incapable of explaining itself, as incapable as the sponsors of a very similar order in *Waiting for Godot* where one boy is punished and another spared, but no reasons are given. Only Warder Regan, the Christian humanist, questions the right of the state to take life: and his lonely position is endorsed among the prisoners solely by a young lad from the Gaeltacht. The others all conspire in a euphemistic language – slang among the prisoners, officialese among the warders – to deflect the enormity of what is about to happen among them, an execution by hanging, planned for the following morning, of the Quare Fellow. He is variously "your man" or "the condemned man", but he is never named and, like Godot, he never appears. In the manner of Beckett's tramps, the prison inhabitants fill the unnerving time of waiting with nervous jokes, verbal routines, and hysterical laughter.

The only moral distinction offered by the play is made at the level of language, in a contrast between those who use words to describe hanging for what it is and those who use them to occlude the facts. On this matter, most of the prisoners are honest, resorting to bitter parodies of the cosy officialese which appears in the newspapers. But the warders are similarly divided between those who evade and confront the event. If the elderly lag Dunlavin is frequently drunk on methylated spirits, the prison visitor Holy Healey is endlessly drunk on alcohol. If Dunlavin refers somewhat casually to "topping", Healey is even more occlusive in talking to Warder Regan of their "sad duty". Regan, who believes that the whole show should be put on in a football stadium for the public which pays for it, asks very savagely "What, neck breaking and throttling, sir?" Healey tries to rationalize his sense of guilt by reminding the warder that the condemned man at least dies a Christian death with the benefit of the sacraments: but Regan responds with a further parody of the official jargon:

> We can't advertise "commit a murder and die a happy death", sir. We'll have them all at it. They take religion very seriously in this country.[6]

In fact, it is Regan alone in this play who takes religion seriously: the others, Holy Healey included, do not. Healey refuses to help Dunlavin secure accommodation after his imminent release on the grounds that he is currently visiting the prison as an official of the Department of Justice; and he makes a clear distinction between this and his charitable work for the Society of St. Vincent de Paul, urging Dunlavin to call on him in the Society's office upon his release. In such an exchange, one can hear echoes of Behan the crusading socialist, mocking all who would separate notions of charity from notions of justice, in the mode of Aneurin Bevan who said that "private charity is no substitute for organized justice".

The ultimate indictment of the prison system in the play lies in the fact that conditions outside are so much harsher for the old lag Dunlavin that he is actually better off inside.[7] This is Behan's none-too-covert critique not just of the British penal system, which so offended Wilde and Synge, but, even more scathingly, of the so-called Irish Free State which blithely persisted with this British model. Dunlavin is old enough to remember the British régime and he recalls how, for want of real cigarettes, he used to smoke its mattress coir in paper rolled from prison Bibles:

> I smoked my way half-way through the book of Genesis and three inches of my mattress. When the Free State came in we were afraid of our life they were going to change the mattresses for feather beds . . . But sure, thanks to God, the Free State didn't change anything more than the badges in the warders' caps.[8]

Three decades after the foundation of the state, Behan's assessment of its progress was as bleak as that to be produced by Rushdie after thirty years of Indian "independence". His analysis of the decay of republican ideals linked him to those socialists who had warned that a nationalist élite might paint the post-boxes green and hoist a tricolour over Dublin Castle, but that it would all mean nothing unless there was a change in the structure of society. That decay is most bitterly exemplified in the clandestine meetings which Prisoner C and the idealistic young warder Crimmin, both from the Kerry Gaeltacht, are forced to resort to if they are to enjoy conversations in the Irish language. Such an ironic use of Irish as a sort of secret, outlaw language in one of the Free State's official institutions is mordant indeed.

Behan himself had begun his literary career writing modernist lyrics in Irish during his time in jail for the republican cause, an exercise which allowed him to fulfil his artistic impulses while carrying on his father's struggle against British imperialism.[9] He was arguably the first poet to introduce the Imagist techniques of Ezra Pound and Hilda Doolittle to Irish, crossing them with those of the *haiku*:

> *Uaigneas*
>
> Blas sméara dubh'
> tréis báisteach
> ar bharr an tsléibhe.
>
> I dtost an phriosúin
> feadail fhuar na traenach.
>   Cogar gáire beirt leannán
>   don aonarán.
>
> The blackberries' taste
> after rainfall
> on the hilltop.
>
> In the silence of the prison
> the train's cold whistle.
> The whisper of laughing lovers
> to the lonely.

Ó Cadhain adjudged Behan and Ó Ríordáin the two best poets in modern Irish:[10] and the former must have felt real pangs of guilt at having reverted to English for the sake of international acclaim in his later writings, mainly novels and plays. It is significant that, at the climactic moment of *The Quare Fellow*, a minor character comes forward with a statement in Irish, as if this were the language of some not-fully-closed-off recess of Behan's mind. Just before the Quare Fellow is hanged, Prisoner C sings the haunting Gaelic song *Is é Fáth mo Bhuartha*, whose first line says "It is the cause of my sorrow, that I have not permission for a visit".

Like others before him, Behan clearly felt, as a result of sojourns there, that the Blasket islands offered something akin to an ideal society which combined social equality with Gaelic cultural values. These values did not include a belief in judicial execution, as Synge had found decades earlier in the story of how islanders had sheltered a murderer in flight from the law. The Aran islanders' philosophy was straightforward: a killer with any human feeling would obviously experience such dreadful remorse for his deed that it could make no sense to add to his burdens the pain and humiliation of physical confinement. He was so punished by his action that he scarcely needed to be punished for it: solitary confinement was hardly necessary to induce such a one to look into his soul, but it would cut him off from those fellow-humans to whom he must ultimately return from his lonely knowledge.[11] Behan's rather caustic brand of Gaelic idealism is manifest in the remark of the Prison Governor in *The Quare Fellow* about the fact that the Free State had to import an English hangman to perform the distasteful duty:

> We advertised for a native hangman during the Economic War. Must be fluent Irish speaker. *Cailíochtaí de réir Meamram a Seacht* (Qualifications in accord with memorandum number seven). There were no suitable applicants.[12]

Whenever he espoused Gaelic ideals, Behan was at pains to fuse them with socialist principles. He reserved great contempt for those profiteers who used the native language in their bid for academic success, financial affluence and social respectability – that is to say, for the conservative wing of the nationalist movement. He knew that the dream of such people was not a free, Gaelic Ireland which would cherish its children equally, but simply to replace their former British overlords and to take over their privileges. He spoke often and with jocular scorn of the silver and gold rings worn in lapels by officially-accredited Irish-speakers as "erseholes". Prisoner D is a tell-tale example of this type in the play. He is incensed by the young prisoner from the Gaeltacht, who had developed a close friendship with Warder Regan. The young islander recalls for the other prisoners Regan's diatribes against capital punishment and against the vice of wealthy judges, and his contention that the prisoners were simply doing penance for the sins of the wealthy and powerful. "As a ratepayer", Prisoner D will stand for no more libellous remarks on the judiciary, for "property must have security". Regan, he alleges, must be an atheist if he disbelieves in capital punishment and should therefore be dismissed from the public service. "I shall take it up with the Minister when I get out of here", says Prisoner D: "I went to school with his cousin".[13]

By now, it is clear in the play that this man is a corrupt government hack who has sailed too close to the wind: so it is no surprise to learn that "he's in for embezzlement; there were two suicides and a by-election over him". He can boast of his grandfather's role in the Land

War, while at the same time prating that his youngest nephew has just gone to Sandhurst, the British military academy. He has the requisite Gold Medal in Irish from school, but is quite flummoxed by the natural conversational Irish of a native speaker like Prisoner C: and so he turns savagely on the youth, reprimanding him for his secret meetings with the young Irish-speaking warder. "How can there be proper discipline between warder and prisoner with that kind of familiarity?" Prisoner C replies in a moving speech, which suggests more powerfully than any other, that both he and his warder-friend are enduring a similar punishment, exile from their own civilization:

> He does be only giving me the news from home and who's gone to America or England; he's not long up here and neither am I . . . the two of us do be each as lonely as the other.[14]

It is no accident that alone among the prisoners, it is this young islander who has developed a real friendship and intimacy with the Quare Fellow.

The absurdism of the prisoners' world leads them to rate a man who killed his wife cleanly with the blow of a silver-topped cane above the Quare Fellow, who apparently used a meat-cleaver to chop his brother to bits. Even more spooky, however, is the fact that such thinking seems to be shared by the authorities, who spare Silver-Top but execute the Quare Fellow. To the warders, he has no more identity than he has to most of the prisoners: even his bureaucratic identity within the crazy system is expendable, as he is changed from E779 to E777, because a seven is easier to carve on stone than a nine. There can be no clear relation between cause and effect in such a world, nor any clear plot-line of development. It has sometimes been complained that *The Quare Fellow* lacks an adequate climax,[15] since the execution happens offstage . . . but this, of course, is exactly Behan's point: that capital punishment continues only because it is so successfully hidden from the public. If there is anticlimax in the ending, it is surely as deliberate as the off-key endings of O'Casey, which served to emphasize the randomness of the fate which overtakes the poor. If the authorities show no deference to the bureaucratic identity of Prisoner E779 in death, the prisoners are even less respectful, fighting for possession of the dead man's letters in hopes of selling them to Sunday scandal-sheets.

This late moment of the play is a grotesque reminder of the soldiers who cast lots for the garments of the dead Jesus: it reinforces the Christian parallel between the Quare Fellow and Regan drawn all through the play, proving that they are doing penance for the sins of the mighty: but it also provides a fitting final image of life as an absurd game of chance, just as O'Casey had done in *The Plough and the Stars*, where the card-game on the coffin-top and the tossing of coins epitomized the appalling arbitrariness of the destiny in store for all on stage. Such a commentary is linked here by Behan to his satire on the anarchic forces of *laissez-faire* capitalism: for it is the establishment embezzler Prisoner D who initiates the sordid squabble for letters. Prisoner B and the young Blasket islander refuse to take any part in this plunder, and the embezzler quickly appropriates their share with the words "We can act like businessmen". To Prisoner A Behan leaves the last word on this, when he has him ask "What's a crook, only a businessman without a shop?"[16] In such a world, where punishment is as random and unaccountable as everything else, the prisoners may be forgiven for finally turning the hanging into a sporting farce, complete with bets, gambling and commentary: for each in his heart must realize that he may well be the next to face the chop.

The play, along with the autobiographical *Borstal Boy*, entitles Behan to high praise as an exponent of prison literature. These texts take their place in a tradition which also includes John Mitchel's *Jail Journal*, Wilde's *De Profundis* and "Ballad of Reading Gaol", and Peadar O'Donnell's *The Gates Flew Open*. But they also subvert this predecessor genre, in the sense that they remain iconoclastic about nationalist pieties: the teenage Behan, masturbating in his lonely cell in an English borstal, asks himself witheringly if great men like de Valera were driven in similar circumstances to do this too.[17] Even rebellion must be rebelled against, if it is to become liberation. Indeed, Behan's understanding of prison literature is so wide, so ecumenical, that there is a valuable sense in which his example reminds us that many other classic Irish texts, from the cellular musings of *Malone Dies* to the babbling voices of *Cré na Cille* should also be considered prison writing, as an organized project of resistance by those in the modern world who stand defeated but not destroyed.

Like other republican prisoners before and since, Behan was branded a common criminal – or as he joked, an ODC, "ordinary decent criminal" – in the eyes of the law: but he had no final objection to that, recognizing that to give some privileged prisoners political status was as absurd as to declare some literary texts above and beyond political influence.[18] In the snobbish jockeying for the three P's – pay, promotion, pension – among the warders, he depicted not only the careerism of the new administrative élites, but also the way in which the state apparatus "may be not only the stake, but the site, of the class struggle".[19] Though his prisoners were sometimes clever at exploiting this division among the warders, he showed that ultimately they succumbed to such thinking themselves. Being in his origins a socialist as well as a republican, he framed a devastating critique of the entire state system which had emerged, in keeping with that later outlined by Herbert Marcuse:

> The robber and the murderer leave the head that can punish them intact and thus give punishment its chance; but rebellion "attacks punishment itself" and thereby not just disparate portions of the existing order, but this order itself.[20]

When Behan was returning to Ireland after release from his jail-sentence in England for bombing activities, a friendly official waved him through customs in Irish with the words "It must be great to be free, Brendan". His laconic reply was "It must". ("Caithfidh sé go bhfuil sé go hiontach bheith saor? Caithfidh".)[21]

Despite the major success of *The Quare Fellow* on its transfer to the London stage, Behan wrote his next play in Irish as *An Giall* (The Hostage). "Irish is more direct than English, more bitter", he explained to bemused British journalists, "it's a muscular, fine thing, the most expressive language in Europe".[22] He had little to gain in terms of commercial success from such a venture, but there were other motivations. In the words of his nephew "no amount of foreign applause could satisfy this facet of his personality: he could no more forget his earlier hopes than he could cut himself off completely from the IRA. He had always wanted, among other things, to serve Ireland and now, as something of a world figure, he was in a strong position to do so".[23]

An Giall was a quiet success in Dublin and the inevitable call to rewrite the play in English for Joan Littlewood's Stratford experimental theatre in London soon followed. What happened next is hotly debated: but the majority view is that Behan never really rewrote his own play, instead ceding it to Littlewood's company, which teased it into a shape calculated to appeal to Princess Margaret and the fashionable, *avant-garde* first-night audience. A spare and simple tragedy thus became something very different, *The Hostage*, a variety-show play complete with topical, newsy references to Prime Minister Macmillan, risky homosexuality and the film-star Jayne Mansfield. Only on the opening night, amid the thunderous applause, did Behan's brother Brian detect that something might be wrong: "I looked at him closely.

He looked suddenly as if he knew he had been taken for a ride, that he had been adopted as a broth of a boy, that they had played a three-card-trick on him".[24]

Many additional characters appeared in *The Hostage*, straight from the scandal-sheets of *News of the World* and *The Sunday People*, but they added little, other than a boozy bravado, to the play itself. Much of the wordplay in *An Giall* proved untranslatable. Great fun was had in it with the double meaning of the word *conradh*, signifying both the Anglo-Irish Treaty of 1921 and the League (i.e., Gaelic League):

KATE: Cad a chuir as a mheabhair é?
PAT: Ó, an Conradh.
KATE: Cén Conradh? Conradh na Gaeilge? Yerra, chuirfeadh an dream sin duine ar bith as a mheabhar.[25]

This is a layered exchange in Irish, for through the words of Kate, Behan mocks that very organization whose members would provide much of the audience for *An Giall*. This effect was all but lost in the London production, though the technique of "insulting the audience" is discernible in *The Hostage* as well. In the following passage, Meg (who has just sung a rebel song) remarks on Behan's notorious fondness for appearing suddenly in his own plays, like other absurdist play-wrights, with a song or a story:

MEG: The author should have sung that one.
PAT: That is, if the thing has an author.
SOLDIER: Brendan Behan, he's too anti-British.
IRA OFFICER: Too anti-Irish, you mean. Bejasus, wait till we get him back home. We'll give him what-for, for making fun of the movement.
SOLDIER: (to audience) He doesn't mind coming over here and taking your money.
PAT: He'd sell his country for a pint.[26]

That exchange, in which Behan displays much self-knowledge, gets the balance of his play about right, poised as it is between healthy insolence towards the theatrical audience and servile deference to British expectations.

Too often, however, complex characterization in *An Giall* declines into mere caricature in *The Hostage*: in the latter, for instance, the IRA men are cruel to the captured British soldier Leslie, whereas in the former they give him cigarettes to calm his nerves. In *An Giall* they grow so fond of Leslie that they hide him in a cupboard during a police raid, and he dies there of suffocation through no fault but sheer bad luck: in *The Hostage*, though the circumstances of his death remain somewhat blurred, the unspoken assumption of the average British audience will be that he was a victim of the IRA.[27] The real complexity of the Irish attitude to the English – which is to suspect them *en masse*, but to warm to them as individuals – is lost.

In a subsequent article, Behan denied that there had been any betrayal of the original text in London: indeed, he suggested that if there had been any betrayal, it had happened in Dublin:

> I saw the rehearsal of *An Giall* and while I admire the producer Frank Dermody tremendously, his idea of a play is not my idea of a play. He's of the school of Abbey Theatre naturalism, of which I'm not a pupil. Joan Littlewood, I found, suited my requirements exactly. She has the same views on the theatre that I have, which is that the music hall is the thing to aim at, in order to amuse people, and any time they get bored divert them with a song or a dance.[28]

If O'Casey had turned a music-hall variety-show into a play, complete with comic duos, tear-jerking routines and periodic songs, Behan seemed intent on reversing that process, stripping down a play to something like a music-hall variety-show, where even members of the audience might get hauled into the act:

> I've always thought that T. S. Eliot wasn't far wrong when he said that the main problem of the dramatist today was to keep his audience amused; and that while they were laughing their heads off, you could be up to any bloody thing behind their backs – and it was what you were doing behind their bloody backs that made your play great.[29]

Just as the vaudeville knockabout was borrowed from O'Casey, so also were many of the underlying themes – his critique of narrow-gauge nationalism, his recording of the decay of republican ideals, and his attempt to provide a perspective on the sufferings of the Dublin poor as being, in essence, no different from that of an unemployed cockney youth driven by economic pressure into the ranks of the British Army. However, Behan goes much further than O'Casey in *The Hostage*, where he delights in stripping off the coverings of his play to reveal its raw, constituent parts, offering it more as process than as product. He itemizes the songs, gags, climaxes and anticlimaxes that might make up a serviceable drama, but refuses to bolt them all finally together in a coherent plot. It has become *de rigueur* to stage it in a set that is only half-built, a house that has the look of incompleteness about it, a building as unvarnished and unfinished as the state itself. Behan wants audiences to note the workings of his contraption: hence that passage already quoted, in which the exchanges between characters sound suspiciously like the reviews in the next morning's papers, as the play discusses itself, its author, and its attitude.

In a scene such as that, Behan beat the critics to the punch, disarming them in advance by incorporating all possible critiques into the play. This is a favourite device of Irish absurdists, to be found also in a novel like *At Swim-Two-Birds*, in which Flann O'Brien renders not just a text but the critical apparatus by which it is to be judged ("A satisfactory novel is a self-evident sham . . ."), or in John Banville's *Doctor Copernicus*, which proclaims itself a machine that deconstructs itself. Such manoeuvres can be viewed in two ways: as attempts to assert the proud self-sufficiency of the text (arguably the case for O'Brien and Banville) or to cope with a fear of public misinterpretation (certainly the case for Behan). Behan's self-consciousness as an artist was the result of his self-doubt, a feeling shared with many artists who had been driven to the edge of society as a result of specialization. From Bohemia, such figures thumbed noses at a bourgeoisie often too philistine even to notice their gestures of revolt: and that nose-thumbing often took the form of wilful obscurity, a cult of obscenity, or outrageous personal behaviour (Behan specialized in the latter two categories). When all this failed to attract attention, such artists often thumbed noses at themselves and one another, in works which turned neurosis into a form of perverse heroism and which were filled with knowing references to other works, other writers.

Hence Behan's clever-clever reference to the play's producer, Joan Littlewood. Hence, too, his rehash of the famous joke from the Cyclops chapter of *Ulysses*:

SOLDIER: What actually is a race, sir?
MONSEWER: A race occurs when a lot of people live in one place for a long period of time.
SOLDIER: I reckon our old sergeant-major must be a race; he's been stuck in that same depot for about forty years.[30]

The Hostage is filled with echoes of previous works, not just of *An Giall.* The plot, insofar as it exists, is a dramatization of Frank O'Connor's

famous short story "Guests of the Nation", and the many references to
O'Casey have been noted. All this should be seen less as the result of
Behan's failure to think up new jokes or an adequate plot of his own,
than as part of his offence of his audience. With the increasing
specialization of art in the mid-twentieth century came an increasingly
specialized audience, which revelled in in-jokes, which enjoyed spotting
back-references to Joyce and others, and which loved above all to be
attacked, so that it could give further evidence not just of learning but
of its own tolerance. The constant breaking of the dramatic illusion by
Behan, onstage and off, may be seen as part of the attempt to induce a
critical, rather than too easily sympathetic, attitude in the viewers.
Behan's reported "anger" with Joan Littlewood may have been as
theatrical as anything enacted on the stage.

The title *The Hostage* seems to refer to the captured Leslie, but may
really indicate the older Irish onstage, all of whom seem to be hostages
to a calcified past. In the case of Monsewer, the oldest, the obsession is
quite ridiculous: the rabid Anglophobia of a nationalist who prefers to
be called "Monsewer" than to be reminded of his origins as a British
public-schoolboy. When he spoke Irish to bus-conductors, we are
gravely informed, he had to bring an interpreter with him, so that the
man would know where to let him off. (Presumably, his British dialect
of Irish was incomprehensible.) Behan here endorses Kavanagh's view
of the revival as a plot by disaffected public-schoolboys; and, like Brian
O'Nolan, he mocks the aristocratic pretensions of the nationalists,
especially their cult of the kilt. This element disgusted the socialist in
Behan. So his satire on de Valera is crudely predictable: when told that
the Taoiseach can speak seven languages, Pat remarks that it's a pity that
English and Irish are not among them, so "we'd know what he was
saying at odd times".[31]

In castigating de Valera for his aloof image, Pat is speaking for all
those disappointed radicals of the republican movement, who were told
that "Labour must wait", that the social question was secondary to the
national question. For Behan, this was the moment when "liberation"
was missed. He has Pat recall, with mingled pride and frustration, the
time when the agricultural labourers of Kerry took over five thousand
acres of land from Lord Tralee. The puritanical IRA officer of the
1950s knows nothing of this radical strand in the earlier history of his
movement, so Pat has to explain how the IRA leadership forbade the
seizure of Lord Tralee's land, sending a message to the effect that "the
social question could be settled when we'd won a thirty-two county
republic". "Quite right too" says the IRA officer: but Pat responds with

a more pragmatic line. "The Kerrymen said they weren't greedy, they didn't want the whole thirty-two counties, their own five thousand acres would do 'em for a start". Pat, being less interested in social questions than in social answers, stayed with the farm labourers in their cooperative, and was court-martialled: "Sentenced to death in my absence – so I said, right, you can shoot me in my absence".[32] As a disillusioned ex-IRA man, Pat in all this speaks for Behan.

His shabby boarding-house-turned-brothel is a fitting metaphor for the decayed ideals of a free Ireland. He is the first character onstage to speak directly to the audience, as if he were mediating between Behan, the actors and onlookers. No sooner has the play begun, than he confides in the audience that Monsewer is an "old idiot", that in 1960 the days of heroes are over and the IRA as dead as the Charleston. Yet he, too, feels the tug of the past. When told that the IRA prisoner in Belfast jail will soon die, he growls "and who asked him to give himself the trouble?"; yet, seconds later, he voices his resolve to stand by Monsewer, "because we were soldiers of Ireland in the old days". In that, he speaks for the Behan who shot at a Free State policeman at the age of nineteen, but he also speaks for the older man, when he says "It's the H bomb. It's such a big bomb it's got me scared of all the little bombs. The IRA is out of date . . . and so is the RAF, Swiss Guards, Foreign Legion, Red Army . . . "[33]

While the other characters in the house seem minor pawns in a power-game between England and Ireland – Leslie is to die if the boy in Belfast Jail is executed – Pat sees the truth: that such a backyard squabble means little. If anyone else onstage shares this realistic view of things, it is Leslie. To his IRA captors he appears less a person than an image: in capturing him, they believe they have someone important, who can force his superiors to the negotiating table. But Leslie knows that in modern warfare a soldier is disposable:

> You're barmy if you think that what's happening to me is upsetting the British government. I suppose you think they're all sitting round in their West End clubs with handkerchiefs over their eyes, dropping tears into their double whiskies . . . Yeah, I can just see the Secretary of State for War now waking up his missus in the night: "Oh, Isabel-Cynthia love, I can hardly get a wink of sleep wondering what's happening to that poor bleeder Williams".[34]

The IRA are accused of being hostages to an outworn belief in military chivalry: amazingly, it is the IRA which believes that British fair-play will see their boy right. As a realist, Leslie agrees with the disillusioned republican Pat's reading: and so, as in earlier playwright's work, the seeming opposite becomes an actual double. Leslie even echoes Pat's view that all modern armies and soldiers are the same. On being introduced to Monsewer, Leslie remarks acidly "Just like our old Colonel back at the depot. Same face, same voice. Gorblimey, I reckon it is him".[35] If the warders in *The Quare Fellow* were finally indistinguishable from the prisoners, so in *The Hostage* kilted rebels are interchangeable with moustachioed colonels.

Leslie drives the parallel home in an even more telling response to his girlfriend Teresa's explanation of the idealism which fires the young republican condemned to death in Belfast:

> TERESA: It's because of the English being in Ireland that he fought.
> LESLIE: And what about the Irish in London? Thousands of them. Nobody's doing anything to them.[36]

Of course, Behan doesn't simply rehash O'Casey's themes, but he updates them in the light of more recent history. In *The Plough and the Stars*, the Covey had asked the British soldier what he was doing in Ireland, and got the rather illogical, if romantic, reply: "defending my country". Four decades later, the response of the British Tommy is more pragmatic:

> RIO RITA: Ah you murdering bastard. Why don't you go back home to your own country?
> LESLIE: You can take me out of it as soon as you like. I never bloody well asked to be brought here.[37]

His freedom from the dead pull of the past is epitomized by the fact that he is an orphan, like Teresa, who rejects the "madness" of Monsewer. She is appalled by the relish with which Monsewer anticipates the martyrdom in Belfast Jail: "he is mad to say that the death of a young man will make him happy". Together, Teresa and Leslie unlearn the remaining clichés about past Anglo-Irish relations. When Teresa suggests that England was exploiting Ireland for hundreds of years, Leslie answers "That was donkey's years ago – Everyone was doing something to someone in those days".[38] The same armies which crushed the Irish also harried the English poor. This cheerful pragmatism contrasts with the stylized gestures of the IRA men who talk little and mostly of the past, while Leslie thinks only of a future with Teresa.

Everything about Leslie is real, from his unheroic reasons for enlisting in the army, to his desire that tea and cigarettes be brought in by Teresa.

To the first Gaelic League audience of *An Giall* – many reared on a narrow conception of the stiff-upper-lipped British soldier – this portrayal must have been a challenge. Leslie has no time for his superiors, and is quick to spot their Irish counterparts. He is being used by the Secretary of State for War as surely as Pat is being exploited by the IRA, which cares little for the socialism to which he has been always committed. So, as Leslie debunked the armchair patriots swigging whiskey in London, Pat mocks the pretensions of his superiors in the republican movement. "Nine years I spent in prisons", he recalls, to which the IRA man says "The loss of liberty is a terrible thing". "That's not the worst thing", says Pat, "do you know what the worst thing is?" "No". "The other Irish patriots in along with you".[39] These narrow-gauge nationalists in their trenchcoats and berets seem to be involved in some puritanical game, which prompts Pat to ask whether they haven't their initials confused: "Are you in the IRA or the FBI?" The IRA men feel obliged to remind Leslie "You are the hostage" and when he questions the rules of the game, they say "This is war".[40] As part of their game, they tell him to stand in a chalk circle drawn on the floor, but Leslie flees this vicious circle in which they would contain him, and is shot dead. The very manner of his death suggests just how unbreakable that cycle of history is, for his death is the predicted reprisal for the execution of the young lad in Belfast Jail.

Prejudices on both sides are inflamed. Pat, who had so often seemed to agree with Leslie, now retreats into the role of hard-line nationalist. Torn between an understandable pride in the past and a realization that such pride may be no longer useful but lethal, Pat is a fair representative of the Irish condition. On the one hand, he tells a distraught Teresa that Leslie's death was unintentional; on the other, he hints that it was somehow deserved, once the boy in Belfast Jail died too. Yet he seems to be heartbroken at the close, at the death of a young Englishman who has been his secret double. It is left to Teresa to point the moral:

> It wasn't the Belfast Jail or the Six Counties that was troubling you, but your lost youth and your crippled leg. He died in a strange land, and at home he had no one. I'll never forget you, Leslie, till the end of time.[41]

One final question remains: in *The Hostage* (though not in *An Giall*), the dead British soldier slowly gets up and sings a last song:

The bells of hell
Go ting-a-ling-a-ling,
For you but not for me.
Oh death where is thy sting-a-ling-a-ling,
Or grave thy victory?
If you meet the undertaker
Or the young man from the Pru,
Get a pint with what's left over.
Now I'll say goodbye to you.

Leslie may simply be repeating his cheerful pragmatism, urging those he leaves to drink a pint with the change left when the funeral money is spent; or he may, indeed, be suggesting that the weeping will be less for the departed than for those doomed to remain. But there may be something more at work here. All through the play, characters had seemed painfully aware of their roles and some had even stepped right out of role for moments to discuss the material: in that sense, it is quite consistent of Leslie to rise, since the actor must do exactly that every night. In music-hall and vaudeville characters slip easily *and on stage* from one role to another: Leslie is but the latest to do so. He may also be making a final point. When alive, he had repeatedly warned the IRA men, who foolishly thought that the British authorities cared for an army private, that this was not the case. The IRA did not heed his warning, nor perhaps did people in the audience. If Leslie arises now, it is not to allay the IRA's feeling of guilty complicity in his death, so much as to remind all, once again, that soldiers are dispensable, that willing cannon-fodder comes easily, and that there are plenty more cheap recruits where he came from.

Read in this way, *The Hostage* seems less a misrepresentation of *An Giall* than a massively different text, one of the first examples of that form of writing more recently titled by Rushdie "The Empire Writes Back". If *John Bull's Other Island* could carry different meanings in Dublin and in London, then Behan was simply taking that contrast onto a new plane with his reworking of *An Giall* for a London audience which included many of the Sloane Street set. Why this need to "write back"? Obviously, Behan felt the urge to dismantle the remains of the imperial agenda, not just in Ireland but in the imperial capital itself. The right of a state to take a life had been seen as absolute in imperial days: that right was thrown into question in the colonies, later still in Britain. The liberals of Britain felt the desire to stand accused in these matters by former colonial subjects, so Behan was almost effortlessly recruited into the ranks of the Angry Young Men in the late 1950s. Though this was a valid enough way of interpreting his work, that work was in the end quite different from that of, say, John Osborne, whose anger was less with imperialism than with its failure to implement itself full-bloodedly. Behan was, instead, one of the first post-colonial writers to impinge on the consciousness of post-war Britain.

In what name does such an artist write? Initially, in the name of his own emergent nation-state. Only later does he come to realize that this very form is itself an artificial imposition which contains, within it, many of the familiar oppressions: and so he must proceed from nationalism to liberation. If Britain had colonized in the name of an imperial self, then a writer like Behan served to initiate a questioning as to how stable or perfect that self really was. His attack on the right of that stable self to take life in *The Quare Fellow* was extended to an assault on the notion of authorship as such in *The Hostage*, and more particularly on the authority of any one text. As a bisexual male[42] who wrote in Irish as well as in English, Behan cheerfully embraced his own hybridity. Aware that the dramatic form in which he worked was largely alien to Gaelic literary traditions, he nonetheless gloried in the sheer artificiality and conventionalism of his adopted medium. One of the first plays in Irish had been Hyde's *Casadh an tSúgáin* (The Twisting of the Rope), and at first he thought of ironically calling his play on capital punishment *The Twisting of Another Rope*.

The dialect in which Behan's characters speak was neither standard Irish nor standard English, and whenever he worked in English, Behan left a number of Gaelic phrases untranslated, as if to remind audiences of all that must be lost in such a carry-over. This was in no way to suggest the feasibility of a return to some pre-colonial identity, merely to resist his own too-facile absorption into the canon of English literature. He sensed, as Synge had before him, that the target language in any translation always enjoyed an excessive status, and so he liked to put that status into question. All of this was of a piece with his incorporation of the act of criticism into the literary text. To the very end, Behan's fear was that his own formal wildness might be domesticated and misinterpreted as literary realism.

Thirty

Beckett's Texts of Laughter and Forgetting

The Easter Rebellion happened when Samuel Beckett was ten. It scarcely touched the lives of his parents and neighbours at all: relations with servants and local shopkeepers went on as they had before. The father's business of quantity-surveying was in no way threatened: indeed, if the destruction of buildings was widespread, it could only have been enhanced. Out in Foxrock, and well away from the fighting, the family treated the event as "something akin to an irritating wildcat strike".[1] Towards the end of the week, Bill Beckett took both of his sons to the top of a local hill, from which the burning inner city could be clearly seen. He began to laugh like someone at a holiday fireworks display, but "Sam was so deeply moved that he spoke of it with fear and horror more than sixty years later".

This vignette has been cited as proof that Samuel Beckett, from the very outset, found himself estranged from the emerging Ireland, but in fact his experience would have been typical of the great majority of Dubliners in Easter Week. They had not voted for (or against) the forces which staged the Rising, just as they would not have a chance to vote for (or against) the Anglo-Irish Treaty of 1921. Theirs was a history which seemed always to happen in their absence, or at least without their active participation: and frequently, large sections of the public had been either too bored or too frightened even to watch for long as powerless spectators. To many, the old Ireland had ceased to exist after the famines of the 1840s and the vast migrations to England and North America: what was left was a tremendous silence, a vast emptiness, which one poet has called "an awful absence moping through the land".[2] The effect of such disasters was to make the Irish feel like strangers in their own country.

For the young Sam Beckett, that sense of estrangement had been even more keen: his parents, unlike many other Protestant families, were not Empire loyalists, but they were certainly not Irish republicans either. They lived in something akin to a cultural vacuum: "Foxrock deliberately avoided much of Irish popular culture, while providing regrettably little English culture, high or low, to put in its place".[3] It is hardly surprising that their son should have eventually set up shop in the void: many decades later, he recalled his sense of decontextualization and bafflement:

> . . . when you started not knowing who you were from Adam trying how that would work or a change not knowing who you were from Adam no notion who I was saying what you were saying whose skull you were clapped up in whose moan you had . . .[4]

Small wonder that the protagonist of his early stories comes to conclude that his true home is "nowhere so far as I can see".[5] Yet such a nowhere would, in time, be revealed as an artistic blessing. It would make of Beckett the first truly Irish playwright, because the first utterly free of factitious elements of Irishness. If Fanon could chide black nationalists for forgetting that "niggers" were disappearing, Beckett could offer a similar service to his native people. In this, too, he was strangely representative of that silent majority of fellow-islanders who remained "too Irish to be nationalists".

What began in the young boy's mind on that Dublin hill in 1916 was what the writer Aijaz Ahmed would much later call "a nationalism of mourning". Beckett himself would joke that if all who claimed to have been in the General Post Office in 1916 had truly taken part, then the building would have burst at the seams. In his first published novel, *Murphy*, he set a mischievous scene there: a Cork mystic named Neary convinces himself that the "deathless rump" of the Cuchulain statue is "trying to stare me down" and so he takes remedial action:

> . . . Neary had bared his head, as though the holy ground meant something to him. Suddenly, he flung aside his hat, sprang forward, seized the dying hero by the thighs and began to dash his head against his buttocks, such as they are.[6]

The book takes similar liberties with a "nobly proportioned" member of the *Garda Siochána* (Civic Guard) and with the new state which he represents: a character is described as being "famous throughout civilized world and Irish Free State".[7]

That jibe was Beckett's repayment in kind for the banning of his first book by the state censors, whose prurience he mocks by supplying the phrase MUSIC MUSIC MUSIC in bold type as a "filthy synecdoche" for the sexual act. At another juncture, after describing a kiss as "the slow-motion osmosis of love's spittle", he adds jocosely "The above passage is carefully calculated to deprave the cultivated reader". In general, his treatment of the new state may be summed up by the book's adage: "Turf may be compulsory in the Saorstát, but one need not bring a private supply of it to Newcastle".[8] Dublin in the 1920s and early 1930s was in the grip of a triumphalist revivalism which grew daily more self-congratulatory and more censorious: and literary nationalism was still the prevailing fashion. Many mediocre poets, fearing that they did not possess the requisite coefficient of Irishness, sought it in mechanical imitations of Gaelic prosody. And Beckett was merciless:

> This view of the matter will not seem strange to anyone familiar with the class of poetaster that Ticklepenny felt it his duty to Erin to compose, as free as a canary in the fifth root (a cruel sacrifice, for Ticklepenny hiccuped in bad rhymes) and at the caesura as hard and fast as his own divine flatus and otherwise bulging with as many minor beauties from the gaelic prosodoturfy as could be sucked out of a mug of Beamish's porter. No wonder he felt a new man washing the bottles and emptying the slops of the better-class mentally deranged.[9]

The answer to these repressions, adopted by many children of Protestant families in the 1920s, was a return to England, which for them was still the parent country: but Beckett, when he went to London, was thoroughly miserable. Patronized as a Paddy, he reportedly found simple actions like ordering a taxi or buying a newspaper a humiliating ordeal.[10] This is the double burden of *Murphy*, which may be in open revolt against Irish revivalism, but which is, if anything, even more critical of 1930s England. The protagonist undergoes that deracination which is the final lot of the post-colonial exile, a predicament defined with cruel clarity in Beckett's elegy for Foxrock and its doomed scions in *All That Fall*: "It is suicide to be abroad. But what is it to be at home, Mr. Tyler, what is it to be at home? A lingering dissolution".[11] That passage, and the feelings which fed into it, represent a radical rewriting of Synge's much more optimistic line from the first decade of the century in *Deirdre of the Sorrows*: "There's no place but Ireland where the Gael can have peace always".[12] In *Murphy* one of the greatest fears of the protagonist is of "falling among Gaels".[13]

Murphy is, among other things, one of the earliest novels of immigrant life in Britain. At home in Foxrock, Beckett might have been deferred to as a young toff, "a well-to-do ne'er-do-well", but in London he was just another unemployed Irishman. His novel is a challenge to the stock English image of the stage Irishman: this is done, in alternating chapters, which play off Murphy's complex psychological self-image against the widespread social view of him as an idiot and a clown. At one point, when Beckett's London publishers were trying to remove some of the more abstract chapters, he wryly joked that he was willing to cut the book down to its very title, if that would help.[14] Murphy, with the most common surname in Ireland, is "the ruins of the ruins of the broth of a boy",[15] i.e. the final, exploded version of the stage Paddy. It is fitting, therefore, that he should have requested in his will that his ashes be deposited in a paper bag "and brought to the Abbey Theatre, Lr. Abbey Street, Dublin, and without pause into what the great and good Lord Chesterfield calls the necessary house, where their happiest hours have been spent, on the right as one goes down into the pit, and I desire that the chain be there pulled upon them, if possible during the performance of a piece, the whole to be executed without ceremony or show of grief".[16] (Cynics will note that it remains unclear from the syntax whether the happiest hours were spent in the lavatory or the auditorium.) The national theatre had been founded to demonstrate that Ireland was not the home of buffoonery, but of an ancient idealism. So the will is a perfectly proper request from one who has been at pains to show that, although many English might see in Paddy a muscular moron, the Irishman's real problem was that he had a mind of his own without the ability to control it at all times. It is brutally ironic that, in the event, Murphy's ashes should find their resting-place not in the Abbey, but in a London pub, one of the venues in which the stage Irishman was depicted during variety-shows of the nineteenth century.

The comedy in *Murphy*, as in all of Beckett's works, derives from his fish-out-of-water predicament, from the discrepancy between the reader's knowledge of him as a sophisticated, angst-ridden intellectual and the common English attitude of "derision tinged with loathing" with which he is greeted on applying for a job as a smart boy:

" 'E ain't smart", said the chandler, "not by a long chork 'e ain't".
"Nor 'e ain't a boy", said the chandler's semi-private convenience, "not to my mind 'e ain't".
" 'E don't look rightly human to me", said the chandler's eldest waste product, "not rightly".[17]

Murphy, we are assured at once, is too familiar with this attitude to make the further blunder of trying to abate it, for he knows that there is no point trying to break into the closed system which is the English stereotype of Irishness.

Indeed, the entire book depicts a world which is run on closed systems. Murphy's own mind is a closed entity, impenetrable by others, even by his lover: and the mind/body split in the book simply takes the estrangement of the emigrant from the host society to its ultimate degree. Murphy, all mind, loves Celia, all body, the woman whose vital statistics include a face which combines the colours of the Irish national flag:

Eyes – Green
Complexion – White
Hair – Yellow

She, too, had left Ireland, but at the early age of four: and the merely physical description bespeaks her standing as a prostitute. Back in Dublin, the red-light districts had been condemned and closed; in official Ireland no prostitutes existed. By the 1930s, many had in fact decamped to London. Murphy, who wishes to cure himself of his "deplorable susceptibility" to Celia, cannot do so; and she, who pro-fesses to love him, really loves the ideal self-image which she sees reflected back to her from his eyes, the image of a prostitute turned respectable housewife.

As a narrative, *Murphy* is at all times fiercely hostile to Irish reviv-alism, whether the target is Gaelic iconography or AE's *Candle of Vision* (read in bed by the appropriately named Miss Carridge): but it remains loyal to a deeper set of literary traditions. In it may be found a Wildean mixture of elegance and desperation ("You saved my life . . . Now palliate it"), as well as a Joycean mockery ("Gas. Could it turn a neurotic into a psychotic? No. Only God could do that").[18] However, ultimately, such wit and word-play serve to undermine the attack on stage Irishry: the diagnosis in the end seems but a version of the disease. Dylan Thomas was being strictly accurate, as well as very funny, when he called the book a strange mixture of Sodom and Begorrah,[19] though were it not for the pun intended, he might have placed the second category first. Being a jester at the London court of his master was hardly the proper role for a writer committed to exploring the void.

Not long after *Murphy*, Beckett began to write in French, a language in which he could create "without style".[20] By this, he may have meant to indicate a language of such exactitude that the search for *le mot juste* offered greater satisfactions than the baroque rhetoric of English, but it seems that he wished most of all to curb in himself the fatal temptation which assailed so many Irish writers of English to exaggerate the coefficient of wit and blarney. The attraction of French for Beckett may not have been its intrinsic character as a language, so much as the fact that he would have to use it with the literal-minded caution of a learner confronted with a second language: it reminded him that a writer is always estranged from the language. French served for Beckett the same function which Irish discharged for Brendan Behan, freeing him from the pressure of an Anglo-American audience and from its attendant temptations. In their respective ways, both men were thus enabled to express rather than exploit their Irish materials, and to transcend the confinements of revivalist eloquence.

The voices which Beckett heard and committed to paper for the rest of his life as an artist were unambiguously Irish. Occasionally, they bore faint Wildean echoes, as in the inversion of a famous quotation or proverb, but more often they were austere, controlled, pared back. The promise of Yeats and Joyce to take revivalist rhetoric and wring its neck was being brought to a strict conclusion. Yet Irish those voices steadfastly remained, in their inflections, their phraseology, their range of reference: ". . . all is dark, there is no one, what's the matter with my head, I must have left it in Ireland . . ."[21] The Irish landscape of south county Dublin in particular was celebrated through famous passages of the trilogy in the concrete, chaste, descriptive style of the Celtic nature poets, without the burden of abstract metaphorical meaning, without any patriotic eroticizing of this or that landscape as a synecdoche for the whole of Ireland. But, as with the Celtic nature poetry, what was offered in such passages was an *exile's* celebration, which seemed once again to illustrate a bleak law: the imaginative possession of the Irish landscape seemed possible only to those who were removed from it.

The instrument which conveyed these Beckettian epiphanies was utterly bardic in tone: "A voice comes to one in the dark. Imagine".[22] The process of composition was carried out by the Gaelic *filí* as they lay on pallets in small, darkened rooms. This dark seclusion protected them from distracting light and noise and recalled the ancient links between art and sorcery.[23] To secure themselves further, some of the poets lay with stones on their bellies or in the hands (a little like Molloy with his sixteen pebbles) or even with plads around their heads:

To one on his back in the dark. This he can tell by the pressure on his hind parts and by how the dark changes when he shuts his eyes and again when he opens them again. Only a small part of what is said can be verified. As for example when he hears, You are on your back in the dark. Then he must acknowledge the truth of what is said . . .[24]

The subject of a bardic exercise was set overnight: the *fili* worked on it all day, each lying on his bed in the dark until night fell, when at last lights were brought in and the words written down. The *pensum* or writing task which had to be discharged by each of the speakers of the trilogy for the approval of an adjudicating master seems to be a clear version of this procedure. "Strange notion . . . that of a task to be performed before one can be at rest".[25] The students of the bardic schools lived a great distance from their homes, so that they might not be distracted by family or friends from their labours; like the younger Krapp, each was warned against the seductions of a female who might "take his mind off his homework".

Such a literature inserts itself into the interstices between speech and writing: if as speech it seems somewhat writerly, then as writing it retains many of the qualities of a speaking voice which issues – unlike the manual effort of writing – from unconscious depths. While speech is assisted in its articulation by tone and emphasis, writing must be more immediately precise, but such precision can then insinuate itself back into the oral mode, in terms reminiscent of Yeats's "written speech" or of Wilde's rehearsed spontaneities. This is the real meaning of those paragraphs in which a seemingly cold, rhetorical claim ("The silence was absolute") is scaled back ("Profound in any case") to something like precision ("All things considered, it was a solemn moment").[26] Orality, however, persists in the love of lists; in the constant rephrasing of similar statements in slightly altered wording (a notable bardic device); and, most of all, in the extraordinary discrepancy between the looseness of the overall structure of a narrative and the almost manic precision of its constituent parts. This aspect of the trilogy – characterized as "chaos in the macrocosm, order in the microcosm"[27] – perfectly repeats the strategies of the bardic lyric, whose quatrains were "individually well-wrought, but often with only a vague, formal connection between them".[28] The effect of Beckett's text is to install the reader in a universe which no sooner threatens to take a particular shape than it dissolves, so that the birth-trauma of the writer, hearing voices as if for the first time, is repeated by the solitary reader: "You are on your back in the dark".

Many of the greatest Gaelic lyrics are broken and gapped because of the difficulty experienced by scholars who sought to reconstitute them: the order in which individually-beautiful quatrains should succeed one another can never be more than arbitrary. This provides a useful clue to students of Beckett's art, which is in these respects very different from that of a writer like Eliot. In *The Waste Land*, for example, each fragment seems radiant, urging the reader to infer the whole of which it was an integral part before the tradition exploded into pieces. But Irish tradition never knew such coherence, with the consequence that in Beckett's texts, the part achieves an internal rigour-without-radiance. As a result, the reader can never infer the whole of which it seldom, if ever, would have constituted a part anyway.

This becomes clear in the broken songs and stories which fill out Beckett's world: like the song about the dog and the cook in *Waiting for Godot*, they are never told to a conclusion. Eliot might in his great poem have lamented the collapse of a tradition and, with it, of a stable subject, but for Beckett these things had never existed to begin with. In *First Love*, he captured the painful problem of those who tell stories and sing songs out of sheer desperation, in the absence of any overarching narrative which might explain them: "All she had done was to sing, *sotto voce*, as to herself and without words fortunately, some old folk songs, and so disjointedly, skipping from one to another and finishing none, that even I found it strange".[29] For Beckett, the Gaelic tradition seemed posited on a void, every poem an utterance in the face of imminent annihilation, every list an inventory of shreds from a culture verging on extinction. Its bards built structures without an overall purpose, in a territory which remained largely unmapped and de-centred, a world which looked weirdly like his own, only more so. At the centre of that Gaelic world – on whose circumference Beckett could locate Oisín, Cuchulain, Maeve, Tír na nÓg, the Táin and the Hag of Beare – there was "no theme".[30] And in the revivalism of the previous generation, all he could discern was an attempt to translate late-Victorian piety into the Irish language. This was not so much a rejection of Gaelic tradition as of various smug misrepresentations of it.

A fuller, more updated rendition of that tradition may be found in the figure of the tramp in *Waiting for Godot*. That figure had already featured in the poetry of Yeats as an image of the now-rootless Anglo-Irish, neither Irish nor English, but caught wandering across the no-man's-land between the two cultures. Synge had developed it further, signing letters to his Catholic girlfriend "your old tramp",[31] and in his essays comparing the artistic son of Protestant families to the youngest son of a farmer who takes to the roads for want of a better inheritance.[32] The temperament of such men was artistic, he claimed, and they could harmonize more easily with the forces of nature than could any member of the settled community. For Synge, the tramp was a gloriously ambivalent presence, more respectable than the universally-despised tinker, but much less compromised than the solid, sedentary citizen: he had his appointed place in the rural economy, as a casual, seasonal labourer or as the bearer of news, but he nonetheless remained a free spirit, a poet who epitomized all that the emerging rural middle class was busily rejecting in itself.

The ultimate roots of this figure were, of course, in the *spailpín* poets cast out onto the roads after the collapse of the old Gaelic order in the seventeenth and eighteenth centuries. Yeats, for example, read the doom of Anglo-Irish poets into the fate of Aogán Ó Rathaille in "The Curse of Cromwell": just as the Gaelic bard had been faced with a new philistine middle class, to whom the Muses were "things of no account",[33] so was he. Ó Rathaille's self-image was aristocratic, haughty, mandarin: he had the learning and training of a bard, entitled to princely patronage, but in actual life he seemed little better than a mendicant seeking alms. It was this tradition which Beckett invoked at the start of *Waiting for Godot*, when Didi laments to Gogo that "we were respectable in those days. Now it's too late".[34] Their dented bowler hats and shabby morning suits proclaim them as men who once had pretensions to gentility and education. "You should have been a poet", says a sardonic Didi: and his partner, gesturing towards his rags in the manner of an Ó Rathaille, says "I was . . . Isn't that obvious?"[35] When a friend complained to Beckett that the tramps at times talked as if they possessed doctorates, he shot back "How do you know they hadn't?"[36] Their self-image is certainly that of an educated class, even if they are leading the life of the hobo.

They are presented as characters without much history, who are driven to locate themselves in the world with reference to geography. But the world in which they live has no overall structure, no formal narrative: instead, it is a dreadful place in which every moment is like the next. Unable to construct a story of the past, the tramps learn nothing from their mistakes, because they can make none of the comparisons which might provide the basis for a confident judgement. Beckett's characters all know the longing to turn their lives into narrative ("it will have been a happy day")[37] and, by this second look at their history, to free themselves of it; but the trick is not so easily done. Even those who think that they "possess" their past on a tape-recording or on a page find that the present invariably flavours it, emphasizing the near-impossibility of entering into a dialogue with their own history.

On the stage of *Waiting for Godot* is enacted the amnesia which afflicts an uprooted people:

VLADIMIR: At the very beginning.
ESTRAGON: The very beginning of WHAT?
VLADIMIR: This evening . . . I was saying . . . I was saying . . .
ESTRAGON: I'm not a historian.[38]

Such lost souls can, paradoxically, be as deadened by habit as by forgetfulness, a recognition sadly voiced by Gogo: "That's the way it is. Either I forget immediately or I never forget". Mostly, however, he forgets everything:

ESTRAGON: We came here yesterday.
VLADIMIR: Ah no, there you're mistaken.
ESTRAGON: What did we do yesterday?
VLADIMIR: What did we do yesterday?
ESTRAGON: Yes.
VLADIMIR: Why . . . (Angrily) Nothing is certain when you're about.
ESTRAGON: In my opinion we were here.
VLADIMIR: (Looking round) You recognize the place?
ESTRAGON: I didn't say that.[39]

As a victim of a history which he does not understand, Gogo must deal with every situation as if it were a wholly new event. In the face of that terror, he enacts – as do all people whose pasts have been denied them – the invention of traditions.

Lacking an assured part, the tramps can have no clear sense of their own future. This is one reason why they cannot persist with any one of their chosen activities for very long. They are waiting without hope for a deliverance from a being in whom they do not really believe, in the manner of the *aisling* poets; and they are doomed to repeat the past precisely because they have never allowed themselves, or been allowed, to know it fully. This explains the paradox of persons who seem at once fixated on the past and supremely indifferent to it. Their surroundings seem decontextualized, because they represent a geography which has been deprived of a history. The historian Louis Cullen has spoken of "the general poverty of tradition in Ireland", which is why the people view their country "uncertainly and apologetically".[40] Another scholar, noting the indifference of country folk to local antiquities, likens them to a people condemned to live without a key in a superbly coded environment.[41] The loss of the ancestral heritage was a major contributory factor in this process.

The tramps try as best they can to restore and reconnect memories which have been taken from them, but there are just too many gaps, caused by a life of poverty, migration and constant interruption. The "dead voices" haunt them with teasing possibilities – they are like leaves, like wings, like sand – but the sheer proliferation of possibilities means that all are annulled, and so they induce only vague feelings of guilt and frustration. The past erupts, again and again, to usurp the present, but never to connect meaningfully with it. Worse still, the forgetfulness is catching, as Pozzo discovers after exposure to the Tramp's confusions:

> VLADIMIR: We met yesterday. (Silence) Do you not remember?
> POZZO: I don't remember having met anyone yesterday. But tomorrow I won't remember having met anyone today. So don't count on me to enlighten you.[42]

Lacking a clear sense of themselves, the tramps invent short-term identities (Let's play Lucky and Pozzo) or counterfeiting real emotion (Let's abuse each other). Like the Irish in England, or the black man in New York, they feel constantly "on". They become obsessed with the performative element in all exploitative relationships: and their curiosity about Pozzo and Lucky centres on the manner in which the master invents (but seldom deigns to notice) his slave, and in which the slave reciprocates by noticing and thus ratifying his master. Pozzo's absolute need is for such ratification ("Is everybody looking at me?"),[43] for if he is not perceived, he will not feel certain that he exists. Hegel, in his writings on the master/slave paradigm, had taught that the one who attains recognition without reciprocating becomes the master, while he who recognizes but is not recognized becomes the slave. The master thus reduces the slave to a mere instrument of his will, yet in that very victory lurks a longer-term defeat. Alienated from human labour, Pozzo loses the means of transforming his world and himself, but the slave who works upon objects thereby transforms himself. Moreover, since the slave is no better than an animal in the eyes of his master, Pozzo finds the recognition which he obtains inauthentic, because he is recognized only by someone unworthy. Hence, in the play, Pozzo cannot go for long without seeking the society of his likes (the tramps must be "human beings none the less . . . Of the same species as Pozzo") but, he hastily adds, to be suitable to his purposes such figures must be degradedly different as well ("even when the likeness is an imperfect one"). He seeks a botched metaphor, a strained theatricality: while the tramps want most of all to literalize, to write their own script and produce their own drama, of a kind which will not be abjectly dependent on an audience.

The even deeper paradox lies in the fact that onto the slave the master projects many of the qualities which his mastery dictates that he must suppress in himself. So Lucky, like many subject peoples, has once pleased his master by his powers in the dance and by his uplifting, beautiful ideas: "But for him, all my thoughts, all my feelings, would have been of common things", or, again, "He even used to think very prettily once, I could listen to him for hours".[44] Pozzo is a specialist who asks Lucky to live out on his behalf those elements which he must deny in himself; and Lucky, like the traditional clown, is given freedom to speak, but if he says too much, he can be patted on the head (or, as the case may dictate, kicked in the shins).

For here is a servant who will not just do your living, but also your dancing and your philosophy for you, and at the same time connive in his own oppression. The inevitable consequence is that the master becomes enslaved to the limitations and disabilities of his subject: and so the rope on which Pozzo "leads" Lucky becomes the cord by which Lucky confines his master. The tyranny of the weak over the strong becomes lasting indeed. In a world whose characters constantly seek and deny "likeness", the final yearning is for an escape from the endless play of metaphor into a pure declarative statement: and beyond that an escape from communication as such. Lucky exercises a strange, spell-binding power, having done just this, but he manages also to belittle the central activity of waiting for Godot with his subversive hint that the existence of a personal God would solve nothing anyway.

The relentless attempt of the tramps to demetaphorize, to stop life turning into literary material, is expressed in their aversion to theatricalization. They compel Pozzo to scale down his rhetorical excesses, in the manner of a Beckettian prose narrator who knows that *style* is less the expression of self than a means for pursuing the self:

POZZO: He wants to impress me, so that I'll keep him.
ESTRAGON: What?
POZZO: Perhaps I haven't got it quite right. He wants to mollify me, so

that I'll give up the idea of parting with him. No, that's not exactly it either.
VLADIMIR: You want to get rid of him?
POZZO: He wants to cod me, but he won't.[45]

Here, already in Act One, the subservient ones (the tramps, as well as
Lucky) are seen to dictate terms to the overlord at a rhetorical level, and
this anticipates the second act in which they will also be his physical
masters. By then, Pozzo will have been punished for his insincere,
metaphorized account of a sunset in Act One by the literal and
permanent fall of night over his eyes: the result, it is often said, of his
refusal to see life as it really is. As Pozzo lies prostrate on the ground,
Didi will deliver over his body just the kind of insincere rhetoric which
Pozzo was guilty of in an earlier scene:

> Let us not waste our time in idle discourse! (Pause. Vehemently.) Let us do
> something, while we have the chance! It is not every day that we are needed.
> Not indeed that we personally are needed. Others would meet the case
> equally well, if not better. To all mankind they were addressed, those cries
> for help still ringing in our ears! But at this place, at this moment of time,
> all mankind is us, whether we like it or not. Let us make the most of it,
> before it is too late! Let us represent worthily for once the foul brood to
> which a cruel fate consigned us![46]

It is a moment of rare poetic justice when such theatricality punishes
the theatrical. Pozzo, the landlord who wears the clothing of English
gentry, is for the moment at the mercy of mere tramps: and Didi's
studied rationalizations might be seen to resemble the neutral pose
adopted by most Irish in the face of England's crisis at the height of the
Second World War. Instead of offering help, Didi makes a pretty
speech; instead of taking upon himself the reality of Pozzo's suffering,
he becomes a professor of the fact that someone else is suffering. Of
course, Pozzo's punishment, like Didi's hypocrisy, is quite undeliber-
ated: it is simply the outcome of a life spent denying the reality of his
own partner's pains, which are invariably treated as mere spectacle. The
atomism of life in an oppressed society leads to such a loss of communal feeling and to a disinclination among people to help one
another: rather, the protagonist retreats into a posture of idiocy, in the
literal sense of *idiot* as a hopelessly private person. And, ultimately, the
overlord joins the underlings in a state of anomie and amnesia, becoming one of the blind from whom the things of time are hidden too.

The *attempt* by each of these protagonists to hold down a role becomes of far more pressing concern to the audience than is any role which each might conceivably play. The feeling which assails the audience is akin to that which might trouble friends of an amateur cast at a rickety production which is constantly verging on breakdown. It is here that the roots of Beckett's human comedy lie: in the Schopenhauerian will which pushes persons forward regardless of their capacities. Desire is idiotic and the Beckettian protagonist is therefore ludicrous not in repose but in motion: Belacqua on his painful walks with spavined gait, Murphy on the job-hunt, Molloy on the crawl, all of them are fishes out of water. The desire of the tramps has thrust them into a locale where they are patently incongruous, and without clues as to any activity which could be other than pointless. Because they are out of role, because they are caught, indeed, between a role and a self, they are forever watching themselves, monitoring their own performances, as if living life at a remove. Their experiences are thus taken away from them even before they are completed. This is but one further reason why the suffering of Pozzo can only strike them as a distant, even ridiculous, spectacle.

In *Waiting for Godot* the attempt to construct a person, or even a script, is finally abandoned. A stage devoid of props can provide no helpful indications as to how the protagonists might interpret their roles. Institutional behaviour, conditioned by easily visible props, might relieve a person of the task of choosing every single action with agonized deliberation, and without that support the tramps face the bleakness of freedom. But beyond all that, there is a deeper problem. The sheer energy which the tramps invest in constructing a context is one of the factors which prevents them from looking within, from "having thought", from becoming themselves. The open, undefined nature of a text, whose lines they didn't write and don't understand, alongside the extremely detailed and coercive stage directions, serves only to emphasize their unfreedom.

No sooner is a thesis or a personal attribute established in Act One than it is annulled in Act Two. Within specific scenes, a rudimentary, tentative portrait of a character might be sketched, but this impulse is always defeated within the play as a whole. The implications of this for the actor are clear: one cannot impersonate a self which just is not there. The lines must be played in the most literal sense, with a tone of irony, distance, even pointlessness. This, after all, merely mimics the authorial technique of one who asks the audience to imagine with him the making of endless "plays" and their subsequent disruption. In such a context, Pozzo's self-confident bluster, his bravura performances, may create a momentary illusion of personality and of presence, but they cannot ultimately conceal his hollowness. Behind the mask there is no face, no authority at all. The tramps, who always suspected this, were willing for a time, as are all dependents, to indulge a superior's prevailing mood; but, in the end, they tire of a man who seems concerned only with the effect he is making. They, at least, are still obsessed with finding a self worth impersonating and, if that is not possible, of scaling down all ridiculous claims:

VLADIMIR: This is becoming really insignificant.
ESTRAGON: Not enough.
(Silence.)[47]

The play, though initially castigated for high pretentiousness, is actually not pretentious at all: it leaves a pure space between contradictory possibilities, which interpreters are wont to fill with their own desires and fore-meanings. It may well be that the safest reading is a merely descriptive account of the workings of a text which is clearly an essay on theatricality: but that will inevitably become an analysis of the power-relations which make theatricalization possible. Nor is the play a helpless diagnosis, devoid of any hope, for, although Godot fails to come, Didi does manage, very late in the proceedings, to voice his care for the sleeping Gogo and his resolution to wake from his own dream to the sufferings of the world. The speech which begins "Was I sleeping while the others suffered? Am I sleeping now?" goes on to consider a wider possibility: "At me too someone is looking, of me too someone is saying, He is sleeping, he knows nothing, let him sleep on".[48]

In the image of that couple, bound in a rare moment of solidarity and linked to a wider chain of caring perceptors, Beckett hints at the possibility of a restored community. Yet, within a few moments, the shepherd boy reappears and reactivates Didi's faith in Godot and the entire illusion. Didi regresses and succumbs for the ignoblest of reasons: that if he didn't, he might be punished. This has been read as Beckett's commentary on the malfunction of an old-time religion based on fear, but it is much more than that. It is an indictment of all-isms – religious, colonial, political – which use the illusion of a perfect future to turn men and women away from suffering in the present.

The critic Vivian Mercier has argued that Pozzo in *Waiting for Godot* is dressed as were wicked landlords in the melodramas of Victorian Ireland (sporty bowler, riding breeches, cloak-overcoat) and Lucky in the unfastened knee-breeches, bare legs and buckled shoes which "recall the nineteenth-century Irish peasant of *Punch* cartoons". He contends that Pozzo's insistence on the goodness of his own heart and the dog-like devotion to him of Lucky are "as familiar in the mythology of the Irish landlord class as they were in that of the plantation owner of the Old South".[49] Undeniably, Lucky conspires in his own oppression, yet, by a sort of cultivated incompetence and foot-dragging, he seems to bring his master down along with him, since even the simplest orders issued by Pozzo take an eternity to perform. Mercier's is a plausible reading, given the well-known aversion among the Irish Protestant middle class to the pretensions of a clapped-out aristocracy.

A fuller treatment of the theme, however, may be found in *Endgame*, whose central figure, the blind Hamm, barks out constant orders while doing nothing himself. He appears the very epitome of a ruling class gone rancid: "It's time it ended . . . And yet I hesitate, I hesitate . . . to end".[50] His servant yearns, on the contrary, for a "terrific" end. Clov speaks at times to Hamm with the ingratitude of a Caliban who knows that his master's language has been the medium in which his yearnings for expressive freedom have been improvised.

What keeps them onstage, however, is an unfinished script, "the dialogue".[51] *Endgame* is, in fact, the most extreme example of a re-peated revivalist theme: the study of the sufferings of characters who make themselves willing martyrs to an approved text. Hamm, true to his name, is a consummate actor, impersonating the sort of authority he feels he ought to be, and Clov the human nail which is driven in by the force of his master's voice. But doubts nag, and they bother Hamm as much as Clov. Hamm senses acutely enough that the authority which he represents may be non-existent, that he can never centre himself at the exact mid-point of the stage, that he is "never there".[52] Clov tells him that he is lucky, for as a slave he *has* suffered and been there. If both men are marooned between an assumed role and an authentic self, then Hamm has gone far more deeply into the role, while Clov hovers painfully near to those zones in which he might become himself, those moments when he will counter what "they said to me" with "I say to myself" and become the subject of his own history.

One of the mysteries of the relationship is why Clov tolerates the tyranny of a man, who is obviously enfeebled and, in any practical sense, powerless. Hamm glories in his remaining control, taunting Clov with the possibility of opening the door to walk towards a free, beautiful landscape beyond their ravaged terrain:

HAMM: Did you ever think of one thing?
CLOV: Never.
HAMM: That here we're down in a hole. (Pause.) But beyond the hills? Eh? Perhaps it's still green. Eh? (Pause.) Flora! Pomona! (Ecstatically.) Ceres! (Pause.) Perhaps you won't need to go very far.[53]

This sounds like a mischievously-devised test. Earlier in their exchanges, Hamm had established that Clov will obligingly repeat whatever he chooses to decree: that there is no more nature, that there is nothing outside their shelter but a devastated landscape.

Of course, in wearily repeating these platitudes, Clov is very likely doing no more than humouring a cranky and demanding master, whose performance of despair ("Can there be misery", he stifles a yawn, "loftier than mine?")[54] expresses more his illusion of disillusion than the real thing. A man who repeats these truisms, day in day out, may finally come to believe them: or he may not. Hamm wants to know and so he propounds his little test, but Clov doesn't take the hint. Perhaps, like Lucky, he is in love with his own servitude and cannot, at such a late stage, face the rigours of change: or perhaps, with some cunning, he divines that Hamm is testing the fidelity of his partner, employing that ultimate blackmail between lovers, when one tells the other to go, the better to savour that secret hold which usually ensures that the partner will stay. When servitude is so extreme that the servant cannot contemplate freedom, then the master knows a final form of control: Clov is as in love with his subjection as Hamm is with his gloom. Beckett, like O'Casey, is scandalized by the apparent willingness of men and women to adapt themselves even to disaster and catastrophe. Winnie, in *Happy Days*, is but the most blatant case, buried up to her chest in sand, hating her existence, but not letting on, and thereby upsetting everybody all the more. But the lineaments of the situation were sketched most fully in *Endgame*, where habit has so deadened the servant that his eye can see only what it has been trained to see: or so it seems.

There is, however, in Clov's responses a mindless, automatic quality which suggests that he knows his assigned script far too well. At times, he jumbles it as if from over-familiarity, supplying rote-answers to questions which Hamm has not yet fully asked. This could be done out of numbed fatigue. Or it could be done to shut a prattling master up. Or it could be a scathing subversion of a smug system, which asks questions in a form which ensures that the answer has already been provided:

HAMM: Have you not had enough?
CLOV: Yes! (Pause.) Of what?[55]

This was the problem which faced the previous generation of Irish writers: they had questions to answer, but, as long as these were asked in forms imposed from without, the answers could only be drearily formulaic. In the play, Clov must unlearn the rhetorical habits of a lifetime in order to look into himself *and* in order to believe in the reality of the boy who suddenly appears at the close, in an apparently destroyed world. *Godot* had ended with the appearance of a boy who distracted the tramps from the task of self-authentication; *Endgame* concludes with the revelation of a boy whose identification confirms Clov's own ability to speak for himself. If the former play was a critique of man's inability to stop hoping against the odds, the latter is a repudiation of those who cannot transcend their own self-induced despair.

Clov is one of those underlings, described by Hegel, who know more than their rulers, but who cannot often or easily pretend to. The kitchen is his zone, that time-honoured preserve of servants, but the master keeps the key to the cupboard. In theory it contains the means of their deliverance; in all probability it holds nothing. The underling knows exactly what is going on, and yet he must accept an obsolete rhetorical account of the world from the current holder of power, a man who is but a broker in outmoded forms. The Marxian application of Hegel's master/slave paradigm is rehearsed in the exchanges between both men, but with a certain weariness, as if the act is wearing thin:

HAMM: Get the sheet. I'll give you nothing more to eat.
CLOV: Then we'll die.
HAMM: I'll give you just enough to keep you from dying. You'll be hungry all the time.
CLOV: Then we shan't die. (Pause.) I'll go and get the sheet.[56]

So threadbare have these routines become that Hamm sometimes shrewdly hints at their stagy inauthenticity, as when he instructs Clov to place a toy dog standing before him in an imploring posture. And Clov's nascent rebellion is clear in the reassuring answer: "Your *dogs* are here".[57]

That looming rebellion is even more obvious in their exchange about religion. When Hamm suggests that they pray, he evokes Clov's derision, and then proceeds to concur with it by calling down a curse on "the bastard", who has the audacity not to exist. Clov's simple, subversive answer is "Not yet."[58] The Irish grudge which he feels against God was summed up by the Gaelic poet Seán Ó Ríordáin, who said in response to the same question "Bhuel, má tá sé ann, is bastard ceart é" (Well, if he does exist, he's a proper bastard). What is rejected in *Endgame* is the old religion of fear satirized also at the end of *Godot*; but Clov's "not yet!" becomes a moving reprimand to those who see prayer as a set of demands rather than a real conversation, as an ultimatum rather than an overture. In his stage directions, Beckett goes to some lengths to mock the "attitudes of prayer", the mechanical hand-joining and the insincere silence of those onstage who seek a sign of God's favour. The artist whose motto was "no symbols where none intended" might have been expected to hate all wicked generations who seek obvious signs; and so the boy whom Clov sees at the end comes unbidden, to one who uttered that tentative, undogmatic phrase "Not yet!".

What is enacted onstage in both *Waiting for Godot* and *Endgame* is the bleakness of a freedom from which there will always be numerous mechanisms of escape. Beckett's is a world whose characters are constantly tempted to allow others to do their thinking for them, to resign their wills to a higher authority (often no more than a polite phrase for tyranny).

> ESTRAGON: Well? If we gave thanks for our mercies.
> VLADIMIR: What is terrible is to *have* thought.
> ESTRAGON: But did that ever happen to us?[59]

Freedom from ancient spiritual authorities will be meaningful only if the character is capable of actual thought. Too often what he calls "freedom" is actually and only the freedom to be like everybody else. As Erich Fromm has written: "the right to express our thoughts means something only if we are able to have thoughts of our own".[60] The problem is that, having cut the cords which connected them to the old authority, the tramps sag like redundant puppets: theirs is the empty freedom of the puppet. Their consequent fear of their own insignificance – joked about because so greatly feared – leads them to make a final surrender to the Old Testament god of fear and loathing, or to a modern variant thereof. All of Beckett's characters worry as to whether or not they have loved or been worthy of love: many assume that this will only be possible on conditions of complete self-surrender. Their attachments to one another are not the free solidarity of equals so much as a sado-masochistic conspiracy of the wounded:

HAMM: Gone from me you'd be dead.
CLOV: And vice-versa.[61]

The psychology at work here is that which fed the fascist cult. There may well be a link between it and the vengeful deity on which Beckett poured such scorn in his post-war plays. Erich Fromm remarks that "once man was ready to become nothing but the means for the glory of a God who represented neither justice nor love, he was sufficiently prepared to accept the role of a servant to the economic machine – and eventually a Führer".[62] Clov is tempted, like the tramps, to make himself dependent on a charismatic authority-figure, in whose aura he can bathe, and from whose confidence he can acquire a measure of the strength in which he is lacking. Because Hamm is so closely identified with his role, he is less conflicted than Clov, and more able (like Pozzo) to give a convincing impersonation. Yet in Clov's listlessness, his inability to maintain a role for any length of time, lies his great hope: the assertion of a still-defiant self.

Students of the sado-masochistic relation report that, in it, feelings of real love and tenderness only assert themselves at the very moment when the relationship is about to break up. This can also be true of the transactions between entire peoples; but it may also be found in the interplay between individuals too. Near the close of *Endgame*, Hamm suddenly finds in himself the grace to thank the Clov whom he believes to be leaving:

HAMM: I'm obliged to you, Clov. For your services.
CLOV: Ah, pardon, it's I am obliged to you.
HAMM: It's we are obliged to each other.[63]

This closing declaration is made against all the odds, and it is one of the most beautiful moments in Beckett's writings.

There is high irony in what follows, as the blind man fixes to die in the belief that Clov has gone. But Clov remains beside him, no longer a speaking servant but a silent partner, aware that there is no need for any rebellion now, because a true freedom never needs to declare or prove itself as such. Having spoken for himself in the first person singular,

Clov is free to stay without objection or to go without cruelty. The compassion, which he finds in himself in these late moments, suggests also that his earlier repetitions of Hamm's platitudes may have been offered as much out of care for a suffering mortal as out of numb acquiescence. This duo, like Didi watching over the sleeping Gogo, take their places alongside all the other couples of O'Casey and Shaw, of Wilde and Synge, as the rudiments from which a real society might yet be built. It may not even take these persons, just a rational being, or, indeed, a flea. For the moment, however, the two wordless men, broken and blasted though they be, point like shattered signposts on a battlefield towards an uncertain but feasible future.

For his own part, Beckett appears to have believed that the conditions of post-war France, in which he wrote his plays, held vital lessons for Irish people, still nursing their own wounds three decades after British withdrawal from the twenty-six counties. In June 1946, he prepared a broadcast for Radio Éireann on the work of an Irish Red Cross hospital, of which he was storekeeper, at St. Lô, a town which had been bombed almost out of existence in a single night. Now, he was happy to report, it was being rebuilt by a combination of German war-prisoners, Irish technical expertise, and French pluck. In a coded rebuke to Irish neutrality during the war, he ended by suggesting that the Irish doctors, nurses and relief-workers at St. Lô "got at least as good as they gave . . . got indeed what they could hardly give, a vision and sense of a time-honoured conception of humanity in ruins, and perhaps even an inkling of the terms in which our condition is to be thought again".[64] The talk was never broadcast. One of the editors at Radio Éireann was Roibeárd Ó Faracháin, a follower of those antiquarian poets whom Beckett had derided in 1934 for their flight from self-perception. In the suppressed broadcast, Bechett clearly stated that the Irish in France were the real inheritors of a national genius for building amid ruins with the shreds and patches, the metal sheeting and the wooden boards, of a shattered society. When asked whether his migration from Dublin, publication in London and domicile in Paris, meant that he was no longer to be considered an Irishman, his reply was laconic enough: "au contraire". To the end, Beckett held onto his green passport.

Perhaps, in the contours of a France remaking itself after the devastation wrought by the Nazis, he saw the image of an ideal Ireland of the future.

Thirty-One

Post-Colonial Ireland – "A Quaking Sod"

Patrick Pearse had always feared that the shapers of an independent Irish state might consolidate the order which they had set out to overthrow. He had, after all, opened *The Murder Machine*, his essay on educational reform, with a warning that freedom was so little experienced or understood that "the very organizations which exist in Ireland to champion freedom show no disposition themselves to accord freedom; they challenge a great tyranny but they erect their own little tyrannies".[1] The danger was that people would mistake a repressive colonial machine for nature itself and proceed, unbidden, to employ many of the old categories of thought upon themselves. When Michael Collins sent for British guns to help the Free State army to defeat the republican insurgents in the Four Courts, he did at the level of action what generations of Irish intellectuals would do at the level of ideas. Years later, after similar experiences in Africa, Fanon was to write:

> . . . In its wilful narcissism, the national middle class is easily convinced that it can advantageously replace the middle class of the mother country. But that same independence which literally draws it into a corner will give rise within its ranks to catastrophic reactions, and will oblige it to send out frenzied appeals for help to the former mother country.[2]

The new élites had, quite simply, arrived too late, missing out on the heroic period of the bourgeoisie in the nineteenth century, that phase when its members learned how to found heavy industries and factories. The new rulers emerged only *after* independence in the twentieth century and the vast majority of them never learned how to produce, only how to consume. In Ireland, they failed to transform the semi-developed economy inherited from the British regime.

The history of independent Ireland bears a remarkable similarity, therefore, to the phases charted by Frantz Fanon in *The Wretched of the*

Earth. In the early decades, the new leaders soothed a frustrated people with endless recollections of the sacred struggle for independence. Commemorations abounded, the Irish version of this disease being the repeated political taunt "Where were you in 1916?"

Poor leadership and scant resources condemned the nation for years to the status of an artisan economy, featuring local products. Shoddy native manufactures were protected by tariff barriers, just as bad writers who played up "local colour" were elevated over talented modernists who refused to follow the approved line. When this way of living was revealed as untenable, the native élite identified its historic role as intermediary for multinational companies: and, thereafter, it modelled its lifestyle on that of the international élite, whose members it invited to visit as tourists in search of the exotic. At this point, the literary exponents of local colour found themselves ratified by a new, even more influential, even more ecstatic, audience.

The new régime created not industries so much as industrial authorities, not factories so much as fixers. Its schools remained obsessed with a hyperacademic form of learning, derived from the colonial period, which tested new recruits for the swelling civil service. The curriculum emphasized languages, not just English and Irish but also Latin and Greek, "resembling that of the English public schools of the mid-Victorian period".[3] Science and technology tended to be secondary. This ruling group mimicked the surface-effects of western consumerism, while its politicians bought votes at election-time with borrowed cash: but it built no infrastructure with which to service the debt. Its educators scarcely concealed their snobbish contempt for those who actually made things with their hands.

This *trahison des clercs* might have been attributed to the failure to overhaul the "murder machine" so that education could instead have served the community's needs. Hence, Nigerian children found themselves sweating through Corneille's *Le Cid* at much the same time that V. S. Naipaul in Trinidad was straining over Dickens and Irish students were picking their way through the essays of Sir Arthur Quiller-Couch.[4] Ngugi reported from 1960s Kenya that its children, after a decade of independence, were still taught to know themselves only through London and New York, and he recalled the complaint of a syllabus committee that "students were still being subjected to alien cultural values which are meaningless to our present needs".[5] Chinua Achebe noted that the post-independence élite of readers, "where they exist at all, are only interested in reading textbooks", and he recalled a pathetic letter from a Ghanaian reader of his *Things Fall Apart*, which took the form of a complaint that he had not included sample questions and answers at its end, "to ensure his success at next year's school examination".[6]

Such a system produced, with dire predictability, a people lacking in self-confidence and easily bullied by outsiders. Doctors, dentists, lawyers, engineers and architects were produced in over-abundance, to meet the career-aspirations of the new élite, but most were then exported as free, instant experts to the First World: and so it is with most Irish critics. The more gifted amongst them were often simply internalizers of the imperial mode. "No Irishman", wrote Denis Donoghue, "can ever assume that he is at the centre of anything".[7]

In the post-colony, school students engaged in rote-learning of the old, familiar texts, on courses often taught by mediocre lecturers from the former colonial power rather than by persons of talent from the independent state. In Nigeria, Achebe noted a similar tendency in college administrators: "Given a chance, they will appoint a European over a Nigerian to teach at their university".[8] Ngugi's account also rejected the widespread notion that Africa was a mere extension of the West. He recollected a question put by young lecturers in 1968: "if there is need for the 'study of the historic continuity of a single culture', why can't this be African? Why can't African literature be at the centre so that we can view other cultures in relation to it?"[9] Eventually, of course, these reforms would be achieved: but one side-effect of the intervening crisis was the extraordinary tardiness in the development of a probing native criticism. The few native-born critics who emerged in the years immediately following independence often specialized in overseas literature, while the leading native writers were most fully explicated by foreigners: and many lower-level postings in universities were occupied by foreign academics hoping desperately for a summons back to a more "prestigious" assignment in the old country. Today, all that has changed, but in the intervening period much psychological damage was done.

"When exams matter so terribly", writes Paul Harrison in *Inside the Third World*, "rote learning is encouraged and creative, adaptable thinking is suppressed. Anyone who has taught in a developing country cannot help noticing the problems of bringing out students' self-confidence and ability to make independent judgements".[10] The student was often taught a covert self-hatred, seeing advancement as the poised imitation of English masters. V. S. Naipaul put this very well in *The Mimic-Men*:

We pretended to be real, to be learning, to be preparing ourselves for life, we mimic men of the New World, one unknown corner of it, with all its reminders of the corruption that came so quickly to the new.[11]

And George Lamming was even more blunt:

Supervising this complexity of learning to be a new man, in a new place, was an authority whose home was elsewhere.[12]

The Irish, being the first English-speakers to decolonize in this century, were inevitably the first to make the expected wrong-turning, before, in Achebe's words, "the great collusive swindle that was independence showed its true face to us".[13] Achebe adds that at least Empire had its glorious heyday, its years of honour, but "its successor, independence, did not even wait to grow old before turning betrayer".

It seemed, at the outset, as if the Irish might genuinely renovate their students' consciousness. Eoin Mac Néill, a brilliant Gaelic scholar and co-founder of the Gaelic League, became the native Minister for Education of whom Pearse had long dreamed, a man who abolished payment of teachers according to examination results and who introduced open courses in literature, without the dead weight of prescribed and approved texts. But he did *not* abolish the hated examination system, and so schools faced the ultimate nightmare, an open course followed by a set test. The bleakness of such a freedom could not long be tolerated and, by June 1940, a new Minister, Éamon de Valera, reintroduced prescribed books. The anthologies of English literature thereafter studied, for the next three decades in Ireland, were described by one teacher as "a monument to an essentially Victorian sensibility".[14] While England in the 1940s and 1950s transformed itself into a welfare state and retuned its syllabi to that modern world, the Irish continued for another decade to model their literary studies on the methods of Quiller-Couch.

The fact that religion, rather than English literature, was held to be the central subject of study in schools helped to prevent the emergence of a movement of literary critics such as followed F. R. Leavis in England. Even more regrettable was the fact that the courses studied paid scant heed to the considerable achievement of modern Irish writers in the English language. It may even have suited certain dogmatists in the Department of Education to misrepresent English culture by antique imperial curiosities, since that helped to feed a pet theory that Irishness was only to be found within the Gaelic tradition. If religion was the central subject in the humanities, then the Irish language and its literature were not far behind. English literature was nothing more than a pretext for the study of historical sensibilities. It was, therefore, hardly surprising that Ireland should have continued to produce some of the foremost exponents of *belles lettres* still working in the English language.

The problem, as Daniel Corkery saw it at the end of the first decade of independence, was that such a system produced in most cases neither an English nor an Irish sensibility, nor any admirable hybrid. It led instead to confusion, the kind that would be found later in Ghana when nationalists sang "Lead, Kindly Light" to welcome their leader Nkrumah back from jail, or in Kenya when the young Ngugi, seeking to visualize Wordsworth's daffodils in a school classroom, reached hopelessly for the image of fish crowded into a lake. In Ireland, too, Corkery detected not just a lack of native forms, but the want of any foundation on which to shape them. "Everywhere in the mentality of the Irish people are flux and uncertainty. Our national consciousness may be described, in a native phrase, as a quaking sod. It gives no footing. It is not English, nor Irish, nor Anglo-Irish ...."[15] That is what Lamming had in mind when he described how the colonized is invariably separated from the original ground on which the colonizer found him: "It is this awareness of distance between what is his and what he has learned to do, it is precisely this awareness which undermines his confidence in what he really was and really could be".[16]

Corkery attributed such self-doubt to the continuing prestige of English culture in Irish scholastic institutions. An English child, reading his or her own literature, finds in it a focus of the minds and instincts of English people; whereas an Irish child, reading English, experiences something very different:

> His education, instead of buttressing and refining his emotional nature, teaches him the rather to despise it, inasmuch as it teaches him not to see the surroundings out of which he is sprung, as they are in themselves, but as compared with alien surroundings: his education provides him with an alien medium through which he is henceforth to look at his native land! At the least his education sets up a dispute between his intellect and his emotions ... So does it happen that the Irishman who would write of his own people has to begin by trying to forget what he has learnt ...[17]

Just as the English turned Ireland into a mock-England, so now the post-colonial student, caught between a reality for which there were no obvious forms and a set of proffered forms which did not cohere with that reality, had to try to convert English locations and characters into Irish versions already known and loved. The outcome was often a student blinded equally to the richness of both inheritances, constantly forgetting what little had been learned. Ngugi's report from Kenya reads in places like a paraphrase of Corkery, a man whose work in all likelihood he did not know.

The apologists for English literature as traditionally understood might argue that such self-estrangement, the production of such a divided consciousness, has been the *object* of all sophisticated literary study since the eighteenth century. As Gauri Viswanathan has written:

> It entails the suppression of the individualistic self, through self-examina-
> tion and self-evaluation, to make way for the idealized self of culture.
> Division is the key to canonical power, inducing the reader to absorb
> another identity and respond in another voice. The tyranny of canons can
> be overcome only by deliberate estrangement from the texts that constitute
> them. But if education remains committed to our "getting into" texts rather
> than viewing them from the outside as strangers, the process of division will
> continue.[18]

This, however, seems only half the story. The British Victorian élite were inspired to self-improvement: they *began* as estranged, but soon separated themselves from the philistine middle class, and thus achieved their ideal selves. The Bombay élite, in contrast, were selected out of their society, and by the study of English literature set into such tension with it that all their efforts at self-elevation were redirected to the reform of that society. Matthew Arnold never dreamed of estrange-ment *from a national culture*, merely from a philistine middle class, the better to pursue the ideal. Two generations after him, his American disciple Lionel Trilling did indeed ask his students so to read the texts of modernism that they took a step "beyond culture", in ways which allowed them to view man as if he were an anthropological witness of himself. Trilling was, however, shrewd and sardonic enough to note the scandalous ease with which his students stepped back inside their charmed circle.[19] Had they stayed outside just a little longer, their understanding of other cultures – for instance, that of Islam – might have been enriched. The readers of English in colonies were asked a rather different question – to step outside their native cultures on the strict understanding that they would never thereafter step back in. *All* became victims of this process, but the spiritual disorientation reported by Ngugi, Achebe and Corkery was far more painful than the kind envisaged by Arnold for English schoolchildren.

It is, nonetheless, one of the recurring paradoxes of a decolonizing culture that Corkery's subtle account of a dispute between a child's intellectual schooling and emotional nature is a reworked version of Eliot's theory of the dissociation of sensibility. It lends a pervasive gloom to Corkery's entire opening chapter in *Synge and Anglo-Irish Literature*, a gloom not to be found in West Indian commentaries on the same crisis. (Perhaps the lack of a native language left the West Indians less prone to depression than their Irish, African or Indian counterparts, who felt that something good had been taken away.) Whereas Corkery can complain quite bluntly that "Ireland has not learned how to express its own life through the medium of the English language"[20] (and this after the decade of *Ulysses, The Tower* and *The Silver Tassie*!), Lamming can welcome the novel as "a way of investigating and projecting the inner experience of the West Indian community".[21] Lamming, indeed, sees this as the positive result of being caught between two cultures, a turning inward to examine the ground of one's perceptions, to find out how one knows what one knows. To him this is an event as important as the very discovery of the islands.

Corkery is equally negative concerning the sheer number of expatriate Irish writers who function as prisoners of overseas markets. Yet Lamming can find exile a "pleasure" rather than a dreary financial necessity: it affords him a welcome relief from a philistine class at home which reads solely for examinations, and an opportunity to discover overseas, perhaps for the first time, what it means to be West Indian. To write an investigation of the sources of West Indian consciousness virtually demands a strategic withdrawal from the place: to write at all is, in effect, to go into exile. This might have been the answer given to Corkery by the Irish writers.

Corkery's piercing insights into aspects of Irish reality are of the kind possible only to one who has blinded himself to nine-tenths of that reality. His essay ends on a note of near-farce, virtually denying the existence of Anglo-Irish literature, except perhaps as an exotic offshoot of the English parent plant.[22] The hothouse image is, nonetheless, very well chosen. This is, of course, an aspect of Fanon's second phase of decolonization, into which so many of the texts treated in this book have fallen, in whole or in part: that moment when a writer attempts to stamp the forms of the colonizer with "a hallmark which he wishes to be national, but which is strongly reminiscent of exoticism".[23] Fanon could make such a critique the basis on which he constructed his model of liberation, that phase which would set all Corkeryesque gloom to rights. Corkery's closing regret in his famous diatribe, that the literary revivalists had failed to throw up a body of criticism which might explain their limitations and point the way ahead, might with some justice be ultimately applied to its own author. He deserves great praise also, for, until the advent of Conor Cruise O'Brien in the 1950s, he was the nearest thing Ireland produced to a post-colonial critic.

The years of the "open syllabus" proved happy ones for the more imaginative teachers and students in Ireland who could afford to think little of examinations; and it may be no accident that they also coincided with that period when Ireland came to be regarded with affection and respect by the peoples of the developing world. In such places, tens of thousands of Irish missionaries were made welcome in the 1920s and 1930s, since they came with no hidden political agenda. When Ireland entered the United Nations after World War Two, its position of non-alignment between the superpowers became a model for other emerging states; and when the foremost architect of that policy, Conor Cruise O'Brien, displeased the European imperial establishment by his handling of affairs in Katanga (formerly part of Belgian Congo) in 1961, that phase in Irish history reached something of a climax. Editors in London were sharpening fangs well bloodied from recent clashes with the Egyptian leader Gamal Abdul Nasser. "And who", sniffed Prime Minister Macmillan in London, "is Conor Cruise O'Brien?" At Dublin Airport, a suddenly jobless O'Brien gave his answer: an unimportant, expendable civil servant. But then, eyebrows arched, he declared that he had just received the backing of a less expendable man, Prime Minister Nehru of India, leader of a sub-continent.[24] That moment in Irish history was soon lost. For his part, O'Brien soon afterward embarked on a revision of the anti-colonialism of his younger years, although it was some time before he went public with it. As late as 1969, in his masterly study of the French Algerian writer Albert Camus, he came out in support of Sartre's attack on French colonialism in Algeria and was suitably caustic about Camus's acquiescence. Camus had said that, if forced to choose between revolutionary justice and his mother, he would in the end opt to save his mother. "Not every intellectual has to make the same choice", commented O'Brien, "but each must realize how he is a product of the culture of the advanced world, and how much there is that will pull him, among the 'Algerias' of the future, towards Camus's fall".[25]

By 1969, however, western intellectuals were repenting of their support for national liberation movements, as the new states of Africa and Asia sank into chaos, censorship and even dictatorship. Those who saw such problems as a predictable legacy of colonialism were drowned out by a new kind of commentator, often from a former colony, who gravely assured his old masters that these troubles were largely due to the inherent incapacity of such peoples to govern their own affairs. Chinua Achebe was scathing about this "bunch of bright ones" who came along in this way to say "We are through with intoning the colonial litany ... We are tough-minded. We absolve Europe of all guilt. Don't you worry, Europe, we were bound to violence long before you came to our shores". Many liberal Europeans were greatly relieved by this exculpation. Achebe called it "this perverse charitableness, which asks a man to cut his own throat for the comfort and good opinion of another": but he did not fail to note how many European thinkers praised the "sophistication" and "objectivity" of these new analysts.[26] Their thesis of the self-inflicted wound proved immensely consoling to readers of the "liberal" western press, especially when penned in the elegant essays of a V. S. Naipaul. "No Indian can take himself to the stage", wrote Naipaul, "where he might perceive that the faults lie within the civilization itself, that the failures and cruelties of India might implicate all Indians".[27] An Indian economist might point to the many effects of colonial undevelopment which this thesis excluded, and might seek to occupy a space somewhere between the secular Naipaul and the militant holy men: but it was the revisionists who held the high ground. Naipaul was feted in western journals, having told their readers that after their rulers withdrew from their holdings, things only went from bad to worse.

In Ireland, Conor Cruise O'Brien began to sing the same song, but in the future tense, by way of justifying a continuing British presence in the six counties of the north. He repented publicly of his anti-partitionist past, becoming a favoured columnist in the London and New York press, "a voice of sanity in the Irish mess". He translated the mess of Ireland into a rational, enlightenment discourse which made good sense to his international readers. Witty, urbane, amusing, he shared with Naipaul a coolly analytical brain and a mind formed by close study of the European classics. After the outbreak of renewed violence in Northern Ireland, he revised his view of the Camus–Sartre debate and concluded that Camus had been right. The man who had once echoed Lenin's disappointment that the 1916 rebels had risen too soon to launch an international revolution now made it very clear that he no longer considered the Easter Rising to have been a positive thing. Yet his career, for all its twists, had an inner logic, that same logic which he had detected in the work of Albert Camus. Both men had found themselves caught on the cusp between Europe and the developing world. Both responded deeply to these twin tugs, because they could feel the pulls so deeply within themselves. What O'Brien said of Camus was, perhaps, even more applicable to himself: "he belonged to the frontier of Europe, and was aware of a threat. The threat also beckoned to him. He refused, but not without a struggle".[28]

The leaders of modern Ireland also "refused", but only after a period of uncertainty and doubt. The roots of this change may be found in the career of O'Brien's own youthful model, the writer and pundit Seán ÓFaoláin. He was a brilliant protégé of Corkery, but one who eventually transcended and repudiated his former teacher in a much-publicized critique. That critique, however, remained unsatisfactory, because it invoked only the values of European individualism, values which, however admirable in themselves, had often been invoked in order to justify the colonial enterprise from which the country was but slowly emerging.[29] ÓFaoláin and Cruise O'Brien represented the ideal of a liberal-European Ireland, but free of its problematic past, whose only tense was the present and its needs: but the persistent injustices in Northern Ireland, and the economic undevelopment of the south, meant that the conditions for such transcendence were never propitious.

It may be doubted, anyway, whether such transcendence, even if achievable, would have been desirable: a post-colonial Ireland had many important differences from a mainly post-imperial Europe. Its people could hardly "play at being Europeans",[30] not because of invincible provincialism but because their traditions linked them to a much wider global network. The years of evolution from the nineteenth century to the twentieth had not been some kind of apprenticeship for an understanding of Europe: rather, the culture of Europe might offer an apprenticeship for a fuller understanding of the writings of Yeats, Joyce and Beckett. All three handled many classic themes of European art, but they did not feel tied to that tradition by any special devotion, and so their handling was irreverent, subversive, even insolent. Of nothing was this more true than of their treatment of English literary culture.

Living at such an angle to official English canons, Irish artists "read England" as a prelude to "writing Ireland". They incorporated many of their re-readings of English authors into their creative texts, and revealed to a new generation of English readers a Shakespeare, Milton, Blake and Shelley richer and more various than the versions of these authors which had been promoted by previous critics. The English, to their lasting credit, took the lesson to heart. It was Irish *academics* who continued to ask their students to read Shakespeare and the others as they would have been interpreted by educated English persons in the year 1922. There was no attempt to imagine how the study of republican poets like Blake or Shelley in a university of Dublin or Cork might constitute a challenge to the Eliotic notion of a royalist, Anglo-Catholic canon. In 1922 the images of national possibility froze, with the country's teachers cast as curators of a post-imperial museum, whose English departments were patrolled by zealous custodians anxious to ensure that nothing changed very much. Down the corridor, many curators of the post-colonial Gaelic museum, known as the Irish Department, made equally certain that no radical revisions occurred, no compromising contacts with other cultures.

All of this required a vast degree of self-repression. If nineteenth-century critics in England had a full-time job stripping Shakespeare and other writers of their radical potentials, the academics of twentieth-century Ireland devoted themselves with equal solicitude to the deradicalization of native writing in both languages. In our journey through the Irish Renaissance we have encountered more than one revolutionary text being turned into a revivalist document. Long before Irish nationalist politicians had erased subversive voices from Irish debate, the critics in the academies had performed parallel feats on the great national writers.

The utopian content of great literature can never be wholly suppressed, however. It can be driven just a little deeper into the unconscious, awaiting, like all despised potentials, for its moment to rise again. At times when an old order of life has lost its meaning, and a new world has not yet been born, Caliban may indeed be tempted to plot the murder of Prospero. Shakespeare's *The Tempest* transcends such negative perspectives, for all that, with its plea for the fulfilment of the entire potential of the person in a world with "no sovereignty", no tyranny of one over another, no sway of humans over nature. What Gonzalo offers is the dream of a liberated world, a vision of anarchist community, to be found in the writings of Caliban, once he puts pen to paper.

RECOVERY AND RENEWAL

RECOVERY AND RENEWAL

The pace of modernization in the 1960s astonished many and no area of Irish life was left untouched.[1] Between 1960 and 1969 over 350 manufacturing enterprises came from overseas to take advantage of the attractive terms offered by the government, not the least of which was an educated and ambitious workforce. At the same time, Ireland became a holiday destination for members of the international jet-set: these tourists brought a touch of glamour and a consumerist philosophy which soon had their hosts in thrall. In 1963 the formal state visit of John F. Kennedy, a Catholic who had become President of the United States, seemed to epitomize the new mood of internationalism and self-confidence: his youth, charisma and urbanity appealed in particular to a generation born after the Rising and Civil War which now felt ready to possess its inheritance. Better still, President Kennedy was a proud Irishman, a glorious illustration that perhaps one could be Irish and modern at the same time.

He appealed to a growing national propensity for having things both ways. His visit – though this only became clear in retrospect – made Ireland safe for western-style consumerism: henceforth, foreign policy would be less independent, less sympathetic to decolonizing peoples and more securely locked within the American sphere of influence. Yet Kennedy praised the Irish for being a nation of rebels, who had achieved great things by a stubborn refusal to conform. In many ways he embodied, as well as appealing to, a national self-deception: for he played the rebel while secretly being a superstraight. The myth of a rugged frontier-style individualism helped to reconcile many latter-day Americans who supported Kennedy to life as tractable consumers of services and goods. For the Irish, however, the gap between myths of rebellion and the consumerist actuality was going to be more difficult to bridge. For one thing, consumer comforts were still not widely or equally distributed: one person in three in the west of Ireland was described as chronically isolated and whole villages continued to die. For another, the actual rebellion was not safely over in the north — merely simmering, unresolved, beneath a queasy surface.

The national television service initiated in 1962 had an immediate effect in encouraging the ventilation of problems which had long gone undiscussed. So irate did one rural politician become at the new free-ranging debates that he famously complained that "there was no sex in Ireland before television".[2] The winds of change were felt with real force inside the Catholic church: the liberalizing presence and policies of Pope John XXIII and the aggiornamento *of his Second Vatican Council led to vernacular and folk masses and much talk about the priesthood of the laity. The enclosed training of priests and nuns in seminaries, isolated from newspapers, electronic media and the modern world, was widely criticized as an unsound basis for a ministry which seemed more and more likely to bring them into contact with areas of social deprivation, at home or overseas. In the face of these developments, many bishops relaxed their older, autocratic styles of address. The bans on late-night dancing were rescinded. Bishops who failed to move with the times were no longer immune to criticism: one was attacked by a student who called him "an immigrant into the twentieth century".[3]*

The bishops were confronted by other, even more challenging, voices. From the heart of the rural community came a Clarewoman, Edna O'Brien, a fine storyteller and gifted stylist, who focused in her work on the sexual passions and betrayed emotions of a whole generation of Irish-women. Books like The Country Girls *won their author an early reputa-tion as a scandalous woman, a sort of Irish Françoise Sagan; but the unerring accuracy of her eye and the deft rightness of her phrase convinced many that here were believable, fallible, flesh-and-blood women, neither paragons nor caricatures. That some of the male characters portrayed in these books were based on noted "pillars of Irish society" added to the cream of the jest. Although a later, openly feminist, generation would become somewhat critical of her fondness for "wounded woman" stereotypes, O'Brien was arguably the writer who made many of the subsequent advances in Irishwomen's writing possible: and she continued to craft a prose of surpassing beauty and exactitude.*

Traditional Ireland remained ambivalent about the changes: as he opened the national television station in 1962, President de Valera ad-mitted that it could be a force for great good, but feared that it might in the end do more harm. Perhaps he sensed that the new media, conducted in prestigious international languages, might seal the doom of minority tongues like Irish. In that he would not have been far wrong, though it is also arguable that the massive revival of traditional music and folk dancing was as much the creation of television as of the counter-cultural movements of the 1960s. Television became the device by which a long-repressed community learned once again how to talk to itself; and in the process that society was forced to confront much that had long gone unadmitted.[4]

Throughout the 1960s there were major discrepancies in the levels of social welfare enjoyed north and south of the border. Although unionist politicians had embraced the welfare state only with reluctance, they were soon happy to cite these discrepancies as another argument against reunification: for instance, in 1960 Northern Ireland spent more on education than the Republic, which had three times the population.[5] *Within the next two decades these discrepancies would largely disappear, not in some disingenuous attempt to woo unionists into the Republic, but simply because its citizens insisted on modern levels of comfort and social security. Accession to the European Economic Community was endorsed by a majority of five to one, despite the warnings of traditional republicans and radical socialists that it might herald further diminutions of national sovereignty. Soon Irish farming would enter into a boom period, brought on by the policy of higher prices for food.*

In the cities, however – and after 1971 more than half the people lived in urban rather than rural settings – reactions were more mixed. Many established industries such as shoe-manufacturing, motor-assembly and milling went under in the face of new trade conditions. (These industries had been traditional centres of militant trade unionism.) Political leaders were, nonetheless, able to sell EEC membership to the electorate on the basis of the large subventions accruing to the country as a peripheral region from central European coffers, subventions which helped to build an infrastructure of roads, redesigned seaports and luxury hotels. Though the employment generated was welcome, fears were expressed that a "dole mentality" long endemic in the depressed west was extending across the whole island, whose leaders and civil servants became expert in the small-print of European hand-outs. While much of the money promoted enterprise, some clearly stunted it. Cynics began to suggest that Shaw's dire prophecy in John Bull's Other Island *was finally coming true: as smaller unviable farms were sucked up by bigger ones whose proprietors seemed more interested in ranching than crop-growing, the future of entire rural areas seemed to lie wholly within the area of tourism. The playwright Brian Friel even wrote a satire,* The Mundy Scheme, *devoted to the idea of Ireland as a gigantic theme-park, retirement commune and cemetery for European industrialists.*

In 1969, inspired by the Civil Rights movement for black emancipation in the United States, a group of activists in the Connemara Gaeltacht launched their own campaign to revitalize the Irish-speaking areas. At that time, the level of unemployment was even higher in Connemara than in the gerrymandered city of Derry, itself under unionist misrule. The demand was for industrial development in the region, for proper schools and villages, for an autonomous local authority, and for a broadcasting service in the native language. It had become sadly clear that, while politicians in Dublin paid lip-service to Irish, they had allowed the Gaeltacht areas to continue their slow dying. Some sardonic souls believed that by 1969 it was simply too late to turn the policy around: to them the argument was no longer about how to revive the language so much as about who exactly was responsible for the disposal of the corpse. Yet the Cearta Sibhialta (Civil Rights) movement was in most respects remarkably successful. Appealing to the idealism of the young in the years following student revolts in Europe and North America, it managed to detach Irish from the purgatorial fires of the school classroom and to present it as part of a global countercultural movement constructed upon "small is beautiful" principles. Many gifted graduates did what few Gaelic Leaguers of Hyde's generation managed: they voted with their feet and settled in the west, offering leadership to rural cooperatives. Young people from the Gaeltach no longer regarded emigration as axiomatic: many stayed and helped to build small industries in their communities.[6]

Meanwhile, in the major cities of Dublin, Cork, Galway and Belfast, a strong parents' movement called for all-Irish language schools in areas of social deprivation: recognizing that Irish was still a passport to educational success, some wanted their offspring to benefit from expert instruction in the language, while others simply believed that without a sound knowledge of Irish their children would have only a two-dimensional understanding of the national culture. These schools soon became centres of excellence and the nucleus of other language-based activities of the wider community. Many of the activists were persons of high culture and soon a revival in the writing and publishing of Irish was under way. Most of its exponents had learned Irish as a second language, and predictable arguments raged as to whether the quality of their work really measured up to that of the previous generation of masters such as Máirtín Ó Cadhain or Máirtín Ó Direáin: but one of the surviving geniuses of the earlier group, Máire Mhac an tSaoi, gave her enthusiastic blessing to Nuala ní Dhomhnaill, whose poetry won an international following in English translation as well as in the original Irish. Other younger authors such as Alan Titley, Michael Davitt and Derry O'Sullivan seemed to confirm that this revival was of real artistic consequence.

Irish continued to enjoy a privileged but strangely precarious position in national life. A book of poems published in the language was likely to have as many intelligent readers as a comparable volume in English, yet Irish was by common consent still in danger of disappearing as a community language within a generation. The incursions of the international media, whose television shows and magazines were conducted in English, meant that the Gaeltacht remained under cultural threat even after some semblance of industrial policy had been formulated for it. Bilingualism became widely practised among the young in such places; and few spoke Irish with the same purity or rigour as did their ancestors. It become clear that if Irish had a long-term future, it was as likely to be in the cities as in the countryside.

The public at large wished the language well, but remained unwilling to make concrete sacrifices to protect it. The decision by the Fine Gael/Labour coalition government of the mid-1970s to make a "pass" in Irish no longer compulsory in state examinations was generally applauded. Many language enthusiasts felt betrayed, however – one said that the move ended "the last vestige of state policy on the language"[7] – but others argued that compulsion had served only to bring Irish into discredit with honest minds. Henceforth, those who studied the language would, it has hoped, come to see it as a gift rather than a threat: those who nursed such ideas pointed to the immense popularity of Gaelic music and folk music among those same young people least inclined to learn compulsory Irish at school.

This paradox seemed to indicate a failure of official policy, yet at a deeper level it may simply have revealed a real ambivalence in national attitudes. A 1975 government report showed that about three-quarters of the people still believed the language essential to Irish identity, but that less than one quarter believed that the language would still be thriving in the next century. The problem of being at once Irish and modern had not been fully solved by John F. Kennedy's ritual phrase or two in Irish. The fate of a people still despondent about its capacity to shape its cultural future became manifest in the tortuous clauses of the government report:

> The average individual . . . feels rather strongly that the Irish language is necessary to our ethnic and cultural integrity, and supports the efforts to ensure the transmission of the language. At the same time, under present policies and progress, he is not really convinced that we can ensure its transmission. He has rather negative views about the way Irish has been taught in school and has a rather low or "lukewarm" personal commitment to its use, although in this latter case, the average person has not sufficient ability in the language to converse freely in it. On the other hand, he strongly supports nearly all government efforts to help the Gaeltacht, but at the same time feels that the language is not very suitable for modern life.[8]

These words were published in 1975, but they still hold true. A government proposal to establish an Irish-language television station won popular support in 1993, though not without opposition from the mass-circulation Independent group of newspapers. Adult classes in Irish remained much in demand: and the Gaelic schools movement, on the basis of superlative results, grew stronger than ever. Yet, for all that, Irish-language programmes on television and Irish-language newspapers were watched and read only by a minority. The "rebels" of John F. Kennedy's imagination were showing a surprising degree of conformism to the world of Dallas and Falcon Crest.

In that, of course, they were no different from other peoples: what disappointed the idealists, however, was that it need not necessarily have been so. Douglas Hyde had hoped to make Ireland again interesting to the Irish: the repossession of a language was to be the prelude to the repossession of a distinctive cuisine, clothing, dance tradition, physical culture, and so on. Though Gaelic games and music grew ever more popular, the language itself remained in an ambiguous position. While some of its partisans could be written off as antiquarians better at home in a Society for Creative Anachronism, many more touched a truly sensitive nerve. By 1989 a best-selling history of the country by J. J. Lee held that at the root of the failure of enterprise lay a lack of self-belief, traceable directly to the loss of the ancestral language.[9] This thesis, which might have been laughed to scorn a decade earlier, was now widely quoted on the airways of a national broadcasting station which many – though not Lee himself – held respon-sible for bringing Ireland into line with international consumerism.

In the decades following the 1960s, the Catholic church implemented much of the aggiornamento. *The censorship of books and films was relaxed, often with the support of the more intellectual priests and nuns. Although individual bishops were still capable of giving errant politicians "the belt of a crozier", most religious debates were internal to the Catholic church, which was confronted with a catastrophic fall in vocations to the religious life. That church retained its controlling interest in most secondary schools, but fewer and fewer priests and nuns could be spared for teaching work: meanwhile, the new community schools, staffed by lay personnel, continued to multiply. The encyclical of Pope Paul VI outlawing contra-ception in 1968 generated much acrimonious debate, but it soon became clear that a new* à la carte *Catholicism was being practised: between 1960 and 1990 the size of the average Irish family was cut by half from 4.6 to 2.3 children.*

Sexual behaviour, within and outside marriage, became markedly more liberal; and many rights denied to women – such as the right to work in the civil service after marriage – were restored. The special position of the

Catholic church in de Valera's constitution was removed by popular consent in 1972, by the self-same electorate which sent Ireland enthusiastically into the EEC. One of the leaders of Catholic opinion, Jeremiah Newman, argued that adaptation to the new reality of life in an industrialized Europe would test Irish mettle to the end of the century. For Newman (who would prove to be a highly traditionalist bishop of Limerick) the question was "how to construct a new culture in a new context, a culture that will at once be new and relevant in that context and at the same time preserve the best of the old. It means a culture that will be considerably industrial yet without losing what is of lasting value in our rural social fabric . . . It means a culture that will be considerably secular yet without losing our religious persuasions".[10] His conclusion was that religion would be more and more a private election rather than a matter of social decorum. The logical inference was that this might produce a more thoughtful sort of Catholic, but that there would be fewer practising. Henceforth, those who went into the religious life would choose it in a most deliberate and conscientious way, rather than seeking social prestige or career opportunity.

One result was that throughout the 1970s and 1980s many Catholic priests and nuns spoke increasingly of their "option for the poor". Some adopted radical positions on social questions concerning travellers, the unemployed, or the rights of children. Many others went to the mission fields of the "developing" world, where they made their own comparisons with the situation in their home country: a significant number returned with new ideas about the democratization of parish life or the need for clergy to enter the regular workforce rather than live as a group apart. These persons, a force for renewal, became a thorn in the side of many a cautious bishop. The spectacle of nuns being jostled by policemen outside the American embassy or of priests being arrested on demonstrations became commonplace.

When the US President Ronald Reagan visited Ireland in 1984, the public response was lukewarm in contrast to that accorded Kennedy, despite the visitor's sentiment that he was "coming home" to the family seat at Ballyporeen. This was largely due to the caustic commentaries on US foreign policy by radical priests and nuns, some of whom had been abused or even imprisoned by CIA-sponsored dictatorships in the Third World. The huge outpouring of support for Irish singer Bob Geldof's Live-Aid musicals for the relief of famine in Africa owed something to folk memories of the Great Hunger, but much also to the campaigns of returned missionaries. Confronted with awful poverty in debt-ridden states, many Irish volunteers reexamined their own motives, preferring to promote social change in these societies rather than seeking religious conversions. A nation whose missionaries had gone forth to teach the poor of the developing world now found many returning with the news that the "Third World" had much to teach them.[11] The "liberation theology" pioneered in Latin America was a major factor, prompting much talk of two churches (an ecclesiocracy of empurpled prelates versus a people's devotional church), though the case should not be overstated, since many priests and nuns remained conservative while some bishops were social radicals.

The response of the institutional church to the loosening of its teaching authority was a call for charismatic renewal, which came to a climax in 1979 with the visit of Pope John Paul II. He preached against the IRA, abortion, divorce and contraception: and, before one million souls in the Phoenix Park, he called on the faithful to remain loyal to their creed in face of secularist attack. The right of married couples to use contraceptives as an aspect of family planning had been upheld by the Supreme Court in 1973: now the focus shifted elsewhere, as strict Catholics demanded that the legal ban on abortion be written into the constitution by special referendum, something which was done after a bitterly acrimonious debate in 1983. The majority Fianna Fáil party was still not ready for a full-scale confrontation with the church in order to separate its domain from that of the state.

Three years later in 1986 the Fine Gael/Labour coalition, led by the social democrat Garret FitzGerald, attempted by referendum to rescind the ban on divorce. The conservatives won again: women, in particular, were said to have been frightened at the implications for property and inheritance in a society of limited means where divorce might easily be available. Foreign correspondents who watched a small majority for divorce turn into a modest majority against it remained unclear as to whether Catholic theory or pragmatic considerations explained the result. In the following decade, Fianna Fáil (now in coalition government with Labour) would confront the clergy on a range of issues, from control of schools to the running of hospitals: when in 1993 they decriminalized homosexuality in a vote of parliament, there was so little dissent that many felt sure that a reform of the law against divorce would not be far off.

What had not been resolved, however, was the question: what kind of society was to replace the pious, mainly rural and Catholic community of an earlier period? Successive government leaders, though they talked glibly of pluralism, never defined it with any clarity. To many it seemed no more than a buzz-word for administrative convenience: if the Catholic ethos of many hospitals seemed under threat, so did the Protestant ethos of still others, both in danger of making way for a soulless, characterless health-service whose governing principle was a value-free efficiency.

Similar debates were conducted on educational reform. That "Catholic ethos" which had pervaded schools for two centuries had never been clearly defined, largely because it was assumed to be unproblematic and all-pervasive. What was to take its place was not at all obvious. Traditional constraints of Catholicism had been set aside by the post-1960s generation: by the early 1990s many church congregations in Dublin were dominated by persons over forty years of age, and that in a city with a markedly youthful demography. The old pieties had been absolutist: in the vacuum left after their breakdown, it became obvious that exponents of the "liberal agenda" had no alternative philosophy beyond vague nostra about "growth" and "GNP". Even in the discipline of economics, some intrepid commentators began to ask the politicians whether they were running a country or just an economy. In the philosophical vacuum, it was all too easy for a "cowboy" ethic to flourish, often to the strains of country-and-western music.[12] To some critics it seemed that the Irish, a most sociable and friendly people, still had not managed to create a truly civil society.

Many people – probably a clear majority – were better fed, educated, housed and cared for than ever before: yet by the 1990s three hundred thousand were unemployed and one in every three lived below the official poverty line. For them the loss of the old coherent codes would prove especially traumatic, for they had few material comforts to make the new spiritual emptiness bearable. This, along with the lack of employment opportunities, high taxation and the burgeoning debt crisis, may have prompted many young people to decide that there was no future for them in the country. Emigration, which had halted during a brief period of affluence in the 1970s, began again to assume chronic proportions, with up to 40,000 leaving in some years. Entire villages in the west of Ireland now had few, if any, inhabitants in their twenties and thirties. Instead, in the absence of that middle generation, the very old began to retreat into a world of nostalgic fantasy, while the very young succumbed often to a rather mindless hedonism. Yet, for all that, the conviction remained that it was from the younger generation that answers must finally come. When many of the more recent emigrants began to return in the 1990s from countries where recessions left alternative employment hard to find, there was a perverse kind of hope that their experiences and energy might have given this generation the impetus to change life at home for the better.

What made such transformation problematic was the obdurate, unyielding nature of the problem of Northern Ireland, a state which seemed unreformable from within or without. To the modernizing élites in the republic, as to public opinion overseas, the opposition of northern unionists to the ecumenical spirit of the 1960s had seemed the worst form of traditionalism. "We are now approaching Aldergrove Airport, Belfast", went a comedians' joke in Dublin: "Please put your watches back three hundred years". Though the immediate portents from the Lemass-O'Neill meetings of 1964 had been good, a more ominous response came from the unionist community, one third of whose members pronounced themselves opposed to any renewed contacts with the Dublin government.[13] When a younger, more self-confident generation of nationalists initiated the Northern Ireland Civil Rights Association (NICRA) in 1967, modelled on Martin Luther King's non-violent movement in the US, the unionist answer was to baton the marchers off the streets. A mildly reformist set of proposals to eliminate discrimination against Catholics in housing, local government and the franchise, led to the toppling of Terence O'Neill from the prime ministry; and by 1969 the British Army had been drafted into Northern Ireland, initially to protect Catholic homes from Protestant gangs.

At the time, a wag wrote tauntingly on a Belfast wall: "IRA = Irish Ran Away". By 1971, however, the same IRA was doing a roaring business, training recruits in the wake of internment without trial. In January of the following year, thirteen unarmed civil rights marchers were shot dead by British paratroopers in Derry on "Bloody Sunday"; and later that year, the IRA killed eleven with bombs in public places on "Bloody Friday". The death-toll began to mount fast. Against this lurid backdrop, the accession of the Republic to the European Economic Community or the ending of compulsory Irish in its schools, seemed events from a different order of reality. To some northern nationalists they must have seemed like further confirmation that the south would betray them and the traditional insignia of national sovereignty. To many southerners, the north seemed a Neanderthal place, caught in a historical time-warp, inhabited by paranoiacs who couldn't trust one another, much less the outside world. The south liked to think of itself as superior, affluent, urbane and forward-looking; the north, according to such thinking, was trapped in a woeful, repetitive past. Although Taoiseach Jack Lynch in the earliest phase of the "Troubles" moved troops nearer to the border and made rhetorical references to the defence of "our people", the longer-term view was that northern nationalists were not really "our people" at all. In theory, of course, this was because such a phrase in good republican parlance should apply to all in the north, separated unionist brethren as well as nationalists; in practice, it was because many southerners had long despaired of accommodating either northern side and simply called down a plague on both houses.[14]

The citizens of the republic had been enjoying a rare period of affluence when Northern Ireland erupted into violence: they feared that the spill-over of such disorder into the south could only threaten their new material well-being. That well-being was, by any previous standard, spectacular. In the 1960s alone the standard of living had doubled. Between 1962 and 1982 Irish industrial growth was the fastest in Europe (admittedly, the baseline from which it started was low, but this only added to the sense of momentum gained). So there was no serious solidarity with the Catholics across the border: in the new, emerging Ireland religion was to be a private affair. Hence, when Jack Lynch dismissed two senior government ministers on suspicion of gun-running (at a time when some people felt that northern Catholics needed arms in the face of a loyalist community armed to its teeth), it soon became clear that there was more support for than opposition to the Taoiseach's hands-off policy. The general attitude to the North in the republic was not unlike the approach to the Irish language: make us pure, Lord, but not quite yet (and certainly not if such purity entails financial or intellectual sacrifice).

In 1972 the political scientist Richard Rose pronounced the Northern Ireland problem intractable: it was one of the few trouble-spots on earth, he said, for which there was no imaginable solution.[15] What followed bore that assessment out: at some point or another almost every remedy has been tried – every one, that is, except a British withdrawal. 1972 was also the year which saw the old regime at Stormont prorogued in favour of direct rule from London: in the following year a power-sharing executive, involving both unionist politicians and the nationalist Social Democratic and Labour Party (SDLP) was set up to fill a political vacuum which had been exploited by terrorists of all sides. It was brought down, however, in 1974 by a loyalist workers' strike, which the British Labour government failed to confront. That same year, over thirty people were killed in the republic by UVF bombs planted, in Dublin and Monaghan, with the alleged collusion of British operatives. If the objective was to panic the coalition government into ever more draconian legislation, it succeeded: at one point in the mid-1970s the government had rebel songs banned from Irish national airwaves; and it opened a file on the editor of The Irish Press (who had been incautious enough to publish letters from republicans critical of the new censorship).

Through the 1970s a balance of terror seemed to be all that either side achieved: the IRA bombed British cities in scenes of horrific carnage, while the security forces perfected techniques of surveillance, espionage and "grassing" (the work of paid informers who provided courts with uncorroborated evidence concocted by the police). In 1981 ten IRA men starved themselves

*to death in a desperate attempt to gain political status within the prison
system: the emotions unleashed by this even in Northern Ireland brought
hundreds of recruits flowing into the Provisional Sinn Féin/IRA movement.
Only a tiny minority could be trained for military activities: the remainder
were drawn into the political process, heralding the rise of the modern Sinn
Féin as a political party, second only to the SDLP within the northern
minority and the largest single party on Belfast City Council. Thereafter,
the IRA/Sinn Féin went forward on a two-track policy "with an armalite
in one hand and a ballot-box in the other", one result of which was the
election of Gerry Adams as MP for West Belfast. In the south, however,
news of the hunger strikes was downplayed by the national broadcasting
station, probably unnecessarily, for the popular reaction was one of bafflement.*

*After the hunger strikes Sinn Féin won almost 42 per cent of the
nationalist vote in Northern Ireland, and relations between Taoiseach
Charles Haughey and the British Prime Minister Margaret Thatcher
soured. In an attempt to reopen debate about the future, the next Taoiseach,
Garret FitzGerald, launched a New Ireland Forum in May 1983, at
which the Republic's parties, the SDLP and some of the unionists gave
evidence. It also heard submissions from a range of politicians, ecclesiastics,
academics, writers and so on. Its report went far – some said too far – in
acknowledging the integrity of the unionist tradition, about which it had
more to say than, for example, about the rights of Irish speakers. It listed
three possible options, (i) a united Ireland, which would necessitate a
replacement for the 1937 constitution, (ii) federation of the two parts of
Ireland, (iii) a system of joint authority with Dublin and London together
responsible for the north. As the Irish had radically revised and reduced the
aspirations of Irish nationalism, it was assumed that the British would
revise their nostra too and attempt to bring the unionists onside. In the
event Mrs. Thatcher said "out, out, out" to all three proposals, much to the
chagrin of the republic and of international commentators. Indeed, so
damaged was she by the ensuing adverse publicity that her advisers urged
her to adopt a more conciliatory line.*

*Accordingly, when the leader of a Fine Gael/Labour coalition, Garret
FitzGerald, signed an Anglo-Irish Agreement with Mrs. Thatcher at
Hillsborough in 1985, there was an audible sigh of relief. The right thing
had been done by the SDLP and northern nationalism: henceforth the
Dublin government would have a recognized consultative voice (though not
a decision-making one) in the conduct of northern policy, and violations of
the civil rights of the minority could be closely monitored. Unionist opinion
was outraged by this unprecedented recognition of a legitimate southern*

interest. Many nationalists on the ground complained that the agreement made little difference to their actual living conditions, but that in the process Dublin had conferred legitimacy on the British interest in Northern Ireland.[16]

In the years that followed, and particularly during the Sinn Féin/SDLP peace initiative of 1993-4, the British government repeatedly stressed that it had no long term strategic or selfish interest in staying in Ireland and would do so only as long as a majority in Northern Ireland wanted it that way. At the same time, war-weary nationalists began to admit that something less than a united Ireland would satisfy them now. They had never expected much from the republic, a place which had often seemed as hostile as London to their aspirations. At the start of the recent phase of "Troubles" in 1968, only 40% of them had supported a united Ireland (though less than 20% were satisfied with the existing constitutional position: which begged a question – what did they want?). By 1993 a large number still pronounced themselves indifferent to final unity with Dublin, but even more disenchanted than ever with the northern state, whose troubles had cost more than 3000 lives in the interim. Though some demographers estimated that Catholic nationalists might outbreed the Protestant unionists by the year 2040, this was sheer fantasy: the contraceptive pill was doing far more to curtail the number of Catholics than the loyalist death-squads. As Northern Catholics grew ever more confident and sophisticated, it seemed unlikely that this group would ever evolve a homogeneous politics or cultural philosophy: they were, in the words of one commentator, "in search of a state".[17] *Moreover, it was very possible that by 2040 the religious and cultural pieties of both sides would have been so diluted by international consumerism as to render any model which sought to reconcile them useless and redundant.*

Through all the "Troubles" Northern Catholics held their heads high: they won a sympathetic hearing in the world, thanks to the astute leadership of John Hume. The IRA, by a combination of ruthlessness and intelligence, remained one of the most feared guerrilla movements in modern history. Though it claimed to be a non-sectarian movement eager to embrace Protestants in the event of a British withdrawal, many of its actions seemed to belie that rhetoric – such as the massacre of eleven Protestants at a service for Remembrance Day in Enniskillen in 1987. For their part, the Sinn Féin/IRA leadership made full political capital out of an alleged "shoot to kill" policy of the British Army in pursuit of unarmed Provisionals: when the British policy officer, John Stalker, probed too closely into this case, he was relieved of his duties. Equally corrupting of due legal process was the widespread use of "supergrasses" from within the nationalist (and, to a lesser extent, unionist) communities: in return for betraying comrades, some rather unsavoury individuals were offered immunity from law and start-up cash for a life elsewhere.

The newly-politicized Sinn Féin/IRA axis exploited such weaknesses to the full before a British audience increasingly ready to believe ill of its police and army. The growing doubts about the safety of convictions for terrorist bombings in the mid-1970s led in time to the release of the Guildford Four and Birmingham Six, after sustained campaigns by their families and friends, much aided by priests, nuns and conscientious members of the British legal profession. For all of their sufferings, nationalists generally conveyed the impression of a group operating to a clear agenda and to some purpose. It was the unionist political leadership which, again and again, gave the sense of an insecure people on the verge of some final betrayal, forever at war with self and circumstance. Unionists excited far more sympathy in the republic (which they nonetheless continued to distrust) than in Britain. This was because the objective interests of the élites in the northern and southern states were now at one.

If southerners liked to think of themselves as happy Europeans who had long outgrown the battles of the past which still engrossed their cousins north of the border, there was much truth in that analysis but also some strain. For they had not so much solved as shelved the problem of creating a liberal nationalism. In their period of national revival, they had identified as essentially Irish precisely those elements of the national heritage which they now seemed most anxious to discard; and, through the years of the northern "Troubles", they had allowed a small, tightly-organized cadre of broadcasters to wish all messy, tribal nationalisms away. Coverage of Northern Ireland through most of the 1980s had substituted a wish – that nationalisms would evaporate – for a fulfillment. The collapse of Stalinism in eastern Europe in 1989 left these commentators in shock. The reemergence of nationalism as a force to be reckoned with meant that the question of how to achieve a humane modernization of national traditions (as opposed to their callous liquidation) loomed more pressingly than ever.

Moreover, the debt crisis which sapped enterprise in the south meant that its citizens still owed more per capita than those of Mexico – and the politicians who had squandered the monies loaned by bankers during the spate of elections between 1977 and 1987 had left no major infrastructures with which to service the debts. At one point all the money collected in personal taxation went to service the interest payment component of the debt.[18] Given that there had been a doubling of jobs in the public service from 1966 to 1985, it was obvious where much of the borrowed money had gone, but there was often little for these employees to do and poor promotional prospects in a service doomed to cutbacks in future decades. Most young people still faced a future as likely to involve a job in London, Dusseldorf or New York as in Dublin, Galway or Cork. They were better educated than ever and by no means convinced that such a prospect was more unfair than that which many east-coast Americans have of being transplanted to work in some western state: but, through all the debates, there remained the strong sense that Ireland was a good place, a preferable place, in which to live and raise a family. Nobody could quite say why: encomia on the "quality of life" were often vague. Perhaps what drew people back to Ireland was the conviction that in a Europe filled with countries which have a glorious past, the Irish are among the very few still exercised by the prospect of an interesting future, by a belief that everything in the country might yet be remade.

That belief was shown to have some basis with the election to the presidency in 1990 of Mary Robinson, a civil rights lawyer and feminist, a woman with a record of speaking out on difficult topics such as censorship, sexual freedom and travellers' rights. She expanded the role and symbolic meaning of her largely ceremonial office, in a series of publicized visits to Buckingham Palace (never before graced by an Irish Head of State), West Belfast (a virtual no-go area to most members of the Dublin élite), Inis Meáin (where she started her campaign) and Somalia (where, in a bold linkage to the Great Famine, she told the Somalis that they were the Irish of Africa, before proceeding on to the United Nations to plead for international aid on their behalf). Mrs. Robinson's election had a galvanizing effect upon all political parties, compelling them to put forward more female candidates: of equal importance was her return to traditional ideas of the nation, such as the notion that Irish people include not only the five million on the island but the many millions more overseas, whom she visited regularly and for whom she kept a light burning in the window of her official residence. In her continuing focus on the "Third World" and on Irish anticipations of that experience, she reinvigorated many debates of the revivalist generation.[19]

All in all she presented another instance of the classic Irish radical in deceptively conservative clothing. She effected a brilliant reconciliation at the level of symbolic politics of the best native traditions with a thoroughly renovated modern consciousness. The problem which was solved by the shapers of Irish literature but unresolved in the world of realpolitik *found in her a national leader who portended a resolution in a fashion that might be meaningful for all inhabitants of the island.*

Thirty-Two

Under Pressure – The Writer and Society 1960–90

Although the Irish Renaissance was largely a celebratory affair, in tone and in mood, it nonetheless shaped a notion of the artist as a person at war with the social consensus, a crusader for some ideal which existed more often in the past or in the future. No matter how ferocious the critique mounted by a writer, he or she could always justify that ferocity by pointing to the patriotic motives which underwrote it.

Independence had not resolved any of these tensions: rather it exacerbated them. Censorship, ostracism and emigration became the lot of the more accomplished artists, proving to Samuel Beckett's satisfaction, at any rate, that the Irish nation never "gave a fart in its corduroys for any form of art whatsoever, whether before the Union or after".[1] With so many modernist masterpieces banned, Irish readers often had to content themselves with cowboy tales. These proved hugely popular with a readership which may have identified with the improvisations of a frontier society: certainly, the recurring legend of a seeming rebel who turns out on inspection to be a pillar of society seemed to sort well with the national condition after 1921.

Yet the underlying paradox was that by censoring modernism the Irish authorities maintained it at the level of an heroic opposition, long after it had begun to lose that status in other countries and especially in the wake of World War Two. Though censorship made it harder than ever for writers to make a living in Ireland, it also managed to endow the profession with a conspiratorial glamour: the writer was easily seen as a subversive, a magician, a user of dark hidden powers. Poets such as Austin Clarke maintained a sharply antagonistic commentary on the timidity of political leaders afraid to enter a Protestant church for the funeral of Douglas Hyde: yet the more sensitive among them feared that the muse might be coarsened by the constant practice of satire which was, as Patrick Kavanagh lamented, "unfruitful prayer".[2]

Deep down, the writers yearned for a *rapprochement* with the new order: yet the fate of the gifted young writer John McGahern, whose novel *The Dark* was banned and whose teaching contract was not renewed in 1965, made such an adjustment seem difficult. The young had already opened themselves to the world of rock-and-roll, in the conviction that it would prove quite compatible with native tradition. If sexual intercourse began in England in 1963, as Philip Larkin had it, it came also to Ireland in that year with the rattle of the *bodhrán* and the beat of the portable radio. John Montague played the role of an Irish Larkin as its somewhat wistful laureate:

The Siege of Mullingar, 1963

At the Fleadh Cheoil in Mullingar
There were two sounds, the breaking
Of glass, and the background pulse
Of music. Young girls roamed
The streets with eager faces,
Shoving for men. Bottles in
Hand, they rowed out a song:
Puritan Ireland's dead and gone,
A myth of O'Connor and O'Faoláin.

In the early morning the lovers
Lay on both sides of the canal
Listening on Sony transistors
To the agony of Pope John.
Yet it didn't seem strange, or blasphemous,
This ground bass of death and
Resurrection, as we strolled along:
Puritan Ireland's dead and gone,
A myth of O'Connor and O'Faoláin.[3]

It took official Ireland and its loyal opposition of writers a few more years to catch the new mood. By 1965 the posture of "inherited dissent" adopted by artists was being castigated by younger critics as a superannuated stereotype, which appealed to "forces of rejection" rather than "forces of affirmation".[4] Writers were enjoined to engage with a new, confident, inclusive Ireland of advance factories, material affluence, liberal education and a self-reforming church. The nay-saying which had once been a challenging form of address was now dismissed as a dead formula; yet even after the censors had been removed, many writers continued to act as if they were still under ban, and portraits of a repressive priesthood still dominated fiction. It took a liberal priest, Peter Connolly of Maynooth, to argue that with the lifting of censorship a truly national criticism could again become a possibility.

In 1967 the Minister for Justice introduced legislation to allow for the "unbanning" of books after a period of twelve years, and thereby thousands of volumes were freed to enter the Irish market.[5] Henceforth, every bookshop would have a well-stocked section featuring "Irish Writing" on permanent display. Many Irish artists who had begun their careers overseas opted to come home and claim their share in the new riches. A returned Pádraic Colum pronounced himself delighted by the smiling faces of young men and women openly holding hands in the city streets.

Yet, among the artists certain uncompromising souls sensed something more than a truce in the war between Bohemian and bourgeois: the defeat of Irish modernism itself. This had been a movement which assumed that the artist must live at an angle to society: now, even the most scathing assaults on that society by people like Patrick Kavanagh and Kate O'Brien were being transformed into facile testimonies to the tolerance of the Irish mind and, worse still, into weekly television entertainments. If in the 1890s a generation of Irish artists had returned to Dublin from a London which seemed determined to reduce them to the role of mere entertainers, now in the 1960s another generation, whose members had trained as artists in foreign lands, found its writers reduced to the status of "gas bloody men" on prime-time television.

The stage Irishman, a fabrication of the British folk mind, might almost be a thing of the past: but the native élites had replaced him with an equally spurious caricature, the stage writer. Doubtless, the legendary drinking feats of Brendan Behan, Flann O'Brien and Patrick Kavanagh had given credence and a prehistory to the stereotype: perhaps their drinking was an attempt to assert in pubs a *machismo* which the very act of writing had put into some doubt, given that theirs was a culture in which words were seen as feminine and deeds as masculine. However, it was the unprecedented affluence of the 1960s and early 1970s which saw the widespread emergence of the phenomenon, a phenomenon by no means peculiar to Ireland. Pondering the numbers of writers in residence on campuses, the American critic Irving Howe observed rather wistfully of their easy domestication: "Modernism must always struggle, but never quite triumph – and in the end it must struggle in order not to triumph".[6] His fear was that in the US, as elsewhere, the bracing enmity between Bohemian and bourgeois had given way to wet embraces.

So it happened in Ireland. The Fianna Fáil government announced a tax holiday for artists, encouraging many English and American authors to settle on the island. In the event, most who came were purveyors of pot-boilers and airport-novels, whose earnings were vast enough to justify living for at least part of the year under rainy Irish skies and making the promised financial killing. The real effect, however, was on the status and self-image of Irish artists, who now felt free to come in from the cold. Even in the bad old days, Kavanagh had jibed that the standing army of Irish poets never fell below five thousand, but that number now seemed conservative as the bards declaimed their verses in the pubs. Each poet was granted a ritual, often drunken, appearance on television; summer schools resounded to their voices; and some government ministers even appeared in newspaper photographs with artists whose work they had once helped to suppress. The more disreputable a writer had once been, the higher (it seemed) the fee now commanded. These newly-visible Bohemians embodied for the Irish élites all those qualities which fifty years of money-grubbing had led the Paudeens to reject in themselves – lyricism, prodigality, spirituality, open-heartedness. There was an element of repressive tolerance at work in this process, alongside a very genuine admiration of the artist's intrepidity of mind. In the climate so created, it was predictable that some more biddable types would prefer to enact in public the role of writer than to confront in private the anguish of actual writing.

One way of avoiding these pressures was the oldest remedy of all: exile. The novelist Brian Moore left his native Belfast during World War Two, took out Canadian citizenship and, after years of struggle, published *The Lonely Passion of Judith Hearne*. It evoked the quiet desperation of drab Belfast lives in a scrupulous rendition of provincialism of mind and body. Thereafter, Moore tended to write cross-cultural novels, often spliced between an Irish and a foreign setting. A similar technique characterizes novels by William Trevor, for instance *Felicia's Journey*, which cuts between the British midlands and a rural Irish community: but this author, who was born in Cork and has done most of his writing in England, is most well-known in Ireland for *The Ballroom of Romance* and *Fools of Fortune*, the first a study in middle-aged disappointment, while the second is a chronicle set in Cork during the war of independence. Both Moore and Trevor are rightly renowned for the cool, crafted clarity of their prose, their wry, wistful ironies, and their use of telling detail; and each has won a substantial overseas readership for many other books of high quality which have nothing to do with Ireland.

Throughout this period Samuel Beckett remained in Paris, a last surviving exponent of the monastic discipline of high modernism: his example inspired many of the less compromising sort, poets such as John Montague, Richard Murphy, Derek Mahon, Seamus Heaney, 'Heaney', Brendan Kennelly Nuala ní Dhomhnaill; playwrights like Brian Friel, Tom Murphy and Thomas Kilroy; novelists including Francis Stuart, John Banville and Máirtín Ó Cadhain. This is not to say that the authors named all endorsed his apparent indifference to society: but it is to suggest that his elevation of the *estranged artist* as a model had immense implications. It fostered a healthy scepticism about the politicians' wet embraces, all the more necessary when in 1980 the Taoiseach Charles Haughey (who had also devised the tax holiday) announced the foundation of *Aosdána*, a self-electing élite of about 150 artists, who would have a basic income guaranteed by the state as well as the prestige of membership.

What followed, however, was in the case of many artists a remorseless privatization of experience, and an art which located its interest in the pathology of the alienated individual. This may explain why so many Irish poets in the period fought shy of politics and of social issues. The decade after the foundation of *Aosdána* saw hunger strikes in the north, vast unemployment in the south, the wrongful imprisonment of suspects in British jails, and the divisive divorce and abortion referenda, yet these events passed without finding their laureate. It would be difficult to imagine a Yeats or an O'Casey failing to use such material. Only a vulgar cynic would accuse the writers of being bought by the politicians for, being a self-elective body, *Aosdána* operates under no direct political constraint, its members being theoretically free to write whatever they wish: but in practice writers were a lot less critical of Haughey than poets like Clarke and Kavanagh had been of Costello or de Valera. Perhaps Haughey's own rather ambiguous relationship with the Irish middle class, which thought of him as rather too raffish for its tastes, gave him a special appeal for artists; or perhaps they were understandably grateful for what was, after all, an imaginative scheme which undid much of the damage caused by the censorship.

Thomas Kinsella was one of the very few artists who refused an invitation to membership of *Aosdána*. An Irish-language scholar himself, he must have smiled wryly at the ambiguity of the title, *aos* meaning a "band" and *dána* either "artistic" or "audacious" (depending on the context). As a student of Eliot and Auden, however, he was also aware of the need to marry modernity to native tradition. When he was a younger man, he had by day earned his living as a civil servant in that Department of Finance which opened up Ireland for overseas trade and investment; by night he wrote poems which worried that Ireland might

> . . . have exchanged
> A trenchcoat playground for a gombeen jungle.
>
> Around the corner, in an open square,
> I came upon the sombre monuments
> That bear their names: MacDonagh & McBride
> Merchants; Connolly's Commercial Arms.[7]

This was not at all like Montague's parody of Yeats on Romantic Ireland: it was more a weary parody of the consumerist present, in a grocer's republic which could never live up to the Ireland of Easter 1916.

Even after a decade of apparent economic success in the 1960s, Kinsella's voice remained troubled, unsure. If one of the cultural contradictions of capitalism was its tendency to produce "functionaries by day and hedonists by night",[8] he seemed to reverse that process, his working career a commitment to that materialistic Ireland which his poems did so much to question:

> Robed in spattered iron
> At the harbour mouth she stands, Productive Investment,
> And beckons the nations through our gold half-door:
> Lend me your wealth, your cunning and your drive,
> Your arrogant refuse; Let my people serve them
> Bottled fury in our new hotels,
> While native businessmen and managers
> Drift with them, chatting, over to the window
> To show them our growing city, give them a feeling
> Of what is possible; our labour pool,
> The tax concessions to foreign capital,

> How to get a nice estate though German,
> Even collect some of our better young artists.[9]

Kinsella's project was representative of a whole generation which sought – as Yeats had at the start of the century – to free Ireland from provincialism by an exacting criticism and European pose. Now, however, there was the added complication of Yeats to be coped with. One way of fighting free of that awesome legacy was to set up shop under the sign of Eliot:

> Domestic Autumn, like an animal
> Long used to handling by those countrymen,
> Rubs her kind hide against the bedroom wall . . .[10]

or else under the sign of Auden:

> I nonetheless inflict, endure,
> Tedium, intracordal hurt,
> The sting of memory's quick, the drear
> Uprooting, burying, prising apart.
> Of loves a strident adolescent
> Spent in doubt and varity.[11]

The influence of Auden on Kinsella, Michael Longley and Derek Mahon was at least as extensive as that of Kavanagh. And there was good reason for this. Auden was, along with Philip Larkin, the artist of post-imperial England, a land of anticlimax and antimacassars, evoked with a desperately self-deprecating suburban wit. Their tone seemed strangely suitable for those Irish poets born too late to partake in the heroic phase, either of Ireland or of modern poetry. By a brutally revealing paradox, Auden's England was an appropriate model for yet another tradition winding down into self-irony. In this, as in so much else, Ireland was disappointing all by turning into a botched version of England. As Montague observed in "Speech for an Ideal Irish Election":

> Who today asks for more
> – Smoke of battle blown aside –
> Than the struggle with casual
> Graceless unheroic things.
> The greater task of swimming
> Against a slackening tide?[12]

In much the same mode, "Casement's Funeral" by Richard Murphy was not just a weary rebuke of those "Rebels in silk hats now" who "exploit the grave with an old comrade's speech",[13] but also a self-confessed example of such exploitation, a superb parody of "Parnell's Funeral" by Yeats. Parody proved itself to be an appropriate mode for trapped post-Yeatsian minds, unsure whether they could engage in acts of radical creation. The new Ireland seemed like a parody of the old.

Where some writers could find continuity in Irish tradition, and a seemingly stress-free carry-over of Gaelic traditions into English, Kinsella remained troubled by the gaps in Irish narrative, and specifically by the traumatic loss of Irish in the nineteenth century. In a 1971 lecture, symptomatically titled "The Divided Mind", he explained that he did not feel fully at home in the English language; that for him Yeats represented the beginning of the Irish line in English; that "silence is the real condition of Irish literature in the nineteenth century"; and that further back beyond that is "a world suddenly full of life and voices, the voices of poets who expect to be heard and understood and memorized", the Hidden Ireland of the ancestral language:

> In all of this I recognize a great inheritance and, simultaneously, a great loss. The inheritance is certainly mine, but only at two enormous removes – across a century's silence and through an exchange of worlds. The greatness of the loss is measured not only by the substance of Irish literature itself, but also by the intensity with which we know it was shared; it has an air of continuity and shared history which is precisely what is missing from Irish literature, in English or Irish, in the nineteenth century and today. I recognize that I stand on one side of a great rift, and can feel the discontinuity in myself. It is a matter of people and places as well as writing – of coming from a broken and uprooted family, of being drawn to those who share my origins and finding that we cannot share our lives.[14]

Like Seamus Heaney and many others, Kinsella tried to bridge that rift by producing translations from Irish poetry and prose: his version of *The Táin* is justly famous, as are his laconic English translations in *An Duanaire: Poems of the Dispossessed* (dedicated with a fine sense of irony to T. K. Whitaker, the Irish speaker who suggested the project). Such translations had an undisputed value in the early years of the Irish renaissance, when readers yearned for a glimpse of the poetry hidden in a language which they had never been encouraged to learn. By the late 1970s, however, and well before Heaney's *Sweeney Astray* (a version of *Buile Shuibhne*) and *An Duanaire* were published, it was possible for

Michael Hartnett to allege that translations from Irish were often conscience-stricken gestures by poets who felt a sense of frustration, or even guilt, at producing their major work in English.

Hartnett bid "A Farewell to English" in 1975, in the course of which he derided Yeats for his use of token Gaelic phrases gleaned from Aogán Ó Rathaille:

> Our commis-chefs attend and learn the trade,
> bemoan the scraps of Gaelic that they know:
> add to a simple Anglo-Saxon stock
> Cuchulainn's marrow-bones to marinate,
> a dash of Ó Rathaille simmered slow,
> a glass of University hic-haec-hoc:
> sniff and stand back and proudly offer you
> the celebrated Anglo-Irish stew.[15]

Hartnett's retreat into Irish-language poetry (in which he never quite emulated the quality of his English work) lasted almost a decade, during which he discovered that it may not be a question of a writer choosing a language, so much as a case of the language choosing to work out its characteristic genius through a writer.

For his part, Thomas Kinsella saved himself this detour, when he announced that Irish no longer had the intellectual subtlety or density of reference to sustain a modern sensibility:

> To write in Irish instead of English would mean the loss of contact with my own present – abandonment of the language I was bred in for one I believe to be dying. It would also mean forfeiting a certain possible scope of language; for English has a greater scope than an Irish which is not able to handle all the affairs of my life.[16]

In view of the high order of Kinsella's achievement in English, this was hardly a surprising conclusion: yet it must not be generalized, for the work of Seán Ó Ríordáin attests that Irish is still a language calibrated to certain kinds of modern sensibility. Anyway, the idea of a necessary choice between languages and traditions may seem excessively melodramatic, given the fact that Hopkins and Eliot were among the strongest influences on Ó Ríordáin. Stronger than either of these, however, was the imprint of Joyce.

Ó Ríordáin's mind was saturated with the symbols of the Roman Catholicism which he had decided to reject; and, like Joyce, he put the repudiated terminology of theology to use in evolving a personal aesthetic theory. If Joyce spoke of epiphanies as moments of sudden spiritual manifestation, Ó Ríordáin wrote of the *beo-gheit* which leaves a person *fé ghné eile* (under a different aspect). If Joyce annexed the Eucharist for his *epicleti*, Ó Ríordáin stole the notion of *Faoistin* (confession) and *Peaca* (sin), reworking these words until they became aesthetic terms. Joyce's surrender to "the whatness of a thing" was recapitulated in Ó Ríordáin's desire to achieve "instress" with his objects. For Ó Ríordáin in his poems, *I* becomes *Thou* and every opposite is revealed to be a double – male blends with female; the poet with his *anima*; and Ó Ríordáin's Gaelic poems may also be seen as an experiment with the English poetic tradition.

There are moments when creation for this poet is indistinguishable from the process of pillaging English, in much the same way as the *anthropophagus* writers of Latin America in the 1920s cannibalized Spanish:

> A Ghaeilge im pheannsa
> Do shinsear ar chaillís?
> An teanga bhocht thabhartha
> Gan sloinne tú, a theanga?
>
> An leatsa na briathra
> Nuair a dheinimse peaca?
> Nuair is rúnmhar mo chroíse
> An tusa a thostann?[17]
>
> O Gaelic in my pen
> Have you lost your ancestry?
> Are you a poor illegitimate,
> Without a surname, O Language.
>
> Are the verbs yours
> When I commit a sin?
> When my heart is secret,
> Is it you who are quiet?

The poet who began by writing sprung rhythms in imitation of Hopkins finally concedes that his ideas are often stolen from the very language which he seeks to escape:

Ag súrac atáirse
Ón striapach allúrach
Is sínim chugat smaointe
A ghoideas-sa uaithi.[18]

You are escaping from
The foreign harlot
And I proffer to you the ideas
Which I stole from her.

The chauvinism underlying the word "harlot" might offend many; but
in general terms, the lines are a graphic illustration of the cultural trap
described by Daniel Corkery as facing every Irish schoolchild in the
1920s and 1930s: a reading in English literature which, instead of
sharpening the child's focus on a neighbourhood, actually distracts
from it. Ó Ríordáin's poems bear palpable traces of his reading of
Hopkins, Eliot and Wordsworth. In such a context, Daniel Corkery's
attack on "the want of native moulds" in Anglo-Irish writing seems
faintly ludicrous, especially in view of his recommendation of the Irish
language as the natural remedy for such a lack. The diagnosis offered
by Corkery had been astute when he said of the aspiring poet that "his
education provides him with an alien medium through which he is
henceforth to look at his native land".[19] But Corkery's mistake had
been to believe that Irish was, by some mysterious privilege, immune to
the incursions of international culture and modern thought. Ó Ríordáin suffered from no such delusion.

   Nor did he suffer from Kinsella's syndrome. Far from feeling dis-
abled by a "divided mind", he took that as a postulate and proceeded to
use Irish in a brilliant diagnosis of the split condition. He particularly
praised those thinkers – Corkery included – who had managed to
reinterpret Gaelic voices for modernity:

Gur thit anuas
De phlimp ar urlár gallda an lae seo
Eoghan béal binn,
Aindrias Mac Craith, Seán Clarach, Aodhgán,
Cith filí.[20]

Until there fell down
With a bang onto the foreign floor of our times
Eoghan of the sweet mouth,

Aindrias Mac Craith, Sean Clárach, Aodhgán,
A shower of poets.

Kinsella was less sure that tradition could be so easily translated. All he could discern around him was an almighty mess, the wreckage of history. With Beckett, however, he shared the bleak consolation of being able to diagnose the mess as such, before going on to accommodate it in exact forms, which derived as much from early Irish literature (especially the *Book of Invasions*) as from contemporary psychology and anthropology. If the *Book of Invasions* posited the Irish experience as one of violent, wrenching assimilations, the intellectual structure provided by Jung and Teilhard de Chardin helped Kinsella to create a sense of order in a world which might otherwise have seemed hopeless. What he said of Joyce was also true of his own achievement: that he took the fragments of Irish experience and somehow found a language in which they could be depicted. He shared Joyce's sense that man is educated most fully by sin, illness and suffering: that one must first go wrong in order to gain some inkling of how later one might go right. Kinsella is, in the words of Seamus Heaney, "the poet who affirms an Irish modernity, particularly in his treatment of psychic material which is utterly Irish Catholic".[21]

That achievement, though hard-won, remains ever-precarious in a land where politics looms around every corner and where "the politics of the last atrocity" can jeopardize the equilibrium of even the foremost poet. The coarseness of Kinsella's *Butcher's Dozen*, a response to the killing of thirteen civil rights marchers on Bloody Sunday 1972, was a reminder of the difficulty of writing poems that are political but, for all that, nonetheless poems.

Of the many talented poets to emerge from Northern Ireland in the period, Seamus Heaney appears to have faced that challenge with notable poise, though for some years after the eruption of violence in 1968, he was forced to "make statements in prose about why he wasn't making them in verse".[22] The attempt underlying Heaney's early work is the same as that made by Kinsella: to translate the violence of the past into the culture of the future. This is never easy and the poet is repeatedly astonished by the way in which violence insinuates itself into even the most everyday activities. The farm of his childhood thus becomes a colony in which unwanted kittens are purged, and the urge is to mock attempts by self-deceiving town-dwellers to convert such carnage into pretty pastoral:

> Still, living displaces false sentiments
> And now, when shrill pups are prodded to drown
> I just shrug, "Bloody pups." It make sense:
>
> "Prevention of cruelty" talk cuts ice in town
> Where they consider death unnatural,
> But on well-run farms pests have to be kept down.[23]

In Heaney's first book, the naturalist dies but death is not yet unnatural; though written by a member of the nationalist minority in the North, that last line has an ominous ring to it. Years were to pass before the artist directly addressed the political violence. However, there is a sense in which the relation between violence and social ritual was always his theme, something acknowledged in "The Betrothal of Cavehill":

> Gunfire barks its questions off Cavehill
> And the profiled basalt maintains its stare
> South: proud, protestant and northern and male.
> Adam untouched, before the shock of gender.
>
> They still shoot here for luck over a bridegroom:
> The morning I drove out to bed me down
> Among my love's hideouts, her pods and broom,
> They fired above my car the ritual gun.[24]

Heaney developed an aesthetic in which the hard, masculine consonants of Protestant English culture "bulled" the softer, feminine words of Gaelic tradition. In the 1960s, at a time when the Lemass/O'Neill courtship promised much and free trade was instituted between Ireland and England, his implication appeared to be that only a fully Anglo-Irish fusion might produce a single, workable language.[25] In other words, what remained a brutal conflict at the level of politics might somehow be resolved at the level of culture. Hence the fetishizing of childhood landscapes which gave an almost pornographic quality to many of Heaney's poems about south Derry, a place in which land is reduced to mere symbol (as in Gaelic *dinnsheanchas*). The part in such poems is loved in the name of the whole, and made to exist at the level of an image rather than for what it truly is.

Yet there is in Heaney's writing a developed ethical sense which causes him constantly to question his own evasions. So, in one poem, when the IRA tars and feathers a woman for fraternizing with British soldiers, he is reminded not only of a parallel case of a Danish woman sacrificed to the land in an ancient fertility rite but also of the more accusing parallel between the IRA and himself, since both are guilty of reducing woman to cultural totem. "Punishment" is as much about pornography as about violence, because pornography is another zone where violence and culture overlap. The poem admits that the logical consummation of the pornographic imagination is death:

> I can feel the tug
> of the halter at the nape
> of her neck, the wind
> on her naked front.
>
> It blows her nipples
> to amber beads,
> it shakes the frail rigging
> of her ribs . . .
>
> I am the artful voyeur
>
> of your brain's exposed
> and darkened combs,
> your muscles' webbing
> and all your numbered bones:
>
> I who have stood dumb
> when your betraying sisters,
> cauled in tar,
> wept by the railings,
>
> who would connive
> in civilized outrage
> yet understand the exact
> and tribal, intimate revenge.[26]

The bog in Heaney's *mythos* preserves not just bodies but consciousness. Every layer, "camped on before", tells its own history in the form of geography, and so the adulteress is paradoxically preserved by the sheer weight of all that culture, all that layered earth which suffocated her. The poet partakes of that duplicity, on the one hand sympathizing with

her plight and even worshipping her as a saint, while on the other hand
repeating his characteristic sin of fetishizing the beaded nipples like a
cheap voyeur, and a voyeur, moreover, whose sin is traceable to his art,
being perhaps as great an outrage as his connivance in the tribal
revenge.

The bog-myth has the effect of distancing contemporary violence.
Some might feel that this is done to come to terms with the strange fact
that readers, inured to newspaper photographs of daily atrocity, can feel
more for the ancient than the modern victim; others would contend
that it is done because feelings about contemporary violence are too
pressing for control and so need the objective correlative of a victim of
a sacrificial cult. With such distancing comes aestheticization and a
seductive conceptual cliché, as the old stereotypes of the "bog Irish" are
reasserted with an unexampled complexity. Denis Donoghue has defended the bog-poems as providing a necessary consolation, a reminder
that, however terrible, the current violence has its part in a wider North
European cycle, releasing minds from the immediate experience to the
comfort of "hearing that there is a deeper, truer life going on beneath
the bombing and murders and torture".[27] The danger is that the
violence may seem to have been sanitized and even prettified by art.
To guard against it, "Punishment" returns in its closing sequence to
current outrages, which refuse to be contained by the mythological
structure devised for them. There is in Heaney a real scruple which
saves his poems, despite their frequent winsomeness, from becoming
too pleased with themselves or with the conclusions they propose.
There is also another scruple, a recognition that while the moral
community must condemn exponents of violence, the artistic community must try to understand its authenticity and its roots.

The fear is that simple, rudimentary souls will foolishly conclude
that to understand violence is to connive in apologizing for it. Inter-
estingly, Heaney uses the word "connive" with the phrase "civilized
outrage" to indicate his sense that there are no easy solutions to the
poetic, as well as the political, problems posed. Despite this, as Ireland's
most celebrated poet, "famous Seamus" has been expected, whenever
he appears on television, to dispense political wisdom. He has answered
the charge of being "soft on the IRA" by signing the book of con-
dolences at the British Embassy after the murder of Ambassador Ewart-
Biggs in 1976: but such gestures have merely prompted critics like the
socialist politician Jim Kemmy to say that the poet would have made a
fine Fianna Fáil town-councillor.

However, the worst that can be said against Heaney always turns out to have been said already of himself by the artist within the poems. So in the ironically-titled "Exposure", he accuses himself of ambivalence, of a two-facedness masquerading as artistic even-handedness. This poem was written in a period after he had resigned his lectureship in Belfast. He had taken up residence in the woods of County Wicklow, rather in the manner of Sweeney, that northern king who fled from the madness of battle to seek a different kind of exposure – to nature, to the poetic quarrel with the self rather than the political quarrel with others:

> I am neither internee nor informer;
> An inner emigré, grown long-haired
> And thoughtful; a wood-kerne
>
> Escaped from the massacre,
> Taking protective colouring
> From bole and bark, feeling
> Every wind that blows;
>
> Who, blowing up these sparks
> For their meagre heat, have missed
> The once-in-a-lifetime portent,
> The comet's pulsing rose.[28]

Again, there is ambiguity, for "wood-kerne" was the very term used by English officers for those Irish rebels and rapparees who sought protection in the woods. The guilt at having, in other poems, dignified deeds done by men of action is qualified here by a guilt at not being a man of action himself.

In *Station Island*, his sixth volume, published in 1984, Heaney finally tired of his own pose of scrupulous neutrality and intermittent empathy, opting instead to offer absolute, unqualified empathy to all, smiters and smitten. Here he achieved a different, more complex kind of even-handedness. At various points in the title-poem all Northern voices are allowed to speak; and the poet no longer professes to speak for or even to them. Instead, they talk at him, accusing him of giving too much relief by his winsome images, of soothing the pain by describing it too beautifully. His shot cousin sees the poet as little better than a traitor, who turns his sordid death into another shapely poem:

> You saw that, and you wrote that – not the fact.
> You confused evasion and artistic tact.
> The Protestant who shot me through the head
> I accuse directly, but indirectly you . . .
> (who) saccharined my death with morning dew.[29]

The artist who had most fully explored the points of intersection between poetry and violence before Heaney was, of course, Synge. His Pegeen discovered how large was the gap between poetry and dirty deeds. Synge's own answer to the aestheticization of violence (which he found in Yeats's writing) was to sharpen rather than soften the focus on that brutality. He went even further, insisting that poetry must become brutal again if it were ever to recover its full humanity. The saccharine of morning dew and Celtic mist must be removed from the "skinny shee", and winsomeness seen for the temptation that it was.

That is also the point to which Heaney came in *Station Island*, a book whose poems are as raw and open as a wound, a book which rejects the distancing frame of the bog poems for a more immediate messiness. The landscapes in it are filled with a technology only half-subsumed back into the earth. In the midst of such jaggedness and indecision, the author becomes a kind of self-critical Christy Mahon, ashamed of his facility with words:

> And there I was, incredible to myself
> among people far too eager to believe me
> and my story, even if it happened to be true.[30]

Heaney's self-image as a poet has never been as high as one might expect of a best-selling, much-prized author: perhaps this is because his work has achieved awesome complexity and mass popularity in ways which would leave anyone, especially a poet, suspicious. He has at various times likened himself to Hamlet the Dane, hand-wringing over graves, dithering, blathering: but like Synge, that other expert on handling skulls, he knows that art is carrion, a barbarian's booty steeped in a violence which it must nevertheless somehow seem to deplore. As he writes in "The First Flight":

> I was mired in attachment
> until they began to pronounce me
> a feeder off battlefields.[31]

i.e. a beneficiary of a violence which he cannot morally support, yet which he can to some degree understand. Conor Cruise O'Brien might contend that this makes him the laureate of the SDLP: and, as a former classmate of John Hume at St. Columb's in Derry, Heaney might respond "so be it". The strain has sometimes shown, especially in his treatment of sexual conquest: but no Irish artist since Synge has given a fuller account of the relation between poetry and violence, and that in a period when such accounts have often been simplified into mere polemics. If some of Heaney's poems are too patently allusive, too obviously destined for the university seminar (as some of his earlier lyrics were for the school anthology), there is a great middle range in his poems which answers the Irish experience in his generation.

Station Island was at once an audacious self-identification with a "Catholic" tradition of writing (from Carleton through Joyce to Kavanagh) and a call for an honourable discharge from political or tribal affiliation. It ended with the ghost of Joyce urging the poet to "fill the element / with signatures on your own frequency" and to forget the old, accumulated grudges:

> You are raking at dead fires,
>
> a waste of time for somebody your age.
> That subject people stuff is a cod's game . . .[32]

Behind that intimation of freedom lay the example of Sweeney, the king who went mad in battle, threw a saint's book into the lake and fled the North, transformed into a bird aloft over the fields of Ireland, voicing his pain and his pleasure in terse, beautiful poems. With his versions in *Sweeney Astray* (1983) Heaney had freed himself. It was, arguably, this encounter with a famous old text which liberated him – as it had Synge and Austin Clarke – into zones where he could soar and sing.

Thereafter Heaney's poems were much less earthed in identifiable locales and less bound by hard-and-fast titles than the earlier work. Now they tended to take off into the sky or across the waters on a voyage into the unknown. That unknown was a dimension in which man could at last become an almost non-human witness of himself. The poet who had once taken up a position in the real world from which he explored analogies of distant metaphor now reversed the process, occupying a world of metaphor from which he could now and then look back upon the real.

In the title poem of the collection *Seeing Things*, images of flying and sailing are conflated in a skyship from which the artist looks down on passengers in a boat committed to the risky buoyancy of Inishbofin's waters. It might be an audacious image from Chagall did it not feature, centuries earlier, in *The Book of Clonmacnoise*. These annals recount how another skyship found its progress halted when its anchor became somehow hooked into the monastery's altar-rail. One of the sailors tried but failed to release the anchor-rope, as Heaney relates in another poem from the volume:

> "This man can't bear our life here and will drown",
>
> The abbot said, "unless we help him". So
> They did, the freed ship sailed, and the man climbed back
> Out of the marvellous as he had known it.[33]

This poses the central question: which is more miraculous, the mythical or the mundane? The poet may be a little like the sailor, glad to escape drowning in the political waters that left him "mired". To be out of one's familiar element is to be drowned and at the same time enriched by new possibilities for marvel. The everyday world will henceforth seem strange to such a one, who writes as if from beyond the grave; but the sailor's return to the skyship does not signify a total rejection of quotidian things, merely a resolution to see them in a new light.

After *Seeing Things* Heaney's poetry veered away from the ideal of portraiture to that of vision, with images that were at once audacious and appropriate:

> His hands were warm and small and knowledgeable,
> When I saw them again last night, they were two ferrets,
> Playing all by themselves in a moonlit field.[34]

The canny Northern urge to check soaring fictions against the available facts was still present (a deflating voice in the collection says "be literal a moment"); but the more powerful poems were undeniably those which allowed the everyday to give way to the crepuscular world of the imagination. The choice was no longer seen as between a metaphor and a real thing but – as the sailor found – between one metaphor and another. In the familiar experience of schoolboys playing an increasingly notional game of football in a deepening twilight, the poet read his new condition:

> Youngsters shouting their heads off in a field
> As the light died and they kept on playing
> Because by then they were playing in their heads
> And the actual kicked ball came to them
> Like a dream heaviness, and their own hard
> Breathing in the dark and skids on grass
> Sounded like effort in another world . . .[35]

Like the poet, those players had marked out a celestial pitch, a field of force constructed to rules which at no point purport to compete with mundane reality.

As Heaney's voice matured, the poet took on an increasingly bardic aura, infusing tight quatrains with a variety of registers. A notable number of elements from Gaelic tradition – especially the lore of place associated with *dinnsheanchas* – were to be found in his work and in that of many contemporaries. This revived fashion for poetic geography was questioned in the 1980s by the critic Vincent Buckley, who detected in it the old Celticist idea of a people foredoomed by landscape and character to an ineffable melancholy. "We should not read into the geography a sadness produced among the human family by history", he warned: "Ireland is a living testimony to the fact that its own people have absorbed history into geography, events into climate".[36] The response of the leading poets to such critiques has been to historicize geography, something which Richard Murphy did as early as *The Battle of Aughrim* and again in *Sailing to an Island*, as did John Montague in *The Rough Field*. Heaney, likewise, excavated each layer of soil for evidence from remoter periods, the spade striking always inward and downward by a poet self-cast as archaeologist. Derek Mahon's answer, even more radical, was to present the poet as anthropologist, engaged in a search for some sign of the persistence of the person. Such an approach had the merit of looking forward as well as back, which may account for a certain jauntiness in Mahon's rhythms:

> Already in a lost hub-cap is conceived
> The ideal society which will replace our own.[37]

But the underlying trajectory is, for all its eloquence, more gloomy, individual and estranged. He is, of course, a poet of Belfast, but often by way of disavowal:

> One part of my mind must learn to know its place.
> The things that happen in the kitchen houses

> And echoing back-streets of this desperate city
> Should engage more than my casual interest,
> Exact more interest than my casual pity.[38]

Mahon's problem is that he never felt that he belonged to a city which he would eventually escape, for as an artist he was destined to take Bohemia rather than Belfast for home:

> Perhaps if I'd stayed behind
> And lived it bomb by bomb
> I might have grown up at last
> And learnt what is meant by home.[39]

Yet there is no final evasion of commitment in the gesture: rather a widened embrace which has room for the dead peoples of earlier holocausts. In "A Disused Shed in County Wexford" – perhaps the finest poem written by his generation of Irish artists – the speaker seems to open a door onto those earlier victims imaged now as mushrooms:

> They are begging us, you see, in their wordless way
> To do something, to speak on their behalf
> Or at least not to close the door again.
> Lost people of Treblinka and Pompeii.
> "Save us, save us", they seem to say,
> "Let the god not abandon us
> Who have come so far in darkness and in pain.
> We too had our lives to live.
> You with your light meter and relaxed itinerary,
> Let not our naïve labours have been in vain!"[40]

If Mahon has turned from his native city to a wider world, Ciaran Carson has in *Belfast Confetti* brilliantly mapped the European architectonics of Walter Benjamin onto the streets and suburbs of that very place. He renders the sights and smells with a real intensity, as if photographing the scenes of a crime; but the emotion is suffused with a conclusive tenderness that can come only from intimate knowledge:

Suddenly as the riot squad moved in, it was raining exclamation marks,
Nuts, bolts, nails car-keys. A fount of broken type. And the explosion
Itself – an asterisk on the map. This hyphenated line, a burst of rapid
fire . . .

I was trying to complete a sentence in my head, but it kept stuttering,
All the alleyways and side-streets blocked with stops and colons.[41]

As remarkable as the revival in the north has been the recent out-pouring of poetry and prose by women writers in the south: if the voices of the northern minority, long repressed, became finally audible, the words of women began to make a similar claim to attention. In an obvious sense, this was a reflection of the re-emergence of the women's movement in the 1970s, following the international success of books like Germaine Greer's *The Female Eunuch* and Kate Millett's *Sexual Politics*: but at a deeper level it was a repossession by women of energies which had informed the Irish renaissance only to be denied in the new state, energies which some connected back to Celtic ideals of womanhood. Perhaps predictably then, the two fore-most women poets of this period worked in Irish, Máire Mhac an tSaoi and Nuala ní Dhomhnaill. The former was already well established by 1960 as a writer of enviable emotional range, who chronicled the frustrations of women spurned in love by cold-hearted males and who appealed by way of consolation to the image of a self-sufficient Celtic woman.

The most technically gifted versifier of her time, Máire Mhac an tSaoi achieved a richness and density of language which nobody could hope to rival. Blessed with such gifts, she was enabled to translate major and minor texts from English, French and Spanish into beautiful, idiomatic Irish, a superb reversal of the more usual trajectory, but one which served and enriched the language which she had wrought to such a pitch of intensity. The difficulties faced by her generation of female artists were pithily summed up in her lyric parody of holy-picture prayers of Irish womanhood:

Cré na Mná Tí

> Coinnibh an teaghlach geal
> Agus an chlann fé smacht,
> Nigh agus sciúr agus glan,
> Cóirigh proinn agus lacht,
> Iompaigh tochta, leag brat,
> Ach, ar nós Sheicheiriseáide,
> Ní mór duit an fhilíocht chomh maith![42]

The Housewife's Credo

Keep the dwelling bright and clean and the children in
order; wash and scour and clean; prepare meal and beverage;
turn mattress – spread cloth – but, like Scheherazade,
you will need to write poetry also.

That contemporary condition was also evident in her admission that
the strong woman of Celtic mythology was no longer a feasible model
in the age of reified bodies in fashion magazines:

AthDheirdre

"Ní bhearrfad m'ingne",
Adúirt sí siúd
Is do thug cúl don saol
De dheascaibh an aonlae sin –
Lena cré
Ni mhaífinnse,
Ná mo leithéidse, gaol –
   Cíoraim mo cheann,
   Is cuirim dath ar mo bhéal.[43]

Another Deirdre

"I shan't cut my nails",
That woman said
And turned her back on life.
In consequence of that one day
– With her clay
I would not claim,
Nor would my sort claim, kindred –
   I comb my hair
   And put rouge on my lips.

So wrought and complex were Máire Mhac an tSaoi's lyrics that they
drew few translators: quite the opposite was the case with her follower
in the next generation, Nuala ní Dhomhnaill. She, too, handled Gaelic
tradition in a more subversive fashion than did the English-language
poets. They, in turn, went to her work and translated it in order to
derive from the experience a sense of greater abandon in the presence of

Gaelic material. Her "An Crann" (The Tree) tells of how a fairy-woman, armed with a Black and Decker power-cutter, hacked down a garden tree, and of how the speaker's husband asked whether *she* would like it if he were to do the same to her. She duly reports his response to the returned fairy-woman:

> "O", ar sise, "that's very interesting".
> Bhí béim ar an *very.*
> Bhí cling leis an *-ing.*
> Do labhair sí ana-chiúin.
> Bhuel, b'shin mo lá-sa,
> Pé ar bith sa tsaol é,
> iontaithe bunoscionn.
> Thit an tóin as mo bholg
> is faoi mar a gheobhainn lascadh cic
> nó leacadar sna baothbáin
> íon taom anbhainne isteach orm
> a dhein chomh lag san mé
> gurb ar éigin a bhí ardú na méire ionam
> as san go ceann trí lá.
>
> Murab ionann is an crann
> a dh'fhan ann, slán.[44]

Paul Muldoon's version is as unbuttoned as the original:

> "O", says she, "that's very interesting".
> There was a stress on the "very".
> She lingered over the "ing".
> She was remarkably calm and collected.
> These are the times that are in it, so,
> all a bit topsy-turvy.
> The bottom falling out of my belly
> as if I had got a kick up the arse
> or a punch in the kidneys.
> A fainting-fit coming over me
> that took the legs from under me
> and left me so zonked
> I could barely lift a finger
> till Wednesday.

> As for the quince, it was safe and sound
> and still somehow holding its ground.

Such a treatment is infinitely more satisfying than Ní Dhomhnaill's
programmatic assaults on the Sean-Bhean Bhocht of national tradition,
an old woman now grown bourgeois, cantankerous and unstoppable:

> is gur ag dul i mínithe is imbréagaí atá gach dream
> dá dtagann: gach seanrá a thagann isteach i mo chloigeann,
> aon rud ach an tseanbhean bhaoth seo a choimeád socair.[45]

or in Ciaran Carson's version:

> Folly, I'm saying, gets worse with every generation:
> Anything, every old cliché in the book, anything at all
> To get this old bitch to shut the fuck up.

These translations from contemporary Irish are very different
from the quieter performances of Kinsella or Heaney – as when
Eiléan ní Chuilleanáin renders "Fear" (Looking at a Man) as a male
striptease:

> Ba chóir go mórfaí tú
> os comhar an tslua,
> go mbronnfaí ort
> craobh is próca óir,
> ba chóir go snoífí tú
> id dhealbh marmair
> ag seasamh romham
> id pheilt is uaireadóir.[46]

> You're the one they should praise
> In public places,
> The one should be handed
> Trophies and cheques.
> You're the model
> For the artist's hand,
> Standing before me
> In your skin and a wristwatch.

Writing in Irish, Ní Dhomhnaill might be forgiven a little piety, a certain rumination on the question of a double colonialism: but rather than lament the wrongs of woman, she assumes equality, even superiority to men, with an ease which may have its roots in Celtic traditions. Nevertheless, she is well aware of the precarious nature of such an achievement in a language which may well be dead as a community tongue before she herself passes on: and so she likens her hope to an infant child placed in a basket on the waters:

> féachaint n'fheadaraís
> cá dtabharfadh an sruth é,
> féachaint, dála Mhaoise,
> an bhfóirfifh iníon Fharóinn?[47]

> only to have it bounce hither and thither,
> not knowing where it might end up;
> in the lap, perhaps,
> of some Pharaoh's daughter.

Ní Dhomhnaill taught her generation that the best way to protect a tradition is to attack and subvert it. So in "The Woman Turns Herself into a Fish" Eavan Boland offers a clear inversion of the fish-into-girl progress of the image in Yeats's "The Song of Wandering Aengus", while at the same time registering in lines which echo Sylvia Plath just how much strain is involved in any conformity to an image:

> It's done:
> I turn,
> I flab upward

> blub-lipped,
> hipless
> and I am

> sexless
> shed
> of ecstasy,

> a pale
> swimmer
> sequin-skinned,

> pealing eggs
> screamlessly
> in seaweed.
>
> It's what
> I set my heart on.
> Yet
>
> ruddering
> and muscling
> in the sunless tons
>
> of new freedoms
> still
> I feel
>
> a chill pull,
> a brightening,
> a light, a light
>
> and how
> in my loomy cold,
> my greens
>
> still
> she moons
> in me.[48]

This is more than a revision of Yeats's lyric, for in it a woman has moved from passivity to self-transformation, from being the object of the poem to becoming its subject. Remaining loyal to the idea of nation, Boland found nevertheless that the fusion of the feminine and the national in previous Irish poetry seemed to simplify both in ways that were unacceptable. Lamenting "the power of nationhood to edit the reality of womanhood", Boland pointed to the fact that the women featured in the work of male Irish poets were "often passive, decorative, raised to emblematic status".[49]

Though this judgement may overlook the strong, self-willed women who are featured in the poems of Yeats, it is informed by Boland's confession that she wrote her own early work in derived modes, as if she were still the object of it:

Rather than accept the nation as it appeared in Irish poetry, with its queens and muses, I felt the time had come to re-work those images by exploring the emblematic relation between my own feminine experience and a national past.

Hence her renegotiation of the mermaid image, her move "with an almost surreal invisibility, from being within the poem to being its maker".[50] The result, in many of Boland's works, is an updating rather than a repudiation of the idea of the nation: a process which has made her the logical laureate of Mary Robinson's presidency. This, however, has not protected Boland from interrogation by northern critics who believe that the age-old equation of woman and nation should be dismantled altogether: "at least unionism does not appropriate the image of woman", proclaims Edna Longley, "or hide its aggressions behind our skirts".[51] To characterize Irish nationalism as female is, in her view, to endow it with a mythic pedigree with conveniently "exonerates it from oppressive and aggressive intent".

Edna Longley goes further, arguing that it is not necessarily *always* a good thing when passive versions of women are transformed into active ones – especially if they buttress notions of warrior-womanhood which may prove helpful to the IRA. In her denationalized landscape, there would be no need for Boland to apologize for her early imitations of Elizabethan court lyrics or of English Movement poets of the 1960s. "To what icon is she apologizing?" asks Longley and answers "In fact, it is to Mother Ireland herself".[52] She accuses Boland of a failure to interrogate the notion of nation, with the result that the poet ends up reinstating some of the very clichés which she set out to question.

Edna Longley does not manage to define any ground other than the nation from which a poet might conduct such an enquiry. Boland, for her part, adopts the view that myths are best dismantled from within. So in one of her most quoted lyrics "Mise Éire", Pearse's refrain "I am Ireland" is rewritten as "I am woman":

> . . . who neither
> knows nor cares that
> a new language
> is a kind of scar
> and heals after a while
> into a passable imitation
> of what went before.[53]

In seeking to free her own voice as a woman, Boland expanded and enriched the definitions of a nation: and she did this by an expressed solidarity with other forgotten communities, including the voteless, voiceless emigrants. In earlier decades leaders such as de Valera had used great festivals to remind those at home of the diaspora overseas. After the 1960s, this went out of fashion and the nation was defined in increasingly shrunken terms as those living on the island or those living in the twenty-six county statelet. When Mary Robinson was inaugurated as president, one of her first actions was to light a lamp in Áras an Uachtaráin as a reminder that the "greater Ireland overseas" also belonged. The inspiration for that gesture she cited as a poem by Boland:

The Emigrant Irish

Like oil lamps we put them out the back,

of our houses, of our minds. We had lights
better than, newer than and then

a time came, this time and now
we need them. Their dread, makeshift example.

They would have thrived on our necessities.
What they survived we could not even live.
By their lights now it is time to
imagine how they stood there, what they stood with,
that their possessions may become our power.

Cardboard. Iron. Their hardships parcelled in them.
Patience. Fortitude. Long-suffering
in the bruise-coloured dusk of the New World.

And all the old songs. And nothing to lose.[54]

The new wave of emigration, especially among the educated young, was a challenge to the older generation to consider whether the national renaissance had been successful: a pervasive sense of failure, too deep for words or open admission, had led many to "solve" that intractable problem simply by refusing to discuss it. Society was characterized by a growing rift between righteous traditionalists and jittery revisionists. It became fashionable to rewrite the key documents of Irish nationalism in bitter acts of dismissive parody. Paul Durcan caught the sourness of the prevailing mood in a short lyric:

> She was America-bound, at summer's end.
> She had no choice but to leave her home –
> The girl with the keys to Pearse's Cottage.[55]

This bleakness of tone was characteristic of many plays and novels in the 1980s. As young Ireland went into a ferocious reaction against the older pieties, it seemed that no aspects of national tradition would be left unscathed. In *The Journey Home* Dermot Bolger took the name of a 1916 patriot, Plunkett, for a corrupt gombeen-politician, and filled the narrative with anger against the Christian Brothers, nuns (who beat girls for possessing such pagan names as Sarah), and rural immigrants in Dublin suburbs who, after three decades in the city, persisted in calling Kerry or Cork "home".[56] *The Woman's Daughter*, his next novel, was equally depressed, but it spoke for the disillusion of many young people who had given up on Ireland, or at least thought they had. Bolger's posture of radical dissent came rather oddly, however, from one who throughout the period was fêted by *The Irish Times* and accorded a seat on the Arts Council. There was in truth something over-determined about his attacks: he represented a movement which fancied itself the voice of a persecuted modernity while in fact already being fully established and empowered.

Moreover, the writing of Bolger and his colleagues was considerably less subversive than it sometimes took itself to be. In its underlying sentimentality about its youthful subjects as victims of social tyranny, it grossly exaggerated the malevolence and the importance of priests, teachers, politicians. Although it prided itself on its realistic engagement with the sordid aspects of Dublin life, it may have unintentionally ratified the old pastoral notion of rural Ireland as real Ireland. The city, in Dermot Bolger's world, was not a place in which a happy, modern life was possible: it was not depicted as the vibrant zone of creativity which Dublin by then had become. His attacks on the clergy furthered the illusion that they were still a force to be reckoned with: but by 1985 even the most conservative bishops had privately conceded to journalists that the battle for traditional Catholicism was lost. The books of Bolger and his colleagues were much admired in England, where they were read as indicating a new cutting-edge realism in Irish writing: but soon the conservative undertow was all too apparent, as well as the conceptual clichés of a strangely caricatured Dublin landscape of horses in high-rise flats and doomed young things in squalid bed-sits.

In *The Lament for Arthur Cleary*, however, Bolger achieved a work of rare command and power. Here he broke free of the prevailing clichés by the simple expedient of translating a famous Irish-language poem into modern terms. It tells of how a young Irishman returns from a sojourn on the Continent only to find the Dublin that he loved now gone forever, and his own doom sealed. When he accepted the Irish past as a basis on which to know the Irish present, Bolger impressed as a writer: but when he went to war against the past, he was left dependent on his own resources, which could never be equal to the challenge. In his texts, he found it difficult to register a variety of voices, and this was symptomatic of a generation which, in its anxiety to redefine the Irish condition, sometimes seemed unwilling to allow any voices other than its own to be heard. In that respect, also, they were all too like the older gang which they were reacting so strongly against.

For the younger artists the surviving hero of the Irish renaissance was Francis Stuart, the "prophet of dishonour" who had always acted as if the writer's duty was to put himself at odds with all consensus viewpoints. His *Black List, Section H* was a wonderfully acerbic account of the revival period, but also an apologia for the author's days in Nazi Germany, from which he had broadcast programmes in the 1940s. This was now "forgiven", however, on the grounds of his exemplary dissident authority: in effect, a fool's pardon was extended to the artist by persons who seemed not at all perturbed by the implicit admission that what such an artist thinks or says is of no consequence, since it will have no social effect. Perhaps this was why so many of the younger generation could portray themselves as dissidents while actually functioning as careerists. Though artists were fêted in Charles Haughey's Ireland, art had in fact lost much of its former social power. The rising generation did not speak with a single voice: and its members were too mobile to solidify into schools. Some, such as Dermot Bolger, repudiated Irish nationalism and declared themselves positively uninterested in having a united Ireland.[57] On the most urgent question facing the people, these took a line even more conservative than that favoured by the Dublin establishment. They did so with the best will in the world, as a warning to the IRA that the killing was not to be construed as done in their name: but this then led them into an obsessive, sometimes paranoid, search for elements in southern culture which might be complicit in the northern carnage.

By contrast, novelists such as Roddy Doyle or Joe O'Connor, who took a more relaxed, even humorous, approach to Irish pieties, often seemed to achieve more as artists and as social analysts. Doyle, in particular, explored in his Barrytown trilogy the life of Dublin housing estates. In *The Commitments* he described the attempt by poor teenagers to succeed as exponents of soul music, on the grounds that "the Irish are the niggers of Europe, and the Dubliners are the niggers of Ireland, and the northside Dubliners are the niggers of Dublin".[58] He was one of the first artists to register the ways in which the relationship between "First" and "Third" Worlds was enacted daily in the streets of the capital city. Even more impressive was his exploration of the inner world of child-hood in *Paddy Clarke Ha Ha Ha* (1993), a book which evinced a nostalgia for the 1960s in which it was set and at the same time checked that tendency with a portrait of a disintegrating marriage. Similarly, Joseph O'Connor's *Desperadoes* (1994), a richly comic novel which cut between the Ireland of the 1950s and the Nicaragua of the 1980s, was another successful investigation of the similarities and dissimilarities between Ireland and the "Third World" – a concern evident also in the rock lyrics of U2 and in the campaigns of musician Bob Geldof.

In drama Brian Friel's *Dancing at Lughnasa* was a huge box-office success: its depiction of a priest returned from the African missions, no longer able to distinguish between Irish harvest rituals and African tribal practices, was a further elaboration on a theme touched on by President Robinson and by the more radical members of the Christian clergy. In poetry, Paul Muldoon's epic masterpiece *Madoc* hinted at an equally suggestive set of connections between the experience of the Irish and of the native Indians of America. A puckish, mischievous post-modernism flickered across the sophisticated lines of Muldoon, and it was this element of wry self-mockery which made his writing immense-ly attractive to many. Traditionally-minded readers found his promis-cuous mingling of codes and narratives often exhausting and mind-numbing: but his refusal of what Beckett once termed "the distortions of intelligibility" was quite deliberate, for he hated and still hates the fixed point of view. Even his sternest critics, however, have had to concede the awesome symmetry of his arrangements:

The Right Arm

I was three-ish
when I plunged my arm into the sweet-jar
for the last bit of clove-rock.

We kept a shop in Eglish
that sold bread, milk, butter, cheese,
bacon and eggs,

Andrews Liver Salts,
and, until now, clove-rock.

I would give my right arm to have known then
how Eglish was itself wedged between *ecclesia* and *église*.

The Eglish sky was its own stained-glass vault
and my right arm was sleeved in glass
that has yet to shatter.[59]

Even more noteworthy, however, were the audacious formal experiments in so many texts, indicating a huge and largely justifiable self-
confidence in their authors. The content of many works might be bleak
enough, but it was often set in dynamic tension with a superb jauntiness of form. The retailing of local gossip in stories of Borgesian
economy by "Nina Fitzpatrick", and the swerve from humorous recollection to sombre conclusion in *Paddy Clarke Ha Ha Ha* were cases in
point. So was the elliptical structure of John Banville's *Kepler* and its
equation of the scientist with an artist whose work deconstructs itself.
Perhaps the most spectacular instance of all was Tom Murphy's construction of *The Gigli Concert* as a form of verbal opera. Murphy's
drama has its roots in the disorder of rural Irish life, yet it moves always
to a moment when routine is elevated to the pitch of sacred ritual: the
desire of a successful house-builder to sing with the sweetness of
Beniamino Gigli being a case in point. In Murphy's world the ideal
and the real never completely lose touch with one another: and in rare
moments of benediction they overlap. He has drawn heavily on the
gangster movies of Hollywood for his prototypes of the Irish gombeen
man, but there is always an element of affection even in his hardest
mockery: and this has meant that he is perhaps the most subtle
chronicler of the embourgeoisification of rural Ireland, whether in *A
Crucial Week in the Life of a Grocer's Assistant* or in the magnificent
Bailegangaire, which presents the reminiscences of a bedridden old
woman. All of these experiments with form, in novels, poems or plays,
indicated that what was afoot was something very like a second literary
renaissance.

The conditions for that renaissance were not so very different from those which had produced the first one – a highly-educated young population, whose intellectual ambitions often exceeded the available career opportunities. Indeed, the immense reputation of Irish writing in overseas capitals was a great help to aspiring artists. Unlike Kavanagh and his contemporaries of the mid-century, who wrote in the intimidating aftermath of Yeats and Joyce, and who often found it hard to believe that their concerns were of interest to any but themselves, this new generation effortlessly assumed the attention of the world as a natural right. Some reputations were, if anything, too easily won: by the 1990s to be an "Irish writer" in London or New York was for some a passport not only to relative comfort but also to complacency. But the advantages of such a warm welcome more than outweighed the dangers. The rapid international recognition of still-young writers, playwrights and film-makers allowed the more gifted among them to pursue extremely mobile careers, which in turn led to a further internationalization of themes and tones.

Evidence for a "second renaissance" was also to be found in the major films (often with strong literary associations) made by Neil Jordan (director of *The Crying Game*) and by Jim Sheridan (director of *My Left Foot*). Unlike their English contemporaries, who often achieved at the age of thirty a technical competence which left them invulnerable to criticism but incapable of development, the Irish artists took risks, improvised, and often brought off quite breath-taking effects. Some indeed were accused of experimentation for its own sake, of engaging in nothing more than a succession of daredevil feats. Most, however, could justly claim that they were driven to test new forms by the exacting nature of their chosen themes. Of no artist was this more true than of Brian Friel, a man whose entire oeuvre achieved early a representative status, as admired in the south as in the north, as often performed overseas as at home, as praised in the academy as it was loved by live audiences.

Thirty-Three

Friel Translating

Translations is the best known of Brian Friel's plays. Set in the Donegal hedge-school of Baile Beag in August 1833, it describes the attempt by the British soldiers of the Royal Engineers and their Irish collaborators to transliterate the local Gaelic placenames and Anglicize them, in the process of mapping the area for the Ordnance Survey. It is a time of transition in every sense, for it becomes clear that the local hedge-school will soon be replaced by a state-sponsored National School providing free education in English for all.

This was but one of a number of modernizing experiments conducted in the colonial laboratory that was Ireland in the mid-nineteenth century before being applied in England. Another was the introduction of a streamlined postal service years before such a thing was enjoyed in England. The postal system was welcome since it vastly improved communications: the National Schools have had a more ambiguous reputation, since they were often cited by nationalist historians as having played a major part in the decline of the Irish language. So rapid was the transition from Irish to English in some rural areas that William Carleton, the novelist and short story writer, reported attending a wedding where the bride spoke no English and the groom no Irish, with the result that "the very language of love cried out for an interpreter".[1] This passage may lie behind the central scene of Friel's play, in which the English officer Yolland and the peasant Máire Chatach enact an identical ritual. The Irish language was fatally associated in the popular mind with poverty, backwardness and defeat.

When *Translations* was first staged in Derry in 1980, to launch the Field Day Company, Irish theatre critics had no doubt that, like Heaney before him, Friel was another canny northerner who chose a remote historical event to throw an oblique light on the present. The pressure on Máire Chatach to learn English as a prelude to emigration seemed a scenario out of the 1950s as much as the 1830s; and the cultural debates in the play seemed to echo resoundingly of the clash between tradition and modernity, between the pastoral Ireland of de Valera and the technological island envisioned by Seán Lemass. The anti-industrial bias of some pastoralists is epitomized in Friel's play by the hedge-schoolmaster Hugh who remarks derisively that few of the towns-folk speak English, and then only for commercial purposes to which the language seems particularly suited. This is certainly a feasible interpreta-tion, given that Friel's own career as an artist has spanned the decades since the First Programme for Economic Expansion in 1958 paved the way for investment by multinationals. Like many northern nationalists, Friel has looked at this modernization with very mixed feelings, since the emergent southern élites seemed to be abandoning the commitment to nationalist *nostra*. Some southern critics have gone so far as to accuse Friel of misrepresenting an economic crisis of the 1960s as a merely cultural and linguistic problem of the 1830s. They allege that this is symptomatic of a general retreat by modern Irish writers from the political complex-ities of modernity into a more private domain of language.[2]

By the time the play was written, P. J. Dowling had proved in *The Hedge-Schools of Ireland* that English rather than Irish was the main subject of study, as well as the major language of instruction,[3] in classes which were hardly the bulwark of Gaelic or indeed Greek civilization portrayed by pious nationalist historians. The school evoked in *Trans-lations* was not typical, but there were establishments of its kind in existence. What proved controversial, however, was Friel's stylized dramatization of adults as pupils in the school. Some literalists, missing the author's irony, complained that the device recalled the imperial theories of the 'childlike' Celts.

Nevertheless, Friel can be defended on the very grounds on which he was attacked. For one thing, his play ends when the hedge-school-master Hugh promises to teach Máire Chatach the English which she needs – as if to demonstrate by dramatic means how the situation described by Dowling came about. Moreover, in locating the debate at the level of language, Friel was not shirking the realities of politics so much as demonstrating the truth of Foucault's thesis that "discourse is the power which is to be seized".[4] The struggle for the power to name oneself and one's state is enacted fundamentally within words, most especially in colonial situations.

So a concern with language, far from indicating a retreat, may be an investigation into the depths of the political unconscious. After all, one of the first policies formulated by the Norman occupiers was to erase Gaelic culture. It was, however, only in the mid-nineteenth century that the native language declined, not as an outcome of British policy so much as because an entire generation of the Irish themselves decided no longer to speak it. O'Connell said that the superior utility of English was such that even a native speaker like himself could witness without a sigh the gradual disuse of Irish, a remark cited by Máire Chatach in *Translations*. To put the matter starkly, Irish declined only when the Irish people allowed it to decline. Brit-bashing mythology which cites the tally-stick, National Schools and Famine as the real causes was designed by politicians to occlude this painful truth, lest it cast a probing light on the contemporary situation, which is that Irish is still dying, still recoverable, but popular will to complete that recovery seems lacking.[5]

The government survey of 1975 reported that, despite a widespread love of Irish, few persons believed that it would survive as a community language into the next century.[6] The statistics were a focus of intense debate in the years that followed, the years in which *Translations* gestated. Far from being an evasion of current debates, the play is an uncompromising reminder that it is Irish, and not English people, who have the power to decide which language is spoken in Ireland. The very fact that audiences are to imagine the play being enacted in Irish is not just a clever double-take, but a conceit which is savagely satiric of those modern audiences which lack proficiency in their own language. If they laugh at the Englishman's halting attempts to express himself to the villagers, they are also in effect laughing at themselves.

Friel, therefore, is no nostalgic revivalist, no exponent of the dreamy backward look. During the controversy which followed *Translations* he said: "the only merit in looking back is to understand how you are and where you are at this moment".[7] He believes that culture can be causative, can have political consequences: so, when he discusses language, he sees it as a specific basis for all the politics which may ensue. Northern Irish writers are more conscious than southern counterparts of this fact, because they grew up in a state where the speaking of Irish was a political act, and where a person who gave a Gaelic version of a name to a policeman might expect a cuff on the ear or worse. The language did not enjoy the levels of support in schools or government which it had in the south. Writers, accordingly, were aware of a cultural deprivation from birth and sought to repair it as best they could.

For them a few token phrases – the *cúpla focal* – were not a perfunctory performance but a glamorous conspiratorial act. Hence the trouble taken by Heaney to provide a version of *Buile Shuibhne*.

Like Friel, Heaney finds a poetry in the Gaelic echoes that survive in placenames like Anahorish (*Anach Fhíor Uisce*), their musicality being connected with their poetic refusal to disclose at once all recoverable meanings. He can therefore describe himself as a tourist in Jutland as if he were recounting a motor-drive through the Donegal Gaeltacht:

> Something of his sad freedom
> As he rode the tumbril
> Should come to me, driving,
> Saying the names
>
> Tollund, Grabaulle, Nebelgard,
> Watching the pointing hands
> Of country people,
> Not knowing their tongue.[8]

Friel's love-scene between Yolland and Máire Chatach is based on the same kind of incantatory ecstasy, as if the two lovers can be invested with a special radiance simply by intoning favoured placenames to one another:

Bun na hAbhann . . . Druim Dubh . . . Lis na nGall . . . Liss na nGrá . . . Carraig an Phoill . . . Carraig na Rí . . . Loch na nÉan . . .[9]

To a northern writer with little Irish, however, the melody of local placenames can seem more a rebuke than a ratification. In "A Lost Tradition", a key poem in *The Rough Field*, John Montague treats of his ancestral homeland in County Tyrone. The map of his native townland is studded with placenames derived from an Irish which has been dead in that area for generations. In an ancient Gaelic manuscript, which no contemporary reader can understand, Montague finds an image of his own geography of disinheritance:

> All around, shards of a lost tradition, . . .
> The whole landscape a manuscript
> We had lost the skill to read,
> A part of our past disinherited;
> But fumbled, like a blind man,
> Along the finger-tips of instinct.[10]

Those lines, published in the mid-1970s, may have been another source for Friel:

OWEN: Do you know where the priest (now) lives?
HUGH: At Lis na Muc, over near . . .
OWEN: No, he doesn't. Lis na Muc, the Fort of the Pigs, has become Swinefort. (NOW TURNING THE PAGES OF THE NAME-BOOK. A PAGE PER NAME.) And to get to Swinefort you pass through Greencastle and Fairhead and Strandhill and Gort and Whiteplains . . . And the new school isn't at Poll na gCaorach – it's at Sheepsrock. Will you be able to find your way?[11]

By the play's end, that geography of disinheritance will be complete when Máire Chatach, the person onstage who wants most of all to learn English, will stumble back into the hedge-school with the words:

I'm back again. I set out for somewhere, but I couldn't remember where. So I came back here.[12]

With cruel irony the master's response to her alienation is not to cure it but to complete it, by teaching her the English which will make her feel at home in the face of these strange roadsigns.

All of these echoes from Heaney and Montague as well as from Joyce and Carleton indicate Friel as exponent of a knowing inter-textuality, and as someone who wishes to inscribe his texts into the contours of a developing national debate. Though *Translations* gathers many threads of that debate together, it also gives rise to many others. Quite late in the play, the hedge-schoolmaster Hugh has decided that every culture must be renewed and that he will learn the new names so as to know his new home. At just that point his son, Owen, who has done most to collaborate with the map-makers, suddenly shouts in a burst of ancestral piety: "I know where I live". His father's response is: "Take care, Owen, to remember everything is a form of madness".[13] Four years after the play's performance, in the poem called *Station Island* which he dedicated to Brian Friel, Seamus Heaney causes Carleton to say: "remember everything and keep your head",[14] i.e. it may be possible to avoid madness and yet recall all. This debate between the members of Field Day often proved far more challenging and even abrasive than the critiques of the movement mounted from without.

That it is the backward-looking hedge-schoolmaster who finally opts for English, modernity and the world of facts suggests how little an exercise in nostalgia Friel's play actually is. Hugh refuses to fossilize past images which had no roots in reality. *Translations* is a tough-minded play about the brutal actualities of cultural power. Some of its peasants may be cunning, others dreamers, but the pragmatists outnumber the dreamers when the chips are down. The sentimental English officer Yolland confesses a sense of guilt for his part in the Ordnance Survey: "it's an eviction of sorts". His Donegal collaborator Owen tersely translates that misty-eyed nostalgia into real words: "We're making a six-inch map of the country. Is there something sinister in that?"[15]

Owen is reminiscent of Shaw's Larry Doyle, a pragmatic fact-facing Irishman who works best with a rather emotional English Celticist, but one who has enough of the rebel in him to sense that, if the Irish are to fight successfully, they had better master the language of their colonizers. By far the most complex character onstage, Owen sees the positive potential in the mapping: for example, placenames lost by natural attrition within the Gaelic culture might be restored. Owen in this play is only seen as abject when he wilfully mistranslates a sentence or a name, or when he wilfully endures such a mistranslation (for instance, submitting to the name Roland). However, a true translation, true to the genius of both traditions, appears to Friel as the least of all evils in the negotiation between tradition and modernity. The problem is that a translator is often a traducer, especially when working out of a minor and into a major imperial language.

Thus Owen becomes Roland and Bun na hAbhann, equally inexplicably, Burnfoot, as an English grid is remorselessly imposed on all Irish complexities. This is a noted feature of imperialism: its desire not so much to translate Irish values into English words as to translate English values into Irish terms.[16] In this fashion they are imposed, much as the citizens of California have, by the assiduous use of watersprinklers, converted the brown grass of the southern parts of that state into a facsimile of the English lawn: a reminder that imperialism can be ecological as well as linguistic. John Dryden's hopeful aphorism – that landmarks are more sacred than words and never to be removed[17] – is well and truly rebutted in Friel's play; at the end even the physical appearance of the landscape is to be changed by a scorched-earth policy.

The iterative image of such imperial designs in this play is Lieutenant Yolland's attempt to draw a map of his native Norfolk for his Irish lover on the wet sands of Baile Beag. The hopeless stupidity of the attempt to impose a foreign grid on Irish reality is manifest in the fact that Yolland's model is etched in shifting sands. His attempt to draw Norfolk on the Donegal seashore is a fair image of what his own government is trying to do in the Ordnance Survey. Such a map, however romantic in this particular context, is the usual occupier's response to what he perceives as uncharted wilderness. And the attempt to write all the new names into a book represents the colonizer's benign assumption that to name a thing is to assert one's power over it and that the written tradition of the occupier will henceforth enjoy primacy over the oral memory of the natives. A map, in short, will have much the same relation to a landscape as the written word has to speech. Each is a form of translation.

Such a translation has always been an aspect of imperialism, for as Edward Said has written:

> . . . cultures have always been inclined to impose concrete transformations on other cultures, receiving these other cultures not as they are but as, for the benefit of the receiver, they ought to be. To the Westerner, however, the Oriental was always *like* some aspect of the West . . . for the Orientalist makes it his work to be always converting the Orient from something into something else . . .[18]

For "Orientalist" read "Celticist". Said adds, in what might be a bleak reference to the name book, that "it seems a common human failing to prefer the authority of a text to the disorientations of direct encounters with the human . . ." The next stage, he says, occurs when all that is in the books is preposterously put into practice, reducing the complexities of a culture to a kind of flatness, in much the same way that Captain Lancey decides to level Baile Beag. No Orientalist text, Said adds, was complete without a ritual infatuation on the part of the narrator with some mysterious woman of the native tribe, much along the lines of Yolland's assignations with Máire Chatach, an infatuation often experienced by the wayward son who is sent to an outpost because he can find no suitable job or partner at home. The woman, like the colony, is a mystery to be penetrated; and the real issue in all this, says Said, is

> whether there can indeed be a true representation, or whether any and all representations, because they *are* representations, are embedded first in the language and then in the culture, institutions and political ambience of the representer.[19]

Of nothing are these observations more true than of an insurgent nationalism, which is perpetually doomed to define itself in the loaded language and hegemonic terms set by the colonizer. So, because England's was an aristocratic, class-ridden culture, the Irish – in order to feel as nobly born – had to claim an aristocratic lineage. One of the peculiarities of the aristocratic English was their growing interest in Ireland, or indeed any colony, where things seemed to have petrified and time to have stood still, even as the home country slowly industrialized. The anti-modern, anti-democratic component of Irish revivalism greatly appealed to, because it was a creation of, the English upper-class mind. Echoes of this aristocratic fetishism may be heard in the revivalist association of England with levelling vulgarity . . . and in Yolland's comment that the English-language version makes the classical Latin of the hedge-school sound only plebeian.

Yolland is in open revolt against this modernization, and against the father who equates the new imperial mission with such modernization. That father was born in 1789, on the very day that the Bastille fell: so he inherited a new world of restless experiment, innovative rationalization, the bustle of an order which placed more emphasis on money than on land, on profit rather than on leisured elegance. Yolland, however, on setting foot in Ireland feels that he has recovered the ease of the *ancien régime*, "a consciousness that wasn't striving nor agitated, but at its ease and with its own conviction and assurance".[20] The account, late in the play, of how Hugh and his friend walked towards the French-inspired rebellion of 1798 only to turn back suggests not so much a fear of the English enemy as a timidity in the face of revolutionary French modernity, a collective decision by the Irish to keep the modern world at bay. Now modernity has caught up with them in the shape of the survey, implemented by a Yolland who scarcely believes in it and by a collaborator who has strong reservations.

The hedge-schoolmaster Hugh seeks to resolve the consequent dilemmas. Having lost his nerve back in 1798, he found that he had opted instead for a world of regressive nostalgias – the kind of foolish dreams epitomized at the end by his star pupil Jimmy Jack as he mumbles through an alcoholic haze about his recent engagement to the goddess Athene. Hugh has learned enough by now to know that a culture which refuses to make some adjustments will eventually find itself mummified. Hence his willingness to take over the post in the new national school – though there is something negative in this gesture, since it will deny the aspirations of his loyal son to a steady job and to marriage with Máire Chatach.

Apart from failing to grow and adapt, the other way in which a culture dies is when it is suffocated and overlain with that of a foreign power. It is surely deliberate that either possible meaning could be inferred from Hugh's statement that

... words are signals, counters. They are not immortal. And it can happen – to use an image you'll understand – it can happen that a civilization can be imprisoned in a linguistic contour which no longer matches the landscape of . . . fact.[21]

Facts were, of course, the tyranny with which the Celt was held unable to cope: but the fact that these most famous lines in the play – culled from George Steiner's *After Babel: Aspects of Language in Translation* – are so ambivalent nicely illustrates Friel's underlying theme: that once Anglicization is achieved the Irish and English, instead of speaking a truly identical tongue, will be divided most treacherously by a common language. This division is literally enacted onstage whenever Owen has to translate Captain Lancey's circumlocutions into homely words.

So, in the final moments it is, most surprisingly, Hugh who voices the pragmatist's willingness to embrace English and the new order, even as Owen indicates that he may join the rebels for one last stand. Holding the name book in his hand, Hugh says

> We must learn where we live. We must learn to make them our own. We must make them our new home.[22]

A shrewd reading of the play would reveal that this realistic tone had been implicit in Hugh's utterances all along. In that earlier scene, wherein he had offered just the kind of Arnoldian explanations of Irish eloquence that Yolland wanted to hear, he had not in fact been speaking literally so much as parodying himself (the stage direction is explicit on this). In saying "we like to think we endure around truths immemorially posited",[23] he was being sarcastic less about Irish self-images than about English self-deception. Nowhere is that thrust more deadly than in his mimicry of the liberal imperialist notion that culture thrives in direct proportion to poverty and sacred simplicity, that those who lose the material wars are consoled by having all the best songs:

> You'll find, sir, that certain cultures expend on their vocabularies and syntax acquisitive energies and ostentations entirely lacking in their material lives. I suppose you could call us a spiritual people.[24]

This isn't just savage anti-pastoralism of the kind practised by Myles na gCopaleen in *An Béal Bocht*; it is also a critique of that Irish revivalism which saw culture as a compensation for squalor. As a hedge-school-master Hugh knows the costs of such eloquence. His circumlocutions –

"vesperal salutations" for "good evening" – are in the familiar mode of long-winded but diplomaless hedge-schoolteachers. The fabled jaw-breakers of Hiberno-English are rooted less in native Irish exuberance than in a tragic defensiveness in the face of a more powerful language.

Seen in that light, Friel's play is a brilliant reconciliation within a single work of two apparently disparate Irish dramatic traditions: the Abbey revivalist and the Shavian socialist. The desire of all early Abbey playwrights was, Lady Gregory said, a theatre with a base of realism and an apex of beauty. That combination eventually came under baleful scrutiny from radical critics who saw in it evidence of the Abbey's neo-colonial position, Lady Gregory's view of poetry as a compensation for poverty being taken as a tell-tale instance. To the radical mind it would never be enough simply to juxtapose the mythical and mundane, unless each was also made to form part of a critique of the other. This is what happens in Friel's play: the pragmatic warnings of Shaw against dreaming as a function of repression are placed alongside the lethal fantasies of Jimmy Jack and those English Yollands who would sentimentalize them. If Friel has in the play been massively influenced by the creative art of Heaney and Montague, as well as by Shaw and Synge, he is perhaps most indebted to the ideas of critics such as George Steiner and Seamus Deane, and particularly to the suspicion which dominates the writings of the younger Deane[25] of all attempts to present high eloquence and rich culture as an adequate consolation for suffering and loss.

Thirty-Four

Translating Tradition

The Irish Renaissance had been essentially an exercise in translation, in carrying over aspects of Gaelic culture into English, a language often thought alien to that culture. Oscar Wilde had predicted as much when he averred that a national literature can only emerge as a result of contact with a foreign literature: what he said, in effect, was that the concept of the "original" comes into existence only after it has been translated. Taken further, this meant that the translator was as often *inventing* as *reflecting* an original Ireland: when writers dubbed Standish O'Grady the father of modern Irish literature, they were recognizing that to translate Ireland was but another way of bringing it into being. This has been true of most of the great creative phases of cultural history: in the words of Octavio Paz, they "have been preceded or accompanied by inter-crossings between different poetic traditions".[1]

Standish O'Grady's versions of the Cuchulain legends were intended for readers who could not understand the Irish-language texts. What is different about Friel's *Translations* is that, although it is to be imagined as enacted in Irish, in fact there is no original. This has not prevented enthusiasts from translating it back with much success into the native language in which it was never written. Perhaps intentionally, it mimics the Irish Constitution of 1937 which, while written in English, asserts Irish as the first official language, whose version should therefore prevail over the English version in the event of a mistranslation. Not for nothing did the philosopher Jacques Derrida warn that "one should never pass over in silence the question of the tongue in which the question of the tongue is raised".[2] Friel is well aware that his play is a post-colonial text to precisely the extent that its powerful diagnosis of a traumatized Irish consciousness nonetheless adds to the glories of the English language.

A root-meaning of "translate" was "conquer": the Romans conquered not only Greece but the Greek past, which they refitted for their present purposes. Yet coded into even this imperial gesture was the recognition that the plundered culture possessed many a quality worth stealing. By a somewhat similar logic, the former greatness of the Celts was established in the first instance by British public servants and translators, who set out to reform and improve the debased contemporary realities of Irish culture. Since the ancient Celtic past was a thinly-disguised version of the British imperial present, acceptance of that present (albeit in the English language) could presage a restoration of former Irish glories. The work of nineteenth-century antiquarians, of defenders of the Anglo-Irish gentry such as O'Grady, provided native readers with a curtailed if potent set of images, available in translation. Yet that golden age was a myth, and a myth moreover which at least some of its sponsors privately saw as such. A Trinity College professor, Robert Atkinson, secretly despised the Celtic literature whose study had made his academic name. His strictures against it in 1899 recalled all too aptly Lord Macaulay's claim that "a single shelf of a good European library was worth the whole native literature of India and Arabia".[3] (That European library was, of course, non-Celtic.)

It was the communication of this idea to the natives which led generations of boys, like those who boarded Charles Trevelyan's steamer at Comercally, to say "Give me any book, all I want is a book".[4] The Irish shared this longing for learning, but with one major difference. In India only a native élite was destined to be improved by the study of English; in Ireland the whole population was not only taught English at school, but even the poor themselves decided to speak English on all possible occasions. Accordingly, rather than learn that language from its native speakers, most of them learned it from one another with the effects of "brogue" and mispronunciation that became a source of easy laughter on the British stage. In short, they opted to become their own translators. This was a violation of one of the tenets of imperialism, which declared it "highly dangerous to employ the natives as interpreters, upon whose fidelity they could not depend".[5] No wonder that Owen in Friel's play is a figure of much ambivalence for the English as well as the Irish; and *Translations* in its conclusion shows that those official doubts were well-grounded.

The cultural violence which underlay this change of languages remained largely invisible, since it presupposed the consent of the Irish to that change. Yet *Translations* shows that Owen is finally more committed to "translating back" into his native language all that has been translated out of it. Seen in this light, his agenda has its roots in Seathrún Céitinn's retranslation of Spenser and Stanyhurst back into "truer" Gaelic terms; and its corollary in the writings of Nuala ní Dhomhnaill, Seán Ó Ríordáin and Máire Mhac an tSaoi. This process – which allows for an *Irish* translation of the Irish past – is something very different from, and far more positive than, the mechanism of imperialist translation. It involves what Nietzsche pithily called "a reversal of the theft".[6] Denying that the colonizer alone has the power to represent the native, it permits the colonized to represent themselves, not alone to the world but also to one another. Instead of the Irish past being pressed into service of a British imperial present, what is discovered by an artist like Synge is the power of the past to disrupt the revivalist present. This is evident in the dynamic uses of Gaelic tradition in *The Playboy*, and more generally in the fact that Synge's oeuvre was a sustained act of translation.

Synge's literary sensibility found its fullest expression in the manoeuvre between Irish and English. His own poetry, composed in English, seems all too often a stilted pastiche of second-rate contemporary styles, whereas the brilliant translations from continental languages into Hiberno-English dialect give us a sense of the man himself. The dialect in which he finally found his desired medium was the bilingual weave, the language of his innermost being, what George Steiner has called "the poet's dream of an absolute idiolect".[7] In the years of dramatic success from 1903 to 1909, Synge's interest in translation was compounded by his desire to test the resources of Hiberno-English. Even towards the end of his life he translated the works of Petrarch, Walter Von der Vogelweide and other continental artists into his dialect. These exercises were far more successful than many standard English versions of the work of these poets. This genius went far deeper than a conventional flair for turning a piece of Irish poetry or prose into English. It involved a capacity to project a whole Gaelic culture in English. Each of Synge's works is an act of supreme translation: the language of his plays is based less on the English spoken in rural Ireland than on the peculiar brand of English spoken in *Gaeltacht* areas. This English is an instantaneous and literal translation from Irish.[8]

Renato Poggioli has argued in an inspired paraphrase that the translator is "a character in search of an author" in whom he can identify a part of himself. His translation of such an author's work is no masquerade in which he deceives his audience by mimicking the original writer; rather ". . . he is a character who, in finding the author without, finds also the author within himself . . . Nor must we forget that such a quest or pursuit may intermittently attract the original writer also, when he too must search for the author in himself".[9] In the example of Seathrún Céitinn, Synge found a reflection of himself and his own concerns. In the native literature and lore, he found all those characteristics for which his artistic soul had longed – intensity, home-liness, wry irony, sad resignation, sensuality and the love of place. His years of writing in Paris had yielded nothing but morbid and intro-spective works; but the discovery of Aran, and the challenge to project its life to the world in English, signalled his discovery of himself as a writer. The English in which he had tried and failed to express himself in those Paris writings had been mannered, weary and effete; only when that language was vitalized by contact with a "backward" oral culture did it offer him the chance of real self-expression.

That Synge's plays should, after his death, have been triumphantly "translated back" into Irish, in the attempt to get even closer to the psychic state of his chosen localities, is but a further confirmation of their authenticity. The lesson seems clear: the more "translated" a work is, the more fully does it seem to perfect its inherent form. It was doubtless a similar kind of thinking which inspired George Moore to suggest to Yeats and Lady Gregory in 1901 that the right way to create a version of the story of Diarmuid and Gráinne was for Moore to compose it in French, for Lady Gregory to translate it into Kiltartanese, for Tadhg Ó Donnchadha to convert that into Irish, and then for Lady Gregory to retranslate it into English.[10] Presumably, his point was an aesthetic one: that Bohemia, more than this or that country, is the artist's true dwelling-place, and that the ceaseless activity of translation expresses the solidarity of the supranational artistic community.

All great works of literature are so because in some way or another they surpass the usual potentials of their own tongue, reaching out to a universal language. At certain moments of high intensity, that surplus potential may entirely escape the entrapments of language, being con-tained between the lines rather than in them. Such a moment is the dumbshow of wordless love between Máire Chatach and Lieutenant Yolland in Friel's *Translations*: in a strict sense it embodies the achieve-ment of the higher ideal underlying every act of translation, for in a language of silence which has no need of recasting is the hope of a privileged space in which resistance to all degrading systems may be possible.

Translation is in the most literal sense a reminder of that high aspiration, for the earliest translators hoped to exceed their originals, to use them as pre-texts for greater inspirations in their own languages. The energies unleashed when one element bonds with another are often volatile, but potent for all that. A translation, therefore, may release qualities which were latent but unexpressed in either the source or the target language. By redeploying ideas, images and structures from English literature in Irish, for instance, Seán Ó Ríordain massively extended its limits, using the lyrics of Wordsworth or Hopkins as a point of release for his own. Similarly, Synge, by allowing his English to be powerfully remodelled by Gaelic syntax, liberated in it yet-unsuspected meanings. This process enacted on a linguistic level the desire of many that in renovating Ireland they should also "save England". For such reasons, Walter Benjamin in a somewhat different context wrote of the translator as one who watches over the maturing process of the original language and the birth-pangs of his own. He saw every translation as an intrepid attempt to reach a little closer toward that lost, prebabelian universal idiom:

> It is the task of the translator to release in his own language that pure language which is under the spell of another, to liberate the language imprisoned in a work in his recreation of that work. For the sake of pure language, he breaks through decayed barriers of his own language.[11]

The new version glances off the original, as a tangent touches a circle, before pursuing its own primary course: yet that course is forever determined by the point of impact.

For Walter Benjamin the great flaw of most nineteenth-century translations was their excessive respect for the conventions of the target language (usually an imperial one), and their refusal to allow its usages to be creatively disrupted by the syntax of the source. This was Synge's theme-song in his critique of most previous translators: they kept turning Irish into English, rather than remodel English as Irish. His alternative programme to release hidden potentials of English was analogous to Wilde's desire to make England a pastoral republic. In effect, both men wished to reverse the trajectory of Spenser and Stanyhurst: instead of a new England called Ireland, they hoped to make a new Ireland called England.

Ultimately, however, only the English could save themselves, by following the examples mapped out for them in the writings of the Irish. "In translating", said Godfrey Lienhardt, "it is not finally some mysterious 'primitive philosophy' that we are exploring, but the further potentialities of our own thought and language".[12] Every society, every culture can only be reformed from within: and the lesson of imperialism is that one's own society is the only society which one can reform without destroying. The aim of the Irish Renaissance was such renovation: saving England turned out to be a mere rehearsal for the work of inventing Ireland. How were the Irish to do this? By performing their own acts of translation and retranslation . . . by writing their own history and then rewriting it. This would be a literal re-membering – not a making whole of what was never whole to begin with, but a gluing together of fragments in a dynamic recasting.[13]

If the past were to be exactly repeated in detail, it would smother the present: this is why Friel's sage says that it is a form of madness to remember *everything*. Indeed, to remember anything at all one must first learn how to forget it; for it is that temporary forgetfulness which gives memory the excitement of surprise, the force of revelation. Marcel Proust knew better than most the vividness of a past recalled after a period of denial. He called it "involuntary memory" which he saw as triggered by associative mechanisms; and he said that it offered "an air which is new precisely because we have breathed it in the past . . . since the true paradises are the paradises that we have lost".[14] Others went further, arguing that in order to act at all – and memory is but another action – one must forget a great deal.[15] Since absolute forgetting is as impossible as total recall, the need is to bring elements of the past into contact with the present in a dynamic constellation. Benjamin called this *citation*, but it could as validly be termed *translation*, for what is suggested is neither a break with the past nor an abject repetition of it, but a rewriting.

"To articulate the past historically", says Benjamin, "does not mean to recognize it as it really was . . . It means to seize hold of a memory as it flashes up at a moment of danger".[16] This memory might be of a legend such as Deirdre and the Sons of Uisneach, or of a major event such as the Easter Rising. The greatest sin one could commit against such past moments, said Yeats, would be to bring the work of the dead to nothing. The other great sin would be to repeat that work exactly. Between these two extremes, it is nevertheless possible to form constellations, to perform translations. That was what Patrick Pearse did in linking the work of his generation to that of 1798, 1848 and 1867. Equally, it is what Friel means in connecting the Ireland of the 1830s with that of the 1970s. His plays show the audience how it must somehow grasp the meaning of the prior moment and learn how to make it also contemporary. No activity is ever more pressing or necessary than self-translation: by recasting its own words a people makes them its own all over again. Owen's reduction in *Translations* of circumlocution to terseness is one version of that need; another is

Friel's imaginative linkage of the 1830s and 1970s. This is why the critique of Friel's "escape" into language or into the nineteenth century is so banal. The playwright is ultimately less interested in the surface details of either past or present moments than in the new constellation between them which he has made. He *is* the angel of history[17] caught in the storm that blows from paradise and propelled into that future to which his back must always be turned, while the mound of debris strewn behind him grows to the sky.

The collapse of the native language, like the great famine which followed it, is an event which remains remarkably unstudied by Irish historians: little research was done on either event for decades and even today there is no classic study by an Irish scholar. Much the same might be said of the Easter Rising and its aftermath: these also lack an adequate narrative history. Large elements of the Irish story need to be written before they can be rewritten. Just as great texts exercise a claim and cry out for translation, so also do great events. A serious translation is usually an indication of fame, of enduring value: such translations owe their existence to the prior work, much as modern Ireland (whether it admits it or not) owes its character to great events, including those neglected by its historians. Of such traumas, as much as of his own immediate fate – he killed himself in flight from the Nazis in 1940 – must Benjamin have been thinking when he wrote:

> . . . One might, for example, speak of an unforgettable life or moment, even if all men had forgotten it. If the nature of such a life or moment required that it be unforgotten, that predicate would not imply a falsehood but merely a claim not fulfilled by men, and probably also a reference to a realm in which it *is* fulfilled: God's remembrance.[18]

Even if texts and events go untranslated, it is their translatability which is significant. Just as in the gospels which show the moment of Jesus in the New Testament as forming a constellation with the moment of ancient prophecies in the Old Testament, there is in this analysis a link between remembrance and redemption: but part of the point, as Patrick Pearse understood very well, is that many people will not notice it. This type of quotation without quotation marks is most exacting, for it rejects the notion of history as continuum, and prefers to unfreeze moments by placing them in suggestive alignments. Central to it is a need, often felt by the Irish, to translate the past, in the sense of displacing it, and to put it into a disturbing relationship with the present. Irish memory has often been derisively likened to those historical paintings in which Virgil and Dante converse in a single frame:[19] but for Friel, it is the *only* method, and so the denizens of his hedge-school quote not only Virgil and Dante but also George Steiner.

This is the same strategy by which James Connolly discovered utopian socialism or Patrick Pearse a child-centred education-system in ancient Ireland. The technical problem posed for artists (as well as apologists) in 1916 was the old one: how to express something unknown in a language dense with precedents? The answer, as has been shown in detail, was also an old one: use the known to express the unknown. This was another useful reminder that all progress depends on translation: even the child learning to speak is learning how to use known words in the attempt to acquire unknown ones. Translation within one's own language is arguably as important as that between languages, and no different in essence. Friel's play on the theme, dealing with the ways in which a child or an adult acquires language, demonstrates that reading and writing are equally versions of this act.

These activities are necessarily painful, fraught with possibilities of humiliation and even defeat: for the familiar word is invariably more confidently used than the acquired, the spoken word more easily summoned than the written or read one. Language itself may be no more than a pale translation of the ideal voices of silence. The translator is by very definition belated, secondary, dependent on the prior text: yet the prior text itself keeps slipping into unavailability. If spoken words are copies, then writing is a copy of a copy, and reading but a further copying. So where is the point of origin? In the exchange of Máire Chatach and Lieutenant Yolland? But *Translations* denies that there is any source text.

This problem is raised even more acutely in Friel's other masterpiece *Faith Healer*. There the protagonist, attempting to turn human pain to balm, is as often con-man as holy healer. A broker in risk, Francis Hardy knows that to be an artist is to fail, to experience only misery punctuated by rare moments of unexpected splendour and, in the end, to know ignominious rejection. Yet the strictures are implied also of the author, for the play is an occluded version of the *Fate of the Sons of Uisneach*: its theme of a well-brought-up girl, destined for a noble calling in the north of Ireland, then spirited away to Scotland by an attractive but feckless man to the dismay of an elderly guardian, is reworked by Friel. So also is its central narrative technique, the lilting listing of place names loved and lost; and so also its consummation, a return to predicted disaster. The play turns out to be about itself, since it, like the healer, veers between confidence trickery and brilliant innovation. And the first audience which the artist must con is himself: for if he becomes overly self-analytical, he may kill his very gift and it will even sooner desert him.[20]

In *Faith Healer* an original text is neither reproduced or imitated, but set in vibration with the present – which is to say that it is decanonized in a free translation or "reverberation". By that act it transforms rather than merely reproduces the original legend, in keeping with the latest artist's expressive needs: but this is also a phase in the further development of the original, which depended for its survival over many centuries on just such translations. So also did Joyce remodel *The Odyssey* of Homer by his translation of it in *Ulysses*.

In *Faith Healer* an ancient myth is creatively misinterpreted so that Brian Friel can redefine heroism for the modern Irish audience. According to the legend Deirdre's name meant "troubler" and she was remembered for the prophecy at her birth that many would die because of her beauty. Grace, the modern Deirdre, is heroic not so much for the suffering which she inflicts (though she has some of the cruelty of the old heroine) as for the pain which she must endure with her partner, the healer. Similarly, the manager Teddy is not allowed the easy "heroic" option of instant death in defence of the man and woman he worships, but is left behind at the end to pick up what pieces remain. The ultimate realism is to deny Deirdre the fake glamour of a romantic death she had in medieval versions, and instead to give her a lonely death as a nervous wreck in a bedsitter. In this respect, Friel returns to the oldest versions of the tale, which had Deirdre dash out her brains on a rock, the hopeless act of a woman crazed with grief, a year and a day after the execution of her lover. Perhaps most significant of all is Friel's decision to give Hardy the central role, just as Naoise was the pivotal figure in the oldest version of the legend in *The Book of Leinster*.

Underlying Friel's depiction of Hardy as a modern Naoise, or for that matter Joyce's account of Bloom as a modern Ulysses, is the conviction that primitive myths are *not* impositions of a culture but innate possessions of every person, who professes to be unique but is in fact a copy, consciously or unconsciously repeating the lives of others. Hence the characteristic modern malaise of inauthenticity, which assails those sophisticated enough to sense the frustrations of a life lived in quotation marks. Hence also the supreme importance of those small differences with which history repeats itself, for they are the sole guarantee of individuality. What applies to persons and characters is also true of authors. Friel retells an old story, borrowing protagonists, situations, even phrases from the tale, and to that extent he is, like

Francis Hardy, a con-man. But like Hardy, he also remoulds his tale and his people to some private standard of excellence of his own . . . and to that extent he is indeed an artist. It adds to the poignancy of Hardy's life that he is quite unaware that he has reenacted the story of Deirdre and the Sons of Uisneach.

Friel's plays are implicit critiques of the value-free approach to history taken by most contemporary Irish historians: and reminders that it is human nature to name as truth what is usually the narrative most flattering to current ruling vanity. Many historians will not admit his implied claim that there is always a crisis of representation, that they (as much as any artist) are at the mercy of their chosen forms and genres. Friel's confrontation with them became most explicit in his 1988 play *Making History*, which asks whether there is any effective difference between a defective personal memory and a distorted public record.

In the play Archbishop Peter Lombard is writing the life of Hugh O'Neill, but what he seeks is neither "interpretation" nor "fact" but "the best possible narrative". Being himself caught up in the events he is to record, he is too wary to define either the historian's function or his method: "History has still to be made before it is remade".[21] This is, perhaps, a cynical reminder that all historians are revisionists, but it is a reminder which hints at a fundamental similarity between a recorder and maker of events. Both are *interpreters*. For the strategist O'Neill an action is an interpretation, an option for a single possibility out of a thousand others; and in seeking by imaginative action to shape a nation-state, he too is a maker of supreme fiction. Both men know, of course, that Lombard will have the last word, since history is not written by winners or losers but by historians. Yet Lombard has the wit to concede that there is no History, just histories, each one produced for persons who think they revere facts while secretly wanting a good story. So the story forgets that O'Neill at one point fought for the Tudors against Irish rebels, or that Kinsale was a one-hour rout. Instead, "the telling of it can still be a triumph".[22] The problem with that is the problem confronted in *Translations*: of what value is a linguistic contour which no longer matches the landscape of fact? Histories may get lost in the very act of being recorded and simplified into "narrative". Every interpretation is an imprisonment and an exclusion, an act of aggression against the multiplicity of life. O'Neill's history becomes Lombard's story, and the Irish historian comes to seem to him an enemy as deadly as the English colonizer, since both would imprison him in *their* fictions.

Many of Friel's earlier plays had enacted a similar dialogue between a high-minded narrator (perhaps a presiding judge, or a script-director) and the cries of those caught up in the fury of lived histories. For the latter official history became a kind of tragic net, and the more they struggled against it, the more it seemed to entrap its sad and laughable antagonists. In *Making History* there is, however, a sense that the net itself may be faintly ridiculous: the stubborn complexity of the person is asserted against social prescriptions. So the war between Gael and Gall seems a minor matter when compared to the struggle within O'Neill between native *pietas* and Renaissance self-fashioner. At times he can feel exhausted by his own versatility: but he knows that, while his "two pursuits" can scarcely be reconciled, yet the attempt must be made. The test of a first-rate mind is, indeed, its ability to hold opposed codes in the head without losing the capacity to function. The impossible, but nonetheless desirable, fusion of Gaelic and English tradition, which characterized the central love-scene in *Translations*, is attempted again in *Making History* in the marriage of O'Neill and Mabel Bagenal.

Those who seek such a reconciliation may be, it seems, either ennobled or debilitated by it. Ennobled, as when one culture repairs the gaps in another in a mutual exchange of golden songs; or debilitated, as when two discrepant codes cancel one another out, leaving only suspicion and distrust to fill the ensuing vacuum. Yeats had called the two pursuits Reality and Justice, and had hoped to hold them "in a single thought". The gap is not fully closed at the end of *Making History*, but it has been bridged by an electric irony, which suggests that the choice is not between reality and illusion, but between one dream and another. The historians who reviewed Friel's play were not impressed, and neither were they amused by such a finding.

John Banville, however, would have understood Friel perfectly, for he had already constructed *Doctor Copernicus* (1976) on a still more radical critique of academic claims to "truth". This novel shows that even a scientist will in the end choose to save the phenomena rather than admit that they have eluded him. Early in the narrative Copernicus discovers that each of his rival scientists is an unwitting artist: they know that Ptolemy's theory is wrong but have too deep an investment in it to admit this, and so they devise working theories which are grounded in Ptolemy's errors, but which can nevertheless be made to account for the superficially-observed motions of the planets. By the end of the book, Copernicus too has opted for his own "superior" falsification. "The past doesn't exist in terms of fact", said Banville himself in an interview shortly after the publication of his book: "It only exists in terms of the way we look at it".[23] What holds a world together is nothing more than a *style*, but for Banville each style excludes far more than it includes: with every structuralization of chaos, chaos itself increases, because each structure detonates new reactions. Those intrepid souls who seek a better, or at least a more aesthetic, explanation are heroes of the mind.

Copernicus, like Marx or Freud or Loyola, becomes the inventor of a new discourse. Copernicus's severance of traditional ties robs him not just of old securities but of nationality too: behind the mask of "Ermlander", says the author, "he was that which no name or nation could claim. He was Doctor Copernicus".[24] In short, he was a type of the pure artist for whom tradition is not a *datum* so much as a personal renegotiation with and reinvention of all that has gone before. Seen in this context, anti-nationalist revisionists are in a number of ways rather like the nationalist historians whom they debunk: both take the world as a given and Irish tradition as a stable element in that handover. Both accept the paradigm of the imperialist in that they overlook the actual violence of the colonial "translation" itself – the nationalist by returning to a point of mythic origin, the revisionist by treating the translator's effect that is the "native" as a cause, both literal and metaphorical. Above all, both agree that Ireland marks the outer limits of their enterprise. Banville, however, feels unable or unwilling to write from within that secure culture, and so he takes up a position beyond it, writing of all those forces which have made the very phrases "Irish tradition" or "German culture" problematic.[25]

The most chastening discovery of Banville's Copernicus is that the space once occupied by God is now filled with a void: and so, the maker of the ultimate fiction having absconded, all secondary fictions become self-enclosed. If the world is not a translation of a more perfect one elsewhere, then art and science can hardly claim any longer to be renditions of the world, being merely stylistic arrangements of experience. Banville once, in a sly parody of Shelley, said that novelists are the unacknowledged historians of the world:[26] the implication, of course, is that the historians will not acknowledge that there is a sense in which they might also be novelists. So he deliberately took for subject a scientist of whose life few facts were known, leaving him free to vivify that life and its setting with an overlaid consciousness which can quote Wallace Stevens or Henry James. In much the same manner, Shaw in *Saint Joan* had his medieval characters talk as if they had already read Marx and Nietzsche.

All of these writers are post-nationalist, insofar as they are committed to a project of perpetual translation. The nationalist, being merely the effect of a single act of translation, mistakenly takes himself for the original cause: but Irish artists have long known that such singularity is a delusion. They have known estrangement from all languages as the natural condition of their work: this has meant that they have been able to make a home in many. Far from being ill-fitted to modernity, they have taken it as the one sure given, and so theirs has been a genius for adjustment. While their people have scattered across the face of the earth, moving from neolithic communities to the hyperreality of Hell's Kitchen, the writers have shown similar gifts of adaptation. Beckett wrote his greatest masterpieces in French before translating some of them "back" into English; and then he reverted wholly to creation in English, but only when French had become "*trop facile*". Liam O'Flaherty began writing in Irish, soon switched to English, and oscillated between them after that. Flann O'Brien and Brendan Behan wrote most of their work in English, but each also wrote major texts of the modern Irish language. Joyce, the greatest of them all, wrote his last text simultaneously in about two dozen languages. Even today *Finnegans Wake* poses stupendous problems for a translator: how is the job to be done? Out of what language? And into what base-language? How can any version begin to render the plurality of the text?

All of these artists repeatedly disproved the widespread delusion that one can produce original work only in one's mother tongue. They recognized that every true translation, every text, must retain for the reader some sense of the foreignness of its originals. Beckett offered the most extreme case of this self-estrangement, but many other writers also sought it – "the most extraordinary form of humiliation that a writer, who is not a bad writer, could inflict upon himself".[27]

These observations suggest that modern Irish writing set up shop under the sign of Babel. That biblical myth rehearsed the forces and themes of Irish art, being at once a story of imperialism and of its counter-image in nationalism, and of the punishments attendant upon either. God the Father, who alone was the origin of a universal language, was driven by anger to punish the Semite imperialists who built their tower "as high as heaven" and their affliction was a proliferation of "mother tongues". Instead of filiation, they knew affiliation. That myth is a warning against all who would seek to impose an official language of enlightenment, whether English in the nineteenth century or Irish in the twentieth. The builders of the tower were guilty, after all, of wanting to make a name for themselves, of wishing to construct themselves solely by the act of self-naming.[28]

Against such hopeful simplicities, the myth insists that identity is dialogic, porous. Friel's *Translations* mocks the notion of a *cordon sanitaire* placed around a self-sufficient Ireland and it accepts that translation, however difficult, is absolutely necessary. The occupants of Babel were punished because of their vain belief that they could do away with evil and create an absolute purity.

Translation, however, allows a people to reach back longingly to a lost universal language, but only in the knowledge that it can never be repossessed. Banville's Copernicus suspects as much: "If such harmony had ever existed, he feared deep down, deep beyond admitting, that it was not to be regained".[29]

REINVENTING IRELAND

Thirty-Five

Imagining Irish Studies

"To restore great things", said Erasmus, "is sometimes a harder and nobler task than to have introduced them".[1] The exponents of the Irish Renaissance shaped and reshaped an ancient past, and duly recalled it, giving rise to an unprecedented surge of creativity and self-confidence among the people. The task facing this generation is at once less heroic and more complex: to translate the *recent* past, the high splendours and subsequent disappointments of that renaissance, into the terms of a new century. Perhaps the greatest wrong committed by the English in Ireland, after their coming, was their refusal to open themselves fully to all the experiences that followed, to achieve a true translation of that culture towards which they nonetheless moved, as if animated by some undeclared need. It was left to Yeats, Hyde and their generation to point to the lesson and to bring to England a knowledge which the colonists themselves had signally failed to glean. There is nothing especially surprising about that blindness: it is a peculiarity of imperialists everywhere that they fail to identify with human experience, "but also fail to see it as human experience".[2]

What *was* surprising, however, was the willingness of large numbers of nationalists to countenance the notion of Irish exceptionality. Preening themselves on some occasions for being "like no other people on earth", arraigning themselves on others, they often failed to regard Irish experience as representative of human experience, and so they remained woefully innocent of the comparative method, which might have helped them more fully to possess the meaning of their lives. As an exceptional instance, Ireland was always there to be studied by others: the narcissistic fantasy of some nationalists was a little like that of the naïve Aran islander who gravely told J. M. Synge that "there are few rich men now in the world who are not studying the Gaelic".[3] The proliferation of courses in Irish Studies in Britain and North America and beyond may have fed such narcissism: but it has not yet prompted

any group of native intellectuals to make a reciprocal gesture by studying the ways in which outsiders choose to see them. For instance, an
institute of British Studies, based in one or other of the universities,
might valuably monitor the ways in which the British constructed their
own world (and the Irish as a vital part of it). Instead of this, however,
many Irish-born scholars have internalized the external models, producing analyses which owe far more to the narrative methods of *Heart of
Darkness* than their authors might care to admit.

The aim of recent Irish historians has been worthy enough: to
replace the old morality-tale of Holy Ireland versus Perfidious Albion
with a less sentimental and simplified account. However, the more
seductive writers among them tended to appeal to the old Manichaean
mentality, choosing simply to invert its workings: whatever the nationalists had extolled, they tended to deride. Nationalism in Ireland, as in
most other countries, was a broad and comprehensive movement,
containing progressive as well as conservative elements. Compelled by
the facts of history to admit that nationalism often found itself in
alliance with socialism, feminism and even pacifism, the historians
tended nevertheless to characterize even cultural nationalism as Anglophobic and anti-Protestant. "To a strong element in the Gaelic
League", wrote Roy Foster in the most influential and brilliant synthesis of this school, "literature in English was Protestant as well as anti-
national". With conclusive eloquence, he deduced that "the emotions
focused by the cultural revolution at the turn of the century were
fundamentally sectarian and even racist".[4]

The motives behind these rather unexpected assertions were of the
highest: the desire of the historians was to invent a more ecumenical
and inclusive definition of Irishness than the one with which many of
them had grown up in the southern state. Denying doctrines of inevitability, they wished to restore to each moment of history the openness
which it once had: hence Foster's claim that the 1916 Rising was not
the outcome of the cultural revival led by Hyde and Yeats, so much as a
discrete event brought on by the conditions pertaining during World
War One. This was a classic "revisionist" denial of that Whig view of
history which sees everything in the light of what followed. It was a
salutary reminder that most protagonists are at the mercy of their
immediate moment: but it can be taken too far. To remove a sense of
linear causality is to deny oneself and one's readers answers to fundamental questions: Why did the English colonize, exploit and terrorize
the Irish? In the name of what values did they put down the 1916
Rising? And why did they so fatally misinterpret the popular mood as

to deliver Ireland into the arms of Sinn Féin? Because he remained incurious about the popular culture which often makes things happen, Foster was reduced in the manner of a *nouveau romancier* to chronicling cataclysmic events without apparent or adequate cause. It can be scarcely surprising that he should have found the Easter Rebellion "irrational". In such a version of history-without-agency, what seem like the impersonal laws of history are often no more than historians' laws, improvised to meet the needs of a moment.

It would be wrong to infer from this, as some nationalist critics of Foster have done, that his is a heartless, value-free practice.[5] If anything, precisely the reverse is true: far from being clinical, his work is the outcome of a deep emotional investment by a patriotic Irishman who believes that the most useful service which he can perform for his people is the devaluation of a nationalism, some of whose disciples are still willing to kill and be killed in its defence. The fact that the rebellion in the north was primarily a protest against economic oppression and political injustice has not prevented the new generation of historians from a scrupulous consideration of whether any links in the chains of events which led to insurrectionary violence might have been forged in their professional smithies. Many of them – Roy Foster and F. S. L. Lyons included – lived as Protestants in an independent southern state which was at times a sponsor of narrow-gauge nationalism and a Catholic triumphalism. These unattractive forces repelled them, as they distressed tens of thousands of liberal Catholics: many thus repelled concluded, against the weight of the evidence, that they must always have been present or at least latent in cultural nationalism. So the Anglophobia and sectarianism of the republic in the mid-century were "read back", in a curiously ahistorical fashion, into the writings and workings of the revolutionary generation. The same historians who had been taught to be sceptical of those, like Yeats, who saw every process in the light of what followed, now suspended that scepticism when it came to their own experience. Yeats was not permitted to "read forward" from the cultural *risorgimento* to 1916, but they could surely "read back" from the frustrations of their own lives.

For all their iconoclasm and for all their overdue revisions, the historians did not in the main challenge the Anglocentric account of the Irish past.[6] Instead, they produced the familiar polar narrative beloved of their nationalist precursors, but on this occasion they viewed it more often from a British than an Irish perspective. Far from seeing the British presence in Ireland as a colonial or imperial exercise, they tended to present it as well-meaning, occasionally inept, but rarely malevolent – very much in keeping with the prevailing view of the role of the military in Northern Ireland. Indeed, one of the historians, Ronan Fannning, remarked with some asperity on the indecent haste with which the authorities in Dublin, confronted by the IRA at a time when membership of the European Economic Community seemed more pressing a concern than rehearsing the wrongs of the British, suddenly accommodated the new history. He remarked that ruling regimes always seek to control the presentation of the past in such a way as to buttress and legitimize their own authority.[7] As it happened, the spread of free secondary education coincided with the moment when a revised history began to appear in school textbooks. A bitter debate ensued between the old-fashioned nationalists and the revisionists, proving little other than the fact that in Ireland the past is never a different country and scarcely even the past: instead it becomes just one more battleground contested by the forces of the present.

Most of the historians, like the British, remained fixated on a nationalism which they repeatedly deplored but could not transcend by any truly innovative methodology. Telling the old story from the other side's viewpoint was scarcely a breakthrough: more an attempt to trick out Tom Broadbent's benevolent imperialism in slightly updated gear. By refusing to countenance a post-colonial analysis, they colluded – quite unconsciously, of course – with the widespread nationalist conceit of Irish exceptionality: the Irish experience was not to be compared with that of other peoples who sought to decolonize their minds or their territory. In exculpating the British, they certainly did justice to some persons who had been unfairly demonized by nationalist historians, but they also passed rather too swiftly over instances of imperial guilt; and, in the process, they invented some new demons of their own. Patrick Pearse, for example, was no longer to be treated as a plaster saint but as a vulgar egomaniac: the consideration that it is not usual for egomaniacs to sacrifice their lives for a cause did not detain the new commentators, most of whom found it hard to imagine any set of values which might transcend the life of the individual. Yet the revisionist enterprise was genuinely useful: Pearse needed rescuing from his uncritical admirers, who had long ceased to read what he actually said, and the historians sent many back to the original texts, which surprised and delighted a whole new generation of readers. If nationalism was the thesis, revisionism was the antithesis: of its nature it was not so much wrong as incomplete. The dialectic needed to be carried through to a synthesis.

Joseph Lee's *Ireland: Politics and Society 1912–86* brought that moment even closer. In rhetoric of high voltage, the author declared his agenda with commendable openness – Ireland has been cursed with those who want to "possess" land, jobs, prestige and bereft of those who can "perform" (entrepreneurs, creative social thinkers, a dynamic middle class).[8] His work appealed to many cultural nationalists, who had no difficulty in endorsing his argument that the loss of the Irish language had a traumatic effect on Irish self-confidence. Yet explicit in Lee's study was an allegation not unlike that implicit in Foster's: that since the English left in 1921 things had only got worse. Lee's theme was the failure of economic nationalism – an ideal he judged to have been sapped by emigration, lack of enterprise, cultural introversion, and the absence of a critical intelligentsia. Readers were beguiled by the author's *brio*, by the patriotism which manifestly informed his rather devastating diagnoses, and by his willingness (so untypical of the academic) to offer prescriptions – but it may well be that he overstated his case.

His comparisons were all with smaller European countries, which did not undergo the long nightmare of colonial expropriation and misrule, much less wave after wave of massive emigration. Had he widened his field of vision, he might have conceded that in many respects the Irish achievement has been remarkable: a great modernist literature, a caring community bound together by a high degree of social consensus, an economy which (for all its undevelopment) still features in the top thirty industrial democracies, a stable multi-party system with sufficient independence to pursue through a number of decades a distinctive foreign policy unbeholden to either superpower. Greece, the other former colony of the European Union, is much less developed than Ireland in most of these respects.

Karl Marx was right to describe Ireland as a crucible of modernity, for in at least two major ways it is arguably more advanced than Britain. It has recognized the need to come to terms with nationalism and has accepted a fully modern form of the state, with a written constitution that has gradually been purged of sectarian accretions. At the start of this century, George Bernard Shaw said that England was still too backward for a Home Rule movement; and, at the end, that remains the case, with English nationalism locked into an archaic multinational state that fails to recognize modern notions of citizenship or of rights. The extraordinary modernity of Irish thinking and writing deserves to be stressed, when too many commentators have emphasized only backwardness. Equally striking are the constant, usually successful, adjustments to an ever-changing situation. It would be hardly too much to say that the Irish, despite their reputation, are one of the least conservative peoples of Europe, to judge by the rate at which they have changed over the past century and a half. The need now is to understand the inner experience of those caught up in the process: and my belief is that literature and popular culture can help us to recover many voices drowned out by official regimes or by their appointed chroniclers.

The historians, with the best intentions in the world, rarely acknowledge that they write at the mercy of literature – that for each there is an appropriate form, which dictates a whole range of exclusions as well as inclusions. If Foster has written the story of his land as a *nouveau roman*, then Lee has chosen the *jeremiad*. Man, it would seem, is finally an aesthetic creature who will choose the most "elegant" model which seems to account for the facts – but literary studies may, somewhat paradoxically, serve to remind people of all those messy phenomena which escape such hopeful thematization. This is not to claim a higher truth-value for literature, merely to recognize that it can complete the picture and at the same time draw attention to what the framer chose to exclude. The myths debunked by revisionist historians were in some cases terribly false; yet, if huge numbers of people believed in them, then they also must be accorded their place as decisive agents of history. Moreover, the trauma of those who suffered and the exaltation of those who struggled deserve our accounting. To creative artists may have fallen the task of explaining what no historian has fully illuminated – the reason why the English came to regard the Irish as inferior and barbarous, on the one hand, and, on the other, poetic and magical.

Perhaps the greatest contribution made by Joseph Lee to Irish scholarship has been his insistence on the value of comparisons (even though most of his are limited to a European frame of reference). Only Raymond Crotty, in his analytic studies of agricultural economics in Ireland and the "underdeveloped" world, went further.[9] Both men stood relatively isolated in a university system which lacked departments of comparative politics or comparative literature. As notable as this lack, however, was the unwillingness of most colleges in the republic to offer holistic courses in Irish Studies. These are widely and successfully taught on an interdisciplinary basis in Belfast, Coleraine, Oxford, Kent, London, Liverpool and in dozens of American, Canadian and Australian universities, but in Ireland the thinking still seems to be that academic rigour would be compromised by such approaches. The result is an extraordinarily insulated set of disciplinary activities, as well as a rather dishonourable suspicion of those few practitioners who have bravely pursued cultural studies in the widest sense. Yet the need for such ecumenical, even impure, practices is far greater there than in most other countries. Imagine the contribution to peace and reconciliation if every unionist child, through an integrated course of cultural study, learned something of the riches of the Gaelic tradition as mediated by such exemplary Protestants as Synge, Gregory and Hyde. Imagine also the potential if many children in the republic were to be challenged by a syllabus which asked them to study the elements of English Protestant tradition which might help them to repair the gaps in their own. An education which used the traditions of neighbouring peoples as a basis for constructing a critique of its own might in due time lead to real progress.

There have been sustained, at times self-lacerating, attempts at just such an autocritique in the republic: but these have been matched by no similar revisions in other places. The unionists of Northern Ireland, perhaps because they feel besieged, consider this a time less for self-scrutiny than for self-assertion, and so they have produced no coherent movement of revisionism – although individual contributions by Christopher McGimpsey and the reverend Martin Smyth have proved illuminating. Equally, the British analysis veers between the traditional "not an inch" of the pro-union conservatives and the rather uncritical "greener than green" sentiment of the labourite left. Unionists have yet to explain the meaning of their union with a Britain now filled with ethnic minorities and a multicultural system: in such a contact, might not the speakers of the Irish language in Belfast claim good treatment as a civil right rather than as a tribal challenge? There is reason to believe that the "union" in which many believe is with a Britain that is now a pre-war curiosity for historians.

The British, for their part, might ask themselves to spell out the implications of their continuing support for the union: they must attempt to explain how for fifty years one of the most civilized peoples of modern Europe maintained a one-party state on its very own doorstep. And they might consider whether the cost of that union has been heavy not just in terms of lives and money, but in the damage done to British democracy by a system of torture, supergrasses and spies. As the forces for a republican Britain gather strength and self-confidence, they may begin to ask whether the links between a triumphalist all-Protestant monarchy and the thinking of loyalist exremists are too close for comfort.

British socialists and radicals might come to question their own longstanding fixation on Irish nationalism, with its colourful array of poets, balladeers, desperadoes, and try instead to make an informed assessment of the deeper aspirations and implications of unionism. Since the days of Matthew Arnold, British liberals have offered mythical readings of the culture which their government is nominally opposing: perhaps it is time for them to conduct a pragmatic analysis of the culture of the northern majority which Westminster is still actually supporting. The link with an exclusively Protestant monarchy has not been an entirely happy one for many unionists, who are painfully aware of the use of that link to an openly sectarian politician like Ian Paisley: and the much-neglected contribution of Ulster Presbyterianism to the building of the United States might prove a better source of inspiration, and of overseas aid, in years to come. One possible explanation for the reluctance of many unionist revisionists to declare themselves may be the widespread view among republicans that Northern Ireland, being constructed on ritual discrimination, is unsalvageable: to reform it, they say, would be in effect to destroy it. Yet the emergence of a strong unionist autocritique might well be the most potent of all defences against such strictures.[10]

Equally, the citizens of the republic need to put some hard questions to themselves. Just how "Gaelic" is the self-image of a country which, within the past decade, has had a Minister for Education who could not speak the Irish language? And just how "Catholic" is a land which no longer produces priests in sufficient quantity to service the increasingly elderly and depopulated parishes of the major archdioceses?

Of their very nature, the problems of the north of Ireland cannot be solved by some bold, imaginative gesture: rather their harsh contours can be softened by a steady chipping-away at the lies fostered by simplified versions of history. Just how tangled the questions of identity have become is apparent in the fact that militant loyalist gunmen have at various times in recent decades threatened to kill British soldiers in defence of a union which – it is feared – the authorities in London might be about to betray. There could scarcely be a more vivid illustration of Douglas Hyde's thesis that Anglophobia was strongest among those who were most Anglicized: what was true of English-imitating Irish nationalists in the 1890s seems now to be true of English-fixated Irish unionists in the 1990s. Hyde took this hatred of England as a sign of lost self-confidence, of a people whose culture lacked an inner dynamic ever since their abandonment of their native language.

Paradoxical it may be, but the recent debate surrounding the Irish language may shed much unexpected light on the current dilemma of unionists. Some unionist militants, as if vaguely sensing this, have taken to learning the Irish language during protracted spells in jail; others have adopted the figure of Cuchulain who, after all, defended the gap of the north against outside attack, as a model to inspire their followers. There is an Orange Lodge which marches under the banner *Oidhreacht Éireann* (Irish Heritage). Some of the more liberal unionists, such as Christopher McGimpsey, have argued strongly for the Irish language as an essential part of their heritage too: and it is a fact that many ancestors of today's loyalists would have been Irish-speaking.

The twin frustrations of twentieth-century Irish life, reflected in the two unachieved aims of the largest political party on the island, are the failure to reintegrate the national territory and to revive Irish as the community language. The second wound is much less discussed in books and newspapers, and nobody has died because of it – but the silence which surrounds it may in large part be due to the fact that it was self-inflicted. In just over a century a language spoken by millions withered to almost nothing. Had such a thing happened in any other small or medium-sized European country, it is probable that the language in question would have disappeared. At the start of the nineteenth century, there were more speakers of Irish than speakers of Dutch, Danish, Norwegian, Swedish or Welsh: yet they coolly abandoned their language in the belief that it was an obstacle to progress. Only later did some of them, led by Douglas Hyde, conclude that with it went a social framework, a hold on a world, a basis for self-belief and, ultimately, economic prosperity.

Few enough people outside the ranks of cultural nationalism have been able to admit to the traumatizing effect of the loss of Irish on the personality of citizens. Roy Foster's *Modern Ireland* offers no separate consideration of it in the course of a very long study. For more than half a century after the foundation of the independent state in 1922, there was no official investigation of public attitudes. Most people congratulated themselves on their eloquence in English, while remaining dumb in Irish.[11] It is hard to avoid the conclusion that even the brilliance of the Irish literary performance in English may have had about it some element of determined compensation. The astonishing speed and stunning success with which the Irish jettisoned their native language has never been fully explained, nor has the unsuccess with which they strove to reclaim it in the twentieth century. After seventy years of official support and daily classes for every school child in the land, only five per cent could claim "frequent user" ability, and only two per cent "native speaker" fluency.[12] Learning a second language is never easy, of course, yet with far fewer institutional supports, the Irish mastered English so comprehensively in the nineteenth century that they produced one of the greatest literary outpourings in that language.

Most other European minorities who learned English did so only when they had settled in major cities of Britain or the new world: but the Irish changeover occurred at home. Other peoples had to trade with speakers of a foreign language and so to acquire some proficiency in it, but this never led them to give up their own. The Irish experience was in this respect unique: they didn't learn English in order to emigrate – rather they learned English, and then many of them emigrated, finding no pressing reasons to stay. Seán de Fréine has argued most convincingly that the Great Famine did not of itself destroy the language: a people with self-belief will recover from even worse cataclysms, as both the Germans and Jews have done in the twentieth century. Rather, the Famine revealed a new helplessness in people who had previously faced adversity with confidence and good spirit: it exposed the fact that they no longer had traditions which might give them sustenance.[13] De Fréine contends that the Penal Laws of the previous century debilitated the Irish, robbing them of an aristocratic leadership. They were willing to adopt English by the 1790s, if that was to be the price of reforms which would permit them to hold onto their religion. So Maynooth was set up in 1795, with classes conducted in English for "young dandies" who were painfully keen to conceal their Irish.[14]

Thereafter, more and more parents who spoke only Irish to one another saw to it that English alone was spoken by their children. A process of "denial" soon followed. Convulsed by guilt at the enormity of what they had done, many found it most convenient to forget that there ever had been such a thing as an Irish language distinct from English. The inferiority-complex which impelled so many to give up Irish was not cured, more often exacerbated, by the gesture: and so a people in denial sought to project their own guilt elsewhere. Hence the rampant Anglophobia among many nationalists in the latter half of the nineteenth century, and the consequent writing of Irish history as a Manichaean morality-tale in the first half of the twentieth.[15] Hence, too, the over-emphasis on Catholicism as definitive of Irishness in the same period. With the native language all but gone, many found it necessary to locate the sole or central meanings of a culture in what *had* survived. Yet the evidence would now suggest that the Irish may be about to jettison Catholicism as unsentimentally as once they disposed of their own language.

By its own admission the Catholic church is already on the retreat in the southern state, unable to find any mainstream daily newspaper to sponsor its values: yet many Protestant unionists remain suspicious of the siren-call of the south. In ancient times, certainly, the seductive powers of Gaelic culture were such that even a group as self-confident as the Normans was assimilated, becoming "more Irish than the Irish themselves": but the evidence from recent centuries all points to the capacity *of the Irish themselves* to be assimilated. The more Anglophobic the leaders of Irish nationalism became, the more fully did they make their country an integral part of a prevailing British culture. At the start of the century Synge had lamented the lack of sufficient Irish readers to sustain native publishing houses or a national school of letters: yet the nationalist politicians who grumbled about a unionist veto on political progress never seemed to worry about the fact that English publishing houses and English tastes largely determined what books by Irish authors got into print.

In more recent decades, native publishing houses have flourished, but the newspaper market has been flooded by cheap British tabloids, which sold widely and did much to coarsen public taste, while the better broadsheet papers were forced to imitate English rivals, which constantly undercut them on the basis of their superior economies of scale. There was little enough reason for unionists to fear cultural assimilation: rather the danger was that both unionists and nationalists were being coopted by the global media network in the English language.

Against that rather bleak backdrop the cultural successes of the past three decades seem positively heartening. There are now thousands of books published in Ireland every year, to a very high standard of writing and design: an indigenous children's literature is but one manifestation of a new-found confidence. Local publishing companies, like local radio stations, have reflected the traditions of their immediate hinterland in ways which help people to resist the globalization of English-language culture. Among the young in particular, ever since the 1960s, the Irish language has been embraced by many as a force for a "counterculture" quite distinct from nationalist attachments. Indeed, anti-English outbursts have been signally absent among those who, speaking Irish on a daily basis, have no reason to worry as to whether what they say or do has the stamp of Irishness or not. Given that only fifty people could write in Irish when the Gaelic League set to work, the current levels of writing in the language are near-miraculous.

The fact that many who learned Irish as a second language are also the ones who have mastered French and German has had its exemplary value in answering negative criticisms of the amount of time devoted to the study of Irish in schools. One of the less admirable features of British culture (aped by many nationalists) was its insularity, when it came to the speaking of continental languages. Arguably, the Irish-speaking lobby has done more than most others to counter this. Equally, the fact that many of the most successful business "achievers" in society have been enthusiastic *Gaeilgeoiri* has strengthened arguments for a connection between cultural self-confidence and economic success. Such self-belief might ultimately prove far more attractive to uncertain unionists in search of a viable identity than the more fretful nationalism which preceded it. The polls in the south show a huge majority against coercing unionists into a united Ireland.[16] At the same time, Irish speakers, rightly resentful of a Southern state whose officials could not always deal with them in their native language, made a new kind of case on the basis of minority rights: and in making it they repeatedly urged unionists to keep a close eye on this "test case", which might have implications for the treatment of a unionist minority in some future "agreed Ireland".

Useful lessons from the Irish experience might be learned and applied in other places and settings. The major moral – it is not too strong a word – is this: that, if the native culture of a people is devalued and destroyed for the sake of material progress, what follows may not be material progress of the kind hoped for, but cultural confusion and a diminished sense of enterprise. The Irish prosper mightily abroad, whenever they are part of a dynamic community with a belief in itself. At home during the earlier decades of the independent state, they often seemed to stagnate through lost self-belief. Given that they had just done the impossible and dislodged a mighty imperial army, this was a remarkable failure – although it seems less astounding now in the light of subsequent failures in Africa and elsewhere. Nevertheless, some significant element in that failure may be traceable to the experience of losing Irish.

The confusion which followed was, in the words of one of Brian Friel's characters, not an ignoble condition.[17] It produced a great experimental literature, which is admired across the world and which has, coded into its texts, many elements which might be helpful in redesigning an Ireland of the future. If other, less original groups in that society were to look to artists for inspiration, and not just for ornament, much could be learned from the scrutiny. Their art shows that the Irish are still, despite all their frustrations, vibrant – a people of immense versatility, sophistication and multiplicity of viewpoint. The past decade has seen a notable emergence of regional theatre companies, of publishing houses devoted to local authors and local history; and the new community radio stations are winning more and more listeners. If "Ireland" is recovering an interest in its constituent parts, that may be all to the good: writers nowadays are more alert to the dangers of overriding real differences of class, region or language. While the peripheries seem ever more vital, the Abbey Theatre – despite the brilliant successes of Friel, Murphy and Frank McGuinness – has found it increasingly difficult to reconcile its "national" duty to perform a largely ruralist canon with its "civic" desire to service its immediate hinterland. Perhaps by redefining the National Theatre as an abstract, federal entity, encompassing vibrant regional companies who might play parts of that canon, the Abbey could be freed to move in that direction. In this way the idea of a national theatre could be defended and updated.

If the notion of "Ireland" seemed to some to have become problematic, that was only because the seamless garment once wrapped like a green flag around Cathleen ní Houlihan had given way to a quilt of many patches and colours, all beautiful, all distinct, yet all connected too. No one element should subordinate or assimilate the others: Irish or English, rural or urban, Gaelic or Anglo, each has its part in the pattern.

NOTES

INTRODUCTION

1. Benedict Anderson, "Exodus", *Critical Inquiry*, Vol. 20, No. 2, Winter 1994, 316.
2. Ibid., 319.
3. Bill Ashcroft, Gareth Griffiths, Helen Tiffin, *The Empire Writes Back: Theory and Practice in Postcolonial Literatures*, London 1989, 33.
4. On the Janus-faced nature of nationalism in the "developing" world, see three brilliant recent interventions: Partha Chatterjee, *Nationalist Thought and the Colonial World: A Derivative Discourse*, London 1986; Kwame Anthony Appiah, *In My Father's House: Africa in the Philosophy of Culture*, London 1993; and Basil Davidson, *The Black Man's Burden: Africa and the Curse of the Nation-State*, London 1992. The increasing influence of African (and Indian) analyses on recent Irish cultural debates may be measured by reading books as different as Desmond Fennell's *Heresy: The Battle of Ideas in Modern Ireland*, Belfast 1993 and Liz Curtis, *The Cause of Ireland*, London 1995.

ONE: A NEW ENGLAND CALLED IRELAND?

1. See Declan Kiberd, "The Fall of the Stage Irishman", *The Genres of the Irish Literary Revival*, ed. R. Schleifer, Norman, Oklahoma 1979, 39–60 where this argument was first elaborated.
2. Edmund Spenser, "A View of the Present State of Ireland" (1596), *The Field Day Anthology of Irish Writing*, 1, Derry 1991, 183 ff.
3. "An Síogaí Rómhánach", *Five Seventeenth Century Political Poems*, ed. C. O'Rahilly, Dublin 1952, 29.
4. Spenser, ibid., 191.
5. See Piaras Béaslaoi, *Éigse NuaGhaedhilge* 1, Dublin n.d., 64.
6. Philip Edwards, *Threshold of a Nation: A Study in English and Irish Drama*, Cambridge 1979, 79.

7. Act 3, scene 2, lines 120–4. Touchiness on matters of national pride was not confined to the Irish. After the disappointments of the Earl of Essex's campaign in Ireland, this passage may have been censored on the Elizabethan stage: certainly it does not exist in the 1600 Quarto. By July 1599 the open discussion of Irish affairs was itself a serious offence: already Ireland was turning into the official English Unconscious. On this see Janet Clare, *Art Made Tongue-Tied by Authority: Elizabeth and Jacobean Dramatic Censorship*, Manchester 1990, 71–2.

8. Quoted by Edwards, 79.

9. Seathrún Céitinn (Geoffrey Keating), *Foras Feasa ar Éirinn* 1, ed. David Comyn, London 1902, 76.

10. Ibid., 30.

11. See Andrew Carpenter, "Double Vision in Anglo-Irish Literature", *Place, Personality and the Irish Writer*, ed. Carpenter, Gerrards Cross 1977, 182–3.

12. See Edmund Burke, *Irish Affairs*, London 1988 (first published 1881).

13. Edmund Burke, *Works*, Boston 1869, Vol. 10, 217.

14. Burke, *Works*, Vol. 2, 222.

15. Burke, *Correspondence*, ed. T. Copeland, Cambridge Mass. 1958, Vol. 5, 255.

16. Burke, *Works*, Vol. 2, 195.

17. Burke, *Works*, Vol. 12, 23–4.

18. Edmund Burke, *Reflections on the Revolution in France* in *Works*, Vol. 2, 320.

19. Burke, *Works*, Vol. 2, 205.

20. Burke, *Works*, Vol. 5, 225.

21. Burke, *Works*, Vol. 5, 148.

22. Conor Cruise O'Brien, introduction to *Reflections on the Revolution in France*, Harmondsworth 1969, 42–9.

23. Burke, *Correspondence*, Vol. 1, 202.

24. Standish O'Grady, *Selected Essays and Passages*, Dublin 1918, 180 ff.

IRELAND: ENGLAND'S UNCONSCIOUS?

1. John Keats, *Letters*, selected by Frederick Page, London 1954, 149.

2. Matthew Arnold, *The Study of Celtic Literature*, London 1891, 115.

3. Ibid., 104.

4. Shaemas O'Sheel, *Jealous of the Dead Leaves*, New York 1928.

5. Arnold, ibid., 92.

TWO: OSCAR WILDE – THE ARTIST AS IRISHMAN

1. Henry Craik, letter to John Forster, Forster MS 48.E.25, British Library.

2. W. B. Yeats, *Autobiographies*, London 1955, 138.

3. Ibid., 138.
4. Ibid., 137.
5. Richard Ellmann, *Oscar Wilde*, Harmondsworth 1987, 11–12.
6. Oscar Wilde, *Plays*, Harmondsworth 1968, 267.
7. Oscar Wilde, *Complete Works*, Glasgow 1994, 770.
8. Wilde, *Plays*, 51.
9. Quoted by H. Montgomery Hyde, *Oscar Wilde*, London 1976, 31.
10. Oscar Wilde, *Selected Letters*, ed. R. Hart-Davis, Oxford 1979, 20–1.
11. Quoted Hyde, 232.
12. Wilde, *Selected Letters*, 100.
13. Quoted by Hyde, 85.
14. Quoted by Richard Ellmann, *James Joyce*, Oxford 1959, 226.
15. Richard Ellmann, *Eminent Domain*, Oxford 1967, 12–13.
16. Wilde, *Selected Letters*, 197.
17. See Hyde, 38 ff.
18. Oscar Wilde, *The Artist as Critic*, ed. R. Ellmann, London 1970, 389.
19. Ibid., 136–40.
20. On this see Lionel Trilling, *Sincerity and Authenticity*, Oxford 1972, 118–22.
21. Wilde, *Plays*, 288.
22. Ibid., 290.
23. James Laver, *The Concise History of Costume and Fashions*, New York 1969, 182.
24. Wilde, *Plays*, 310.
25. On Wilde's critique of determinism, see Christopher Nassaar, *Into the Demon Universe*, New Haven 1974, 135–7.
26. Quoted by Rodney Shewan, *Oscar Wilde: Art and Egotism*, London 1977, 193.
27. Wilde, *Plays*, 263.
28. Ibid., 277.
29. See L. P. Curtis Jnr., *Anglo-Saxons and Celts: A Study of Anti-Irish Prejudice in Victorian England*, Bridgeport 1968.
30. Wilde, *Selected Letters*, 50.
31. Otto Rank, *The Double: A Psychoanalytic Study*, New York 1971.
32. Wilde, *Plays*, 262.
33. Eric Stern, review of Rank's *The Double*, *Die Literatur* XXIX, 1926–7, 555.
34. Rank, *The Double*, 48 ff.
35. Wilde, *Plays*, 284.
36. Quoted by Harry Tucker, introduction, Rank, *The Double*, xvi.
37. G. W. F. Hegel, *The Phenomenology of Mind*, London 1966, 229–40.
38. Ashis Nandy, *The Intimate Enemy: Loss and Recovery of Self Under Colonialism*, Bombay 1983, 7–8.
39. Ibid., 79–113.
40. Ibid., 11.

41. Wilde, *The Artist as Critic*, 403.
42. Quoted by R. K. R. Thornton, *The Decadent Dilemma*, London 1983.
43. Quoted by H. Kingsmill-Moore, *Reminiscences and Reflections*, London 1930, 45.
44. Nandy, 32–5.
45. Almy, "New Views of Mr. O. W.", *Theatre*, London 1894, 124.
46. Wilde, *Plays*, 268.
47. Ibid., 268.
48. Quoted Ellmann, *Oscar Wilde*, 20.
49. Quoted by Hyde, 71.
50. Wilde, *Selected Letters*, 29.
51. Ellmann, *Oscar Wilde*, 186.
52. Quoted by Tom Nairn, *The Enchanted Glass: Britain and its Monarchy*, London 1988, 328.
53. Quoted ibid., 332.
54. Ibid., 340.
55. Wilde, *Selected Letters*, 112.
56. Wilde, *The Artist as Critic*, 396.
57. Ibid., 373.
58. Wilde, *The Artist as Critic*, 405.
59. Jorge Luis Borges, *Labyrinths*, Harmondsworth 1970, 216.
60. George Russell, *Letters from AE*, ed. Alan Denson, London 1961, 20.
61. Wilde, *The Artist as Critic*, 130.
62. Quoted by Ellmann, 186.
63. Wilde, *The Artist as Critic*, 386.

THREE: JOHN BULL'S OTHER ISLANDER – BERNARD SHAW

1. G. B. Shaw, *John Bull's Other Island*, in *The Field Day Anthology of Irish Writing*, Vol. 2, Derry 1991, 438.
2. G. B. Shaw, *The Matter with Ireland*, ed. David H. Greene and Dan H. Laurence, London 1962, 33.
3. Shaw, *John Bull's Other Island*, 432.
4. Ibid., 429.
5. Ibid., 427.
6. Ibid., 426.
7. Ibid., 459.
8. Ibid., 440.
9. Ibid., 436.
10. Ibid., 433.
11. Shaw, *Matter*, 16.
12. On this see Alfred J. Turco Jnr., *Shaw's Moral Vision: The Self and Salvation*, Ithaca 1976, 178 ff.

13. Frantz Fanon, *The Wretched of the Earth*, tr. by Constance Farrington, Harmondsworth 1967, 124.
14. Shaw, *John Bull's Other Island*, 439.
15. Ibid., 470–1.
16. Ibid., 460.
17. Ibid., 431.
18. Ibid., 425.
19. Ibid., 467.
20. Ibid., 467.
21. Ibid., 469.
22. Ibid., 436.
23. Ibid., 467.
24. Shaw, *Matter*, 99.
25. Shaw, *John Bull's Other Island*, 461.
26. Ibid., 471.
27. Shaw, *Matter*, 35.
28. Ibid., 149.
29. Ibid., 252.

FOUR: TRAGEDIES OF MANNERS – SOMERVILLE AND ROSS

1. Quoted by Gifford Lewis, *Somerville and Ross: The World of the Irish RM*, Harmondsworth 1987, 165.
2. Lewis, ibid., 9.
3. E. Oe. Somerville and Martin Ross, *The Real Charlotte*, London 1977, 11.
4. Quoted by Gifford Lewis, 104.
5. Gifford Lewis ed., *Selected Letters of Somerville and Ross*, London 1989, 252.
6. E. Oe. Somerville, *Irish Memories*, Chapter 8.
7. Quoted by Gifford Lewis, *Somerville and Ross*, 127.
8. Charles Lever, *Tom Burke of Ours*. Dublin 1844, 71.
9. Somerville and Ross, *The Real Charlotte*, 67.
10. Ibid., 117.
11. Ibid., 45.
12. Ibid., 79.
13. Ibid., 124.
14. Somerville, *Irish Memories*, Chapter 20.
15. Quoted by Hilary Robinson, *Somerville and Ross: A Critical Appreciation*, Dublin 1980, 87.
16. Lewis, *Somerville and Ross*, 196.
17. Quoted by Lewis, ibid., 134.
18. The phrase is D. W. Harding's from the essay of that title in *Scrutiny* VIII (1940), 346–62.
19. Quoted by Robinson, 88.

20. Quoted ibid., 88.
21. John Cronin, "The Real Charlotte", *The Anglo-Irish Novel*, Belfast 1980, 146.
22. Somerville and Ross, *The Real Charlotte*, 327.
23. Ibid., 42.
24. C. S. Lewis, "A Note on Jane Austen", *Jane Austen: A Collection of Critical Essays*, ed. Ian Watt, New Jersey 1963, 33.
25. Somerville and Ross, *The Real Charlotte*, 223.
26. Ibid., 344.
27. Ibid., 198.
28. Ibid., 338.
29. Ibid., 198.
30. Ibid., 338.
31. Ibid., 80.
32. Ibid., 178.
33. Ibid., 24.
34. Lewis, *Somerville and Ross*, 44.
35. Quoted ibid., 195.
36. Somerville and Ross, *The Real Charlotte*, 50–1.
37. Ibid., 245.

FIVE: LADY GREGORY AND THE EMPIRE BOYS

1. Augusta Gregory, *Seventy Years 1852–1922*, ed. Colin Smythe, Gerrards Cross 1974, 1.
2. Gregory, Holograph Diary, Vol. 12, 11 April 1896, Berg Collection, New York.
3. Mary Lou Kohfeldt Stevenson, "The Cloud of Witnesses", *Lady Gregory: Fifty Years After*, eds. Ann Saddlemyer and Colin Smythe, Gerrards Cross 1987, 60.
4. Holograph Diary, Vol. 2, Berg.
5. George Moore, *Vale*, New York 1920, 184.
6. See *Lady Gregory: Fifty Years After*, 197 and 195.
7. Brian Jenkins, "The Marriage", ibid., 79.
8. Gregory, *Seventy Years*, 34.
9. Ibid., 35.
10. Ibid., 36.
11. Ibid., 38.
12. Ibid., 59, 35.
13. Mary Lou Kohfeldt, *Lady Gregory: The Woman Behind the Irish Renaissance*, London 1985, 62–3.
14. *Seventy Years*, 44.
15. Ibid., 49.
16. Ibid., 54.

17. Kohfeldt, *Lady Gregory*, 65.
18. Augusta Gregory, "A Woman's Sonnets", *Lady Gregory: Fifty Years After*, 105.
19. Kohfeldt, *Lady Gregory*, 74–5.
20. Quoted ibid., 75, 80.
21. Quoted ibid., 79.
22. Quoted ibid., 82–3.
23. *Seventy Years*, 95–6.
24. "A Woman's Sonnets", 106.
25. Augusta Gregory, "Dervorgilla", *Selected Plays*, Gerrards Cross 1983, 155.
26. Ibid., 156.
27. Ibid., 158–9.
28. Ibid., 161.
29. The lines are by Aogán Ó Rathaille, from "Bhailintín Brún".
30. *Selected Plays*, 165.
31. Ibid., 166.
32. Ibid., 168.
33. Ibid., 169.
34. W. B. Yeats, *Memoirs*, ed. D. Donoghue, London 1972, 190.
35. Quoted by Kohfeldt, *Lady Gregory*, 213.
36. Augusta Gregory, "Grania", *Selected Plays*, 189.
37. *Seventy Years*, 91.
38. *Selected Plays*, 190.
39. Ibid., 197.
40. Ibid., 187.
41. Ibid., 205.
42. Ibid., 210.
43. Ibid., 212.
44. Ibid., 214.
45. Ibid., 213.

YEATS: INTERCHAPTER

1. Karl Marx, Friedrich Engels, *Selected Correspondence 1846–95*, London 1934, 92, 94.
2. John Mitchel, *Jail Journal*, Dublin 1913, 357.

SIX: CHILDHOOD AND IRELAND

1. G. K. Chesterton, *The Autobiography of G. K. Chesterton*, New York 1936, 139.
2. W. M. Murphy, *Prodigal Father: The Life of John Butler Yeats*, Ithaca 1978, 161.
3. W. B. Yeats, *Autobiographies*, London 1955, 31.

4. Ibid., 49.
5. Ibid., 27.
6. W. B. Yeats, *Collected Poems*, London 1950, 233.
7. W. B. Yeats, *Collected Plays*, London 1952, 55.
8. Peter Coveney, *The Image of Childhood*, Harmondsworth 1967, 193.
9. F. Marryat, *Masterman Ready*, London 1878, 140.
10. Yeats, *Autobiographies*, 11.
11. Quoted *Prodigal Father*, 87.
12. Yeats, *Collected Poems*, 266.
13. Ibid., 340.
14. Yeats, *Autobiographies*, 5.
15. Letter to J. P. Fitzgerald, April 1947; quoted by Michael Holroyd, "GBS and Ireland", *Sewanee Review* LXXXIV, No. 1, Winter 1976, 46.
16. Yeats, *Autobiographies*, 35.
17. Ibid., 3.
18. Yeats, *Collected Poems*, 136–7.
19. Yeats, *Autobiographies*, 280.
20. Yeats, *Collected Poems*, 199.
21. Ibid., 347.
22. Ibid., 381.
23. Yeats, *Autobiographies*, 47.
24. Ibid., 461.
25. Yeats, *Collected Poems*, 392.
26. Yeats, *Autobiographies*, 106.
27. Yeats, *Collected Poems*, 113.
28. Quoted in *Prodigal Father*, 446.
29. Allan Wade ed., *Letters of W. B. Yeats*, London 1954, 63.
30. Yeats, *Autobiographies*, 305.
31. Yeats, *Collected Poems*, 21.
32. Ibid., 204.
33. Ibid., 205.

SEVEN: THE NATIONAL LONGING FOR FORM

1. William Henry Curran, *The Life of John Philpott Curran*, ed. R. Shelton Mackenzie, Chicago 1882, 523.
2. Patrick O'Farrell, *Ireland's English Question: Anglo-Irish Relations 1534–1970*, New York 1971, 14.
3. W. B. Yeats, *Collected Poems*,
4. Ibid., 241.
5. Matthew Arnold, *The Study of Celtic Literature*, 144.
6. Gilles Deleuze and Felix Guattari, *Kafka: Toward a Minor Literature*, Minneapolis 1986, 28.
7. Chinua Achebe, *Hopes and Impediments*, London 1988, 56.
8. Oscar Wilde, *The Artist as Critic*, 300.

9. Yeats, *Collected Poems*, 57.
10. Achebe, *Hopes*, 43.
11. Yeats, *Autobiographies*, 515.
12. Ibid., 515.
13. Ibid., 531.
14. Ibid., 244.
15. Ibid., 473.
16. Ibid., 438.
17. Ibid., 437.
18. Ibid., 93.
19. Ibid., 485.
20. W. B. Yeats, *Anima Mundi*, 347–8.
21. Yeats, *Autobiographies*, 457.
22. Ibid., 58.
23. Ibid., 166.
24. Ibid., 166.
25. Ibid., 273.
26. Ibid., 194, 254.
27. Deleuze and Guattari, *Kafka*, 17.
28. Yeats, *Autobiographies*, 263.
29. Ibid., 321.
30. Ibid., 461.
31. Ibid., 476.
32. Ibid., 463.
33. Ibid., 493.
34. W. B. Yeats, "First Principles", *Samhain*, December 1904, 20.
35. Walt Whitman, preface to *Leaves of Grass*, *The Portable Walt Whitman*, ed. Mark van Doren, New York 1969, 56.
36. W. B. Yeats, *Samhain*, December 1904, 20.
37. On this see Louis MacNeice, *The Poetry of W. B. Yeats*, London 1967, 41 ff. Biographical sources for Whitman here include Justin Kaplan, *Walt Whitman: A Life*, New York 1980; and Paul Zweig, *Walt Whitman: The Making of the Poet*, New York 1984.

RETURN TO THE SOURCE? INTERCHAPER

1. P. H. Pearse, "About Literature", *An Claidheamh Soluis*, 26 May 1906, 6.
2. J. M. Synge, Manuscripts, Trinity College Dublin, Ms 4387, 14ff.

EIGHT: DEANGLICIZATION

1. W. B. Yeats, *Ideas of Good and Evil*, London 1903, 337.

2. W. J. O'Neill Daunt, *Personal Recollection of the late Daniel O'Connell*, London 1848, 14–15.

3. Maureen Wall, "The Decline of the Irish Language", *A View of the Irish Language*, ed. Brian Ó Cuív, Dublin 1969, 86.

4. Benedict Anderson, *Imagined Communities*, London 1983, 122.

5. W. B. Yeats, *Samhain*, October 1901, 9.

6. Harold Bloom, *Yeats*, New York 1970, 87.

7. W. B. Yeats, *Uncollected Prose 1*, ed. J. P. Frayne, London 1970, 361.

8. J. M. Synge, "National Drama: A Farce", *Plays 1*, ed. Ann Saddlemyer, Oxford 1968, 221–2.

9. Quoted by Diarmuid Coffey, *Douglas Hyde: President of Ireland*, Dublin 1938, 18.

10. On ascendancy attitudes to Irish, see Janet Egleson Dunleavy and Gareth W. Dunleavy, *Douglas Hyde: A Maker of Modern Ireland*, Berkeley 1991, 1–136.

11. George Moore, *Hail and Farewell*, ed. R. Cave, Gerrards Cross 1976, 238.

12. W. B. Yeats, *Samhain*, 1905, 5–6.

13. W. B. Yeats, postscript, *Ideals in Ireland*, ed. Lady Gregory, London 1901. See also *Essays and Controversies*, 10.

14. Ibid., 38.

15. Eric Hobsbawn and Terence Ranger eds., *The Invention of Tradition*, Cambridge 1983, 263–81.

16. Douglas Hyde, "The Necessity for Deanglicizing Ireland", *The Revival of Irish Literature*, London 1894, 120.

17. W. B. Yeats, *Essays and Introductions*, London 1961, 248.

28. James Joyce, *Stephen Hero*, London 1977, 52.

19. Hyde, "Necessity", 119.

20. D. P. Moran, "The Battle of Two Civilizations", *Ideals in Ireland*, 28, 30.

21. Ibid., 36.

22. Hyde, "Necessity", 123, 129.

23. Quoted by David Greene, "The Founding of the Gaelic League", *The Gaelic League Idea*, ed. Seán Ó Tuama, Cork 1972, 10.

24. Hyde, "Necessity", 129, 128.

25. *Ideals in Ireland*, 55.

26. John Berger, *About Looking*, London 1980, 35.

27. Hyde, "Necessity", 138, 159.

28. W. B. Yeats, "The Literary Movement in Ireland", *Ideals in Ireland*, 85–90.

29. Quoted by Tomás Ó Fiaich, "The Great Controversy", *The Gaelic League Idea*, 67. This is the best account and I rely on it accordingly.

30. Ibid., 68.

31. Augusta Gregory, *Seventy Years*, 359.

32. Edward Martyn, *Beltaine*, No. 2, February 1900.

33. See Declan Kiberd, *Synge and the Irish Language*, London 1993, 224–5.

34. Thomas Babington Macaulay, "Indian Education", 2 February 1835 minute: in *Prose and Poetry*, ed. G. M. Young, Cambridge, Mass. 1967, 729.
35. Stephen Gwynn, *Today and Tomorrow in Ireland*, Dublin and London 1903, 59.
36. Kevin B. Nowlan, "The Gaelic League and Other National Movements", *The Gaelic League Idea*, 45.
37. Letter from J. O. Hannay to Hyde, 15 April 1907; Tadhg McGlinchey papers.
38. Nowlan quotes this, *The Gaelic League Idea*, 47.
39. Sean O'Casey, *Drums Under the Windows*, London 1945, 73.
40. Caoimhghín Ó Góilidhe ed., *Dánta Árdteastais*, Dublin 1967, 8.
41. Seán de Fréine, *The Great Silence*, Dublin 1965, 108.
42. Eric Hobsbawm, "Inventing Traditions", *The Invention of Tradition*, 15–22.
43. Quoted in *The United Irishman*, 22 June 1901.
44. Robert Kee, *The Green Flag*, London 1972, 432.
45. James Joyce, *Dubliners*, Harmondsworth 1992, 135.
46. Ruth Dudley Edwards, *Patrick Pearse: The Triumph of Failure*, London 1979, 178 (The Coming Revolution), 229 (From a Hermitage).
47. Quoted by Myles Dillon, "Douglas Hyde", *The Shaping of Modern Ireland*, ed. Conor Cruise O'Brien, London 1960, 59.
48. Quoted by Lady Gregory, *Seventy Years*, 417.
49. George Moore, *Hail and Farewell*, 587.
50. Michael Collins, *The Path to Freedom*, Dublin 1922. For a finely detailed study of the links between language revival and creative expression see Philip O'Leary, *The Prose Literature of the Gaelic Revival 1881–1921*, Pennsylvania 1994. Similar studies of poetry, sport, political discourse, and philosophy would in all likelihood yield equally rich results to researchers possessed of O'Leary's imaginative daring and scholarly scruple.

NINE: NATIONALITY OR COSMOPOLITANISM?

1. W. B. Yeats, *Uncollected Prose 1*, 255.
2. George Moore, "Literature and the Irish Language", *Ideals in Ireland*, 47.
3. D. P. Moran, *The Philosophy of Irish Ireland*, Dublin 1905, 37 ff.
4. Stopford A. Brooke, *The Need and Use of Getting Irish Literature into the English Tongue*, London 1893, 65.
5. John Eglinton, in *Literary Ideals in Ireland* (Eglinton et al.), London 1899, 11.
6. George Russell, ibid., 81–2.
7. George Russell, *Thoughts for a Convention*, Dublin and London 1917, 7.
8. *Literary Ideals in Ireland*, 86.
9. John Eglinton, *Bards and Saints*, Dublin 1906, 11.

10. John Eglinton, "A Word for Anglo-Irish Literature", *United Irishman*, 22 March 1902.
11. Quoted by Moore, *Hail and Farewell*, 166; Eglinton, *Bards and Saints*, 12, 7.
12. *United Irishman*, 31 March 1902.
13. John Eglinton, *Irish Literary Portraits*, 26.
14. *United Irishman*, 8 February 1902.
15. A. P. Thornton, *The Imperial Idea and Its Enemies*, London 1959, 210–11.
16. E. A. Boyd, *Appreciations and Depreciations*, Dublin 1918, 152.
17. Ibid., 157.
18. George Eliot, *Middlemarch*, Harmondsworth 1965, 110.
19. D. H. Lawrence, *Women in Love*, Harmondsworth 1960, 444.
20. Quoted by Hyde, *Oscar Wilde*, 506.
21. W. B. Yeats, *Plays and Controversies*, 197–8.
22. J. M. Synge, *Prose*, ed. Alan Price, Oxford 1968, 400.
23. D. P. Moran, *The Leader*, 2 November 1901.
24. W. B. Yeats, *Samhain*, October 1902, 8.
25. Thomas MacDonagh, *Literature in Ireland*, Dublin 1916, 47–8.
26. W. B. Yeats, *Samhain*, October 1902, 9.
27. W. B. Yeats, *Samhain*, October 1903, 8.
28. Frantz Fanon, *A Dying Colonialism*, Harmondsworth 1970, 73.
29. Salman Rushdie, *Imaginary Homelands*, London 1992, 124.
30. Quoted in *Samhain*, 1903, 35.
31. W. B. Yeats, *Samhain*, 1904, 20.
32. Rushdie, *Imaginary Homelands*, 124–5, 210, 149.
33. W. B. Yeats, *Samhain*, 1908, 7.

TEN: J. M. SYNGE – REMEMBERING THE FUTURE

1. All phrases from J. M. Synge, "The Playboy of the Western World", *Plays 2*, ed. Ann Saddlemyer, Oxford 1968.
2. Ibid., 75.
3. Ibid., 161.
4. René Girard, *Violence and the Sacred*, translated by Patrick Gregory, Baltimore 1977, 77–80.
5. P. H. Pearse, *Political Writings and Speeches*, Dublin 1924, 145–6.
6. Synge, *Plays 2*, 173.
7. Ibid., 73.
8. W. B. Yeats, *Collected Poems*, 226.
9. J. M. Synge, preface to *Poems*, ed. R. Skelton, London 1962, xxxvi.
10. Yeats, *Autobiographies*, 531.
11. Kay Dick ed., "Ernest Hemingway", *Writers at Work: The Paris Review Interviews*, Harmondsworth 1972, 188.

12. J. M. Synge, *Collected Letters 1: 1871–1907*, ed. Ann Saddlemyer, Oxford 1983, 297.
13. Synge, *Plays 2*, 59.
14. Ibid., 81.
15. Ibid., 81.
16. Ibid., 149.
17. Ibid., 153.
18. Ibid., 173.
19. Ibid., 169.
20. See Michael J. Sidnell, "Synge's Playboy and the Champion of Ulster", *Dalhousie Review*, XLV, Spring 1965, 51–9; and Diane E. Bessai, "Little Hound in Mayo", ibid., XLVIII, Autumn 1968, 372–83.
21. Mary C. King, *The Drama of J. M. Synge*, London 1985, 49.
22. Synge, *Plays 1*, 19.
23. Oliver Goldsmith, "The Deserted Village", *Field Day Anthology 1*, Derry 1991, 450.
24. W. B. Yeats, "Notes and Opinions", *Samhain*, November 1905; also *Samhain*, October 1902, 3–7.
25. Quoted by Nowlan, *The Gaelic League Idea*, 48–9.
26. Seamus Deane, "Synge and Heroism", *Celtic Revivals*, London 1985, 51–62.
27. David H. Greene and Edward M. Stephens, *J. M. Synge 1871–1909*, New York 1961, 66.
28. Synge, *Plays 2*, 63.
29. Fanon, *A Dying Colonialism*, 83–5.
30. Synge, *Plays 2*, 63.
31. Ibid., 89.
32. Ibid., 103.
33. Ibid., 95.
34. John Berger, *Ways of Seeing*, Harmondsworth 1972, 51.
35. Synge, *Plays 2*, 99.
36. Art Mac Cumhaigh, "Bodaigh na hEorna", *Dánta*, ed. Tomás Ó Fiaich, Dublin 1981, 102.
37. Dónal Ó Colmáin, *Parliament na mBan*, ed. B Ó Cuív, Dublin 1970, 11. I have modernized spelling in this passage.
38. Donncha Ó Corráin, "Women in Early Irish Society", *Women in Irish Society*, eds. Margaret MacCurtain and Donncha Ó Corráin, Dublin 1978, 11.
39. Synge, *Prose*, 143.
40. Synge, *Plays 2*, 97.
41. Ibid., 28.
42. See Declan Kiberd, *Synge and the Irish Language*, 122–50.
43. Synge, *Plays 2*, 151.
44. Green and Stephens, 241.
45. Synge, *Plays 2*, 167.
46. Lady Gregory, *Cuchulain of Muirthemne*, Gerrards Cross 1970, 33.
47. Synge, *Plays 2*, 167.

48. Interview, *Freeman's Journal*, 30 January 1907, 7.
49. Mary Colum, *Life and the Dream*, London 1947, 139.
50. Green and Stephens, 148.
51. Fanon, *The Wretched of the Earth*, 119–49.
52. Jacques Lacan, *Ecrits: A Selection*, New York 1977, 2.
53. The Jungian methodology has been most lucidly explained by Helen M. Luke, "Mirrors", *Parabola: The Magazine of Myth and Tradition*, Vol. XI, No. 2, Summer 1986, 56–63.
54. Synge, *Plays 2*, 127.
55. Ibid., 169.
56. Fanon, *The Wretched of the Earth*, 180.
57. Synge, *Prose*, 398.
58. Synge, *Poems*, 49.
59. Fanon, *Wretched*, 181.

REVOLUTION AND WAR: INTERCHAPTER

1. Richard Davis, *Arthur Griffith and Non-Violent Sinn Fein*, Tralee 1974.
2. Brian Murphy, *Patrick Pearse and the Lost Republican Ideal*, Dublin 1991.
3. Sean O'Casey, *The Story of the Irish Citizen Army*, Dublin 1919.
4. C. Desmond Greaves, *The Easter Rising as History*, London 1966.
5. Quoted by Mary Kotsonouris, *Retreat from Revolution: The Dail Courts 1920–24*, Dublin 1994, 21.
6. Tim Pat Coogan, *Michael Collins: A Biography*, London 1990.
7. Lord Craigavon (Sir James Craig), Northern Ireland Parliamentary Debates, Hansard, House of Commons, Vol. 16, Col. 1095.
8. Michael Farrell, *Northern Ireland: The Orange State*, London 1980.

ELEVEN: UPRISING

1. Standish O'Grady, *History of Ireland: Heroic Period*, London 1878, v.
2. Quoted by Yeats, *Autobiographies*, 424.
3. Yeats, *Collected Poems*, 393.
4. George Russell, *The Living Torch*, ed. Monk Gibbon, London 1937, 134–44.
5. Yeats, *Collected Poems*, 375.
6. V. I. Lenin, *On Ireland*, London 1949, 32–3.
7. Conor Cruise O'Brien, "The Embers of Easter", *1916 The Easter Rising*, ed. Owen Dudley Edwards and Fergus Pyle, London 1968, 227. Connolly quotation ibid.
8. On this phenomenon in other revolutionary situations see Crane Brinton, *The Anatomy of Revolution*, New York 1965, 34, 42, 53, 68 ff.
9. Russell, *Thoughts for a Convention*, 7.
10. Yeats, *Essays and Controversies*, 24. There are *some* anti-English outbursts in the writings of Pearse, but even Fr Francis Shaw – no admirer of Pearse

– comments that "nowhere does Pearse teach as explicitly as Tone the duty of hate", "The Canon of Irish History: A Challenge", *Studies*, Summer 1972, LXI, 126.

11. Shaw, *The Matter with Ireland,* 112.
12. Yeats, *Collected Poems*, 205.
13. Thomas MacDonagh, "Language and Literature in Ireland", *The Irish Review,* IV, March-April 1914, 176–82.
14. P. H. Pearse, *Plays, Stories, Poems*, Dublin 1924, 336.
15. *Letters of W. B. Yeats,* 295.
16. Quoted by Conor Cruise O'Brien, *Ancestral Voices*, Dublin 1994, 68.
17. Pearse, *Plays, Stories, Poems*, 44.
18. Joseph Mary Plunkett, *Poems*, Dublin 1916, 59–60.
19. Yeats, *Collected Plays*, 591.
20. Richard Sennett, *The Fall of Public Man: On the Social Psychology of Capitalism*, New York 1978, 184, 184, 186.
21. Ibid., 192.
22. Yeats, *Plays and Controversies*, 161.
23. Ibid., 158.
24. J. P. Sartre, *Life/Situations*, New York 1977, 167.
25. Beltaine, No. 3, April 1900.
26. Yeats, *Collected Poems*, 373.
27. Jose Ortega Y Gasset, *España Invertebrada*, Madrid 1922, 3, 146–50.
28. Yeats, *Collected Plays*, 431–46.
29. Harold Rosenberg, "The Resurrected Romans", *The Tradition of the New,* Chicago 1982, 155 ff.
30. Brinton, 203.
31. Máire nic Shiubhlaigh, *The Splendid Years*, Dublin 1955, 87.
32. Quoted Coogan, *Michael Collins*, 53–4.
33. On this see Robert Wohl, *The Generation of 1914*, Cambridge, Mass. 1979.
34. Pearse, *Plays, Stories, Poems*, 323.
35. Yeats, *Collected Poems*, 206.
36. Desmond FitzGerald, *Memoirs 1913–16,* London 1968, 142–3.
37. Pearse, *Plays, Stories, Poems*, 324.
38. Max Weber, *The Protestant Ethic and the Spirit of Capitalism*, London 1985, 104 ff.
39. Quoted by Bruce Mazlish, *The Revolutionary Ascetic*, New York 1976, 85.
40. J. J. Horgan, *From Parnell to Pearse*, Dublin 1948, 285.
41. Shaw, *Studies*, Summer 1972, 123.
42. P. H. Pearse, "The Coming Revolution", November 1913, 91–2.
43. See Eric Hobsbawn, "Mass-Producing Traditions: Europe 1870–1914", *The Invention of Tradition*, 271.
44. Ronald Paulson, *Representations of Revolution 1789–1820*, New Haven 1983, 14.
45. Tom Paine, *The Rights of Man*, Harmondsworth 1969, 71, 73.

46. Bernard MacLaverty, *Cal*, Belfast 1984, 73.
47. Yeats, *Collected Poems*, 202–5.
48. Yeats, "The Tragic Theatre", *Essays and Introductions*, 245.

TWELVE: THE PLEBEIANS REVISE THE UPRISING

1. Joseph Holloway, *Impressions of a Dublin Playgoer: A Selection*, eds. Robert Hogan and Michael J. O'Neill, London 1967, 215.
2. David Krause, *Sean O'Casey: the Man and his Work*, London 1967, 22 ff; and Robert G. Lowery, "Sean O'Casey: Art and Politics", *Sean O'Casey; Centenary Essays*, eds. Krause and Lowery, Gerrards Cross 1980, 123 ff.
3. Citations from Krause, 4–7.
4. Sean O'Casey, *Drums Under the Windows*, 115–30. Reference to the shilling fee is on 130.
5. Samuel Beckett, "Sean O'Casey", *Disjecta*, New York 1984, 82.
6. O'Casey, *Drums*, 73.
7. Quoted by Herbert Coston, "Prelude to Playwriting", *Sean O'Casey Modern Judgements*, ed. R. Ayling, London 1969, 49, 50.
8. Quoted by Onwuchekwa Gemie, *Langston Hughes: An Introduction*, New York 1976, 28.
9. Sean O'Casey, *Three Plays*, London 1957, 111.
10. Ibid., 110.
11. Ibid., 110–11.
12. Ibid., 27.
13. Ibid., 8.
14. Ibid., 70.
15. Nic Shiubhlaigh, *The Splendid Years*, 145.
16. O'Casey, *Innishfallen, Fare Thee Well* (with *Rose and Crown, Sunset and Evening Star*), London 1963, 125–38.
17. Bertolt Brecht, *The Life of Galileo*, London 1963, 107–8.
18. Capt. David Platt in a letter to his wife Jane, May 1916.
19. *Three Plays*, 178.
20. This is the argument put, with some qualifications, by William Irwin Thompson, *The Imagination of an Insurrection: Dublin Easter 1916*, 114 ff.
21. *Three Plays*, 46.
22. Yeats, *Mythologies*, 331.
23. *Three Plays*, 169.
24. Ibid., 208.
25. Ibid., 164, 193, 193–4.
26. O'Casey, *Drums*, 273. Connolly ordered that looters be shot.
27. Seamus Deane, *Celtic Revivals*, 109. See also Greaves, *Sean O'Casey: Politics and Art*, 116–22.
28. Patrick Pearse, *Political Writings*, Dublin 1924, 371, 376.
29. O'Casey cites this as the major reason in his autobiography, but his history of the Citizen Army refers favourably to uniforms. See Greaves, 74.

30. Karl Marx, *Surveys from Exile*, ed. David Fernbach, Harmondsworth 1973, 94.
31. Quoted Marshall Berman, *All That is Solid Melts into Air*, London 1983, 22–3.
32. Pearse, *Political Writings*, 216.
33. See Declan Kiberd, "Inventing Irelands", *The Crane Bag*, Vol. 8, No. 1, 1984, 11–25.
34. Wohl, *The Generation of 1914*, 5.
35. Pearse, *Political Writings*, 216.
36. Wohl, 236.
37. Francis Sheehy Skeffington, "An Open Letter to Thomas MacDonagh", *1916 The Easter Rising*, eds. Edwards and Pyle, 150.
38. Coston, *O'Casey: Modern Judgements*, 54.
39. In this I follow the analysis of Ramond Williams, *Drama from Ibsen to Brecht*, Harmondsworth 1973, 161–9.
40. C. S. Andrews, *Man of No Property*, Dublin 1982, 53–5.
41. They were the most popular of all plays in the Abbey repertoire and *The Plough* was the most often revived: Ernest Blythe, *The Abbey Theatre*, Dublin 1963, 9. T. R. Henn says they offered audiences "a defence mechanism against the rawness of their recent memories of the 'Troubles'", *The Harvest of Tragedy*, London 1956, 212.
42. Alexander Pope, public letter to John Gay, *Daily Journal*, 23 December 1731.
43. *Three Plays*, 185.
44. Lennox Robinson ed., *Lady Gregory's Journals*, London 1946, 97.
45. Quoted by Una Ellis-Fermor, "Poetry in Revolt", *Sean O'Casey: Modern Judgements*, 108.
46. *Three Plays*, 215.

THIRTEEN: THE GREAT WAR AND IRISH MEMORY

1. Francis Ledwidge, "Lament for Thomas MacDonagh", *Field Day Anthology of Irish Writing*, 2, 774.
2. Reproduced in *1916: The Easter Rising*, 220.
3. There is a good account of the epistolary controversy in "The Silver Tassie: Letters", *Sean O'Casey: A Collection of Critical Essays*, ed. Thomas Kilroy, New Jersey 1975, 113–17.
4. Bertrand Russell, *Autobiography*, London 1975, 283.
5. Sean O'Casey, *Three More Plays*, London 1965, 34.
6. Ibid., 41.
7. Paul Fussell, *The Great War and Modern Memory*, London 1975, 26–8.
8. *Three More Plays*, 38.
9. This point is well argued by Krause, 109–22.
10. *Three More Plays*, 59.

11. Ibid., 51.
12. Ibid., 53, 48.
13. Ibid., 105.
14. Ibid., 97.
15. Ibid., 67.
16. D. H. Lawrence, *Kangaroo*, Harmondsworth 1951, 241.
17. Fussell, 86–8, 196.
18. The phrase is used by Dick Diver in *Tender is the Night*, Harmondsworth 1955, 125.
19. *Letters of W. B. Yeats*, 874.
20. Henry James, *Letters 2*, ed. Percy Lubbock, New York 1920, 384.
21. Wohl, 115.

FOURTEEN: IRELAND AND THE END OF EMPIRE

1. Conor Cruise O'Brien, foreword, *The Shaping of Modern Ireland*, London 1960, 10.
2. See *The Gonne–Yeats Letters 1893–1938*, eds. McBride and Jeffares, London 1992, 293–4.
3. W. B. Yeats, *Explorations*, New York 1962, 401. On the theme see Ganesh Devi, "India and Ireland: Literary Relations", J. McMinn ed., *The Internationalism of Irish Literature and Drama*, Gerrards Cross 1992, 300–3.
4. Yeats, *Essays and Introductions*, 515.
5. Dhananjay Keer, *Veer Savakar*, Popular Prabakashan, Bombay 1950–66, 77.
6. Eamon de Valera, *India and Ireland*, speech to Friends of the Freedom of India, New York 1920, 3.
7. Ibid., 6, 8, 11, 16–17, 24.
8. See C. Desmond Greaves, *Liam Mellows and the Irish Revolution*, London 1971, 205, 216; Ramesa-Chandra Majumdar, *History of the Freedom Movement of India*, Vol. 2, 387–91, 398–402; and Liz Curtis, *The Cause of Ireland*, London 1995, 124–5, 175–6, 315–16.
9. British Cabinet Papers, 458, 15 Jan 1920, CAB 24/96, 13(185).
10. H. A. L. Fisher's diary, 1921. Information from Tim Pat Coogan.
11. A. P. Thornton, *The Imperial Idea and its Enemies*, 217.
12. Dáil Éireann debates, August 1921, private sessions, 12: Sean T. O'Kelly's report.
13. Anthony Babington, *The Devil to Pay: The Mutiny of the Connaught Rangers, India, July 1920*, London 1991, 3–4.
14. Ibid., 7, 10, 27, 28, 63, 65, quoted 86, quoted 26.
15. Sean T. O'Kelly, *India and Ireland*, New York 1924, 2.
16. Ibid., 3, 4, 9.
17. *The Collected Works of Mahatma Gandhi*, Vol. XXII (1921–2), New Delhi 1966, 17–18.
18. O'Kelly, 11.

19. On this see George Gilmore, *The Irish Republican Congress*, Dublin. Rev. ed. 1978, 30, which alleges that de Valera refused Patel's request for support for his Indian Congress in its anti-imperial struggle in 1932. The IRA also seemed uninterested: Patel recorded that only Maud Gonne was keen to help.

INVENTING IRELANDS: INTERCHAPTER

1. Kotsonouris, *Retreat from Revolution*, 99–105 for O'Higgins's role.
2. Terence Brown, *Ireland: A Social and Cultural History 1922–79*, London 1981, 42.
3. W. R. Rodgers, *Irish Literary Portraits*, London 1972, 10.
4. Yeats, *Autobiographies*, 533.
5. Máirtín Ó Cadhain, "Irish Prose in the Twentieth Century", *Literature in Celtic Countries*, Cardiff 1971, 150 ff.

FIFTEEN: WRITING IRELAND, READING ENGLAND

1. Appendix 1, "*The Irish Times* on the Easter Rising", *1916: The Easter Rising*, 247.
2. *Letters of W. B. Yeats*, 349.
3. Edward Dowden, "The Teaching of Literature", *New Studies in Literature*, London 1895, 445.
4. Yeats, *Essays and Introductions*, 104.
5. Yeats, "The Literary Movement in Ireland", *Ideals in Ireland*, 101.
6. Yeats, *Essays and Introductions*, 108.
7. Yeats, *Explorations*, 222.
8. For more on Crashaw's 1610 sermon see Edwards, *Threshold of a Nation*, Cambridge 1979, 98–100.
9. A. P. Rossiter, quoted by Kenneth Muir, introduction, *Richard II*, New York 1963, xxviii.
10. Quoted by John Devitt, "English for the Irish", *The Crane Bag*, Vol. 6, No. 1, 1982, 108.
11. James Joyce, *Ulysses*, Harmondsworth 1992, 271, 272.
12. Nicholas Mansergh, *The Irish Question 1840–1921*, 88–9.
13. Holloway, diaries, National Library manuscripts.
14. Quoted by Ellmann, *Oscar Wilde*, 41.
15. Sankaran Ravindran, *W. B. Yeats and Indian Tradition*, Delhi 1990, 19–32.
16. James Joyce, *A Portrait of the Artist as a Young Man*, Harmondsworth 1992, 228.
17. Edward Dowden, "The Serenity of *The Tempest*", *The Tempest: A Selection of Critical Essays*, ed. D. J. Palmer, London 1968, 75.
18. Edward Dowden, "The Scientific Movement and Literature", *Studies in Literature*, London 1878, 114.

19. Joyce, *Portrait*, 205–6.
20. Synge, preface to *The Playboy*, *Plays 2*, 53–4.
21. Deane, *Celtic Revivals*, 48.
22. Cited David Reed, *Ireland: The Key to the British Revolution*, London 1984, 9–11.
23. See Paul Buhle, *C. L. R. James: The Artist as Revolutionary*, London 1988, 160.
24. See Roberto Fernandez Retamar, *Caliban and Other Essays*, translated by Edward Baker, Minneapolis 1989.
25. William Shakespeare, *The Tempest*, ed. Robert Langbaum, New York 1964, 55.
26. Samuel Beckett, *Endgame*, London 1964, 32.
27. *The Tempest*, 54.
28. Ibid., 89.
29. G. Wilson Knight, *The Crown of Life*, London, 138.
30. *The Tempest*, 121.
31. Ibid., 110.
32. George Lamming, *The Pleasures of Exile*, London 1984, 110.
33. Seamus Heaney, *North*, London 1975, 65.
34. *Ulysses*, 235.
35. Wilde, *The Artist as Critic*, 235.
36. Ibid., 307.
37. *Ulysses*, 6.
38. Ellis-Fermor, *The Irish Dramatic Movement*, 59–90.
39. Shakespeare, *The Winter's Tale*,
40. Wilde, *The Artist as Critic*, 291.
41. Yeats, *Autobiographies*, 89.
42. Séamus Ó Buachalla, ed., *A Significant Irish Educationalist: Educational Writings of Patrick Pearse*, Cork 1980, 353–4.
43. Buhle, *C. L. R. James*, 18.
44. Lamming, *Pleasures*, 27.
45. *Significant Irish Educationalist*, 354–5.
46. Lamming, *Pleasures*, 42.
47. *Significant Irish Educationalist*, 372.
48. Aimé Césaire, *Discourse on Colonialism*, translated by Joan Pinkham, New York 1972, 21.
49. The comparison was first made by Tomás Bán Ó Concheanainn; and later taken up by Douglas Hyde.
50. *Letters of W. B. Yeats*, 414.
51. Both *Earnest* and *Intentions* contain ideas of educational reform.
52. *Significant Irish Educationalist*, 374, 377.
53. Ibid., 377.
54. Yeats, *Autobiographies*, 291.
55. Chris Baldick, *The Social Mission of English Criticism 1848–1932*, Oxford 1983.

SIXTEEN: INVENTING IRELANDS

1. Quoted by R. Poirier, *A World Elsewhere*, Wisconsin 1985, 210.
2. Tomás Ó Criomhthainn, *Allagar na hInse*, Dublin 1928, 115.
3. Muiris Ó Súilleabháin, *Fiche Blian ag Fás*, Maynooth 1976, 196.
4. Synge, *Prose*, 140.
5. Weldon Thornton, *J. M. Synge and the Western Mind*, Gerrards Cross 1979, 98 ff.
6. These features are all discussed in, for instance, Edward Said's *Orientalism*, New York 1978.
7. Synge, *Prose*, 50–1, 140, 140.
8. Jean-Paul Sartre, *Anti-Semite and Jew*, New York 1968, 78.
9. W. B. Yeats, *Letters to the New Island*, Cambridge, Mass. 1934, 109.
10. Sartre, 97.
11. Yeats, *Essays and Introductions*, 372–3, 357.
12. Yeats, *Samhain*, 1908, 8–9.
13. On this see Thomas R. Whitaker, *Swan and Shadow: Yeats's Dialogue with History*, Chapel Hill 1964, 95–6.
14. The phrase is Aijaz Ahmed's: see *In Theory: Classes, Nations, Literatures*, London 1992, 95–122.
15. Yeats, *Essays and Introductions*, 317.
16. Yeats, *John Sherman and Dhoya*, 116.
17. Yeats, *Plays and Controversies*, 95.
18. Yeats, *Explorations*, 345.
19. Whitaker, 221.
20. Carlos Fuentes, "Remember the Future", *Salmagundi*, Fall 1985/Winter 1986, No. 68–9, 338–43.
21. Ibid., 338.
22. Walter Benjamin, "Theses on the Philosophy of History", *Illuminations*, tr. Harry Zohn, London 1973, 263.
23. Friedrich Nietzsche, *On the Advantage and Disadvantage of History for Life*, tr. Peter Preuss, Indianapolis 1980.
24. Fanon, *The Wretched of the Earth*, 135.
25. The phrase is Ernie O'Malley's, *On Another Man's Wound*, Kerry 1979, 41.
26. Quoted by Bernard Ransome, *Connolly's Marxism*, London 1980, 18.
27. Sigmund Freud, *A General Introduction to Psychoanalysis*, tr. Joan Rivière, New York 1920, 325.
28. George Russell, *The National Being*, Dublin 1916, 81.
29. Yeats, *Collected Poems*, 233.
30. Ibid., 225.
31. Yeats, *Uncollected Prose 2*, ed. John P. Frayne, 452.
32. Yeats, *Collected Poems*, 166–7.
33. Lionel Trilling, *Sincerity and Authenticity* 1–52 for main thesis.
34. Jean-Paul Sartre, *Words*, tr. Irene Clephane, Harmondsworth 1967, 71.
35. Wilde, *The Artist as Critic*, 358.

36. Ibid., 375.
37. Quoted by Isaiah Berlin, *Vico and Herder*, London 1976, 203.
38. Yeats, *Letters to the New Island*, 174.
39. Fred Jameson, *The Political Unconscious: Narrative as a Socially Symbolic Act*, London 1981, 68.
40. Yeats, *Collected Plays*, 133.
41. Ibid., 111–12.
42. Jameson, *The Political Unconscious*, 81.
43. Northrop Frye, *Anatomy of Criticism*, Princeton 1957, 193.
44. Synge, *Prose*, 350.
45. Synge, *Poems*, 34.
46. Ibid., 38.
47. Synge Manuscripts TCD, MS 4382, f69v.
48. Wilde, *The Artist as Critic*, 398.
49. Ibid., 283–4.

SEVENTEEN: REVOLT INTO STYLE – YEATSIAN POETICS

1. Yeats, *Collected Poems*, 8.
2. Ibid., 9.
3. Ibid., 35.
4. Yeats, *Essays and Introductions*, 195.
5. Yeats, *Collected Poems*, 71.
6. Yeats, *Plays and Controversies*, 161.
7. Yeats, *Collected Poems*, 88.
8. Ibid., 89.
9. Ibid., 126.
10. Ibid., 141.
11. On this see *Autobiographies*, 330–2; *Essays and Introductions*, 111–45.
12. Yeats, *Collected Poems*, 151–2.
13. Ibid., 197.
14. Ibid., 232.
15. Yeats, *Collected Plays*, 206.
16. Ibid., 235.
17. Ibid., 241.

EIGHTEEN: THE LAST *AISLING* – *A VISION*

1. Yeats, *Collected Poems*, 240.
2. W. B. Yeats, *A Vision*, New York 1966, 10–11.
3. Ibid., 24–5.
4. The words are William Blake's, quoted by Peter Coveney, *The Image of Childhood*, 54.
5. F. Scott Fitzgerald, *The Crack-Up with Other Pieces and Stories*, Harmondsworth 1965, 39.

6. See *A Vision*, 23–7.
7. For a superb analysis of the greatest exponent see Seán Ó Tuama, *Fili'faoi Sceimhle*, Dublin 1979.
8. Quoted by Ellmann, *Yeats: The Man and the Masks*, London 1965, 249.
9. Yeats, *A Vision*, 8.
10. Quoted by Ellmann, *The Man and the Masks*, 6.
11. *Letters of W. B. Yeats*, 656.
12. Yeats, *Explorations*, 336.
13. *A Vision*, 52.
14. Ibid., 52.
15. Ibid., 84.
16. On this see Alfred Cobban, "The Revolt against the Eighteenth Century", *Romanticism and Consciousness*, ed. H. Bloom, New York 1972, 64.
17. Yeats, *Explorations*, 333–4.
18. I take this from T. J. Diffey, "The Roots of Imagination", *The Romantics*, ed. Prickett, London 1981, 165–72.
19. Quoted ibid., 190.
20. Yeats, *Collected Poems*, 240–1.
21. Yeats, *Essays and Introductions*, 158.
22. Ibid., 341.
23. *A Vision*, 114.
24. Whitaker, 95. The phrase glossed is from *Autobiographies*.
25. Yeats, *Collected Poems*, 266.
26. Quoted by Jeffares, *A Commentary on the Collected Poems of W. B. Yeats*, Stanford 1968, 352.
27. *A Vision*, 263.
28. Ibid., 205–6.

NINETEEN: JAMES JOYCE AND MYTHIC REALISM

1. Gerald Griffin, *The Wild Geese*, London 1938, 24.
2. For more contemporary examples see Gayatri Chakravorty Spivak, *The Postcolonial Critic*, London 1990, 165.
3. Ellsworth Mason and Richard Ellmann, *The Critical Writings of James Joyce*, New York 1959, 174.
4. Ibid., 198.
5. Djuna Barnes, "James Joyce", *Vanity Fair*, XVIII, April 1922, 65.
6. Quoted Ellmann, *James Joyce*, 403.
7. Deleuze and Guattari, *Kafka*, 41.
8. R. Ellmann ed., *Letters of James Joyce 2*, London 1966, 134.
9. Joyce, *A Portrait of the Artist as a Young Man*, 274.
10. Ibid., 205.
11. Ibid., 220.
12. Ibid., 274.

13. James Joyce, *Finnegans Wake*, Harmondsworth 1992, 171.
14. Salman Rushdie, *Imaginary Homelands*, London 1992, 11.
15. *Letters of James Joyce 1*, 63.
16. Joyce, *A Portrait*, 228.
17. Joyce, *Critical Writings*, 196.
18. Ibid., 224, 212.
19. Ibid., 163.
20. Ibid., 168.
21. Ibid., 188.
22. Ibid., 195.
23. Vincent Tucker, "The Myth of Development", Unpublished paper, Dept. of Sociology, University College Cork 1993.
24. Joyce, *Critical Writings*, 173.
25. This was the allegation made by John Eglinton against revivalist representations of the western peasant.
26. Joyce, *Critical Writings*, 166.
27. Yeats, *Collected Poems*, 167.
28. Benedict Anderson, *Imagined Communities*, 127–46.
29. Rushdie, *Imaginary Homelands*, 376.
30. Gerald Martin, *Journeys Through the Labyrinth: Latin American Fiction in the Twentieth Century*, London 1989, 206.
31. Octavio Paz, "A Literature of Foundation", in J. Donoso and W. Henkins eds., *The Triquarterly Anthology of Latin American Literature*, New York 1969, 8 (tr. Laysander Kemp).
32. Jorge Luis Borges, *Labyrinths*, Harmondsworth 1970, 221–4.
33. Roberto Ferñandez Retamar, *Caliban and Other Essays*, tr. Edward Baker, Minneapolis 1989, 28.
34. Joyce, *Ulysses*, 248.
35. Rushdie, *Imaginary Homelands*, 420.
36. R. A. Breatnach, "The End of a Tradition", *Studia Hibernica*, 1961, 142.
37. On this see Cathal Ó Háinle, "An tÚrscéal nár Tháinig", *Promhadh Pinn*, Dublin 1978, 74–98.
38. *Ulysses*, 449.
39. Linda Hutcheon, *A Theory of Parody: The Teaching of Twentieth Century Art Forms*, London 1985, 35.
40. Jameson, *The Political Unconscious*, 146.
41. Tucker, ibid.,
42. Spivak, *The Postcolonial Critic*, 8.
43. See Emer Nolan, *James Joyce and Nationalism*, London 1994.
44. *Ulysses*, 42.
45. Ibid., 49.
46. Ibid., 56.
47. Ibid., 55.
48. Ibid., 45.
49. Ibid., 181.

50. Ibid., 248.
51. Ibid., 235.
52. Ibid., 258.
53. Ibid., 239–40.
54. Ibid., 272.
55. On the decline in deference see David Fitzpatrick, *Politics and Irish Life 1913–21*, Dublin 1977; and J. J. Lee, *The Modernisation of Irish Society 1848–1918*, Dublin 1973.
56. *Ulysses*, 427.
57. Ibid., 432.
58. Ibid., 445.
59. Ibid., 401.
60. Ibid., 434.
61. Ibid., 435–6.
62. Ibid., 539.
63. W. B. Yeats, *Samhain*, December 1906, 6.
64. *Ulysses*, 60.

SEXUAL POLITICS: INTERCHAPTER

1. Michael O'Sullivan, *Sean Lemass: A Biography*, Dublin 1994, 55.
2. For a good survey see Francis McManus ed., *The Years of the Great Test 1926–39*, Cork 1967.
3. Yeats, *Collected Poems*, 377–81.
4. On de Valera's rivalry with Collins, and for a full assessment of his 1937 constitution, see Tim Pat Coogan, *De Valera: Long Fellow, Long Shadow*, London 1993, 197–229 and 489–99.
5. The strongest case for viewing Yeats as fascist is Conor Cruise O'Brien, *Passion and Cunning*, London 1988 (1965); but Elizabeth Cullingford's answer in *Yeats, Ireland and Fascism*, London 1981, is decisive.
6. W. B. Yeats, "Divorce", *The Senate Speeches of W. B. Yeats*, ed. Donald R. Pearce, Indiana 1960, 157.
7. Ibid., 104–5.
8. Yeats, *Uncollected Prose 1*, 462–3.
9. Yeats, *Autobiographies*, 333.
10. Yeats, *Uncollected Prose 1*, 462–3.
11. On this see C. L. Innes, *Women and Nation in Irish Literature and Society 1880–1935*, Athens, Georgia 1993, 9–62.
12. Francis Sheehy Skeffington, *1916 The Easter Rising*, 151.

TWENTY: ELIZABETH BOWEN – THE DANDY IN REVOLT

1. Elizabeth Bowen, *The Shelbourne*, London 1951, 128.
2. Elizabeth Bowen, *The Last September*, Harmondsworth 1987, 46.

3. Elizabeth Bowen, *Bowen's Court*, London 1942, 22.
4. Ibid., 97.
5. Quoted by Victoria Glendinning, *Elizabeth Bowen: Portrait of a Writer*, Harmondsworth 1985, 12.
6. Quoted by Edwin J. Kenney, *Elizabeth Bowen*, Lewisburg 1975, 23.
7. Ibid., 92–3.
8. Quoted Glendinning, 120–1.
9. Ibid., 164–5.
10. Ibid., 117.
11. Elizabeth Bowen, *Pictures and Conversations*, London 1975, 23.
12. *Bowen's Court*, 15.
13. *The Last September*, 89.
14. Quoted Kenney, 38.
15. *The Last September*, 131.
16. Ibid., 32–3.
17. *The Last September*, 98.
18. Ibid., 34.
19. Ibid., 60.
20. Ibid., 46.
21. Ibid., 134.
22. Ibid., 44.
23. Ibid., 49.
24. Ibid., 49.
25. Glendinning, 206.
26. Quoted Glendinning, 160.
27. *The Last September*, 44.
28. Ibid., 58.
29. Walter Benjamin, *Charles Baudelaire: A Lyric Poet in the Era of High Capitalism*, tr. Harry Zohn, London 1983, 74.
30. *The Last September*, 98.
31. Benjamin, 75.
32. *The Last September*, 187.
33. Ibid., 161.
34. Ibid., 82.
35. Benjamin, 95–6.
36. *Bowen's Court*, 194.
37. Elizabeth Bowen, *The House in Paris*, London 1935, 94.
38. Elizabeth Bowen, *Collected Impressions*, London 1950, 161.
39. Ibid., 198.
40. *Bowen's Court*, 338.
41. Quoted Kenney, 18.
42. Quoted Kenney, 23–4.
43. Quoted Glendinning, 139.
44. Quoted Ibid., 139.

TWENTY-ONE: FATHERS AND SONS

1. Albert Memmi, *The Colonizer and the Colonized*, tr. Howard Greenfeld, Boston 1967, 95–100.
2. Ibid., 101.
3. Patrick Kavanagh, "The Great Hunger", *Collected Poems*, London 1972, 36.
4. Sean O'Casey, *Three Plays*, 71.
5. Joyce, *A Portrait*, 262.
6. Joyce, *Ulysses*, 798.
7. Ibid., 266.
8. Ibid., 33.
9. Synge, *Plays 2*, 97.
10. Ibid., 151.
11. Ibid., 85.
12. Ibid., 149.
13. Matthew Bruccoli, *As Ever, Scott-Fitz*, London 1973, 184.
14. Fanon, *A Dying Colonialism*, tr. Haakon Chevalier, Harmondsworth 1970, 81.
15. Ibid., 83, 85.
16. Ibid., 86.
17. B. C. Rosset, *Shaw of Dublin: The Formative Years*, Pennsylvania 1964, 55, 102.
18. The phrase was used by Michael Holroyd, lecture, Carlow, 11 May 1992.
19. *Dublin Evening Mail*, 21 September 1923, 4.
20. Stanley Weintraub ed., *Shaw: An Autobiography 1856–98*, London 1969, 52.
21. Ibid., 24.
22. Salman Rushdie, *Midnight's Children*, London 1981, 108.
23. Ibid., 111.
24. Fanon, *A Dying Colonialism*, 82.
25. Ibid., 83.
26. *Letters of W. B. Yeats*, 589.
27. Yeats, *Autobiographies*, 28.
28. Ibid., 66.
29. *Letters of W. B. Yeats*, 583.
30. Joyce, *Portrait*, 3.
31. Ibid., 89.
32. Hannah Arendt, *Between Past and Future: Six Exercises in Political Thought*, London 1961,
33. Deleuze and Guattari, *Kafka*, 10.
34. Quoted by Takeo Doi, *The Anatomy of Dependence*, Tokyo 1986, 157.
35. Joyce, *Portrait*, 3.
36. Ibid., 5.
37. Carl E. Schorske, *Fin-de-Siécle Vienna: Politics and Culture*, New York 1981, 191–7.

38. Yeats, *Collected Poems*, 105.
39. Peter Gay, *Weimar Culture: The Outsider as Insider*, New York 1970, 141.
40. Ibid., 142.
41. Robin Skynner and John Cleese, *Families and How to Survive Them*, London 1983, 189 ff.
42. Virginia Woolf, "Mr. Bennett and Mr. Brown", *The Captain's Death Bed*, 110.
43. Erich Fromm, *The Fear of Freedom*, London 1984, 148–9.
44. Ibid., 142.
45. Fanon, *The Wretched of the Earth*, 135.
46. Norman O. Brown, *Life against Death: The Psychoanalytical Meaning of History*, Middletown, Connecticut, 1959, 92.
47. This is Wohl's summary of the ideas of Karl Mannheim, *The Generation of 1914*, 77.
48. Cited Wohl, 196.
49. Ibid., 196.
50. David Fitzpatrick, *Irish Emigration 1801–1921*, Dundalk 1984, 41.

TWENTY-TWO: MOTHERS AND DAUGHTERS

1. Carol Coulter, *The Hidden Tradition: Feminism, Women and Nationalism in Ireland*, Cork 1993, 12.
2. See Margaret Ward, *Unmanageable Revolutionaries: Women and Irish Nationalism*, London 1983, 4–39.
3. Joseph J. Lee, "Women and the Church since the Famine", *Women in Irish Society: The Historical Dimension*, 41.
4. Rosemary Cullen Owens, *Smashing Times: A History of the Irish Women's Suffrage Movement 1889–1922*, Dublin 1984, 31–5.
5. Quoted Margaret MacCurtain, "Women, the Vote and Revolution", *Women in Irish Society*, 49.
6. Mary Colum, *Life and the Dream*, New York 1947, 174.
7. Hanna Sheehy Skeffington, quoted by Leah Levenson and Jerry H. Natterstad, *Hanna Sheehy-Skeffington: Irish Feminist*, Syracuse 1986, 29.
8. Rosemary Cullen Owens, 63.
9. Ibid., 42.
10. Constance Markievicz, *Bean na hÉireann*, Vol. 1, No. 4, February 1909, 2.
11. Hanna Sheehy-Skeffington, ibid., Vol. 2, No. 13, November 1909, 5–6.
12. D. P. Moran, *The Leader*, 19 March 1910.
13. 'Maca", *Bean na hÉireann*, July 1909; cited Owens 104.
14. Editorial, *The Irish Citizen*, 2 May 1914.
15. Ward, 91.
16. Cited by Levenson-Natterstad, 75.
17. MacCurtain, *Women in Irish Society*, 55.
18. Cullen Owens, 85.
19. Quoted C. L. Innes, *Woman and Nation*, 143.

20. Ward, 111.
21. *An Phoblacht*, 16 July 1932.
22. Ward, 109.
23. Ibid., 111–17.
24. Coulter, *The Hidden Tradition*, 18.
25. Levenson and Natterstad, 116.
26. Cited Ward, 123.
27. *Irish Citizen*, October 1916.
28. Ward, 145.
29. Quoted Levenson and Natterstad, 135.
30. "Reprisals Condemned", *Freeman's Journal*, 19 February 1921, 5.
31. Levenson and Natterstad, 135.
32. Ward, 167; also Levenson and Natterstad, 139 ff.
33. Ward, 176.
34. Ibid., 178.
35. Quotations in Levenson and Natterstad, 112.
36. Cullen Owens, 130–1.
37. Ward, 179 ff.
38. Ibid., 193.
39. Ibid., 192.
40. Mary Robinson, "Women and the New Irish State", *Women in Irish Society*, 63.
41. Levenson and Natterstad, 161.
42. Statement by Sean Lemass, *Daily Express*, 7 May 1930.
43. Cited Ward 244.
44. Quoted Tim Pat Coogan, *De Valera: Long Fellow, Long Shadow*, 497.
45. Maurice Manning, "Women in Irish National and Local Politics 1922–72", *Women in Irish Society*, 95–6.
46. Quoted by Coogan, 497.
47. Helena Molony, "James Connolly and Women", *Dublin Labour Year Book*, 1930.
48. Carol Coulter, "Ireland: Between First and Third Worlds", *A Dozen Lips*, Dublin 1994, 111.
49. Quoted by Coogan, *De Valera*, 497.
50. Quoted by Jeffares, *A Commentary on the Poems of W. B. Yeats*, 370.
51. C. L. Innes, *Woman and Nation*, 35.
52. Andrew Parker, Mary Russo, Doris Sommer and Patricia Yaeger, introduction, *Nationalisms and Sexualities*, London 1992, 5.
53. Ann McClintock, quote ibid., 6.
54. Geraldine Heng and Ganadas Devan, "State Fatherhood: the Politics of Nationalism, Sexuality and Race in Singapore", *Nationalisms and Sexualities*, 343.
55. Ibid., 343.
56. Basil Davidson, "On Revolutionary Nationalism: The Legacy of Cabral", *Race and Class*, 27, No. 3, Winter 1986, 43.

57. Adele Dalsimer, *Kate O'Brien: A Critical Study*, Dublin 1990, xiv.
58. See Dalsimer, 59–72; and Eibhear Walshe ed., *Ordinary People Dancing*, Cork 1993.
59. See Seamus Deane, "Mary Lavin", *The Irish Short Story*, eds. Patrick Rafroidi and Terence Brown, Lille 1978, 237–48; and A.A. Kelly, *Mary Lavin: Quiet Rebel*, Dublin 1980.

PROTESTANT REVIVALS: INTERCHAPTER

1. Patrick Buckland, *Irish Unionism 1: The Anglo-Irish and the New Ireland 1886–1922*, Dublin 1973, 288.
2. Donald R. Pearce ed., *The Senate Speeches of W. B. Yeats*, 52, 94, 97, 98, 101, 158, 177–8, 160.
3. W. B. Yeats, *Explorations*, 337.
4. See Michael Farrell, *Arming the Protestants*, Dingle 1983, 89–92, 114–15.
5. Michael Farrell, *Northern Ireland: The Orange State*, London 1976, 97 ff.
6. Quoted ibid., 93–4.
7. Paddy Devlin, *Straight Left: An Autobiography*, Belfast 1993, chaps. 1–3.
8. National Council for Civil Liberties, Commission of Enquiry into purposes and effect of the Civil Authorities (Special Powers) Acts 1922 and 1933: London 1936, 11.
9. On the general attitude of Protestants, see F. S. L. Lyons, "The Minority Problem in the 26 Counties", *The Years of the Great Test 1926–39*, 92–103.
10. Conor Cruise O'Brien, *States of Ireland*, London 1972, 117.

TWENTY-THREE: PROTHOLICS AND CATHESTANTS

1. G. B. Shaw, *The Matter with Ireland*, 32.
2. Ibid., 72.
3. Edmund Burke, *Irish Affairs*, 350.
4. G. B. Shaw, *Autobiography 1856–98*, 14.
5. Ibid., 68.
6. E. M. Forster, *A Passage to India*, London 1965, 269.
7. Edward Said, *Culture and Imperialism*, London 1993, 1–50.
8. Hubert Butler, *Escape from the Anthill*, Mullingar 1985, 114–21.
9. George Moore, *Hail and Farewell*, 391.
10. Synge, *Prose*, 13.
11. Synge, *Plays 2*, 65.
12. Ibid., 73.
13. Synge, *Plays 1*, 133.
14. Synge, *Plays 2*, 215.
15. Ibid., 267.
16. G. M. Young, *Victorian England: Portrait of an Age*, London 1936, 5.

17. Vivian Mercier, "Evangelical Revival in the Church of Ireland 1800–69", *Modern Irish Literature: Sources and Founders*, Oxford 1994, 64.
18. Standish O'Grady, *All Ireland Review*, No. 4, 1903, 340.
19. Yeats, *Autobiographies*, 115.
20. The terms were devised by Brendan Kennelly in a lecture at Kavanagh's Yearly, Monaghan, 1990.
21. Quoted by W. M. Murphy, *Prodigal Father*, 137.
22. Quoted ibid., 249–50.
23. James Joyce, *Poems and Exiles*, Harmondsworth 1992, 107.
24. G. B. Shaw, *Autobiography: 1856–98*, 1–66.
25. Shaw, *The Matter with Ireland*, 69, 71, 73.

TWENTY-FOUR: SAINT JOAN – FABIAN FEMINIST, PROTESTANT MYSTIC

1. Shaw, *Autobiography 1856–98*, 19.
2. Shaw, *Autobiography 1898–1950*, New York 1970, 161.
3. Shaw, *Autobiography 1856–98*, 33.
4. G. B. Shaw, *Saint Joan*, Harmondsworth 1946, 83.
5. Marina Warner, *Joan of Arc: The Image of Female Heroism*, London 1981, 145–6.
6. Ibid., 147: St. Paul, epistle to Galatians, 3.28.
7. Ibid., 148.
8. *Saint Joan*, 73.
9. H. L. Mencken, *The Nature and Origin of Religion*, New York 1905, 67.
10. Ibid., 68, 76.
11. John Milton, "Areopagitica", *Prose Writings*, London 1958, 158.
12. Holly Hill ed., *Playing Joan*, New York 1987, 127 ff.
13. Eric Bentley, *Bernard Shaw*, New York 1985, 116–19.
14. James Connolly, *Labour in Irish History*, Dublin 1966, esp. 1–15.
15. *Saint Joan*, 98, 99.
16. Ibid., 112.
17. Ibid., 131.
18. Ibid., 148, 149.
19. Ibid., 154.
20. Ibid., 159.

TWENTY-FIVE: THE WINDING STAIR

1. Brian Tyson, *The Story of Shaw's Saint Joan*, Montreal 1982, 6–8.
2. Yeats, *Autobiographies*, 3.
3. Yeats, *Plays and Controversies*, 33.
4. Ibid., 217.

5. Yeats, *Collected Poems*, 282.
6. Ibid., 285.
7. Ibid., 285.
8. R. P. Blackmur, "Between Myth and Philosophy", *Yeats: A Collection of Critical Essays*, ed. J. Unterecker, New Jersey 1963, 64–74.
9. Yeats, *Collected Poems*, 280.
10. Ibid., 281.
11. Frank Kermode, *Romantic Image*, London 1971, 40.
12. Yeats, *Collected Poems*, 280.
13. Ibid., 275–6.
14. Ibid., 278–9.
15. Ibid., 228.
16. Yeats, *Autobiographies*, 11–12.
17. Ibid., 86.
18. Ibid., 473.
19. David Daiches, *Some Late Victorian Attitudes*, London 1969, 97.
20. Yeats, *Collected Poems*, 267.
21. Ibid., 266.
22. Max Weber, *The Protestant Ethic and the Spirit of Capitalism*, 106.
23. Yeats, *Collected Poems*, 284.
24. J. C. Beckett, *The Anglo-Irish Tradition*, London 1976, 65.
25. W. M. Murphy, *Prodigal Father*, 249–50, 618.
26. Louis MacNeice, *The Poetry of W. B. Yeats*, 97.
27. Synge, *Prose*, 231.
28. Yeats, *Collected Poems*, 73.
29. Ibid., 140.
30. Yeats, *Essays and Introductions*, 339.
31. Ibid., 339.
32. Yeats, *Plays and Controversies*, 120.
33. Quoted by Darcy O'Brien, *W. R. Rodgers*, Lewisburg 1970, 19–20.
34. Quoted by John Wilson Foster, "The Dissidence of Dissent: John Hewitt and W. R. Rodgers", *Across a Roaring Hill*, eds. E. Longley and G. Dawe, Belfast 1985, 150.
35. Ibid., 142.
36. Ibid., 141.
37. Donald Harman Akenson, *A Mirror to Kathleen's Face*, Monteal 19, 35–62.
38. Deirdre Bair, *Samuel Beckett: A Biography*, London 1978, 38.

TWENTY-SIX: RELIGIOUS WRITING: BECKETT AND OTHERS

1. Samuel Beckett, *More Pricks than Kicks*, London 1970, 21.
2. Samuel Beckett, Communication with present author, August 1985.
3. Samuel Beckett, *Endgame*, 35.

4. Samuel Beckett, *Waiting for Godot*, London 1965, 52.
5. Beckett, *Endgame*, 38.
6. Beckett, *More Pricks*, 146.
7. Ibid., 184.
8. John Milton, *Poetical Works*, ed. D. Bush, London 1966, 218.
9. *More Pricks*, 81.
10. Samuel Beckett, *Murphy*, London 1973, 36.
11. Ibid., 102.
12. Ibid., 42.
13. Ibid., 42.
14. Harvey Cox, *Turning East*, Boston, 1987
15. *Murphy*, 49.
16. Samuel Beckett, *Watt*, London 1963, 254.
17. On this see Theodor Adorno, "Toward an Understanding of *Endgame*", *Endgame: A Collection of Critical Essays*, ed. Bell Gale Chevigny, New Jersey 1971, 106 ff.
18. Lecture to Clifden Community Arts Festival, Co Galway, September 1984.
19. Samuel Beckett, *Proust*, New York 1970, 8.
20. Hugh Kenner, *A Reader's Guide to Samuel Beckett*, London 1973, 134.
21. Quoted by Bair, *Samuel Beckett*, 198.
22. Samuel Beckett, *Molloy: Malone Dies: The Unnamable*, London 1959, 152.
23. Ibid., 170.
24. Weber, *The Protestant Ethic*, 148 ff.
25. Samuel Beckett, *Disjecta*, 74.
26. Thomas MacGreevy, *Collected Poems*, ed. T. D. Redshaw, Dublin 1971, 17.
27. Thomas MacGreevy, "Gloria de Carlos V", *Collected Poems*, ed. S. Schreibman, Dublin 1991, 36.
28. Anthony Cronin, *Heritage Now: Irish Literature in the English Language*, Dingle 1982, 155.
29. Brian Coffey, "Nightfall, Midwinter, Missouri", *Field Day Anthology 3*, 158.
30. Denis Devlin, "Lough Derg", ibid., 151.
31. Ibid., 152.
32. Beckett, *Disjecta*, 70.
33. Quoted by Susan Halperin, *Austin Clarke: His Life and Works*, Dublin 1974, 55.
34. Austin Clarke, *Collected Poems*, Dublin 1974, 189.
35. Ibid., 252.
36. Ibid., 318.
37. Synge, *Plays 2*, 4.
38. Beckett, *Disjecta*, 68.

UNDERDEVELOPMENT: INTERCHAPTER

1. See Terence Brown, *Ireland: A Social and Cultural History 1922–79*, 141–70.
2. For interesting perspectives see Joseph Lee and Gearóid Ó Tuathaigh, *The Age of de Valera*, Dublin 1982.
3. For the general cultural climate in the war years and their aftermath see Kevin B. Nowlan and T. Desmond Williams eds., *Ireland in the War Years and After 1939–51*, Dublin 1969; Anthony Cronin, *Dead as Doornails*, Dublin 1976 and *No Laughing Matter: The Life and Times of Flann O'Brien*, London 1989; and John Ryan, *Remembering How We Stood: Bohemian Dublin at the Mid-Century*, Dublin 1975.
4. Louis MacNeice, *Collected Poems*, London 1966.
5. Ibid., 133, 131.
6. Louis MacNeice, *The Strings are False*, London 1965, 17.
7. MacNeice, *Collected Poems*, 164.
8. Letter to E. R. Dodds, quoted in *Across a Roaring Hill*, 99.
9. Quoted by Cronin, *Heritage Now*, 202.
10. For a fuller elaboration of this thesis see Raymond Crotty, *Ireland in Crisis: A Study in Capitalist Colonial Underdevelopment*, Dingle 1986; and *A Radical's Response*, Dublin 1988.
11. Saamir Amin, *Eurocentrism*, tr. Russell Moore, London 1989, 112.
12. For an inspiring account of one family's struggle, and of the prevailing temper of the times, see Noel Browne, *Against the Tide*, Dublin 1986.
13. Patrick Kavanagh, *Collected Poems*, 37.
14. Ibid., 52.
15. Patrick Kavanagh, *Collected Poems*, London 1973, 19.
16. Kavanagh, *Collected Poems*, xiv.
17. On Lemass, see Brian Farrell, *Sean Lemass*, Dublin 1983; and more generally J. J. Lee, *Ireland 1912–1985: Politics and Society*, Cambridge 1989, 329–410.
18. See John Montague, "The Impact of International Poetry on Irish Writing", *Irish Poets in English*, ed. Sean Lucy, Cork 1973, 144–58.

TWENTY-SEVEN: THE PERIPHERY AND THE CENTRE

1. Conor Cruise O'Brien, *States of Ireland*, 71–2.
2. Yeats, *Explorations*, 187.
3. Yeats, *Collected Poems*, 359.
4. Ibid., 152.
5. Ibid., 369.
6. John McGahern, *High Ground*, London 1985, 23.
7. Quoted in Maurice Goldring, *Faith of Our Fathers: The Foundation of Irish National Ideology 1890–1920*, Dublin 1982, 62 ff.
8. Synge, *Prose*, 286.

9. Yeats, *Explorations*, 232. The passage was written in 1908.

10. Quoted by Frank O'Connor, *The Big Fellow*, London 1965, 20.

11. Tomás Ó Criomhthainn, *An tOileánach*, Dublin 1929, 51.

12. Synge, *Prose*, 95–6.

13. Synge, *Collected Letters 2*, 116–17.

14. David Fitzpatrick, *Politics and Irish Life 1913–21*, 234.

15. Synge, *Prose*, 132–3.

16. The text has been restored by Seán Ó Coileáin of University College Cork in what promises to be a definitive edition.

17. Yeats, Preface to *The King of the Great Clock Tower*, Dublin 1934.

18. G. B. Shaw, *The Matter with Ireland*, 156.

19. Ibid., 136.

20. On the phenomenon see Alexander J. Humphreys, *New Dubliners*, London 1966.

21. John Meagher, quoted *The Irish Times*, 9 December 1986, 10.

22. Declan Kiberd, "The Moral Superiority of Rural Villages", *The Irish Times*, 9 December 1986, 10.

23. Fintan O'Toole, "Going West: The Country versus the City in Irish Writing", *The Crane Bag*, Vol. 9, No. 2, 1985, 111–16.

24. Ellmann, *James Joyce*, 169.

25. Ibid., 170.

26. Interview with present author, 12 November 1985 "Exhibit A", RTE Television.

TWENTY-EIGHT: FLANN O'BRIEN, MYLES, AND THE POOR MOUTH

1. David Krause, introduction, *The Dolmen Boucicault*, Dublin 1964, 32.

2. Quoted by Anne Clissmann, *Flann O'Brien: A Critical Introduction to His Writings*, Dublin 1975.

3. Flann O'Brien, *At Swim-Two-Birds*, Harmondsworth 1967, 25.

4. Jack White, "Myles, Flann and Brian", *Myles: Portraits of Brian O'Nolan*, ed. Timothy O'Keeffe, London 1973, 63.

5. Brian O'Nolan, "De Me", *New Ireland*, March 1964, 41.

6. Clissmann, 3.

7. Myles na gCopaleen, *An Béal Bocht*, Dublin 1964, 30; Flann O'Brien, *The Poor Mouth*, tr. Patrick Power, London 1978, 23. Hereafter *BB*, *PM*.

8. *BB* 23; *PM* 30–1.

9. *BB* 25; *PM* 34.

10. *BB* 42; *PM* 51–2.

11. James Joyce, *Stephen Hero*, London 1966, 54.

12. Brendan Kennelly, "An Béal Bocht", *The Pleasures of Gaelic Literature*, ed. J. Jordan, Dublin 1977.

13. *BB* 10; *PM* 14–15.

14. *PM* 63; *BB* 52.

15. L. Perry Curtis Jnr., *Apes and Angles: The Irishman in Victorian Caricature*, London 1971, 31.
16. Bernard Partridge, *Punch*, 24 December 1919; 18 February 1920; 13 October 1920.
17. *PM* 36; *BB* 27.
18. Curtin, 60.
19. *PM* 110–11; *BB* 98–9.
20. *PM* 100; *BB* 87.
21. *PM* 13; *BB* 8.
22. *PM* 78; *BB* 67.
23. James W. Redfield, *Comparative Physiognomy*, New York 1852, 253–8.
24. *PM* 89; *BB* 75.
25. Adam Smith, *The Wealth of Nations*, 1, 201–2.
26. *PM* 98; *BB* 85.
27. Curtis, 102.
28. Myles na gCopaleen, "Cruiskeen Lawn", *Irish Times*, 30 July 1953.
29. Ibid., 2 March 1966.
30. Curtis, 95.
31. Kevin O'Connor, *The Irish in Britain*, London 1974, 22.
32. Brian O'Nolan, "A Bash in the Tunnell", *Envoy* v, 17, May 1951, 11.
33. Niall Sheridan, "Brian, Flann and Myles", 40.
34. Ibid., 53.
35. R. N. Cooke, *Centenary History of the Literary and Historical Society of University College Dublin*, ed. J. Meenan, Kerry 1955, 242. For an extended consideration of wasted talent see Anthony Cronin, *No Laughing Matter: The Life and Times of Flann O'Brien*, London 1989.

TWENTY-NINE: BRENDAN BEHAN – THE EMPIRE WRITES BACK

1. Ted E. Boyle, *Brendan Behan*, New York 1969, 31.
2. Ulick O'Connor, *Brendan Behan*, London 1972, 61–85.
3. Máirtín Ó Cadhain in conversation with the present author, April 1969.
4. Ted E. Boyle, 63.
5. Quoted ibid., 64.
6. Brendan Behan, *The Quare Fellow*, London 1960, 29.
7. Colbert Kearney, *The Writings of Brendan Behan*, Dublin 1977, 75–6.
8. *Quare Fellow*, 21.
9. Kearney, *The Writings*, 48.
10. See Máirtín Ó Cadhain, *As an nGéibheann*, Dublin 1973, 201.
11. Synge, *Prose*, 95.
12. *Quare Fellow*, 74.
13. Ibid., 56.
14. Ibid., 57, 58.

15. Ted E. Boyle, 67.
16. *Quare Fellow*, 86.
17. The references in the published version of *Borstal Boy* were toned down and made much less explicit than those in earlier versions: see Boyle, 104.
18. Brendan Behan, *Borstal Boy*, London 1961, 302–3.
19. Barbara Harlow, *Resistance Literature*, New York 1987, 143.
20. Quoted ibid., 152.
21. *Borstal Boy*, 379.
22. Ulick O'Connor, *Brendan Behan*, 193.
23. Kearney, *The Writings*, 119.
24. Brian Behan, quoted in O'Connor, 208.
25. Brendan Behan, "An Giall", *Poems and a Play in Irish*, Dublin 1981.
26. Brendan Behan, *The Hostage*, London 1962, 76.
27. For an extended contrast see Richard Wall, "*An Giall* and *The Hostage* Compared", in E. H. Mikhail ed., *The Art of Brendan Behan*, London 1979, 138–46.
28. Quoted in O'Connor, 207.
29. Quoted Boyle, 86.
30. *The Hostage*, 61.
31. Ibid., 35.
32. Ibid., 33, 34.
33. Ibid., 5.
34. Ibid., 89.
35. Ibid., 61.
36. Ibid., 58.
37. Ibid., 52.
38. Ibid., 58.
39. Ibid., 51.
40. Ibid., 78. On this element of play-acting see Paul M. Levitt, "Hostages and History: Title as Dramatic Metaphor in *The Hostage*, *The Art of Brendan Behan*, 146–55.
41. *The Hostage*, 108, 108.
42. On this aspect see O'Connor, 96–9.

THIRTY: BECKETT'S TEXTS OF LAUGHTER AND FORGETTING

1. Deirdre Bair, *Samuel Beckett: A Biography*, 26.
2. Brendan Kennelly, "My Dark Fathers", *Field Day Anthology 3*, 1361.
3. Vivian Mercier, *Beckett/Beckett*, London 1977, 37.
4. Samuel Beckett, *That Time*,
5. Beckett, *More Pricks Than Kicks*, 146.
6. Beckett, *Murphy*, 28.
7. Ibid., 22.
8. Ibid., 47, 69, 111.

9. Ibid., 53.
10. Bair, 212.
11. Samuel Beckett, *All That Fall*, London 1965, 10–11.
12. Synge, *Plays 2*, 223.
13. *Murphy*, 6.
14. Bair, 241.
15. *Murphy*, 126.
16. Ibid., 151.
17. Ibid., 47, 10.
18. Ibid., 36, 101.
19. Dylan Thomas, *New English Weekly*, XII, 17 March 1938, 454–5.
20. Niklaus Gessner, *Die Unzulänglichkeit der Sprache*, Zurich 1957, 32.
21. Samuel Beckett, *Texts for Nothing*, Collected Shorter Prose, London 1984, 74.
22. Samuel Beckett, *Company*, London 1982, 7.
23. My sources on this are Eleanor Knott, U. Caerwyn Williams and James Carney.
24. *Company*, 7.
25. Beckett, *Molloy: Malone Dies: the Unnamable*, 313.
26. Ibid., 159.
27. Hugh Kenner, *A Reader's Guide to Samuel Beckett*, London 1973, 98, 100.
28. David Greene, lecture on "Bardic Poetry", Trinity College Dublin, 11 March 1967.
29. Samuel Beckett, *First Love*, London 1974, 17.
30. Beckett, *Disjecta*, 71.
31. See Ann Saddlemyer ed., *Letters to Molly: John M. Synge to Maire O'Neill*, Harvard 1971.
32. Synge, *Prose*, 202.
33. Yeats, *Collected Poems*, 350.
34. Beckett, *Waiting for Godot*, 10.
35. Ibid., 12.
36. Vivian Mercier *Beckett/Beckett*, 46.
37. Samuel Beckett, *Happy Days*, London 1966, 46.
38. *Waiting for Godot*, 65, 61.
39. Ibid., 14–15.
40. Quoted by Vincent Buckley, *Memory Ireland*, 98.
41. Vincent Buckley, ibid., 98.
42. *Waiting for Godot*, 88.
43. Ibid., 30.
44. Ibid., 33, 39.
45. Ibid., 31.
46. Ibid., 79.
47. Ibid., 68.
48. Ibid., 91.
49. Mercier, *Beckett/Beckett*, 53.

50. *Endgame*, 12, 34.
51. Ibid., 39.
52. Ibid., 47.
53. Ibid., 30.
54. Ibid., 12.
55. Ibid., 13.
56. Ibid., 13–14.
57. Ibid., 30.
58. Ibid., 38.
59. *Waiting for Godot*, 64.
60. Erich Fromm, *The Fear of Freedom*, London˙1984, 207.
61. *Endgame*, 45.
62. Fromm, *The Fear of Freedom*, 96.
63. *Endgame*, 51.
64. The text is reproduced in Eoin O'Brien, *The Beckett Country*, Dublin 1986, 337.

THIRTY-ONE: POST-COLONIAL IRELAND

1. Patrick Pearse, *A Significant Irish Educationalist*, 352.
2. Frantz Fanon, *The Wretched of the Earth*, 120.
3. D. H. Akenson, *A Mirror to Kathleen's Face*, 76.
4. Paul Harrison, *Inside the Third World*, Harmondsworth 1981, 325 ff.
5. Ngugi wa Thiong'o, *Decolonizing the Mind: The Politics of Language in African Literature*, London 1986, 97, 100.
6. Chinua Achebe, *Hopes and Impediments*, 27–8.
7. Quoted by Vincent Buckley, *Memory Ireland*, Victoria 1985, 175.
8. Achebe, *Hopes and Impediments*, 64.
9. Ngugi, *Decolonizing the Mind*, 89 ff.
10. Paul Harrison, *Inside the Third World*, 317.
11. V. S. Naipaul, *The Mimic-Men*, Harmondsworth 1969, 146.
12. George Lamming, *Caribbean Essays*, ed. Andrew Salkey, London 1973, 11.
13. Achebe, *Hopes and Impediments*, 58, 84.
14. John Devitt, "English for the Irish", *The Crane Bag*, Vol. 6, No. 1, 1982, 106.
15. Daniel Corkery, *Synge and Anglo-Irish Literature*, Cork 1966, 14.
16. George Lamming, *The Pleasures of Exile*, 157.
17. Corkery, *Synge and Anglo-Irish Literature*, 15.
18. Gauri Viswanathan, "The Empire Within", *Voice Literary Supplement*, New York, January-February 1989, 22.
19. Lionel Trilling, "On the Teaching of Modern Literature", *Beyond Culture: Essays on Literature and Learning*, Oxford 1980, 3–27.
20. Corkery, *Synge and Anglo-Irish Literature*, 12.

21. Quoted by Gareth Griffiths, *A Double Exile: African and West Indian Writing Between Two Countries*, London 1978, 91.
22. Corkery, *Synge and Anglo-Irish Literature*, 11.
23. Fanon, *The Wretched of the Earth*, 180.
24. On this episode see Conor Cruise O'Brien, *To Katanga and Back: A UN Case History*, London 1965.
25. Conor Cruise O'Brien, *Camus*, London 1970, 85.
26. Achebe, *Hopes and Impediments*, 64.
27. V. S. Naipaul, *India: A Wounded Civilization*, Harmondsworth 1979, 148.
28. Conor Cruise O'Brien, *Camus*, 84.
29. Within these general constraints, O'Brien was sometimes capable of adopting a somewhat oedipal attitude to Ó Faoláin; see Donald Harman Akenson, *Conor: A Biography*, Montreal 1994, 120–3.
30. The phrase was used by Jorge Luis Borges, *Labyrinths*. See footnote 59, Chapter 2.

RECOVERY AND RENEWAL: INTERCHAPTER

1. An excellent source on which I have repeatedly drawn is Fergal Tobin, *The Best of Decades: Ireland in the 1960s*, Dublin 1984.
2. Ibid., 66.
3. The speaker was Brian Trevaskis, of the University Philosophical Society, Trinity College, Dublin in 1968.
4. On television see Lelia Doolan, Jack Dowling and Bob Quinn, *Sit Down and Be Counted*, Dublin 1969. For its effect on Irish language policy see Terence Brown, *Ireland: A Social and Cultural History*, 271 ff.
5. Tobin, 30.
6. On these developments, see Declan Kiberd, editorial, *The Crane Bag: Irish Language and Culture – An tEagrán Gaelach*, Vol. 5, No. 2, 1981; and passim.
7. Gearóid Ó Tuathaigh, historian; quoted by Brown, 269.
8. *Report of the Committee on Irish Language Attitudes and Research*, Dublin 1975, 24.
9. J. J. Lee, *Ireland 1912–1985: Politics and Society*, 658–74.
10. Jeremiah Newman, "Ireland in the Eighties" Our Responsibility", *Christus Rex*, Vol. XXV, No. 3, 1971, 190.
11. On this, see Peadar Kirby, *Ireland and Latin America: Links and Lessons*, Dublin 1992; and *Has Ireland a Future?*, Cork 1988.
12. See Fintan O'Toole, *A Mass for Jesse James*, Dublin 1989.
13. Tobin, 196.
14. For a mordant southern viewpoint, see Conor Cruise O'Brien, *States of Ireland*, esp. 147–294.
15. His subsequent book was Richard Rose, *Northern Ireland: A Time of Choice*, London 1976.

16. On the Northern Ireland "Troubles" see Tim Pat Coogan, *The IRA*, London 1995; and J. J. Lee, *Ireland 1912–1985*, 411–57; and Dermot Keogh, *Twentieth Century Ireland*, Dublin 1994, 295–388.
17. Fionnuala O'Connor, *In Search of a State*, Belfast 1993.
18. Raymond Crotty, *Ireland in Crisis*, see back.
19. Michael O'Sullivan, *Mary Robinson*, Dublin 1993.

THIRTY-TWO: UNDER PRESSURE

1. Letter to Thomas MacGreevy, 31 January 1938.
2. Patrick Kavanagh, *Collected Poems*, 132.
3. John Montague, *Selected Poems*, Winston-Salem 1982, 62.
4. The phrase is Augustine Martin's; for the surrounding debate, see issue of *Studies* in the period 1965.
5. Brown, *Ireland: A Social and Cultural History*, 297.
6. Irving Howe, "The Idea of the Modern", *Literary Modernism*, ed. Howe, New York 1968, 13.
7. Thomas Kinsella, *Downstream*, Dublin 1962, 48.
8. Daniel Bell, *The Cultural Contradictions of Capitalism*, London 1979, esp. 33–174.
9. Thomas Kinsella, *Nightwalker and Other Poems*, Dublin 1968, 59.
10. Thomas Kinsella, "Another September", *Field Day Anthology 3*, 1341.
11. "Baggot Street Deserta", ibid., 1342.
12. John Montague, *Selected Poems*, 10.
13. Richard Murphy, "Casement's Funeral", *Field Day Anthology 3*, 1338.
14. Thomas Kinsella, *The Irish Writer*, MLA New York 1966, 58–9.
15. Michael Hartnett, *A Farewell to English*, Dublin 1978, 64.
16. Thomas Kinsella, "The Divided Mind", *Irish Poets in English*, 209.
17. Seán Ó Ríordáin, "A Ghaeilge im Pheannsa", *Brosna*, Dublin 1964, 9–10.
18. Seán Ó Ríordáin, ibid.
19. Corkery, *Synge and Anglo-Irish Literature*, 6, 14.
20. Seán Ó Ríordáin, "Do Dhomhnall Ó Corcora", *Eireaball Spideoíge*, Dublin 1952, 51.
21. Seamus Deane, "Unhappy and At Home: Interview with Seamus Heaney", *The Crane Bag*, 1, No. 1, Spring 1977, 64.
22. Anthony Heaney, "A Gift for Being in Touch", *Quest*, January-February 1978, Vol. 2, No. 1, 42.
23. Seamus Heaney, *Death of a Naturalist*, London 1966, 23.
24. Seamus Heaney, *North*, London 1975, 51.
25. David Lloyd, who first made this connection, discusses it in a very critical essay, "Pap for the Dispossessed: Seamus Heaney and the Poetics of Identity", *Anomalous States: Irish Writing and the Post-Colonial Moment*, Dublin 1993, 13–40.
26. Seamus Heaney, *North*, 37–8.

27. Denis Donoghue, "Now and in Ireland: the Literature of Trouble", *Hibernia* (Dublin), 11 May 1978, 17.
28. Heaney, *North*, 73.
29. Seamus Heaney, *Station Island*, London 1984, 83.
30. Ibid., 98.
31. Ibid., 102.
32. Ibid., 93.
33. Seamus Heaney, *Seeing Things*, London 1991, 62.
34. Ibid., 21.
35. Ibid., 8
36. Vincent Buckley, *Memory Ireland*, 105–6.
37. Derek Mahon, *Poems 1962–78*, Oxford 1979, 69.
38. Ibid., 4.
39. Ibid., 58.
40. *Field Day Anthology 3*, 1384.
41. Ciaran Carson, *Field Day Anthology 3*, 1406.
42. Máire Mhac an tSaoi, *An Cion go dti' Seo*, Dublin 1987, 81. Translation by the poet.
43. Ibid., 20. Translation by Declan Kiberd
44. Nuala ní Dhomhnaill, *Pharaoh's Daughter*, Oldcastle 1990, 36, 38.
45. Ibid., 130, 131.
46. Ibid., 142, 143.
47. Ibid., 154, 155.
48. Eavan Boland, *Field Day Anthology 3*, 1395–6.
49. Eavan Boland, "A Kind of Scar: The Woman Poet in a National Tradition", *A Dozen Lips*, Dublin 1994, 80–1.
50. Ibid., 89, 91.
51. Edna Longley, "From Cathleen to Anorexia: The Breakdown of Irelands", *A Dozen Lips*, 177, 180.
52. Ibid., 178.
53. Eavan Boland, "Mise Éire", *A Dozen Lips*, 72.
54. Eavan Boland, "The Emigrant Irish", *Field Day Anthology 3*, 1397–8.
55. *The Selected Paul Durcan*, Belfast 1985, 26.
56. Dermot Bolger, *The Journey Home*, London 1990, 7–8; *The Woman's Daughter*, London 1991.
57. In the wake of the 75th anniversary of the 1916 Rising, Dermot Bolger wrote articles in *The Sunday Press* strongly promoting this line.
58. Roddy Doyle, *The Barrytown Trilogy*, Secker and Warburg, London 1992, 13.
59. Paul Muldoon, *Field Day Anthology 3*, 1414–15.

THIRTY-THREE: FRIEL TRANSLATING

1. See Benedict Kiely, *Poor Scholar*, London 1947, 47.

2. For such a critique see Fintan O'Toole, "Island of Saints and Silicon", *Cultural Contexts and Literary Idioms in Contemporary Irish Literature*, ed. Michael Kenneally, Gerrards Cross 1988, 15–18.

3. P. J. Dowling, *The Hedge Schools of Ireland*, Cork 1968.

4. Michel Foucault, "The Order of Discourse", *Untying the Text: A Post-Structuralist Reader*, London 1981, 53.

5. On this see Maureen Wall, "The Decline of the Irish Language", *A View of the Irish Language*, 81–90.

6. *Report of the Committee on Irish Language Attitudes and Research*, 293–305.

7. Programme note to *Translations*, Field Day 1980.

8. Seamus Heaney, *Wintering Out*, London 1972, 48.

9. Brian Friel, *Translations*, London 1981, 51–2.

10. John Montague, *Selected Poems*, 108.

11. Friel, *Translations*, 42.

12. Ibid., 67.

13. Ibid., 66–7.

14. *Station Island*, 66.

15. *Translations*, 43.

16. On this see Walter Benjamin, *Illuminations*, 81 ff.

17. John Dryden, "On Translation", *Theories of Translation*, eds. R. Schutte and J. Biguenet, Chicago 1992, 28.

18. Edward Said, *Orientalism*, 67.

19. Ibid., 93, 272.

20. *Translations*, 40.

21. Ibid., 43.

22. Ibid., 66.

23. Ibid., 42.

24. Ibid., 42.

25. See especially some of the essays collected in *Celtic Revivals*.

THIRTY-FOUR: TRANSLATING TRADITION

1. Octavio Paz, "Translation: Literature and Letters", *Theories of Translation*, 160.

2. Jacques Derrida, "Des Tours de Babel", *Theories of Translation*, 219.

3. Macaulay, *Prose and Poetry*, 722.

4. Charles Trevelyan, *On the Education of the People of India*, London 1838, Chapter 2.

5. William Jones, *A Grammar of the Persian Language*, London 1771, vii.

6. Friedrich Nietzsche, "On the Problem of Translation", *Theories of Translation*, 69–70.

7. George Steiner, *After Babel: Aspects of Language and Translation*, London 1975, 321.

8. On this see Declan Kiberd, *Synge and the Irish Language*, 54–94.

9. Renato Poggioli, "The Added Artificer", *On Translation*, ed. Reuben A. Brower, Harvard 1959, 142.

10. See Declan Kiberd, "George Moore agus an Ghaeilge", *Idir Dhá Chultúr*, Dublin 1993, 129–30.

11. Walter Benjamin, *Illuminations*, 80.

12. Godfrey Lienhardt, "Modes of Thought", *The Institutions of Primitive Society*, Oxford 1961, 97.

13. The image is from Benjamin's essay on translation.

14. Marcel Proust, *Remembrance of Things Past*, Book 3, 903.

15. Friedrich Nietzsche, *On the Advantage and Disadvantage of History for Life*, Trans. I. Ellis, Carbondale 1984, 35.

16. Benjamin, *Illuminations*, 257.

17. Ibid., 259.

18. Ibid., 70.

19. See David Lowenthal, *The Past is a Foreign Country*, Cambridge 1985, 250.

20. See Declan Kiberd, "Brian Friel's *Faith Healer*", *Irish Writers and Society at Large*, Gerrards Cross 1985, 106–21.

21. Brian Friel, *Making History*, London 1989, 9.

22. Ibid., 65.

23. John Banville, with Ronan Sheehan and Francis Stuart, "Novelists on the Novel", *The Crane Bag*, Vol. 3, No. 1, 1979, 84.

24. John Banville, *Doctor Copernicus: A Novel*, London 1976, 94.

25. Banville, "Novelists on the Novel", 79–80.

26. In conversation with the present writer, October 1985.

27. Friedrich Schleiermacher, "On the Different Methods of Translating", *Theories of Translation*, 46–7.

28. Derrida, *Theories of Translation*, 218–27.

29. Banville, *Doctor Copernicus*, 27.

THIRTY-FIVE: IMAGINING IRISH STUDIES

1. Erasmus to Leo X, 1 February 1516, letter 384, *Correspondence*, 3, 221–2.

2. Said, *Orientalism*, 328.

3. Synge, *Prose*, 60.

4. R. F. Foster, *Modern Ireland 1600–1972*, London 1988, 453, 453.

5. See, for instance, the strictures of Brendan Bradshaw, "Nationalism and Historical Scholarship in Modern Ireland", *Interpreting Irish History: The Debate on Historical Revisionism*, Dublin 1994, 191–216.

6. See Kevin O'Neill, "Revisionist Milestone", *Interpreting Irish History*, 217–21.

7. Ronan Fanning (quoting Bernard Lewis), "The Great Enchantment: Uses and Abuses of Modern Irish History", *Interpreting Irish History*, 156.

8. J. J. Lee, *Ireland: Politics and Society 1912–86*, 390 ff.

9. Crotty, *Ireland in Crisis*, Dingle 1986.

10. Some hopeful trends are recorded by Alvin Jackson, "Unionist History", *Interpreting Irish History*, 253–68.
11. See Seamus Deane, "Remembering the Irish Future", *The Crane Bag*, Vol. 8, No. 2, 1984, 81–92.
12. Pádraig Ó Riagáin, Micheál Ó Gliasáin, *National Survey on Languages 1993*: Preliminary Report, Dublin 1994, esp. 5–15.
13. Seán de Fréine, *The Great Silence*, esp. 61–74.
14. Ibid., 144–6.
15. Ibid., 188–90.
16. A poll in *Sunday Independent* in late 1993 showed that almost 80% of the Republic's citizens had no wish to coerce unionists into a united Ireland.
17. *Translations*, 67.

INDEX

Abbey Theatre (Irish National Theatre Company), 57, 70, 87, 89, 100, 128, 149, 153, 164, 168, 171, 183, 187, 203, 220, 221, 224, 232, 233, 241, 245, 259, 270, 271, 272, 338, 340, 400, 493–4, 496, 513, 522, 533, 623, 653
Achebe, Chinua, 118, 120, 552–3, 557, 559; *Things Fall Apart*, 552–3
Adams, Gerry, 576
Adorno, Theodor, 144
aesthetic movement, 201
Africa, 4, 15, 118, 120, 135, 143, 157, 160, 197, 251, 268, 272, 287, 335, 340, 392, 407–8, 465, 480, 553, 559, 579, 611, 652
Ahmed, Aijaz, 531
Aisling (vision poem), 18, 210, 317, 362, 539
Alexandria, 85
Algeria, 163, 276, 296, 558
Allgood, Molly, 176
Allingham, William, 102
Amritsar, 254, 256
Anabaptists, 434
anarchists, 351, 436, 490; *L'Anarchie*, 175
Anderson, Benedict, 2, 3, 137, 338
Andrews, C.S., 233
androgyny, 35, 38–41, 59, 84, 124, 175–7, 181, 182–3, 300, 307, 344, 385, 406–7, 429–32, 439
Anglicization, 11, 69
Anglo-Irish Agreement, 576
Anglo-Irish aristocracy, 21, 23–5, 33–4, 36, 49–50, 51, 67, 68–82, 83–95, 138, 153, 159, 174, 175, 217, 273, 274, 301–3, 317, 318–26, 350, 363, 364–79, 414, 416, 438, 443–4, 449, 482–4, 491, 499, 545, 621
Anglo-Irish relations, 1–20, 29–63, 124, 251–2, 279, 317, 367–79, 521–9, 592
Anglo-Irish Treaty, 194, 218, 255, 401–2, 521, 530
Anglophobia, 142, 524, 642, 648, 650; paucity of in 1916 writing, 199

Anglo-Saxon, 354
anima, animus, 41, 181–2, 307
Annam, 197
Anthropophagus (Brazilian movement), 589
Aosdána, 584–5
Aran Islands, 107, 120, 161, 169, 287–8, 289, 476, 516–17, 579, 627, 641
Archaeological Society, 133
Arendt, Hannah, 387
Argentina, 49, 339
Aristotle, 214, 511
Arnold, Matthew, 30–2, 42, 48, 60, 116, 124, 138, 139, 157, 233, 269, 272, 318, 349, 425, 556–7, 615, 622–3, 648
Arts Council (Ireland), 609
Asia, 135, 143, 162, 197, 252
Asquith, H. H., 192
Atkinson, Robert, 146, 265, 625
Auden, W. H., 477, 585–6
Austen, Jane, 68, 72, 75, 76, 199, 397; *Emma*, 76; *Mansfield Park*, 68, 72

Balcombe, Florence, 34
Balfour, Arthur, 61
Balzac, Honoré de, 44, 494
Bande Mataran, 253
Banville, John, 523, 584, 634–5, 637; *Doctor Copernicus*, 523, 634–5, 637; *Kepler*, 612
Beardsley, Aubrey, 361
Beckett, J. C., 449
Beckett, Samuel, 1–2, 12, 126, 220, 265, 266, 276, 299, 421–2: on O'Casey, 220; removal of silences from *Godot*, 237; compared with Bowen, 377–8; and with Yeats, 441, 443–5, 446–9, 459; and A. A. Luce, 452–3; and religious art, 454–61; and Shaw, 454; on suffering, 454–5; on art as stain, 455; and Protestant contradictions, 456–7; and eastern religion, 457; puritan approach to drama, 458–9; stage directions, 458–9; art as prayer, 461; on MacGreevy, 461, 464, 467; and Coffey, 462, 464; and

Beckett, Samuel (*contd*)
Devlin, 463–4; mocks Clarke, 464; prefers wartime France to Ireland, 471; on Irish neutrality, 473, 542, 550; and Kavanagh, 478; on Victorian Gael, 484; compared with Behan, 513; and Easter Rising, 530–1; youthful character of, 531; and censorship, 531; *Murphy* on emigration, 533; source of comedy, 533–4; writing in French, 534–5; and Gaelic tradition, 535–8; orality, 536; fragmentary art, 537; compared with T. S. Eliot, 537; and Ó Rathaille, 538; on postcolonial amnesia, 539; on lack of tradition in Ireland, 539–40; on subject peoples and art, 541; on master-slave paradigm, 541–2, 545–50; role versus self, 543; on idiocy of desire, 543; *Godot* on impossibility of selfhood, 543–4; compared to O'Casey, 546; and hope, 548; on sado-masochism, 549; as republican, 550; and Europe, 560; on Irish nation, 580; as last of moderns, 584; and Kinsella on fragmentation, 591; and tradition, 636; *More Pricks than Kicks*, 454–6, 543; *Murphy*, 448, 456–7, 464, 531–3, 543; *First Love*, 537; *Molloy*, 459–60, 535, 543; *Malone Dies*, 519; *The Unnamable*, 460, 494; *Waiting for Godot*, 455, 458–9, 514, 537–45, 547, 548; *Endgame*, 276, 455, 458, 545–50; *Happy Days*, 546; *Krapp's Last Tape*, 536
Beckett, William, 530
Beethoven, Ludwig van, 455
Behan, Brendan, 6: birth, 513; as republican, 513; and Alan Simpson, 513; and prison system, 514–15; and Beckett, 514, 535; and socialism, 514–15; compared to Rushdie, 515; poetry, 515–16; and Blaskets, 516–17; and capital punishment, 517; socialist republicanism, 517–19; and prison literature, 519–20; on Irish, 520; *An Giall* recast as *The Hostage*, 520–2; on Abbey techniques, 523; contrasted with O'Casey, 522; autocritic, 523; and *Ulysses*, 523; and Frank O'Connor, 523–4; and Kavanagh's anti-revivalism, 524; critique of republican failures, 524–6; updates O'Casey, 526; challenges stereotypes of Englishness, 527; ending of *Hostage*, 527–8; literary radicalism of, 529; as postcolonial artist, 529;

bisexuality, 529; as 'gas bloody man', 582; and translation, 636; *The Quare Fellow*, 513–19, 520, 526, 529; *An Giall*, 520; *The Hostage*, 520–9; *Borstal Boy*, 519
Behan, Brian, 521
Bell, The (literary magazine), 366
Beltaine (theatrical magazine), 146
Benjamin, Walter, 4, 293, 374–9, 600, 628–30
Bennett, Arnold, 285
Berger, John, 144
Berkeley, Bishop George, 322–3, 449, 452
Besant, Annie, 252
Bevan, Aneurin, 515
Bey, Arabi, 84–6
Bible, The, 404, 423, 424, 429–30, 455, 460, 548, 630, 636
bilingualism, 146
big house culture, 67–82, 99, 365–79, 416, 449
Birrell, Augustine, 141
'Black and Tans', 194, 218, 236, 401
Blackmur, R. P., 441
Blasket islands, 286–7, 289, 487–8, 490, 516–17
Blueshirts, 360
Blunt, Wilfrid Scawen, 84–95, 252; *Ideas on India*, 87; *In Vinculis*, 88
blutbrüderschaft, 95
Boland, Eavan, 605, 606, 608–9
Bolger, Dermot, 609–10
Bombay, 556
Borges, Jorge Luis, 49, 339, 343
Bow Bells, 144
Bowen, Elizabeth, 6, 363, 364–79: *Bowen's Court*, 364–5, 372–3, 378–9; on Easter Rising, 364; and Catholics, 365; childhood, 365; on Anglo-Irish landowners, 365–6; on style, 367; on Troubles, 368; on behaviour, 368–9; and Somerville & Ross, 369; on big house as enervating, 370; on England, 370; father's book, 371; decorum, 371; and dandy figure, 373–9; on nonchalance, 375; on property, 376; Anglo-Irish attitudes, 376; on 'poor mouth', 376–7; compared to Beckett, 377; on romantic desperation, 377; collapse of dandy, 377–8; spiritual hyphenation, 378; and ruined Gaelic aristocrats, 378; leaves Bowen's Court, 379; *The Last September*, 365–79

Bradley, A.C., 234
Brecht, Bertolt, 225
Brehon law, 151, 178–9, 398
British Foreign Service, 86
British Museum, 137
British Raj, 254
Brontë, Emily, 397
Brooke, Charlotte, 30, 271: *Reliques of Ancient Irish Poetry*, 30, 271
Brooke, Stopford A., 156
Brown, Norman O., 393
Browne, Noel C., 478–9
Brugha, Cathal, 263, 400–1
Buckley, Vincent, 599
Buddhism, 460
Bunyan, John, 272, 426; *The Pilgrim's Progress*, 272
Burke, Edmund, 17–20, 32, 212, 321–3, 419–20, 449; *Reflections on the Revolution in France*, 18; *Enquiry into...the Sublime*, 322
Byron, Lord Gordon, 123

Cabral, Amilcar, 252
Cairo, 84–6, 88, 336
camogie, 472
Campbell, Lady Colin, 35
Campion, Thomas, 199
Camus, Albert, 558–60
Canada, 375, 471, 646
Carleton, William, 136, 342, 597, 614, 618
Carson, Ciaran, 600, 604; *Belfast Confetti*, 600
Carson, Lord Edward, 192, 414
Casement, Sir Roger, 47, 198, 352, 587
Cathleen ní Houlihan (image of Ireland), 16, 57, 183, 200, 217, 294, 298, 315, 403, 439, 607, 653
Catholic Emancipation, 20, 29
Ceannt, Éamon, 224
Céitinn, Seathrún (Geoffrey Keating), 6, 11, 13–15, 19, 32, 191: *Trí Biorghaoithe an Bháis*, 146, 625–7
Celtic Society, 133
Celtic Studies, 386, 398, 498, 505–6
Celticism, 29, 30–1, 37–8, 42, 47, 49, 52–3, 58, 61, 94, 99, 103, 113, 116, 128, 137, 143, 151, 156, 179, 183, 269–70, 280, 285, 317–26, 348, 349, 425, 441, 464, 510, 535, 599,

601–2, 605, 619, 620, 622–3, 625
censorship, 161, 264, 297–8, 333–4, 361, 390, 404, 414, 472–3, 575, 579, 580
Cervantes, Miguel de, 341
Césaire, Aimé, 5, 186, 251, 278, 283
Ceylon, 86
Chagall, Marc, 598
Chardin, Teilhard de, 591
Chatterjee, Mohini, 253, 325
Chekhov, Anton, 366
Chesterfield, Lord, 533
Chesterton, G. K., 101
Childers, Erskine, 198
China, 339
Christianity, 60, 94, 109, 211, 226–7, 310, 317, 329, 335, 354, 360–1, 419–27
Church of Ireland (Anglican), 23, 81–2, 419, 474: disestablishment of, 423
Churchill, Winston, 393, 472
Cinderella, 83
Civil War (Irish), 129, 194, 218–19, 257, 263, 315, 359, 384, 403, 513, 551, 566
Claidheamh Soluis, An (*The Sword of Light*), 146, 151, 264
Clan na Gael, 253
Clarke, Austin, 464–6, 580, 584
Clarke, Kathleen, 400, 403
Clissmann, Anne, 512
Coffey, Brian, 462
Coleridge, Samuel Taylor, 20, 348, 443, 447, 491; 'Kubla Khan', 348; *The Rime of the Ancient Mariner*, 443, 447
Collins, Michael, 4, 99, 154, 194–5, 207, 286, 392, 402, 413–14, 463, 481, 486, 489, 451
Colmcille, 284
colonialism, 5, 6, 30, 43–5, 49–50, 60, 68, 85–8, 101, 104, 114–15, 118, 123, 137, 144, 148, 163, 166, 170, 179, 180, 186, 237, 251–9, 275, 279–85, 286, 292, 315, 322, 334–5, 344, 349, 351, 354, 380–1, 387–8, 389, 395, 426, 435–7, 438–9, 475, 494, 529, 540–50, 551–2, 556–7, 559, 614–23, 633–4, 641–3, 651–3; reverse colonialism, 35, 62, 271–2, 425, 475
Colum, Mary, 265, 397, 398
Colum, Pádraic, 582
Comercally, 625
Congested Districts, 485
Congo, 335, 352, 480, 558

Congress of Berlin, 157
Connaught Rangers, 265–8
Connolly, Cyril, 477
Connolly, James, 3–4, 140, 192–3, 207,
208, 212, 218, 227, 230, 247, 259, 293,
294, 319, 399, 407, 435, 476, 479, 631;
Labour in Irish History, 293, 319, 435
Connolly, Peter, 582
Connolly, Seán, 203–4
Conrad, Joseph, 266, 344, 642; *Heart of
Darkness,* 266, 344, 642
conscription, 193
Conservative Party, 192, 335
Coole Park, 70, 85, 88, 89, 215, 443–4
Copernicus, Nicholas, 634–5
Corkery, Daniel, 264, 555–8, 560,
590
Corneille, 532, 552
Cosgrave, William T., 359–60
cosmopolitanism, 7, 155–65
Costello, John A., 476, 584
Council for Civil Liberties, 416
Craik, Henry, 33
Crashaw, William, 270
cricket, 282
Cromer, Lord, 159
Cromwell, Oliver, 17, 211, 483, 538
Crotty, Raymond, 646
Cuchulain, 25, 31, 44, 151, 156, 162, 169,
171, 180, 183, 196, 197, 203, 206, 208,
212, 213, 217, 224, 229, 230, 285, 293,
484, 500, 537, 624, 649
Cullen, Louis, 539–40
Cultural Studies, 145, 641–53
Cumann na mBan, 398–400, 402, 404
Cumann na nGael, 195, 263, 360, 471
Cumberland, 43
Curragh Internment Camp, 513
Curtis, L. Perry (Jnr.), 104
Cusack, Michael, 350
Cyprus, 480

Dáil Eireann, 151, 193, 256, 359, 401–2,
404, 476, 484, 576–7; First Dáil's
Democratic Programme, 401
Daly, James, 256
dandy, 74, 299; as tragic figure, 373–9;
Wilde and Yeats on, 374; collapse of,
377–9.
Dante, Alighieri, 445–6, 631
Darwin, Charles, 329, 414, 497, 509;
Darwinism, 424
David, Jacques Louis (painter), 212

Davidson, Basil, 407–8
Davis, Thomas, 22, 24, 102, 134, 137,
156, 158, 160, 162
Davitt, Michael, 51, 294, 351, 490; *Fall of
Feudalism in Ireland,* 51, 490
Davitt, Michael (poet), 568
Deane, Seamus, 174–5, 186, 228, 274,
623
deanglicization, 135, 136–54, 155, 157,
186: of clothing, 10–11, 35, 38, 144,
151–2, 177, 229, 430–2, 502, 524; of
sexuality, 177–82; difficulty of, 251–2,
265; of political structures, 359–60, 476;
Behan on failure of, 513–29, 561; Pearse
on challenge, 551; Naipaul and
Lamming on, 552–3; "translating back",
625–6
Defoe, Daniel, 178, 272
Deleuze, Gilles, 117, 125, 331, 388
Dench, Judi, 434–5
Dermody, Frank, 522
Derrida, Jacques, 624
de Valera, Éamon, 4, 183, 194, 195,
208, 254–5, 257, 259, 286, 295, 296,
359–60, 362, 392, 393, 399–400,
404–6, 416–17, 471–80, 481, 519, 524,
554, 566, 571, 584, 615
Devlin, Denis, 462–6
Devlin, Paddy, 415
Dickens, Charles, 103, 282, 397
Dilke, Charles, 46–7, 139
Dillon, John, 149, 400
dinnsheanchas, 107, 592, 599
Disraeli, Benjamin, 509
divorce, 361, 413–14, 416, 572
Donoghue, Denis, 553, 594
Dostoevsky, Fyodor, 383
Double (literary device), 41–4, 184–5, 278,
317, 526
Dowden, Edward, 121, 123, 128, 159–60,
161, 269–70, 273, 277–8, 281, 386,
445–6
Dowling, P. J., 615
Doyle, Roddy, 611
Dryden, John, 619
Dublin Castle, 145, 218, 515
Dublin Daily Express, 156
Dublin Lock-Out, 152, 192, 220
Dublin Opinion, 265
Duffy, Louise Gavan, 363
duo (literary couple), 12, 38–44, 76, 220,
299, 544, 548–50
Durcan, Paul, 609

Dyer, General, 254, 256
Easter Rising 1916, 92, 99, 113–14, 152, 154, 193, 196–217; reaction to, 193, 199; alleged irrationalism of, 198, 200; radical proclamation, 400, 402; as theatre, 203–4; artistic and ethical issues raised, 204–12, 229; Yeats's 'Easter 1916', 213–17; O'Casey and, 223; looting, 227–8, 231; as social advance, 229–30, 489; Plunkett in Egypt, 252; *Irish Times* and, 268; Shakespeare and, 269–70; as poets' production, 285; as utopian moment, 293; and *Ulysses*, 330; and Shelbourne Hotel, 365, 400; leaders' ideas ignored later, 389; links to Great War, 394; women in, 399–400; Ulster unionists on, 414; and masculinism, 438; 1966 commemoration, 480; and Beckett, 530–1; use of by later politicians, 552; Lenin on, 559; Cruise O' Brien on, 560; forgetting of, 566; Kinsella and, 585; mocked by Bolger, 609; and Benjamin's idea of citation, 629–30; Roy Foster on, 642–3
Eckhardt, Meister, 435
Economic War, 360
ecumenism, 147, 153, 158
Edgeworth, Maria, 71, 342; *Castle Rackrent*, 71
Edward VII, 61
Eglinton, John, 157–65
ego, 185, 291
Egypt, 68, 84–7, 88, 159, 197, 252, 255, 256–8, 272, 276
Eliot, George, 74, 160
Eliot, T. S., 339, 464, 471–2, 522, 537, 557, 561, 585–6, 588–90, 610
Ellmann, Richard, 345
Elpis nursing home, 175
Emerson, Ralph Waldo, 4, 61, 99, 128, 138
emigration, 2, 51–2, 53, 99, 107, 164–5, 180, 264-5, 295, 328, 333, 530; missing middle generation, 394; of intellectuals, 403; of Protestant people, 416, 532; Samuel Beckett on, 532–4, 540; and West Indians, 557; returns in 1980s, 573, 578–9; Eavan Boland on, 508; Friel on, 614–15
Emmet, Robert, 20, 414
Empire Writes Back, The, 4–5
Engels, Friedrich, 99, 175, 230, 271, 320, 530

England, 2, 6, 9, 16, 23–4, 29, 32, 34–6, 44, 48, 51, 60, 62, 67, 107, 122, 124, 135, 140, 142, 160–1, 164, 194, 198, 211, 215–16, 217, 258, 275, 279, 284, 289, 307, 337, 352, 370, 402, 418, 420, 477, 586, 614, 628–9, 642
Englishness, 9–10, 11, 15, 38, 39–40, 44–7, 62, 140, 151, 160–1, 179, 251, 268, 279, 315, 322, 346, 418, 420, 464, 527, 555
epic, 342–3, 355
Erasmus, 641
Eton college, 25
Eucharistic Congress 1932, 360
Eurocentrism, 49, 160, 161, 287, 340, 343, 345–7, 553, 559–60
European Economic Community (EEC), 480, 567, 573–4, 644
European Union, 645
evictions, 88, 166
Ewart-Biggs, Ambassador Christopher, 592
expressionism, 242ff
'External Association', 194

Fabians, 145, 431
fairyland, 1–2, 112–14
famine, 21–2, 115, 133, 180, 254, 497, 530, 571, 579, 616, 650
Fanning, Ronan, 644
Fanon, Frantz, 5, 43, 55, 59, 184–6, 251, 276, 383–4, 389, 392, 531; *The Wretched of the Earth*, 55, 59, 551–2, 557–8
Farquhar, George, 16
Farr, Florence, 123
fascism, 320, 360–1, 416, 471, 550, 610, 630
fellaheen (fellahin), 84, 88, 336
feminism, 40, 79–81, 175, 177, 179, 281, 362, 395–410, 431–2, 435, 566, 579, 601–8, 642
Fenian brotherhood (IRB), 21–3, 144, 149, 212, 335, 351, 497, 509; *see also* Irish Republican Brotherhood
Ferguson, Sir Samuel, 446
Fianna Fáil, 359, 404, 583, 594
Field Day Theatre Company, 618
Fine Gael, 476, 479, 569
Fisher, H. A. L., 255
FitzGerald, Desmond, 99, 209, 210, 328
Fitzgerald, F. Scott, 246, 317, 383
FitzGerald, Garrett, 572, 576
Fitzgerald, Gerald, 85

Flaubert, Gustave, 78, 367, 377, 414
Forster, E. M., 44, 344, 350, 420
Foster, Roy, 642–3, 645, 646, 649
Foucault, Michel, 615
Franco, General, 472
Free Trade Agreement, 480
Fréine, Sean de, 151, 650
French Revolution, 206, 211–12, 273, 293, 621
Freud, Sigmund, 40, 176, 205, 231, 295, 308–9, 431, 635
Friel, Brian, 496, 567, 584, 613, 614–23, 652, 653; and Anglicization, 614; and modernization, 615, 620–1; on hedge schools, 615; and language as index of power, 615–16; on decline of Irish, 616; and northern background, 616; and intertextuality, 617–18, 622–3; translation, 619; cultural colonialism, 619–20; and French Revolution, 621; and George Steiner, 622; and eloquence, 622–3; on madness of total recall, 629; on translation of tradition, 625–33; *Translations*, 614–23, 624–6, 627, 629–31, 633, 637; *Faith Healer*, 631–3; *Making History*, 633–4; *Dancing at Lughnasa*, 611
Fromm, Erich, 392–3, 548–9; *The Fear of Freedom*, 392–3, 548–9
Froude, James Anthony, 37, 52–3; *The English in the West Indies*, 37

Gaelic American, 253
Gaelic Athletic Association (GAA), 25, 44, 99, 350, 570
Gaelic football, 151
Gaelic League, 2, 3, 7, 99, 134, 135, 141–54, 155, 158, 162, 182, 191, 193, 201, 205, 221, 228, 268, 283, 331–2, 352, 364, 396, 398, 501–2, 521, 527, 554, 568, 592, 642, 651
Gaelic tradition, 10, 11, 16–18, 31, 87, 91, 107, 118, 121, 126, 224, 275, 277, 284, 286, 300, 328, 331–2, 336–7, 364, 378–9, 394, 396, 402, 413–14, 424, 435, 464–6, 483, 500–12, 516–17, 532, 535–9, 561, 570, 587, 588, 599, 601–8, 164–23, 625–6, 629–30
Gaelic Union, 133, 141
Gaeltacht (Irish-speaking area), 142, 146, 149, 265, 286–7, 297, 336, 490, 514, 515, 517, 617; Civil Rights movement, 567–8; threat to

quality of Irish, 569; spoken English of, 626
Galileo, 225
Galsworthy, John, 285
Gandhi, Mahatma, 259, 337, 397
Garda Síochána (Guardians of the Peace – police), 415, 531
Gauguin, Paul, 264
Gay, Peter, 390
Geldof, Bob, 571, 611
generation, concept of, 205, 393–4
Genet, Jean, 513
George, David Lloyd, 195, 255
Georgian houses, 229
Georgian poetry, 245–6
Ghadar party (India), 254
Ghana, 552–3, 555
Ghosh, Aurobindo, 253
Gifford, Grace, 224
Gladstone, William E., 24, 31, 47, 86, 191
Gladstone's Land Act, 1870, 23–4
God, 1, 92, 109, 215, 306, 429, 432–5, 454–5, 460, 462–3, 635
Gogarty, Oliver St. John, 264
Gogol, Nikolai, 366
Goldsmith, Oliver, 16, 173–4, 322–3, 449, 452
Gonne, Maud, 139, 182, 214, 215, 225, 254, 363
Gosse, Edmund, 386; *Father and Son*, 386
Gramsci, Antonio, 144, 394
Grattan, Henry, 414
Great War, 1914–18, 139, 192–3, 197–9, 207, 239–47; effect on civilians, 242–4; theatricality of, 246; literature largely silent on, 246; devalues quotidian, 266; influence on Joyce, 328–30; decline of deference, 350, 394, 489; England after, 370; threat of conscription, 401; Kate O'Brien on, 408; and masculinism, 438; and MacGreevy, 461, 469; Foster on, 642
Greece, 148, 476, 645; Greeks, 202, 225, 414, 624–5; Greek language, 552, 615
Greene, Herbert, 75
Greer, Germaine, 601
Gregory, Lady Augusta, 6, 68, 70, 83, 107, 153, 172, 183, 252, 449; birth and early life, 83; adolescence, 84; marriage, 85; affair with Blunt, 84–95; cultural nationalism emerges, 86–7; poetry about Blunt, 88–9; growing self-confidence, 88–9; androgyny, 89; belief in English

good faith, 90; on colonial wound, 90–1; on her infidelity, 91–2; vow of purity with Blunt, 93; on strong women, 94–5; autobiographical element in *Grania*, 95; on theatre, 280; on republican women, 403; and religion, 425; and Yeats, 443; *Dervorgilla*, 89–93; *Grania*, 93–5; *A Woman's Sonnets*, 87–9; *Cuchulain of Muirthemne*, 183

Gregory, Robert, 84, 482
Gregory, Sir William, 84–95, 89
Griffin, Gerald, 342
Griffith, Arthur, 191, 193, 194–5, 259, 479
Guattari, Felix, 117, 125, 331, 388
Guildford Four, 578
Gwynn, Stephen, 148

Hannay, Canon James ('George Birmingham'), 149, 153
Harrison, Paul, 553
Hartnett, Michael, 588; *Farewell to English*, 588
Hastings, Warren, 17–18
Haughey, Charles, 576, 584, 610
Hawes, Joe, 256
Hawthorne, Nathaniel, 127, 272
Hayden, Mary, 396
Heaney, Seamus, 279, 584, 587, 614, 616–17: as translator, 587; on Kinsella, 591; on northern crisis, 591–2; and pastoral, 591–2; and Derry, 592; on IRA, 593; on bog and consciousness, 593–4; and violence, 594; Donoghue on, 594; as political seer, 594; as self-critic, 595; compared to Synge, 596–7; and postcolonial stress, 597; visionary turn, 597; bardic aura, 599; and translation, 604; and intertextuality, 618; and Friel, 623; 'Death of a Naturalist', 591–2; 'Betrothal of Cavehill', 592; 'Punishment', 593–4; 'Exposure', 595; *Station Island*, 595–7, 618; 'The First Flight', 596–17; *Sweeney Astray*, 587, 597, 616–17; *Seeing Things*, 597–9
hedge schools, 19, 615–23
Hegel, G. W. F., 43–4, 320, 540, 547
Heliopolis, 85
Hemingway, Ernest, 169
Henn, T. R., 175
Hercules, 375
Herder, 300

Hewitt, John, 451–2
Hiberno-English, 120–1, 122, 126, 153, 155, 162–3, 173–5, 187–8, 303, 331, 333, 450, 529, 622–3, 625, 626
Hindu, 259
Hitler, Adolf, 472, 513
Holloway, Joseph, 218, 271
Holloway prison, 400
Hollywood, 612
Home Rule, 24, 31, 56, 62, 71, 72, 86–9, 153, 166, 191, 192, 239, 334–5, 419, 479, 492, 645; for England, 62
Homer, 129, 207, 306, 338, 343, 353–4, 355, 441, 632
homophobia, 270
homosexuality, 39, 47
Hopkins, Gerard Manley, 588–90, 627
Horgan, J. J., 211
Howe, Irving, 583
Hughes, Langston, 221
Hugo, Victor, 203
Hume, David, 322
Hume, John, 577, 597
hunger-striking, 222, 397, 402, 576, 584
hurling, 25, 151, 296, 472
Huxley, Aldous, 264
Huxley, T., 424
hybridity, 10–11, 48–50, 142, 162–5, 173–5, 187–8, 253, 337, 408, 529, 555–8, 588–92 625–37, 651–2
Hyde, Douglas, 3, 7, 21, 22, 122, 138–54, 155, 182, 183; 'The Necessity for deanglicizing Ireland', 140; Gaelic League, 140–52; on English culture, 141–3; on colonial education, 144, 148; on mass culture, 144–5; on national education, 145–6; on religious songs, 147; battle with Trinity College, 148; contradictions in philosophy, 149; revivalism of, 150; on clothes, 151–2; disillusion with League, 153; chair at NUI, 153; *Love Songs of Connacht*, 155, 180, 182–3; Eglinton on, 158; difficulty of deanglicization, 251–2; President of Ireland, 361; as Protestant, 416–17; and religion, 425; mocked by Flann O'Brien, 501–2; *Casadh an tSúgáin*, 529; and later movements, 568–70; funeral, 580; on colonial misrule, 641; and unionism, 648; and national revival, 649

Ibsen, Henrik, 169
Igpo people, 120
imperialism, 5, 19, 25, 30, 38–40, 45, 52, 56, 84–7, 92, 114, 134–5, 140–1, 157, 159, 160, 194, 197, 198–9, 222–3, 230, 237, 251–9, 270, 275–6, 330–7, 340–4, 348, 350, 351, 353, 395, 397–8, 418–27, 435–7, 442, 464, 516, 530, 555, 619–23, 651–2, 625, 628–9
interior monologue, 345, 347, 348, 350
Ionesco, Eugène, 513
Irish Christianity, 60, 159, 360
Irish Citizen Army, 193, 218–19, 221–4, 229–30; women in, 400; *History of the Citizen Army,* 221
Irish Citizen, 231, 398–9
Irish Constitution (1922), 361, 403–4; (1937), 361–2, 404–5, 477, 576, 624
Irish Free State, 7, 154, 207, 244, 257, 263, 296, 402, 413–17, 450–1, 484, 515, 525, 531, 532, 551; securing boundaries of, 405–7; and Protestants, 413, 419
Irish Homestead, The 494
Irish Ireland movement, 69, 134, 138, 156, 162
Irish joke, 36
Irish Labour Party, 194, 221
Irish language, 1, 2, 10, 13–15, 31, 115, 133, 138–52, 157–8, 162, 183, 221, 253; books in, 145; grammar, 146, 265, 296; in education, 265; and Victorianism, 275, 286; Joyce on, 331–3, 354; lip-service to, 476, 484, 568; and Flann O'Brien, 497, 502, 508; and Behan, 520–1, 524, 529; and television, 566–7, 570; current revival of, 568–9; *see also* 515, 520, 535, 552, 561
Irish Literary Society, 99, 146
Irish Literary Theatre, 146
Irish Medical Organization, 476
Irish Party (at Westminster), 140, 149, 191, 253, 334, 335, 400
The Irish Press, 575
Irish Red Cross, 550
Irish Republic, 200, 203, 296, 476, 574; Proclamation of, 206–7, 224; economic development of, 574–7; cultural policy, 648
Irish Republican Army, 236, 360, 368ff, 438, 449, 471, 476, 513, 520, 522, 524–5, 526–8, 574; Provisional

IRA, 575, 576–8, 593, 594, 607, 610, 644
Irish Republican Brotherhood (IRB), 191, 225, 400; *see also* Fenians
Irish Review, The 200
Irish Studies, 30, 641–53
Irish Transport and General Workers' Union, 192
Irish Volunteers, 192–3, 218, 398–9
irony as narrative technique, 77–9
Islam, 556

James, C. L. R., 5–6, 276, 282
James, Henry, 246, 635
Jameson, Fredric, 301, 342–3
Jefferson, Thomas, 100, 259, 295
Jesus Christ, 109, 140, 180, 211, 212, 230, 290, 311, 351, 361, 362, 429, 430, 463, 518, 630
John XXIII, Pope, 566
John Paul II, Pope, 572
Johnson, Samuel, 239
Jordan, Neil, 613
Joyce, James, 3, 35, 52, 71, 122, 126, 128, 140, 147, 152, 160, 161, 186, 222, 264, 265, 270–1, 276, 277; on language, 276, 279; journalism, 334–8; and Great War, 328–30; and Irish modernism, 329–30; and short story form, 330–1; and Irish, 331–2; as postcolonial, 33–4; on misrule in Ireland, 335; on revivalism, 335–6; as postcolonial artist, 333–4; and *bildungsroman,* 336; and Gaelic tradition, 336–7; and magic realism, 338–44; and Europe, 340; and epic, 342–3; and parody, 343–4; and modernism, 344–5; provincialism and style, 345–6; interior monologue, 345, 347; on Jewishness, 347–8; and orality, 348, 355; on style, 348–9; on Shakespeare, 349; anti-colonial *Ulysses,* 350–4; on de Valera, 359; and Bowen, 378; on Irish male, 381; on fatherhood, 382, 385; on language of father, 387; and anti-Oedipus, 388–9; Woolf on, 392; and religion, 421–3, 425, 459; influence on MacGreevy, 462; on new élites, 484–5; and rural stereotypes, 494; as antipastoralist, 503; and Behan, 523–4; and early Beckett, 534–5; influence on Ó Ríordáin, 588–9; Kinsella on, 591; and Heaney, 597; and successors, 612; and

intertextuality, 618; art as perpetual translation, 636; *Dubliners*, 140, 152, 161, 292, 331–3, 334, 383, 390–1, 476, 495; *Stephen Hero*, 141, 503; *A Portrait of the Artist as a Young Man*, 119, 272–3, 299, 331–4, 335–6, 380, 381–2, 387–8, 421; *Ulysses*, 52, 118, 126–7, 135, 207, 270–1, 273, 280, 293, 327–55, 382–5, 392, 484–5, 490, 494, 523, 557, 632; *Finnegans Wake*, 332, 636

Kafka, Franz, 331
Kant, Immanuel, 320
Karnak, 85
Katanga, 558
Kavanagh, Patrick, 381, 472, 476–8, 481, 492, 498, 503, 512, 524, 581, 582, 584, 586, 597, 613
Keane, John B., 476
Keats, John, 20, 29, 34, 121, 122
Kemmy, Jim, 594
Kennedy, John F., 565, 569–70, 571
Kennelly, Brendan, 503
Kenner, Hugh, 459
Kenya, 554–6
Kettle, Thomas, 240, 397
Kickham, Charles, 174, 481
Kilmainham jail, 400
Kilroy, Thomas, 584
kilt, 15, 502, 524, 526
King, Martin Luther, 574
Kinsale, battle of, 13, 633
Kinsella, Thomas, 584–8, 590–1, 604
Kipling, Rudyard, 253
Knight, G. Wilson, 277–8
Koran, The, 49

Labour Party (Britain), 47, 197, 275
Ladies' Land League, 395–6
Laforgue, Jules, 464
Lamming, George, 279, 282–3, 553, 555, 557; *The Pleasures of Exile*, 279, 282–3, 553, 555
Land League, 23, 24, 51, 85, 87–8, 166, 234, 273, 355; Land Acts, 55, 67, 74, 192, 490–1
Larkin, James, 152, 192, 220
Larkin, Philip, 581, 586
Larminie, William, 156
Latin, 265, 296, 552, 621
Latin America, 129, 272, 297, 340, 449, 572, 589
Lavin, Mary, 363, 409–10

Lawrence, D. H., 160–1, 244, 383; *Lady Chatterley's Lover*, 156; *Women in Love*, 160–1, 266; *Kangaroo*, 244
Leader, The, 398
League of Nations, 359, 471
Leavis, F. R., 144, 554
Ledwidge, Francis, 239–40
Lee, Joseph J., 396, 570, 644–5, 646
Lee, Sir Thomas, 10
Lee, Vandaleur, 385
Lenin, V. I, 197, 559
Leonard, Father, 438
Lever, Charles, 33, 73
Lewis, C. S., 78
Liberal Home Rule Association, 398
Liberal Party (Britain), 191–2, 335, 528–9, 569, 575, 648
'liberation theology', 572
liberationism, 44, 59, 181–6, 289, 291–300, 301, 351, 393, 405, 559, 579
Lienhardt, Geoffrey, 628
Littlewood, Joan, 520, 522, 523–4
Locke, John, 322–3
Lombard, Peter (Bishop), 633
Longley, Edna, 607
Longley, Michael, 586
Lover, Samuel, 49
Loyola, Ignatius, 635
Luce, A. A., 452–3
Luther, Martin, 434, 454, 460; Lutheranism, 450
Lynch, Jack, 574–5
Lynn, Kathleen, 400
Lyons, F.S.L, 643

Macardle, Dorothy, 404–5
Macaulay, Thomas Babington, 148, 625
MacBride, John, 214, 225
MacCraith, Aindrias, 590
MacCumhaigh, Art, 177–8: 'Bodaigh na hEorna', 177–8
MacDiarmada, Seán, 212
MacDomhnaill, Seán Clárach, 590
MacDonagh, Thomas, 114, 198, 199, 200–1, 214, 224, 226, 231, 240, 247, 328, 363, 399
MacDonald, Ramsay, 275
McDonald, Walter, 147
McGahern, John, 485, 496, 581
McGimpsey, Christopher, 647, 649
MacGreevy, Thomas, 265, 460–4, 466
McGuinness, Frank, 653
Macken, Mary, 404

MacKenna, Stephen, 264
Macmillan, Harold, 520, 558
McMurrough, Dermot, 89, 91, 206, 345
MacNeice, Louis, 449, 473–4
MacNeill, Eoin, 554
McQuaid, John Charles (Archbishop), 405–6
MacSwiney, Mary, 402
MacSwiney, Terence, 222, 258, 402
magic realism (mythic realism), 60, 242, 281, 338–9, 440
Mahaffy, John Pentland, 145, 327
Mahon, Derek, 584, 586, 599–600
'Máire' (Séamas Ó Grianna), 498, 503
Manet, 472
Mann, Thomas, 266, 339, 383; *The Magic Mountain*, 266
Mansfield, Jayne, 520
Marcuse, Herbert, 520
Maritain, Jacques, 462
Markievicz, Constance, 182, 200, 214, 215, 363, 397–8, 399, 400, 401–2
Márquez, Gabriel García, 342, 503
Marryat, Captain, 104
martial law, 193
Martin, Robert, 71
Martin, Violet ('Martin Ross'), 68, 69–82, 363; with Edith Somerville writes *The Real Charlotte*, 65–82; compared with Bowen, 369; on Dublin life, 71; landlord background, 71; family decline, 71; relations with wider community, 72; on flawed heroine, 76; as ironist, 77; novelistic technique, 75–8; destiny of Ireland, 78–80; on women, 80–1
Martinique, 186
Marx, Karl, 38, 40, 59, 62, 99, 175, 202, 206, 229, 230, 275, 320, 414, 489, 635, 645; *Kapital*, 175, 414, 489; *Communist Manifesto*, 175; *Eighteenth Brumaire of Louis Bonaparte*, 229
Marxism, 206, 211, 235, 281, 319–20, 321, 435, 547
mask, 36, 121, 128–9, 203, 299, 308–10, 321, 324, 329
maternity, 380–4, 395–400
matriarchy, 401
Matura, Mustafa, 188; *Playboy of the West Indies*, 188
Maynooth College, 147, 422, 582, 650
Mazzini, Giuseppe, 116–17, 158, 336
meitheal oibre (work party), 288
Mellows, Liam, 255, 286

melodrama, 219–20
Melville, Herman, 127; *Moby-Dick*, 127
Memmi, Albert, 5, 380–1, 389
Mencken, H. L., 433–4
Mercier, Vivian, 423, 544–5
Merriman, Brian, 177–9: *Cúirt an Mheáin Oíche*, 177–9
Mhac an tSaoi, Máire, 568, 601–2
middle class, 51, 81, 175, 334, 392, 403; Protestants, 449, 545; rural, 51, 55, 491; urban, 233–4; Catholic women, 363
Middleton, William, 106
Millett, Kate, 601
Milton, John, 272, 426, 434, 456. 561: *Paradise Lost*, 456
mirror, 160, 176–86, 280, 290, 306, 324, 333, 389
missionaries, 465, 471–2, 571–2
Mitchel, John, 99, 259, 519; *Jail Journal*, 519
modernist literature, 23–4, 134, 266–7, 295, 330–55, 374–9, 383, 515–16, 580, 583, 645–6
modernization, 59, 140, 197, 566, 568–78, 580–613, 615–23, 636–7, 645
Mohammed, 49; Mohammedans, 259
Molony, Helena, 400, 405
monster meetings, 136–7
Montague, John, 581, 584, 585–7, 599, 617–18, 623
Montessori, Maria, 134, 283–4, 293
Moore, Brian, 583–4
Moore, George, 84, 99, 119, 138, 151, 153, 156, 161, 162, 279, 342, 422, 627
Moore, Col. M., 413–14
Moore, Sturge, 442
Moran, D. P., 142, 156, 162, 174, 398
Morris, William, 141, 172, 175, 284
Muldoon, Paul, 603–4, 611–12
multiculturalism, 145, 339
multinationals, 566, 615
Munster Women's Franchise League, 81
Murphy, Richard, 584, 587, 599
Murphy, Tom, 496, 584, 612, 653
Murphy, William Martin, 192
Musil, Robert, 266
mysticism, 433–4: mystical poetry, 200, 207

na gCopaleen, Myles, 497–500
Naipaul, V.S., 282, 327, 329, 552, 553–4, 559
Nandy, Ashis, 5, 44–5, 251

Nasser, Gamal Abdul, 558
Napoleon, 272
Nation, The, 22
National Council, 191
National Gallery of Ireland, 462
National Schools, 133, 614, 616
National University, 147, 273, 326, 396–7
nationalism, 49, 53, 55, 63, 81, 86, 116,
    123–4, 128–9, 137, 141, 142, 147–8,
    153, 158, 168, 175, 183, 185, 192, 196,
    213, 217, 222, 223, 230, 233–4, 237,
    259, 270, 281, 288–9, 290–300, 301–3,
    321–2, 330–40, 344–5, 350, 351–2,
    389–90, 399, 406, 418, 420–7, 522,
    531, 576–7, 578; *see also* 434, 438–9,
    448, 606–8, 610, 635, 642–4
Nationalisms and Sexualities, 407
négritude, 186
Nehru, President of India, 395, 558
Nelson, Admiral, 362
Neruda, Pablo, 129
neutrality, 472–3, 479–83, 542
New Ireland Forum, 576
New Testament, 211
New Yorker, The, 494
Newman, Jeremiah (Bishop), 571
News of the World, The, 521
Newton, Sir Isaac, 322, 326
Ní Chuilleanáin, Eiléan, 604
Ní Dhomhnaill, Nuala, 568, 584, 601,
    603–5, 625
Nicaragua, 611
Nietzsche, Friedrich, 7, 46, 230, 293, 294,
    388, 626, 635
Nkrumah, of Ghana, 555
Noble, Margaret, 252
Norfolk, 619
Normans, 9, 10, 143, 159, 206, 615, 651
Norwegian, 649
Northern Ireland, 192, 194, 195, 414–16,
    473, 476, 480, 573–8, 559, 560, 567,
    591, 616–17, 643–4, 647–8; poets of,
    454, 473–4, 527
Northern Ireland Civil Rights Association
    (NICRA), 574
Ngugi wa Thiong'o, 552, 555–7

oaths of allegiance, 257, 359
O'Brien, Conor Cruise, 19, 197, 393, 558–
    60, 597
O'Brien, Edna, 566; *The Country Girls*, 566
O'Brien, Flann (aka Brian O'Nolan, Myles
    na gCopaleen), 497–512; and

Boucicault, 497; and stage Irishry, 498;
    antipastoral, 498; and pseudonym,
    498–500; and *Irish Times*, 499,
    511–12; Anne Clissmann on, 500; on
    erosion of Gaelic identity, 500–1;
    mocks revivalists, 501–2; on kilt, 502;
    and poor mouth, 503; and stage Gaels,
    503–4; and 'porcine' Irish, 505; and
    stage Irish tradition, 505–6; and
    Victorian racism, 507–8; and Adam
    Smith, 508; and animality, 509; and
    Victorianism, 510; and Celtic
    helplessness, 511; artistic frustration
    of, 511–12; and Behan, 523; both
    artists mock revival, 524; and Friel,
    622; and translation, 636; *An Béal Bocht*,
    497–512, 622; *At Swim-Two-Birds*, 266,
    494; *The Third Policeman*, 512
O'Brien, Kate, 363, 408–9, 472, 582
Ó Cadhain, Máirtín, 482, 487, 498, 568,
    584; *Cré na Cille*, 482, 487–8, 498, 513,
    516, 519
O'Casey, Seán, 12, 71, 149, 150, 152, 153,
    212, 218–47, 421–2, 442; background,
    218–20; combines farce and tragedy,
    220; influence on Beckett, 220; Shavian
    method, 221; rhetorical style, 221; ex-
    republican, 222; on Trade Unionism,
    223; sentimentalises victims, 223; on
    communal failure, 223; against
    theatricality, 224; nurses mother in 1916,
    225; drama as self-justification, 226,
    228–9; technical challenge of 1916, 227;
    critique by Deane, 228; on clothing and
    revolution, 229; formal problems, 230;
    on Francis Sheehy-Skeffington, 231–2;
    flaws in *Plough*, 232–3; language of, 232;
    urban pastoralist, 232–3; strong women,
    233; critique of heroism, 234; as satirist,
    235; inauthentic form, 236; on sexual
    relations in Ireland, 236; theatre riots
    contrasted, 236–7; end of *Plough*, 237;
    sentimentality of, 237–8; on survival
    skills, 237–8; and Great War, 240; Yeats
    rejects *Silver Tassie*, 240–1; solves formal
    questions, 242; religious symbolism,
    243–4; *Tassie* a Yeatsian play, 245; on
    Irish male, 381; on Protestant ethos, 439;
    confined by ruralist forms, 493;
    compared to Behan, 513, 518–19, 522;
    Plough updated by *Hostage*, 526; and
    hunger strikes, 584; *The Plough and the
    Stars*, 212, 222, 225, 226, 228, 231,

O'Casey, Séan (*contd*)
232–3, 234–5, 237, 243–4, 422, 519,
526; protests against, 234; and
Protestantism, 439; *The Shadow of a
Gunman*, 218, 220, 221–2; *Juno and the
Paycock*, 219, 222–3, 226, 237, 244,
380–1, 422; *The Silver Tassie*, 240–7,
557; *Red Roses for Me*, 245, 422; *Purple
Dust*, 245
Ó Colmáin, Dónal, 178
Ó Conaire, Pádraic, 100
O'Connell, Daniel, 20–3, 133, 136, 142,
180, 203, 291, 362, 616
O'Connor, Frank, 107, 119, 382, 472,
523–4, 581
O'Connor, Joseph, 611
Ó Criomhthainn, Tomás, 286–7, 487, 490,
498; *An tOileánach*, 286–7, 487, 490
Ó Direáin, Máirtin, 568
Ó Donnchadha, Tadhg, 627
O'Donnell, Peadar, 519
Odyssey, 207, 266, 293, 338, 343, 353, 632
Ó Faoláin, Seán, 365, 372, 472, 560, 581
O'Farrell, Patrick, 116
O'Farrelly, Agnes, 360, 404
O'Flaherty, Liam, 234, 476, 490, 636
O'Grady, Standish J., 24–5, 122, 196–7,
424, 624, 625
O'Hegarty, P. S., 200, 403
O'Hickey, Dr, 147
O'Higgins, Kevin, 263, 403
O'Kelly, Sean T., 255, 257, 258–9
Old Testament, 211
O'Leary, John, 21
O'Leary, Father Peter, 146
Ó Neachtain, Seán, 341–2
O'Neill, Hugh, Earl of Tyrone, 12, 633–4
O'Neill, Terence, 480, 574, 592
Orangeism, 22
Ó Rathaille, Aogán, 91, 317, 378, 538,
588, 590
Ordnance Survey, 614, 619
Orientalism, 287, 620–1
Ó Ríordáin, Seán, 516, 548, 588–91, 627
O'Rourke, King of Breffny, 89–90, 91
Ortega Y Gasset, 205
Osborne, John, 529
O'Shea, Kitty, 24, 345, 413
O'Sheel, Shaemas, 31
Ó Súilleabháin, Muiris, 287, 487
O'Sullivan, Derry, 568
O'Sullivan, Owen Roe (Eoghan Rua Ó
Súilleabháin), 170

O'Toole, Fintan, 493
Owen, Wilfred, 245–6
Oxford University, 30, 33, 35–7, 48, 51,
56, 271, 351, 646
Oxford Union, 401
Oxford Book of Modern Verse, 246

Pairlement Chloinne Tomáis, 150, 277,
483–4
Paisley, Revd. Ian, 648
Parnell, Anna, 395–6
Parnell, Charles Stewart, 23–5, 37, 87, 136,
137, 140, 180, 191, 205, 291
Parnellism, 43, 87
parody, 341–3, 350, 498–512, 581, 585,
587
Parsons, Sir William, 10
partition, 230, 335, 404–8
Partridge, Bernard, 505
pastoralism, 51, 59, 233, 234, 287–8, 303,
481–96; antipastoral, 477–8, 498–512,
591–2; unintentionally ratified, 609;
Friel on, 615
Pater, Walter, 164
paternity, 380–94, 395, 426
patriarchy, 182–3, 389–91, 426
Patrick, Saint, 60, 134
Paul, Saint, 431
Paul VI, Pope, 570
Payne, Ben Iden, 89
Pearse, Patrick, 4, 103, 114, 134, 141,
152, 158, 162, 167–8, 191, 193, 196,
198, 200, 205, 208–9, 214, 224,
225–8, 293: proclamation of republic,
206–7; 'The Singer', 201; on cyclical
history, 207; on Ireland, 208; 'Mise Éire',
208; 'Fornocht' (Naked I Saw Thee),
209–10; revolutionary asceticism, 210;
on revolution, 211; use of Christian
language, 211; accused of heresy, 211;
as Jacobin, 211–12; speechmaker,
212–13; Yeats recycles his words, 217; as
poseur, 224; treatment by O'Casey,
226–7; radical, 228; St. Enda's College,
252; collaborates with Yeats, 272,
275; anti-imperialist, 276; on
education, 281–5; and future, 293;
on mother-son relation, 381;
supports Hanna Skeffington's hunger-
strike, 397; betrayal of his vision, 476;
duo as basis of a society, 550; on
postcolonial pitfalls, 551; *The Murder
Machine*, 551–2; on educational reform,

554; Eavan Boland revises 'Mise Éire', 607–8; and Benjamin, 629–30; as utopian, 631; devalued by some historians, 644

peasantry, 137, 139–40, 142, 147–8, 167–88, 192, 219, 220, 234, 235–6; *see also* 43, 54–5, 67, 70, 72–3, 77–9, 90–1, 104–5

Pegasus, 215

Péguy, Charles, 230–1

Penal Laws, 16–17, 20, 650

Peter Pan, 103, 113

Petrarch, 626

Petrie, George, 326

Phoenix Park, 572

phrenology, 129

Pigot, E. F. Smyth, 161

Pike theatre, 513

Pius XI, Pope, 428

plantation of Munster, 9

Plato, 361

Poe, Edgar Allan, 164, 252

Poggioli, Renato, 626

Police Intelligence, 144

Poole, Hewitt, 80

'poor mouth', 376–7, 503–12

Pope, Alexander, 235

postcoloniality, 5, 6, 19, 55–6, 59–60, 99, 117–18, 135, 164, 186, 197–8, 212, 240, 251–9, 289–97, 315, 319, 322–3, 326, 333–4, 343, 359, 391–3; and women, 395–410; and emigration, 474–6; and commemoration, 480, 491; and capital, 492–6; in Ireland, 515–29; and amnesia, 539–40; and minority languages, 624–5; and failure, 645; pitfalls of, 551–61; and Irish poetry, 588–91; and Heaney, 597

post-nationalism, 636

Pound, Ezra, 446, 464

Powell, York, 145

Power, Arthur, 265

Prescott, Marie, 41

Principes du Socialisme, 175

prison system, 436, 493, 513–14, 584

Protestantism, 7, 17, 21, 40, 67, 81–3, 107, 122, 126, 147–8, 153, 159, 207–8, 211, 338, 352; idea of election, 83; and Northern Ireland, 195, 360, 404; dissenting tradition, 272, 334; and imperialism, 352; and Roman Catholic majority, 365; civil rights of, 404; and sexual desire, 406; and autobiography,

428; Irish Protestantism, 429, 446, 449, 451, 452, 530–1, 537–8, 642–3, 647; and Beckett, 454–61; and Eastern religion, 457; Beckett and O'Casey on, 546; in Northern Ireland, 573–8, 592; and monarchy, 648; *see also* 413–17, 418–27

Proust, Marcel, 339, 414, 463, 629

provincialism, 22, 78, 121, 125, 135, 138, 157, 160–1, 289, 334, 346–7, 362, 386, 392, 395–6, 413–14, 445–6, 486, 491, 560, 586–7

Ptolemy, 634

Punch magazine, 45, 505, 545

Pythagoras, 313

Quadragesimo Anno, 405

Quakers, 460

Queen's Theatre, 220

Quiller-Couch, Sir Arthur, 554

Quinn, John, 425

Rabelais, François, 343

Radio Éireann, 472, 550; Radio Telefís Éireann, 566–7, 578–9, 582, 653

Raftery, Anthony (Antoine Ó Reachtabhra), 313

Ralegh, Sir Walter, 11

Rank, Otto, 41–3, 389

Raphael (painter), 361

Reagan, Ronald, 571

Redfield, James W., 507–8: *Comparative Physiognomies*, 507–8

Redmond, John, 141, 191–3, 339

Renan, Ernest, 31, 280, 349

republicanism, 46–7, 63, 119–20, 139, 142, 147, 194–5, 200, 202, 211, 219, 222, 234, 244, 263, 272, 286–7, 296, 360, 361–3, 414, 419–27, 438–9, 476, 514–29, 551, 574, 621, 628

Retamar, Roberto, 340

revivalism, 21, 32, 47, 49, 51, 55–6, 101, 105, 107, 142–3, 144, 150, 152, 156, 162, 172, 180–1, 187, 251–2, 255, 275; Eglinton on flaws of, 159; lack of comparative method, 255; as oedipal drama, 388; as an end in itself, 389; revivalist psychology, 391–3; pastoral element, 491ff; mocked by Flann O'Brien, 498; mocked by Behan and Kavanagh, 524; after independence, 532; mocked by Beckett, 534; loses critical edge, 561; *see also* 288–9, 335–7, 351

Richards, I. A., 466
Robinson, Lennox, 280
Robinson, Mary, 404, 579, 607, 611
Rodgers, W. R., 451–2
Roman Catholicism, 16, 17, 20, 23–4, 36–
    7, 90, 107, 153, 159, 168, 207, 209–12,
    227, 256, 350, 352, 354, 360–1, 365,
    396, 404, 406, 408, 409–10: effect of *Ne
    Temere* decree, 421, 429–30, 432, 435;
    and bishops, 436–8; Yeats on folk
    spirituality, 449–51; and Protestantism,
    452–3; 456–60; in art, 461–6; Synge on
    clergy, 466; Mother and Child crisis,
    479; and Pope John XXIII, 566; Pope
    Paul VI and contraception, 570; radical
    elements in, 571–3; and Ó Ríordáin,
    588–9; and Kinsella, 591; and Heaney,
    597; and Bolger, 609; and revisionism,
    643; and national identity, 650–1
Romans, 202, 316, 414, 624–5
romantic lyric, 117, 201–2, 280
Roosevelt, Franklin Delano, 472
Rose, Richard, 575
Rose of Lima, Saint, 361
'Ross, Martin', *see* Martin, Violet
Rossa, Jeremiah O'Donovan, 228
Rossetti, Dante Gabriel, 81, 169
Rothenstein, William, 272
Rouault (painter), 472; 'Christ Crowned
    with Thorns', 472
Round Table, 255
Rousseau, Jean-Jacques, 211, 339
Roxborough House, 95
Royal Ulster Constabulary (RUC), 415;
    'B-Specials', 415
Rugby school, 25, 31
Rushdie, Salman, 163–5, 329, 333, 343,
    385, 515, 528; *Imaginary Homelands*,
    164–5, 333, 339; on hybridity, 163–5;
    Midnight's Children, 385
Ruskin, John, 45, 59, 61, 141, 284
Russell, Bertrand, 241
Russell, George ('AE'), 49, 153, 156, 196;
    on nationality versus cosmopolitanism,
    156–65; on imperialism, 198; advised by
    Yeats, 200; compares 1916 Rising and
    Great War, 240; and American writers,
    252; eastern mysticism, 253; emigrates,
    264; on dangers of revolutionary spirit,
    296; questions visions, 316; and East,
    457; and pastoralism, 481; mocked by
    Beckett, 534
Russian Revolution, 315

Ryan, W. P., 100

Said, Edward W., 5, 14, 46, 420, 620
Saint Enda's College, 252, 484
Samhain (theatrical magazine), 128, 164
Sanger, Margaret, 264
Sartre, Jean-Paul, 43, 203, 288, 299,
    558–9; *Words*, 299; *Anti-Semite and Jew*,
    288–9
Sassoon, Siegfried, 245
satire, 234–5
Schopenhauer, Arthur, 460, 543
Scott, Walter, 397
secularization, 571–4
self-invention, 7, 46, 84, 121, 205–6, 212,
    291, 293, 384–6, 426
Senghor, Leopold, 252
Sennett, Richard, 203
separatism, 19, 22, 81, 116, 145, 191,
    252–4, 274
Shakespeare, William, 13, 35, 80, 121,
    129, 181, 213, 268–82, 284, 285, 300,
    317, 349, 426, 430–1, 445, 561; *Henry
    the Fifth*, 12–13, 213, 271; *Two
    Gentlemen of Verona*, 270; *Richard the
    Second*, 268–9; *Merchant of Venice*, 276;
    Hamlet, 122, 162, 280, 349, 386, 596;
    Othello, 276; *King Lear*, 270; *The
    Winter's Tale*, 281; *The Tempest*, 270–82,
    300, 561
Shaw, Father Francis, 211
Shaw, George Bernard, 3, 6, 24, 47–8, 51–
    63, 67, 107, 161, 200, 221, 233, 240; on
    agrarian reforms, 51; on Anglo-Irish
    images, 52; and socialism, 54; on Land
    Acts, 55; predicts neocolonial future, 56;
    on 'liberal' imperialism, 56–7; a Celticist
    critique of Celticism, 58–9; on imperial
    mindset, 60; magic realism as alternative,
    60; as social visionary, 61; self-cancelling
    prescriptions, 62; on Wilde, 61–2; on
    Yeatsian revivalism, 62; on British, 61–3;
    on English censorship of Wilde, 161; on
    Easter Rising, 199; on Yeats's rejection of
    Silver Tassie, 241; criticism of English,
    252; criticised by de Valera, 254–5; on
    Ireland and India, 274; on Trinity
    College Dublin, 281; as jester, 321; and
    fatherhood, 382–4; 'GBS', 384–5; on
    education, 385; on Protestantism, 418–
    27; on northern Protestants, 419; and
    Burke, 420; and religion, 422–5; art as
    biography, 428; childhood and religion,

432–3; Joan of Arc, 430; androgyny, 431–3; against specialist priesthood, 432–3; and saintliness, 433; on republicanism, 438–9; on disobedience as progress, 436; on prisons, 436; on heretics, 436–7; Protestant-nationalist connection, 446, 450; on peasant proprietors, 482, 484–5; Synge confirms Shaw's diagnosis of rural Ireland, 485; effects of Land Acts, 490; on Irish Question, 451–2; and Friel's *Translations*, 623; on Home Rule for England, 645; *Arms and the Man*, 433; *Mrs Warren's Profession*, 59, 433; *John Bull's Other Island*, 51–63, 347, 418, 482, 528, 567, 619–44; *Saint Joan*, 418–27, 420, 426–7, 428–37, 438–9, 635

Shaw, George Carr, 384–5
Sheehy, Father, 438
Sheehy-Skeffington, Francis, 193, 231, 362–3
Sheehy-Skeffington, Hanna, 3, 234, 255, 286, 363, 397–9, 400–5
Shelley, Percy Bysshe, 38, 123, 272, 317, 445, 561, 635; *The Cenci*, 38
Sheridan, Jim, 613; *My Left Foot* (film), 613
Sheridan, Richard Brinsley, 16, 449
shoneens (seoinini), 69–70, 151
Shyamaji, 253
Sidney, Sir Philip, 270
Silone, Ignazio, 463
Sinn Féin, 1, 62, 149, 154, 191, 193–5, 254, 350, 352, 359, 398, 401, 472, 473, 643; Sinn Féin courts, 193–4, 263, 401; Provisional Sinn Féin, 576, 577–8; *see also* 419
Simpson, Alan, 513
Skinnider, Margaret, 400
slang, 126
slavery, 343
Smith, Adam, 508
Smyllie, R. M., 499–500, 512
Smyth, Revd Martin, 647
Social Democratic and Labour Party (SDLP), 575–7, 597
'Soldier's Song', 222
Somalia, 579
Somerville, Edith, 68, 69–82, 363–4; compared with Elizabeth Bowen, 369; on her suitor Hubert Greene, 75; her mother's verdict on *Real Charlotte*, 76; on marginalization of women, 75; as ironist, 77; novelistic technique, 75–8; on

destiny of Ireland, 78–80; on role of women, 80–1; ill-fated love affair, 80; on female friendship, 80; President of Munster Women's Franchise League, 81; on contemporary writers, 81; *The Real Charlotte*, 69–82; *see also* Martin, Violet
Sophocles, 181
Southey, Robert, 20
spalpeen (spailpín), 378, 538
Special Powers Act (Northern Ireland), 415
Spender, Stephen, 477
Spenser, Edmund, 9, 10, 13–14, 30, 625, 628; *View of the Present State of Ireland*, 10–11, 30
stage Englishman, 53, 57, 59
stage Irishman, 12–13, 29, 52, 69, 136, 163, 186–7, 220, 271, 288, 456, 483, 497, 500, 503, 582, 625; stage Gael, 498, 503–4
stage writer, 582–3
Stalker, John, 577
Stanley, explorer, 268
Stanyhurst, Richard, 13, 148, 625, 628
Steiner, George, 622–3, 626, 631; *After Babel*, 622, 626
Stephens, James, 144
stereotype, 12–20, 29–30, 32, 52, 54–61, 104, 136, 163, 186–7, 220, 233, 288–90, 483, 504–12, 532–5
Stern, Erich, 42
Stevens, Wallace, 635
Stoker, Bram, 34
Stormont, parliamentary house of Northern Ireland, 415, 575
Stratford Theatre, London, 520
Stuart, Francis, 584, 610; *Black List Section H*, 610
style, 117–26
suffragism, 81, 175, 397–8, 399–403, 408, 432
Sunday People, newspaper, 521
Supreme Court (Irish Republic), 572
surrealism, 274–5, 347
Swedish language, 649
Sweeney, king, 587, 595, 597
Swift, Jonathan, 16, 67, 291, 322–3, 449, 452; *Drapier's Letters*, 16; *A Modest Proposal*, 16
Swinburne, Algernon Charles, 169, 349
Synge, John Millington, 6, 62, 70, 102, 107, 110, 120–1, 122, 126, 134, 138, 153, 162, 166–88, 200, 219, 232–3, 301, 311, 421, 515, 532, 646; and

Synge, John Millington (*contd*)
dialect, 120–1; Aran, 121; on
educational reforms, 147; on colonial
culture, 166–7; on violence, 166–73;
on scapegoating, 167; Pearse on, 167–8;
and religion, 168; influence on Yeats,
169; on Aran islands, 169, 179;
distinguished from Lady Gregory, 172;
on island modernization, 172–3; death
of Gaelic culture, 173–4; on
Hiberno-English, 173–4, 279, 302; as
radical, 175; as ascendancy eavesdropper,
174; gender reversals, 176–7; and Gaelic
poetic tradition, 177–9; use of Hyde's
Love Songs, 180; frustration of
liberationist aims, 181; riots, 183–4;
on androgyny and integration, 185; stage
Irishry criticised, 186; O'Casey as heir to,
219, 232; later productions of *Playboy*,
237; on Elizabethan English, 274;
cynical about revivalism, 275; 'reality
and joy', 280; and islanders, 287;
antipastoralism, 287–8; tradition and
modernity, 295; art as collaboration,
301; influence of Wilde, 303; parodied
by Joyce, 333; and anti-Oedipus,
388–9; on Catholic philistines, 414;
handling of religious themes, 422–3,
425; Yeats's praise of, 445, 450; on big
house decline, 449; on peasant penury,
486; Synge-song influences O'Casey,
493; as island utopian, 488–9; attitude to
capital punishment, 516; and Behan's
idiom, 529; and tramp figure, 537–8;
compared to Heaney, 596–7; influence
on Friel, 623; translation and art, 626;
and Céitinn, 627; and Gaelic syntax,
628; on Ireland as exceptional case, 641;
on lack of readers in Ireland, 651; *The
Shadow of the Glen*, 177, 485; *Riders to
the Sea*, 172–3; *The Well of the Saints*,
423; *The Tinker's Wedding*, 423, 466,
485; *The Playboy of the Western World*,
166–88, 224, 236, 290, 298–9, 324,
347, 381, 382–8, 395, 422–3, 490, 596,
626; riots at, 89, 164, 167, 171, 175,
183–4, 224–5, 236, 301, 481; compared
with *Plough* riots, 381; *Deirdre of the
Sorrows*, 173, 288, 301–2, 423, 532;
Collected Poems, 169; 'The Curse', 187;
'Queens', 301–2; 'Passing of the Shee',
302; *The Aran Islands*, 172–3, 486,
489–90

Tagore, Rabindranath, 129, 252, 258,
272; *The Post Office*, 252, 272; *Gitanjali*,
272
Táin, 537
tally-stick, 143
tax-holiday for artists, 583
Tel-el-Kebir, 86
Tenniel, Sir John, 35
Thackeray, William Makepeace, 81
Thatcher, Margaret, 576
Theosophists, 316
Thermidor, 203
Thomas, Dylan, 534
Thomas Aquinas, Saint, 361
Thompson, Francis, 199
Thomson, George (Seoirse MacThomáis),
488
Thoreau, Henry David, 272; *Walden*, 272
Thornton, Weldon, 287
Tilak, Lokmanya, 252
Time (magazine), 479
Times, The (London), 47, 85–6, 510
Tír na nÓg (Land of Young), 103, 112,
241, 537
Titbits, 348
Titley, Alan, 568
Tone, Theobald Wolfe, 17, 21, 140,
211–12, 259, 294
tourism, 30, 49, 51–2, 59, 60, 149, 172–3,
287–8, 294, 336, 552, 566–7
translation, 163, 614–23, 624–39
travellers, 571, 579
Treblinka, 600
Trevelyan, Charles, 625
Trevor, William, 583–4
Trilling, Lionel, 298, 556; *Sincerity and
Authenticity*, 298; *Beyond Culture*, 556
Trinity College Dublin, 2, 121, 138, 145–
8, 161, 192, 273, 281, 327, 396, 452–3,
625
Trollope, Anthony, 81
Tunisia, 381
Twain, Mark, 105
Tynan, Kenneth, 455

U2, 611
Ulster Volunteer Force (UVF), 192, 420,
575
unconscious, 16–19
underdevelopment, 329, 477–8, 646
unionism, 6, 22, 124, 133, 148, 153,
192, 194, 222, 237, 335, 360,
415–16, 568, 575, 576–7; Loyal

Orange Association, 397; unionists on Easter Rising, 414; future of unionism, 647–52
Unionist Party, 415, 567, 577–9
United Irishman, 159, 191, 193
United Irishmen, 504
United Nations, 479, 558, 579
United States, 21, 35, 50, 100, 101, 105, 114–19, 123, 128, 164, 194–5, 253–9, 272, 284, 294, 475, 545, 567, 571, 646, 648
University College Dublin, 512
Upanishads, 253
urbanization, 492–6, 567
utopia, 12, 41–2, 48–50, 59–60, 293, 304, 310, 338, 367, 424, 561

Vatican, 439; Second Vatican Council, 566
vers libre, 461–2
Victoria, Queen, 47, 72, 85, 92, 139–40, 352, 397, 476
Victorianism, 30–1, 35–9, 43, 54, 83–4, 104, 179, 183, 220, 233–4, 269, 273, 275, 299, 329, 348, 383, 464, 488, 497, 507–11, 544, 552, 554; on Gaelic Victorianism, 464, 537
Vienna, 389
Viking power, 21, 143
Virgil, 630
Virgin Mary, 92, 109, 237, 316, 361, 440–1
Viswanathan, Gauri, 556
Vogelweide, Walter Von der, 626
Vorster, B. J., south African minister, 415

Walkley, A. B., 164
War of Independence, 416ff
Warner, Marina, 430
Washington, George, 100
Weber, Max, 447; *The Protestant Ethic and the Spirit of Capitalism*, 447
Weil, Simone, 435
Weimar culture, 390
Wells, H. G., 285
Welsh language, 649
West Britons', 144, 151, 289, 398
West Indies, 37, 276, 279–83, 407, 552, 557
Westminster (House of Commons), 19, 23, 58, 62, 140, 145, 191, 192, 401, 441–2, 648; (House of Lords), 192
Whitaker, T. K., 479, 587
Whitaker, Thomas R., 324

White, William Hale, 446; *The Autobiography of Mark Rutherford*, 446
Whitelaw, Billie, 458
Whitman, Walt, 4, 21, 100, 115, 117–19, 123–9, 157, 164, 252, 272, 324
Wild Geese, 327, 394
Wilde, Oscar, 33–51, 120–6, 145, 161, 192, 200–3, 233; parents of, 33–4; identity, 34–5; Oxford, 35–6; religion, 36; Anglo-Irish strains, 37–9; Irish Question, 42–3; as critic of imperial psychology, 44–5; as republican, 46–7; and Irish Renaissance, 47–8; against literary realism, 48; love of English culture, 48; as decolonizing artist, 49–50; trial of, 192; on Celt in art, 266; on upper-class attitudes, 271; on dissenters, 272; on Shakespeare and romantics, 280; on failures of modern education, 281; and mask, 299, 308; and revisionism, 300; art as the future, 304; as jester, 321; and dandyism, 374; on property, 376; on pose, 378; on respect for youth, 384; on self-invention, 384; and anti-Oedipus, 389; use of religious themes, 424–5; on faith versus good works, 444; compared to early Beckett, 456, 458, 534–6; and prison, 515; duo as basis of a society, 550; on national consciousness, 624; desire to make England a republic, 628; *The Importance of Being Earnest*, 34, 38–50, 61–2, 283; *Salomé*, 161; *The Picture of Dorian Gray*, 425; *Lady Windermere's Fan*, 47; *Intentions*, 280; 48–51; 'Ballad of Reading Gaol', 519; *De Profundis*, 36, 519; *The Soul of Man Under Socialism*, 45–6
Wilde, Lady ('Speranza'), 33–4, 46
Wilde, Sir William, 33–9, 143, 382
Windisch (Celtic scholar), 145
Wohl, Robert, 231
Wollstonecraft, Mary, 397
Woman's World, The, 45
Women's Irish Education League, 255
Woolf, Virginia, 392
Wordsworth, William, 103, 199, 428, 486, 491, 555, 590, 627; *The Prelude*, 103, 428
Workers' Education Movement, 145
World Peace Conference, 257
World War Two, 393, 408, 471, 473–4, 542, 550, 558, 580, 583
Wyndham's Land Act (1903), 51

Yeats, Mrs George, 103, 318
Yeats, Jack (painter), 485
Yeats, John Butler, 101, 105, 110, 123, 317, 382, 386–71, 425, 449
Yeats, Lily, 101, 106
Yeats, Mrs Susan, 110–1
Yeats, William Butler, 3, 6, 21, 22–3, 33, 36, 62, 70, 71, 84, 92, 133, 200, 223, 233, 252, 305–26; childhood, 101–3; early London career, 100–1; and English Romantics, 102, 108–10; *Land of Heart's Desire*, 103–4; on romantic image of child, 103ff; autobiography, 105, 107–8, 122; on Pollexfen inheritance, 105–6; imaginative capacity, 106; on landscape and identity, 107; philosophy of marriage, 109; on expression, 110; on education, 110–11; innocence, 112; on cultural colonialism, 115–16; on genre, 115; romantic quest, 116; on style as redemption, 117–26; on magic realism, 118–19; art as process, not product, 120; deAnglicization, 122; on literary affectation, 123; against bookishness, 123–4; unity of Being, 284–5; unity of Culture, 125; on gathering an audience, 126, 136; on self-criticism, 126–7; Whitman's influence, 127–9, 324–5; as late Romantic, 137; on English literary forms, 137–8; folk origins of art, 138–9, 180, 306; Gaelic League and educational reform, 146–7, 281; and Hyde, 153; on deAnglicizing literature, 155; on nationality versus cosmopolitanism, 156–65; Eglinton on his flaws, 158–9; against provincialism, 161, 486, 586; collaboration with Moore, 162; on Hiberno-English, 162–3, 174; on hybridity, 163; on national culture, 163–5; on violence, 168–9; Synge's influence on, 169; and *Playboy* riots, 183, 236–7; antiself, 185; eloquence and terseness, 186; on Easter Rising, 196–205; influence on O'Casey, 212; repeats Pearse's words, 217; compared to O'Casey, 223ff; break with nationalism, 225, 286–97; on rhetoric, 226; on *Silver Tassie*, 241–5; on war as theatre, 246; *Oxford Book of Modern Verse* edited, 246; and decolonization, 251–2; on Ireland and Asia, 252; studies mysticism, 253; Nobel Prize, 264; Irish coinage, 265; self-defeating heroism, 266; on

Shakespeare, 268–70; on Dowden, 269–70, 273; on American writing, 272; anti-imperialism, 276–7, 279–80; in US, 284; on nation, 289–91; on tradition and modernity, 295; Wildean mask, 299; in search of a lyric style, 305–26; on form, 310–11; and Dancer, 311–12, 444; and feminists, 312; scepticism, 316–17; Arnold and Celticism, 318; *A Vision* as Celtic Constitution, 318; accused of fascism, 320; on Georgian Ireland, 322–4; on self-becoming, 324–5; rote memory, 340; *personae*, 347; on print versus orality, 355; songs for Blueshirts, 360–1; opposes ban on divorce, 361–2; and Catholic education, 361–2; influence on Bowen, 367; on dandy, 374; on youth and fatherhood, 384–7; on Irish leaders, 394; on Sinn Féin and English law, 401; on 'hysterical' women, 403; on women's rights, 404; Crazy Jane, 406; and Free State, 413–14; diary in 1930, 414; and Protestant identity, 421–2, 439–53; folk spirituality, 425, 449–50; distrust of mimesis, 439–43; self-interrogation, 441, 444–9; on Coole Park, 443–4; Synge and Ireland, 450; need for fusion of Irish traditions, 451; and Northern poets, 451–3; MacNeice on, 474; and pastoralism, 481–3; on free-thinking in art, 490; on coinage, 491; and tramp, 537–8; and hunger strikes, 584; Montague's parody of, 587; Hartnett on his use of Gaelic tradition, 588; and aestheticization of violence, 596; Boland's revision of 'Wandering Aengus', 605–6; and successors, 612; and translation, 627; and forgetfulness of past, 629; on cultural fusion, 634; reading of histc challenged by Foster, 643; 'Song of Happy Shepherd', 306; 'Song of th Shepherd', 306–7, 309; 'Indian up God', 306; 'Indian to His Love', 3('Stolen Child', 112–14, 217; 'Lake I Innisfree', 120, 272; 'To Ireland in Coming Times', 119; 'Moods', 306; 'Song of Wandering Aengus', 307; ' and Bells', 301, 321; 'Valley of the Pig', 450; *Wind Among the Reeds*, 3' *the Seven Woods*, 309; 'Never Give Heart', 388; 'Adam's Curse', 308–9 'Mask', 309–10; 'At the Abbey Th

153; 'Cold Heaven', 450; 'Magi', 310, 313; 'Coat', 112; 'In Memory of Major Robert Gregory', 310–11; 'Irish Airman Foresees his Death', 482; 'Fisherman', 298, 311, 337; 'Easter 1916', 112–14, 213–17, 224ff, 235, 325; 'Sixteen Dead Men', 199; 'Second Coming', 312, 314, 442; *The Tower*, 313, 443, 557; 'Sailing to Byzantium', 313, 441; 'Meditations in Time of Civil War', 312; 'Leda and the Swan', 92, 312–15, 439; 'Among School Children', 108, 310, 313, 443, 444–5; *The Winding Stair and Other Poems*, 439–53; 'Dialogue of Self and Soul', 325, 446–8; 'Choice', 444, 448; 'Byzantium', 441–2; 'Mother of God', 440–1; 'Vacillation', 312, 441, 448; 'Remorse for Intemperate Speech', 448;

'Meru', 112; 'What Then?', 109–10; 'Long-legged Fly', 110, 125; 'Circus Animals' Desertion', 112, 312; *Land of Heart's Desire*, 103–5, 109; *Cathleen ni' Houlihan*, 200–2; *On Baile's Strand*, 162, 212, 266–9; *Deirdre*, 320–1; *Dreaming of the Bones*, 206; *Resurrection*, 202; *A Vision*, 128, 284–5, 290, 316–26, 451; *Autobiographies*, 105, 281, 284, 386–7, 439, 441; *Explorations*, 320; 'Anima Mundi', 122

Young Ireland movement, 22, 46, 83, 102, 137

Ypres, 240

Zen, 457–8
Zimmer, Heinrich, 145
Zola, Émile, 169

Other books in the *Convergences* series:

Jeffrey Kallberg, *Chopin at the Boundaries: Sex, History, and Musical Genre*

Jane Miller, *Seduction: Studies in Reading and Culture*

Masao Miyoshi, *Off Center: Power and Cultural Relations between Japan and the United States*

Tom Paulin, *Minotaur: Poetry and the Nation State*

Richard Poirier, *Poetry and Pragmatism*

Jacqueline Rose, *The Haunting of Sylvia Plath*

Tony Tanner, *Venice Desired*

Tzvetan Todorov, *On Human Diversity: Nationalism, Racism, and Exoticism in French Thought*